OXFORD EC LAW LIBRARY

General Editor: F.G. Jacobs
Formerly Advocate General, The Court of Justice of the European Communities

THE EC COMMON FISHERIES POLICY

OXFORD EC LAW LIBRARY

The aim of this series is to publish important and original studies of the various branches of EC Law. Each work provides a clear, concise, and original critical exposition of the law in its social, economic, and political context, at a level which will interest the advanced student, the practitioner, the academic, and government and Community officials.

Other Titles in the Library

The European Union and its Court
of Justice
Second edition
Antony Arnull

The General Principles of EU Law
Second edition
Takis Tridimas

EC Company Law
Vanessa Edwards

EU Anti-Discrimination Law
Evelyn Ellis

EC Competition Law
Fourth edition
Daniel G. Goyder

EC Agricultural Law
Second edition
J.A. Usher

Intellectual Property Rights in the EC
Volume 1 Free Movement and
Competition Law
David T. Keeling

EC Customs Law
Second edition
Timothy Lyons

EC Employment Law
Third edition
Catherine Barnard

EU Justice and Home Affairs Law
Second edition
Steve Peers

Directives in EC Law
Second edition
Sacha Prechal

External Relations of the European Union
Legal and Constitutional Foundations
Piet Eeckhout

The Law of Money and Financial Services
in the EC
Second edition
J.A. Usher

Workers, Establishment, and Services
in the European Union
Robin C.A. White

The EC Common Fisheries Policy

ROBIN CHURCHILL AND DANIEL OWEN

OXFORD
UNIVERSITY PRESS

OXFORD
UNIVERSITY PRESS

Great Clarendon Street, Oxford OX2 6DP

Oxford University Press is a department of the University of Oxford.
It furthers the University's objective of excellence in research, scholarship,
and education by publishing worldwide in

Oxford New York

Auckland Cape Town Dar es Salaam Hong Kong Karachi
Kuala Lumpur Madrid Melbourne Mexico City Nairobi
New Delhi Shanghai Taipei Toronto

With offices in

Argentina Austria Brazil Chile Czech Republic France Greece
Guatemala Hungary Italy Japan Poland Portugal Singapore
South Korea Switzerland Thailand Turkey Ukraine Vietnam

Oxford is a registered trade mark of Oxford University Press
in the UK and in certain other countries

Published in the United States
by Oxford University Press Inc., New York

British Library Cataloguing in Publication Data

Data available

Library of Congress Cataloging in Publication Data

Data available

Typeset by MPS Limited, A Macmillan Company
Printed in Great Britain
on acid-free paper by
CPI Antony Rowe

ISBN 978–0–19–927584–7

1 3 5 7 9 10 8 6 4 2

General Editor's Foreword

The Common Fisheries Policy is one of the least understood of the European Union's policies. The policy is of great importance, both politically and economically, in some Member States, while of little or no importance in others. Yet the rules are, inevitably, highly specialized and technical in character. The policy is also widely condemned; and—more than is the case with other policies—the blame for the CFP's alleged failings, and especially its adverse impact on the environment and on fish stocks, is routinely placed on the European Commission rather than on the Member States' governments, where it truly belongs.

Yet whatever its merits and defects, the CFP is legally, and even constitutionally, of great importance. The origins of the policy, in the original EEC Treaty, are fragmentary. Its development has been the result of an impressive body of legislation by the Council and of an abundant case-law of the European Court of Justice. The key elements of these are explored and discussed, with great clarity, in this book.

In the Member States the fisheries policy has generated constitutional disputes, and in the United Kingdom it gave rise to the *Factortame* litigation in which the United Kingdom Supreme Court (then known as the House of Lords) recognized and established the primacy of European law over Acts of Parliament. Indeed many cases on fisheries involving the United Kingdom have given rise to constitutional rulings by the European Court of Justice of the highest importance. In addition, the wider international dimension is important: the interaction of EU law and policy with international law and policy is of especial interest in relation to fisheries: there are here, after all, no natural boundaries, and the world must share limited and endangered stocks.

The substance of the law is also of great interest. There are, broadly speaking, two main aspects: the management of fisheries, and the regulation of markets and trade in fishery products. The authors give an exceptionally clear and objective analysis of the main issues, often placing them in a broader context.

With effect from 1 December 2009 the Common Fisheries Policy is given a new Treaty basis, and new legislative procedures, with a new role for the European Parliament as co-legislator with the Council. That is one of the effects of the Treaty of Lisbon, whose provisions are touched upon in this book. Efforts should now be redoubled to improve the policy and to give still greater attention to conservation and the environment. A common policy, though far from perfect, may be preferable to independent actions by the Member States.

It is a pleasure to welcome this latest addition to the Oxford EC Law Library, where it will stand alongside John Usher's book on Agricultural Law. As I step down as general editor of the series, which I took on almost 25 years ago on the initiative of Oxford University Press, I can express also a more general pleasure that the series has attracted so many books of an extremely high standard, and give my thanks and congratulations to their many authors and to OUP.

Francis G. Jacobs
November 2009

Preface

The Common Fisheries Policy (CFP) is one of the longest established and most developed of the common policies of the European Community (EC). Its principal concerns are the conservation and management of fishery resources, relations between the EC and third States in fisheries matters, the marketing of and trade in fishery products, financial assistance to the fisheries sector, and aquaculture. Although dealing with a rather specialized sector of economic activity, and thus at first sight appearing to be of interest only to economic actors within that sector (notably producers, processors, wholesalers, and traders) and their regulators, the CFP has in fact much broader ramifications. It raises issues concerning the management of natural resources, the impact of fishing on the wider marine environment, and relations between developed and developing States, and as such is of interest to many outside the fisheries sector, including environmental and development non-governmental organizations. From the perspective of EC policy and law, it raises general issues about the ability of the EC to formulate, implement, and secure compliance with common policies; the division of competence between the EC and its Member States; the role of the EC as an international actor; and whether the EC and its Member States together are capable of managing an important natural resource sustainably, effectively, and equitably. In writing this book, an account of the CFP from a legal perspective, we have tried to remain aware of these broader issues, even though our focus is on the law. We hope, therefore, that this book will appeal not just to those mentioned above, but also to those with a more general interest in EC law and policy-making, natural resource management, and marine affairs.

The first steps to adopt a CFP were taken more than forty years ago, and since then the CFP has undergone substantial development and change. We thought that it would be useful to provide the reader at the outset (in Chapter 1) with a brief sketch of the development of the CFP from its origins through to the present day, in the hope that such a bird's eye view will aid understanding of the subsequent chapters. The questions of to what, where, and to whom the CFP applies do not have straightforward answers, and these preliminary and necessary matters therefore form a topic in their own right in Chapter 2. Much of the CFP takes place against the backdrop of, and has been influenced by, the international law of the sea in general and international fisheries law in particular. Those areas of law are examined in Chapter 3. The remaining chapters deal with substantive aspects of the CFP. Chapter 4 looks at fisheries management in Community waters (ie the waters falling under the sovereignty or jurisdiction of EC Member States). The Community's external relations regarding fisheries management form the subject of Chapter 5. Chapters 6 and 7 cover the marketing of, and trade in, fishery products. Chapter 8 deals with public expenditure in the fisheries sector, while the last chapter, Chapter 9, addresses aquaculture.

A few remarks should be made here about two issues of terminology arising in this book. The first concerns the question of when to use 'European Union (EU)' and when to use 'European Community (EC)'. The legal basis of the CFP is the EC Treaty. As such it is a policy of the EC specifically, and the references in this book to the CFP and its associated legislation reflect this. There are some occasions in the book when, strictly speaking, it would have been appropriate to refer to the EU rather than the EC, such as references to the organization joined by new Member States since 1992. However, to avoid possible confusion, we have opted not to use the term 'EU' at all, other than in quoted material.

The other point of terminology concerns the numbering of the articles in the EC Treaty. As EC lawyers will be only too well aware, the articles of the EC Treaty were renumbered by the Treaty of Amsterdam in 1997. Given that the new numbering system has been in existence for more than a decade, we have decided generally to refer solely to the new numbers of EC Treaty articles. The old numbers are referred to only where not to do so would cause confusion, or when quoting from judgments of the European Court of Justice.

At the time of writing it was uncertain whether the Treaty of Lisbon would enter into force. For this reason we have discussed the Treaty only rather briefly. On such occasions, we have referred to the article numbering used in the consolidated version of the Treaty on the Functioning of the European Union (as the EC Treaty would be renamed), published in OJ 2008 C115.

This book is based on material available in the public domain as at 30 November 2008 and does not consider anything that became available after that date. For example, any Commission Communication issued after 30 November 2008 or any Regulation published in the *Official Journal* after that date has not been considered. Regulations and other secondary legislation published in the OJ on or before 30 November 2008 but not entering into force or applying until subsequently have been taken into account. Our references in the text to 'at the time of writing', 'current', and 'currently' mean as at 30 November 2008.

We have, at many points throughout this book, referred to material found on a variety of websites. In such instances we have not given detailed website references, on the ground that they often become out of date quite quickly, but instead have simply stated that the material may be found on the website of a particular organization. We have assumed that readers will then be able to find those websites easily themselves by using internet search engines.

Finally, there are various people we would like to thank. First, the authors would like to thank Dr Urfan Khaliq for reading and commenting on drafts of Chapters 5 and 7. Secondly, various individuals in the world of fisheries and marine affairs have been kind enough to discuss points or to respond to queries arising during the writing of the manuscript and this has been much appreciated.

Thirdly, and above all, the authors are very grateful to the staff of Oxford University Press, in particular Gwen Booth, Chris Champion, Alex Flach, and Fiona Stables, as well as the copyeditor Cheryl Prophett and the proofreader Lynn Aitchison, for all their assistance in the production of this book, and for their unfailing courtesy and patience.

In addition, Robin Churchill would like to thank his former employer, Cardiff Law School, for funding a period of academic leave to work on this book during 2005/6; and the European University Institute and what was then the Centre for Maritime Policy (now the Australian National Centre for Ocean Resources and Security) at the University of Wollongong, where that leave was spent, for providing him with extremely congenial facilities for writing early drafts of parts of this book. He would also like to express his heartfelt thanks to his wife, Maggi, for her understanding and forbearance as he spent more of his 'spare time' than he should have done shut away in his office working on this book.

Daniel Owen would like to thank his clients, as well as his fellow barristers and the staff at Fenners Chambers, for their interest in this project and for their patience and understanding when the workload associated with the book threatened to swamp all else in his professional diary. In addition, he would like to thank his friends and family, who have been a wonderful source of support and encouragement. He would also like to take this opportunity to thank Innes Cuthill and Michael Davey, for their teaching and guidance at certain points over the years. Daniel would like to dedicate this book to his mother.

Robin Churchill and Daniel Owen
Dundee and Cambridge

Contents—Summary

Contents

Contents

List of Abbreviations

(This list contains only those abbreviations that are not explained in the text or footnotes of this book.)

AG	Advocate General
CFI	Court of First Instance
CML Rev	Common Market Law Review
COM	Communication [from the European Commission]
Court	European Court of Justice
DG	Directorate-General [of the European Commission]
DG Mare	Directorate-General for Maritime Affairs and Fisheries
ft	feet
ICLQ	International and Comparative Law Quarterly
IJECL	International Journal of Estuarine and Coastal Law
IJMCL	International Journal of Marine and Coastal Law
ILM	International Legal Materials
JO	*Journal officiel des Communautés européennes*
m	metres
nm	nautical miles
OCM	Ocean and Coastal Management
ODIL	Ocean Development and International Law
OJ	Official Journal of the European Communities/Union
SEC	Internal documents of the European Commission
UNTS	United Nations Treaty Series

Table of Cases

EUROPEAN COURT OF HUMAN RIGHTS

INTERNATIONAL TRIBUNAL FOR THE LAW OF THE SEA

PANELS AND APPELLATE BODY OF THE WORLD TRADE
ORGANIZATION

ARBITRATION

Table of EC Legislation

Table of Treaties

Part I

Introductory issues

1

The origins and development of the Common Fisheries Policy

1 Introduction

In the four decades that have elapsed since its birth in the late 1960s, the Common Fisheries Policy (CFP) of the European Community (EC) has undergone substantial development and modification. The authors feel that it would be helpful to provide the reader at the outset with an overview of the history of the CFP which, it is hoped, will aid understanding of the detailed discussion of specific aspects of the CFP in the chapters that follow. In this chapter the various actors, interests, and processes involved in the formulation, adoption, and development of the CFP are also outlined.

The history of the CFP falls fairly naturally into five periods: the years 1957–73 (covering the conception, birth, and early development of the CFP); 1973–83 (the adoption of an EC system of fisheries management in response to major changes in the international law of the sea); 1983–92 (the challenge of Iberian accession and the consolidation of the EC's fisheries management system); 1993–2002 (the second decade of the fisheries management system); and the period since 2002, which has seen major reform of the CFP and an almost doubling of the EC's membership. Each of these five periods will be looked at in turn.[1] In reading the account that follows (and later chapters), two matters will rapidly become apparent. The first is that the CFP is based on a high degree of regulation. There is a vast mass of legislation, emanating from the Council of the European Union (the Council) and the European Commission (the Commission), that governs most aspects of the fishing industry. Secondly, when considering what regulatory action to take, the Council and Commission have not been able to act purely with reference to the situation in the Community, but have had to take account of, and have been significantly influenced by, external factors, notably the first and third enlargements of the EC, the changing international law of the sea, and international concerns about the state of the world's fish stocks.

---

[1] For more detailed accounts of the development of the CFP up to the late 1990s, see Berg, A, *Implementing and Enforcing European Fisheries Law* (The Hague: Kluwer Law International, 1999), chs 2 and 3; Holden, M, *The Common Fisheries Policy* (Oxford: Fishing News Books, 1996); and Long, RJ and Curran, PA, *Enforcing the Common Fisheries Policy* (Oxford: Fishing News Books, 2000), ch 1.

2 The conception, birth, and early development of the CFP, 1957–73

It is a cardinal principle of EC law that the Community has the competence to adopt common policies and legislation only to the extent that such competence is conferred upon it by the Treaty establishing the European Community (EC Treaty).[2] As originally drafted (in 1957), the Treaty did not explicitly authorize the EC to adopt a CFP: such a competence was not expressly articulated until the extensive amendment of the EC Treaty by the Treaty on European Union in 1992, when Article 3 of the Treaty was amended to read: 'the activities of the Community shall include ... (e) a common policy in the sphere of agriculture *and fisheries*' (the words in italics being added by the Treaty on European Union). Nevertheless, authorization to adopt a CFP can be found, albeit not very obviously, in the original version of the Treaty, in its provisions dealing with agriculture. Those provisions, described immediately below, are still in force and unchanged, apart from the Treaty Article numbers, which have been renumbered (as indicated). Article 38(1) of the Treaty (now Article 32(1)) provided that the 'common market shall extend to agriculture and trade in agricultural products'. 'Agricultural products' were defined as including the products of fisheries and the products of first stage processing directly related to fisheries products. That the agriculture provisions of the Treaty (Articles 38–47, now 32–38) included fisheries was reinforced by Article 38(3) (now 32(3)), which stipulated that the products subject to those provisions were the products listed in Annex II to the Treaty (now Annex I): that list included, *inter alia*, fish, crustaceans, and molluscs (see further Chapter 2). Article 38(4) (now 32(4)) went on to provide that '[t]he operation and development of the common market for agricultural products must be accompanied by the establishment of a common agricultural policy'. The consequence of those provisions of the original version of the Treaty was, therefore, that the EC had to develop a common agricultural policy (CAP) that would also include fisheries. Article 40 (now 34) envisaged that the CAP would be developed by degrees, and by agricultural sector, over the period 1958–70, and that the Policy was to include the establishment of one or more common organizations of agricultural markets. Article 43 (now 37) provided that measures implementing the CAP were to be adopted by the Council, acting on a proposal from the Commission and after consulting the European Parliament.

Given that fisheries in the original six Member States of the EC were of far less economic and political importance in the late 1950s and early 1960s than most sectors of their agriculture, it is not surprising that the Commission was in no great hurry to exercise its responsibility to initiate steps towards the adoption of a CFP. Not until 1966 did it take its first action in this matter, when it published a *Report*

---

[2] Lenaerts, K and Van Nuffel, P, *Constitutional Law of the European Union* (2nd edn, London: Sweet & Maxwell, 2005), 86–100.

on the Situation in the Fisheries Sector of EEC Member States and the Basic Principles for a Common Policy.[3] The Commission followed this up two years later with three draft Regulations, dealing with structural policy, a common organization of the market in fishery products, and trade with third States.[4] In the Council, Member States had widely differing views about the desirability of the Commission's proposed Regulations. What eventually induced a compromise agreement was the prospect of the EC's first enlargement. In 1969 General de Gaulle resigned as president of France, thus unblocking the applications of Denmark, Ireland, Norway, and the UK to join the EC. As a principle of enlargement, the original six Member States decided that States wishing to join the EC must accept the so-called '*acquis communautaire*' (ie the body of EC legislation existing at any given time, in this case the point just prior to the new States joining) and that any derogations from the *acquis* could only be temporary—a principle that has been followed in all subsequent enlargements of the EC. It therefore became desirable for the original Member States to have an *acquis* for fisheries in place before the negotiations with the four applicant States began. To that end the Council eventually succeeded in adopting amended versions of the Commission's draft Regulations in June 1970 (the second and third draft Regulations being combined in one),[5] the day before formal negotiations with the four applicant States began.

That action was not well received by the applicants, whose fisheries interests collectively were far greater than, and somewhat different from, those of the original six Member States (hereafter, 'the Six'). In particular, all the applicants were very unhappy with a provision in Regulation 2141/70 that gave fishing vessels registered in one Member State the same access to the maritime zones of any other Member State as vessels registered in the latter Member State (a provision known as the 'equal access principle').[6] This matter proved one of the toughest in the entire enlargement negotiations.[7] In the end the Six were prepared to agree to a ten-year derogation from the equal access principle in the inner 6 nm of Member States' then 12 nm fishing limits, which was extended to the whole of the 12 nm limit in certain regions where the local population was

---

[3] COM(66) 250, partially reproduced in [1967] JO 862. The Report is in French.

[4] JO 1968 C91/1 (French-language version; there is no English-language version).

[5] Council Regulation (EEC) No 2141/70 of 20 October 1970 laying down a common structural policy for the fishing industry, OJ S Ed 1970 (III) 703; and Council Regulation (EEC) No 2142/70 of 20 October 1970 on the common organisation of the market in fishery products, OJ S Ed 1970 (III) 707.

[6] Reg 2141/70, Art 2(1). Art 4 authorized the Council, by way of derogation from Art 2(1), to limit access for a five-year period to certain zones within the 3 nm limit from the baselines to the local population of the zone concerned if it was essentially dependent on coastal fishing. In practice, the Council never made use of that power, either before or after enlargement.

[7] For a contemporaneous account of the negotiations, see a series of anonymous notes at *CML Rev* 8 (1971), 227–8 and 503–43 *passim*, and 9 (1972) 82, 181–7, 191–8, and 206–19 *passim*.

heavily dependent on fishing.[8] It was also agreed that this derogation should be re-examined at the end of the ten-year period.[9] That concession appears not to have been sufficient in the case of Norway, however, as the fisheries provisions of the Act of Accession are widely believed to have been a leading factor in the decision by a majority of Norwegians to vote against EC membership in a referendum. Norway did not therefore join Denmark, Ireland, and the UK when they became members of the EC on 1 January 1973.

3 The challenge of 200 nm limits—producing a fisheries management policy, 1973–83[10]

In the same year that the EC underwent its first enlargement, the first session of the Third United Nations Conference on the Law of the Sea was held. That Conference, and the treaty that it eventually produced in 1982 (the UN Convention on the Law of the Sea), were to have a profound impact on the development of the CFP. By 1976 it was clear that one of the central elements of any treaty that the Conference might produce would be a 200 nm exclusive economic zone (EEZ), within which a coastal State would, *inter alia*, have sovereign rights to exploit, conserve, and manage the living resources. It was also clear that many States intended to press ahead and unilaterally claim 200 nm EEZs without waiting for the Conference to adopt a treaty. Such States included a number in the North Atlantic. Canada, Norway, and the USA all announced by mid-1976 that they would extend their fisheries jurisdiction from their existing 12 nm limits to 200 nm from the beginning of 1977. Iceland, in fact, had already extended its fishery limits to 200 nm in 1975. In the absence of any countervailing action by the EC and its Member States, those developments signalled a potential double disadvantage for EC Member States. First, there was a risk that many EC distant-water fishing vessels that had traditionally fished in waters that were to fall within the 200 nm fishery limits of third States in the North Atlantic and off West Africa (such fishing accounting for nearly a third of the total EC catch at that time[11]) would no longer be able to continue to do so, or only at reduced levels. Secondly, there was a risk that distant-water vessels of both EC and third States that became excluded from the 200 nm zones of other States would turn to fish off the coasts of EC Member States, thus putting increasing pressure on fish stocks that were for the

---

[8] 1972 Act of Accession, JO 1972 L73, Arts 100–101.   [9] 1972 Act of Accession, Art 103.

[10] For more detailed studies of the evolution of the CFP during this period, see Farnell, J and Elles, J, *In Search of a Common Fisheries Policy* (Aldershot: Gower, 1984); Leigh, M, *European Integration and the Common Fisheries Policy* (Beckenham: Croom Helm, 1983); and Wise, M, *The Common Fisheries Policy of the European Community* (London: Methuen, 1984), chs 6–11.

[11] Wise, *The Common Fisheries Policy*, 145.

most part fully exploited or close to it,[12] unless EC Member States themselves claimed 200 nm fishing limits.

In September 1976 the Commission responded to this potential double threat by publishing an ambitious four-point package of proposals.[13] First, Member States should extend their fishing limits off their North Sea and North Atlantic coasts to 200 nm in concert from 1 January 1977. Secondly, the management of fish stocks within those new limits (hereafter, 'Community waters'[14]) should be undertaken by the EC and not by individual Member States. Thirdly, the EC (and not individual Member States) should negotiate agreements with third States that would permit vessels of EC Member States (hereafter, 'Community fishing vessels'[15]) to fish inside the new limits of third States, and would also permit some third States' vessels that had traditionally fished within what were to become Community waters to continue to do so. Lastly, the EC should provide financial aid to enable the restructuring of the Community fishing fleet that would be necessary following the general extension of limits to 200 nm. In particular, the capacity (ie size in terms of tonnage and engine power) of the Community fleet needed to be reduced if there was not to be overfishing in Community waters. In addition, many distant-water fishing vessels, being no longer able to fish on their traditional grounds off third States, would need to be adapted if they were to fish in Community waters.

The Council readily agreed to the first of the Commission's proposals. On 3 November 1976 it adopted a resolution (known as the Hague Resolution[16]) in the second paragraph of which it agreed that EC Member States would extend their fishing limits in concert from their existing 12 nm to 200 nm off their North Sea and North Atlantic coasts from 1 January 1977. That was duly done.[17] The Council also reached agreement easily on the third element of the Commission's package. The final three paragraphs of the Hague Resolution gave the Commission a mandate to negotiate agreements with those third States off whose coasts Community vessels had traditionally fished and/or whose vessels had traditionally fished off the coasts of EC Member States. Many of those negotiations were successful, and from 1978 onwards the EC was able to conclude agreements both with States in the North Atlantic (Canada, Denmark (in respect of the Faroe Islands), Norway, and

---

[12] ICES, *Reports of the Liaison Committee of ICES, November 1976 to October 1977*, Cooperative Research Report No 73 (Charlottenlund: International Council for the Exploration of the Sea, 1978), *passim*.

[13] *Commission Communication to the Council. Future external fisheries policy and internal fisheries system*, COM(76) 500, 21.9.1976.

[14] In fact, this term did not become part of the official terminology of the CFP until the early 1980s, but it is used here for convenience.

[15] In fact, this term did not become part of the official terminology of the CFP until the mid-1980s, but it is used here for convenience.   [16] OJ 1981 C105/1.

[17] For details of the legislation of Member States extending fishing limits, see Churchill, RR, *EEC Fisheries Law* (Dordrecht: Martinus Nijhoff Publishers, 1987), 71–2.

the USA) and with some African States such as Guinea-Bissau and Senegal.[18] The EC also became a member of a number of regional fisheries management organizations around this time, including the Northwest Atlantic Fisheries Organization (in 1979), the North-East Atlantic Fisheries Commission (in 1982) and the Commission for the Conservation of Antarctic Marine Living Resources (also in 1982).[19]

The second aspect of the Commission's 1976 package of proposals—an EC system of fisheries management for Community waters—was by far and away the most difficult on which to reach agreement. The major difficulties were questions of allocation and access. In order to conserve stocks, it was necessary to limit catches. The existing fishing fleets of Member States were too large for all vessels to be able to fish economically and sustainably for the resources available. It would thus not be possible to allocate to all Member States the size of quotas that they desired for their fleets. There was intense debate as to what the criteria for allocation should be. As for access, some Member States with larger fishery zones than others (notably the UK) wished to be able to reserve a substantial part of their zone for their own fishermen. Not until January 1983, more than six years after the Commission put forward its proposals, was the Council able to reach agreement on an EC system of fisheries management (for details, see below). In the end two principal factors ultimately persuaded Member States to agree in the Council. The first was the fact that the ten-year derogation from the equal access principle laid down in the 1972 Act of Accession was due to expire at the end of 1982, which meant that without a further derogation the principle would apply fully to all inshore waters covered by the 1972 derogation, a consequence that many Member States wished to avoid. The second factor was the prospect of further enlargement of the EC to include two States with major fishing interests, namely Portugal and Spain, which had each applied for EC membership in 1977. Most of the existing Member States felt that it was highly desirable to have a system of fisheries management in place before negotiations for Iberian membership got underway in earnest.

During the six years between the extension of Member States' fisheries jurisdiction to 200 nm in 1977 and the adoption of the EC system of fisheries management in 1983, fishing in Community waters was regulated by a mixture of short-term EC and national measures, which collectively failed to provide effective management. At this time the Court played an important role in determining the permissible scope of national fishery measures.[20] Its most important judgment in this respect was in *Commission v United Kingdom*, delivered in 1981.[21] In this case the Court addressed the meaning of Article 102 of the 1972 Act of Accession, which required the Council to 'determine conditions for fishing with a view to ensuring protection of the fishing grounds and conservation of the biological

---

[18] These and other agreements are discussed in Chapter 5.
[19] EC membership of these and other organizations is discussed in Chapter 5.
[20] For a detailed analysis of the relevant case law, see Churchill, *EEC Fisheries Law*, 85–110.
[21] Case 804/79 *Commission v United Kingdom* [1981] ECR 1045.

resources of the sea' by the end of 1978. The Court held that this provision meant that as from the beginning of 1979 the EC had exclusive competence to adopt conservation measures for Community waters and that the Member States no longer possessed such competence, even though the Council had not in fact exercised its duty under Article 102 by the time of the Court's judgment.[22] Thus, an EC system of fisheries management for Community waters was transformed from something that at that time was widely considered to be no more than politically desirable to a legal necessity.

The EC system of fisheries management adopted in 1983 was contained in a number of Regulations. The basic Regulation was Regulation 170/83,[23] which began by setting out the objectives of the system, defining them as being 'to ensure the protection of fishing grounds, the conservation of the biological resources of the sea and their balanced exploitation on a lasting basis and in appropriate economic and social conditions'.[24] Regulation 170/83 went on to provide that each year the Council was to adopt total allowable catches (TACs) for the main fish stocks of commercial interest found in Community waters. TACs were to be divided into quotas allocated to individual Member States.[25] As regards the criterion by which such allocation was to be made, Article 4(1) provided that '[t]he volume of catches available to the Community ... shall be distributed between the Member States in a manner which assures each Member State relative stability of fishing activities for each of the stocks concerned'. In practice, 'relative stability of fishing activities' was determined by the combining of three elements—past catches, preferential treatment for regions particularly dependent on fishing, and losses of catch resulting from the exclusion of Community vessels from the waters of third States following the extension of fishing limits to 200 nm.[26] One of the other 1983 Regulations, Regulation 172/83,[27] set out quotas (expressed in tonnages) for the stocks for which TACs had been set, based on the principle of

---

[22] Case 804/79 *Commission v United Kingdom*, paras 17–18. Were the Treaty of Lisbon to enter into force, it would reflect the Court's ruling. Art 3(1)(d) of the Treaty on the Functioning of the European Union (as the EC Treaty would be renamed) provides that the EU has exclusive competence in relation to 'the conservation of marine biological resources under the common fisheries policy'; Art 4(2)(d) provides that the EU and the Member States share competence as regards 'fisheries, excluding the conservation of marine biological resources'. See further Chapter 2.

[23] Council Regulation (EEC) No 170/83 of 25 January 1983 establishing a Community system for the conservation and management of fishery resources, OJ 1983 L24/1, as amended and corrected (and now repealed).   [24] Reg 170/83, Art 1.

[25] Reg 170/83, Art 3.

[26] Churchill, *EEC Fisheries Law*, 115–16. See also the 5th to 7th recitals of Reg 170/73.

[27] Council Regulation (EEC) No 172/83 of 25 January 1983 fixing for certain fish stocks and groups of fish stocks occurring in the Community's fishing zone, total allowable catches for 1982, the share of these catches available to the Community, the allocation of that share between the Member States and the conditions under which the total allowable catches may be fished, OJ 1983 L24/30, as corrected (and now no longer applicable). Although this Regulation formally (and retrospectively) set TACs and quotas for 1982, it was in practice applied in 1983.

relative stability. Apart from relatively minor adjustments, each Member State's quotas, in terms of a percentage share of the TAC for each of the stocks concerned, has remained more or less unchanged ever since (see further Chapter 4).[28] The basic Regulation, Regulation 170/83, also provided that the Council should adopt what are known in EC fisheries law as 'technical conservation measures' or 'technical measures', such as closed seasons and areas to protect spawning and immature fish, limits on the minimum size of fish that could be landed, and restrictions on the use of fishing gear.[29] A set of technical conservation measures was contained in another of the 1983 Regulations, Regulation 171/83.[30] On access, Regulation 170/83 provided that the derogation to the equal access principle contained in the 1972 Act of Accession was to continue for a further ten years, although it was extended to cover the waters out to 12 nm from the baselines off all coasts rather than just in regions heavily dependent on fishing, with the position to be reviewed at the end of this ten-year period in 1992.[31] Beyond this 12 nm limit, the equal access principle applied, although the effect of the quota system diminished its impact. The final principal element of the EC system of fisheries management was a set of rules on enforcement of the system. Such rules were not contained in the January 1983 set of measures, but had been adopted some months previously.[32]

The fourth element of the Commission's package of September 1976, it will be recalled, was a set of proposals for financial aid to restructure the fishing industry to take account of the new world of 200 nm limits, and, in particular, to adjust the capacity of the Community fleet to the resources available. The Council did not reach agreement on those proposals until October 1983, when it adopted two Regulations and a Directive which provided EC aid for: (a) modernizing, laying-up, and scrapping vessels; (b) encouraging fishing in new areas and for new species; (c) encouraging joint ventures with companies from third States; and (d) developing aquaculture.[33]

One of the original two CFP Regulations adopted in 1970 established a common organization of the market in fishery products. In 1978 the Commission undertook a review of that Regulation to see whether changes were necessary as a

---

[28] Long and Curran, *Enforcing the Common Fisheries Policy*, 15.   [29] Reg 170/83, Art 2.

[30] Council Regulation (EEC) No 171/83 of 25 January 1983 laying down certain technical measures for the conservation of fishery resources, OJ 1983 L24/14, as amended and corrected (and now repealed).   [31] Reg 170/83, Arts 6 and 8.

[32] Council Regulation (EEC) No 2057/82 of 29 June 1982 establishing certain control measures for fishing activities by vessels of the Member States, OJ 1982 L220/1, as amended (and now repealed).

[33] Council Regulation (EEC) No 2908/83 of 4 October 1983 on a common measure for restructuring, modernizing and developing the fishing industry and for developing aquaculture, OJ 1983 L290/1, as amended (and now repealed); Council Regulation (EEC) No 2909/83 of 4 October 1983 on measures to encourage exploratory fishing and cooperation through joint ventures in the fishing sector, OJ 1983 L290/9, as amended (and now repealed); and Council Directive 83/515/EEC of 4 October 1983 concerning certain measures to adjust capacity in the fisheries sector, OJ 1983 L290/15, as amended (and now repealed).

result of the establishment of 200 nm fishing limits and experience in the operation of the system since its establishment. Some relatively minor changes were made as a result of that review and the existing Regulation replaced,[34] but the main elements of the system—price support (which operated by withdrawing products from the market when they fell below a certain price); marketing standards (to ensure that fish were of good quality); financial support for producer organizations (which operated the price support arrangements); equal access for Community fishing vessels to the ports of Member States; and rules on trade with third States—remained much as before.

The final development of note during the period 1973–83 was the EC's second enlargement. On 1 January 1981, while the EC was still in the throes of trying to reach agreement on a system of fisheries management, Greece became a member of the EC. Unlike the first enlargement, the second enlargement was unproblematic as far as fisheries were concerned. There were several reasons for that: Greece's small fishing fleet largely confined its activities to Greece's own waters; few, if any, vessels from other Member States fished in those waters; Greece, like virtually all Mediterranean States at that time, had no aspirations to claim an EEZ or exclusive fishing zone, the extent of its fisheries jurisdiction thus being limited (as it still is) to its 6 nm territorial sea; and the EC system of fisheries management then under negotiation was not intended to apply to the Mediterranean Sea.[35]

4 Iberian accession and consolidation of the CFP, 1983–92

No sooner had the Council managed at last to reach agreement on an EC system of fisheries management, than it was faced with a further and equally knotty fisheries issue—the applications of Portugal and Spain to become members of the EC. The main problem was that the Iberian fishing fleets were very large (the Spanish fleet alone was nearly three-quarters of the size of the combined fishing fleets of all ten existing Member States), while Portugal and Spain had few resources in their own waters to contribute to the 'Community pond'.[36] The main reason for the latter was that although Portugal and Spain had established 200 nm EEZs (except, in the case of Spain, in the Mediterranean Sea), the continental shelf in the geological (as opposed to the legal) sense off the Iberian peninsula is quite narrow, and yet it is the waters overlying continental shelves that are by far the most productive areas of

---

[34] Council Regulation (EEC) No 3796/81 of 29 December 1981 on the common organization of the market in fishery products, OJ 1981 L379/1, as amended and corrected (and now repealed).

[35] Leigh, *European Integration and the Common Fisheries Policy*, 177–82; and Wise, *The Common Fisheries Policy*, 20 and 56.

[36] House of Lords Select Committee on the European Communities, *The Common Fisheries Policy* (HL Paper (1984–85) 39, 99).

the sea for fish.[37] The mismatch between Iberian fleet size and resources was compounded by the fact that Portuguese vessels had not fished in the waters of the existing Member States since limits were extended to 200 nm at the beginning of 1977 and, although Spain had had an agreement with the EC permitting its fishermen to fish in Community waters,[38] the amounts of fish that could be taken under that agreement were quite small. Thus, if Portugal and Spain were to be given access to fish in the waters of the existing Member States above the levels that they had previously fished, it would require existing Member States to reduce their catches (because stocks were generally fully exploited[39]) and it would risk upsetting the hard-won agreement on the principle of relative stability as the criterion of catch allocation. Nor could any possible increase in Iberian access to existing Community waters be offset by offering significant quotas to Community vessels in Iberian waters because of the lack of resources there. Negotiations between the EC and Portugal and Spain were therefore particularly tough, and the compromise agreement that eventually resulted was complex. It gave Portuguese and Spanish vessels very limited access to the waters of the existing Member States until 2002, with the possibility for some adjustment from 1996.[40]

Once Portugal and Spain became members of the EC at the beginning of 1986, it was possible for the CFP to enter a period of consolidation and for its four main elements—fisheries management, relations with third States, structural adjustment, and organization of the market—to operate routinely. As to the first of those elements, the Council succeeded in setting TACs and quotas each year, as intended by Regulation 170/83, although all too frequently TACs were set at levels considerably above those recommended by fisheries scientists in order to try to satisfy at least some of the demands of EC fishermen.[41] The original 1983 set of technical conservation measures was amended on points of detail several times, and replaced in 1986 by a consolidating Regulation.[42] The 1982 Regulation on enforcement was also amended several times, and replaced by a consolidating version in 1987.[43] The

---

[37] Barston, RP and Birnie, PW (eds), *The Maritime Dimension* (London: George Allen & Unwin, 1980), 27–30.

[38] Agreement on Fisheries between the Government of Spain and the European Economic Community, 1980, OJ 1980 L322/3.

[39] House of Lords Select Committee on the European Communities, *The Common Fisheries Policy* (HL Paper (1984–85) 39, 99).

[40] 1985 Act of Accession, OJ 1985 L302/23, Arts 156–166 and 347–353. See further Long and Curran, *Enforcing the Common Fisheries Policy*, 19–20 and 24–5.

[41] For a detailed analysis, see Churchill, RR, 'Fisheries in the European Community: Sustainable Development or Sustained Mismanagement?' in Couper, A and Gold, E (eds), *The Marine Environment and Sustainable Development: Law, Policy and Science* (Honolulu, Hawaii: Law of the Sea Institute, 1993), 141 at 150–77.

[42] Council Regulation (EEC) No 3094/86 of 7 October 1986 laying down certain technical measures for the conservation of fishery resources, OJ 1986 L288/1, as amended and corrected (and now repealed).

[43] Council Regulation (EEC) No 2241/87 of 23 July 1987 establishing certain control measures for fishing activities, OJ 1987 L207/1, as amended and corrected (and now repealed).

EC system of fisheries management adopted in 1983 in practice (although not for-mally) originally applied only to the North Sea and north-east Atlantic, but during the 1980s the EC began to expand the geographical application of the system by adopting a set of technical conservation measures for the Baltic Sea in 1986.[44]

Turning now to the other elements of the CFP, on the external plane the EC continued to negotiate agreements for the access of Community fishing vessels to the waters of third States, a particular stimulus being provided by Iberian accession. At the time of their accession, Portugal and Spain had fisheries access agreements with quite a number of States with which the EC did not have agreements. Under the 1985 Act of Accession those agreements were due to be replaced by EC agreements.[45] By 1992 the EC had concluded a total of some thirty fisheries access agreements with third States in the North Atlantic, Baltic, and Africa since it had begun negotiating such agreements in the late 1970s. It had also become a member of a further number of regional fisheries management organizations. As regards structural measures, the 1983 measures were replaced by a fresh set of measures in 1986 that put more emphasis on adjusting capacity to catch potential and less on modernizing vessels.[46] Such emphasis was necessary not only because the 1983 measures had done very little to reduce excess capacity but also because Portuguese and Spanish accession had exacerbated the problem of over-capacity. Efforts to reduce excess capacity were centred on Multi-Annual Guidance Programmes, which required the size of each Member State's fishing fleet to be adjusted to the resources available over a set period. The first programme ran from 1983 to 1986 and the second from 1987 to 1991. The fourth element of the CFP, the common organization of the market in fishery products, operated fairly routinely during the 1980s, on the one hand helping producers, by means of a price intervention mechanism, and, on the other hand, consumers, through quality standards for fish.

Regulation 170/83, it will be recalled, provided that the derogation to the equal access principle relating to coastal waters within 12 nm of the baselines should be reviewed in 1992. Accordingly, as required, the Commission published a report on the matter in 1991.[47] In fact, the Commission's report ranged much more widely than the question of access, and considered the whole of the CFP. Its broad

---

[44] Council Regulation (EEC) No 1866/86 of 12 June 1986 laying down certain technical measures for the conservation of fishery resources in the waters of the Baltic Sea, the Belts and the Sound, OJ 1986 L162/1, as amended (and now repealed).   [45] 1985 Act of Accession, Arts 167 and 354.

[46] Council Regulation (EEC) No 4028/86 of 18 December 1986 on Community measures to improve and adapt structures in the fisheries and aquaculture sector, OJ 1986 L376/7, as amended and corrected (and now repealed).

[47] *Report 1991 from the Commission to the Council and the European Parliament on the Common Fisheries Policy*, SEC(91) 2288, 18.12.1991. The Commission had also published a report on the crisis in the fishing industry the previous year (*Communication from the Commission to the Council and the European Parliament on the Common Fisheries Policy*, SEC(90) 2244, 06.12.1990). As part of its review of the CFP, the Commission published a separate report in 1992 on monitoring of the implementation of the CFP (*Report from the Commission to the Council and the European Parliament on monitoring implementation of the Common Fisheries Policy*, SEC(92) 394, 06.03.1992).

conclusion was that Member States' fishing industries faced a crisis unless the CFP was radically improved. The system of TACs and quotas had failed to prevent the overfishing of many stocks; there was still substantial over-capacity in Member States' fishing fleets in spite of the EC's structural measures; there was poor compliance with EC conservation measures as a result of weak enforcement; and there was insufficient coordination between the management of resources and the structural and marketing aspects of the CFP.

In response, and following a legislative proposal from the Commission, the Council adopted a new basic Regulation, Regulation 3760/92, in December 1992 to replace Regulation 170/83.[48] Much of the new Regulation was similar to Regulation 170/83, in particular its provisions on the adoption of TACs and quotas (allocation still being based on the principle of relative stability), technical conservation measures, and access (with the existing derogation to the equal access principle being extended for a further ten-year period). However, parts of the Regulation, in their wording at least, marked an advance on Regulation 170/83 to reflect some of the concerns expressed by the Commission in its report. Thus, Article 2 added references to sustainability and the implications of fishing for the marine ecosystem in its statement of the objectives of the CFP (in part reflecting the fact the Regulation was adopted only a few months after the UN Conference on Environment and Development at which sustainable development was a central concern); Article 5 called for the introduction of a system of licensing; Article 8 envisaged management being on a multi-annual and, 'where appropriate', multi-species basis, and exploitation being limited, where necessary, by effort as well as or instead of by catch (reflecting the Commission's concerns that single species TACs were inadequate as the sole form of harvesting restriction other than technical conservation measures); Article 11 called on the Council to 'set the objectives and detailed rules for restructuring the Community fisheries sector with a view to achieving a balance on a sustainable basis between resources and their exploitation'; and Article 12 called for a new control system applying to the entire sector. Under Article 14(2) the Commission was to carry out a review of Regulation 3760/92 before the end of the ten-year period following its adoption, on the basis of which the Council would decide on 'any necessary adjustments' to be made, particularly as regards access.

5 The second decade of the EC's fisheries management system, 1993–2002

As mentioned above, the 1985 Iberian Act of Accession envisaged that some adjustment to its fisheries provisions could be made from 1996. In the event, far-reaching adjustments were made, terminating the original arrangements

---

[48] Council Regulation (EEC) No 3760/92 of 20 December 1992 establishing a Community system for fisheries and aquaculture, OJ 1992 L389/1, as amended (and now repealed).

completely and further integrating Portugal and Spain into the CFP.[49] In waters where access had been restricted under the Act of Accession, a system of managed fishing effort for the fishing vessels of all Member States was introduced with effect from 1 January 1996, establishing the maximum annual effort that each Member State could employ to take the quotas available to it under the EC's general system of TACs and quotas in the waters concerned. Such effort could be prosecuted only by named vessels. Nevertheless, those arrangements did not lead to any increase in the overall permitted level of effort, compared with the position at accession, for the Portuguese and Spanish fishing fleets in existing Community waters.[50]

This system of fishing effort management, and a system introduced for Community waters in the Baltic Sea in 1997,[51] represented one of the differing forms of harvesting restriction for which Regulation 3760/92 called. Nevertheless, the main management tool used by the Council throughout the 1990s continued to be annual single species TACs, which continued frequently to be set at levels above those recommended by fisheries scientists. However, in the late 1990s the EC agreed on multi-annual management objectives for some of the fish stocks that it shared with Norway.[52] The Council also took action to implement several of the other matters called for by Regulation 3760/92. Among such measures were a system of vessel licensing (introduced in 1993/94);[53] a new enforcement system,

---

[49] The adjustments were made by the following Regulations: (a) Council Regulation (EC) No 1275/94 of 30 May 1994 on adjustments to the arrangements in the fisheries chapters of the Act of Accession of Spain and Portugal, OJ 1994 L140/1; (b) Council Regulation (EC) No 685/95 of 27 March 1995 on the management of the fishing effort relating to certain Community fishing areas and resources, OJ 1995 L71/5; and (c) Council Regulation (EC) No 2027/95 of 15 June 1995 establishing a system for the management of fishing effort relating to certain Community fishing areas and resources, OJ 1995 L199/1, as amended. Regs 685/95 and 2027/95 were repealed and replaced pursuant to: (a) Council Regulation (EC) No 1954/2003 of 4 November 2003 on the management of the fishing effort relating to certain Community fishing areas and resources and modifying Regulation (EC) No 2847/93 and repealing Regulations (EC) No 685/95 and (EC) No 2027/95, OJ 2003 L289/1; and (b) Council Regulation (EC) No 1415/2004 of 19 July 2004 fixing the maximum annual fishing effort for certain fishing areas and fisheries, OJ 2004 L258/1 (and see further Chapter 4). At the time of writing Reg 1954/2003 was the subject of ongoing litigation in the Court: see further Chapter 4.

[50] Reg 1275/94, recitals and Art 3(3).

[51] Council Regulation (EC) No 779/97 of 24 April 1997 introducing arrangements for the management of fishing effort in the Baltic Sea, OJ 1997 L113/1, as corrected (and now repealed). Management of fishing effort is discussed in more detail in Chapter 4.

[52] See further Chapters 4 and 5.

[53] Council Regulation (EC) No 3690/93 of 20 December 1993 establishing a Community system laying down the rules for minimum information to be contained in fishing licences, OJ 1993 L341/93 (now repealed); Commission Regulation (EC) No 109/94 of 19 January 1994 concerning the fishing vessel register of the Community, OJ 1994 L19/5, as amended (and now repealed); Council Regulation (EC) No 1627/94 of 27 June 1994 laying down general provisions concerning special fishing permits, OJ 1994 L171/7, as amended; and Council Regulation (EC) No 3317/94 of 22 December 1994 laying down general provisions concerning the authorization of fishing in the waters of a third country under a fisheries agreement, OJ 1993 L350/13 (now repealed).

adopted in 1993, that provided an integrated and comprehensive approach to control and enforcement of all aspects of the CFP, and not simply, as hitherto, conservation and management measures;[54] a new set of technical conservation measures for the Atlantic and North Sea, adopted in 1997, which was stricter, but more straightforward, than the measures that it replaced;[55] and a new set of technical measures for the Baltic Sea, adopted in 1998.[56] In 1994 the EC expanded the geographical application of the Community system of fisheries management by adopting a first set of conservation measures for the Mediterranean Sea.[57] From the late 1990s onwards, influenced by discussions in such fora as the North Sea Conferences[58] and the insertion of Article 6 into the EC Treaty by the Treaty on European Union (which requires environmental protection requirements to be integrated into various Community policies), the Commission published a number of policy papers on integrating environmental considerations into fisheries management.[59]

On the external plane during the decade 1993–2002, the EC continued to negotiate bilateral access agreements with developing States, as well as renewing existing agreements. At the beginning of that decade there were increasing concerns as to whether the fisheries provisions of the UN Convention on the Law of the Sea provided an adequate framework for fisheries management, especially on the high seas. During the mid-1990s the EC was heavily engaged in negotiations with other States for a number of new global and regional fisheries instruments to

---

[54] Council Regulation (EC) No 2847/93 of 12 December 1993 establishing a control system applicable to the common fisheries policy, OJ 1993 L261/1, as amended, discussed further in Chapter 4.

[55] Council Regulation (EC) No 894/97 of 29 April 1997 laying down certain technical measures for the conservation of fishery resources, OJ 1997 L132/1, as amended, largely replaced from the beginning of 2000 by Council Regulation (EC) No 850/98 of 30 March 1998 for the conservation of fishery resources through technical measures for the protection of juveniles of marine organisms, OJ 1998 L125/1, as amended and corrected. These two Regulations are discussed further in Chapter 4.

[56] Council Regulation (EC) No 88/98 of 18 December 1998 laying down certain technical measures for the conservation of fishery resources in the waters of the Baltic Sea, the Belts and the Sound, OJ 1998 L9/1, as amended and corrected (and now repealed).

[57] Council Regulation (EC) No 1626/94 of 27 June 1994 laying down certain technical measures for the conservation of fishery resources in the Mediterranean, OJ 1994 L171/1, as amended (and now repealed).

[58] See, for example, the *Statement of Conclusions from the Intermediate Ministerial Meeting on the Integration of Fisheries and Environmental Issues*, Bergen, 1997, available on the website of the Internet Guide to International Fisheries Law.

[59] See, for example, *Communication from the Commission to the Council and the European Parliament: Fisheries management and nature conservation in the marine environment*, COM(1999) 363, 14.07.1999; *Communication from the Commission to the Council and the European Parliament: Elements of a Strategy for the Integration of Environmental Protection Requirements into the Common Fisheries Policy*, COM(2001) 143, 16.03.2001; *Communication from the Commission to the Council and the European Parliament: Biodiversity Action Plans in the area of Conservation of Natural Resources, Agriculture, Fisheries and Development and Economic Co-operation*, COM(2001) 162, 27.03.2001; and *Communication from the Commission setting out a Community Action Plan to integrate environmental protection requirements into the Common Fisheries Policy*, COM(2002) 186, 28.05.2002. See further Chapter 4.

address some of the perceived shortcomings of the Convention.[60] In 1992 the EC concluded the Agreement on the European Economic Area with the EFTA States, which extended EC rules on intra-Community trade in fishery products to trade between the EC and EFTA States and increased access for Community fishing vessels to EFTA States' waters.[61]

On the structural side, the EC adopted the third and fourth Multi-Annual Guidance Programmes for the periods 1992–96 and 1997–2002 against the backdrop of a report from a group of independent experts in 1991, which recommended a reduction of 40 per cent in the capacity of the Community fishing fleet.[62] However, the two Programmes resulted in an overall reduction in capacity of far less than the recommended figure.[63]

Major changes to the common organization of the market in fishery products were made with effect from 1993 with the adoption of a new Regulation.[64] In particular, the role of producer organizations was strengthened; the system of price support changed (particularly in order to aid producers) and was made less wide-ranging in its coverage; and a temporary system of import prices was introduced. Further changes, to take account of market developments, altered patterns of fishing activity, and shortcomings in the existing rules, were made in 1999, the changes being sufficiently wide-ranging to justify a new Regulation replacing and repealing the 1992 Regulation.[65]

In 1995 the EC underwent its fourth enlargement, when Austria, Finland, and Sweden all joined. As far as fisheries were concerned, the membership of Austria posed no problems because of its limited interests in the matter: as regards sea fisheries, it is landlocked and has no fishing vessels registered under its flag.[66] Finland's membership was also straightforward, as its fishing industry is small and its fleet largely confines its activities to Finland's own waters. Sweden's fishing industry is larger, and at the time of accession its vessels fished not only in Swedish waters but also in the waters of the existing Member States under an agreement with the EC[67] and in Norwegian waters under an agreement with Norway. However, it proved a straightforward matter to incorporate Sweden into the CFP by including the quotas that it had received under its agreement with the EC in the

---

[60] See further Chapters 3 and 5.   [61] See further Chapters 5 and 7.

[62] The report is annexed to the 18th Report of the Scientific and Technical Committee for Fisheries, Appendix, SEC(91) 279.   [63] See further Chapter 4.

[64] Council Regulation (EC) No 3759/92 of 17 December 1992 on the common organization of the market in fishery and aquaculture products, OJ 1992 L388/1, as amended (and now repealed).

[65] Council Regulation (EC) No 104/2000 of 17 December 1999 on the common organisation of the markets in fishery and aquaculture products, OJ 2000 L17/22, as amended and corrected, discussed in detail in Chapters 6 and 7.

[66] Commission, *Facts and Figures on the CFP: Basic Data on the Common Fisheries Policy* (2008), 12, available on the website of DG Mare.

[67] Agreement on Fisheries between Sweden and the European Economic Community, 1977, OJ 1980 L226/2.

general system of Community TACs and quotas, and by including the quotas that it had received under its agreement with Norway in the quotas that the EC received under its own agreement with Norway.[68] The accession of Finland and Sweden meant that the EC began to set TACs and quotas for the Baltic Sea. Norway had applied (for a second time) to join the EC at the same time as Austria, Finland, and Sweden. Although negotiations over fisheries were tough, agreement was reached on the terms of Norwegian accession. However, for the second time the Norwegian electorate rejected EC membership in a referendum.

6 CFP reform and further EC expansion—developments since 2002

As mentioned earlier, Regulation 3760/92 provided that a review of the EC's system of fisheries management was to take place by the end of 2002, initiated by the Commission. Accordingly, the Commission published a number of documents on the matter in 2001 and 2002, of which the two most important were the *Green Paper on the Future of the Common Fisheries Policy*,[69] published in March 2001, and a 'Roadmap' on reform of the CFP in May 2002.[70] As well as publishing those reports, the Commission also engaged in extensive consultations with stakeholders and other interested parties in preparing its proposals for reform.

Like its 1991 report, the Commission's reports in 2001 and 2002 ranged more widely than the EC system of fisheries management and addressed all aspects of the CFP apart from marketing and trade. They were also candid and critical of the functioning of the CFP. The Commission's principal conclusion was that the EC's system of fisheries management had failed to ensure sustainable exploitation of resources. Many stocks had been overfished and were (almost) outside safe biological limits as a result of TACs being set at levels above those recommended by scientists[71] and poor enforcement of quotas and conservation measures. The size of many stocks (especially of high value demersal species such as cod and hake) were at the lowest levels ever recorded. In addition, there was still substantial over-capacity in Member States' fishing fleets because existing measures to reduce capacity had been inadequate.[72] These conclusions of the Commission, it will be noted, are similar to those that it had reached a decade earlier, in its 1991 report.

---

[68] 1994 Act of Accession, OJ 1994 C241/21, Arts 118–124.

[69] *Green Paper on the Future of the Common Fisheries Policy*, COM(2001) 135, 20.3.2001.

[70] *Communication from the Commission on the reform of the Common Fisheries Policy ('Roadmap')*, COM (2002) 181, 28.5.2002.

[71] Although the Commission does not say so, it is not only the Council in adopting TACs which is to blame for this state of affairs, but also the Commission when proposing TACs. See WWF, *Mid-term Review of the EU Common Fisheries Policy* (Brussels: WWF, 2007), 13–15. Although the latter refers to Commission practice only in 2006 and 2007, there is no reason to suppose that it was any different in earlier years.   [72] COM(2001) 135, pp 7–9, 10–11, and 12–13.

Thorough and urgent reform of the CFP was therefore required. Accordingly, the Commission put forward a wide-ranging set of proposals for reform, which, it hoped, would lead to a CFP 'capable of providing sustainable development in environmental, economic and social terms'.[73] Among its proposed reforms were fresh objectives for the CFP; a new multi-annual framework of fishery conservation and management; strengthening technical conservation measures; incorporating environmental considerations into fisheries management; reducing the capacity of Member States' fishing fleets; an improved system of enforcement; measures to address the socio-economic impacts of effort limitation and fleet reduction; and greater involvement of stakeholders in decision-making.[74]

In response to the Commission's reports and its legislative proposal,[75] the Council adopted a new basic Regulation at the end of 2002, Regulation 2371/2002,[76] which repeals and replaces the previous basic Regulation, Regulation 3760/92. Some of the new Regulation is similar to its predecessor, but much is new, reflecting, at least in part, the Commission's proposals. Article 1 enlarges the scope of the CFP. First, it does so in relation to subject matter. After setting out the scope of the CFP in Article 1(1) in broad terms as being concerned with the conservation, management, and exploitation of living aquatic resources, aquaculture, and the processing and marketing of fishery and aquaculture products, in language similar to that of Article 1 of Regulation 3760/92, Article 1(2), which has no equivalent in Regulation 3760/92, goes on both to clarify and to some extent amplify the rather broad formulation of Article 1(1). Thus, it stipulates that the CFP shall provide for 'coherent measures' concerning conservation, management and exploitation of living aquatic resources; limitation of the environmental impact of fishing; conditions of access to waters and resources; structural policy and the management of fleet capacity; control and enforcement; aquaculture; common organization of the markets; and international relations. Secondly, Article 1(1) of Regulation 2371/2002 enlarges the scope of the CFP in terms of those to whom it applies. Like Article 1 of Regulation 3760/92, it states that the CFP shall cover fisheries activities where they are practised on the territory of Member States, in Community waters, and by Community fishing vessels, but then goes on to add that the CFP also covers nationals of Member States, 'without prejudice to the primary responsibility of the flag State'. The main purpose of this addition appears to be to cover Member State nationals who may be engaged in illegal, unreported, and unregulated (IUU) fishing (a phenomenon explained in Chapter 3), but who are not doing so on Member State territory, in Community waters, or from a

---

[73] COM(2002) 181, p 5.

[74] COM(2001) 135, pp 20–33 and COM(2002) 181, pp 5–16 and 19–26.

[75] *Proposal for a Council Regulation on the conservation and sustainable exploitation of fisheries resources under the Common Fisheries Policy*, COM(2002) 185, 28.5.2002.

[76] Council Regulation (EC) No 2371/2002 of 20 December 2002 on the conservation and sustainable exploitation of fisheries resources under the Common Fisheries Policy, OJ 2002 L358/59, as amended and corrected.

Community fishing vessel. Article 2 of Regulation 2371/2002 deals with the objectives of the CFP. It begins by setting out those objectives in general terms in much the same way as Article 2 of Regulation 3760/92, by stating that the CFP 'shall ensure exploitation of living aquatic resources that provides sustainable economic, environmental and social conditions', but then goes on to make a number of significant additions. For the purpose of ensuring the sustainable exploitation of resources, the EC is to apply the precautionary approach, and must aim at a 'progressive implementation of an eco-system-based approach to fisheries management'. It must also 'aim to contribute to efficient fishing activities within an economically viable and competitive fisheries and aquaculture industry, providing a fair standard of living for those who depend on fishing activities and taking into account the interests of consumers'. In addition, the CFP is to be guided by principles of good governance, including a 'clear definition of responsibilities at the Community, national and local levels'; timely decision-making based on sound scientific advice; 'broad involvement of stakeholders at all stages of the policy from conception to implementation'; and consistency with other Community policies, especially environmental, social, regional, development, health, and consumer protection policies.[77] Here, and elsewhere in much of Regulation 2371/2002, there is reflection of the requirement of Article 6 EC (referred to above) for the integration of environmental protection into, *inter alia*, the CFP.

Article 4 of Regulation 2371/2002 sets out the types of management measures that may be used. Many of them are similar to those in Regulation 3760/92 (although interestingly the new Regulation makes no mention of TACs, simply referring to catch limits[78]), but there are some significant additions. They include, *inter alia*, the adoption of recovery and management plans (as detailed in Articles 5 and 6), the establishment of targets for the sustainable exploitation of stocks, the adoption of specific technical measures to reduce the impact of fishing activities on marine ecosystems and non-target species, and conducting pilot projects on alternative types of fisheries management techniques.[79] The provisions on access and allocation in Regulation 2371/2002[80] are similar to those in Regulation 3760/92. Unlike Regulation 3760/92, which had simply required the Council subsequently to adopt rules on the adjustment of capacity and enforcement, Regulation 2371/2002 itself contains detailed rules on those matters.[81] Like Regulation 3760/92, Regulation 2371/2002 delegates certain powers to Member States to adopt fisheries conservation measures, but enlarges

---

[77] For a detailed, and critical, discussion of the provisions on good governance, see Gray, T and Hatchard, J, 'The 2002 Reform of the Common Fisheries Policy's System of Governance—Rhetoric or Reality?' *Marine Policy* 27 (2003), 545.   [78] See further Chapter 4 on this point.

[79] Most of these matters are discussed in more detail in Chapter 4.

[80] Arts 17 and 20, respectively, discussed in detail in Chapter 4.

[81] Arts 11–16 and 21–28, respectively, discussed in detail in Chapter 4. The rules on enforcement are largely taken from the then existing principal Regulation dealing with enforcement, Reg 2847/93 (referred to in section 5 above).

the scope of those powers.[82] In response to the Commission's calls for the greater participation of stakeholders in the operation of the CFP, and in implementation of the principles of good governance set out in Article 2 of Regulation 2371/2002, Article 31 provides for the establishment of Regional Advisory Councils.[83] Articles 35 and 17(2) provide for a review of Chapters II and III of Regulation 2371/2002 (on 'conservation and sustainability' and adjustment to fishing capacity, respectively), as well as some of its provisions on access, in 2011/2012.

In the event, the foresaid review process has begun a good deal earlier than originally envisaged. In September 2008 the Commission proposed that a full-scale review of the CFP should be launched immediately in order to prepare the ground for a major reform of the institutional framework of EC fisheries management. Although, in the view of the Commission, the 2002 reform had done much to improve the way that EC fisheries were managed (including greater credibility and transparency of the scientific basis of the CFP, improved dialogue with stakeholders, increasing use of long-term management plans, and action to reduce illegal fishing), the CFP still faced considerable challenges, including overcapacity, the need to make fishermen properly accountable, prioritizing ecological sustainability ahead of economic and social sustainability, simplified regulation at EC level combined with greater regional management, and aligning the CFP with the Marine Strategy Framework Directive that was adopted in 2008.[84] The Commission's initiative received broad support from the Member States at an informal meeting of the Council held in September 2008.[85] At that time the Commission stated that it intended to undertake a broad-based consultation with the fisheries sector, other stakeholders, and the wider public, and would table a Green Paper early in 2009. In early 2010 it would publish the results of its consultation and later that year it would table reform proposals with a view to their entry into force in 2012.[86]

The remaining notable development of the period since 2002 has been the expansion of EC membership to almost twice its previous size. On 1 May 2004 ten States, most of them former Communist States from central and eastern Europe, became members. In terms of their fisheries interests, those States are a diverse group. Three—the Czech Republic, Hungary, and Slovakia—are landlocked and have no sea-fishing industry. A further three—Cyprus, Malta, and Slovenia—are Mediterranean Sea States with small fishing fleets that fish largely or wholly in their own coastal waters.[87] For that reason, and also because existing Member States

---

[82] Reg 2371/2002, Arts 8–10, discussed further in Chapter 4.

[83] These bodies are discussed in more detail in the following section of this chapter and in Chapter 4.

[84] See further Commission press release, 17 September 2008 and *Reflections on further reform of the Common Fisheries Policy* (both available on the website of DG Mare). See also Chapter 4.

[85] Commission press release, 26 September 2008 (available on the website of DG Mare).

[86] Ibid.

[87] Commission, *Facts and Figures on the CFP*, *passim*; Commission, *Facts and Figures on the EU Fishing Fleet*, *passim*; and Eurostat, *Fishery Statistics: Data 1990-2006* (Luxembourg, 2007), *passim*. All are available on the website of DG Mare.

fished relatively little in the waters of those three States and because at the time of their accession the EC had adopted few conservation and management measures for the Mediterranean Sea, the membership of Cyprus, Malta, and Slovenia posed no real difficulties as far as fisheries were concerned. The remaining four States— Estonia, Latvia, Lithuania, and Poland—all lie in the Baltic Sea and, in the days of Communism (when Estonia, Latvia, and Lithuania were part of the then Soviet Union) and before the general expansion of fishing limits to 200 nm, were all major fishing nations with important distant-water interests. However, by the time that they joined the EC, their fishing industries had declined dramatically, largely as a result of the exclusion of their fishing fleets from former distant-water grounds, although they still engaged in some distant-water fishing, mainly in the North Atlantic.[88] Prior to their accession, Estonia, Latvia, and Lithuania had each had agreements with the EC providing for the reciprocal access of the parties' vessels to each other's waters.[89] Thus, for the same reasons as in the case of Sweden (as explained in section 5 above), the three States were easily incorporated into the CFP. Even though Poland had not had a similar agreement with the EC, its absorption into the CFP proved relatively straightforward. The accession of the four Baltic States to the EC means that in fisheries terms the Baltic Sea is now almost entirely Community waters.[90]

At the beginning of 2007 Bulgaria and Romania became members of the EC. The history of their sea-fishing industries is similar to that of Poland, although their decline since the late 1970s has been greater and they no longer have any distant-water interests.[91] Since neither Bulgaria nor Romania fished in the waters of existing Member States and vice versa, their inclusion in the CFP was straight-forward. The accession of Bulgaria and Romania means that for the first time there are now Community waters in the Black Sea, and there are, accordingly, EC fisheries management measures applying there (see further Chapter 4).

Three States—Croatia, the Former Yugoslav Republic of Macedonia, and Turkey—are currently engaged in negotiations for EC membership, but it is likely to be some time before any of them become EC members. If or when they do, their membership should not pose major problems as far as fisheries are concerned. Macedonia is landlocked and without a sea-fishing industry. Croatia has a small fishing industry, its total catch of marine fish in 2005 being only 0.6 per cent of the total catch of the current 27 Member States. The whole of the Croatian catch was

---

[88] Ibid.

[89] EEC–Estonia Agreement on Fisheries Relations, 1992, OJ 1993 L56/1; EEC–Latvia Agreement on Fisheries Relations, 1992, OJ 1993 L56/5; and EEC–Lithuania Agreement on Fisheries Relations, 1992, OJ 1993 L56/9. In 1996 these agreements were replaced by three new agreements, OJ 1996 L332/2, 7, and 17.

[90] See further Chapters 4 and 5. For a detailed study of the 2004 enlargement and fisheries, see Ørebech, P, 'The Fisheries Issues of the 2004 Second European Union Accession Treaty: A Comparison with the 1994 First Accession Treaty' *IJMCL* 19 (2004), 93.

[91] Eurostat, *Fishery Statistics, passim.*

taken in the Mediterranean Sea.[92] Turkey, by contrast, has a sizeable fishing industry. Its total catch of marine fish in 2005 was exceeded only by the catches of Denmark, France, the Netherlands, Spain, and the UK, of current Member States, and was 6.9 per cent of the total EC catch. The whole of the Turkish marine catch was taken in the Black and Mediterranean Seas.[93] As far as the authors are aware, Turkey has no right to fish in the waters of existing EC Member States, nor do the latter have any fishing rights in Turkish waters. Turkish accession would significantly increase the EC's fishing presence in the Black Sea.

7 Actors, interests, and processes involved in the formulation, adoption, and development of the CFP[94]

The final section of this chapter pulls together and expands upon some of the threads in the earlier sections so as to present a more systematic picture of the actors, interests, and processes involved in the formulation, adoption, and development of the CFP which, it is hoped, will aid understanding of the subsequent chapters.

The two principal actors involved in the CFP are the Member States, both when acting individually and when acting collectively in the Council, and the Commission. The Council is the principal decision-maker in the operation and development of the CFP. Thus, it is the Council that adopts all major fisheries legislation and that decides whether the Community is to become a party to fisheries treaties with third States. The Council takes its decisions on these matters by qualified majority.[95] The voting behaviour of Member States in the Council on fisheries matters is largely determined by their fisheries interests. It is beyond the scope of this book to attempt to analyse those interests.[96] What may be briefly pointed out here is that the fisheries interests of the Member States differ widely, from Member States that have no interest in sea fisheries (at least as far as their own fishing operations are concerned) because they are landlocked and do not operate a fishing fleet (Austria, Czech Republic, Hungary, Luxembourg, and Slovakia) to those for whom fisheries is a significant economic activity (at least for certain of

---

[92] Eurostat, *Fishery Statistics*, 2, 30, and 38.   [93] Ibid.

[94] For a more detailed discussion of this issue, from a political science perspective, see Lequesne, C, *The Politics of Fisheries in the European Union* (Manchester: Manchester University Press, 2004), ch 2; and Lequesne, C, 'Fisheries Policy: Letting the Little Ones Go?' in Wallace, H, Wallace, W, and Pollack MA (eds), *Policy-Making in the European Union* (Oxford: Oxford University Press, 2005), 353 at 358–64.

[95] Art 37 EC. For what constitutes a qualified majority vote, see Art 205 EC.

[96] For such analyses, see Lequesne, *The Politics of Fisheries*, 5–14; Long and Curran, *Enforcing the Common Fisheries Policy*, 47–55; Commission, *Facts and Figures on the CFP*; Commission, *Facts and Figures on the EU Fishing Fleet*; and Eurostat, *Fishery Statistics*.

their regions) (eg Denmark, France, Ireland, Spain, and the UK). Some Member States have important interests in distant-water fishing (eg France, Portugal, and Spain), while others have interests only in near-water fishing (eg Cyprus, Finland, Greece, and Malta).

Member States play an important role in the CFP not only in the Council but also in their individual capacities. Although the EC has exclusive competence to adopt fisheries conservation legislation in Community waters, it has, as mentioned above, delegated certain legislative powers to the Member States. For example, Articles 8–10 of the current basic Regulation, Regulation 2371/2002, provide that Member States may adopt certain types of measure in certain circumstances and subject to certain procedures, as will be explained in Chapter 4. Member States also have various other powers (and duties), including, *inter alia*, stipulating which fishing vessels may have their nationality and thus fly their flag; determining how their quotas are to be allocated between such vessels;[97] administering certain aspects of the EC's programmes of structural measures;[98] and carrying out various tasks in relation to the common organization of the market in fishery products.[99] In addition, Member States play a significant role in the enforcement of the CFP.[100]

Apart from the Member States, the Commission is the other principal actor in the operation of the CFP. It has a variety of important functions. As already indicated, it is the initiator of all fisheries legislation. Since the late 1970s, and perhaps especially since the late 1990s, it has published a stream of proposals for legislation and many important policy papers (some of which have already been referred to in this chapter and others of which are discussed in later chapters). Although its right of initiative gives it the power to shape the CFP agenda, by no means all of the Commission's proposals are adopted by the Council, and those that are, are often significantly amended. As well as proposing legislation, the Commission also has widespread powers, delegated to it by the Council, to legislate on more detailed matters or in cases of emergency. When exercising such delegated legislative powers, the Commission, as is generally the case in EC law, normally has to consult a committee comprising representatives of the Member States.[101] The Commission is responsible for the negotiation of fisheries treaties with third States, but it does so within the limits of a mandate laid down by the Council and subject to the latter's approval of the results of its negotiations. The Commission is responsible for administering the considerable amounts of financial assistance that the EC provides to the fisheries sector (including aquaculture) through the European Fisheries Fund and other financial instruments, and for

---

[97] Reg 2371/2002, Art 20(3), discussed in Chapter 4.   [98] See Chapters 4 and 8.
[99] See Chapter 6.   [100] See further Chapter 4.
[101] See, for example, Reg 2371/2002, Art 30; Reg 2847/93, Art 36; Reg 104/2000, Art 38; and Council Regulation (EC) No 1198/2006 of 27 July 2006 on the European Fisheries Fund, OJ 2006 L223/1, Art 101. But cf Reg 2371/2002, Art 7 (on the Commission's emergency powers). Generally on the procedures by which the Commission exercises its delegated legislative powers, see Lenaerts and Van Nuffel, *Constitutional Law*, 611–18.

monitoring aid to the fishing industry from individual Member States (see further Chapter 8). The Commission also has a variety of administrative duties in relation to many individual pieces of EC fisheries legislation, as will be seen in later chapters. As the general guardian of the Community interest, the Commission has overall responsibility for monitoring the operation of the CFP and seeking to ensure compliance with its rules, especially by the Member States and the Council. Where it believes a Member State or the Council to be breaching EC fisheries law, it may bring it before the Court,[102] and in practice has frequently done so in the case of Member States.

In terms of internal organization, the Commission has a Directorate-General for Maritime Affairs and Fisheries, dubbed DG Mare (formerly the Directorate-General for Fisheries and Maritime Affairs (DG Fisheries)). Since 2008 DG Mare has been divided into six directorates concerned with: policy development and coordination; international affairs and markets; Atlantic, outermost regions, and Arctic; Mediterranean and Black Seas; Baltic Sea, North Sea, and landlocked Member States; and resources. The Commission is assisted in its work by various expert bodies. The Scientific, Technical and Economic Committee for Fisheries (STECF), consisting of between 30 and 35 scientific experts sitting in an individual capacity, advises the Commission on issues of conservation and management, as well as publishing an annual report on the state of fisheries resources relevant to the EC.[103] That Committee, and DG Mare more generally, are assisted by the International Council for the Exploration of the Sea (ICES), an inter-governmental marine research organization, which provides information on the state of fish stocks relevant to the EC and advice on their management. The Advisory Committee on Fisheries and Aquaculture (ACFA), which consists of 21 members representing fishermen, processors, traders, and the interests of consumers, the environment, and development, advises the Commission on all aspects of the CFP.[104] Regional Advisory Councils (RACs), currently seven in number, are composed of representatives from the fisheries sector and other interest groups affected by the CFP. Their main function is to advise the Commission (and Member States) on matters of fisheries management in a particular region, including problems relating to the implementation of Community rules.[105]

---

[102] Arts 226 and 230 EC.

[103] The Committee was first established (under a slightly different name) in 1979 by Commission Decision 79/572/EEC, OJ 1979 L156/29. Its current composition and functions are set out in Commission Decision 2005/629/EC of 26 August 2005 establishing a Scientific, Technical and Economic Committee for Fisheries, OJ 2005 L225/18, as corrected. See also Reg 2371/2002, Art 33.

[104] The Committee was first established in 1971: see Commission Decision 71/128, JO 1971 L68/18, subsequently repealed and replaced by Commission Decision 1999/478/EC of 14 July 1999 renewing the Advisory Committee on Fisheries and Aquaculture, OJ 1999 L187/70, as amended. The Committee is discussed in detail in Chapter 4.

[105] The establishment of RACs is provided for by Reg 2371/2002, Arts 31 and 32. They are discussed in detail in Chapter 4.

In contrast to the Council and Commission, the other principal institutions of the EC—the European Parliament, the Court, and the Court of Auditors—all play a rather modest role in the CFP. Turning first to the European Parliament, as mentioned in section 2 above, the procedure for the adoption of fisheries legislation during the early days of the CFP (set out in Article 37 EC) was the consultation procedure. That meant that the Council was to consult the European Parliament before adopting legislation proposed by the Commission. In spite of the fact that most of the original provisions of the EC Treaty stipulating use of the consultation procedure for the adoption of legislation have subsequently been amended to increase the legislative powers of the European Parliament, substituting the cooperation or co-decision procedures for the consultation procedure, Article 37 EC has not yet been so amended. Thus, the enactment of fisheries legislation remains subject to the consultation procedure. (However, if the Treaty of Lisbon were to come into force, the legislative procedure for fisheries would be changed to one of co-decision.[106]) Although the European Parliament must currently be consulted on fisheries legislation, there is no obligation on the Council (or Commission) to heed its opinion. Furthermore, there are occasions when the Parliament plays no role at all in the legislative processes of the CFP. One such situation is when the Commission is exercising its delegated legislative powers.[107] Another form of delegation was introduced by the 1983 basic Regulation under which annual TACs and quotas, technical conservation measures, and enforcement rules were all to be adopted by the Council acting on a proposal from the Commission,[108] in other words without any obligation to consult the European Parliament. However, since 1992 the basic CFP Regulations have stipulated that the consultation procedure is to be the normal process for the enactment of fisheries legislation.[109] Nevertheless, there is still some legislation, notably the annual and biennial fishing opportunities Regulations and various measures concerned with the common organization of the markets in fishery products,[110] which is to be adopted by the delegated procedure just described. The Court has held that this form of delegation is valid provided that it is restricted to matters of detail and that the basic elements of the CFP have been adopted by the consultation procedure.[111] The European Parliament must also be consulted before the Council concludes

---

[106] Treaty on the Functioning of the European Union, Art 43(2). Note, however, that under Art 43(3) the European Parliament would have no role at all in the adoption of measures on 'the fixing and allocation of fishing opportunities'.

[107] The European Parliament must, however, be kept informed of proceedings in the committee which the Commission consults: see Council Decision 1999/468/EC of 28 June 1999 laying down the procedures for the exercise of the implementing powers conferred on the Commission, OJ 1999 L184/23, as amended, Art 7(3). See also Art 5(4).   [108] Reg 170/83, Art 11.

[109] Reg 3760/92, Arts 4(1), 5(1), 8(3), 11, and 12; and Reg 2371/2002, Art 29.

[110] Reg 2371/2002, Art 20(1); and Reg 104/2000, Arts 18(3), 24(7), 26(1), 28(3), and 31.

[111] Case 46/86 *Romkes v Officier van Justitie for the District of Zwolle* [1987] ECR 2671. See also Art 202 EC, third indent, third sentence. On this form of delegation, see further Churchill, *EEC Fisheries Law*, 39–41.

fisheries treaties with third States.[112] The Parliament has for many years been anxious to play a much greater role in the development of the CFP. It also seeks to monitor the operation of the CFP, principally through its Committee on Fisheries.[113] Over the years the Parliament has issued a stream of opinions, some in response to consultation by the Council, others on its own initiative.

Turning to the next institution, the Court played a major role in the evolution of the CFP in the late 1970s and early 1980s, principally in its determination of the respective competences of the EC and its Member States in the fisheries sector. The Court found that the EC was exclusively competent both to adopt fisheries conservation measures in Community waters (in *Commission v United Kingdom*; see section 3 above and Chapter 4) and to negotiate treaties with third States relating to fisheries conservation (in the *Kramer* case[114]). Since the adoption of the EC system of fisheries management in 1983, the Court has played a more routine role, interpreting EC fisheries law and determining whether the Member States and EC institutions have acted in accordance with their obligations under Community law.

The remaining principal EC institution is the Court of Auditors. The function of the Court of Auditors is not only to examine whether the EC's finances are being properly administered, but also to look at the broader issue of whether EC policies are giving value for money. As part of the latter function, the Court of Auditors has on a number of occasions examined particular aspects of the CFP that involve EC expenditure, from time to time publishing detailed, and often highly critical, reports on the functioning of particular aspects of the CFP, such as enforcement, structural policy, and relations with third States. Some of those reports are referred to in later chapters.

Apart from the five principal institutions, as well as the STECF, the ACFA, and the RACs (mentioned above) there are a number of other EC bodies involved in the CFP. The European Economic and Social Committee has occasionally been consulted on proposals for fisheries legislation (for example, on what was to become the basic Regulation of 1992, Regulation 3760/92, and on the Commission's 2002 'Roadmap' paper that led to Regulation 2371/2002), but there is no obligation on either the Council or Commission to do so; and if they do choose to do so, there is no obligation on them to take the Committee's views into account. Like the European Parliament, the Committee also issues own-initiative opinions on particular aspects of the CFP from time to time. Another EC body concerned with the CFP is the Community Fisheries Control Agency, which was set up by the Council in 2005 to improve enforcement of the CFP by coordinating the enforcement activities of individual Member States.[115]

---

[112] Art 300(3) EC. See further Chapter 5. If the Treaty of Lisbon comes into force, the European Parliament will not merely be consulted but required to give its consent to fisheries treaties with third States: Treaty on the Functioning of the European Union, Art 218(6)(a)(v).

[113] See further Lequesne, 'Fisheries Policy', 363–4.

[114] Joined Cases 3, 4, and 6/76 *Officier van Justitie v Kramer* [1976] ECR 1279, discussed in Chapter 5.

[115] Council Regulation (EC) No 768/2005 of 26 April 2005 establishing a Community Fisheries Control Agency, OJ 2005 L128/1. The Agency is discussed in Chapter 4.

So much for EC bodies: there are also, of course, many private interest actors, principally those engaged in the fishing industry (fishermen, processors, wholesalers, traders etc). Such interests, to be effective, need to be organized. There has long been organization of fishing interests at the national level. Since the early 1970s there has also been organization at the European level. Such European organizations lobby the Commission, fisheries ministers in the Council, and the European Parliament. In addition, they may from time to time be consulted by the Commission when it is formulating policy proposals, and they are also represented on bodies such as the ACFA and the RACs. The main organizations at the European level are Europêche (representing producers), the EU Fish Processors Association (AICPE), the EU Federation of National Organisations of Importers and Exporters of Fish (CEP), the European Association of Fish Producers Organisations (EAPO), and the Federation of European Aquaculture Producers (FEAP). In the view of one writer, national fisheries organizations have had more influence on the development of the CFP than European organizations.[116]

Little interest was shown in the CFP during its early years by environmental and development non-governmental organizations (NGOs). However, since the 1990s, when the impact of European fishing not just on fish stocks but also on the wider marine environment and developing countries was becoming more obvious, environmental NGOs (such as BirdLife International, Greenpeace, and WWF) and development NGOs (such as the Coalition for Fair Fisheries Arrangements) have taken an increasing interest in the CFP, lobbying the European institutions and Member States, responding to consultations, and publishing critiques of the Policy. They are represented on the ACFA and the RACs, albeit with significantly smaller membership opportunities than the fishing industry.

As will be apparent from this brief overview of actors and processes, the CFP is currently very much based on a 'command and control', top-down, technocratic system of regulation, administered principally by the Council and the Commission. There is only limited democratic involvement in the form of the European Parliament's modest role in the legislative process. There is some provision for consultation of stakeholders through the ACFA and the RACs. Experience to date suggests that such consultation has so far had little influence on the substance of the CFP, but that situation may be changing with ongoing engagement by the RACs in the CFP process and with the current review of the CFP. If so, it remains to be seen whether a more participatory system of decision-making will lead to significant improvements in the CFP.

---

[116] Lequesne, *The Politics of Fisheries*, 43–53. In May 2006 the Commission published proposals for increasing consultation with stakeholders: see *Communication from the Commission to the Council and the European Parliament: Improving consultation on Community fisheries management*, COM(2006) 246, 24.5.2006, discussed further in Chapter 4.

2

The scope of the Common Fisheries Policy

1 Introduction

This chapter addresses the scope of the Common Fisheries Policy (CFP), from three angles. After a brief introduction, it looks at the species and products covered by the CFP, known as the 'material scope'. Then it considers the CFP's geographical scope, ie the land and maritime areas to which the CFP applies. Thirdly, it addresses the 'personal scope' of the CFP, meaning the various entities to which the CFP applies. Although the chapter focuses on the EC Treaty, it also considers the potential effects of the Treaty of Lisbon on the CFP's material and geographical scope.

As was seen in Chapter 1, the CFP has its origins in the EC Treaty. Under the EC Treaty the activities of the EC, in achieving its purposes, are to include, *inter alia*, 'a common policy in the sphere of agriculture *and fisheries*' (emphasis added).[1] However, there is no express reference to a 'common fisheries policy' anywhere in the EC Treaty. Instead, that term has arisen through practice. That contrasts with the situation for agriculture: the EC Treaty refers to 'a common policy in the sphere of *agriculture* and fisheries' (emphasis added) but then later, in the Agriculture Title, it refers expressly to a 'common agricultural policy' (CAP). The Agriculture Title comprises Articles 32–38 EC. Of those, Article 37 provides the legal basis for Council measures implementing the CAP and Article 33(1) sets out the objectives of the CAP (see below).

Fisheries is included within the Agriculture Title. That arises because: (a) Article 32(1) EC states that the term 'Agricultural products' means 'the products of the soil, of stockfarming *and of fisheries* and products of first-stage processing directly related to these products' (emphasis added); and (b) Article 32(3) EC states that '[t]he products subject to the provisions of Articles 33 to 38 are listed in Annex I to this Treaty', Annex I in turn including products arising from fisheries (on which, see subsection 2.1 below). The result of the inclusion of fisheries within the Agriculture Title of the EC Treaty is that, as with the CAP, the legal basis for Council measures implementing the CFP is Article 37 EC and the objectives of the CFP are those set out in Article 33(1) EC.

Article 33(1) EC states that the objectives of the CAP are: '(a) to increase agricultural productivity by promoting technical progress and by ensuring the rational development of agricultural production and the optimum utilisation of the factors of production, in particular labour; (b) thus to ensure a fair standard of living for the agricultural community, in particular by increasing the individual

---

[1] Art 3(1)(e) EC.

earnings of persons engaged in agriculture; (c) to stabilise markets; (d) to assure the availability of supplies; (e) to ensure that supplies reach consumers at reasonable prices'.

Translated from agricultural into fisheries terminology, and broadly speaking, the objectives listed in Article 33(1) may be read as being to increase fisheries productivity; ensure a fair standard of living for, *inter alia*, fishermen; stabilize markets in fishery and aquaculture products; assure the availability of supplies of fishery and aquaculture products; and ensure that supplies of fishery and aqua-culture products reach consumers at reasonable prices.

As can be seen, there is no express reference in Article 33(1) to fisheries con-servation. However, the central role for fisheries conservation within the CFP (on which, see Chapters 4 and 5) may be implied from the reference in Article 33(1) to ensuring 'the rational development of agricultural production' and assuring 'the availability of supplies'; furthermore, its central role has been acknowledged and endorsed by the Court from an early stage in the CFP's existence (see Chapter 4).

It is also necessary to bear in mind Article 6 EC, which states that: 'Environ-mental protection requirements must be integrated into the definition and implementation of the Community policies and activities referred to in Article 3 [EC], in particular with a view to promoting sustainable development.' The CFP is one of the Community policies referred to in Article 3 EC. The Court has held that, in view of Article 6 EC, environmental protection 'must be regarded as an objective' of the common transport policy.[2] It is therefore strongly arguable that the same applies to the CFP.

2 Material scope

2.1 Annex I to the EC Treaty

Introduction

As noted in section 1 above, Article 32(3) EC identifies the products subject to Articles 33–38 EC as being those listed in Annex I to the EC Treaty. Annex I to the EC Treaty, entitled 'List referred to in Article 32 of the Treaty', contains a wide variety of 'products', each listed opposite the chapter number from the so-called 'Brussels nomenclature' (BN) relating to that product. The product descriptions in Annex I are often very short, and no guidance is provided in the Annex itself on their interpretation. The listed products related to fisheries include, *inter alia*, 'Fish, crustaceans and molluscs', 'Fats and oil, of fish and marine mam-mals, whether or not refined', and 'Preparations of meat, of fish, of crustaceans or molluscs'.

---

[2] Case C-440/05 *Commission v Council* [2007] ECR I-9097, para 60.

The BN was established by the 1950 Convention on Nomenclature for the Classification of Goods in Customs Tariffs.[3] However, the BN has been superseded by the Harmonized Commodity Description and Coding System, generally referred to as the 'Harmonized System' (HS). The HS was developed by the World Customs Organization, and States' functions with regard to the HS are set out in the 1983 International Convention on the Harmonized Commodity Description and Coding System.[4] The HS is accompanied by Explanatory Notes.

The EC has in turn adopted a nomenclature known as the 'Combined Nomenclature' (CN), which is based on the HS but with further EC subdivisions known as 'CN subheadings'.[5] The CN was established by Regulation 2658/87. The CN itself is contained in Annex I to that Regulation,[6] and the most recent reissue of that Annex as at the time of writing was in 2008 (entering into force at the beginning of 2009).[7] Part One of Annex I comprises preliminary provisions, including general rules for the interpretation of the CN. Part Two contains the CN itself, including some notes within each chapter.

Regulation 2658/87 is supplemented by a code of conduct for the management of the CN[8] and by further explanatory notes.[9] Both those documents are issued by the Commission. The Commission's explanatory notes include, *inter alia*, identification guidelines for particular species or species groups and some cross-references to the HS Explanatory Notes.

In view of the developments since the BN, it is appropriate to consider whether the products listed in Annex I to the EC Treaty should now be interpreted by reference to the CN, and its explanatory notes, rather than the original BN. That question arose in *Parliament v Council*,[10] a case concerning the correct legal basis for two Regulations providing protection for forests from atmospheric pollution and forest fires.

The Court in *Parliament v Council* had cause to seek to interpret the phrase 'Live trees and other plants; bulbs, roots and the like; cut flowers and ornamental foliage' as used in Annex I (then Annex II) to the EC Treaty. The Court, referring to the

---

[3] 347 UNTS 127, as amended.

[4] 1503 UNTS 167, as amended. See Council Regulation (EEC) No 2658/87 of 23 July 1987 on the tariff and statistical nomenclature and on the Common Customs Tariff, OJ 1987 L256/1, as amended and corrected, 3rd recital.   [5] Reg 2658/87, 3rd and 5th recitals and Art 1(1) and (2).

[6] Reg 2658/87, Art 1(3).

[7] Commission Regulation (EC) No 1031/2008 of 19 September 2008 amending Annex I to Council Regulation (EEC) No 2658/87 on the tariff and statistical nomenclature and on the Common Customs Tariff, OJ 2008 L291/1.

[8] *Commission Communication: Code of Conduct for the Management of the Combined Nomenclature*, OJ 2000 C150/4.

[9] *Commission: Explanatory Notes to the Combined Nomenclature of the European Communities*, OJ 2008 C133/1, as amended.

[10] Joined Cases C-164/97 and C-165/97 *Parliament v Council* [1999] ECR I-1139.

CILFIT case,[11] held that '[s]ince there are no Community provisions explaining the concepts contained in that annex, it is appropriate to refer to the established interpretations and the methods of interpretation relating to the Common Customs Tariff in order to interpret the annex'.[12]

Accordingly, the Court turned to the CN annexed to Regulation 2658/87. 'Live trees and other plants; bulbs, roots and the like; cut flowers and ornamental foliage' are covered by Chapter 6 of the CN. Chapter 6 has four principal headings. The one relating to live trees reads 'Other live plants (including their roots), cuttings and slips, mushroom spawn'. This heading has several subheadings, including, *inter alia*, 'Trees, shrubs and bushes, grafted or not, of kinds which bear edible fruit or nuts' (CN code 0602 20) and 'Other' (0602 90). Note 1 at the start of Chapter 6 states that, subject to a reservation that did not apply in the case in question, the Chapter covers 'only live trees and goods (including seedling vegetables) of a kind commonly supplied by nursery gardeners or florists for planting or for ornamental use . . .'.

In the light of its consideration of Chapter 6 of the CN, the Court held that (what is now) Annex I to the EC Treaty *'cannot be regarded as covering in general terms trees and forestry products* even though some of those products, taken in isolation, may fall within the scope of Articles 39 to 46 of the [EC] Treaty' (emphasis added).[13] The Court seems to have reached that conclusion on the basis of a very brief consideration of the headings and subheadings within Chapter 6 of the CN and consideration of Note 1 at the beginning of Chapter 6. Interestingly, the Court did not expressly consider the subheading 'Other' (CN code 0602 90) referred to above, perhaps because of the clarity of Note 1 in explaining what types of live trees are (and hence are not) included within the scope of Chapter 6.

The case of *Parliament v Council* illustrates that the Court is willing to turn to the CN, including the notes within the chapters of the CN, to interpret the wording used in Annex I to the EC Treaty. That approach will therefore be used in this subsection to analyse whether particular groups of species fall within the scope of the CFP. The groups that will be considered are fish, crustaceans and molluscs, other aquatic invertebrates, and marine mammals. (Space does not permit consideration of other groups, for example sea turtles or marine algae.)

Before carrying out the said analysis, four general points need to be considered. First, may legislation adopted under the CFP apply to products *not* listed in Annex I to the EC Treaty? In principle, in view of the wording of Article 32(3) EC (see above), the answer should be 'no'. However, in *Commission v Council* the Court held that secondary legislation that applies 'essentially' to products in (what is now) Annex I and that is 'an essential factor in increasing agricultural productivity' but

---

[11] Case 77/83 *Srl CILFIT and others and Lanificio di Gavardo SpA v Ministero della sanità* [1984] ECR 1257, para 7.   [12] Joined Cases C-164/97 and C-165/97 *Parliament v Council*, para 18.
[13] Ibid. Arts 39–46, as referred to by the Court, are now Arts 33–38 EC (on which, see section 1 above).

that also refers 'incidentally' to certain products not included in that Annex may, and indeed must, be adopted under (what is now) Article 37 EC.[14] This finding was endorsed by the Court in *United Kingdom v Commission*;[15] however, in that case the Court referred more generally to the objectives set out in (what is now) Article 33(1) EC rather than just that of 'increasing agricultural productivity'.[16]

One implication from *Commission v Council* and *United Kingdom v Commission* is that the Court may be willing to uphold the validity of a Regulation adopted under the CFP even if it covers 'incidentally' products not included in Annex I. To the authors' knowledge, this specific point has not been tested in the Court in the context of the CFP. Perhaps the way to summarize the situation is that products not included in Annex I to the EC Treaty are not subject to the provisions of Articles 33–38 EC and hence fall outside the scope of the CFP unless: (a) their inclusion within the scope of secondary legislation made under the CFP is merely 'incidental'; and (b) such legislation applies 'essentially' to products included in Annex I and is 'an essential factor' in meeting the objectives of the CFP.

Secondly, it is important to note that the primary focus in the CN is on products rather than on, say, individual species. For example, in Chapter 3 of the CN, on 'Fish and crustaceans, molluscs and other aquatic invertebrates', one of the seven principal headings is 0302 entitled 'Fish, fresh or chilled, excluding fish fillets and other fish meat of heading 0304'. The wording of that heading illustrates the product focus of the CN. Under that heading, many of the entries are for named fish species. However, such species are only covered by that heading to the extent that they are made available to the market as 'fresh or chilled' fish.

The product-based focus of the CN has implications for deciding whether, or how, particular species are covered by the CFP and hence to what extent they may be the subject of secondary legislation adopted under the CFP. For example, if fish species [x] was only listed in the CN under heading 0302, ie 'fresh or chilled' fish, and was not covered by any inclusive 'Other' category in the CN, species [x] in other forms (for example, frozen or converted to oil) would not, in principle, be covered by the CFP. That in turn has implications for whether or how that species should be covered by the CFP at, say, the catching stage, ie the extent to which the EC is entitled, under the CFP, to adopt fisheries conservation rules for the fishery for that species.

In principle, the answer may depend on whether the tests established by the Court in *Commission v Council* and *United Kingdom v Commission* (see above) are met. Arguably, on the basis of those cases, it would be acceptable for a fisheries conservation Regulation adopted under the CFP to apply to fish species [x] irrespective of the type of product it was destined for if those products not covered by Annex I to the EC Treaty were merely 'incidental' in terms of, say, the amount to

---

[14] Case C-11/88 *Commission v Council* [1989] ECR 3799 (summary publication).
[15] Case C-180/96 *United Kingdom v Commission* [1998] ECR I-2265, paras 134 and 135 (and see generally paras 131–136).   [16] Case C-180/96, para 135.

which they contributed to the market or the amount of fish that were caught for those products. In practice, this issue may not arise often in respect of fish species. That is because, as noted below, fish are fairly comprehensively covered by Chapter 3 of the CN. However, that is not to say that the issue would never arise. Furthermore, the situation may potentially also arise for species other than fish, as is considered further below in respect of invertebrates.

The third general point to make is one arising from *Parliament v Council*. In that case the Court considered whether the live trees comprising forests were covered by (what is now) Annex I to the EC Treaty, by virtue of the phrase 'Live trees and other plants; bulbs, roots and the like; cut flowers and ornamental foliage' as used in the Annex. The Court excluded such trees, in general terms, from the scope of Annex I, by means of its interpretation of Chapter 6 of the CN (see above). However, by analogy, the question arises whether live animals in the marine environment might be covered in certain ways by the CFP by virtue of the phrase 'Live animals' used in Annex I to the EC Treaty.

The phrase 'Live animals' is also used in the heading of Chapter 1 of the CN. The notes to Chapter 1 state that the chapter covers all live animals except 'fish and crustaceans, molluscs and other aquatic invertebrates, of heading 0301, 0306 or 0307', 'cultures of micro-organisms and other products of heading 3002', and 'animals of heading 9508'. Chapter 1 expressly includes, *inter alia*, 'Whales, dolphins and porpoises (mammals of the order Cetacea); manatees and dugongs (mammals of the order Sirenia)' (CN code 0106 12 00) and turtles (0106 20 00). It also includes an 'Other' category (0106 90 00). Chapter 1 could therefore potentially include all living marine animals not covered by the exceptions set out in the notes to Chapter 1.

As such, it is arguable that Chapter 1 provides a means for the CFP to apply to the catching phase of such species, whilst they are still alive and present in the marine environment, irrespective of the products into which those species would then be converted. However, that result would broaden significantly the scope of the CFP and is likely to be highly contentious in some quarters.

In a policy document issued in 2007 on Community action in relation to whaling, the Commission stated that '[a]s "Live animals", cetaceans fall within the scope of Annex I to the EC Treaty and are subject to Articles 33 to 38 thereof'.[17] This raises some interesting points. The first is that the Commission is willing to invoke the inclusion of 'Live animals' in Annex I to the EC Treaty as a basis for inclusion of species within the scope of the CFP. If it is willing to do so in respect of cetaceans, would it be willing to do so with respect to other groups of animals not covered by the exceptions set out in the notes to Chapter 1 of the CN (see above)? The second point is that, in the case of cetaceans, the Commission did not

---

[17] *Communication from the European Commission to the European Parliament and to the Council on Community action in relation to whaling*, COM(2007) 823, 19.12.2007, para 19, p 7.

instead invoke the other means by which cetaceans are covered by Annex I (see further below).

The stance taken by the Commission in its 2007 policy document appears to have been carried through to a legislative proposal issued on the same date. The proposal in question was for a Council Decision establishing the position to be adopted on behalf of the EC in relation to the International Convention for the Regulation of Whaling. The Commission proposed that the Decision be based on Article 37 EC (and, *inter alia*, Article 175(1) EC), stating that 'cetaceans fall within the scope of Annex I to the EC Treaty and are subject to Articles 33 to 38 thereof' (although not mentioning the 'Live animals' consideration).[18] The Council did in turn adopt a Decision,[19] but this appears to have been solely on the basis of Article 175(1) EC to the exclusion of Article 37 EC, indicating that the Council rejected the Commission's proposed use of Article 37 EC.[20]

In its proposal for a similar Decision in 2008, the Commission decided not to seek to base the measure on Article 37 EC. The reason for the change of approach is not made explicit, but the Commission was careful to state that its decision was 'without prejudice' to the EC's exclusive competence 'in the field of the resources of the sea . . .' (see further Chapter 4) and did 'not create a precedent for any future negotiations about the conservation and management of living aquatic resources falling under the [Basic Regulation]'.[21] Presumably the Commission changed its approach in the 2008 proposal in view of its experience with the 2007 proposal. The fate of the 2007 proposal and the wording of the 2008 proposal suggest that, overall, the Council is concerned by the Commission's attempt to invoke Annex I to the EC Treaty, whether through the 'Live animals' route or otherwise, as a basis for adopting secondary legislation on cetaceans and is happier with reliance on Article 175(1) EC.

It is not impossible that EC secondary legislation on cetaceans, if it were to be based on the 'Live animals' heading in Annex I to the EC Treaty, might end up before the Court for a ruling on its validity (for example by a reference for a preliminary ruling under Article 234 EC). At that point, the Court would presumably turn to the CN, as it did in *Parliament v Council*. In the latter case, the Court was able to avoid considering the policy implications of the inclusion of live

---

[18] *Proposal for a Council Decision establishing the position to be adopted on behalf of the European Community with regard to proposals for amendments to the Schedule of the International Convention on* [sic] *the Regulation of Whaling*, COM(2007) 821, 19.12.2007, explanatory memorandum, para (5); see also proposed preamble.

[19] Council of the European Union, 2874th Council meeting, Environment, 5 June 2008, press release, 9959/08 (Presse 149), 15.

[20] Council of the European Union, document no 9818/08 (ENV 317, PECHE 114), 2 June 2008, pp 3 and 9.

[21] *Proposal for a Council Decision establishing the position to be adopted on behalf of the European Community with regard to proposals for amendments to the International Convention on* [sic] *the Regulation of Whaling and its Schedule*, COM(2008) 711, 6.11.2008, explanatory memorandum, para (11) and proposed recital (10).

trees comprising forests within the scope of the CAP by virtue of the clear exclusion in Note 1 at the start of Chapter 6 of the CN (see above). In the case of Chapter 1 of the CN, on 'Live animals', cetaceans are expressly *included* (see above). It remains to be seen what the Court would decide. An interpretation of the kind used by the Commission in relation to cetaceans in its 2007 policy document (see above) would potentially have implications for other groups of marine animals covered by Chapter 1 of the CN. An alternative, but more conservative, possibility would be to find that the phrase 'Live animals' in Annex I related only to animals that reached the market in live form.

The fourth general point to be made relates to Article 6 EC (see section 1 above), ie the duty to integrate environmental protection requirements into the definition and implementation of the CFP. The implementation of that duty is addressed in Chapter 4. However, the point to be made here is that environmental integration may result in a species being protected under the CFP despite the fact that the species in question does not itself fall within the products listed in Annex I to the EC Treaty.

There are some conceptual similarities between the application of the CFP to certain species by virtue of the implementation of Article 6 EC and the application of the CFP to certain products by virtue of the Court's conclusions in *Commission v Council* and *United Kingdom v Commission*. In particular, both in effect allow the material scope of secondary legislation adopted under the CFP to be expanded beyond Annex I products. However, there are also some important differences. Article 6 EC is a duty on the EC institutions, whereas the cases of *Commission v Council* and *United Kingdom v Commission* (merely) provide a power to those institutions to include non-Annex I products. The Court's case law referred to above relates to 'products' specifically, whereas the operation of Article 6 EC does not rely on that concept. The Court's case law requires any non-Annex I products covered by a measure to be 'incidental'. In contrast, Article 6 EC contains no equivalent requirement. However, in cases where Article 6 EC is being relied on to adopt a measure under the CFP that restricts the activities of fishing vessels exclusively or primarily for the purposes of environmental protection, questions may arise as to whether Article 37 EC is the appropriate legal basis for such a measure.[22]

Fish

Fish are covered by, *inter alia*, the following phrases used in Annex I to the EC Treaty: 'Fish, crustaceans and molluscs' (listed opposite a reference to Chapter 3 of the BN); 'Animal products not elsewhere specified or included; dead animals of Chapter 1 or Chapter 3, unfit for human consumption' (Chapter 5, heading 05.15);

---

[22] See further Owen, D, *Interaction Between the EU Common Fisheries Policy and the Habitats and Birds Directives*, IEEP Policy Briefing (Brussels: IEEP, 2004), available on the website of the Institute for European Environmental Policy (IEEP).

'Fats and oil, of fish and marine mammals, whether or not refined' (Chapter 15, heading 15.04); 'Preparations of meat, of fish, of crustaceans or molluscs' (Chapter 16); and 'Residues and waste from the food industries; prepared animal fodder' (Chapter 23). Of these five phases, the following text, for reasons of space, will address only the first, ie 'Fish, crustaceans and molluscs'.

The phrase 'Fish, crustaceans and molluscs' in Annex I to the EC Treaty has its equivalent in the heading of Chapter 3 of the CN, which reads 'Fish and crustaceans, molluscs and other aquatic invertebrates'. Thus, although one phrase is broader than the other in respect of invertebrates, both refer to 'Fish'. Chapter 3 of the CN does not contain a succinct definition of the term 'Fish'. Instead, it starts by setting out some categories, or products, of fish that are not covered by the chapter. Thus it states that the chapter does not cover, *inter alia*, 'fish (including livers and roes thereof) . . . dead and unfit or unsuitable for human consumption by reason of either their species or their condition' (because such products are covered by Chapter 5) or 'flours, meals or pellets of fish . . . unfit for human consumption' (because that is covered by Chapter 23).

Chapter 3 is structured by way of seven principal headings, the first five of which relate exclusively to fish. All five of those headings are focused on fish as products. They comprise: 'Live fish' (heading 0301); 'Fish, fresh or chilled, excluding fish fillets and other fish meat of heading 0304' (0302); 'Fish, frozen, excluding fish fillets and other fish meat of heading 0304' (0303); 'Fish fillets and other fish meat (whether or not minced), fresh, chilled or frozen' (0304); and 'Fish, dried, salted or in brine; smoked fish, whether or not cooked before or during the smoking process; flours, meals and pellets of fish, fit for human consumption' (0305). In practice, the products named in those headings appear to encompass the majority of fish products for human consumption.

The listings under each of the above five headings set out various groups or taxa of fish. In the case of headings 0302, 0303, and 0304, those listings are extensive. By virtue of the use of various levels of 'Other' categories, the overall impression is that all species of fish, whether marine or freshwater and whether bony or cartilaginous, are covered within each of the five headings and hence that the term 'Fish' in the phrase 'Fish, crustaceans and molluscs' in Annex I to the EC Treaty includes all fish species so long as they are in the form of products named in the headings 0301, 0302, 0303, 0304, and 0305 of the CN.

Crustaceans and molluscs

Crustaceans and molluscs are covered by, *inter alia*, the following phrases listed in Annex I to the EC Treaty: 'Fish, crustaceans and molluscs' (listed opposite a reference to Chapter 3 of the BN); 'Animal products not elsewhere specified or included; dead animals of Chapter 1 or Chapter 3, unfit for human consumption' (Chapter 5, heading 05.15); 'Preparations of meat, of fish, of crustaceans or molluscs' (Chapter 16); and 'Residues and waste from the food industries; prepared animal fodder' (Chapter 23). Of these four phrases, the following text, for reasons of space, will address only the first, ie 'Fish, crustaceans and molluscs'.

The phrase 'Fish, crustaceans and molluscs' in Annex I has its equivalent in the heading of Chapter 3 of the CN, which reads 'Fish and crustaceans, molluscs and other aquatic invertebrates'. Thus both refer to 'crustaceans' and 'molluscs'. (The additional reference in Chapter 3 to 'other aquatic invertebrates' is dealt with separately below.) As with 'Fish', Chapter 3 starts by setting out some types, or products, of crustaceans and molluscs that are not covered by the chapter. Thus it states that the chapter does not cover, *inter alia*, 'crustaceans, molluscs or other aquatic invertebrates, dead and unfit or unsuitable for human consumption by reason of either their species or their condition' (because such products are covered by Chapter 5) or 'flours, meals or pellets . . . of crustaceans, molluscs or other aquatic invertebrates, unfit for human consumption' (because that is covered by Chapter 23).

As noted above, Chapter 3 is structured by way of seven principal headings. Although the first five headings relate exclusively to fish, the last two, ie 0306 and 0307, relate to crustaceans and to molluscs and other aquatic invertebrates, respectively. Heading 0306, regarding crustaceans, reads as follows: 'Crustaceans, whether in shell or not, live, fresh, chilled, frozen, dried, salted or in brine; crustaceans, in shell, cooked by steaming or by boiling in water, whether or not chilled, frozen, dried, salted or in brine; flours, meals and pellets of crustaceans, fit for human consumption'.

Heading 0306 is in turn divided into 'Frozen' and 'Not frozen' categories. The subheadings in each of the those two categories are the same, namely 'Rock lobster and other sea crawfish (*Palinurus* spp., *Panulirus* spp., *Jasus* spp.)'; 'Lobsters (*Homarus* spp.)'; 'Shrimps and prawns'; 'Crabs'; and 'Other, including flours, meals and pellets of crustaceans, fit for human consumption'. The last of those headings comprises 'Freshwater crayfish', 'Norway lobsters (*Nephrops norvegicus*)', and 'Other'.

Heading 0307, regarding molluscs and other aquatic invertebrates, reads as follows: 'Molluscs, whether in shell or not, live, fresh, chilled, frozen, dried, salted or in brine; aquatic invertebrates other than crustaceans and molluscs, live, fresh, chilled, frozen, dried, salted or in brine; flours, meals and pellets of aquatic invertebrates other than crustaceans, fit for human consumption'.

The subheadings within heading 0307 comprise 'Oysters'; 'Scallops, including queen scallops, of the genera *Pecten*, *Chlamys* or *Placopecten*'; 'Mussels (*Mytilus* spp., *Perna* spp.)'; 'Cuttle fish (*Sepia officinalis*, *Rossia macrosoma*, *Sepiola* spp.) and squid (*Ommastrephes* spp., *Loligo* spp., *Nototodarus* spp., *Sepioteuthis* spp.)'; 'Octopus (*Octopus* spp.)'; 'Snails, other than sea snails'; and 'Other, including flours, meals and pellets of aquatic invertebrates other than crustaceans, fit for human consumption'.

By virtue of the use of various levels of 'Other' categories, the overall impression is that all species of crustacean and mollusc, whether marine or freshwater, are

covered within the two headings 0306 and 0307 and hence that the terms 'crustaceans' and 'molluscs' in the phrase 'Fish, crustaceans and molluscs' in Annex I to
the EC Treaty include all crustacean and mollusc species so long as they are in the
form of products named in the headings 0306 and 0307. In practice, the products
named in those headings probably encompass the majority of crustacean and
mollusc products for human consumption.

Other invertebrates

Annex I to the EC Treaty uses the phrase 'Fish, crustaceans and molluscs' whereas
Chapter 3 of the CN is entitled 'Fish and crustaceans, molluscs *and other aquatic
invertebrates*' (emphasis added). It is relevant to consider whether reference to the
CN could be used to imply that, today, the phrase 'Fish, crustaceans and molluscs'
in Annex I includes all aquatic invertebrates. That would widen the material scope
of the CFP considerably, since there is a huge array of marine invertebrate species
of potential commercial interest other than just crustaceans and molluscs (for
example corals, sea cucumbers, sea urchins, sponges, and tunicates).

Within Chapter 3 of the CN, 'other aquatic invertebrates' are addressed with
molluscs in heading 0307. The subheadings within 0307 have already been mentioned above. The one covering 'other aquatic invertebrates' follows six others
dealing exclusively with molluscs and reads: 'Other, including flours, meals and
pellets of aquatic invertebrates other than crustaceans, fit for human consumption'.
That subheading is in turn divided into two categories, namely 'Live, fresh or
chilled' and 'Other'. The use of various levels of 'Other' categories implies that the
subheading could cover any non-crustacean species of aquatic invertebrate so long
as they are in the form of products named in the heading 0307.

As noted above, the Court in *Parliament v Council* referred back to the *CILFIT*
case. In that case, the Court had stated: 'Since there are no Community provisions
explaining the concepts contained in [Annex I] to the [EC] Treaty *and that Annex
adopts word for word certain headings of the Common Customs Tariff*, it is appropriate to
refer to the established interpretations and methods of interpretation relating to the
Common Customs Tariff in order to interpret the Annex.'[23] (Emphasis added.)

Thus, in *CILFIT*, the Court had been prepared to look to the Common Customs Tariff (CCT) because the wording in (what is now) Annex I was, 'word for
word', the same as that in the CCT. Likewise, the Court in *Parliament v Council*
was dealing with a phrase from Annex I that was, word for word, the same as in the
CN. In endorsing reference to the CN, the Court in *Parliament v Council* was not
seeking to expand a phrase in Annex I to the EC Treaty to include a whole new
group. Instead, it was just seeking to understand whether the term 'Live trees [etc]'
in Annex I included living trees comprising forests.

It is notable that the Court in *Parliament v Council*, when referring to the *CILFIT*
case, did not itself note that the Annex 'adopts word for word certain headings of

---

[23] Case 77/83 *CILFIT*, para 7.

the Common Customs Tariff'. That perhaps suggests that the Court may not have regarded that particular aspect as so important. Thus it is arguable that the Court has developed the principle established by the *CILFIT* case such that resort to the CN for the purposes of interpretation no longer requires word for word parity between the phrases in Annex I to the Treaty and the chapter headings in the CN.

However, that does not necessarily equate to being prepared to imply inclusion of whole new groups into phrases in Annex I that, by their wording, do not relate to such groups. In other words, for example, it does not necessarily equate to being prepared to imply inclusion of 'other aquatic invertebrates' into the phrase 'Fish, crustaceans and molluscs' in Annex I. Such an approach could be regarded as seeking, in effect, to amend the EC Treaty by means of secondary legislation. Instead, the Court's approach in *Parliament v Council* may simply be allowing the terms 'Fish', 'crustaceans', and 'molluscs' to be interpreted by reference to the CN to the extent that those terms occur in the CN (as has been done above).

An example of a Regulation adopted under the CFP that refers to aquatic invertebrates other than crustaceans or molluscs is Regulation 104/2000 on the common organization of the markets in fishery and aquaculture products.[24] That Regulation states that 'fishery products' include, *inter alia*, 'aquatic invertebrates *other than* crustaceans and molluscs . . .' (emphasis added).[25] However, that reference (and others of a similar kind in the same Regulation) is effected merely by means of a cross-reference to the relevant CN code. Regulations in turn implementing the common organization of the markets (see Chapter 6) do not appear to address any specific aquatic invertebrates other than crustaceans or molluscs. A further example is provided by Regulation 3880/91.[26] This Regulation requires the submission by Member States to the Statistical Office of the European Communities of data on catches by their vessels of various species, including, *inter alia*, certain species of aquatic invertebrates other than crustaceans or molluscs.[27] However, whereas Regulation 3880/91 was adopted under the CFP, it is notable that the Commission has proposed that the successor for Regulation 3880/91 should be based on Article 285(1) EC,[28] which is the legal basis for 'measures for the production of statistics where necessary for the performance of the activities of the Community'.

---

[24] Council Regulation (EC) No 104/2000 of 17 December 1999 on the common organisation of the markets in fishery and aquaculture products, OJ 2000 L17/22, as amended and corrected.

[25] Reg 104/2000, Art 1, table.

[26] Council Regulation (EEC) No 3880/91 of 17 December 1991 on the submission of nominal catch statistics by Member States fishing in the north-east Atlantic, OJ 1991 L365/1, as amended. See also Reg 2597/95, OJ 1995 L270/1, as amended.   [27] Reg 3880/91, Arts 1 and 2 and Annex I.

[28] *Proposal for a Regulation of the European Parliament and of the Council on the submission of nominal catch statistics by Member States fishing in the north-east Atlantic (Recast)*, COM(2007) 763, 29.11.2007. See also COM(2007) 760, 29.11.2007.

To obtain certainty on whether or not aquatic invertebrates other than crustaceans or molluscs are covered by Annex I to the EC Treaty, a ruling of the Court would be required. The opportunity for such a ruling might arise if, by means of a direct action under Article 230 EC or a reference for a preliminary ruling under Article 234 EC, the Court were to be asked to rule on the validity of an act of the Commission or the Council, adopted under the CFP, aiming to regulate fisheries or markets for aquatic invertebrates other than molluscs and crustaceans. The existence of any such act to date does not necessarily mean that such practice is valid in EC law. Meanwhile, for the purposes of this chapter, it will be assumed that the products covered by the CFP do not include those of invertebrate species other than crustaceans or molluscs except to the extent that their inclusion within the scope of secondary legislation made under the CFP meets the tests established by the Court in *Commission v Council* and *United Kingdom v Commission* (see above).

Marine mammals

Introduction   When considered other than as 'Live animals' (on which, see above), marine mammals are covered by, *inter alia*, the following phrases listed in Annex I to the EC Treaty: 'Meat and edible meat offal' (listed opposite a reference to Chapter 2 of the BN); 'Animal products not elsewhere specified or included; dead animals of Chapter 1 or Chapter 3, unfit for human consumption' (Chapter 5, heading 05.15); 'Fats and oil, of fish and marine mammals, whether or not refined' (Chapter 15, heading 15.04); and 'Residues and waste from the food industries; prepared animal fodder' (Chapter 23).

'Meat and edible meat offal'   The phrase 'Meat and edible meat offal' in Annex I reads the same as the heading of Chapter 2 of the CN. One of the headings within Chapter 2 of the CN is 'Other meat and edible meat offal, fresh, chilled or frozen' (0208), which in turn includes the subheading 'Of whales, dolphins and porpoises (mammals of the order Cetacea); of manatees and dugongs (mammals of the order Sirenia)' (0208 40). Heading 0208 also includes the subheading 'Other' (0208 90), which in turn includes 'Seal meat' (0208 90 55).

Another of the headings within Chapter 2 is 'Meat and edible meat offal, salted, in brine, dried or smoked; edible flours and meals of meat or meat offal' (0210), which, after subheadings relating to pigs and cows, includes the subheading 'Other, including edible flours and meals of meat or meat offal'. That in turn includes, *inter alia*, 'Of whales, dolphins and porpoises (mammals of the order Cetacea); of manatees and dugongs (mammals of the order Sirenia)' (0210 92 00). It also includes an 'Other' category (0210 99) that could potentially include seals.

The implication is that the phrase 'Meat and edible meat offal' in Annex I to the EC Treaty, as it relates to marine mammals, includes, *inter alia*, all species of cetacean and sirenian so long as they are in the form of products covered by the CN codes 0208 40 and 0210 92 00 and all species of seal so long as they are in the form of products covered by the CN codes 0208 90 55 and 0210 99.

'Animal products not elsewhere specified or included [etc]'   The phrase 'Animal products not elsewhere specified or included; dead animals of Chapter 1 or Chapter 3, unfit for human consumption' in Annex I reads virtually the same as heading 0511 of Chapter 5 of the CN. Heading 0511 does not include ivory (including tusks of narwhal and walrus and teeth of marine mammals in general), whalebone, whalebone hair, or ambergris since those products are covered by other headings within Chapter 5 (ie 0507 and 0510 00 00).

Heading 0511 itself has the potential to cover some marine mammal products because of its use of 'Other' categories. However, the notes within Chapter 5 make it clear that the chapter does not cover 'hides or skins (including furskins)' (with some exceptions). Overall, the implication is that the phrase 'Animal products not elsewhere specified or included; dead animals of Chapter 1 or Chapter 3, unfit for human consumption' in Annex I to the EC Treaty has very limited application to marine mammals.

'Fats and oil, of fish and marine mammals, whether or not refined'   The phrase 'Fats and oil, of fish and marine mammals, whether or not refined' in Annex I has its equivalent in heading 1504 of Chapter 15 of the CN, which reads 'Fats and oils and their fractions, of fish or marine mammals, whether or not refined, but not chemically modified'. Thus, although the latter is both more expansive (by expressly including 'fractions') and more restrictive (by expressly requiring that the fats and oils are 'not chemically modified'), both phrases refer to fats and oil of marine mammals.

In respect of marine mammals, heading 1504 includes the subheading 'Fats and oils and their fractions, of marine mammals' (1504 30) which in turn is divided into 'Solid fractions' and 'Other'. The implication is that the phrase 'Fats and oil, of fish and marine mammals, whether or not refined' in Annex I to the EC Treaty, as it relates to marine mammals, includes all species of marine mammal so long as they are in the form of products covered by the CN code 1504 30.

'Residues and waste from the food industries; prepared animal fodder'   The phrase 'Residues and waste from the food industries; prepared animal fodder' in Annex I reads the same as the title of Chapter 23 of the CN. Chapter 23 includes nine principal headings. Those potentially relating to marine mammals include 'Flours, meals and pellets, *of meat or meat offal*, of fish or of crustaceans, molluscs or other aquatic invertebrates, unfit for human consumption; greaves' (2301; emphasis added) and 'Preparations of a kind used in animal feeding' (2309). The latter includes various 'Other' categories that could potentially apply to marine mammals, but it also includes a specific category entitled 'Fish or marine mammal solubles' (2309 90 10). The implication is that the phrase 'Residues and waste from the food industries; prepared animal fodder' in Annex I to the EC Treaty, as it relates to marine mammals, includes all species of marine mammal so long as they are in the form of products covered by the CN codes 2301 and 2309.

2.2 The term 'living aquatic resources'

The definition of the material scope of the CFP has been further developed by secondary legislation including, in particular, Regulation 2371/2002 (hereafter, 'the Basic Regulation').[29] The Basic Regulation introduces the term 'living aquatic resources'. That term is deployed initially in Article 1(1), which states, *inter alia*, that the CFP 'shall cover conservation, management and exploitation of *living aquatic resources*, aquaculture, and the processing and marketing of fishery and aquaculture products' (emphasis added).

Thus Article 1(1) of the Basic Regulation confines the use of the term 'living aquatic resources' to that part of the CFP dealing with 'conservation, management and exploitation'. The term is not associated with the other activities listed in Article 1(1), namely aquaculture and processing and marketing. In the case of aquaculture, no qualifying term is used. In the case of processing and marketing, those activities are linked to 'fishery and aquaculture products'. That in turn suggests that the term 'living aquatic resources' is intended to relate to the catching stage rather than subsequent stages in the supply chain and is not intended to limit the species that may be the subject of aquaculture.

The term 'living aquatic resources' is defined by Article 3(b) of the Basic Regulation as 'available and accessible living marine aquatic species, including anadromous and catadromous species during their marine life'. (The term is not formally defined in the Commission's legislative proposal for the Basic Regulation;[30] the definition provided in Article 3(b) was also used in the predecessor to the current Basic Regulation, albeit for the term 'resources'.[31]) This subsection will focus on several aspects of the definition in Article 3(b).

First, it is necessary to point out that the term 'living aquatic resources' must be interpreted in the light of the EC Treaty. Thus the term cannot lead to the inclusion of species within the scope of the CFP other than those that anyway fall within the CFP's scope by virtue of the EC Treaty and its interpretation by the Court (on which, see subsection 2.1 above). For example, subject to any 'incidental' inclusion permissible pursuant to *Commission v Council* and *United Kingdom v Commission*, the term cannot, on the basis of the assumption made in subsection 2.1 above, apply to species of aquatic invertebrates other than crustaceans or molluscs. That is corroborated by the explanatory memorandum to the Commission's legislative proposal for the Basic Regulation, which states that '[t]he

---

[29] Council Regulation (EC) No 2371/2002 of 20 December 2002 on the conservation and sustainable exploitation of fisheries resources under the Common Fisheries Policy, OJ 2002 L358/59, as amended and corrected.

[30] *Proposal for a Council Regulation on the conservation and sustainable exploitation of fisheries resources under the Common Fisheries Policy*, COM(2002) 185, 28.5.2002, explanatory memorandum, p 2.

[31] Council Regulation (EEC) No 3760/92 of 20 December 1992 establishing a Community system for fisheries and aquaculture, OJ 1992 L389/1, as amended (and now repealed), Art 3(b).

Common Fisheries Policy . . . should cover all activities which exploit fish, crustaceans and molluscs (referred to in the proposal as living aquatic resources)'.[32]

Secondly, the term is defined by reference to aquatic species that are marine or are in the marine phase of their lifecycle. Thus, despite the possibilities provided by the CN for the CFP to cover the conservation of freshwater species, the definition of 'living aquatic resources' appears to indicate a political decision by the Council for the time being for the conservation provisions of the CFP to relate only to the marine environment. This contrasts with the approach taken in respect of the European Fisheries Fund, the regulation of aquaculture, and the common organization of the markets in fishery and aquaculture products (on which, see subsection 3.2 below).

However, that limitation may be changing. In a Communication on the *Development of a Community Action Plan for the management of European Eel* issued in 2003[33] the Commission proposed action at the EC level to conserve and manage European eel. This species is catadromous, meaning it migrates regularly between the marine environment and fresh water and breeds in the former. The Commission noted that the definition of 'living aquatic resources' in the Basic Regulation 'would seem to exclude the management of eels during their fresh water life from the scope of [the Basic Regulation]'.[34] However, that observation did not deter the Commission. It stated that:[35]

Community management of eels during their marine life alone would clearly be insufficient, since most human activities that affect eels take place in fresh waters. It must be said, in this context, that the spirit of [the Basic Regulation] is clearly to bring all living aquatic resources, including catadromous species, under the scope of Community action *when and where necessary*. From that point of view, the Commission believes that [the Basic Regulation] *does not constitute a barrier* to the management of eels, including during their fresh water life, at Community level. [Emphasis added.]

The Commission's position seems confused. On the one hand, it is saying that the definition of 'living aquatic resources' *is* a barrier and, on the other hand, it is saying that it is *not*. The Commission goes on to state that 'Community competence in the management of eels may be inferred *directly* from the EC Treaty (in particular, Article 37)' (emphasis added).[36] It is correct that ultimately EC competence under the CFP stems from the EC Treaty. However, as noted above, the Council has chosen to limit its own powers in the field of 'conservation, management and exploitation' to 'living aquatic resources', with the constraints that the definition of the latter term brings. In any event, the Commission seems rather unsure of its stated position because it goes on to state that, 'in order to bring more clarity to the relevant legal texts', it intends to propose an amendment to the

---

[32] COM(2002) 185, explanatory memorandum, p 2.

[33] *Communication from the Commission to the Council and the European Parliament: Development of a Community Action Plan for the management of European Eel*, COM(2003) 573, 01.10.2003.

[34] COM(2003) 573, section 5.1, p 6.   [35] Ibid.   [36] Ibid.

definition of 'living aquatic resources' to remove the words 'during their marine life' in respect of catadromous species.[37]

In 2005, the Commission issued a legislative proposal for a Council Regulation establishing measures for the recovery of the stock of European eel.[38] The explanatory memorandum to that proposal makes no reference to the limitations imposed by the definition of 'living aquatic resources' in the Basic Regulation. Instead the only mention of legal basis is as follows: 'Measures to protect eel stocks fall under Article 37 of the Treaty, as are [sic] considered to be agricultural products for the purposes of this Treaty Article.'[39] Thus the Commission appears to be relying on its view, expressed in its 2003 policy paper, that EC competence in eel management 'may be inferred *directly* from the EC Treaty (in particular, Article 37)' (see above; emphasis added).

In 2007 the Council adopted a Regulation based on the Commission's legislative proposal.[40] Like the latter, it was based on Article 37 EC—the standard basis for secondary legislation adopted under the CFP. Furthermore, reflecting the legislative proposal, it contained no amendment to the Basic Regulation's definition of 'living aquatic resources' to remove the words 'during their marine life' in respect of catadromous species. The Regulation clearly applies to the conservation of eels in, *inter alia*, the freshwater environment. For example, its stated purpose to establish 'a framework for the protection and sustainable use of the stock of European eel . . . in Community waters, in coastal lagoons, in estuaries, *and in rivers and communicating inland waters* of Member States that flow into the seas in ICES areas III, IV, VI, VII, VIII, IX or into the Mediterranean Sea' (emphasis added).[41]

If, as it appears, the Regulation does indeed seek to side-step the constraint arising from the definition of 'living aquatic resources' in the Basic Regulation, and if the Commission and the Council believe that this constraint can be avoided as and when necessary, one wonders what other constraining aspects of the Basic Regulation may be avoided in the future by the EC institutions when it suits them. It remains to be seen whether the Commission will seek to use the current review of the CFP (on which, see Chapters 1 and 4) to amend the definition of 'living aquatic resources', or any equivalent term adopted pursuant to the Treaty of Lisbon, to remove the constraint that currently applies in respect of the freshwater environment. In the interests of legal certainty, such an amendment would perhaps be preferable to the EC institutions making derogations at will from the Basic Regulation.

It should be added that at least two fisheries conservation Regulations unrelated to European eel include reference to freshwater species. Regulation 2103/2004

---

[37] Ibid.

[38] *Proposal for a Council Regulation establishing measures for the recovery of the stock of European Eel,* COM (2005) 472, 6.10.2005.   [39] COM(2005) 472, explanatory memorandum, section 3, p 4.

[40] Council Regulation (EC) No 1100/2007 of 18 September 2007 establishing measures for the recovery of the stock of European eel, OJ 2007 L248/17.   [41] Reg 1100/2007, Art 1(1).

envisages that freshwater fish may be the target of fisheries in subdivisions 22–32 of the Baltic Sea and hence establishes codes for the reporting of effort in such fish-eries.[42] Regulation 2847/93 likewise requires, or required, effort reports relating to fisheries for freshwater fish in the Baltic Sea.[43] The inclusion of reference to freshwater fish in these two Regulations may be attributable to the fact that in parts of the Baltic Sea the salinity is so low that freshwater fish may be present and, as such, are regarded for the sake of convenience as 'marine' species.

A third point to make about the definition of the term 'living aquatic resources' is that it relates to species that are 'available and accessible'. That term is not defined in the Basic Regulation. Of note, it was not present at all in the Com-mission's legislative proposal for that Regulation[44] although it had been used previously in the definition of the term 'resources' in Regulation 3760/92.[45] One possibility is that the Commission may have wished to drop the term during the 2002 reform of the CFP but that it then got reintroduced by the Council.

The term 'available and accessible' (or 'available or accessible') is used in EC legislation in fields other than the CFP, for example in the context of informa-tion,[46] technology,[47] media for information transfer to the public or consumers,[48] data,[49] and evidence.[50] However, none of those usages throws much light on the interpretation of the term in the context of fisheries resources. In the fisheries context, 'available' could mean available in terms of the resource base itself, and 'accessible', as a qualification to 'available', could mean accessible in terms of the regime governing access to that resource base (for example catch and effort limits, technical measures, and nature conservation designations).

It should also be added that some Regulations adopted under the CFP use variants on the theme of 'living aquatic species'. Regulation 1967/2006,[51] on the

[42] Commission Regulation (EC) No 2103/2004 of 9 December 2004 concerning the transmission of data on certain fisheries in the western waters and the Baltic Sea, OJ 2004 L365/12, Annex III, Tables 2 and 4 and Annex IV, Table 2.

[43] Council Regulation (EEC) No 2847/93 of 12 October 1993 establishing a control system applicable to the common fisheries policy, OJ 1993 L261/1, as amended, Art 19i. The provisions cited in this footnote and the previous one are linked to Reg 779/97, OJ 1997 L113/3, as corrected, which was repealed by Reg 1098/2007, OJ 2007 L248/1. The ongoing validity of the cited provisions is therefore not entirely clear.   [44] COM(2002) 185.

[45] Reg 3760/92, Art 3(b).   [46] Reg 62/2006, OJ 2006 L13/1, Annex, para 4.2.12.1.

[47] Commission Decision of 21.12.2004 declaring a concentration to be compatible with the com-mon market (Case No COMP/M.3605—Sovion/HMG) according to Council Regulation (EC) No 139/2004, para 141.

[48] Dir 2002/92, OJ 2003 L9/3, as corrected, Art 13(1)(a); Dir 2002/65, OJ 2002 L271/16, as amended, Arts 5(1) and 6(6); Dir 1999/44, OJ 1999 L171/12, Art 6(3).

[49] Reg 322/97, OJ 1997 L52/1, as amended, Art 6; Dec 93/464, OJ 1993 L219/1, Art 5.

[50] Reg 1768/95, OJ 1995 L173/14, as amended and corrected, Art 14(1)(b).

[51] Council Regulation (EC) No 1967/2006 of 21 December 2006 concerning management meas-ures for the sustainable exploitation of fishery resources in the Mediterranean Sea, amending Regulation (EEC) No 2847/93 and repealing Regulation (EC) No 1626/94, OJ 2006 L409/11, as corrected (corrected version reissued as OJ 2007 L36/6).

Mediterranean Sea, uses the term 'living aquatic *organisms*' (emphasis added) in addition to 'living aquatic resources'. The former term is used on three occasions, all of which are rather specific.[52] It is not clear whether the use of that term, as an alternative to 'living aquatic resources', is intentional or a drafting error. Despite the occasional use of the term 'living aquatic organisms', the scope of Regulation 1967/2006 with regard to conservation, management, and exploitation activities is still defined by reference to 'living aquatic resources' (as with the Basic Regulation).[53]

Regulation 708/2007, on 'use of alien and locally absent species in aqua-culture',[54] uses the term 'aquatic organism'. In dealing with aquaculture specific-ally, it is not surprising that the Regulation does not use the term 'living aquatic resources' at all (see above). Instead, the Regulation is to cover 'all alien and locally absent aquatic organisms farmed'.[55] The term 'aquatic organisms' is defined very broadly, as 'any species living in water belonging to the animalia, plantae and protista kingdoms, including any part, gametes, seeds, eggs or propagules of their individuals that might survive and subsequently reproduce'.[56] Despite its apparent inclusiveness, this term would need to be interpreted compatibly with Annex I to the EC Treaty and its interpretation by the Court (on which see subsection 2.1 above) in view of the Regulation having been adopted under the CFP.

2.3 Treaty of Lisbon

The Treaty of Lisbon, which is known in full as the Treaty of Lisbon amending the Treaty on European Union and the Treaty establishing the European Commu-nity,[57] sets out many changes to the current Treaty on European Union and the current EC Treaty. The EC Treaty itself would become the Treaty on the Functioning of the European Union (hereafter, 'the FEU Treaty').[58] This book is concerned with developments as at the end of November 2008, and at that time the Treaty of Lisbon, and hence the FEU Treaty, was not in force. However, this subsection will nonetheless examine briefly some aspects of the Treaty of Lisbon that, if or when it enters in force, would be relevant to the material scope of the CFP.

First, the Treaty of Lisbon would make changes to the Agriculture Title of the EC Treaty. In the resulting FEU Treaty, the 'Agriculture' Title would become the 'Agriculture and Fisheries' Title.[59] Articles 32, 36, and 37 EC would be amended

---

[52] Reg 1967/2006, Art 20(1) and (2) and Art 21.   [53] Reg 1967/2006, Art 1(1)(a).
[54] Council Regulation (EC) No 708/2007 of 11 June 2007 concerning use of alien and locally absent species in aquaculture, OJ 2007 L168/1, as amended.   [55] Reg 708/2007, Art 2(3).
[56] Reg 708/2007, Art 3(4).   [57] Signed at Lisbon, 13 December 2007, OJ 2007 C306.
[58] Treaty of Lisbon, Art 2(1).   [59] Treaty of Lisbon, Art 2(46).

by the Treaty of Lisbon.[60] However, the amendments would not remove the existing reference, in (what is currently) Article 32(3) EC, to Annex I to the EC Treaty; that reference would likewise be present in the FEU Treaty. Thus, under the FEU Treaty, the products subject to the provisions of the Agriculture and Fisheries Title would continue to be those listed in Annex I (on which see sub-section 2.1 above). Annex I itself would not be changed by the Treaty of Lisbon.

Secondly, as noted in Chapter 1, the FEU Treaty would include a provision listing the areas in which the EU 'shall have exclusive competence'.[61] One of the listed areas is 'the conservation of marine biological resources under the common fisheries policy'. The FEU Treaty would also include a provision listing areas of shared competence, to include, *inter alia*, 'agriculture and fisheries, excluding the conservation of marine biological resources'.[62]

The term 'marine biological resources' is not used in the EC Treaty or in the Basic Regulation. However, it will be recalled from Chapter 1 that the 1972 Act of Accession, in Article 102, uses the term 'the biological resources of the sea'. As can be seen, the latter is very similar to 'marine biological resources'. Equally, the French version of the Treaty of Lisbon, for 'marine biological resources', uses 'ressources biologiques de la mer'; the latter term—word-for-word—is used in the French version of Article 102 of the 1972 Act of Accession. This evidence, although not representing a comprehensive tour of the relevant languages prevailing in 1972, suggests that the term 'marine biological resources' in the Treaty of Lisbon is merely intended to continue the approach taken in the 1972 Act of Accession.

It should be added that, as noted above, the FEU Treaty uses the term 'marine biological resources' in the phrase 'the conservation of marine biological resources *under the common fisheries policy*' (emphasis added). The reference to the CFP is a link to the Agriculture and Fisheries Title of the FEU Treaty, implying that the term 'marine biological resources' is to be construed in the light of that Title which, as noted above, retains a reference to Annex I. In other words, consistent with the above language-based evidence, it is strongly arguable that the term 'marine biological resources' in the FEU Treaty is to be interpreted as meaning only those products that fall within the material scope of the CFP by virtue of Annex I.

3 Geographical scope

3.1 Territories to which the CFP applies

Introduction

In principle, the territorial scope of the CFP is the same as that of the EC Treaty. That proposition was confirmed by the Court in 1978 in *Commission v Ireland*, a

---

[60] Treaty of Lisbon, Art 2(47)–(49).   [61] Treaty of Lisbon, Art 2(12); FEU Treaty, Art 3.
[62] Treaty of Lisbon, Art 2(12); FEU Treaty, Art 4.

fisheries case. In that case, in relation to EC Regulations in general and Regulation 101/76 (now no longer in force) in particular, the Court stated that: 'As institutional acts adopted on the basis of the [EC] Treaty, the Regulations apply in principle to the same geographical area as the [EC] Treaty itself.'[63]

Provisions on the territorial scope of the EC Treaty are contained in its Article 299. Those provisions will be addressed in turn in this subsection. The starting point is Article 299(1), which states that the EC Treaty applies to the twenty-seven Member States listed therein.[64] The remaining provisions of Article 299 relate to localities, inside or outside Europe, that are linked to the Member States to varying degrees.

Article 299(2) EC

Article 299(2) relates to the French overseas departments, the Azores, Madeira, and the Canary Islands, which are often referred to in secondary legislation and in policy documents as 'the outermost regions'. The French overseas departments comprise French Guiana, Guadeloupe, Réunion, and Martinique. The Azores and Madeira are part of Portugal; the Canary Islands are part of Spain.

Article 299(2) confirms that the EC Treaty's provisions apply to the outermost regions.[65] However, its second paragraph requires the Council, acting by the consultation procedure, to 'adopt specific measures aimed, in particular, at laying down the conditions of application of the present Treaty to those regions, including common policies'.[66]

In doing so, the Council is to take into account: (a) 'the structural social [sic] and economic situation of the [outermost regions], which is compounded by their remoteness, insularity, small size, difficult topography and climate, economic dependence on a few products, the permanence and combination of which severely restrain their development';[67] and (b) 'the special characteristics and constraints of the outermost regions without undermining the integrity and the coherence of the Community legal order, including the internal market and common policies'.[68]

The application of Article 299(2) to fisheries is expressly mandated by the third paragraph of that provision, which states that:

The Council shall, when adopting the relevant measures referred to in the second subparagraph, take into account areas such as customs and trade policies, fiscal policy, free zones, *agriculture and fisheries policies*, conditions for supply of raw materials and essential consumer goods, State aids and conditions of access to structural funds and to horizontal Community programmes. [Emphasis added.]

Thus the CFP does apply to the outermost regions, but its application there is to take into account the factors set out in Article 299(2). In cases where Regulations

---

[63] Case 61/77 *Commission v Ireland* [1978] ECR 417, para 46.
[64] 2005 Act of Accession, OJ 2005 L157/203, Art 17.   [65] Art 299(2) EC, 1st para.
[66] Art 299(2) EC, 2nd para.   [67] Art 299(2) EC, 2nd para.   [68] Art 299(2) EC, 4th para.

adopted by the Council under the CFP apply exclusively or primarily to the outermost regions, the cited legal basis for such Regulations is usually both Article 37 EC and Article 299(2) EC.[69] In cases where the outermost regions are covered as part of a broader approach by a Council Regulation made under the CFP it is quite common for only Article 37 EC to be specified as the legal basis.[70] However, some Regulations establishing a broad approach as well as including one or more specific provisions on the outermost regions specify both Article 37 EC and Article 299(2) EC as the legal basis.[71]

A good example of how the application of the CFP to the outermost regions differs compared to its conventional application is provided by Regulation 1954/2003 on so-called 'Western waters' (see further Chapter 4). Article 5(1) of that Regulation provides that: 'In the waters up to 100 nautical miles from the baselines of the Azores, Madeira and the Canary Islands, the Member States concerned may restrict fishing to vessels registered in the ports of these islands, except for Community vessels that traditionally fish in those waters in so far as these do not exceed the fishing effort traditionally exerted.' In contrast, the access restriction in 'metropolitan' Community waters is far less generous to coastal Member States (see Chapter 4).

Article 299(3) EC

The first paragraph of Article 299(3) states that: 'The special arrangements for association set out in Part Four of this Treaty shall apply to the overseas countries and territories listed in Annex II to this Treaty.' The abbreviation 'OCT' is often used to describe the overseas countries and territories listed in Annex II, and will be used in this book. There are currently twenty-one OCTs, including twelve linked to the UK,[72] six linked to France,[73] two linked to the

---

[69] See, for example, Council Regulation (EC) No 791/2007 of 21 May 2007 introducing a scheme to compensate for the additional costs incurred in the marketing of certain fishery products from the outermost regions the Azores, Madeira, the Canary Islands, French Guiana and Réunion, OJ 2007 L176/1; and Council Regulation (EC) No 639/2004 of 30 March 2004 on the management of fishing fleets registered in the Community outermost regions, OJ 2004 L102/9, as amended.

[70] See, for example, Council Regulation (EC) No 1198/2006 of 27 July 2006 on the European Fisheries Fund, OJ 2006 L223/1; and Reg 104/2000 (on the common organization of the markets in fishery and aquaculture products).

[71] See, for example, Council Regulation (EC) No 1954/2003 of 4 November 2003 on the management of the fishing effort relating to certain Community fishing areas and resources and modifying Regulation (EC) No 2847/93 and repealing Regulations (EC) No 685/95 and (EC) No 2027/95, OJ 2003 L289/1 (at the time of writing this Regulation was the subject of ongoing litigation: see further Chapter 4); and Reg 708/2007.

[72] Anguilla, Cayman Islands, Falkland Islands, South Georgia and the South Sandwich Islands, Montserrat, Pitcairn, Saint Helena and Dependencies, British Antarctic Territory, British Indian Ocean Territory, Turks and Caicos Islands, British Virgin Islands, and Bermuda.

[73] New Caledonia and Dependencies, French Polynesia, French Southern and Antarctic Territories, Wallis and Futuna Islands, Mayotte, and Saint Pierre and Miquelon.

Netherlands,[74] and one linked to Denmark (ie Greenland, which was part of the EC until 1985).

The 'special arrangements for association' referred to in Article 299(3) are those set out in Articles 182–188 EC. In order to understand whether or not the CFP applies to the OCTs, it is therefore necessary to analyse briefly Articles 182–188 EC, and any relevant secondary legislation made under them, to see whether or not the association they provide for includes any application of the CFP.

Article 182 states that the Member States agree to associate the OCTs with the EC. It notes that the purpose of association is to 'promote the economic and social development of the countries and territories and to establish close economic relations between them and the Community as a whole'.[75] Association is to 'serve primarily to further the interests and prosperity of the inhabitants of these countries and territories in order to lead them to the economic, social and cultural development to which they aspire'.[76]

Article 183 sets out five objectives of association. Those relate to trade between the Member States and the OCTs, investment in the OCTs, participation in tenders and supplies in respect of investments financed by the EC, and the right of establishment. In general, the focus of the objectives is on equal treatment. Regarding fisheries, the objectives have the potential to relate to, in particular, trade in fishery products between the OCTs and the Member States as well as the development of fishing infrastructure within the OCTs.

Articles 184 and 185 relate to customs duties, the former affording some special treatment to the OCTs. The provisions of Articles 184 and 185 have the potential to relate to trade in fishery products (on which, see Chapter 7). Article 186 relates to freedom of movement of workers. Article 187 requires the Council to 'lay down provisions as regards the detailed rules and the procedure for the association of the [OCTs] with the Community'. It is to do so acting unanimously and 'on the basis of the experience acquired under the association of the [OCTs] with the Community and of the principles set out in this Treaty'.

The current Council Decision made under Article 187 is Decision 2001/822,[77] which will remain in force until 2013.[78] That Decision responded in part to a Declaration adopted in 1997 in which the conference of the Member States adopting the Treaty of Amsterdam invited the Council, acting in accordance with

---

[74] Aruba and Netherland Antilles.   [75] Art 182 EC, 2nd para.

[76] Art 182 EC, 3rd para. See further EC Treaty, 7th recital and Art 3(1)(s) EC.

[77] Council Decision 2001/822/EC of 27 November 2001 on the association of the overseas countries and territories with the European Community, OJ 2001 L314/1, as amended and corrected. See also derogations regarding fishery products in Commission Decs 2007/767, OJ 2007 L310/19; 2007/167, OJ 2007 L76/32; 2005/578, OJ 2005 L197/31; 2003/673, OJ 2003 L243/106; 2002/644, OJ 2002 L211/16; and 2001/936, OJ 2001 L345/91.   [78] Dec 2001/822, Art 63.

(what is now) Article 187, 'to review the association arrangements by February 2000'.[79] Bermuda is not included within the scope of Decision 2001/822, at its own request.[80]

The Decision comprises four parts, of which the two major ones address 'The Areas of OCT-EC Cooperation' and 'Instruments of OCT-EC Cooperation'. The Decision starts by stating that the association of OCTs with the EC 'shall have as its basis the purpose set out in Article 182 [EC]' and 'shall pursue the objectives laid down in Article 183 [EC] . . . in accordance with the principles set out in Articles 184 to 188 [EC] . . . by focusing on the reduction, prevention and, eventually, eradication of poverty and on sustainable development and gradual integration into the regional and world economies'.[81]

A principal area of OCT-EC cooperation is trade including, in principle, trade in fishery products.[82] Fisheries merit express mention as one of several listed sectors for which '[c]ooperation shall support . . . policies and strategies that facilitate access to productive activities and resources'.[83] For fisheries, the areas to be supported include 'fishing policy and institution building, fish stock protection and rational management of fish stocks; fish farming and artisanal fisheries; fishery transport; cold storage and fish marketing and preservation'.[84]

The instruments of OCT-EC cooperation are development finance cooperation[85] and economic and trade cooperation.[86] Many of the Decision's provisions on those instruments are, in principle, applicable to fisheries. More specifically, one of the objectives of development finance cooperation is, 'through the provision of adequate financial resources and appropriate technical assistance',[87] to 'support the efforts of the OCTs to achieve economic diversification, *inter alia* by contributing to sustainable exploration, conservation, processing and exploitation of their natural resources'.[88] On economic and trade cooperation, the Decision makes some specific references to fisheries and fishery products (see further Chapter 7).[89]

Article 188 EC relates to Greenland (the OCT linked to Denmark). It states that: 'The provisions of Articles 182 to 187 shall apply to Greenland, *subject to* the specific provisions for Greenland set out in the Protocol on special arrangements

---

[79] Declaration on the Overseas Countries and Territories (Declaration No 36, annexed to the Final Act of the Conference of the Representatives of the Governments of the Member States signed in Amsterdam in 1997). See also Dec 2001/822, recital (2).

[80] Dec 2001/822, recital (22), Art 1(2), and Annex I A.   [81] Dec 2001/822, Art 1(1).

[82] Dec 2001/822, see, *inter alia*, Arts 12 and 14.   [83] Dec 2001/822, Art 11.

[84] Dec 2001/822, Art 11(c).   [85] Dec 2001/822, Part Three, Title I (Arts 18–33).

[86] Dec 2001/822, Part Three, Title II (Arts 34–60).   [87] Dec 2001/822, Art 18.

[88] Dec 2001/822, Art 18(f).

[89] Dec 2001/822, *inter alia*, Art 36(3)(a), Art 35 and Annex III (Art 3(1)(e), (f) and (g) and Art 3(2) and (3)), and Art 28(1) and Annex II A (Art 3(2)). See also Art 38(2), 1st para and Annex III (Art 4(1) and Appendix 2).

for Greenland, annexed to this Treaty.' (Emphasis added.) The said Protocol is very short. Part of it relates to fishery products.[90] The products in question are those subject to the common organization of the market in fishery products (on which, see Chapter 6). Such products, when originating in Greenland and imported into the EC, and if 'complying with the mechanisms of the common market organisation', may enjoy 'exemption from customs duties and charges having equivalent effect and the absence of quantitative restrictions or measures having equivalent effect' (on which, see Chapter 7). However, this is conditional on 'the possibilities for access to Greenland fishing zones granted to the Community pursuant to an agreement between the Community and the authority responsible for Greenland' being 'satisfactory to the Community'. Agreements on access by the EC to Greenland fishing zones are discussed further in Chapter 5.

Overall, it can be seen that Articles 182–188 EC, in combination with Decision 2001/822, provide for an important association between the OCTs and the EC. In the context of fisheries, both development finance cooperation and economic and trade cooperation are relevant to that association. However, it can be seen from the above brief survey that the association, despite addressing fisheries, does not include the application of the CFP to the OCTs. Since Article 299(3) applies the EC Treaty to the OCTs only by reference to Articles 182–188 EC, it can therefore be concluded that the CFP does not apply to the OCTs.

That does not mean, of course, that the CFP has no relevance to OCTs. For example there is trade in fishery products between the EC and OCTs. Chapter 7 considers the role of the CFP in regulating trade. The EC has a Fisheries Partnership Agreement with one of the OCTs, Greenland (on which, see Chapter 5). Community fishing vessels and Member State nationals, when operating in the waters of OCTs, are still potentially subject to CFP measures of general application, such as certain measures on conservation and on monitoring, control, and surveillance. However, in the latter respect, OCT waters are no different to third State waters.

The exclusion of the OCTs from the geographical scope of the CFP is reflected by secondary legislation made under the CFP. The Basic Regulation defines the term 'Community waters' (see subsection 3.2 below) as 'the waters under the sovereignty or jurisdiction of the Member States *with the exception of waters adjacent to the territories mentioned in Annex II to the [EC] Treaty*' (emphasis added).[91] It is notable that the above exception refers only to 'the territories' in Annex II, rather than to 'the territories and countries' therein. However, it seems more likely that this is a drafting error rather than reflecting an intention to make a distinction between, on the one hand, Annex II 'territories' and, on the other hand, Annex II

---

[90] EC Treaty, Protocol (No 15) on special arrangements for Greenland (1985), Art 1(1).
[91] Reg 2371/2002, Art 3(a).

'countries'. Regulation 1005/2008,[92] on illegal, unreported, and unregulated (IUU) fishing, refers to overseas 'territories and countries'. It states that 'IUU fishing within maritime waters of the overseas territories and countries referred to in Annex II of the [EC] Treaty shall be treated as taking place within maritime waters of third countries'.[93]

The second paragraph of Article 299(3) EC states that: 'This Treaty shall not apply to those overseas countries and territories having special relations with the United Kingdom of Great Britain and Northern Ireland which are *not* included in the aforementioned list [ie Annex II].' (Emphasis added.) It is not immediately clear which non-Annex II 'overseas countries and territories' are being referred to here. Article 299(4) EC (see below) deals with 'the *European* territories for whose external relations a Member State is responsible' (emphasis added), which implies that the second paragraph of Article 299(3) EC relates to *non*-European localities. Since the UK no longer has 'special relations' with any non-European countries or territories other than those listed in Annex II, the second paragraph of Article 299(3) EC would now appear to be redundant (but see further below, regarding the Treaty of Lisbon).

Article 299(4) and (5) EC

Article 299(4) states that: 'The provisions of this Treaty shall apply to the European territories for whose external relations a Member State is responsible.' There are various territories that fall into that category. In the case of the UK, such territories comprise Gibraltar, the Channel Islands, and the Isle of Man.

The Channel Islands and the Isle of Man are dealt with by a separate part of Article 299, on which see below. Gibraltar is not dealt with separately by Article 299; the implication is that the EC Treaty applies in its entirety to Gibraltar. However, Article 28 of the 1972 Act of Accession[94] sets out a specific provision on Gibraltar, whereby:

Acts of the institutions of the Community relating to the products in Annex II to the EEC Treaty and the products subject, on importation into the Community, to specific rules as a result of the implementation of the common agricultural policy, as well as the acts on the harmonisation of legislation of Member States concerning turnover taxes, shall *not* apply to Gibraltar unless the Council, acting unanimously on a proposal from the Commission, provides otherwise. [Emphasis added.]

The reference in Article 28 to 'Annex II' is a reference to what is now Annex I to the EC Treaty. Thus the wording '[a]cts of the institutions of the Community relating to the products in Annex II to the EEC Treaty' covers, *inter alia*,

---

[92] Council Regulation (EC) No 1005/2008 of 29 September 2008 establishing a Community system to prevent, deter and eliminate illegal, unreported and unregulated fishing, amending Regulations (EEC) No 2847/93, (EC) No 1936/2001 and EC No 601/2004 and repealing Regulations (EC) No 1093/94 and (EC) No 1447/1999, OJ 2008 L266/1.   [93] Reg 1005/2008, Art 1(3).

[94] 1972 Act concerning the conditions of accession and the adjustments to the treaties, OJ 1972 L73.

Community measures adopted under the CFP (see subsection 2.1 above). Furthermore, the Council has not, to the authors' knowledge, acted to amend the effect of Article 28. Since Article 299(4) EC remains subject to Article 28,[95] the result in principle is that the CFP does not currently apply to Gibraltar.

However, in *Commission v United Kingdom*, the Court stated that '[a]s an exception to the application of Community law in the territory of the Community, [Article 28] must be given an interpretation which limits its scope to that which is strictly necessary to safeguard the interests which it allows Gibraltar to protect' and that '[Article 28] must also be read in the light of the second sentence of the first paragraph of Article 10 EC, pursuant to which the Member States are required to facilitate the achievement of the Community's tasks'.[96] It remains to be seen whether the Commission might seek to use those points to justify, say, fisheries conservation measures for the waters adjacent to Gibraltar.

Article 299(5) states that: 'The provisions of this Treaty shall apply to the Åland Islands in accordance with the provisions set out in Protocol 2 to the Act concerning the conditions of accession of the Republic of Austria, the Republic of Finland and the Kingdom of Sweden.' The Åland Islands are located in the Baltic Sea, and are subject to the sovereignty of Finland.

The Protocol in question starts by stating that '[t]aking into account the special status that the Åland islands enjoy under international law, the Treaties on which the European Union is founded shall apply to the Åland islands with the following derogations . . .'. The derogations that follow relate to certain forms of taxation[97] as well as the right to acquire and hold real property, the right of establishment, and the right to provide services.[98] Although the derogations regarding rights may be relevant to certain CFP commercial operators, it can be seen that, other than that, the Protocol does not prevent the application of the CFP to the Åland Islands.

Article 299(6) EC

The provisions of Article 299(6) are all stated to apply '[n]otwithstanding the preceding paragraphs' of Article 299. In other words, Article 299(6) applies despite the provisions of Article 299(1) to (5). Article 299(6)(a) relates to the Faroe Islands, which are located in the north-east Atlantic and are an autonomous region of Denmark. It states simply that 'this Treaty shall not apply to the Faroe Islands'. Thus, despite the inclusive effect of Article 299(4), the CFP does not apply to the Faroe Islands. The EC has a fisheries access agreement with the Faroe Islands (see Chapter 5).

Article 299(6)(b) relates to the United Kingdom Sovereign Base Areas of Akrotiri and Dhekelia in Cyprus (hereafter, 'the SBAs'). Both the SBAs have

---

[95] Eg see Case C-349/03 *Commission v United Kingdom* [2005] ECR I-7321, paras 41 and 42 and Case C-145/04 *Spain v United Kingdom* [2006] ECR I-7917, para 19.
[96] Case C-349/03, para 43.   [97] 1994 Act of Accession, Protocol No 2, OJ 1994 C241, Art 2.
[98] 1994 Act of Accession, Protocol No 2, Art 1.

coastlines and an adjacent territorial sea.[99] Article 299(6)(b) states that 'this Treaty shall *not* apply to the United Kingdom Sovereign Base Areas of Akrotiri and Dhekelia in Cyprus *except* to the extent necessary to ensure the implementation of the arrangements set out in [Protocol No 3 to the 2003 Act of Accession] and in accordance with the terms of that Protocol' (emphasis added).

The full title of Protocol No 3 is 'Protocol No 3 on the Sovereign Base Areas of the United Kingdom of Great Britain and Northern Ireland in Cyprus'. One effect of the protocol is to include the SBAs within the customs territory of the EC and to apply certain customs and common commercial policy acts to them.[100] However, Article 3(a) of Protocol No 3 adds that, *inter alia*, 'Title II of Part Three of the EC Treaty, on agriculture, and provisions adopted on that basis' apply to the SBAs. Since fisheries is included within the Agricultural Title of the EC Treaty (see section 1 above), Article 3(a) implies that the CFP applies to the SBAs. On that basis, the EC has the power to adopt CFP measures applicable to the SBAs. Such measures could include, for example, fisheries conservation measures for the territorial sea adjacent to the SBAs.

However, the Commission, in a statement about what provisions of EC law it understands to be included within the meaning of Article 3(a),[101] lists only two Regulations, one relating to trade in certain goods resulting from the processing of agricultural products and one relating to rural development in the SBAs. That suggests that, notwithstanding the wider language of Article 3(a), the Commission may only have in mind a very limited application of the Agriculture Title of the EC Treaty to the SBAs. It should be added that under certain conditions, the Council has a power to amend, *inter alia*, Article 3(a) or apply other provisions of EC legislation to the SBAs.[102]

The Protocol is careful to point out that: 'The arrangements provided for in this Protocol shall have the sole purpose of regulating the particular situation of the Sovereign Base Areas of the United Kingdom in Cyprus and shall not apply to any other territory of the Community, nor serve as a precedent, in whole or in part, for any other special arrangements which either already exist or which might be set up in another European territory provided for in Article 299 of the [EC] Treaty.'[103]

Article 299(6)(c) relates to the Channel Islands and the Isle of Man (hereafter, 'the Islands'). It states that 'this Treaty shall apply to the Channel Islands and the Isle of Man only to the extent necessary to ensure the implementation of the arrangements for those islands set out in the [1972 Treaty of Accession]'. As noted above, Article 299(6)(c) applies notwithstanding the previous paragraphs in Article

[99] 1960 Treaty concerning the establishment of the Republic of Cyprus, 382 UNTS 3, Annex C, section 1, para 1(g) and Annex A, section 3.

[100] 2003 Act of Accession, Protocol No 3, OJ 2003 L236/940, Art 2(1).

[101] Declaration by the European Commission, annexed to Protocol No 3 to the 2003 Act of Accession, OJ 2003 L236/944.   [102] 2003 Act of Accession, Protocol No 3, Art 6.

[103] 2003 Act of Accession, Protocol No 3, Art 8.

299, including, *inter alia*, Article 299(4). Therefore, the inclusive effect of Article 299(4) does not apply to the Islands, which are instead covered by Article 299(6)(c).

In practice, the 'arrangements' referred to in Article 299(6)(c) are those set out in 'Protocol No 3 on the Channel Islands and the Isle of Man' attached to the 1972 Act of Accession. The provision of Protocol No 3 of primary relevance to fisheries is Article 1. Article 1(1) states, *inter alia*, that: 'The Community rules on customs matters and quantitative restrictions . . . shall apply to [the Islands] under the same conditions as they apply to the United Kingdom.' One consequence of this is that the Islands are part of the customs territory of the EC, as confirmed most recently by Regulations 2913/92 and 450/2008,[104] which refer to 'the territory of the United Kingdom of Great Britain and Northern Ireland and of the Channel Islands and the Isle of Man' as being part of the EC customs territory.[105]

In *Jersey Produce Marketing Organisation*, the Court noted that Article 1(1) of Protocol No 3 'makes no distinction according to the nature of the goods concerned' and therefore concluded that 'the rules to which it refers are to be applied to all the goods usually covered by them. Since agricultural products listed in Annex II to the EEC Treaty (now Annex I to the EC Treaty) are not subject to any particular treatment in that regard, they fall within the scope of that paragraph'.[106] Impliedly, the same can be said of fishery products listed in Annex I to the EC Treaty (see subsection 2.1 above).

Article 1(2) of the Protocol states, in respect of 'agricultural products and products processed therefrom which are the subject of a special trade regime', that: (a) 'the levies and other import measures laid down in Community rules and applicable by the United Kingdom shall be applied to third countries';[107] and (b) '[s]uch provisions of Community rules . . . as are necessary to allow free movement and observance of normal conditions of competition in trade' are to be applicable.[108]

The Court in *Jersey Produce Marketing Organisation* held that '. . .Article 1(2) reflects, essentially, a concern to take proper account of the fact that, within the Community, agricultural products fall under the Common Agricultural Policy and may be subject in that regard to a certain number of specific rules. It is in view of that fact that Article 1(2) provides for the adoption of the measures judged necessary to ensure the proper operation of the regime put in place as regards the Channel Islands and the Isle of Man, in particular by making certain of those rules

---

[104] Council Regulation (EEC) No 2913/92 of 12 October 1992 establishing the Community Customs Code, OJ 1992 L302/1, as amended and corrected; Regulation (EC) No 450/2008 of the European Parliament and the Council of 23 April 2008 laying down the Community Customs Code (Modernised Customs Code), OJ 2008 L145/1.

[105] Reg 2913/92, Art 3(1); Reg 450/2008, Art 3(1).

[106] Case C-293/02 *Jersey Produce Marketing Organisation Ltd v States of Jersey and Jersey Potato Export Marketing Board* [2005] ECR I-9543, para 36.

[107] 1972 Act of Accession, Protocol No 3, Art 1(2), 1st para.

[108] 1972 Act of Accession, Protocol No 3, Art 1(2), 2nd para.

applicable to those territories'.[109] Again, impliedly, the same can be said of fishery products.

The Council, acting by a qualified majority on a proposal from the Commission, is to determine the conditions under which the provisions referred to in Article 1(2) of the Protocol are to be applicable to the Islands,[110] and indeed did so in respect of trade in agricultural products in Regulation 706/73 (which is still in force).[111] The latter, in Article 1, provides that EC rules applicable to the UK for trade in, *inter alia*, 'agricultural products covered by Annex II [now Annex I]' to the EC Treaty apply to the Islands, with some limited exceptions. Article 3 adds that EC provisions in certain fields apply under the same conditions as in the UK to Annex I products 'imported into [the Islands] or exported from [the Islands] to the Community', again with some limited exceptions. The fields in question are veterinary legislation; animal health legislation; plant health legislation; marketing of seeds and seedlings; food legislation; feedingstuffs legislation; and quality and marketing standards.

The statement in Article 299(6)(c) that the EC Treaty applies to the Islands 'only to the extent necessary to ensure the implementation of the arrangements for those islands set out in the [1972 Treaty of Accession]', coupled with the scope of Protocol No 3 and Regulation 706/73, implies that the only parts of the CFP applicable to the Islands are those relating to trade as well as those fields set out in Article 3 of Regulation 706/73 that fall under the CFP. On that basis, EC fisheries conservation rules do not apply to the Islands. Some doubt on this conclusion is, however, cast by the judgment of the Court in 1980 in *Commission v United Kingdom*.[112] In that case the Court had to rule on, *inter alia*, whether a UK measure establishing a quota and licensing system for herring fishing by UK and Manx vessels around the Isle of Man was contrary to EC law.

The UK government argued that the effect of Article 299(6) (or Article 227(5), as it then was) and Protocol No 3 was that 'only the provisions relating to the free movement of goods are applicable in relations with the Isle of Man so that the measures adopted by the Community relating to the protection of fish stocks do not extend to that territory and to the waters under its jurisdiction'.[113] The Commission, on the other hand, argued that '[i]n view of the close link as regards fisheries between the organization of the market and structural measures . . . Protocol No 3 must be interpreted as meaning that the conservation measures adopted by the Community are also applicable to Isle of Man waters'.[114]

[109] Case C-293/02 *Jersey Produce Marketing Organisation*, para 38.

[110] 1972 Act of Accession, Protocol No 3, Art 1(2), 3rd para.

[111] Regulation (EEC) No 706/73 of the Council of 12 March 1973 concerning the Community arrangements applicable to the Channel Islands and the Isle of Man for trade in agricultural products, OJ 1973 L68/1, as amended and corrected.

[112] Case 32/79 *Commission v United Kingdom* [1980] ECR 2403.   [113] Case 32/79, para 41.

[114] Case 32/79, para 42.

The Court avoided addressing either of these arguments, simply observing that '[i]t does not seem necessary to consider the constitutional position of the Isle of Man and the relationship of that territory to the Community'. Since the measure at issue was adopted by the UK government under UK legislation, 'the United Kingdom must take responsibility for that measure *vis-à-vis* the Community'.[115] The Court did not elaborate on that ambiguous statement. However, its subsequent points and its eventual finding against the UK measure in question imply that it was not prepared to accept that EC law regarding fisheries conservation, including procedural law, does not apply to the waters of the Isle of Man.

If the Court really did consider that EC law relating to fisheries conservation applied to Isle of Man waters, it should have reached such a conclusion explicitly through an interpretation of Protocol No 3. It is probably best to regard the Court's judgment as being of its time. During the period in question, which was before the Council adopted an EC fisheries management system in January 1983 (see Chapter 1), the Court was trying to limit the scope for unilateral management measures by Member States.

Support for a restrictive application of the CFP to the Islands, ie one constrained by the terms of Protocol No 3 and its implementing legislation, is provided by the case of *Barr and Montrose*, where the Court held in 1991 that Article 4 of Protocol No 3 (which provides that the authorities of the Islands 'shall apply the same treatment to all natural and legal persons of the Community') 'cannot be interpreted in such a way as to be used as an indirect means of applying on the territory of the Isle of Man provisions of Community law which are not applicable there by virtue of Article 227(5)(c) of the EEC Treaty [now Article 299(6)(c) EC] and Article 1 of Protocol No 3'.[116]

Evidence from the practice of the EC institutions and the Member States is ambiguous on the matter of whether or not EC fisheries conservation rules apply to the Islands. One Council Regulation adopted in 1977, and no longer applicable, contained fisheries conservation measures relating to Isle of Man waters.[117] Several

---

[115] Case 32/79, para 43. The Court made a similar observation in Case 804/79 *Commission v United Kingdom* [1981] ECR 1045 (para 40), the subject matter of which was much the same as that in Case 32/79.

[116] Case C-355/89 *Department of Health and Social Security v Barr and Montrose Holdings Ltd* [1991] ECR I-3479, para 16. The Court repeated its view, this time in respect of the Channel Islands, in Case C-171/96 *Roque v Lieutenant Governor of Jersey* [1998] ECR I-4607, paras 34 and 47.

[117] Regulation (EEC) No 1779/77 of the Council of 2 August 1977 laying down interim conservation and management measures for herring fishing in the Irish Sea, OJ 1977 L196/4, as amended. See also Case 32/79 *Commission v United Kingdom*: in para 44, the Court stated that Reg 1779/77 'involved the fixing of catch quotas and a seasonal fishing ban from 1 October to 19 November 1977 in a limited zone *covering the Isle of Man waters* and the waters between that island and the coast of Great Britain' (emphasis added).

Council Regulations define herring fisheries zones by reference to the Isle of Man,[118] but it is not clear from any of those Regulations whether the herring fisheries measures in question actually relate to Isle of Man waters. It should also be noted that the Isle of Man is one of the areas covered by the Hague Preferences (on which, see further Chapter 4).

As far as the practice of Member States is concerned, the UK has concluded three treaties with France relating to fishing by French fishermen in the waters around the Channel Islands and fisheries conservation and management in these waters.[119] Such agreements would not be legally possible if EC fisheries conservation measures applied to the Islands (see Chapter 5). As far as the authors are aware, the Commission has not objected to any of these agreements.

In conclusion, as already noted, the analysis above of Article 299(6)(c), Protocol No 3, and Regulation 706/73 suggests that EC fisheries conservation rules do *not* apply to the Islands. The case of *Barr and Montrose* and the practice of the UK regarding treaties with France corroborates that finding. However, the case of *Commission v United Kingdom*, the practice of the EC in terms of fisheries Regulations, and the inclusion of the Isle of Man as one of the Hague Preferences areas creates some doubt about whether EC fisheries conservation rules are not applicable. Overall, on the basis of the foregoing analysis, it must be concluded that it is not entirely clear whether or not EC fisheries conservation rules apply to the Islands.

Treaty of Lisbon

The Treaty of Lisbon was introduced in subsection 2.3 above. The following text will examine very briefly some aspects of the Treaty of Lisbon that, if or when it enters into force, would be relevant to the territories to which the CFP applies. As a result of the Treaty of Lisbon, the content of Article 299 EC would become covered by Article 52 of the (amended) Treaty on European Union and Articles 349 and 355 of the FEU Treaty. In general terms, the content of Article 299 EC as applied to the FEU Treaty would remain unchanged by the Treaty of Lisbon. The main difference compared to Article 299 EC is the list of outermost regions. In

---

[118] Reg 2723/99, OJ 1999 L328/9, Art 1(1); Reg 48/99, OJ 1999 L13/1, Art 13(4); Reg 850/98, OJ 1998 L125/1, Art 20(1)(f) and (g); Reg 894/97, OJ 1997 L132/1, Art 7(5) and (6); Reg 1796/94, OJ 1994 L187/1, Art 1(1); Reg 3676/93, OJ 1993 L341/1, Art 6(3) and (4); Reg 3919/92, OJ 1992 L397/1, Art 6(3) and (4); Reg 4047/89, OJ 1989 L389/1, Art 6(3) and (4); Reg 4194/88, OJ 1988 L369/3, Art 6(3) and (4); Reg 2756/85, OJ 1985 L259/68, Art 1(2); Reg 1/85, OJ 1985 L1/1, Art 6(5); Reg 320/84, OJ 1984 L37/1, Art 8(4); Reg 3624/83, OJ 1983 L365/1, Art 8(5); Reg 172/83, OJ 1983 L24/30, Art 8(7). (Many of these Regulations have since been repealed or amended.)

[119] Exchange of Notes concerning the Activities of Fishermen in the Vicinity of the Channel Islands and the French Coast of the Cotentin Peninsula and, in particular, on the Schole Bank, 1992, UK Treaty Series 1993 No 66; Exchange of Notes regarding Activities by Local Coastal Fishermen in the Vicinity of Guernsey and the French Coasts of the Cotentin Peninsula and of Brittany, 1994, UK Treaty Series 1995 No 37; and Agreement concerning Fishing in the Bay of Granville, 2000, UK Treaty Series 2004 No 9.

2007 Saint-Barthélemy and Saint-Martin voted to no longer be part of Guade-loupe; however, they have themselves become outermost regions. Therefore the FEU Treaty, when listing the outermost regions,[120] would include, Saint-Bar-thélemy and Saint-Martin in addition to Guadeloupe and the other existing out-ermost regions. It is noteworthy that the second paragraph of Article 299(3) EC would be reproduced in the second paragraph of Article 355(2) of the FEU Treaty, despite currently appearing to be redundant (see above). The FEU Treaty would include a provision enabling the European Council, on the initiative of the Member State concerned, to 'adopt a decision amending the status, with regard to the [European] Union' of a French outermost region or a Danish, Dutch, or French OCT.[121]

3.2 Zones under Member State jurisdiction to which the CFP applies

Having considered the territories to which the CFP applies, it is now necessary to consider the zones of such territories to which it applies. Article 1(1) of the Basic Regulation states that:

The Common Fisheries Policy shall cover conservation, management and exploitation of living aquatic resources, aquaculture, and the processing and marketing of fishery and aquaculture products where such activities are practised on the territory of Member States or in Community waters or by Community fishing vessels or, without prejudice to the primary responsibility of the flag State, nationals of Member States.

Thus the CFP covers 'conservation, management and exploitation of living aquatic resources', 'aquaculture', and 'the processing and marketing of fishery and aquaculture products'. It covers those things where they are practised: (a) 'on the territory of Member States'; (b) 'in Community waters'; (c) 'by Community fishing vessels'; or (d) 'by . . ., without prejudice to the primary responsibility of the flag State, nationals of Member States'. Of those, (a) and (b) will be discussed in this subsection and (c) and (d) will be discussed in section 4 below.

The phrase 'on the territory of Member States' is relatively straightforward. It means those parts of the Member State that are subject to its territorial sovereignty. In general, that includes the land territory, internal waters, and the territorial sea. The CFP's application to non-marine internal waters merits a mention here. Certain parts of the CFP, notably the common organization of the markets in fishery and aquaculture products, provisions regulating aquaculture, and the Euro-pean Fisheries Fund (EFF), clearly apply to such waters or to the products arising from them. (The matter of fisheries conservation in relation to non-marine internal waters is discussed in subsection 2.2 above.)

---

[120] FEU Treaty, Arts 355(1) and 349, 1st para.
[121] Treaty of Lisbon, Art 2(293)(e); FEU Treaty, Art 355(6).

The common organization of the markets in fishery and aquaculture products is discussed in Chapter 6. It will merely be pointed out here that the term 'fishery products' as used in Regulation 104/2000, which (re-)establishes the said common organization, is defined as 'both products caught at sea *or in inland waters* and the products of aquaculture listed below' (emphasis added).[122] Thus the common organization of the markets in fishery products includes, *inter alia*, certain products caught in inland waters.[123] As noted above, the CFP's provisions regulating aquaculture also apply to such waters; aquaculture is discussed in Chapter 9 and will not be dealt with further here.

The EFF is discussed in general terms in Chapter 8. Its application to non-marine internal waters will be mentioned briefly here. The EFF was established by Regulation 1198/2006 (hereafter, 'the EFF Regulation'). One provision of specific relevance to inland fishing is Article 33, in priority axis 2, which defines the term 'inland fishing' for its purposes as 'fishing carried out for commercial purposes by vessels operating exclusively in inland waters or by other devices used for ice fishing'.[124] However, other more general provisions of the EFF Regulation are also potentially relevant to non-marine internal waters. These include priority axis 4 on sustainable development of fisheries areas,[125] in view of the term 'fisheries area' being defined as including, *inter alia*, 'an area with . . . lake shore or including ponds',[126] priority axis 3 on measures of common interest,[127] and priority axis 2,[128] which addresses not just inland fishing (as noted above) but also aquaculture and processing and marketing of fishery and aquaculture products.

Having considered the phrase 'on the territory of Member States', this subsection will now look at the term 'Community waters'. That term is defined in Article 3(a) of the Basic Regulation as 'the waters under the sovereignty or jurisdiction of the Member States with the exception of waters adjacent to the territories mentioned in Annex II to the Treaty'. Several points arising from that definition will be addressed here. The first is that the term 'Community waters' overlaps in scope with the phrase 'the territory of Member States', in that both formulations cover the internal waters and territorial sea of a Member State. That is because the internal waters (whether freshwater or marine) and territorial sea are both: (a) 'waters under the sovereignty . . . of the Member States'; and (b) part of 'the territory of Member States'.

Secondly, the definition of Community waters excludes 'waters adjacent to *the territories* mentioned in Annex II to the [EC] Treaty' (emphasis added). As noted in subsection 3.1 above, it seems more likely that the reference in this exclusion to

---

[122] Reg 104/2000, Art 1.   [123] See also Reg 104/2000, Art 4(1)(b).

[124] Reg 1198/2006, Art 33(1). On 'inland fishing' specifically, see also Arts 1, 4(c), and 15(2)(d).

[125] Reg 1198/2006, Arts 43–45.   [126] Reg 1198/2006, Art 3(e).

[127] Reg 1198/2006, Arts 36–42. Art 38(2)(b) makes specific reference to 'the rehabilitation of inland waters, including spawning grounds and migration routes for migratory species'.

[128] Reg 1198/2006, Arts 28–35.

just Annex II 'territories' rather than Annex II 'countries and territories' is a drafting error rather than reflecting an intention to make a distinction between 'territories' and 'countries'. The exclusion in the definition of Community waters reflects the fact that the CFP does not apply to the OCTs. It is notable that the definition makes no mention of any of the other countries or territories referred to in Article 299 EC in respect of which the CFP either does not apply or has some limited application (see subsection 3.1 above). However, the Basic Regulation, as secondary legislation, is subordinate to Article 299. Therefore, the Regulation's definition of Community waters remains subject to the provisions of Article 299.

Thirdly, the definition of Community waters relates to 'the waters under the sovereignty or *jurisdiction* of the Member States' (emphasis added). The reference to jurisdiction means that Community waters include waters beyond the territorial sea that are subject to coastal State jurisdiction.[129] As such, they include, *inter alia*, the exclusive economic zone (EEZ) and/or exclusive fishing zone (EFZ) (see Chapter 3). A 'Table of claims to maritime jurisdiction (as at 28 May 2008)' published by the Division for Ocean Affairs and the Law of the Sea (DOALOS) of the Office of Legal Affairs of the United Nations[130] shows that, of the twenty-two coastal Member States, seventeen have an EEZ[131] and six, including four of the previous seventeen, have a 'fisheries zone' (which the authors assume means an EFZ).[132] Greece has no EEZ or EFZ. Italy and Slovenia each have an 'ecological protection zone' instead of an EEZ or EFZ. Although not mentioned in the DOALOS table, the authors understand that France, like Italy and Slovenia, has an 'ecological protection zone' in the Mediterranean Sea.[133]

Lastly, the definition of Community waters relates to 'the *waters* under the sovereignty or jurisdiction of the Member States' (emphasis added). The reference to 'waters' raises a question about the extent to which the seabed, as opposed to the water column, is covered by the term 'Community waters'. This is not an issue with respect to the seabed of marine internal waters or the territorial sea, since these zones are anyway covered by the phrase 'the territory of Member States' in Article 1(1) of the Basic Regulation (see above). It may be an issue with respect to the seabed of the EEZ (or EFZ) because that zone is not part of 'the territory of

---

[129] See also Case 61/77 *Commission v Ireland* [1978] ECR 417, paras 38–51.

[130] The Table is available on the website of the DOALOS. The Table's 'Introductory note' states, *inter alia*, that the Table 'may not always reflect the latest developments' and 'is unofficial and for informational purposes only'.

[131] Belgium, Bulgaria, Cyprus, Denmark, Estonia, Finland, France (not Mediterranean), Germany, Ireland, Latvia, Lithuania, Netherlands, Poland, Portugal, Romania, Spain (not Mediterranean), and Sweden.

[132] Belgium (in addition to EEZ), Finland (in addition to EEZ), Ireland (in addition to EEZ), Malta (25 nm), Spain (in Mediterranean), and the UK. It is rather surprising that, according to the Table, Belgium, Finland, and Ireland each have a 'fisheries zone' in addition to an EEZ. In principle, an EEZ under international law would anyway encompass a 'fisheries zone'.

[133] Regarding the maritime jurisdiction of coastal Member States in the Mediterranean Sea, see further Chapter 4.

Member States'; however, it is quite likely that the Court would if necessary adopt a purposive interpretation of the term 'waters' and so include within it the seabed of the EEZ (or EFZ).

Questions about whether the seabed is included within the meaning of 'Community waters' may be less easily resolved in respect of the continental shelf beyond the 200 nm limit, ie the so-called 'outer' continental shelf (see Chapter 3). The continental shelf comprises the seabed and subsoil and has no water column element. It is therefore harder to regard seabed comprising the continental shelf, when it is not otherwise the bed of the EEZ or EFZ, as 'waters'. Exclusion of the outer continental shelf from the geographical scope of the CFP would potentially exclude some very large areas of seabed.

As will be noted in Chapter 3, under international law a coastal State has exclusive sovereign rights to exploit sedentary species on its continental shelf, including the outer shelf. Even if one assumes that invertebrates other than crustaceans and molluscs are not covered by the CFP (see subsection 2.1 above), there may still be scope for commercially relevant sedentary species of molluscs or crustaceans to occur on the outer shelf.

Examples of EC legislation made under the CFP and referring expressly to the continental shelf in the sense used above are very rare. One of the few examples is Council Decision 2001/431,[134] which provides for, *inter alia*, enhanced EC funding for fisheries enforcement by 'Member States which have to control an extensive Exclusive Economic Zone, Exclusive Fishing Zone *or continental shelf* or which have to deal with disproportionate obligations arising in connection with the control of fishing at sea' (emphasis added).[135] Although that example relates to enforcement, it could still be used as an example of EC practice to argue that the outer continental shelf does fall within 'Community waters'.

An example, albeit not under the CFP, of where the EC has been more explicit about whether seabed is covered by the term 'waters' is the Marine Strategy Directive.[136] The Directive states that it 'shall apply to all marine waters as defined in Article 3(1)',[137] which in turn states that the term 'marine waters' means, *inter alia*, 'waters, *the seabed and subsoil* on the seaward side of the baseline from which the extent of territorial waters is measured extending to the outmost reach of the area where a Member State has and/or exercises jurisdictional rights, in accordance with the Unclos [sic]' (emphasis added).[138]

---

[134] Council Decision 2001/431/EC of 28 May 2001 on a financial contribution by the Community to certain expenditure incurred by the Member States in implementing the control, inspection and surveillance systems applicable to the common fisheries policy, OJ 2001 L154/22.

[135] Dec 2001/431, Art 9(3)(a).

[136] Directive 2008/56/EC of the European Parliament and of the Council of 17 June 2008 establishing a framework for community action in the field of marine environmental policy (Marine Strategy Framework Directive), OJ 2008 L164/19.   [137] Dir 2008/56, Art 2(1).

[138] Dir 2008/56, Art 3(1)(a).

The Marine Strategy Directive provides an example of where the EC legislature has sought to be clear about the marine geographical scope of secondary legislation. An example, also from EC environmental law, of where it has been less clear in that respect is the Habitats Directive.[139] The Habitats Directive contains no provision explicitly setting out the extent of its application to the marine environment. Instead, it refers to 'the European territory of the Member States to which the [EC] Treaty applies'.[140] A debate has ensued, at the political level and via litigation, on the precise extent of the Directive's application beyond the territorial sea.

In *Commission v United Kingdom*, the Advocate General concluded that '[t]he Habitats Directive is . . . to be transposed in respect of areas outside territorial waters, in so far as the Member States or the Community exercise sovereign rights there'.[141] The Court, after noting that 'it is common ground between the parties that the United Kingdom exercises sovereign rights in its exclusive economic zone [sic] and on the continental shelf and that the Habitats Directive is to that extent applicable beyond the Member States' territorial waters', went on to conclude that 'the directive must be implemented in that exclusive economic zone'.[142] Thus the Court, in its express conclusion, fails to mention the continental shelf. But, in its reasoning, it implies that the Habitats Directive applies to the shelf to the extent that Member States exercise sovereign rights there.

Overall, it would seem that it is currently unclear whether the outer continental shelf is included within the meaning of 'Community waters'. Yet the relevance of the outer continental shelf is increasing as more and more coastal States, including Member States of the EC, make submissions to the UN Commission on the Limits of the Continental Shelf (see Chapter 3). It will be interesting to see whether the European Commission seeks to use the current review of the CFP (see Chapters 1 and 4) to make it clearer in the successor to the current Basic Regulation whether or not 'Community waters', or any equivalent term adopted pursuant to the Treaty of Lisbon, includes the outer continental shelf.

4 Personal scope

4.1 Introduction

The CFP is implemented mainly by means of Regulations. Decisions also play an important role, whereas Directives are used only very rarely. Regulations adopted under the CFP are directly applicable in all twenty-seven Member States, whether

[139] Council Directive 92/43/EEC of 21 May 1992 on the conservation of natural habitats and of wild fauna and flora, OJ 1992 L206/7, as amended and corrected.   [140] Dir 92/43, Art 2(1).
[141] Case C-6/04 *Commission v United Kingdom* [2005] ECR I-9017, AG Opinion, para 135.
[142] Case C-6/04, para 117.

landlocked or coastal. The powers and duties set out in any given Regulation apply to a variety of actors, including the Member States and economic operators, as well as, *inter alia*, EC institutions (notably the Commission and the Council) and the various bodies established under the CFP. The roles of these assorted actors were introduced in Chapter 1 and will be discussed in subsequent chapters of this book. In this section, the focus will be on the application of the CFP, in general terms, to vessels and nationals.

4.2 Application of the CFP to vessels

Under Article 1(1) of the Basic Regulation, the activities covered by the CFP are: (a) conservation, management, and exploitation of living aquatic resources; (b) aquaculture; and (c) the processing and marketing of fishery and aquaculture products. The scope for the CFP to apply to vessels undertaking any of those activities arises via three principal means.

First, the CFP covers those activities when they are practised 'on the territory of Member States'. As noted in subsection 3.2 above, that term encompasses, *inter alia*, internal waters and the territorial sea. The CFP thus covers vessels undertaking the above activities in internal waters and the territorial sea irrespective of their flag State and irrespective of their nature (for example fishing vessel or not), subject to the right of innocent passage of third State vessels through the territorial sea.[143]

Secondly, the CFP covers the said activities when they are practised 'in Community waters'. Again, the CFP therefore covers vessels undertaking the activities in question in Community waters irrespective of their flag State and their nature, subject to third State vessels' right of innocent passage through the territorial sea as well as their freedom of navigation in the EEZ or EFZ. Fishing by third State vessels in Community waters is discussed in Chapter 4.

Thirdly, the CFP covers the activities in question when they are practised 'by Community fishing vessels'. The term 'fishing vessel' is defined by Article 3(c) of the Basic Regulation as 'any vessel equipped for commercial exploitation of living aquatic resources'. The term 'living aquatic resources', as used in the definition of fishing vessel, is discussed in subsection 2.2 above. The term 'Community fishing vessel' is in turn defined in Article 3(d) as 'a fishing vessel flying the flag of a Member State and registered in the Community'.

As can be seen, for a fishing vessel to be a 'Community fishing vessel', it must be a fishing vessel: (a) 'flying the flag of a Member State'; and (b) 'registered in the Community'.[144] This implies that there may be fishing vessels flagged to Member States but not necessarily 'registered in the Community' (see below). Such vessels

---

[143] In some very limited circumstances, there is also a right of innocent passage in marine internal waters. The right of innocent passage is discussed in general terms in Chapter 3.

[144] On Community law and the nationality of fishing vessels, see Chapter 4.

would not be covered by the term 'Community fishing vessel' and hence, if operating beyond Community waters, would not be covered by the CFP. This in turn raises the question of what is meant by the phrase 'registered in the Community'. The phrase is not defined in the Basic Regulation.

Article 15 of the Basic Regulation states that the Commission 'shall set up a Community fishing fleet register' containing certain information that it receives from the Member States.[145] Does 'registered in the Community' mean the act of placing a fishing vessel on the Community fishing fleet register? The information to be provided by the Member States comprises 'the minimum information on vessel characteristics and activity that is necessary for the management of measures established at Community level'. However, this information is to be provided from a national register, to be maintained by each Member State, 'of the *Community* fishing vessels flying its flag' (emphasis added).[146] This implies that fishing vessels are already 'Community fishing vessels' *before* the Member State submits the vessel information to the Commission for the purpose of its inclusion in the Community fishing fleet register. The same implication arises from Regulation 26/2004 on the Community fishing fleet register, which establishes detailed rules for the application of Article 15.[147] This militates against the argument that Member States' fishing vessels become 'Community fishing vessels' by virtue of being entered on the Community register.

One possibility is that 'registered in the Community' means registered in a territory to which the EC Treaty applies (on which, see subsection 3.1 above). On that basis, a fishing vessel registered in the metropolitan territory of a Member State or in one of its outermost regions *would* be a Community fishing vessel, whilst a fishing vessel registered in an OCT or in the Faroe Islands would *not* be a Community fishing vessel. Whether a fishing vessel registered in one of the other localities referred to in Article 299 EC was a Community fishing vessel would depend on the extent to which the EC Treaty, and the CFP, applied to that locality. Some uncertainties about such application have been discussed in subsection 3.1 above. The authors have not been able to inspect the Community fishing fleet register to see whether it supports the interpretation put forward here. In passing it is worth noting that it would presumably not be in a Member State's interest to include in the said register fishing vessels registered in those of its countries or territories to which the EC Treaty does not apply because, in particular, that would make it more onerous for the Member State concerned to meet its capacity reduction obligations (on which, see Chapter 4).

---

[145] Reg 2371/2002, Art 15(3).   [146] Reg 2371/2002, Art 15(1) and (2).

[147] Commission Regulation (EC) No 26/2004 of 30 December 2003 on the Community fishing fleet register, OJ 2004 L5/25, as amended, Arts 4 and 7(1) (albeit cf Art 1(1)(a), which in contrast to Art 15 of Reg 2371/2002, refers to 'the fishing vessels flying its flag' rather than 'the Community fishing vessels flying its flag').

The application of the CFP to Community fishing vessels, specifically, has particular relevance to occasions when such vessels are operating outside Community waters. That is because vessels operating inside such waters are anyway covered by the application of the CFP to the territory of Member States and/or Community waters. In other words, the particular benefit of making the CFP applicable to Community fishing vessels is that it enables the CFP to apply to such vessels even when they are beyond Community waters (for example on the high seas, in the waters of a third State, or in the waters of an OCT).

With the adoption of Regulation 1005/2008, on IUU fishing (hereafter, 'the IUU Regulation'), the application of the CFP to vessels has evolved. The Regulation makes much use of the term 'fishing vessel'. Whereas in the Basic Regulation this term means 'any vessel *equipped for commercial exploitation* of *living aquatic resources*' (see above),[148] in the IUU Regulation it means 'any vessel of any size *used or intended for use for the purposes of commercial exploitation* of *fishery resources*, including support ships, fish processing vessels, vessels engaged in transhipment and carrier vessels equipped for the transportation of fishery products, except container vessels' (emphasis added).[149]

This raises the question whether there is any difference between being 'equipped for commercial exploitation' and 'used or intended for use for the purposes of commercial exploitation'. The term 'equipped for' is not defined in the Basic Regulation. Arguably, being 'equipped for' commercial exploitation has a narrower meaning than being 'used . . . for the purposes of' such exploitation. The two different definitions of 'fishing vessel' also raise the question whether there is any difference between 'living aquatic resources' and 'fishery resources'. As noted above, the former term is defined as 'available and accessible living marine aquatic species, including anadromous and catadromous species during their marine life'.[150] The term 'fishery resources' is not defined in the IUU Regulation, and is not used in the Regulation's Articles other than in the definition of 'fishing vessel'. Overall it is strongly arguable that the definition of 'fishing vessel' in the IUU Regulation is broader than that in the Basic Regulation.

The IUU Regulation makes several references to 'Community fishing vessels'.[151] It defines that term in the same way as in the Basic Regulation (see above), but does so by repeating the latter's definition rather than simply making a cross-reference to it.[152] Because of the IUU Regulation's arguably broader definition of 'fishing vessel' (see above), the term 'Community fishing vessel' as used in the IUU Regulation is therefore presumably correspondingly broad. This has implications for the personal scope of the CFP. In principle, the CFP's personal scope is defined by Article 1(1) of the Basic Regulation. The application of the CFP to 'Community fishing vessels', as defined in the Basic Regulation, is the primary

---

[148] Reg 2371/2002, Art 3(c).   [149] Reg 1005/2008, Art 2(5).
[150] Reg 2371/2002, Art 3(b).   [151] Reg 1005/2008, Arts 27(7) and (8), 38(5), and 41(2).
[152] Reg 1005/2008, Art 2(6).

means for the CFP to apply beyond Community waters. If the term 'Community fishing vessel' as used in the IUU Regulation is broader than the term as used in the Basic Regulation, does the IUU Regulation broaden the CFP's personal scope beyond that provided for by the Basic Regulation? If the answer were 'no' then the IUU Regulation could presumably only apply to Community fishing vessels beyond Community waters to the extent that such vessels were 'fishing vessels' as defined in the potentially narrower sense of the Basic Regulation.

In principle, the potentially broader definition of the term 'Community fishing vessel' in the IUU Regulation is confined in terms of its effect to that Regulation. In practice, the situation is more complicated because the IUU Regulation, in the context of 'Community fishing vessels', make a cross-reference to another Regulation that uses the same term.[153] Furthermore, regarding fishing vessels flying the flag of Member States, the IUU Regulation does not limit itself to references to 'Community fishing vessels'. It makes several references to 'fishing vessels flying the flag of a Member State'.[154] It is not clear whether that phrase is intended to be synonymous with 'Community fishing vessel'. Either way, the point made above about an extension to the personal scope of the CFP by virtue of the IUU Regulation applies likewise to such vessels. For example, Article 37(4) requires that 'fishing vessels flying the flag of a Member State' must not, *inter alia*, in any way 'assist' fishing vessels on the Community IUU vessel list. The IUU Regulation's definition of 'fishing vessel' includes, *inter alia*, 'support ships' (see above).[155] If such vessels are not covered by the Basic Regulation's definition of 'fishing vessel', and if the prohibition in question is intended to apply, *inter alia*, beyond Community waters, Article 37(4) could only work regarding support ships beyond Community waters if the IUU Regulation is accepted as broadening the CFP's personal scope beyond that provided for by the Basic Regulation.

The IUU Regulation's definition of the term 'fishing vessel' may create some problems, or at least uncertainty, as far as the Community fishing vessel register is concerned. The latter register is established by the Basic Regulation, where the term 'fishing vessel' arguably has a narrower meaning than in the IUU Regulation (see above). How does the IUU Regulation's arguably broader definition of 'fishing vessel' affect the types of vessel that are to be included on the Community register? Is, say, a support ship, or a carrier vessel 'equipped for the transportation of fishery products', if flying the flag of a Member State, to be entered on the Community register? Or is the content of the Community register to be limited to 'fishing vessels' as defined in the Basic Regulation, ie vessels 'equipped for commercial exploitation of living aquatic resources'? The latter outcome seems more justifiable, on the basis that the scope of the Community register should be defined by reference to the Basic Regulation, which establishes the register, and hence by

---

[153] Reg 1005/2008, Art 27(8), which cross-refers to Reg 2847/93.
[154] Reg 1005/2008, Arts 2(13), 4(3) and (4), 15, 28(1)(b), 36(2)(b) and (c), 37(4) and (5), and 38(3), (6), and (7).   [155] Reg 1005/2008, Art 2(5).

reference to the definition of 'fishing vessel' contained therein. If that is the case, it supports the case for the phrase 'registered in the Community' *not* being a reference to the Community fishing fleet register (see above). Otherwise, the phrase 'registered in the Community' as used in the definition of 'Community fishing vessel' in the IUU Regulation could not be applied to any types of 'fishing vessel' covered by the definition of that term as used in the IUU Regulation but falling outside the definition of the same term as used in the Basic Regulation.

4.3 Application of the CFP to nationals

As with vessels, the CFP can be applied to nationals (ie natural or legal persons) undertaking any of the activities listed in Article 1(1) of the Basic Regulation (ie conservation, management, and exploitation of living aquatic resources, aquaculture, or the processing and marketing of fishery and aquaculture products) by three principal means. The first two means are the same as for vessels, ie by nationals, irrespective of their nationality, practising the activities in question 'on the territory of Member States' or 'in Community waters' (subject to any restrictions imposed by international law).

The third means arises because the CFP applies, albeit 'without prejudice to the primary responsibility of the flag State', to 'nationals of Member States' practising such activities. This means has particular relevance where the nationals concerned are practising: (a) outside the territory of Member States and/or outside Community waters; and (b) on vessels other than Community fishing vessels.

The application of the CFP to 'nationals of Member States' can be seen as a direct response to the threat posed by IUU fishing. IUU fishing is particularly an issue on the high seas, where it is carried out by, *inter alia*, vessels flagged to States that fail to join, or otherwise cooperate with, the relevant regional fisheries management organizations. The CFP's application to 'nationals of Member States' allows the CFP to reach nationals of Member States involved with such vessels.

The scope for applying the CFP to 'nationals of Member States' is a new development in the current Basic Regulation: no such provision was present in the previous Basic Regulation, ie Regulation 3760/92.[156] Until the adoption of the IUU Regulation, little use had been made of that possibility.[157] With the adoption

---

[156] Reg 3760/92, Art 1.

[157] See: (a) Council Regulation (EC) No 601/2004 of 22 March 2004 laying down certain control measures applicable to fishing activities in the area covered by the Convention on the conservation of Antarctic marine living resources and repealing Regulations (EEC) No 3943/90, (EC) No 66/98 and (EC) No 1721/1999, OJ 2004 L97/16, as amended, Art 31 (Reg 1005/2008 repeals Art 31—see Reg 1005/2008, Art 56); and (b) Reg 1967/2006, Arts 1(1)(a)(iii) and 24(6)(d). See also Council Regulation (EC) No 1936/2001 of 27 September 2001 laying down control measures applicable to fishing for certain stocks of highly migratory fish, OJ 2001 L263/1, as amended, Art 19; Reg 1936/2001, and hence Art 19, was adopted before Reg 2371/2002 was adopted.

of the IUU Regulation, the potential for application of the CFP to 'nationals of Member States' has been more fully realized. A Chapter of the Regulation deals specifically with '[n]ationals subject to the jurisdiction of Member States'.[158] That Chapter, as well as some other provisions of the Regulation,[159] place various obligations on such nationals directly, as well as on Member States in respect of their nationals, with a view to fulfilling the objectives of the IUU Regulation.

---

[158] Reg 1005/2008, Chapter VIII (Arts 39 and 40).
[159] Reg 1005/2008, Arts 38(6) and 41(2). See also Arts 43, 44, and 47.

Part II

Fisheries management

3

The international framework of fisheries management

1 Fisheries management: issues and challenges

Fisheries management is a key concern of the Common Fisheries Policy (CFP), arguably its most important concern. Fisheries management in Community waters is the subject of Chapter 4, while external aspects of fisheries management are considered in Chapter 5. In order to aid understanding of those chapters, this chapter begins by trying to explain what is meant by, and what is involved in, fisheries management.

According to the Food and Agriculture Organization (FAO), the UN's specialized agency with responsibility for fisheries, '[t]here are no clear and generally accepted definitions of fisheries management'.[1] The FAO offers the following as a 'working definition':

The integrated process of information gathering, analysis, planning, consultation, decision-making, allocation of resources and formulation and implementation, with enforcement as necessary, of regulations or rules which govern fisheries activities in order to ensure the continued productivity of the resources and accomplishment of other fisheries objectives.[2]

It is impossible in the space available to do justice to a topic as complex as fisheries management, nor, as lawyers, are the authors equipped to do so since fisheries management primarily involves matters of biology, economics, and politics rather than law. Here no more will be done than briefly highlight some issues of fisheries management that the authors consider particularly germane to management by the EC. In doing so, the authors acknowledge that there may be considerable over-simplification of non-legal matters.

Fisheries management is, in considerable part, about regulating the impact of human harvesting activities on fish with the aim of ensuring that stocks of fish are maintained at levels that will sustain their continued exploitation as a resource indefinitely, an aim that is stressed by the FAO.[3] This may require various

---

[1] FAO, *FAO Technical Guidelines for Responsible Fisheries No 4. Fisheries Management* (Rome: FAO, 1997), 7 (hereafter, '*Guidelines*'), available on the website of the Fisheries and Aquaculture Department of the FAO.   [2] Ibid.

[3] Code of Conduct for Responsible Fisheries, FAO Doc 95/20/Rev 1 (1995) (available on the website of the Fisheries and Aquaculture Department of the FAO), Arts 6.2, 7.1.1, and 7.2.1. The Code is discussed in section 5 below.

measures to be taken. In general terms, responsible fishing 'should not allow more of the resource to be harvested on average than can be replaced by net growth in the stock'.[4] Limits may therefore need to be placed on fishing. Such restriction may take the form of limiting the amount of fish that may be caught, or limiting the number or size of vessels that may fish, or limiting the amount of time that vessels may spend fishing for a particular stock.[5] It may also be necessary to take measures to avoid adverse impacts on the rate of reproduction of a particular stock by, *inter alia*, protecting spawning fish (for example, by prohibiting fishing in areas where, and at times when, spawning takes place) and by preventing the catching of sexually immature fish (for example, by closing nursery areas to fishing and by regulating the size of the mesh in nets so that immature fish may escape).[6]

However, fish that are the target of harvesting are just a part of a much wider marine ecosystem. The concept or principle of an 'ecosystem-based approach' to human activities seeks to address this fact. Further reference to this approach is made in section 8 below and also in Chapter 4. Ecosystem effects of fisheries may be direct or indirect. Examples include the impact of fishing gear on seabed habitats (eg bottom trawling over cold-water corals), on non-commercial species (eg through seabird by-catch or, indirectly, through depletion of seabirds' prey species), and on commercial species (eg through by-catch of juveniles of other commercial species). At the broadest level, choices need to be made by society (not just fisheries managers) about how a particular marine ecosystem is to be used. At the narrower level of fisheries management, measures are needed to reflect such choices. What is frequently required, but seldom done in practice, is the adoption of measures based on a multi-species approach that reflects the relevant ecosystem. As is seen in Chapter 1, one of the criticisms made of the EC's system of fisheries management is that up to now it has been very largely based on single species management.

There are a number of particular difficulties in trying to manage marine fisheries. The first relates to scientific knowledge. To manage a fish stock effectively, it is necessary to have considerable knowledge of the stock, including its size, the proportion of mature individuals, the rates of mortality and reproduction, and so on.[7] Such knowledge cannot be acquired through direct observation. Instead, fisheries scientists have to try to obtain this knowledge through sampling and by studying the size and composition of catches over many years. Clearly this is not an exact science. It suggests a need to be cautious in deciding on permitted levels of fishing, lest an over-generous decision lead to a serious decline of the population of the fish stock(s) concerned. Such an approach has been characterized (and more precisely defined, in a way that is explained in section 3 below) as the 'precautionary approach', and is strongly advocated by the FAO.[8] A precautionary approach is particularly necessary in the case of fisheries directed at stocks about

---

[4] *Guidelines*, 9.   [5] *Guidelines*, 13, 45–6, and 48–51.   [6] *Guidelines*, 46–8.
[7] *Guidelines*, 31–6 and 41–3.   [8] Code of Conduct, Arts 6.5 and 7.5.

whose population dynamics little is known, such as sharks, deep-water species (which have generally only become the object of exploitation in recent years), and fish stocks in the waters of many developing States which have lacked the resources to engage in anywhere near the same level of scientific research on fisheries as in most developed States.[9] Problems about the lack of scientific knowledge and the need for a precautionary approach apply equally to the impact of fisheries on the wider marine environment.

A second complication in the management of marine fisheries is the fact that many fish are migratory in nature, and some are highly so. Consequently it is often the case that a fish stock at the harvestable stage does not spend its entire time in just one of the man-made zones into which the sea is legally divided (and which are explained in the following section of this chapter). Thus, in many cases, a fish stock will migrate into the waters of one or more neighbouring States, and/or onto the high seas that lie beyond national waters, so that two or more States may well be attempting to manage the same stock of fish. It is quite possible for the management measures of such States to be incompatible. For example, one State may pursue a long-term strategy of trying to build up a depleted stock through strict limits on catches and rigorous controls on the mesh size of nets in order to protect immature fish, whereas another State, whose fishermen may be struggling economically, may permit higher levels of catch for that stock in order to help its fishing industry through lean times. Unless the measures adopted by two or more States trying to manage the same stock are compatible, management undertaken by one State risks being undermined by the management measures of other States, as in the example given.[10] This therefore points to the need for States to cooperate over the management of migratory stocks in which they share an interest.[11] The same is true of a stock with a population that, while not migratory, straddles the boundary between two or more States or between national waters and the high seas, and of discrete high seas stocks, where no one State has the competence to manage such stocks (as explained in section 2 below).

A third factor complicating fisheries management is the fact that in most legal systems fish are not actually owned by anyone until they are caught, at which point they become the property of the fisherman or fishing vessel that caught them. This leads to fish frequently being described as a common property natural resource, although in fact, since fish are not owned in common, it would be more accurate

---

[9] For further discussion of the precautionary approach to fisheries management, see FAO, *FAO Technical Guidelines for Responsible Fisheries No 2. Precautionary Approach to Capture Fisheries and Species Introductions* (Rome: FAO, 1996); Garcia, SM, 'The Precautionary Principle: its Implications in Capture Fisheries Management' *OCM* 22 (1994), 99; Garcia, SM, 'The Precautionary Approach to Fisheries: Progress Review and Main Issues (1995–2000)' in Nordquist MH and Moore, JN (eds), *Current Fisheries Issues and the Food and Agriculture Organization of the United Nations* (The Hague: Martinus Nijhoff, 2000), 479–560; and Hewison, GJ, 'The Precautionary Approach to Fisheries Management: An Environmental Perspective' *IJMCL* 11 (1996), 301.   [10] *Guidelines*, 18.
[11] *Guidelines*, 45.

to refer to them as being an unowned resource. This characteristic has traditionally meant that anyone with the necessary means could engage in fishing, whether in national waters or on the high seas. This open-access nature of marine fisheries has major drawbacks. In a new fishery, those first fishing will normally make a decent profit. Seeing this, other vessels will enter the fishery. Before long, the number of vessels will be so great that none is making any profit: in other words, there will be more vessels engaged in the fishery than are necessary economically to take the available catch.[12] This phenomenon is known as 'over-capitalization' or 'over-capacity'. It has been present in many, if not most, of the world's fisheries over at least the past thirty or forty years, and has frequently been exacerbated by the extensive subsidies that many States give to their fishing vessels.[13] Over-capacity is not only undesirable on economic grounds, it is also undesirable on conservation grounds because the presence of too many vessels in a fishery, each anxious to make money, will encourage them to break the rules and take more than the allowed catch of fish or ignore regulations on mesh size, closed areas, closed seasons, and so on.[14] Some States restrict entry to their fishing fleets, but open access still persists in many national fleets and on the high seas (although in the latter case compliance measures adopted by regional fisheries management organizations are helping to curtail access). In the view of many, reducing over-capacity is the single biggest challenge facing fisheries managers today.[15]

Fourthly, marine fisheries are difficult to manage because many of the various management measures that may be required, and which were outlined above, are often difficult and costly to enforce, especially at sea because of the problem of detecting offences in the extensive marine areas where fishing takes places and because of the cost of operating fisheries inspection vessels. In recent years at sea enforcement has been increasingly supplemented by greater use of the powers of control of port States (see further sections 3 and 6 below). Effective enforcement is essential if fisheries management is to be successful.[16]

It will be apparent from the discussion so far that fisheries management has a considerable international dimension, both because management frequently requires cooperation between States and because a good deal of fishing takes place beyond the waters subject to national jurisdiction. Before the First UN Conference on the Law of the Sea, held in 1958, fisheries were regulated to a limited degree by treaties and customary international law. The four Geneva Conventions on the law of the sea, adopted at that Conference, marked the start of the development of a comprehensive international legal framework for fisheries management. The

---

[12] *Guidelines*, 16–17 and 52; and Troadec, J-P, *Introduction to Fisheries Management: Advantages, Difficulties and Mechanisms*, FAO Fisheries Technical Paper 224 (Rome: FAO, 1983), 6–9.

[13] *Guidelines*, 17 and 52.

[14] Brown, J, *Fishing Capacity Management in the EU post 2002 CFP Reform* (London: Institute for European Environmental Policy, 2006), 1; and *Guidelines*, 13.

[15] FAO, *The State of World Fisheries and Aquaculture 2008* (Rome: FAO, 2009), 9 and 66–7, available on the website of the Fisheries and Aquaculture Department of the FAO.   [16] *Guidelines*, 34 and 39–40.

aim of the rest of this chapter is to examine that framework. The latter, or at least its basic elements, is currently contained in the 1982 UN Convention on the Law of the Sea (hereafter, 'the Convention'),[17] the relevant provisions of which are analysed in the following section of this chapter. Although the Convention did not enter into force until 1994, its fisheries provisions have in practice been applied since their drafting was more or less finalized in the late 1970s, even before negotiations on the rest of the Convention had been completed and the Convention adopted.

By the early 1990s, there were serious concerns about the state of the world's fish stocks, about 70 per cent of which were fully exploited or over-exploited,[18] and about the adequacy of the Convention as a framework for their management.[19] Those concerns found particular expression at an International Conference on Responsible Fishing, held at Cancun, Mexico in May 1992,[20] and at the UN Conference on Environment and Development, held the following month.[21] In response to calls made at those conferences, three instruments were adopted in the mid-1990s to supplement the Convention—the 1993 Agreement to Promote Compliance with International Conservation and Management Measures by Fishing Vessels on the High Seas[22] (generally known as the Compliance Agreement), the 1995 Code of Conduct for Responsible Fisheries, and the 1995 Agreement for the Implementation of the Provisions of the United Nations Convention on the Law of the Sea of 10 December 1982 relating to the Conservation and Management of Straddling Fish Stocks and Highly Migratory Fish Stocks[23] (hereafter, 'the Fish Stocks Agreement'). Those instruments, which develop many aspects of the fisheries regime of the Convention and aim to encourage better fisheries management, are the subject of sections 3 to 5 of this chapter. The various instruments mentioned so far are all global in scope. They are supplemented, and to a degree implemented, by a number of treaties that establish regional fisheries management organizations or arrangements with the power to take legally binding decisions. Those treaties and bodies are discussed in section 6. Although not having any formal law-creating powers, the UN General Assembly has, through its resolutions, played a role in stimulating various significant developments in international fisheries law such that the relevant resolutions, which are examined in section 7, may be said to have a soft-law character. Increasingly, as

---

[17] 1833 UNTS 396.   [18] FAO, *The State of Fisheries and Aquaculture* (Rome: FAO, 1995), 8.

[19] Hey, E, 'Global Fisheries Regulations in the First Half of the 1990s' *IJMCL* 11 (1996) 459 at 460–4.

[20] See, in particular, the Cancun Declaration on Responsible Fishing, reproduced in UN Doc A/CONF.151/15, Annex. Also available on the website of the Fisheries and Aquaculture Department of the FAO.

[21] See, in particular, Agenda 21, Chapter 17, Programme Area C. Agenda 21 is available on the website of the UNEP; Chapter 17 is also reproduced in *IJECL* 7 (1992), 296–329.

[22] 2221 UNTS 91.   [23] 2167 UNTS 3.

already hinted at, international fisheries law is being influenced by more general environmental considerations, and this development is charted in section 8.

The discussion that follows is particularly relevant to the following two chapters of this book. Chapter 4 looks at fisheries management in Community waters. The development of the EC's system of fisheries management was heavily influenced by the Third UN Conference on the Law of the Sea and the resulting Convention (see further Chapter 1), and its substantive content has had to take account of the provisions of the Convention and the later instruments adopted during the 1990s, to all of which the EC is a party. Chapter 5 deals with the EC's international fisheries relations. After examining the EC's participation in the Convention and later fisheries instruments, that chapter focuses on the agreements that the EC has concluded with third States for the access of its fishing vessels to the waters of those States, the basic framework for which is provided by the Convention, and on the EC's participation in regional fisheries management organizations. These organizations are also the subject of section 6 of this chapter.

2 UN Convention on the Law of the Sea

2.1 Introduction

The Convention was adopted on 10 December 1982 and entered into force on 16 November 1994. At the time of writing, it had 157 parties, including all twenty-seven Member States of the EC and the EC itself.[24] Unless otherwise stated, references to particular Articles or Annexes in this section, including in the footnotes, are references to the Convention. Provisions of the Convention dealing with the effects of fishing on the wider marine environment are also discussed, albeit only briefly, in section 8 below.

The Convention requires that the EC 'shall exercise the rights and perform the obligations which its member States which are Parties would otherwise have under this Convention, on matters relating to which competence has been transferred to it by those member States'.[25] The corollary is that the EC Member States 'shall not exercise competence which they have transferred to' the EC.[26] (See further Chapter 5.)

Thus the power of EC Member States to make rules for fisheries conservation is restricted not only by virtue of EC law but also by virtue of the Convention. Of course, if the EC chooses to delegate some powers for rule-making back to the Member States (as it has done in some limited respects: see Chapter 4), it is arguable that the restriction on Member State action provided for in the Convention should

---

[24] See the website of the Division for Ocean Affairs and the Law of the Sea (DOALOS) of the Office of Legal Affairs of the United Nations.   [25] Annex IX, Art 4(3).

[26] Annex IX, Art 4(3).

not apply to the Member States to the extent of their delegated powers. The following description of the Convention's provisions concerning fishing will address the coastal State in general, rather than focusing on the division of competence between the EC and its Member States.

Although this section focuses on the provisions of the Convention, it is important to note that much customary international law on fisheries also exists. It is true that much of that has been codified by the Convention. However, it is probably not accurate to state that all of the fisheries provisions in the Convention represent codified customary international law. For example, Churchill and Lowe question whether the coastal State's fisheries management duties set out in Articles 61 and 62 have become part of customary international law.[27]

2.2 Fishing in internal waters and the territorial sea

Internal waters are those waters landward of the baseline from which the breadth of the territorial sea is measured.[28] The normal baseline is 'the low-water line along the coast as marked on large-scale charts officially recognized by the coastal State',[29] and the Convention contains rules for the establishment of other types of baseline.[30] Where straight baselines have been established, the area of marine internal waters can potentially be significant. The territorial sea is a belt of sea extending up to 12 nm from the baseline.[31]

In its internal waters and territorial sea, the coastal State has territorial sovereignty over the seabed and subsoil, the water column, and the airspace.[32] That sovereignty is subject to: (a) the right of innocent passage of foreign-flagged vessels in the territorial sea;[33] and (b) the same right in internal waters in cases where the valid establishment of a straight baseline 'has the effect of enclosing as internal waters areas which had not previously been considered as such'.[34]

Passage by vessels is not innocent if it includes, *inter alia*, 'any fishing activities'.[35] So the territorial sovereignty of the coastal State in its internal waters and territorial sea means that the coastal State has exclusive rights in respect of fishing activities in those waters. Foreign-flagged vessels may not fish there without the consent of the coastal State and there is no requirement for the coastal State to provide access to surplus fish stocks in the waters in question. (On the meaning of 'surplus', see further below.)

The exclusive rights of the coastal State in respect of fishing activities are also made clear by Article 21 by which the coastal State may 'adopt laws and regulations, in conformity with the provisions of this Convention and other rules of

---

[27] Churchill, RR and Lowe, AV, *The Law of the Sea* (3rd edn, Manchester: Manchester University Press, 1999), 290.   [28] Art 8(1).
[29] Art 5.   [30] Arts 6–14.   [31] Art 3.   [32] Art 2(2).   [33] Art 17.
[34] Art 8(2).   [35] Art 19(2)(i).

international law, relating to innocent passage through the territorial sea, in respect of . . . [*inter alia*] . . . (d) the conservation of the living resources of the sea; (e) the prevention of infringement of the fisheries laws and regulations of the coastal State; (f) the preservation of the environment of the coastal State . . .'.

Likewise, no foreign-flagged vessel may carry out exploratory fishing in the internal waters or territorial sea of a coastal State under the guise of 'marine scientific research'. That is because coastal States 'have the exclusive right to regulate, authorize and conduct marine scientific research in their territorial sea' (and hence likewise in their internal waters) and such research 'shall be conducted only with the express consent of and under the conditions set forth by the coastal State'.[36]

The Convention does not establish duties on the coastal State relating expressly to fisheries management in internal waters and the territorial sea. However, Part XII of the Convention, on protection and preservation of the marine environment, contains several general duties that are potentially applicable to fishing activities in such waters (for example, Articles 194(5), 197, and 206). In addition, many provisions in Part XII are potentially relevant to reducing the impact on fisheries resources of activities generating pollution.

2.3 Fishing in the exclusive economic zone

The exclusive economic zone (EEZ) is a zone extending from the seaward limit of the territorial sea out to a maximum of 200 nm from the baseline from which the breadth of the territorial sea is measured.[37] In that zone the coastal State may claim certain rights and jurisdictions. However, such rights and jurisdictions, even if claimed in their entirety, do not amount to territorial sovereignty. Furthermore, they must be exercised with due regard to the rights of other States.[38] The EEZ comprises the subsoil, seabed, and superjacent water column,[39] although EEZ rights and jurisdiction with respect to the seabed and subsoil must be exercised in accordance with Part VI of the Convention, on the continental shelf (on which, see subsection 2.4 below).[40]

Among the rights available in respect of the EEZ are 'sovereign rights for the purpose of exploring and exploiting, conserving and managing the natural resources, whether living or non-living, of the waters superjacent to the seabed and of the seabed and its subsoil'.[41] The term 'natural resources', in the context of the EEZ, is not defined in the Convention. However, it is clear that fish stocks are a type of living natural resources and are therefore covered by the above category of rights. Where the coastal State chooses to claim only sovereign rights for the purpose of exploring, exploiting, conserving, and managing fisheries resources,

---

[36] Art 245.   [37] Arts 55 and 57.   [38] Art 56(2).   [39] Art 56(1)(a).
[40] Art 56(3).   [41] Art 56(1)(a).

rather than any of the other rights available under the EEZ regime, the zone in question tends to be referred to as an exclusive *fishing* zone (EFZ).

In practice, the large majority of coastal States claiming rights beyond the territorial sea now claim an EEZ rather than just an EFZ.[42] The EEZ or EFZ is of great importance for commercial fisheries. For example, Churchill and Lowe reported in 1999 that '[t]he universal establishment of 200-mile EEZs and EFZs would embrace an area where about ninety per cent of commercial fishing currently takes place'.[43]

In contrast to internal waters or the territorial sea, the Convention contains many provisions relating expressly to management of fisheries in the EEZ. Those provisions may be regarded as applying equally to an EFZ. Most of the provisions are found in Part V of the Convention, although others are located in Part XII (on protection and preservation of the marine environment), Part XIII (on marine scientific research), and Part XV (on settlement of disputes). Of note, Part V does not apply to sedentary species (on which, see subsection 2.4 below).[44]

General provisions for the conservation and utilization of fish stocks are laid down in Articles 61 and 62. (Subsection 2.6 below addresses the Convention's provisions on particular species and stocks.) Article 62 establishes a duty on coastal States to promote 'the objective of optimum utilization' of fish stocks.[45] This duty is without prejudice to various conservation duties set out in Article 61, including the obligation to ensure, through proper conservation and management measures, that maintenance of fish stocks 'is not endangered by over-exploitation'.[46]

The said measures are to be 'designed to maintain or restore populations of harvested species at levels which can produce the maximum sustainable yield, as qualified by relevant environmental and economic factors, including the economic needs of coastal fishing communities and the special requirements of developing States, and taking into account fishing patterns, the interdependence of stocks and any generally recommended international minimum standards, whether sub-regional, regional or global'.[47] In taking the measures, the coastal State is to take into consideration effects on associated or dependent species.[48]

The coastal State is required to determine the total allowable catch (TAC) of fish stocks in its EEZ or EFZ.[49] Where it does not have the capacity to harvest the entire TAC, the coastal State must give other States access to that surplus by means of 'agreements or other arrangements'.[50] In doing so, it must have 'particular regard to the provisions of articles 69 and 70 [on the rights of land-locked and geographically disadvantaged States], especially in relation to the developing States mentioned therein'.[51]

In giving other States access to fisheries in its EEZ, the coastal State is to take into account 'all relevant factors', including '*inter alia*, the significance of the living

---

[42] See the website of the DOALOS.   [43] Churchill and Lowe, *The Law of the Sea*, 288.
[44] Art 68.   [45] Art 62(1).   [46] Art 61(2).   [47] Art 61(3).   [48] Art 61(4).
[49] Art 61(1).   [50] Art 62(2).   [51] Art 62(2).

resources of the area to the economy of the coastal State concerned and its other national interests, the provisions of articles 69 and 70, the requirements of developing States in the subregion or region in harvesting part of the surplus and the need to minimize economic dislocation in States whose nationals have habitually fished in the zone or which have made substantial efforts in research and identification of stocks'.[52]

The coastal State, in providing access, is entitled to impose certain conditions on the vessels in question.[53] A non-exhaustive list of the types of conditions is provided in Article 62(4), with the qualification that they must be 'consistent with this Convention'. The conditions may include, *inter alia*, the payment of fees and other forms of remuneration as well as conservation and management measures for the stock in question.[54] The vessels granted access to the EEZ must comply with those conditions.[55] The use by the EC of fisheries access arrangements is discussed in detail in Chapter 5.

With a significant exception, Part XV of the Convention requires disputes concerning the interpretation or application of the Convention's fisheries provisions to be settled in accordance with the Convention's provisions in section 2 of Part XV on compulsory procedures entailing binding decisions.[56] The said exception, set out in section 3 of Part XV, states that:[57]

the coastal State shall not be obliged to accept the submission to such settlement of any dispute relating to its sovereign rights with respect to the living resources in the [EEZ] or their exercise, including its discretionary powers for determining the allowable catch, its harvesting capacity, the allocation of surpluses to other States and the terms and conditions established in its conservation and management laws and regulations.

As can be seen, the exception is broad in that it relates to 'any dispute' relating to the coastal State's 'sovereign rights with respect to the living resources in the [EEZ] or their exercise'. Thus, for example, the coastal State would not be required to accept the application of the section 2 procedures to any dispute over whether or not its particular conservation and management regime had ensured that maintenance of fish stocks is not endangered by over-exploitation. However, the exception does not preclude a coastal State invoking the section 2 procedures against, say, a flag State whose vessels were fishing in its EEZ in breach of the Convention.

A dispute covered by the exception is not totally exempt from the Convention's dispute resolution procedures. The Convention implies that the parties are still required to attempt settlement of the dispute by recourse to section 1 of Part XV.[58] That section contains general provisions on peaceful settlement but none regarding compulsory procedures entailing binding decisions. Failing settlement by recourse to section 1, a dispute regarding any of the following specific allegations is to be

[52] Art 62(3).   [53] Art 62(2) and (4).   [54] Art 62(4).   [55] Art 62(4).
[56] Art 297(3)(a).   [57] Art 297(3)(a).   [58] Art 297(3)(b).

submitted to conciliation under section 2 of Annex V to the Convention at the request of any party to the dispute:[59]

   (i) a coastal State has manifestly failed to comply with its obligations to ensure through proper conservation and management measures that the maintenance of the living resources in the [EEZ] is not seriously endangered;

  (ii) a coastal State has arbitrarily refused to determine, at the request of another State, the allowable catch and its capacity to harvest living resources with respect to stocks which that other State is interested in fishing; or

 (iii) a coastal State has arbitrarily refused to allocate to any State, under articles 62, 69 and 70 and under the terms and conditions established by the coastal State consistent with this Convention, the whole or part of the surplus it has declared to exist.

The conciliation commission may not 'substitute its discretion for that of the coastal State'[60] and, in any event, such conciliation does not entail binding decisions.[61] Nonetheless, the possibility of scrutiny by a conciliation commission may be some incentive to a coastal State to, for example, avoid an allegation of manifest failure to adopt appropriate conservation and management measures. In practice, the Convention's provisions on conciliation have not yet been employed.

It is also possible that a breach by the coastal State of the conservation duties for fish stocks in the EEZ could be pursued by means of arguing a breach of the duty in Article 300 on States Parties to, *inter alia*, 'fulfil in good faith the obligations assumed under this Convention'. However, such an argument has not so far been tested. Overall, it is probably fair to say that compliance by coastal States with the Convention's conservation requirements for EEZ fish stocks is not likely to be driven primarily by the threat of recourse to the Convention's dispute resolution provisions.

Article 73 sets out the enforcement powers of the coastal State in the exercise of its sovereign rights to explore, exploit, conserve, and manage the living resources in the EEZ. In the exercise of such rights, the coastal State may 'take such measures, including boarding, inspection, arrest and judicial proceedings, as may be necessary to ensure compliance with the laws and regulations adopted by it in conformity with this Convention'.[62] Thus boarding, inspection, and arrest by the coastal State of foreign-flagged vessels fishing in the EEZ, and legal proceedings, are expressly permitted by the Convention. Those powers are supplemented by the provisions on hot pursuit in Article 111.

Article 73 also contains provisions on prompt release, non-permissible sanctions (namely 'imprisonment, in the absence of agreements to the contrary by the States concerned, or any other form of corporal punishment'), and prompt notification to the flag State of any arrest or detention. Regarding prompt release, the Convention requires that '[a]rrested vessels and their crews shall be promptly released

---

[59] Art 297(3)(b).   [60] Art 297(3)(c).   [61] Annex V, Arts 14 and 7(2).   [62] Art 73(1).

upon the posting of reasonable bond or other security'.[63] The International Tribunal for the Law of the Sea (ITLOS) has decided five cases on prompt release of fishing vessels where the original arrest of those vessels related to their alleged fishing activities in the EEZ[64] and two cases on prompt release of vessels allegedly associated with fishing activities in the EEZ.[65] In each case, the jurisdiction of the ITLOS arose by virtue of Article 292 in Part XV of the Convention.

The sovereign rights of the coastal State to explore, exploit, conserve, and manage the living natural resources of the EEZ are reflected in Part XIII of the Convention, on marine scientific research. Thus Article 246 permits coastal States to withhold their consent to the conduct of a marine scientific research project by a third State in the EEZ if, *inter alia*, that project 'is of direct significance for the exploration and exploitation of natural resources, whether living or non-living'.[66]

Just as for internal waters and the territorial sea (see subsection 2.2 above), Part XII of the Convention, on protection and preservation of the marine environment, contains several general duties that are potentially applicable to fishing activities in the EEZ (supplementing the fisheries management duties in Part V) as well as many provisions that are potentially relevant to reducing the impact on fisheries resources of activities generating pollution.

2.4 Fishing on the continental shelf

The term 'continental shelf' has both a legal meaning and a meaning derived from geology and geomorphology. In this section, the terms 'continental shelf' or 'shelf' will be used to mean the continental shelf in its legal sense. The Convention's regime for the continental shelf is provided mainly by Part VI, although there are also important provisions in Parts V, VII, XI, XII, and XIII.

The continental shelf consists of the seabed and subsoil.[67] It extends from the seaward limit of the territorial sea.[68] Assuming no geographical constraints created by the proximity of neighbouring States,[69] it extends out to at least 200 nm from the baseline from which the breadth of the territorial sea is measured.[70] However, given appropriate geology and geomorphology (as defined by Article 76(2)–(6)), it may extend further than that to an overall limit of 350 nm from the baseline or 100 nm

---

[63] Art 73(2).

[64] ITLOS Case No 5, *The 'Camouco' Case (Panama v France)*; ITLOS Case No 6, *The 'Monte Confurco' Case (Seychelles v France)*; ITLOS Case No 11, *The 'Volga' Case (Russian Federation v Australia)*; ITLOS Case No 14, *The 'Hoshinmaru' Case (Japan v Russian Federation)*; and ITLOS Case No 15, *The 'Tomimaru' Case (Japan v Russian Federation)*. The judgments of the ITLOS are available on its website.

[65] ITLOS Case No 1, *The M/V 'SAIGA' Case (Saint Vincent and the Grenadines v Guinea)*; and ITLOS Case No 13, *The 'Juno Trader' Case (Saint Vincent and the Grenadines v Guinea-Bissau)*.

[66] Art 246(5)(a).   [67] Art 76(1). See also Art 76(3).   [68] Art 76(1).

[69] Arts 76(10) and 83.   [70] Art 76(1).

beyond the 2,500 m isobath.[71] The Convention does not use a specific term to describe the part of the shelf lying beyond 200 nm from the baseline; this section will use the terms 'outer continental shelf' or 'outer shelf' to refer to that part of the shelf.

Article 77(1) states that: 'The coastal State exercises over the continental shelf sovereign rights for the purpose of exploring it and exploiting its natural resources.' As with the EEZ, such sovereign rights do not amount to territorial sovereignty. In contrast to the EEZ, the continental shelf rights 'do not depend . . . on any express proclamation'. Furthermore, no occupation of the shelf is required.[72] The coastal State's sovereign rights in relation to the continental shelf 'are *exclusive* in the sense that if the coastal State does not explore the continental shelf or exploit its natural resources, no one may undertake these activities without the express consent of the coastal State' (emphasis added).[73]

The rights of the coastal State over the continental shelf 'do not affect the legal status of the superjacent waters'[74] and their exercise 'must not infringe or result in any unjustifiable interference with navigation and other rights and freedoms of other States as provided for in this Convention'.[75] That is particularly significant with regard to the outer shelf. The waters superjacent to the outer shelf are the high seas, in which there is, *inter alia*, a qualified freedom of fishing. The interaction between the rights of the coastal State regarding the outer shelf and the high seas freedom of fishing is addressed in subsection 2.5 below.

The term 'natural resources', in the context of the continental shelf, is defined as 'the mineral and other non-living resources of the seabed and subsoil together with living organisms belonging to sedentary species'.[76] It is the 'living organisms belonging to sedentary species', rather than the 'non-living resources', that are of interest in this book. The term 'sedentary species' is in turn defined as 'organisms which, at the harvestable stage, either are immobile on or under the seabed or are unable to move except in constant physical contact with the seabed or the subsoil'.[77]

Commonly cited examples of sedentary species for which there may be fisheries include abalone, clams, and oysters.[78] In some cases, it may be unclear whether a particular target species is sedentary or not (for example, lobsters or scallops). That is unlikely to be problematic in cases where that species occurs on the shelf within the 200 nm limit. That is because if it is a sedentary species, it is covered by the continental shelf regime and if it is not, it is covered by the EEZ regime (assuming that appropriate EEZ rights have been claimed by the coastal State).

However, any uncertainty is likely to be problematic in cases where the species occurs on the outer shelf: if it is not a sedentary species, it is not covered by the continental shelf regime and cannot be covered by the EEZ regime either because

---

[71] Art 76(5).   [72] Art 77(3).   [73] Art 77(2).   [74] Art 78(1).   [75] Art 78(2).
[76] Art 77(4).   [77] Art 77(4).   [78] See Churchill and Lowe, *The Law of the Sea*, 151.

the maximum seaward limit of the EEZ is 200 nm from the baseline. Instead, in such cases the species is subject to the qualified freedom of fishing on the high seas.

Although the sovereign rights of the coastal State in relation to its continental shelf extend to the exploitation of sedentary species, it is notable that Part VI itself does not establish a conservation regime for such species. That is in contrast to Part V on the EEZ (see subsection 2.3 above). What is more, by virtue of the exclusion of sedentary species from the scope of Part V,[79] the general provisions for the conservation and utilization of living resources set out in Articles 61 and 62 in Part V do not apply to such species either.

However, that does not necessarily mean that sedentary species must or may be exploited without limit. As noted above, the coastal State's sovereign rights for the exploitation of sedentary species are exclusive, with the result that the coastal State may choose *not* to exploit such species on certain parts of its shelf or may choose to attach conditions to the exploitation of such species. Such choices may be motivated by a desire to conserve the species or to protect the wider marine environment from the exploitation activity.

Furthermore, Part XII of the Convention, on protection and preservation of the marine environment, contains several general duties that are potentially applicable to fishing activities for sedentary species on the continental shelf as well as many provisions that are potentially relevant to reducing the impact on fisheries resources of activities generating pollution (as is likewise the case in respect of internal waters, the territorial sea, and the EEZ—see subsections 2.2 and 2.3 above).

It was noted in subsection 2.3 above that the Convention's compulsory dispute resolution procedures entailing binding decisions, as set out in section 2 of Part XV, apply to disputes concerning the interpretation or application of its fisheries provisions, with an exception relating only to the EEZ. Thus disputes concerning interpretation or application of provisions regarding fisheries for sedentary species on the shelf remain subject to the section 2 procedures.

The Convention establishes a mechanism to provide certainty about the limits of the outer shelf. Thus Article 76(8) states that:

Information on the limits of the continental shelf beyond 200 nautical miles from the baselines from which the breadth of the territorial sea is measured shall be submitted by the coastal State to the Commission on the Limits of the Continental Shelf set up under Annex II on the basis of equitable geographical representation. The Commission shall make recommendations to coastal States on matters related to the establishment of the outer limits of their continental shelf. The limits of the shelf established by a coastal State on the basis of these recommendations shall be final and binding.

Several EC Member States potentially have outer shelves. However, at the time of writing, to the authors' knowledge, no Member State had established limits to the

---

[79] Art 68.

outer shelf that are final and binding in accordance with Article 76(8). Of the EC Member States, France, Ireland, Spain, and the UK had made submissions to the Commission on the Limits of the Continental Shelf (CLCS), such submissions comprising (in respect of territories to which the CFP applies): (a) one joint sub-mission by the four Member States in May 2006 (which is only a partial submission for each State); (b) a separate submission by Ireland in May 2005 (which, again, is only a partial submission, and on which the CLCS adopted recommendations in spring 2007); and (c) a separate submission by France in May 2007 (regarding French Guiana).[80]

The deadline in the Convention for submitting information on the shelf limits to the CLCS is 'within 10 years of the entry into force of this Convention for that State'.[81] However, in May 2001 the States parties to the Convention decided that for a State party for which the Convention had entered into force before 13 May 1999, the deadline would be ten years from 13 May 1999—thus falling in May 2009.[82] In June 2008, a further decision by the States parties to the Convention allowed the ten-year time period referred to in both the Convention and the May 2001 decision to be satisfied by submission of, amongst other things, 'preliminary information indicative of the outer limits' of the outer shelf.[83] In practice, the CLCS may well be inundated with submissions by the May 2009 deadline referred to above and may need considerable time to deal with them all. Furthermore, there is clearly scope for the coastal State to disagree with the CLCS's recom-mendations. In case of disagreement, the Convention requires that 'the coastal State shall, within a reasonable time, make a revised or new submission to the [CLCS]'.[84]

Thus it may be quite some time before a coastal State is able to establish final and binding limits on the basis of the CLCS's recommendations and hence be certain about the seaward limits of its outer shelf. In the meantime, practice is likely to vary between States as to the extent to which they are willing to exercise shelf rights on the shelf beyond 200 nm. Some States may be very cautious about exercising such rights; others may be less cautious. The need for coastal State action may be precipitated by, for example, the activities of third State fishing vessels undertaking bottom trawling on the outer shelf (see further subsection 2.5 below).

Whereas Part V of the Convention, on the EEZ, contains a provision (Article 73) giving express powers to the coastal State to enforce its laws and regulations regarding living resources, the Convention contains no equivalent provision regarding enforcement of laws and regulations regarding sedentary species on the continental shelf. Despite the absence of such a provision, the power of the coastal

---

[80] See the website of the DOALOS.   [81] Annex II, Art 4.

[82] Document SPLOS/72, Meeting of States Parties [to the United Nations Convention on the Law of the Sea], Eleventh Meeting, New York, 14–18 May 2001.

[83] Document SPLOS/183, Meeting of States Parties [to the United Nations Convention on the Law of the Sea], Eighteenth Meeting, New York, 13–20 June 2008.   [84] Annex II, Art 8.

State to enforce such laws and regulations against, *inter alia*, third State fishing vessels operating in the high seas superjacent to the outer shelf can probably reasonably be implied. Hot pursuit, pursuant to Article 111, may be undertaken in respect of violations of continental shelf laws and regulations.

The sovereign rights of the coastal State to explore the shelf and exploit its natural resources are reflected in Part XIII of the Convention, on marine scientific research. Thus Article 246 permits coastal States to withhold their consent to the conduct of a marine scientific research project by a third State on the continental shelf if, *inter alia*, that project 'is of direct significance for the exploration and exploitation of natural resources, whether living or non-living' (subject to a limited exception regarding the outer shelf).[85] The living natural resources of the shelf referred to in Article 246 are the living organisms belonging to sedentary species.

2.5 Fishing on the high seas

The high seas comprise 'all parts of the sea that are not included in the [EEZ], in the territorial sea or in the internal waters of a State, or in the archipelagic waters of an archipelagic State'.[86] The seabed and its subsoil lying beneath the high seas comprise, for the greater part, 'the Area'[87] and, for the lesser part, the outer continental shelf. The high seas and the Area are commonly referred to jointly as 'areas beyond national jurisdiction'.

Part VII of the Convention, on the high seas, states that the high seas are open to all States but adds that freedom of the high seas is 'exercised under the conditions laid down by this Convention and by other rules of international law'.[88] Freedom of the high seas is stated to comprise, *inter alia*, 'freedom of fishing, subject to the conditions laid down in section 2 [of Part VII]'.[89] Thus the high seas freedom of fishing is qualified both by a specific reference to section 2 of Part VII as well as a more general reference to 'the conditions laid down by this Convention and by other rules of international law'. The conditions laid down by the Convention clearly include section 2 of Part VII, but they also include, *inter alia*, Articles 87(2) and 147(3) and Part XII.

Article 87(2) requires high seas freedoms to be exercised 'with due regard for the interests of other States in their exercise of the freedom of the high seas'. Article 87(2) also requires the same freedoms to be exercised 'with due regard for the rights under this Convention with respect to activities in the Area'. Likewise, Article 147(3) requires that: 'Other activities in the marine environment shall be conducted with reasonable regard for activities in the Area.'

---

[85] Art 246(5)(a), (6), and (7).   [86] Art 86.

[87] The term 'the Area' is defined by the Convention as 'the seabed and ocean floor and subsoil thereof, beyond the limits of national jurisdiction' (see Art 1(1)).   [88] Art 87(1).

[89] Art 87(1)(e).

Part XII of the Convention contains many environmental protection duties. Just as for internal waters, the territorial sea, the EEZ, and the continental shelf (see subsections 2.2, 2.3, and 2.4 above), Part XII contains several general duties that are potentially applicable to fishing activities on the high seas (as well as many provisions that are potentially relevant to reducing the impact on fisheries resources of activities generating pollution).

Section 2 of Part VII comprises Articles 116–120. Article 116 states that the freedom of fishing is subject to: (a) States' treaty obligations; (b) coastal States' rights, duties and interests provided for, *inter alia*, in Articles 63(2), 64, 65, 66, and 67 (on which, see subsection 2.6 below); and (c) the provisions of section 2 itself. Article 117 requires States to take, or cooperate with other States in taking, 'such measures for their respective nationals as may be necessary for the conservation of the living resources of the high seas'.

The cooperation theme in Article 117 is continued in Article 118. After reiterating a general duty to cooperate, Article 118 focuses on the specific instance where States' nationals 'exploit identical living resources, or different living resources in the same area'. In that instance, those States are to 'enter into negotiations with a view to taking the measures necessary for the conservation of the living resources concerned'. As appropriate, the States are to 'cooperate to establish subregional or regional fisheries organizations' for that purpose.

Article 119 sets out some requirements for States when they are determining the allowable catch and establishing other conservation measures for the living resources in the high seas, including the measures referred to in Articles 117 and 118. As with the EEZ, the measures are to be designed to maintain or restore maximum sustainable yield (with some qualifications similar to those for the EEZ) and States are to take into consideration effects on associated or dependent species.[90] However, in contrast to the EEZ, there is no underlying duty to ensure, through proper conservation and management measures, that maintenance of high seas fish stocks is not endangered by over-exploitation. Article 119 also prohibits discrimination on grounds of nationality.[91] Article 120 applies Article 65, on marine mammals, to the high seas (on which, see subsection 2.6 below).

Part VII of the Convention makes it clear that a ship on the high seas, so long as it is flagged to one State only, is subject to the exclusive jurisdiction of its flag State 'save in exceptional cases expressly provided for in international treaties or in this Convention'.[92] The exceptions provided for in the Convention do not include verifying compliance with high seas fisheries conservation regimes. That is generally accepted as meaning that boarding, inspection, or arrest of a fishing vessel on the high seas by a third State for that purpose would require an express provision in some other treaty (for example, a treaty establishing a regional fisheries management organization).

---

[90] Art 119(1)(a) and (b).   [91] Art 119(3).   [92] Art 92(1).

As noted in subsection 2.3 above, the Convention's compulsory dispute resolution procedures entailing binding decisions apply to disputes concerning the interpretation or application of its fisheries provisions, with an exception relating only to the EEZ. Thus disputes concerning interpretation or application of provisions regarding high seas fisheries remain subject to the Convention's compulsory procedures entailing binding decisions. Those procedures have been invoked on three occasions to date,[93] although, for a variety of reasons, none of the resulting cases has been determined on its merits.

As noted earlier, there will be places where the seabed and its subsoil lying beneath the high seas will comprise the outer continental shelf of a coastal State. In such places, there is scope for interaction between the high seas freedom of fishing and a coastal State's sovereign rights regarding sedentary species on its outer shelf. That interaction could arise by, for example, a fishing vessel on the high seas overlying the shelf using bottom trawling to target demersal non-sedentary species on the shelf.

Despite targeting non-sedentary species, it is possible to imagine that the bottom trawling in question could involve a high by-catch of sedentary species or significant damage to the sedentary species or their habitats. Article 77(2) requires that no one may exploit the natural resources of the shelf without the express consent of the coastal State. It is arguable that high by-catch, or significant damage of species or habitats, is a form of exploitation. However, even if that were not the case, that does not mean that the bottom trawling may necessarily continue unchallenged by the coastal State.

Taking a step back, the example in question would be a case of the exercise of a high seas freedom coming into conflict with the exercise of coastal State rights. If the fishing were to continue unchecked, the coastal State might argue that its natural resources were being damaged. If the coastal State were to prevent the fishing, the flag State might argue that it was unable to exercise its high seas freedom of fishing.

The Convention anticipates this type of conflict. Article 78(2) requires that the exercise by the coastal State of its rights over the natural resources of the shelf must not 'infringe or result in any unjustifiable interference with' the high seas freedom of fishing. Of note, the 1958 Convention on the Continental Shelf[94] (a predecessor to the 1982 Convention) requires only that the exercise of coastal State rights must not 'result in any unjustifiable interference' with high seas freedoms;[95] it does not include a requirement not to 'infringe' such freedoms. At the Third UN Conference on the Law of the Sea, the additional requirement not to 'infringe' was introduced informally into the negotiations by the (then) USSR in 1979.[96]

---

[93] ITLOS Cases Nos 3 and 4, *Southern Bluefin Tuna Cases (New Zealand v Japan; Australia v Japan)*; Annex VII Arbitral Tribunal (2000), *Southern Bluefin Tuna Case (Australia and New Zealand v Japan)*; and ITLOS Case No 7, *Case concerning the Conservation and Sustainable Exploitation of Swordfish Stocks in the South-Eastern Pacific Ocean (Chile/European Community)*. Case No 7 is discussed briefly in Chapter 5.

[94] 499 UNTS 311.   [95] Art 5(1).

[96] Nandan, SN, Rosenne, S, and Grandy, NR, *United Nations Convention on the Law of the Sea 1982—A Commentary*, Vol II (Dordrecht: Martinus Nijhoff Publishers, 1993), 905.

Attard infers from the addition of the requirement not to 'infringe' high seas freedoms in the Convention (compared to the 1958 Convention) that 'the concept of "unjustifiable interference" was not felt to be sufficient to safeguard the international community's interests in view of the new extensive EEZ powers allocated to the coastal State'.[97] If that is right, one can suppose that flag States wanted to guard against the possibility that numerous justifiable interferences over time might end up infringing their high seas freedoms.

On that basis, it would be open to the coastal State to show that an action to prohibit high seas bottom trawling on its outer shelf is a justifiable interference with the high seas freedom of fishing so long as overall that freedom is not infringed. The point at which infringement of the freedom of fishing might occur is open to debate. Perhaps there would be no infringement if vessels flagged to third States were still permitted to fish using other gears or in other locations on the outer shelf.

Subject to the meaning of infringement, it would be necessary for the coastal State to show that its interference was justifiable. Using an example based on potential conflict between oil exploitation and the freedom of navigation in relation to the shelf within 200 nm, Attard states that:[98]

It must also be pointed out that interference, even if substantial, may be justified, whilst certain forms of interference, even if insignificant, may be unjustifiable and may constitute an infringement of the freedom to navigate in the EEZ. In such cases an assessment must be made of the interests involved. Thus, for example, the estimated value of the resource-deposit and the cost to shipping of alternative routes are just two elements which would have to be considered.

On the basis that an assessment of the interests involved must be made, the coastal State might argue that the bottom trawling in question was destroying the resource that was the very subject matter of its rights and was doing so in a zone under its jurisdiction. The coastal State might also argue that the bottom trawling was preventing it from fulfilling some of its environmental protection duties set out in Part XII of the Convention (for example, Article 194(5)) as well as any duties agreed through organizations referred to in Article 197 (for example, regional seas organizations). In principle, a dispute arising from this kind of scenario could be resolved in accordance with Part XV of the Convention.

2.6 Fishing for particular species and stocks

Introduction

This subsection will consider the provisions in Part V of the Convention on shared stocks, straddling stocks, highly migratory species, marine mammals, anadromous

---

[97] Attard, DJ, *The Exclusive Economic Zone in International Law* (Oxford: Clarendon Press, 1987), 144.
[98] Ibid.

stocks, and catadromous species as well as the provisions in Part VII on marine mammals. The Convention's provisions on sedentary species have already been discussed in subsection 2.4 above.

Shared stocks

Shared stocks are addressed by Article 63(1), which relates to situations '[w]here the same stock or stocks of associated species occur within the [EEZs] of two or more coastal States'. In such situations, the coastal States in question 'shall seek, either directly or through appropriate subregional or regional organizations, to agree upon the measures necessary to coordinate and ensure the conservation and development of such stocks without prejudice to the other provisions of this Part'.

Thus Article 63(1) does not actually use the term 'shared stocks'; however, that term, or 'transboundary stocks', has come to be used to describe the stocks referred to in that provision. Of note, Article 63(1) does not apply to stocks shared between coastal States' internal waters or territorial seas. In such cases, the Convention does not establish any duty to cooperate for fisheries conservation specifically. However, there still remains the duty in Article 197 in Part XII to cooperate for the purposes of environmental protection in general whereby:

States shall cooperate on a global basis and, as appropriate, on a regional basis, directly or through competent international organizations, in formulating and elaborating international rules, standards and recommended practices and procedures consistent with this Convention, for the protection and preservation of the marine environment, taking into account characteristic regional features.

The cooperation duty in Article 63(1) is weak in that States need only 'seek . . . to agree' upon the necessary measures. Burke observes that '[t]he substantive obligation imposed by Article 63(1) cannot fairly be described as awesome, imposing, or, even, perhaps, very consequential'.[99] Churchill and Lowe describe some State practice on shared stocks and conclude that 'there still exist many shared stocks for which no co-operative arrangements have yet been agreed by the States concerned'.[100] Owen provides an analysis of the legal and institutional aspects of thirty-nine arrangements relevant to the management of shared stocks.[101]

Straddling stocks

Straddling stocks are addressed by Article 63(2), which relates to situations '[w]here the same stock or stocks of associated species occur both within the

---

[99] Burke, WT, 'Annex 1–1982 Convention on the Law of the Sea Provisions on Conditions of Access to Fisheries Subject to National Jurisdiction' in FAO, *Report of the Expert Consultation on the Conditions of Access to the Fish Resources of the Exclusive Economic Zones, Rome, 11–15 April 1983: A Preparatory Meeting for the FAO World Conference on Fisheries Management and Development*, FAO Fisheries Report 293 (Rome: FAO, 1983).   [100] Churchill and Lowe, *The Law of the Sea*, 294–6.

[101] Owen, D, 'Legal and Institutional Aspects of Management Arrangements for Shared Stocks of Marine Fish' in Fitzmaurice, M and Szuniewicz, M (eds), *Exploitation of Natural Resources in the 21st Century* (The Hague: Kluwer Law International, 2003), 247–87.

[EEZ] and in an area beyond and adjacent to the zone'. In such situations, 'the coastal State and the States fishing for such stocks in the adjacent area shall seek, either directly or through appropriate subregional or regional organizations, to agree upon the measures necessary for the conservation of these stocks in the adjacent area'.

Thus Article 63(2) does not actually use the term 'straddling stocks', but that is the term that has come to be used to describe the stocks referred to in that provision. The provision relates to stocks that straddle the boundary between the EEZ and the high seas. Thus it applies not only to coastal States but also to third States that are fishing on the high seas. As with Article 63(1), the cooperation duty in Article 63(2) is weak in that States need only 'seek . . . to agree' upon measures. Furthermore, any resulting measures are to relate only to the high seas, rather than to the EEZ.

Article 63(2) is referred to in Part VII of the Convention, on the high seas. Thus Article 116 states that the right of all States for their nationals to engage in fishing on the high seas is subject to 'the rights and duties as well as the interests of coastal States provided for, *inter alia*, in article 63, paragraph 2, and articles 64 to 67'. So the right to fish on the high seas is subject to, *inter alia*, the cooperation duty set out in Article 63(2) (as well as being subject to the provisions in Articles 64–67). Article 63(2) has been implemented by means of the Fish Stocks Agreement (see section 3 below). Some regional fisheries management organizations addressing straddling stocks are introduced in section 6 below and are discussed further in Chapter 5.

Highly migratory species

Highly migratory species are addressed by Article 64. The highly migratory species to which Article 64 relates are those listed in Annex I to the Convention. That list includes, *inter alia*, several tuna species, swordfish, several species and families of oceanic sharks, and seven families of cetaceans. In contrast to Articles 63 and 66, but in common with Articles 67 and 68, Article 64 refers to 'species' rather than 'stocks'. Article 64 applies to '[t]he coastal State and other States whose nationals fish in the region' for the Annex I species. It contains two duties to cooperate.

The principal duty is that the States concerned 'shall cooperate directly or through appropriate international organizations with a view to ensuring conservation and promoting the objective of optimum utilization of such species throughout the region, both within and beyond the [EEZ]'. Thus the duty to cooperate is not qualified by any weakening caveat like 'seek', 'try' or 'endeavour', in contrast to Article 63(1) and (2). However, the wording 'with a view to ensuring conservation', rather than just 'to ensure conservation', weakens the duty somewhat.

In contrast to Article 63(2), the desired outcome is not just conservation but also the promotion of 'the objective of optimum utilization', which reflects the general duty in Article 62 (see subsection 2.3 above). Furthermore, the desired outcome of conservation is to apply not just to the high seas portion of the region in question but 'throughout the region, both within and beyond the [EEZ]'. Birnie and Boyle imply from this that: 'The coastal state thus cannot exercise its right to make decisions until it has discharged its duty to co-operate with other states in promoting conservation and use.'[102]

The second cooperation duty in Article 64 is that '[i]n regions for which no appropriate international organization exists', the States concerned 'shall cooperate to establish such an organization and participate in its work'. The duty to cooperate to establish a new body is relatively strong, but the duty to in turn 'participate' raises the question whether such participation entails the same tasks as are included in the first duty or something less. In requiring the establishment of new organizations where none currently exists, Article 64 contrasts with Article 63(2) which is silent in that regard.

Article 64(1) has been implemented by means of the Fish Stocks Agreement (see section 3 below). Some regional fisheries management organizations addressing highly migratory species are introduced in section 6 below and are discussed further in Chapter 5. Article 64(2) adds that: 'The provisions of paragraph 1 apply in addition to the other provisions of this Part.' In other words, the provisions of Article 64(1), insofar as they relate to the EEZ, are supplemental to, rather than an alternative for, the other provisions of Part V—notably the general duties set out in Articles 61 and 62.

Marine mammals

Marine mammals are addressed primarily by Article 65. Marine mammals include, *inter alia*, cetaceans (ie whales and dolphins), seals, and sirenians. Article 65 has two parts. The first states that: 'Nothing in this Part restricts the right of a coastal State or the competence of an international organization, as appropriate, to prohibit, limit or regulate the exploitation of marine mammals more strictly than provided for in this Part.'

The reference to '[n]othing in this Part' relates, *inter alia*, to the requirement in Article 62 to 'promote the objective of optimum utilization' and, in the case of cetaceans specifically, the same requirement in Article 64. The express disapplication of such requirements and others in Part V promoting exploitation, together with the express allowance of a prohibition on exploitation, makes it clear that marine mammals are an exception among living resources and may legitimately be protected from exploitation in the EEZ irrespective of their abundance.

The second part of Article 65 has two components. The first relates to marine mammals in general and states that 'States shall cooperate with a view to the conservation of marine mammals'. That general duty is phrased in the same way as the principal duty in Article 64: although the duty to cooperate is not qualified by

---

[102] Birnie, PW and Boyle, AE, *International Law and the Environment* (2nd edn, Oxford: Oxford University Press, 2002), 666.

any weakening caveat like 'seek', 'try' or 'endeavour', the wording 'with a view to the conservation of', rather than just 'to conserve', is a weakening influence.

The other component of the second part of Article 65 relates to cetaceans specifically and requires that States 'in the case of cetaceans shall in particular work through the appropriate international organizations for their conservation, management and study'. That provision endorses the use of international organizations 'in particular', and contrasts with Articles 63 and 64 which expressly provide for States to either work through organizations or to work with each other directly. However, the reference to international organizations, in the plural form, indicates that the International Whaling Commission is not necessarily the only international organization that may be used. Some international organizations and agreements addressing marine mammals are introduced in section 6 below and discussed further in Chapter 5.

Marine mammals are also singled out for attention in Part VII of the Convention, on the high seas. Article 120 states that: 'Article 65 also applies to the conservation and management of marine mammals in the high seas.' In contrast to Part V, Part VII does not contain any express requirement to promote optimum utilization. However, it does nonetheless promote exploitation (for example, Article 119(1)(a)). So one effect of Article 120 is to allow international organizations regulating conservation and management of marine mammals on the high seas to prescribe zero exploitation irrespective of the abundance of the species in question (on which, see further Chapter 5).

Anadromous stocks

Anadromous stocks are addressed by Article 66. Anadromous species are those that migrate regularly between the marine environment and fresh water and breed in the latter. They include, *inter alia*, sea trout and species of salmon. Article 66 introduces the concept of 'State of origin', meaning the State 'in whose rivers anadromous stocks originate', ie breed.[103] The State of origin has 'the primary interest in and responsibility for such stocks' and is given various conservation duties.[104]

However, Article 66 takes into account that: (a) third States may, to avoid 'economic dislocation', need to fish for anadromous stocks in waters beyond the EEZ (although otherwise there is a prohibition on fishing for anadromous stocks beyond the EEZ); and (b) anadromous stocks may migrate via the waters of one or more coastal States (other than the State of origin), which may or may not target such stocks. In turn, paragraphs (2)–(5) of Article 66 regulate the relationship between the State of origin and such States. There is an emphasis on cooperation. The State of origin and other States fishing the stocks in question are to 'make arrangements for the implementation of the provisions of this article, where appropriate, through regional organizations'.[105] An example of such an

---

[103] Art 66(1) and (2).   [104] Art 66(1) and (2).   [105] Art 66(5).

organization is the North Atlantic Salmon Conservation Organization (NASCO), which is discussed in Chapter 5.

Catadromous species

Catadromous species are addressed by Article 67. Catadromous species are those that migrate regularly between the marine environment and fresh water and breed in the former. They include some eel species. Article 67 does not use the concept of 'State of origin' because catadromous species originate at sea, including the high seas, rather than in fresh water. Instead, it uses the phrase 'coastal State in whose waters catadromous species spend the greater part of their life cycle'.[106]

That category of coastal State has 'responsibility for the management of these species',[107] rather than just 'the *primary* interest in and responsibility for such stocks' (emphasis added) as is the case under Article 66 for States of origin of anadromous stocks. However, '[i]n cases where catadromous fish migrate through the [EEZ] of another State, whether as juvenile or maturing fish', their management is to be regulated by agreement between the two States concerned.[108] The corollary of management of catadromous species falling exclusively to coastal States is that no harvesting of those species may take place beyond EEZs.[109]

3 UN Fish Stocks Agreement[110]

The Fish Stocks Agreement (hereafter, in this section, the 'Agreement'),[111] as its full title implies, is concerned with two broad categories of fish stocks only: straddling fish stocks and highly migratory fish stocks (see further subsection 2.6 above). By the early 1990s a number of disputes relating to straddling

---

[106] Art 67(1).   [107] Art 67(1).   [108] Art 67(3).   [109] Art 67(2).

[110] Agreement for the Implementation of the Provisions of the United Nations Convention on the Law of the Sea of 10 December 1982 relating to the Conservation and Management of Straddling Fish Stocks and Highly Migratory Fish Stocks, 1995, 2167 UNTS 3. The Agreement entered into force on 11 December 2001. For fuller discussion of the Agreement, see, from a considerable literature, Anderson, DH, 'The Straddling Stocks Agreement of 1995: An Initial Assessment' *ICLQ* 45 (1996), 463; Balton, DA, 'Strengthening the Law of the Sea: The New Agreement on Straddling Fish Stocks and Highly Migratory Fish Stocks' *ODIL* 27 (1996), 125; Hayashi, M, 'The Straddling and Highly Migratory Fish Stocks Agreement' in Hey, E (ed), *Developments in International Fisheries Law* (The Hague: Kluwer, 1999), 55; Juda, L, 'The 1995 United Nations Agreement on Straddling Fish Stocks and Highly Migratory Fish Stocks: A Critique' *ODIL* 28 (1997), 147; Lodge, MW and Nandan, SN, 'Some Suggestions towards Better Implementation of the United Nations Agreement on Straddling Fish Stocks and Highly Migratory Fish Stocks of 1995' *IJMCL* 20 (2005), 345; and Tahindro, A, 'Conservation and Management of Transboundary Fish Stocks: Comments in Light of the Adoption of the 1995 Agreement for the Conservation and Management of Straddling Fish Stocks and Highly Migratory Fish Stocks' *ODIL* 28 (1997) 1.

[111] Unless otherwise stated, references to particular Articles in this section, including in the footnotes, are to those of the Agreement.

fish stocks—notably in the Barents Sea, Bering Sea, the north-west Atlantic, and the Sea of Okhotsk—suggested that the provisions of the Convention relating to straddling stocks (which do no more than call on interested States to seek to agree on necessary conservation measures) were inadequate for the effective management of such stocks.[112] That was certainly the view taken in Agenda 21, adopted at the UN Conference on Environment and Development in 1992, which called for an inter-governmental conference 'with a view to promoting effective implementation of the provisions of' the Convention on straddling and highly migratory fish stocks,[113] a call that was endorsed by the UN General Assembly.[114] The conference called for was held between 1993 and 1995, and at its conclusion adopted the Agreement.

The Agreement, which develops Articles 63(2) and 64 of the Convention, as well as section 2 of Part VII, does not contain provisions regulating particular straddling or highly migratory fish stocks. Rather, it establishes a general framework of principles and rules within which, given the necessary political will, particular straddling and highly migratory fish stocks may be better managed at the regional level. The success of the Agreement therefore depends on how well it is implemented at the regional level, as well as on the extent to which high seas fishing States and relevant coastal States become parties to it.

The Agreement begins by setting out, in Article 5, the principles that are to govern the conservation and management of straddling and highly migratory stocks. Although in general the Agreement applies only to the high seas, Article 5, along with Articles 6 and 7, also applies to coastal State management of straddling and highly migratory stocks within areas under national jurisdiction.[115] The principles set out in Article 5 include, *inter alia*: ensuring the long-term sustainability and promoting the optimum utilization of the stocks concerned; applying the precautionary approach; minimizing pollution, waste, discards,[116] catch by lost or abandoned gear, catch of non-target species, and impacts on associated or dependent species; protecting biodiversity; preventing or eliminating overfishing and excess fishing capacity; collecting data concerning fishing activities; promoting scientific research; and implementing and enforcing measures through effective monitoring, control, and surveillance. The precautionary approach listed among those principles is spelt out in detail in Article 6 and Annex II. It requires States as fisheries managers to be 'more cautious when information is uncertain, unreliable or inadequate' and not to postpone the adoption of conservation and management measures because of an 'absence of adequate scientific information'.[117] States must

---

[112] Churchill and Lowe, *The Law of the Sea,* 305–8.   [113] Agenda 21, Chapter 17, para 17.50.
[114] UN General Assembly Resolution 47/192 (1992), reproduced in *Law of the Sea Bulletin* 23 (1992), 14.   [115] Art 3(1) and (2).
[116] Ie organisms that are thrown back into the sea after being caught because they are too small, surplus to quota, or the wrong species. Discarded organisms are usually dead, or at least damaged, as a result of the catching process.   [117] Art 6(2).

apply the guidelines set out in Annex II and determine, on the basis of the best scientific information available, reference points for each stock that they manage. They must ensure that when such reference points are approached, they are not exceeded.[118] The principles set out in Articles 5 and 6 are the most detailed of their kind yet found in a global treaty on fisheries management. If properly applied, they would lead to a significant improvement in the management of straddling and highly migratory fish stocks.

One of the biggest potential obstacles to the effective management of straddling and highly migratory fish stocks is inconsistency between the management measures taken by the coastal State(s) and those taken by high seas fishing States. If their measures are not compatible, there is a likelihood that the management efforts of one will be undermined by the other. This issue is addressed in Article 7 of the Agreement. The Article begins, in its first paragraph, by setting out general obligations of cooperation on the relevant coastal States and the States whose nationals fish for straddling and highly migratory stocks on the high seas. In the case of straddling stocks, such States are to 'seek, either directly or through' regional fisheries management organizations or arrangements, 'to agree upon the measures necessary for the conservation' of such stocks on the high seas. In the case of highly migratory stocks, such States 'shall cooperate, either directly or through' regional fisheries management organizations or arrangements, 'with a view to ensuring conservation and promoting the objective of optimum utilization of such stocks throughout the region, both with and beyond areas under national jurisdiction'. These provisions use very similar wording to that found in the Convention's provisions on straddling stocks and highly migratory species (see subsection 2.6 above). Article 7(2) goes on to provide that conservation and management measures taken by the coastal State(s) in respect of particular straddling or highly migratory stocks in areas under national jurisdiction and the measures adopted for those stocks for the high seas 'shall be compatible in order to ensure conservation and management of . . . stocks in their entirety' (ie both within areas under national jurisdiction and on the high seas). To that end 'coastal States and States fishing on the high seas have a duty to co-operate for the purpose of achieving compatible measures' in respect of straddling and highly migratory stocks. Various factors are listed that are to be taken into account in order to determine such compatibility. States must make every effort to agree on compatible conservation and management measures 'within a reasonable period of time'.[119] If they do not succeed in doing so, any of the States concerned may invoke the Agreement's dispute settlement procedures (discussed below).[120] Pending agreement on compatible conservation and management, the States

---

[118] For further discussion of this aspect of the Agreement, see Freestone, D, 'Implementing Precaution Cautiously: The Precautionary Approach in the Straddling and Highly Migratory Fish Stocks Agreement' in Hey (ed), *Developments in International Fisheries Law*, 287–325.   [119] Art 7(3).
[120] Art 7(4).

concerned 'shall make every effort to enter into provisional arrangements of a practical nature'.[121]

The Agreement envisages that the primary mechanism for giving effect to the duty to cooperate referred to in Article 7(1) will be a regional fisheries management organization or arrangement.[122] If an appropriate organization or arrangement does not exist in a particular region, one must be created.[123] The terms of participation in such organizations or arrangements must not preclude States 'having a real interest in the fisheries concerned' from becoming members or participating.[124] Requirements as to the scope and functions of both new and existing organizations are spelt out in Articles 9–13.

Articles 8(3) and (4) and 17 are crucial provisions of the Agreement. They provide that where a regional organization or arrangement has the competence to establish conservation and management measures for particular straddling or highly migratory stocks, a State wishing to fish on the high seas for stocks to which such measures apply must be a member of that organization or arrangement or agree to apply its measures. If not, it must not authorize its vessels to fish for those stocks. If it fails to prevent its vessels from fishing for such stocks, members of the relevant regional organization or arrangement must take 'measures consistent with th[e] Agreement and international law to deter activities of such vessels which undermine the effectiveness of subregional or regional conservation and management measures'.[125] These provisions should prevent States parties to the Agreement from being free-riders. (A free-rider in this context would be a State whose vessels enjoyed the potential benefits resulting from the conservation and management measures adopted by the organization or arrangement without having to bear the potential burden of complying with those measures.) In relation to potentially free-riding States that are not parties to the Agreement, Article 33(2) requires States parties to the Agreement to take measures 'consistent with th[e] Agreement and international law to deter the activities of vessels flying the flag of non-parties which undermine the effective implementation of th[e] Agreement'.[126]

Parts V and VI of the Agreement deal with the duties of flag States and with compliance and enforcement. A flag State must take such measures as may be necessary to ensure that vessels flying its flag that fish on the high seas comply with the conservation and management measures of regional organizations and arrangements and that they do not engage in any activity that would undermine

---

[121] Art 7(5). See also Art 7(6). For a detailed discussion of the Agreement's provisions relating to compatibility, see Oude Elferink, A, 'The Determination of Compatible Conservation and Management Measures for Straddling and Highly Migratory Fish Stocks' *Max Planck Yearbook of United Nations Law*, 5 (2001), 551.   [122] Art 8(1).
[123] Art 8(5).
[124] Art 8(3). For a discussion of the concept of 'real interest', see Molenaar, EJ, 'The Concept of "Real Interest" and Other Aspects of Co-Operation through Regional Fisheries Management Mechanisms' *IJMCL* 15 (2000), 475.   [125] Art 17(4). See also Art 20(7).
[126] Arts 17(4) and 20(7) are also potentially applicable against non-parties to the Agreement.

the effectiveness of such measures.[127] Where non-compliance is suspected, the flag State must investigate the matter immediately and fully, institute legal proceedings if satisfied that sufficient evidence of a violation exists,[128] and, if the alleged violation is proved, impose sanctions 'adequate in severity to be effective in securing compliance and to discourage violations wherever they occur' and which must also 'deprive offenders of the benefits accruing from their illegal activities'.[129]

Under Article 20 other States are to cooperate with the flag State in the enforcement of conservation and management measures adopted by regional organizations or arrangements, for example by providing evidence of alleged violations. Under Article 21(1) and (2) members of a regional organization or arrangement are to establish schemes whereby any member that is a party to the Agreement may, on the high seas, board and inspect vessels of any other State party to the Agreement, even if the latter State is not a member of the organization or arrangement concerned, for the purpose of ensuring compliance with the conservation and management measures adopted by that organization or arrangement. If within two years of the 'adoption' of the Agreement such schemes have not been established, the Agreement itself (in Article 21(3)) authorizes boarding and inspecting in the same circumstances as under Article 21(1). The Agreement does not define the term 'adoption', but it presumably means the date on which the text of the Agreement was adopted by the UN conference at which the Agreement was negotiated. If that is correct, it has the curious consequence that the second anniversary of the adoption of the Agreement, which activates the authorization in Article 21(3), actually occurred four years before the entry into force of the Agreement in 2001. As far as the authors are aware, Article 21(3) has not been applied in practice. Where a regional organization or arrangement has established 'an alternative mechanism' which effectively discharges the obligation under the Agreement to ensure compliance with the conservation and management measures of that organization or arrangement, its members may agree to limit the application of Article 21(1) as between themselves in respect of the measures that have been established in the relevant high seas area.[130]

Where a vessel has been boarded and inspected, and the inspection reveals that there are 'clear grounds' for believing that the vessel has engaged in any activity contrary to the conservation and management measures of the relevant regional organization or arrangement, the inspecting State must, where appropriate, secure evidence and promptly inform the flag State.[131] The latter must either without delay investigate and, if the evidence so warrants, take enforcement action, or authorize the inspecting State to investigate: in the latter situation the flag State must either take enforcement action or authorize the

---

[127] Art 18(1).   [128] Art 19(1).   [129] Art 19(2).   [130] Art 21(15).
[131] Art 21(5).

inspecting State to do so.[132] If, following a boarding and inspection, there are clear grounds for believing that a vessel has committed a 'serious violation',[133] and if the flag State takes no action, the inspectors may remain on board and secure evidence and, if appropriate, conduct the vessel to an appropriate port.[134]

The above provisions also apply, *mutatis mutandis*, to boarding and inspection by a State which is both a party to the Agreement and a member of a regional organization or arrangement and which has clear grounds for believing that a fishing vessel flying the flag of another party to the Agreement has engaged in any activity contrary to the conservation and management measures of that organization or arrangement while on the high seas and that vessel has subsequently, during the same fishing trip, entered into an area under the national jurisdiction of the first-mentioned State.[135] The Agreement further provides that where a vessel on the high seas is reasonably believed to have engaged in unauthorized fishing within an area under national jurisdiction, the flag State shall investigate the matter at the request of the coastal State and may authorize the latter to board and inspect the vessel on the high seas.[136]

The Agreement gives an enforcement role not only to flag and coastal States, but also to port States. Article 23 provides that a port State has 'the right and the duty' to take measures, in accordance with international law, to promote the effectiveness of regional and global conservation and management measures. In particular, it may inspect vessels that are voluntarily in its ports and may prohibit the landing or transhipment of catches that have been taken in a manner that undermines the effectiveness of regional and global conservation and management measures on the high seas.

Article 30(1) of the Agreement applies the dispute settlement provisions of Part XV of the Convention, *mutatis mutandis*, to any dispute relating to the interpretation and application of the Agreement, whether or not parties to the Agreement are also parties to the Convention. Disputes of a technical character may be referred to an ad hoc panel established by the parties to the dispute.[137] Article 30(2) of the Agreement is a remarkable provision. It extends the Convention's dispute settlement machinery to disputes concerning the interpretation or application of a regional or global agreement 'relating to' straddling or highly migratory stocks, including therefore those agreements establishing regional fisheries management organizations and arrangements of the kind referred to above, where the parties to the dispute are parties both to the Agreement and to the regional or global agreement in question, again whether or not they are parties to the Convention. There are over twenty agreements of the kind referred to in Article 30(2), many of which previously had no machinery for

---

[132] Art 21(6) and (7).   [133] This term is defined in Art 21(11).   [134] Art 21(8).
[135] Art 21(14).   [136] Art 20(6).   [137] Art 29.

settling disputes compulsorily.[138] None of the dispute settlement procedures under the Agreement has yet been invoked.[139]

At the time of writing the Agreement had seventy-two parties, including the EC and all its Member States.[140] The remaining forty-four States constitute a diverse group. Significantly, they do not include a number of major high seas fishing States, such as China and Thailand, or a number of significant coastal States (such as Argentina, Chile, Ecuador, and Peru).

Despite the fact that it took six years to enter into force and the relatively limited number of its parties, the Agreement has had a significant impact since it was adopted in 1995. Several treaties establishing new regional fisheries management organizations or arrangements have been concluded that show many influences of, and incorporate principles from, the Agreement, such as the treaties establishing the South East Atlantic Fisheries Organisation[141] and the Commission for the Conservation and Management of Highly Migratory Fish Stocks in the Western and Central Pacific Ocean (see further section 8 below).[142] In addition, many existing organizations have changed their practices to accord with the provisions of the Agreement.

As provided for by Article 36, a conference to review the Agreement was held in May 2006. The conference showed considerable support for the Agreement and provoked much discussion as to how it might be developed. It resulted in the adoption of a document that assesses the Agreement and makes recommendations for future action.[143]

4 FAO Compliance Agreement[144]

As indicated in the preceding section, much high seas fishing is regulated and managed through regional fisheries management organizations (RFMOs). One of

---

[138] See further Churchill, R, 'The Jurisprudence of the International Tribunal for the Law of the Sea relating to Fisheries: Is there much in the Net?' *IJMCL* 22 (2007), 383 at 394–400.

[139] For detailed discussion of the dispute settlement provisions of the Agreement, see Boyle, AE, 'Problems of Compulsory Jurisdiction and the Settlement of Disputes relating to Straddling Fish Stocks' *IJMCL* 14 (1999), 1; McDorman, TL, 'The Dispute Settlement Regime of the Straddling and Highly Migratory Fish Stocks Convention' *Canadian Yearbook of International Law* 35 (1997), 57; and Treves, T, 'The Settlement of Disputes according to the Straddling Stocks Agreement of 1995' in Boyle, AE, and Freestone D (eds), *International Law and Sustainable Development* (Oxford: Oxford University Press, 1999), 253.

[140] Information as to the parties to the Agreement may be found on the website of the DOALOS. The issue of EC and Member State participation in the Agreement is considered further in Chapter 5.

[141] Convention on the Conservation and Management of Fishery Resources in the South-East Atlantic Ocean (hereafter, 'SEAFO Convention'), 2001, 2221 UNTS 189.

[142] Convention on the Conservation and Management of Highly Migratory Fish Stocks in the Western and Central Pacific Ocean (hereafter, 'WCPFC Convention'), 2000, 2275 UNTS 43.

[143] For a detailed account of the conference, see Takei, Y, 'Unfinished Business: Review Conference on the 1995 Fish Stocks Agreement' *IJMCL* 21 (2006), 551.

[144] For fuller discussion of the Compliance Agreement, see Balton, DA, 'The Compliance Agreement' in Hey (ed), *Developments in International Fisheries Law*, 31; Moore, G, 'The FAO Compliance

the problems faced by RFMOs since the early 1980s has been the practice of some fishing vessel owners changing the registration and flag of their vessels from a member State of an RFMO to a non-member State (often a flag of convenience) in order to avoid being bound by the measures of the RFMO, thus undermining the latter's management efforts.[145] One of the principal reasons for embarking on the negotiation of what became the Compliance Agreement (hereafter, in this section, 'the Agreement') was to tackle this problem of reflagging. At an early stage of the negotiations, an attempt was made to deal with the problem by proposing that a State should not grant the right to fly its flag to a vessel unless there was a genuine link between that State and the vessel, and the State believed that the vessel would not be used to undermine the effectiveness of international con-servation and management measures. However, no agreement could be reached on that or any other measure to tackle directly the issue of reflagging.[146]

Instead the Agreement, which entered into force on 24 April 2003, focuses on the need for vessels fishing on the high seas to be authorized and on the duties of their flag States. Those duties are similar to, although less detailed than, those found in the later Fish Stocks Agreement. Thus, a flag State shall prohibit its vessels from fishing on the high seas unless it has authorized them to do so,[147] and shall only authorize a vessel to fish if it is satisfied that 'it is able, taking into account the links that exist between it and the fishing vessel concerned, to exercise effectively its responsibilities under this Agreement in respect of that fishing vessel'.[148] With some exceptions, no party shall authorize any vessel previously registered in another State that has undermined the effectiveness of international conservation and management measures unless any period of suspension by the previous flag State of an authorization to fish has expired and no authorization has been with-drawn during the previous three years.[149] This provision is intended to limit the ability of vessels with a bad compliance record (such as those involved in the reflagging problem) to shop around for a new flag. A vessel that has been authorized by a party to fish on the high seas may only fish in accordance with the conditions laid down in that authorization, must be marked in a way that permits ready identification, and must provide its flag State with such information on its operations as will enable the latter to fulfil its obligations under the Agreement.[150] A flag State must maintain a record of all those vessels that it has authorized to fish on the high seas.[151]

Flag States must enforce the Agreement in respect of their vessels and provide sanctions for breaches of the Agreement of sufficient gravity to be effective in securing compliance and to deprive offenders of the benefits of their illegal

---

Agreement' in Nordquist and Moore, *Current Fisheries Issues*, 77–91; and Grainger, R., 'High Seas Fishing Vessel Database' in ibid, 93–106.   [145] See further section 6 below.
    [146] For a more extended discussion of this aspect of the negotiations, see Balton, 'The Compliance Agreement', 34–44.   [147] Art III(2).
    [148] Art III(3).   [149] Art III(5).   [150] Art III(2), (6), and (7).   [151] Art IV.

activities; in the case of serious breaches, sanctions must include suspension or withdrawal of the authorization to fish.[152] Other parties shall assist the flag State in exercising its enforcement responsibilities, for example by providing 'evidentiary material'.[153] Such assistance includes, for the first time in a multilateral fisheries agreement, a degree of port State control. Where a party to the Agreement reasonably believes that a fishing vessel voluntarily in one of its ports has been used for an activity that undermines the effectiveness of international conservation and management measures, it shall promptly notify the flag State. 'Parties may make arrangements regarding the undertaking by port States of such investigatory measures as may be considered necessary to establish whether the fishing vessel has indeed been used contrary to the provisions of this Agreement.'[154] It may be noted that these provisions on port State control do not go as far as the corresponding provisions of the later Fish Stocks Agreement, discussed in section 3 above.

Apart from setting out the responsibilities of flag States, the other major concern of the Compliance Agreement is promoting the free flow of information about high seas fishing activities, the lack of which has been an obstacle to effective fisheries management in the past. To that end the Agreement provides that every flag State party must provide information to the FAO about the vessels that it has authorized to fish on the high seas, including action taken against vessels engaging in activities that undermine the effectiveness of international conservation and management measures.[155] The FAO is to circulate that information to other parties and to international fisheries organizations.[156] Apart from increasing knowledge of high seas fishing activities, such information could also be used, for example, by a coastal State to exclude a vessel with a poor high seas compliance record from fishing in its EEZ.

As noted above, the Compliance Agreement entered into force in April 2003, nearly ten years after it was adopted. At the time of writing it had thirty-six parties, including the EC (but not its Member States),[157] as well as a number of major high seas fishing States, such as Japan and South Korea (though not China, Russia, or Thailand).[158] Unsurprisingly, hardly any flag of convenience States, at whom much of the Agreement is aimed, have become parties to the Agreement. Without much wider participation, the Agreement is unlikely to make much contribution to improving the management of high seas fisheries. To be effective, the Agreement is also dependent on there being international conservation and management measures in place, something that is not always the case at present.

There is perhaps a rather limited incentive for States to become parties to the Compliance Agreement because its provisions duplicate, to a considerable degree,

---

[152] Art III(8).   [153] Art V(1).   [154] Art V(2).

[155] Art VI(1), (2), (5), (6), (7), (8)(a), and (9).   [156] Art VI(4) and (10).

[157] The question of EC and Member State participation in the Agreement is discussed in Chapter 5.

[158] Information about the parties to the Agreement may be found on the website of the Fisheries and Aquaculture Department of the FAO.

many of those of the Fish Stocks Agreement, especially as regards the duties of flag States. The Fish Stocks Agreement, unlike the Compliance Agreement, does not apply to discrete high seas stocks, but this limitation may not be so very important in practice because most RFMOs that manage straddling stocks also manage the discrete high seas stocks of the region concerned.[159] On the other hand, the Fish Stocks Agreement has in some respects a wider ambit, as it applies to all vessels fishing for straddling and highly migratory stocks on the high seas, whereas under the Compliance Agreement its parties may, under certain circumstances and subject to certain conditions, exempt vessels of less than 24 m in length from many of its provisions.[160] The major aspect of the Compliance Agreement that has no corresponding provision in the Fish Stocks Agreement is the requirement for its parties to provide the international community, through the FAO, with information on high seas fishing activities. It is therefore a matter of regret that as at the beginning of 2006 only fifteen of the then thirty-two parties to the Compliance Agreement had done so.[161]

5 FAO's Code of Conduct for Responsible Fisheries, and International Plans of Action

As was noted in section 1 above, the FAO adopted the Code of Conduct for Responsible Fisheries in 1995.[162] The Code is wide-ranging in scope, dealing not only with fisheries management (both within national jurisdiction and on the high seas), but also with aquaculture development, integration of fisheries into coastal area management, post-harvest practices and trade, and fisheries research. The Code is not legally binding: essentially it takes the form of a series of exhortations and guidance to States (whether members of the FAO or not), 'fishing entities' (probably a reference to Taiwan), governmental and non-governmental organizations, and all others involved in fisheries.[163] As the Introduction to the Code puts it, the Code 'sets out principles and international standards of behaviour for responsible practices with a view to ensuring the effective conservation, management and development of living aquatic resources, with due respect for the ecosystem and biodiversity'. Although the Code is not legally binding, parts of it are

---

[159] Further on the management of discrete high seas stocks, see Lodge and Nandan, 'Some Suggestions', 369–73.   [160] Compliance Agreement, Art II.

[161] See the website of the Fisheries and Aquaculture Department of the FAO. No more up-to-date information was publicly available on the website at the time of writing.

[162] For more detailed discussion of the Code, see Edeson, WR, 'The Food and Agriculture Organization of the UN Code of Conduct for Responsible Fisheries: An Introduction' *IJMCL* 11 (1996), 233; Moore, G, 'The Code of Conduct for Responsible Fisheries' in Hey (ed), *Developments in International Fisheries Law*, 85–105; and Doulman, DJ, 'Code of Conduct for Responsible Fisheries: Development and Implementation Considerations' in Nordquist and Moore, *Current Fisheries Issues*, 307–30.   [163] Art 1.

based on, and to a degree replicate, existing treaties, including the Convention, the Compliance Agreement, and the Fish Stocks Agreement. Furthermore, it is to be interpreted and applied 'in conformity with' the Convention; 'in a manner consistent with' the Fish Stocks Agreement; and 'in accordance with other applicable rules of international law'.[164] There is an expectation that States and others will apply and implement the Code, notwithstanding its voluntary nature; the FAO will monitor such implementation.[165] The FAO has adopted a number of technical guidelines to support implementation of the Code,[166] as well as a *Strategy for Improving Information on Status and Trends of Capture Fisheries* within the framework of the Code.[167]

Since this chapter is concerned only with fisheries management, discussion of the Code will be confined to those of its provisions that deal with this matter. Articles 6, 7, and 8 of the Code set out various principles for fisheries conservation and management. According to those principles, conservation should be on a long-term and sustainable basis, founded on a precautionary approach and the best scientific advice available; management measures should ensure the conservation not only of target species but also of associated or dependent species or species belonging to the same ecosystem; States should prevent overfishing and eliminate excess fishing capacity; selective and environmentally safe fishing gear should be developed and applied, and waste and catches of non-target species should be minimized; and States should effectively monitor and control the activities of fishing vessels so as to ensure compliance with their management measures, and impose sanctions of adequate severity for violations of those measures. States should establish an effective legal and administrative framework for giving effect to these principles. In addition, and most importantly, States should promote awareness of responsible fisheries through education and training, and ensure that fishermen are involved and consulted on the formulation and implementation of policy.[168] A number of the technical guidelines adopted to promote implementation of the Code deal with fisheries management.

The principles, guidance, and best practice set out in the Code are very sound, if at a considerable level of generality and somewhat repetitive: the technical guidelines relating to implementation of the Code are, however, more detailed and precise. The crucial question is whether States (and others) will follow the Code. As Doulman explains, the Code assumes that governments desire better managed fisheries and are prepared to take the difficult decisions necessary to that end. Governments, however, may have short-term planning and policy horizons and therefore may seek 'to minimize social and economic disruption through their fishery policy interventions, even when it is recognized that such intervention is

---

[164] Art 3.   [165] Art 4.

[166] Available on the website of the Fisheries and Aquaculture Department of the FAO.

[167] Ibid.   [168] See Arts 6.16, 7.1.2, and 7.1.10.

required to improve' management.[169] In 2007 the FAO reported that more than 90 per cent of its members had national policies and legislation in place that either totally or partially conformed to the Code, and, in the case of partial conformity, were working towards achieving complete conformity.[170]

The Code has been supplemented by four International Plans of Action (IPOAs), which are also non-binding. The first three were adopted by the FAO in 1999. The first is the IPOA for Reducing Incidental Catch of Seabirds in Longline Fisheries.[171] It was prompted by concerns about the impact on their populations of the increasing incidental catch of seabirds in various longline fisheries in different parts of the world. The objective of the IPOA is to reduce that catch.[172] To that end States with longline fisheries that have a significant incidental catch of seabirds should adopt a national plan of action for reducing such catch.[173] Such a plan should include mitigation measures, as well as plans for research into mitigation measures, raising awareness of the issue among fishermen and others, and data collection. Recognizing that each longline fishery is unique, the IPOA does not recommend any particular measures, but instead simply lists a number of measures that States may find it appropriate to take.[174] States should also cooperate, including through RFMOs, to reduce incidental seabird catches.[175] The adoption of national plans of action has so far been a slow process. By 2008 only ten such plans had been developed, while a number of others were in draft stage or awaiting government implementation (see further Chapter 5).[176]

The second IPOA is that for the Conservation and Management of Sharks.[177] The IPOA was prompted by concerns over the substantial increase in shark catches in recent years, concerns that were heightened by a lack of knowledge of the biology of sharks and a lack of data on catches and landings. Although not a motivation for the IPOA, there is also considerable concern over the practice of finning, whereby sharks' fins are removed for use in trade, and the remainder of the shark is then discarded at sea. The objective of the IPOA is to ensure the conservation and management of sharks and their long-term sustainable use.[178] To that end States whose vessels conduct directed fisheries for sharks or regularly take sharks as by-catch were exhorted to adopt a national plan of action for the conservation and management of shark stocks by 2001. Guidance for such plans is set out in an appendix to the IPOA.[179] National shark plans should, *inter*

---

[169] Doulman, 'Code of Conduct', at 320–1.

[170] FAO Committee on Fisheries, *Progress in the Implementation of the 1995 Code of Conduct for Responsible Fisheries, Related Plans of Action and Strategy*, COFI/2007/2, para 6, available on the website of the Fisheries and Aquaculture Department of the FAO.

[171] Available on the website of the Fisheries and Aquaculture Department of the FAO.

[172] Para 10.   [173] Para 12.   [174] Para 16.   [175] Paras 19 and 20.

[176] *Report of the Expert Consultation on Best Practice Technical Guidelines for IPOA/NPOA-Seabirds, Bergen, Norway, 2–5 September 2008*, FAO Fisheries and Aquaculture Report No 880, Appendix E, para 5.   [177] Available on the website of the Fisheries and Aquaculture Department of the FAO.

[178] Para 16.   [179] Para 18.

alia, ensure that shark catches are sustainable; assess threats to shark populations; determine and protect critical habitats; and minimize waste and discards from shark catches.[180] States should also cooperate, including through RFMOs, to ensure the effective conservation and management of sharks and the sustainability of shark stocks.[181] Only about a third of those States with vessels whose activities fall within the scope of the IPOA have so far adopted national plans.[182] A number of RFMOs have taken measures to conserve sharks.[183]

As explained in section 1 above, over-capacity is a major problem in many of the world's fisheries. The IPOA on the Management of Fishing Capacity[184] has, as its immediate objective, the achievement by 2005 of an efficient, equitable, and transparent management of fishing capacity by States.[185] To that end States should have carried out an assessment of their capacity by 2000, and identified national fleets requiring urgent measures by the end of the following year.[186] Within a further year they should have adopted a national plan for the management of fishing capacity, giving due consideration to socio-economic requirements, including alternative sources of employment and livelihood to fishing communities that may have to bear the brunt of reductions in fishing capacity.[187] Where there is over-capacity, States should endeavour initially to limit capacity to existing levels, and then gradually reduce it: to the latter end States should reduce and eliminate all factors, including subsidies and economic incentives, that contribute to the build-up of excess capacity.[188] In the case of high seas fisheries, States are urged to cooperate, including through RFMOs, to ensure the effective management of fishing capacity. In particular, States should take immediate steps to address the management of capacity in international fisheries for stocks that are significantly over-fished.[189] If properly implemented, the IPOA would lead to a major reduction of excess capacity, and thus probably to significant improvements in fisheries management globally. Unfortunately, however, implementation of the IPOA remains 'weak': by 2007 less than 10 per cent of FAO members had completed the initial assessment of their fleet's capacity that was due by the end of 2000.[190]

One of the biggest threats to world fish stocks is illegal, unreported, and unregulated (IUU) fishing. This term refers to a number of different kinds of illegal or undesirable fishing practices, including, *inter alia*, fishing in national waters without the permission of the coastal State or in contravention of its laws; fishing by a member contrary to the conservation and management measures of an RFMO;

---

[180] Para 22.   [181] Paras 25 and 26.

[182] FAO Committee on Fisheries, *Progress in the Implementation*, para 31.   [183] Ibid, para 47.

[184] Available on the website of the Fisheries and Aquaculture Department of the FAO. For detailed comment, see Gréboval, D, 'The International Plan of Action for the Management of Fishing Capacity: Retrospect and Prospect' in Nordquist and Moore, *Current Fisheries Issues*, 561–82. See also FAO, *FAO Technical Guidelines for Responsible Fisheries No 4, Supplement 3. Managing Fishing Capacity* (Rome: FAO, 2008).

[185] Para 7.   [186] Paras 13 and 14.   [187] Paras 21 and 22.   [188] Paras 7 and 26.

[189] Paras 27 and 39.   [190] FAO Committee on Fisheries, *Progress in the Implementation*, para 30.

fishing that is not reported to the relevant national authorities or RFMO; fishing by vessels whose flag States are not members of an RFMO in an area regulated by that RFMO that is not consistent with or contravenes the latter's measures; and fishing in other high seas areas in a manner inconsistent with general conservation obligations under international law.[191] IUU fishing undermines the management efforts both of coastal States within their national jurisdiction and of RFMOs on the high seas, and harms vessels fishing legitimately because it reduces the amount of fish available for them to catch. In 2001 the FAO estimated IUU fishing to account for as much as 30 per cent of the world catch.[192]

An IPOA to Prevent, Deter and Eliminate Illegal, Unreported and Unregulated (IUU) Fishing was adopted by the FAO in 2001.[193] Although applying to both areas within national jurisdiction and the high seas, the IPOA is primarily aimed at high seas fishing. The objective of the IPOA is to 'prevent, deter and eliminate IUU fishing by providing all States with comprehensive, effective and transparent measures by which to act, including through appropriate' RFMOs.[194] To that end, all States should, inter alia, take all possible steps to discourage their nationals and vessels from engaging in IUU fishing; impose sanctions for such fishing of sufficient severity effectively to deter, and deprive offenders of the benefits of, such fishing; undertake comprehensive and effective monitoring, control, and surveillance of fishing from its commencement, through the point of landing, to final destination; develop by 2004 national plans of action to further achieve the objectives of the IPOA and give full effect to its provisions; and cooperate with other States to prevent, deter, and eliminate IUU fishing.[195] More specific measures are then set out for flag States (including provisions on the registration, authorization, and maintenance of records of their vessels); coastal States; port States (including provisions on inspection and prohibition of the landing of catches similar to those in the Fish Stocks Agreement);[196] research on ways of identifying

---

[191] IPOA to Prevent, Deter and Eliminate Illegal, Unreported and Unregulated (IUU) Fishing, para 3.

[192] Juda, L, 'Rio Plus Ten: The Evolution of International Marine Fisheries Governance' *ODIL* 33 (2002), 109 at 119. Further on the problems of IUU fishing, see Baird, R, 'Illegal, Unregulated and Unreported Fishing: An Analysis of the Legal, Economic and Historical Factors Relevant to its Development and Persistence' *Melbourne Journal of International Law* 5 (2004), 299; and Riddle, KW, 'Illegal, Unregulated and Unreported Fishing: Is International Cooperation Contagious?' *ODIL* 37 (2006), 265, especially at 266–9.

[193] Available on the website of the Fisheries and Aquaculture Department of the FAO. For comment, see Edeson, WR, 'The International Plan of Action on Illegal, Unreported and Unregulated Fishing: The Legal Context of a Non-Legally Binding Instrument' *IJMCL* 16 (2001), 603. On the background to the IPOA, see Bray, K, 'Illegal, Unreported and Unregulated (IUU) Fishing' in Nordquist and Moore, *Current Fisheries Issues*, 115–35.   [194] Para 8.

[195] Paras 10–33.

[196] Further on port State measures, see FAO, *Report of the FAO Technical Consultation to Review Port State Measures to Combat Illegal, Unreported and Unregulated Fishing*, FAO Fisheries Report No 759 (2004). The Consultation adopted a Model Scheme on Port State Measures to Combat IUU Fishing. At the time of writing the FAO was engaged in the process of drafting a Legally Binding Instrument on

fish species from samples of processed products; assistance to developing States; RFMOs; and the FAO. If all of those measures do not prove adequate, States should seek to prevent trade in fish caught in IUU fishing, subject to their World Trade Organization (WTO) obligations.[197] States and RFMOs should report biennially to the FAO on their plans to combat IUU fishing.[198] Implementation of the IPOA has been quite slow: by 2007 only about half of the FAO's members had taken steps to develop a national plan of action to combat IUU fishing.[199] The FAO has published guidelines to assist States in their implementation of the IPOA.[200]

The EC's participation in, and implementation of, the four IPOAs is discussed in Chapter 5.

6 Regional fisheries management organizations[201]

As has been seen earlier in this chapter, a fish stock at the harvestable stage often does not spend its entire time in the waters of just a single State. This, together with the fact that on the high seas jurisdiction over a vessel may in principle be exercised only by its flag State, means that States need to cooperate if there is to be any possibility of effective management of shared, anadromous, straddling, highly migratory, or high seas fish stocks.[202] Because it is desirable that such cooperation should take place fairly regularly and frequently, and thus preferably be institutionalized, a number of bodies

---

Port State Measures to Prevent, Deter and Eliminate Illegal, Unreported and Unregulated Fishing: see FAO, *The State of World Fisheries and Aquaculture 2008*, 72. See also Ministerially led Task Force on IUU Fishing on the High Seas, *Closing the Net* (2006), 78–80; and Lodge, M, Anderson, D, Løbach, T, Munro, G, Sainsbury, K, and Willock, A, *Recommended Best Practices for Regional Fisheries Management Organizations* (London: Chatham House, 2007), 54–7.   [197] Paras 65–76.

[198] Para 87.

[199] FAO Committee on Fisheries, *Progress in the Implementation*, para 29. Note also the proposals for action to combat IUU fishing made by the Ministerially led Task Force on IUU Fishing on the High Seas, *Closing the Net*.

[200] FAO, *FAO Technical Guidelines for Responsible Fisheries No 9. Implementation of the International Plan of Action to Prevent, Deter and Eliminate Illegal, Unreported and Unregulated Fishing* (Rome: FAO, 2002).

[201] For more detailed studies of such organizations, see *inter alia*, Applebaum, B and Donohue, A, 'The Role of Regional Fisheries Management Organizations' in Hey (ed), *Developments in International Fisheries Law*, 217; Barston, R, 'The Law of the Sea and Regional Fisheries Organisations' *IJMCL* 14 (1999), 333; Henriksen, T, Hønneland, G, and Sydnes, A, *Law and Politics in Ocean Governance: the UN Fish Stocks Agreement and Regional Fisheries Management Regimes* (Leiden: Martinus Nijhoff, 2006); Lodge *et al*, *Recommended Best Practices*; Lugten, GL, *A Review of Measures taken by Regional Marine Fishery Bodies to address Contemporary Fishery Issues*, FAO Fisheries Circular No 940 (1999); Meltzer, E, 'Global Overview of Straddling and Highly Migratory Stocks: Maps and Charts detailing RFMO Coverage and Implementation' *IJMCL* 20 (2005), 571; and Swan, J, *Summary Information on the Role of International Fishery Organizations or Arrangements and Other Bodies concerned with the Conservation and Management of Living Aquatic Resources*, FAO Fisheries Circular No 985 (2003).

[202] Catadromous stocks are not considered here because fishing for such stocks on the high seas is prohibited (see subsection 2.6 above) and the only cooperative arrangement relating to the management

have been set up over the years to manage such stocks. As seen earlier, the Convention, the Fish Stocks Agreement, the Code of Conduct for Responsible Fisheries, and the International Plans of Action all encourage States to cooperate through regional organizations, while the Compliance Agreement assumes their existence.

Some of those organizations are concerned only with the management of shared stocks (on which, see subsection 2.6 above). The focus here is on organizations that are concerned with the management of other kinds of stocks. Such organizations may be divided into two broad categories—those that have the competence to prescribe fishery conservation and management measures that are binding on their members (ie RFMOs), and those that have no regulatory powers and whose role is primarily to advise on the status of fish stocks within their region and possibly also to recommend and/or coordinate management measures which are not legally binding. Because of their relatively limited role, the latter are not considered further here. Such organizations of which the EC is a member are discussed briefly in Chapter 5.

At the present time the principal RFMOs are as follows:
Organizations concerned with the management of straddling stocks and/or discrete high seas fish stocks: the Commission for the Conservation of Antarctic Marine Living Resources (CCAMLR),[203] the General Fisheries Commission (formerly Council) for the Mediterranean (GFCM),[204] the North-East Atlantic Fisheries Commission (NEAFC),[205] the Northwest Atlantic Fisheries Organization (NAFO),[206] and the South East Atlantic Fisheries Organisation (SEAFO).[207] Negotiations are also proceeding to establish an RFMO for straddling and discrete high seas stocks in the South Pacific.[208] *Organizations concerned with the management of highly migratory species*: the Commission for the Conservation and Management of Highly Migratory Fish Stocks in the Western and Central Pacific Ocean (WCPFC),[209] the Commission for

---

of such stocks within areas of national jurisdiction of which the authors are aware is an EC measure, Council Regulation (EC) No 1100/2007 of 18 September 2007 establishing measures for the recovery of the stock of European eel, OJ 2007 L248/17, which is discussed in Chapters 2 and 4.

[203] Established by the 1980 Convention on the Conservation of Antarctic Marine Living Resources (hereafter, 'the CCAMLR Convention'), 1329 UNTS 47.

[204] Established by the 1949 Agreement for the Establishment of a General Fisheries Council for the Mediterranean (hereafter, 'the GFCM Agreement'), 126 UNTS 237. The Agreement was amended significantly in 1997 (including renaming the organization). For the text of the amendments, see 2275 UNTS 157 and 187.

[205] Established by the 1980 Convention on Future Multilateral Cooperation in North-East Atlantic Fisheries (hereafter, 'the NEAFC Convention'), 1285 UNTS 129. Extensive amendments to the Convention were adopted in 2004 and 2006: for the text of these amendments, see the website of the NEAFC. See further section 8 below.

[206] Established by the 1978 Convention on Future Multilateral Cooperation in the Northwest Atlantic Fisheries (hereafter, 'the NAFO Convention'), 1135 UNTS 369. In 2007 far-reaching amendments to the Convention were adopted which, when they enter into force, will effectively replace the present Convention with a new Convention: for the text of the amendments, see the website of the NAFO. See further section 8 below.   [207] Established by the SEAFO Convention.

[208] See the website of the South Pacific RFMO.
[209] Established by the WCPFC Convention.

the Conservation of Southern Bluefin Tuna (CCSBT),[210] the Indian Ocean Tuna Commission (IOTC),[211] the Inter-American Tropical Tuna Commission (IATTC),[212] and the International Commission for the Conservation of Atlantic Tunas (ICCAT).[213] *Organizations concerned with anadromous species*: the North Atlantic Salmon Conservation Organization (NASCO)[214] and the North Pacific Anadromous Fish Commission.[215]

The above list does not include what would be considered 'regional fisheries management arrangements' under the Fish Stocks Agreement, ie where no formal organization is established. The main such arrangements include the 1994 Convention on the Conservation and Management of the Pollock Resources in the Bering Sea,[216] the 2006 Southern Indian Ocean Fisheries Agreement,[217] and a series of annual agreements relating to the management of blue whiting, Norwegian spring-spawning (Atlanto-Scandian) herring, and mackerel in the north-east Atlantic.[218] In the case of the first and third of these arrangements, the participants meet regularly to adopt and review management measures.

There are also a number of organizations concerned with cetaceans. Although cetaceans are not, of course, fish, organizations concerned with cetaceans are frequently discussed in the literature on RFMOs because they share many of the characteristics of RFMOs. The main organizations concerned with cetaceans are the International Whaling Commission (IWC)[219] and the North Atlantic Marine Mammal Commission (NAMMCO).[220] Although operating through conferences/meetings of the parties rather than an organization as such, the 1979 Convention on the Conservation of Migratory Species of Wild Animals[221] and two of the agreements concluded under its auspices, the 1992 Agreement on the Conservation of

[210] Established by the 1993 Convention for the Conservation of Southern Bluefin Tuna (hereafter, 'the CCSBT Convention'), 1819 UNTS 360.

[211] Established by the 1993 Agreement for the Establishment of the Indian Ocean Tuna Commission (hereafter, 'the IOTC Convention'), 1927 UNTS 329.

[212] Established by the 1949 Convention for the Establishment of an Inter-American Tropical Tuna Commission (hereafter, 'the IATTC Convention'), 80 UNTS 3. The Convention will be replaced by the 2003 Convention for the Strengthening of the Inter-American Tropical Tuna Commission (hereafter, 'the Antigua Convention'), OJ 2005 L15/9, when the latter enters into force.

[213] Established by the 1966 International Convention for the Conservation of Atlantic Tunas (hereafter, 'the ICCAT Convention'), 673 UNTS 63.

[214] Established by the 1982 Convention for the Conservation of Salmon in the North Atlantic Ocean, 1338 UNTS 33.

[215] Established by the 1992 Convention for the Conservation of Anadromous Stocks in the North Pacific Ocean, *Law of the Sea Bulletin* 22 (1993), 21.   [216] ILM 34 (1995), 67.

[217] OJ 2006 L196/15. The Agreement is not yet in force.

[218] For details of such arrangements, see Henriksen *et al*, *Law and Politics in Ocean Governance*, ch 8.

[219] Established by the 1946 International Convention for the Regulation of Whaling, 161 UNTS 72. The IWC is a global, rather than a regional, organization.

[220] Established by the 1992 Agreement on Co-Operation on Research, Conservation and Management of Marine Mammals in the North Atlantic, *Law of the Sea Bulletin* 26 (1994), 318.

[221] 1651 UNTS 333.

Small Cetaceans of the Baltic, North East Atlantic, Irish and North Seas[222] and the 1996 Agreement on the Conservation of Cetaceans of the Black Sea, Mediterranean Sea and Contiguous Atlantic Area,[223] as well as the 2006 Memorandum of Understanding for the Conservation of Cetaceans and Their Habitats in the Pacific Islands Region,[224] are concerned with the conservation and management of cetaceans.

The EC is a member of many of the RFMOs listed above. The issue of such membership and the EC's participation in those bodies is reviewed in Chapter 5.

Most RFMOs have broadly similar powers to adopt conservation and management measures. Thus, each year they usually establish TACs for at least some of the fish stocks for whose management they are responsible. Those TACs are then often divided into quotas allocated to individual members of the RFMO. TACs and quotas are frequently supplemented by other conservation measures, such as fishing gear regulations (eg minimum mesh sizes), minimum fish sizes, and by-catch levels. In addition, most RFMOs have the competence to take various steps to promote compliance with their conservation and management measures, such as the adoption of international inspection and observer schemes and vessel reporting requirements. Some RFMOs also have the power to take measures to protect the wider marine environment from the adverse consequences of fishing (see further section 8 below).

In spite of having quite extensive powers, most RFMOs have faced similar problems in managing the fish stocks for which they are responsible. Such problems include inadequate scientific knowledge of the fish stocks for which they are responsible; the inability of their members to agree on adequate conservation and management measures, of which part of the cause is the difficulty in agreeing on criteria for allocating fishing opportunities among members; the possibility in most RFMOs for members to invoke objection procedures and so opt out of such measures as are adopted; an inability or unwillingness on the part of members properly to enforce an RFMO's conservation and management measures; a failure to take sufficient account of the impact of fishing on the wider ecosystem; and the undermining of RFMO measures as a result of fishing by vessels flying the flag of non-member States (which are often flags of convenience), sometimes operated by nationals of member States of the RFMO who have re-registered their vessels under such flags specifically to avoid being bound by the RFMO's measures. Many of these problems have been exacerbated by over-capacity in many of the fishing fleets of RFMO member States.

In recent years steps have been taken in a number of RFMOs to try to overcome some of these problems. This development has been prompted especially by the various global fisheries instruments adopted in the mid-1990s which were surveyed earlier in this chapter. As far as the problem of members

---

[222] 1772 UNTS 217.   [223] 2183 UNTS 303.

[224] The text of the Memorandum of Understanding is available on the website of the Convention on Migratory Species.

invoking an RFMO's objection procedure is concerned, it has been made more difficult to invoke the objection procedures in some RFMOs, such as the SEAFO and the NEAFC, by including in, or adding to, their constitutive treaties a requirement that any member proposing to object to a measure must give reasons for its objection (and in the case of the SEAFO such objections may be made on only a limited number of grounds). Furthermore, an objecting member must indicate any alternative measures that it intends to take.[225] Going further, the WCPFC Convention unusually, and uniquely for an RFMO in which decisions may be taken by majority vote (although only if consensus cannot be obtained), contains no possibility for members to object to its measures, the coastal States of the region having successfully resisted attempts made by distant-water fishing States to include such a possibility when negotiating the WCPFC Convention.[226]

As far as the problem of non-compliance by members of an RFMO is concerned, a number of steps have been taken to improve compliance with RFMO management measures. Many RFMOs (for example, the CCAMLR, NAFO, NEAFC, and WCPFC) have adopted international inspection schemes, whereby a fishing vessel registered in one RFMO member State may be inspected by a fisheries enforcement vessel belonging to any other member State of that RFMO. Usually in such schemes an inspector must notify the flag State of any apparent infringement and may prohibit the vessel from further fishing. The flag State must investigate such allegations of illegal fishing promptly (including ordering the vessel to a nearby port if justified), and prosecute where the evidence so warrants. For any RFMOs that do not have such schemes, the Fish Stocks Agreement gives similar powers of inspection, as was seen in section 3 above. Secondly, some RFMOs (for example, the CCAMLR, IATTC, NAFO, and WCPFC) have adopted international observer schemes under which observers must be placed on board fishing vessels. The task of observers is to monitor a vessel's compliance with the RFMO's measures. Mere presence of an observer may induce compliance. In some schemes (such as that of the NAFO) an observer must report any apparent infringements to an inspector and send a report to the RFMO and the flag State. Thirdly, many RFMOs require vessels fishing in their area of competence to report on their movements and activities within and into and out of the area. At their most sophisticated, such reporting schemes require vessels to be fitted with transponders to record their movements and send the information in near 'real time' to the RFMO concerned. Fourthly, a number of

---

[225] See SEAFO Convention, Art 23; and Recommendation concerning the Procedures of Articles 12 and 13 of the NEAFC, adopted by the NEAFC in November 2004, NEAFC, *Report of the 23rd Annual Meeting, 8–12 November 2004* (2004), vol I, 37–8 and vol II, 28.

[226] Juda, 'Rio Plus Ten', 128. Further on objection procedures, see McDorman, TL, 'Implementing Existing Tools: Turning Words into Actions—Decision-Making Processes of Regional Fisheries Management Organizations (RFMOs)' *IJMCL* 20 (2005), 423, especially at 430–2; and Schiffman, HS, *Marine Conservation Agreements: The Law and Policy of Reservations and Vetoes* (Leiden: Martinus Nijhoff Publishers, 2008), see especially chs 4 and 5.

RFMOs (such as the NAFO and NEAFC) have adopted schemes that require port States to inspect the vessels of RFMO member States using their ports and prohibit the landing of catches that appear to have been taken in contravention of RFMO management measures. Other means used to induce compliance include the investigation and publicizing by an RFMO of the action taken by flag States in response to allegations of non-compliance by their vessels with that RFMO's measures (a measure employed by the NAFO and NEAFC); blacklisting member States' vessels that have engaged in IUU fishing (done, for example, by the CCAMLR, ICCAT, and SEAFO); and reducing an RFMO member's future quotas where it has exceeded its existing quotas (done so far only by the CCSBT and ICCAT).[227]

RFMOs have also taken various steps to combat the activities of non-members. Some RFMOs (such as the CCSBT, ICCAT, IOTC, and NEAFC) have introduced cooperating non-member schemes whereby they will allocate small quotas to those non-members that are prepared to cooperate and observe the management measures of the RFMO concerned. For non-members that are not willing to cooperate (especially flags of convenience), tougher measures have been introduced by the CCAMLR, ICCAT, NAFO, NEAFC, and others. Such measures include, *inter alia*, requiring members of an RFMO to prohibit the landing in their ports of catches taken by non-member vessels in the RFMO's area; the blacklisting of non-member vessels that have engaged in IUU fishing (such vessels may not then, for example, have access to RFMO member ports or be authorized to fish within the national jurisdiction of RFMO members); and regulating transhipment by prohibiting transhipment between RFMO member vessels and non-member vessels or by permitting transhipment only to authorized vessels.[228]

The other problems of RFMOs referred to above have been the object of less action and are less susceptible to solution. There are two provisions in the global fisheries instruments discussed earlier that could help to address some of these problems. The first such provision is the requirement in the Fish Stocks Agreement and the Code of Conduct for Responsible Fisheries to apply a precautionary approach to fisheries management. Quite a number of RFMOs have already embraced or are in the process of adopting such an approach. They include the CCAMLR, IATTC, ICCAT, NAFO, NASCO, and NEAFC,[229] as well as the more recently established SEAFO and WCPFC and the reformed GFCM

---

[227] For more detailed discussion of the measures outlined in this paragraph, including some of their drawbacks, see Rayfuse, R, 'To Our Children's Children's Children: From Promoting to Achieving Compliance in High Seas Fisheries' *IJMCL* 20 (2005), 509, especially at 516–23 and 525–31; and Lodge *et al*, *Recommended Best Practices*, 44–66.

[228] See further Lodge *et al*, *Recommended Best Practices*, 62–6; and Owen, D, *Practices of RFMOs regarding Non-Members*, Recommended Best Practices for Regional Fisheries Management Organizations, Technical Study No 2 (London: Chatham House, 2007).

[229] See further Lugten, *A Review of Measures*, section IV, 13–29; Garcia, 'The Precautionary Approach', 488–500; and Mooney-Seus, ML and Rosenberg, AA, *Progress in Adopting the Precautionary*

whose constituent treaties require them to adopt a precautionary approach.[230] Some RFMOs are also beginning to employ an ecosystem approach (see further section 8 below). The second provision that may help is the requirement in Article 12 of the Fish Stocks Agreement for RFMOs to be transparent in their decision-making processes and to permit the representatives of non-governmental organizations (NGOs) to attend their meetings as observers. The participation of NGOs in their meetings may put pressure on RFMOs to be more conservation- and sustainability-minded. Many RFMOs concerned with straddling or highly migratory fish stocks, such as the ICCAT, NAFO, SEAFO, and WCPFC, have taken steps to give effect to Article 12.

If every RFMO were to adopt the best practices of the most advanced RFMOs outlined above,[231] there is a good chance that the management by RFMOs of the fish stocks for which they are responsible would overall be significantly improved.

7 UN General Assembly resolutions

As is well known, UN General Assembly resolutions are not legally binding, except on internal organizational matters such as adoption of the UN budget and the admission of new members to the UN. Nevertheless, it is widely recognized that some General Assembly resolutions are of legal significance; for example, because they may form part of practice establishing a rule of customary international law or because they may prompt the adoption of legally binding acts in other fora.[232] In this sense we may speak of General Assembly resolutions as being a form of soft law.[233] The General Assembly has adopted a considerable number of resolutions relating to fisheries. Since the late 1980s it has adopted annually or biennially a resolution devoted exclusively to fisheries. In addition, the Assembly's annual Law of the Sea resolutions usually contain some paragraphs addressing fisheries. These resolutions cover many different aspects of fisheries, but there are two particular matters that have been the subject of resolutions that appear to have acquired a soft-law character. The first relates to the use of driftnets, the second to vulnerable marine ecosystems.

Approach and Ecosystem-Based Management, Recommended Best Practices for Regional Fisheries Management Organizations, Technical Study No 1 (London: Chatham House, 2007). According to Lodge and Nandan, most RFMOs have yet to apply the provisions of Annex II of the Fish Stocks Agreement: see Lodge and Nandan, 'Some Suggestions', 359–60.

[230] SEAFO Convention, Art 7; WCPFC Convention, Arts 5(c) and 6; and GFCM Agreement, Art III(2).

[231] See also the summary of best practices in Lodge *et al*, *Recommended Best Practices*, 117–28.

[232] See further Shaw, M, *International Law* (6th edn, Cambridge: Cambridge University Press, 2008), 114–17.

[233] Boyle, AE and Chinkin, C, *The Making of International Law* (Oxford: Oxford University Press, 2007), 211–17.

A driftnet is, in broad terms, a type of net that is suspended vertically near the surface of the sea to a depth of about 30 ft and left to drift for some time before being hauled out of the water. Driftnets were often many miles in length. By the late 1980s such nets were causing widespread concern because of their indiscriminate nature, as they caught not only their target species (usually tuna, salmon, or squid) but also large numbers of other species of fish, marine mammals (particularly dolphins), turtles, and birds.[234] That concern led the UN General Assembly in 1989 and 1991 to adopt resolutions that called for a moratorium on 'large-scale' driftnet fishing on the high seas by the end of 1992 unless it could be shown for a particular region that effective conservation and management measures to prevent the unacceptable impact of such fishing had been adopted.[235] The resolutions prompted a considerable amount of legislative action prohibiting high seas driftnet fishing, including a regional treaty (the 1989 Wellington Convention for the Prohibition of Fishing with Long Driftnets in the South Pacific[236]), measures adopted by various RFMOs, and national legislation.[237] It has been argued that as a result of such action the moratorium for which the General Assembly resolutions call has become part of customary international law, and thus legally binding.[238] EC legislation banning driftnet fishing is examined in Chapters 4 and 5.

The second matter that has been addressed in General Assembly resolutions in a way that suggests that the relevant parts of the resolutions have attained a soft-law character is the protection of high seas vulnerable marine ecosystems (VMEs) from damaging fishing practices. In recent years various kinds of marine ecosystem have increasingly attracted the attention of the international community because of their vulnerability to certain kinds of fishing practices. The ecosystems particularly identified are those associated with cold-water coral reefs, seamounts, and hydrothermal vents. Those three features are found mainly, but not exclusively, in the high seas. Although physically very different, they have certain things in common: in particular, they are areas rich in biological diversity, little is known about most of the plant and animal species living on or near them, and they are particularly vulnerable to damage

---

[234] Miller, B, 'Combating Driftnet Fishing in the Pacific', in Crawford J and Rothwell DR (eds), *The Law of the Sea in the Asian-Pacific Region* (Dordrecht: Martinus Nijhoff Publishers, 1995), 155.

[235] General Assembly Resolution 44/225, Large-scale pelagic driftnet fishing and its impact on the living marine resources of the world's oceans and seas, adopted on 22 December 1989; and General Assembly Resolution 46/215, Large-scale pelagic drift-net fishing and its impact on the living marine resources of the world's oceans and seas, adopted on 20 December 1991, both available on the website of the DOALOS.   [236] ILM 29 (1990), 1449.

[237] Details of this legislative action may be found in the UN Secretary General's annual reports on fisheries, available on the website of the DOALOS.

[238] Hewison, GJ, 'The Legally Binding Nature of the Moratorium on Large-Scale High Seas Driftnet Fishing' *Journal of Maritime Law and Commerce* 25 (1994), 557.

caused by certain kinds of deep-sea fishing practices, in particular bottom trawling. The concerns of the international community over this last matter have been reflected, to a considerable extent, in various General Assembly resolutions.

The first significant resolution is Resolution 59/25, adopted in 2004.[239] The Resolution called on States, acting individually or through RFMOs, to take action 'urgently' to consider on a case-by-case basis the interim prohibition of destructive fishing practices, including bottom trawling, that had adverse impacts on VMEs until 'appropriate' conservation and management measures had been adopted,[240] which should be done by RFMOs 'urgently'.[241] Two years later the General Assembly adopted Resolution 61/105,[242] in which it called on States to take action 'immediately', both individually and through RFMOs or regional fisheries management arrangements, to protect VMEs, including the three kinds of features mentioned above, 'from destructive fishing practices, recognizing the immense importance and value of deep sea ecosystems and the biodiversity they contain'.[243] The Resolution goes on to call on RFMOs or arrangements with the competence to regulate bottom fisheries, as a matter of priority but by the end of 2008 at the latest, to identify VMEs and assess the damage that bottom fishing causes to them; to 'close . . . areas [around VMEs] to bottom fishing and ensure that such activities do not proceed unless conservation and management measures have been established to prevent significant adverse impacts on [VMEs]'; and to 'require' their members to 'cease bottom fishing activities in areas where, in the course of fishing operations, [VMEs] are encountered, and to report the encounter so that appropriate measures can be adopted in respect of the relevant site'.[244] Resolution 61/105 also calls on flag States to adopt the same measures, *mutatis mutandis*, or cease to authorize their vessels to conduct bottom fisheries in areas beyond national jurisdiction where there is no RFMO or arrangement in operation,[245] and to inform the FAO of those vessels that have been authorized to conduct bottom fisheries in areas beyond national jurisdiction and the measures that they have adopted.[246] As can be seen, the language of the Resolution is somewhat repetitive and not entirely consistent, reflecting perhaps

---

[239] General Assembly Resolution 59/25, Sustainable Fisheries, including through the 1995 Agreement for the Implementation of the Provisions of the United Nations Convention on the Law of the Sea of 10 December 1982 relating to the Conservation and Management of Straddling Fish Stocks and Highly Migratory Fish Stocks, and related instruments, adopted on 17 November 2004, available on the website of the DOALOS.   [240] Res 59/25, para 66.

[241] Res 59/25, para 67.

[242] General Assembly Resolution 61/105, Sustainable Fisheries, including through the 1995 Agreement for the Implementation of the Provisions of the United Nations Convention on the Law of the Sea of 10 December 1982 relating to the Conservation and Management of Straddling Fish Stocks and Highly Migratory Fish Stocks, and related instruments, adopted on 8 December 2006, available on the website of the DOALOS.   [243] Res 61/105, para 80.

[244] Res 61/105, para 83.   [245] Res 61/105, para 86.   [246] Res 61/105, para 87.

its compromise nature and the fact that it does not contain the clear-cut prohibition on bottom fishing in areas beyond national jurisdiction that some UN member States and environmental NGOs had sought.[247]

Nevertheless, Resolutions 59/25 and 61/105, or at least the same concerns that prompted them, have led to action to protect VMEs being taken in other fora. A number of RFMOs, notably the CCAMLR, GFCM, NAFO, NEAFC, and SEAFO, have adopted measures to restrict or prohibit fishing in the vicinity of certain specifically identified VMEs. Secondly, the FAO has been working on producing guidelines for the management of deep-sea fisheries in the high seas. A set of guidelines was produced at the end of a Technical Consultation held in August 2008[248] and was forwarded to the FAO's Committee on Fisheries with a view to its adoption at the next biennial meeting of the Committee in March 2009. The role of the *Guidelines*, according to paragraph 6, is 'to provide tools, including guidance on their application, to facilitate and encourage the efforts of States and RFMOs towards sustainable use of marine living resources exploited by deep-sea fisheries, the prevention of significant adverse impacts on deep-sea VMEs and the protection of marine biodiversity that these ecosystems contain'. 'Deep-sea fisheries' are defined as fisheries that occur beyond national jurisdiction where the total catch includes 'species that can only sustain low exploitation rates' and where the fishing gear used is 'likely to contact the seafloor during the normal course of fishing operations'.[249] The concepts of VMEs and 'significant adverse impacts' are explained in paragraphs 14–16 (and Annex 1) and 17–20, respectively. The *Guidelines* then go on to address governance and management (paragraphs 21–29); 'management and conservation steps' (including: (a) data, reporting, and assessment; (b) identifying VMEs and assessing significant adverse impacts; (c) enforcement and compliance; (d) management and conservation tools; and (e) assessment and review of effectiveness of measures) (paragraphs 30–83); special requirements of developing countries (paragraphs 84–85); and additional considerations of implementation (paragraphs 86–89). The *Guidelines* are discussed in more detail in section 8 below in respect of environmental protection. The EC has adopted its own legislation in response to the General Assembly's resolutions.[250] That legislation is examined in Chapter 5.

---

[247] *Proposal for a Council Regulation on the protection of vulnerable marine ecosystems in the high seas from the adverse impacts of bottom fishing gears*, COM(2007) 605, 17.10.2007, pp 2–3.

[248] *Report of the Technical Consultation on International Guidelines for the Management of Deep-sea Fisheries in the High Seas, Rome, 4–8 February and 25–29 August 2008*, FAO Fisheries and Aquaculture Report No 881 (2008), available on the website of the Fisheries and Aquaculture Department of the FAO, Appendix F.   [249] *Guidelines*, paras 8 and 9.

[250] Council Regulation (EC) No 734/2008 of 15 July 2008 on the protection of vulnerable marine ecosystems in the high seas from the adverse impacts of bottom fishing gears, OJ 2008 L201/8.

8 Importing environmental issues into fisheries management

Fisheries management is no longer solely about the conservation of the target fish stocks. Instead, international fisheries management is moving towards an ecosystem-based approach, whereby the focus is the structure, processes, and functions of the relevant ecosystem as a whole rather than merely the population size of a given fish stock. A discussion of the meaning of the so-called 'ecosystem approach', and the means to make it operational, is beyond the scope of this chapter, but a large amount of material is now available on the subject,[251] and the ecosystem approach in an EC context is discussed in Chapter 4. Instead, this section will simply seek to illustrate how consideration of species beyond the target fish stock, and their habitats, has come to play a role in international fisheries management. It does this by focusing almost entirely on the wording of certain global and regional treaties, but without any consideration of the practice under those treaties.

At a global level, the UN Convention on the Law of the Sea (see section 2 above) expressly acknowledges the interaction between fisheries and the wider environment in its Articles 61 and 119 on the EEZ and the high seas respectively. Both those provisions require States to establish fisheries conservation measures that produce maximum sustainable yield albeit 'as qualified by relevant *environmental* and economic factors' (emphasis added)[252] and to 'take into consideration the effects on species associated with or dependent upon harvested species with a view to maintaining or restoring populations of such associated or dependent species above levels at which their reproduction may become seriously threatened'.[253]

In its Part XII, the Convention on the Law of the Sea also contains more general provisions on environmental protection including an obligation to take measures 'necessary to protect and preserve rare or fragile ecosystems as well as the habitat of depleted, threatened or endangered species and other forms of marine life'.[254]

The need to integrate environmental protection into, *inter alia*, the fisheries sector has also been significantly promoted by the 1992 Convention on Biological Diversity,[255] in that Article 6 requires each party, 'in accordance with its particular conditions and capabilities', to '[i]ntegrate, as far as possible and as appropriate, the

---

[251] See, for example, the following, both available on the website of the Fisheries and Aquaculture Department of the FAO: (a) FAO, *FAO Technical Guidelines for Responsible Fisheries No 4, Suppl 2, The Ecosystem Approach to Fisheries* (Rome: FAO, 2003); and (b) Garcia, SM, Zerbi, A, Aliaume, C, Do Chi, T, and Lasserre, G, *The Ecosystem Approach to Fisheries*, FAO Fisheries Technical Paper No 443 (Rome: FAO, 2003).   [252] UN Convention on the Law of the Sea, Arts 61(3) and 119(1)(a).

[253] UN Convention on the Law of the Sea, Arts 61(4) and 119(1)(b).

[254] UN Convention on the Law of the Sea, Art 194(5).   [255] 1760 UNTS 79.

conservation and sustainable use of biological diversity into relevant sectoral or cross-sectoral plans, programmes and policies'. The accompanying Rio Declaration on Environment and Development[256] and Agenda 21[257] give additional, albeit non-legally binding, weight to that obligation.

Subsequent to the Convention on the Law of the Sea and the Convention on Biological Diversity, the Fish Stocks Agreement (see section 3 above) includes provisions reiterating, and perhaps supplementing, the Law of the Sea Convention's provisions on environmental integration. It reiterates the points from Articles 61 and 119 about maximum sustainable yield 'as qualified by relevant environmental and economic factors'[258] and contains various provisions on species associated with or dependent upon target stocks and on protection of the wider environment.[259]

Of note, the treaty introduces the term 'species belonging to the same ecosystem', which is potentially broader than a reference merely to associated or dependent species. For such species, as well as for associated and dependent species, the parties are to 'assess the impacts of *fishing*, other human activities and environmental factors' (emphasis added)[260] and to 'adopt, where necessary, conservation and management measures . . . with a view to maintaining or restoring populations of such species above levels at which their reproduction may become seriously threatened'.[261]

The Fish Stocks Agreement also uses the term 'non-target species', which is expressly stated as including both fish and non-fish species.[262] Again, that term is potentially broader in scope than references to associated or dependent species. Regarding non-target species, assessments of the impact of fishing are to be undertaken by parties and by RFMOs,[263] catch recording, reporting, and verification requirements are to be established by flag States,[264] complete and accurate catch data are to be shared among the parties in a timely manner,[265] and uncertainties regarding the impact of fishing activities are to be taken into account in implementing the precautionary approach.[266]

More substantively, catch of non-target species is to be minimized 'through measures including, to the extent practicable, the development and use of selective, environmentally safe and cost-effective fishing gear and techniques'[267] and conservation plans for such species are to be adopted where necessary.[268] Enhanced monitoring, both of species' status and efficacy of conservation measures, is to be undertaken in cases of concern.[269] With some exceptions or

---

[256] See, in particular, Principle 4 (available on the website of the UNEP).
[257] See, in particular, Chapters 8 and 17 (available on the website of the UNEP).
[258] Fish Stocks Agreement (abbreviated in the footnotes to this section as 'FSA'), Art 5(b).
[259] See, *inter alia*, FSA, Arts 5(d)–(g) and (j), 6(1), 6(3)(c)–(d), 6(5), 7(2)(f), 10(d), and 18(3)(e)–(f) and (i).   [260] FSA, Art 5(d).
[261] FSA, Art 5(e).   [262] FSA, Art 5(f).   [263] FSA, Arts 6(3)(d) and 10(d).
[264] FSA, Art 18(3)(e) and (f).   [265] FSA, Art 5(j) and Annex I.
[266] FSA, Art 6(3)(c) and Annex II.   [267] FSA, Art 5(f).   [268] FSA, Art 6(3)(d).
[269] FSA, Art 6(5).

slight modifications, the above duties likewise relate to species associated with or dependent upon the target stocks.

As well as its provisions on associated or dependent species, on 'species belonging to the same ecosystem', and on 'non-target species', the Fish Stocks Agreement also refers at one point to the protection of 'habitats of special concern'[270] and to a general principle to 'protect biodiversity in the marine environment'.[271] Overall, the Agreement is clearly an important step in developing States' duties to protect the wider environment in the course of fishing activities. That said, the Agreement is of course focused on fisheries for a relatively narrow group of stocks, namely straddling stocks and highly migratory stocks.

The provisions in the Fish Stocks Agreement on protection of the wider environment have been reflected in treaties establishing RFMOs after 1995, the year in which the Fish Stocks Agreement was adopted. Examples include the WCPFC Convention,[272] the SEAFO Convention,[273] and the Antigua Convention (not yet in force),[274] all of which replicate wording, with some adaptations, from the Fish Stocks Agreement, as well as introducing new terminology. The same applies to the 2006 Southern Indian Ocean Fisheries Agreement.[275] The SEAFO Convention defines the term 'marine living resources' as 'all living components of marine ecosystems, including seabirds',[276] which of course has consequences where that term is used later in the treaty.

In addition, some RFMO treaties that were adopted prior to 1995 have recently been amended or replaced in order to provide their corresponding RFMOs with a firmer legal basis to adopt environmental protection measures. The amended version of the NEAFC Convention, which is not yet in force but is meanwhile being applied provisionally,[277] uses relatively concise amendments to the previous treaty to provide the North-East Atlantic Fisheries Commission with the necessary environmental protection powers.[278] As with the SEAFO Convention, the amended NEAFC Convention defines the term 'marine living resources' broadly as 'all living components of marine ecosystems'.[279] In contrast, the 2007 amendments to the NAFO Convention, which are yet to enter into force, involve

---

[270] FSA, Art 6(3)(d).   [271] FSA, Art 5(g).

[272] See, inter alia, Arts 5(d) (cf FSA, Art 5(d)), 5(e) (cf FSA, Art 5(f)), 5(f) (cf FSA, Art 5(g)), 5(i) (cf FSA, Art 5(j)), 6(1)(b) (cf FSA, Art 6(3)(c)), 6(1)(c) (cf FSA, Art 6(3)(d)), 6(4) (cf FSA, Art 6(5)), 8(2)(e) (cf FSA, Art 7(2)(f)), 10(1)(c) (cf FSA, Art 5(e)), 12(2)(c)–(e) and (g), 13(3)(b)–(c), and Annex III, Art 5.

[273] See, inter alia, Arts 3(c), 3(d) (cf FSA, Art 5(e)), 3(f) (cf FSA, Art 5(g)), 6(3)(c) and 14(3)(e) (cf FSA, Art 18(3)(e)).

[274] See, inter alia, Arts IV(3) (cf FSA, Art 6(5)), VII(1)(a), VII(1)(f) (cf FSA, Art 5(e)), VII(1)(g) and (k) (cf FSA, Art 5(f)), and XV(3).

[275] See, inter alia, Arts 4(a), 4(e) (cf FSA, Art 5(f)), 4(f) (cf FSA, Art 5(g)), 6(1)(b), 6(1)(c) (cf FSA, Art 5(d)), 6(1)(d), 7(1)(a)(i), and 13(4)(b).   [276] SEAFO Convention, Art 1(n).

[277] See the website of the NEAFC.

[278] See, inter alia, amended Arts 1(c) and (d), 2, 4(1), 4(2)(c)–(d), and 4(3).

[279] NEAFC Convention, amended Art 1(c).

replacement of entire articles.[280] Like the SEAFO and NEAFC Conventions, the 2007 amendments define the term 'living resources' as 'all living components of marine ecosystems'.[281]

Some RFMO treaties pre-dating the Fish Stocks Agreement already contained express references to species other than the target species. The IATTC Convention, adopted in 1949, requires the IATTC to, *inter alia*, '[m]ake investigations concerning the abundance, biology, biometry, and ecology of . . . the kinds of fishes commonly used as bait in the tuna fisheries, especially the anchovetta, and of other kinds of fish taken by tuna fishing vessels; and the effects of natural factors and human activities on the abundance of the populations of fishes supporting all these fisheries'.[282] However, the reference to investigations concerning bait fish may well reflect an interest in having sufficient bait for tuna fisheries rather than any broader ecosystem concern. Related to the IATTC Convention, and highly relevant to the impact of fishing on the wider environment, is the 1998 Agreement on the International Dolphin Conservation Program (AIDCP) which is discussed in Chapter 5.

The CCAMLR Convention, adopted in 1980, is well known for its early incorporation of an ecosystem approach. It defines the term 'Antarctic marine living resources' as 'the populations of fin fish, molluscs, crustaceans and all other species of living organisms, including birds, found south of the Antarctic Convergence',[283] and states its objective as being the conservation of such resources.[284] Many of the treaty's provisions reflect the relationship between target species and the rest of the Antarctic marine ecosystem.

The CCSBT Convention, adopted in 1993, also contains language regarding the wider environment. It uses the term 'ecologically related species', defined as 'living marine species which are associated with southern bluefin tuna, including but not restricted to both predators and prey of southern bluefin tuna'.[285] Express duties regarding such species include a requirement on parties to: (a) provide to the CCSBT, for collection and accumulation,[286] scientific information, catch and effort statistics, and other data relevant to those species, as appropriate;[287] and (b) cooperate in collection and direct exchange, when appropriate, of fisheries data, biological samples, and other information relevant for scientific research on those species.[288]

In addition, the Scientific Committee is to, *inter alia*, report to the CCSBT its findings or conclusions on the status of such species, where appropriate.[289] In turn, the CCSBT is to take 'full account' of, *inter alia*, any report of the Scientific Committee on the status of 'ecologically related species' when deciding upon: (a)

---

[280] See the website of the NAFO. See, *inter alia*, 'new' Arts I(k) and (l), II, III(d), (e) and (i), VI(6)(c), VI(7), VI(8)(b), VII(8)(a) and (d), VII(10)(a) and (b), and X(1)(d).
[281] NAFO Convention, 'new' Art I(k).   [282] IATTC Convention, Art II(1).
[283] CCAMLR Convention, Art I(2).   [284] CCAMLR Convention, Art II(1).
[285] CCSBT Convention, Art 2(a).   [286] CCSBT Convention, Art 8(1)(a).
[287] CCSBT Convention, Art 5(2).   [288] CCSBT Convention, Art 5(3).
[289] CCSBT Convention, Art 9(2)(c).

the total allowable catch and, if necessary, any additional binding measures for the conservation, management, and optimum utilization of southern bluefin tuna; and (b) recommendations to the parties in order to further the attainment of the treaty's objective.[290]

The analysis so far has focused on treaties. Some soft-law instruments also address the wider impact of fishing. Central amongst these is the FAO Code of Conduct for Responsible Fisheries (see section 5 above). The Code does not expressly refer to the ecosystem approach but contains many provisions consistent with it. The FAO's International Plans of Action for Reducing Incidental Catch of Seabirds in Longline Fisheries and for the Conservation and Management of Sharks (on which, see again section 5 above) are also clearly relevant to the wider impact of fishing. In 2001, the Reykjavik Declaration on Responsible Fisheries in the Marine Ecosystem was adopted by a conference jointly organized by the FAO and Iceland and attended by representatives of fifty-nine members of the FAO.[291] The Declaration uses the term 'ecosystem considerations' and recognizes that 'sustainable fisheries management incorporating ecosystem considerations entails taking into account the impacts of fisheries on the marine ecosystem and the impacts of the marine ecosystem on fisheries'.[292]

The Plan of Implementation of the World Summit on Sustainable Development,[293] adopted in 2002, notes that ensuring the sustainable development of the oceans requires actions at all levels to '[e]ncourage the application by 2010 of the ecosystem approach, noting the Reykjavik Declaration . . . and decision V/6 of the Conference of Parties to the Convention on Biological Diversity'.[294] However, the Plan itself fails to elaborate on the meaning of the term 'ecosystem approach'. The United Nations General Assembly resolutions on driftnet fishing and vulnerable marine ecosystems (see section 7 above) may also be seen as a response to the need to address the wider impact of fishing.

In August 2008, as noted in section 7 above, an FAO technical consultation adopted International Guidelines for the Management of Deep-sea Fisheries in the High Seas,[295] aimed at States and regional fisheries management organizations and arrangements.[296] With a focus on fishing gear that routinely touches the seafloor,[297] the *Guidelines* deal with conservation of the relevant fish stocks and prevention of 'significant adverse impacts' by relevant fishing activities on so-called 'vulnerable marine ecosystems' (VMEs).[298] Many of the *Guidelines'*

---

[290] CCSBT Convention, Art 8(6).

[291] The Reykjavik Declaration is available on the website of the Fisheries and Aquaculture Department of the FAO.   [292] Reykjavik Declaration, 10th recital.

[293] Report of the World Summit on Sustainable Development, Chapter 1, Resolution 2, Plan of Implementation, available on the website of the UN Department of Economic and Social Affairs, Division for Sustainable Development.   [294] Ibid, para 30(d); see also paras 32(c) and 44(e).

[295] Available on the website of the Fisheries and Aquaculture Department of the FAO.

[296] See, for example, paras 1 and 6 of the *Guidelines*.   [297] *Guidelines*, para 8(ii).

[298] See, for example, paras 6 and 11 of the *Guidelines*.

sections deal with both these elements.[299] However, there are also sections specifically on VMEs, namely on the meaning of the terms 'vulnerable' and 'significant adverse impact',[300] on the identification of VMEs and the assessment of significant adverse impacts,[301] and on the types of species and so on comprising VMEs.[302]

The *Guidelines* are a blend of the general and the specific, and are rather unclear in places by virtue of variations in terminology from one provision to the next. An important example of a specific measure is the use of impact assessments 'to establish if deep-sea fishing activities are likely to produce significant adverse impacts in a given area'.[303] The *Guidelines* state that the relevant fishing activities should be 'managed to prevent such impacts [on VMEs] or not authorized to proceed, if it is assessed . . . that they would have significant adverse impacts'.[304] The latter provision is somewhat ambiguous. However, one interpretation is that if the assessment reveals that the fishing activities, despite any mitigation measures, would have significant adverse impacts on one or more VMEs, those activities should not be authorized to proceed. If the presence of VMEs or the likelihood of significant adverse impacts 'cannot be adequately determined', some specific precautionary measures are to be employed.[305] Pending the development of 'a functioning regulatory framework' to, *inter alia*, prevent significant adverse impacts on VMEs, interim measures should include, amongst others, 'closing of areas to [the relevant fishing activities] where VMEs are known or likely to occur, based on the best available scientific and technical information'.[306]

A strong focus of the *Guidelines* is data collection and analysis in order to identify the location of VMEs.[307] This is not surprising given the current lack of knowledge in this regard. In principle, Decision IX/20 of the conference of the parties to the Convention on Biological Diversity, adopted in May 2008, is likely to be highly relevant to the identification of VMEs, and hence to the implementation of the *Guidelines*, because it includes 'scientific criteria for identifying ecologically or biologically significant marine areas in need of protection in open-ocean waters *and deep-sea habitats*' (emphasis added).[308]

Lastly, in this brief survey, it should be mentioned that a wide variety of instruments on environmental protection that are not directly or primarily related to fishing nonetheless contain provisions that are potentially relevant to the conduct of fishing activities in relation to the wider environment. Some examples

---

[299] See, in particular, sections 4.1 (General management considerations), 4.2 (Governance framework), 5.1 (Data, reporting and assessment), 5.3 (Enforcement and compliance), and 5.4 (Management and conservation tools). [300] *Guidelines*, sections 3.2 and 3.3.

[301] *Guidelines*, section 5.2. [302] *Guidelines*, Annex 1.

[303] *Guidelines*, para 47; see also paras 48–53. [304] *Guidelines*, para 73; see also paras 70–2.

[305] *Guidelines*, para 74. [306] *Guidelines*, para 63(i); see also paras 66 and 61.

[307] See, for example, paras 12(ii), 21(ii), 32, 34, 44–45, and 49 of the *Guidelines*.

[308] See, for example, paras 2, 17, 19, and 28 of Decision IX/20 (available on the website of the CBD).

are the 1992 Convention on Biological Diversity (see, for instance, Decision IX/20 referred to above), the 1979 Convention on the Conservation of Migratory Species of Wild Animals, and various agreements made under the latter treaty. Some such instruments are discussed in Chapter 5.

9 Conclusions

According to the most recent biennial report of the FAO on the state of world fisheries and aquaculture, the proportion of the world's fish stocks that is over-exploited and depleted increased from about 10 per cent in the mid-1970s to around 25 per cent by the early 1990s, since when it has remained stable. Furthermore, since the early 1990s about half of all stocks have been fully exploited and so producing catches at or close to their maximum sustainable limits, with no room for further expansion. In the view of the FAO, around 80 per cent of the world's fish stocks require effective, precautionary, and more controlled management.[309]

It is clear from those figures that fisheries management, both national and international, has not been successful over the past thirty years or more. Various reasons for this lack of success have been suggested during the course of this chapter. They include lack of the necessary scientific knowledge; the adoption of inadequate management measures, often as a result of short-term political and socio-economic pressures which are frequently caused by over-capacity in fishing fleets and the open access nature of many fisheries; and inadequate compliance with and enforcement of management measures, both within national jurisdiction and on the high seas. The Plan of Implementation adopted by the World Summit on Sustainable Development, held at Johannesburg in 2002, calls on States to 'maintain or restore stocks to levels that can produce the maximum sustainable yield with the aim of achieving these goals for depleted stocks on an urgent basis and where possible not later than 2015'[310]—a goal that the FAO has described as 'a high-order challenge'.[311] While the various international instruments adopted during the 1990s that were surveyed above may not yet have led to major improvements in fisheries management, it is to be hoped that they will do so and enable States to meet the challenge set by the World Summit on Sustainable Development.

---

[309] FAO, *The State of World Fisheries and Aquaculture 2008*, 7–8 and 30.

[310] Plan of Implementation, para 31(a).

[311] FAO, *The State of World Fisheries and Aquaculture 2004* (Rome: FAO, 2004), 32–4, available on the website of the Fisheries and Aquaculture Department of the FAO.

4

Fisheries management in Community waters

1 Introduction

This chapter examines the legal regime governing the management of fisheries in Community waters, ie those waters under the sovereignty or jurisdiction of EC Member States. An initial issue is the question of how far the competence to adopt management measures for Community waters falls within the competence of the EC and how far within the competence of Member States. It will be clear from the discussion at the beginning of Chapter 2 that Article 37 EC gives the EC the competence to adopt legislation to give effect to the objectives of the Common Fisheries Policy (CFP) set out in Article 33(1) EC. As argued in Chapter 2, those objectives, particularly to increase fisheries productivity by ensuring the rational development of fisheries production and to assure the availability of supplies of fishery products, are broad enough to encompass fisheries conservation. While that position has never seriously been contested, during the 1970s and early 1980s when the EC was trying to agree on an EC system of fisheries management for Community waters (see Chapter 1), there were considerable differences of opinion between the Commission on one side and some Member States on the other (notably the UK) over the scope of the EC's competence and whether its competence, whatever that scope, was exclusive. The issue was the subject of several cases before the Court, culminating in *Commission v United Kingdom*,[1] in which the Court held that the EC had exclusive competence to adopt fisheries conservation measures in Community waters. The Court based that finding on Article 102 of the 1972 Act of Accession (providing for the accession of Denmark, Ireland, and the UK to the EC). Article 102 required the Council to 'determine conditions for fishing with a view to ensuring protection of the fishing grounds and conservation of the biological resources of the sea' by the end of 1978. The Court held that the effect of that provision was that as from the beginning of 1979:

power to adopt, as part of the common fisheries policy, measures relating to the conservation of the resources of the sea has belonged fully and definitively to the Community. Member States are therefore no longer entitled to exercise any power in the matter of conservation measures in the waters under their jurisdiction. The adoption of such

---

[1] Case 804/79 *Commission v United Kingdom* [1981] ECR 1045.

measures, with the restrictions that they imply as regards fishing activities, is a matter, as from that date [ie the beginning of 1979], of Community law.[2]

Four comments may be made about the Court's conclusion. First, the Court expresses the EC's exclusive competence in terms of 'conservation'. The Court does not say what it means by 'conservation' and the term is not defined in EC fisheries legislation. Conservation is not a term of art. In international fisheries law it is frequently coupled with 'management' in references to 'conservation and management measures' (see further Chapter 3). Regulation 2371/2002[3] (hereafter, 'the Basic Regulation') also couples 'conservation' with 'management', referring to the scope of the CFP as covering, *inter alia*, 'conservation, management and exploitation of living aquatic resources'.[4] As noted at the beginning of Chapter 3, 'management' does not have a precise meaning either. 'Management' is often considered to include 'conservation', but is potentially considerably wider in scope. Given that, and given the language used by the Court, the EC's exclusive competence must be taken to relate only to 'fisheries conservation', and not to 'fisheries conservation and management'. However, that does not mean that the EC does not have competence in relation to at least some matters of fisheries 'management' that go beyond 'conservation': it may well do so, but any such competence will not be exclusive.

A second point is that international law makes a distinction between the legislative competence (or jurisdiction) of States, ie the competence to prescribe rules, and States' enforcement competence (or jurisdiction), ie the competence to enforce those rules. It is clear from the language of the Court's ruling, particularly the reference to 'measures', that the EC's exclusive competence in relation to fisheries conservation relates only to legislative competence. The general scheme of EC law endows the EC with only limited enforcement competence, and that competence is never exclusive. That general position applies equally to fisheries.[5]

Thirdly, the fact that the EC has exclusive legislative competence for fisheries conservation in Community waters does not in principle prevent the EC from delegating some of that competence to the Member States, and in fact it has done so, as is explained in subsection 2.4 below.

Fourthly, if the Treaty of Lisbon were to come into force, it would reflect the Court's judgment in *Commission v United Kingdom*. Article 3(1)(d) of the Treaty on the Functioning of the European Union (as the EC Treaty would be renamed) would provide that the EU (as the EC would become) had exclusive competence

---

[2] Case 804/79 *Commission v United Kingdom*, paras 17–18.

[3] Council Regulation (EC) No 2371/2002 of 20 December 2002 on the conservation and sustainable exploitation of fisheries resources under the Common Fisheries Policy, OJ 2002 L358/59, as amended and corrected.   [4] Reg 2371/2002, Art 1(1).

[5] See Berg, A, 'Enforcement of the Common Fisheries Policy, with Special Reference to the Netherlands' in Harding, C and Swart, B, *Enforcing European Community Rules* (Aldershot: Dartmouth, 1996), 62–82, especially at 64–7. See further subsection 2.7 below.

in relation to 'the conservation of marine biological resources under the common fisheries policy', while Article 4(2)(d) would provide that the EU and the Member States shared competence as regards 'fisheries, excluding the conservation of marine biological resources'.[6] It is noteworthy that the Treaty of Lisbon, like the Court, frames exclusivity in terms of 'conservation', and does not use the term 'management'.

The EC's system of fisheries conservation and management for Community waters comprises various elements, including the limitation of catches and fishing effort, technical conservation measures, Member States' delegated powers, access, enforcement, and the adjustment of fishing capacity to the fishing opportunities available, as well as a system of governance involving stakeholders.

At any given time, EC law regulating those matters is contained in a body of legislation comprising: (a) a Regulation setting out the framework of the EC's management system, often referred to as the 'Basic Regulation'; (b) a number of other Regulations containing the main rules of each of the principal elements of the system that are not regulated in their totality by the Basic Regulation; and (c) a mass of separate more detailed legislation implementing those provisions of the Regulations referred to in '(a)' and '(b)' above that require such implementation. As noted in Chapter 1, the first Basic Regulation was adopted in 1983. However, the discussion in this chapter is focused on the current Basic Regulation, Regulation 2371/2002, and its accompanying body of legislation, a good deal of which pre-dates it but is still applicable. Where appropriate, reference is also made to older legislation that has been repealed and/or replaced.

Under the Basic Regulation, and reflecting the objectives set out in Article 33(1) EC, the objectives of the CFP are to ensure exploitation of living aquatic resources that 'provides sustainable *economic, environmental and social* conditions' (emphasis added).[7] As a result, in principle there is discretion for the Commission and Council, when adopting fisheries management measures, to take into account not just scientific advice on the status of fish stocks and the wider environment but also economic and social conditions. However, the increasing use of long-term plans featuring harvesting rules (on which, see subsection 2.1 below) should reduce the amount of discretion that has previously been available to decision-makers. In addition, in the context of the latest reform of the CFP, the Commission observed in 2008 that: 'The long term ecological sustainability of fisheries must be the first priority because the past development of the CFP has demonstrated that healthy fish stocks and healthy marine ecosystems are a *sine qua non* for an economically and socially healthy fisheries sector.'[8]

---

[6] On the term 'marine biological resources' in the context of the Treaty of Lisbon, see further Chapter 2.   [7] Reg 2371/2002, Art 2(1).

[8] *Commission Working Document, Reflections on further reform of the Common Fisheries Policy*, section 4, p 7 (and see also section 3, p 6, 2nd bullet point), available on the website of DG Mare and discussed further in subsection 9.2 below.

The next section of this chapter (section 2) is concerned with general aspects of fisheries management in relation to Community waters. It considers in turn TACs and quotas, effort management, technical measures, Member States' delegated powers, access to fishing grounds, the nationality of fishing vessels, enforcement, and capacity adjustment. Some EC fisheries management measures apply only to particular regions of Community waters, namely the Baltic, Mediterranean, and Black Seas. Such measures are discussed in sections 3–5. (Measures applying to the North Sea and north-east Atlantic are covered in section 2.) Sections 6 and 7 deal, respectively, with the integration of environmental protection into the CFP and the role of Regional Advisory Councils and the Advisory Committee on Fisheries and Aquaculture. Most fishing in Community waters is done by Community fishing vessels (a term explained in Chapter 2 and in subsection 2.6 below), but there is also some fishing by vessels from a small number of third States.[9] EC law governing the latter group of vessels differs in some respects from that governing Community fishing vessels. For that reason fishing by third State vessels in Community waters is discussed separately in section 8. The final section of this chapter considers reform of the EC system of fisheries management.

The concern of this chapter is fisheries management in Community waters, and several sections of this chapter (such as sections 3, 5, and 8) are concerned solely with Community waters. However, it must be acknowledged that some matters discussed in this chapter (such as parts of sections 2, 4, 6, 7, and 9) also have some application outside Community waters. Where that is the case, it is either self-evident from the subject matter (eg nationality of fishing vessels, capacity adjustment) or is pointed out at appropriate points below. There are also cross-references in Chapter 5 (which deals with external aspects of fisheries management) to particularly apposite legislation discussed in this chapter that also applies outside Community waters.

2 General aspects of Community fisheries management

2.1 TACs and quotas

Introduction

Total allowable catches (TACs) and quotas, although complemented by technical measures (see subsection 2.3 below) and increasingly being supplemented with effort management (see subsection 2.2 below), remain the principal fisheries conservation tool used by the EC in respect of Community waters. Not all stocks

---

[9] Currently from the Faroe Islands and Norway in Community waters in the North Sea and north-east Atlantic; from Venezuela in the waters off French Guiana; and from Dominica in the waters off Guadeloupe and Martinique. See further Chapter 5.

fished in Community waters are subject to TACs; however, in such cases technical measures and effort management may still regulate the fisheries to some degree.

The EC's system of TACs and quotas also has some application outside Community waters, in particular where catch limits for the EC are set through regional fisheries management organizations (RFMOs) in relation to the high seas or through negotiations with neighbouring third States in relation to those States' waters. This subsection will consider the EC's system of TACs and quotas in general terms, rather than with specific reference to its use in Community waters.

TACs remain of fundamental importance as a fisheries conservation tool at the EC level not least because, through their division into Member States' quotas, they are currently the 'carriers' of the politically important principle of relative stability (on which, see below).[10] However, TACs as a conservation measure are not without their disadvantages. They can be difficult to enforce and, particularly in a mixed fishery, they can lead to significant discarding (see further below).

In EC vocabulary, TACs are quantitative limits on *landings* (on which, see further below), almost always expressed in tonnes,[11] that are set at the level of stocks or groups of stocks. Each TAC is then divided into one or more quotas allocated to particular Member States. The term 'stock' is defined in the Basic Regulation as 'a living aquatic resource that occurs in a given management area'.[12] The Court has defined the term as 'fish of a particular species located within a specified geographical area' or similar.[13] This subsection will explain: (a) the legal basis for setting TACs and quotas; (b) the process for setting TACs and dividing them into quotas; (c) the administration of TACs and quotas; and (d) the links between the TAC and quota system and discarding.

Legal basis for setting TACs and quotas

The principal legal basis for the EC to set TACs and quotas is the Basic Regulation. Article 4 states that measures to be adopted by the Council for achieving the objectives of the CFP may, in particular, include 'measures for each stock or group of stocks to limit fishing mortality and the environmental impact of fishing activities by . . . [*inter alia*] . . . limiting catches'.[14] Article 20(1) states, *inter alia*, that '[t]he Council, acting by qualified majority on a proposal from the Commission,

---

[10] Regarding the concept of TACs being the 'carriers' of relative stability see House of Lords, European Union Committee, 21st Report of Session 2007–08, *The Progress of the Common Fisheries Policy*, Vol II, Evidence, HL Paper 146-II (London: The Stationery Office Ltd, 2008), p 176 (European Commission's evidence).

[11] For one or two stocks, TACs are expressed by number of individual fish. See, for example, Council Regulation (EC) No 1404/2007 of 26 November 2007 fixing the fishing opportunities and associated conditions for certain fish stocks and groups of fish stocks applicable in the Baltic Sea for 2008, OJ 2007 L312/1, as amended, Annex I, TACs for Atlantic salmon.

[12] Reg 2371/2002, Art 3(g). On the term 'living aquatic resource', see Chapter 2.

[13] Eg Case C-73/90 *Spain v Council* [1992] ECR I-5191, para 28.

[14] Reg 2371/2002, Art 4(2)(d).

shall decide on *catch* and/or fishing effort *limits*' (emphasis added). This power is reiterated in various ways elsewhere in the Basic Regulation,[15] including in relation to recovery plans and management plans which will be mentioned below.

As noted in Chapter 1, the Basic Regulation does not actually use the term 'total allowable catch'. Instead it uses the term 'catch limit'. That term is defined as 'a quantitative limit on *landings* of a stock or group of stocks over a given period unless otherwise provided for in Community law' (emphasis added).[16] The reference to 'landings', rather than 'catches', is significant and is discussed further below in relation to discards. Catch limits, along with fishing effort limits (see subsection 2.2 below), are referred to collectively as 'fishing opportunities'.[17] The term 'fishing opportunity' is in turn defined as a 'quantified legal *entitlement* to fish' (emphasis added),[18] rather than a guarantee of a certain catch of fish.

The term 'total allowable catch' is, however, used and defined in the annual fishing opportunities Regulations (introduced more fully below). In Regulation 40/2008, the term is defined as 'the quantity that can be taken *and landed* from each stock each year' (emphasis added).[19] In Regulations 1404/2007 (for the Baltic Sea) and 1139/2008 (for the Black Sea) it is defined less precisely as 'the quantity that can be *taken* from each stock each year' (emphasis added),[20] ie with no reference to landing. However, to the authors' knowledge, TACs in the Baltic Sea and the Black Sea are anyway interpreted as restrictions on landings, irrespective of the definition used. The term 'quota' is defined as 'a proportion of the TAC allocated to the Community, Member States or third countries'.[21]

Until fairly recently, TACs (and the resulting quotas) in respect of Community waters were set by the Council in the absence of any strategic aim for the particular stock in question. Two things have changed that. First, the Commission has adopted its own (non-binding) rules for the setting of TACs generally (see further below). More significantly, pursuant to enabling powers in the Basic Regulation,[22] an increasing number of long-term recovery plans and management plans are being adopted which establish a strategic approach to setting TACs.

---

[15] Reg 2371/2002, Arts 4(2)(a), (b), and (d), 5(4), and 6(4).   [16] Reg 2371/2002, Art 3(m).

[17] Reg 2371/2002, Art 3(q). See also Arts 11(1), 14(1), 20(1)–(5), and 23(4).

[18] Reg 2371/2002, Art 3(q).

[19] Council Regulation (EC) No 40/2008 of 16 January 2008 fixing for 2008 the fishing opportunities and associated conditions for certain fish stocks and groups of fish stocks, applicable in Community waters and, for Community vessels, in waters where catch limitations are required, OJ 2008 L19/1, as amended and corrected, Art 3(a).

[20] Reg 1404/2007, Art 3(c); Council Regulation (EC) No 1139/2008 of 10 November 2008 fixing the fishing opportunities and the conditions relating thereto for certain fish stocks applicable in the Black Sea for 2009, OJ 2008 L308/3, Art 3(c).

[21] Reg 40/2008, Art 3(b). A slightly different formulation is used in Art 3(d) of Reg 1404/2007 and in Art 3(d) of Reg 1139/2008.   [22] Reg 2371/2002, Arts 5(4) and 6(4).

Recovery plans and management plans are now an important part of the CFP. Their importance is likely to grow if the Commission's policy of getting to, and maintaining, stock sizes that produce maximum sustainable yield (see subsection 9.4 below) gains momentum. The plans as a concept are introduced in this subsection, where they will be referred to generically as 'long-term plans'. Their introduction is followed by a summary of the TAC elements of such plans. The effort management and technical measures elements of long-term plans are summarized in subsections 2.2 and 2.3 below. For reasons of space, the merits and effectiveness of individual plans cannot be addressed here.

Long-term plans have arisen under the CFP in several ways to date. First, there are those which are adopted in the form of a Regulation at the initiative of the EC pursuant to Articles 5 and/or 6 of the Basic Regulation. Secondly, there are recovery plans which are adopted by RFMOs and then transposed into EC legislation by means of a Regulation and which are nominally linked to Article 5 of the Basic Regulation. Thirdly, there are those which are adopted through negotiations between the EC and one or more neighbouring coastal States in respect of shared stocks. Lastly, there is a recovery plan for European eel, which was adopted at the initiative of the EC but is somewhat different to the plans mentioned in the first category above and should probably be regarded as *sui generis*.[23] For the sake of completeness and simplicity, unless otherwise stated, long-term plans will be considered here, and also in subsections 2.2 and 2.3 below, without distinction being made as to whether they relate to Community waters, non-Community waters, or both.

The long-term plans in the third of the above categories have all been labelled as 'management plans', rather than 'recovery plans', but make no mention of Article 5 or 6 of the Basic Regulation. The plans are set out in the annexes of 'agreed records of conclusions of fisheries consultations' and have not been transposed into EC secondary legislation. The legal status of these plans, including whether or not they are binding on the EC, is therefore not entirely clear.

Between the EC and Norway there is a 'long-term management plan' for haddock in the North Sea and Skagerrak, for saithe in the Skagerrak, North Sea, and west of Scotland, and for North Sea herring. There is also a long-term management plan for cod to apply once certain stock conditions are met, and there are basic principles for a still-awaited long-term management plan for plaice.[24] In addition,

---

[23] Council Regulation (EC) No 1100/2007 of 18 September 2007 establishing measures for the recovery of the stock of European eel, OJ 2007 L248/17. See also Commission Decision 2008/292/EC of 4 April 2008 establishing that the Black Sea and the river systems connected to it do not constitute a natural habitat for European eel for the purposes of Council Regulation (EC) No 1100/2007, OJ 2008 L98/14. Regarding Reg 1100/2007, see also Chapter 2.

[24] Agreed Record of Conclusions of Fisheries Consultations between the European Community and Norway for 2008, Brussels, 26 November 2007. See, *inter alia*, Annexes I, II, III, IV, and V (available on the website of the Norwegian government's Ministry of Fisheries).

between various combinations of coastal States in the north-east Atlantic including the EC, there is a long-term management plan for blue whiting,[25] the Norwegian spring-spawning (Atlanto-Scandian) herring stock,[26] and the mackerel stock.[27]

Between the EC and Norway there was also a 'harvest control rule' for sandeel in 2008.[28] Within the EC, and in contrast to the management plans mentioned above, this rule was transposed into EC secondary legislation.[29] For reasons of space, the management plans established in the various 'agreed records', as well as the harvest control rule for sandeel, will not be discussed further here.[30]

The long-term plans in the first two categories referred to above comprised nine in total as at the end of November 2008. Two (regarding Greenland halibut[31] and bluefin tuna[32]) implement agreements reached within RFMOs and the rest are at the initiative of the EC. The latter (in date order, from the most recent) relate to Baltic Sea cod,[33] plaice and sole in the North Sea,[34] sole in the Western

[25] Agreed Record of Conclusions of Fisheries Consultations between the European Community, the Faroe Islands, Iceland and Norway on the Management of Blue Whiting in the North-East Atlantic in 2009, London, 11 November 2008, para 5 and Annex II (available on the website of the Faroe Islands government's Ministry of Fisheries).

[26] Agreed Record of Conclusions of Fisheries Consultations on the Management of the Norwegian Spring-Spawning (Atlanto-Scandian) Herring Stock in the North-East Atlantic for 2009, London, 13 November 2008, para 2 and Annex II (available on the website of the Norwegian government's Ministry of Fisheries).

[27] Agreed Record of Conclusions of Fisheries Consultations between the Faroe Islands, the European Community and Norway on the Management of Mackerel in the North-East Atlantic for 2009, London, 31 October 2008, para 2 and Annex II (available on the website of the Faroe Islands government's Ministry of Fisheries).

[28] Agreed Record of Conclusions of Fisheries Consultations between the European Community and Norway for 2008, Brussels, 26 November 2007. See Annex X.

[29] Reg 40/2008, Annex IID, paras 6 and 7.

[30] The EC's fisheries management relations with its neighbours are discussed further in subsection 8 below and in Chapter 5.

[31] Council Regulation (EC) No 2115/2005 of 20 December 2005 establishing a recovery plan for Greenland halibut in the framework of the Northwest Atlantic Fisheries Organisation, OJ 2005 L340/3.

[32] Council Regulation (EC) No 1559/2007 of 17 December 2007 establishing a multi-annual recovery plan for bluefin tuna in the Eastern Atlantic and Mediterranean and amending Regulation (EC) No 520/2007, OJ 2007 L340/8.

[33] Council Regulation (EC) No 1098/2007 of 18 September 2007 establishing a multiannual plan for the cod stocks in the Baltic Sea and the fisheries exploiting those stocks, amending Regulation (EEC) No 2847/93 and repealing Regulation (EC) No 779/97, OJ 2007 L248/1.

[34] Council Regulation (EC) No 676/2007 of 11 June 2007 establishing a multiannual plan for fisheries exploiting stocks of plaice and sole in the North Sea, OJ 2007 L157/1.

Channel,[35] sole in the Bay of Biscay,[36] southern hake and Norway lobster in the Cantabrian Sea and the western Iberian peninsula,[37] northern hake,[38] and various cod stocks other than those in the Baltic Sea.[39] The last of these plans is commonly referred to as the 'cod recovery plan' and is the most significant of the EC's long-term plans in terms of its effect on fishing activities.

The cod recovery plan and the long-term plans for Baltic Sea cod, North Sea plaice and sole, Western Channel sole, Bay of Biscay sole, southern hake and Norway lobster, and northern hake are typically structured into chapters on introductory matters (including the plan's objective), TACs, effort limitation, control, and final provisions, although there are some important variations on this theme.

Article 5 of the Basic Regulation calls for recovery plans to be adopted 'as a priority'.[40] The Basic Regulation entered into force on 1 January 2003,[41] and the first recovery plan pursuant to the Basic Regulation (the cod recovery plan) was adopted just over one year later on 26 February 2004. However, this first plan has already been subject to a review and a legislative proposal for amendment was issued in April 2008 (see further below).[42] In addition to the plans listed above, a plan regarding herring west of Scotland has been proposed by the Commission[43] and various other plans are under discussion.

The remit of recovery plans is distinctly different to that of management plans. Recovery plans are for fisheries exploiting stocks which are outside so-called 'safe biological limits', their objective being to ensure the recovery of stocks to within such limits.[44] In contrast, management plans are to be adopted 'as far as necessary to

---

[35] Council Regulation (EC) No 509/2007 of 7 May 2007 establishing a multi-annual plan for the sustainable exploitation of the stock of sole in the Western Channel, OJ 2007 L122/7.

[36] Council Regulation (EC) No 388/2006 of 23 February 2006 establishing a multiannual plan for the sustainable exploitation of the stock of sole in the Bay of Biscay, OJ 2006 L65/1.

[37] Council Regulation (EC) No 2166/2005 of 20 December 2005 establishing measures for the recovery of the Southern hake and Norway lobster stocks in the Cantabrian Sea and Western Iberian peninsula and amending Regulation (EC) No 850/98 for the conservation of fishery resources through technical measures for the protection of juveniles of marine organisms, OJ 2005 L345/5.

[38] Council Regulation (EC) No 811/2004 of 21 April 2004 establishing measures for the recovery of the Northern hake stock, OJ 2004 L150/1, as corrected.

[39] Council Regulation (EC) No 423/2004 of 26 February 2004 establishing measures for the recovery of cod stocks, OJ 2004 L70/8. This Regulation was the basis of Case T-91/07 *WWF-UK Ltd v Council*, Order of the Court of First Instance, 2 June 2008 (summary publication only; full text available on the website of the Court). The Order in that case was appealed by the applicant in Case C-355/08 P (see OJ 2008 C260/10). The outcome of the appeal was not known at the time of writing.

[40] Reg 2371/2002, Art 5(1).   [41] Reg 2371/2002, Art 36.

[42] *Proposal for a Council Regulation amending Regulation (EC) No 423/2004 as regards the recovery of cod stocks and amending Regulation (EEC) No 2847/93*, COM(2008) 162, 2.4.2008. The Council reached political agreement in relation to this proposal on 18.11.2008: see Council of the European Union, 2904th meeting of the Council, Agriculture and Fisheries, 18–20 November 2008, press release, 15940/08 (Presse 335), 20–3.

[43] *Proposal for a Council Regulation establishing a multi-annual plan for the stock of herring distributed to the West of Scotland and the fisheries exploiting that stock*, COM(2008) 240, 6.5.2008.

[44] Reg 2371/2002, Art 5(1) and (2). The term 'safe biological limits' is defined in Art 3(l) (see also Art 3(j)).

maintain stocks within safe biological limits for fisheries exploiting stocks at/or within safe biological limits'.[45]

Both types of plan must be drawn up on the basis of the precautionary approach and must ensure 'the sustainable exploitation of stocks and that the impact of fishing activities on marine eco-systems is kept at sustainable levels'.[46] The plans are to be 'multi-annual' and must 'indicate the expected time frame for reaching the targets established'.[47] They must include 'conservation reference points',[48] such as targets against which stock recovery or maintenance, as appropriate, is to be assessed. Targets may also be set for 'other living aquatic resources and the maintenance or improvement of the conservation status of marine eco-systems'.[49] The plans must take into account 'limit reference points'[50] recommended by relevant scientific bodies (such as the International Council for the Exploration of the Sea). They may 'cover either fisheries for single stocks or fisheries exploiting a mixture of stocks' and must 'take due account of interactions between stocks and fisheries'.[51]

In terms of measures, there are some subtle differences between the permitted or required content of recovery plans and management plans. The former may contain any of the measures set out in Article 4(2)(c)–(h) of the Basic Regulation (ie in summary, targets, catch limits, specifications about number and type of vessels, effort limits, technical measures, and incentives to promote selective or low impact fishing).[52] Management plans may contain any of the measures set out in Article 4(2)(d)–(i) of the Basic Regulation,[53] ie the same as recovery plans minus targets and with the addition of pilot projects. The reason for the exclusion of targets is not clear, especially when they are expressly called for in Article 6(2). It can be seen that both types of plan may contain effort limits. However, in addition, Article 5(4) states that recovery plans *must* include effort limits 'unless this is not necessary to achieve the objective of the plan' (see further subsection 2.2 below).

The included measures must take into account, *inter alia*, 'the economic impact of the measures on the fisheries concerned'.[54] The socio-economic effects of long-term plans are potentially far-reaching, and there have been calls for legislative proposals to be accompanied by full impact assessments. The Commission's response appears to have been patchy, the authors being aware of only three legislative proposals for recovery plans or management plans that have been accompanied by separate impact assessments.[55]

---

[45] Reg 2371/2002, Art 6(1).   [46] Reg 2371/2002, Arts 5(3) and 6(3).

[47] Reg 2371/2002, Arts 5(3) and 6(3).   [48] This term is defined in Reg 2371/2002, Art 3(k).

[49] Reg 2371/2002, Arts 5(2) and 6(2). Regarding marine ecosystem targets in long-term plans, see further subsection 9.3 below.   [50] This term is defined in Reg 2371/2002, Art 3(j).

[51] Reg 2371/2002, Arts 5(3) and 6(3).   [52] Reg 2371/2002, Art 5(4).

[53] Reg 2371/2002, Art 6(4).   [54] Reg 2371/2002, Arts 5(4) and 6(4).

[55] *Commission Staff Working Document: Impact Assessment regarding the Commission's proposal establishing revised measures for the recovery of cod stocks*, SEC(2008) 386, 2.4.2008; *Commission Staff Working Paper: Proposal for a Council Regulation establishing measures for the recovery of the sole stocks in the Western Channel and Bay of Biscay (ICES divisions VIIe and VIIIa, b)—Extended Impact Assessment*, SEC(2003) 1480, 23.12.2003; *Commission Staff Working Paper: Proposal for a Council Regulation establishing measures for the recovery of the Southern hake stock and the Norway lobster stocks in the Cantabrian Sea and Western Iberian waters (ICES divisions VIIIc and IXa)—Extended Impact Assessment*, SEC(2003) 1481, 23.12.2003.

Both types of plan may include 'harvesting rules which consist of a predetermined set of biological parameters to govern catch limits'.[56] The inclusion of such rules is discretionary rather than mandatory. Harvesting rules, if well-designed and robust, are potentially very important because they reduce the scope for ad hoc decisions of a political nature by the EC institutions, particularly the Council, regarding catch limits. However, the reliance upon 'a predetermined set of biological parameters' implies a need for data to establish the existence of such parameters. Harvesting rules are therefore potentially susceptible to data deficiency. This is potentially a significant problem in view of the poor state of knowledge of many stocks. For example, the Commission's 2008 policy statement (see further below) stated that of a total of ninety-six stocks under consideration in 2008 the 'state of the stock is unknown due to poor data' for fifty-five of those.[57]

In its proposal for a revision of the cod recovery plan, the Commission noted that data deficiency for the cod stocks in question had constrained scientists' ability 'to provide the parameters to strictly apply the current plan', which had 'led to ad hoc decisions by Council [sic]'. In response, the Commission's proposed revision sought 'to provide clear rules to apply when and where scientists cannot provide precise estimates of stock status'.[58] The proposal was that where, 'due to lack of sufficiently accurate and representative information', the Scientific, Technical and Economic Committee for Fisheries (STECF) is not able to give advice allowing the Council to set the TAC in accordance with the specified harvesting rules, the Council is to do one of two things: in cases where the STECF advises that cod catches 'should be reduced to the lowest possible level' the Council is to set the TAC 'according to a 25% reduction compared to the TAC in the previous year', and in all other cases the Council is to set the TAC at 15 per cent less than the previous year.[59]

Sometimes it is not entirely clear whether a particular plan is a 'recovery' plan under Article 5 of the Basic Regulation or a 'management' plan under Article 6. Indeed, as indicated by the brief analysis which follows, it may be said that the various plans adopted to date leave a lot to be desired in terms of how they are labelled and categorized with reference to Article 5 or Article 6. Overall, despite the uncertainties in categorization, it appears that most activity to date has been focused on developing recovery, rather than management, plans.

As noted above, the plans for Greenland halibut and bluefin tuna implement international agreements. They each refer to 'recovery plan' in their titles, and each states that '[i]t is . . . necessary to implement [the relevant internationally agreed plan] on a permanent basis by means of . . . a recovery plan as provided for

---

[56] Reg 2371/2002, Arts 5(4) and 6(4).

[57] *Communication from the Commission: Fishing Opportunities for 2009—Policy Statement from the European Commission*, COM(2008) 331, 30.5.2008, section 2 and Annex I.

[58] COM(2008) 162, explanatory memorandum, p 3.

[59] COM(2008) 162, proposed new Art 6a. See also proposed new Art 7(2)(a).

in [or 'by'] Article 5 [of the Basic Regulation]'.[60] It is unclear why Article 5 is cited as a 'necessary' basis for the implementation of such international agreements, although in the case of the bluefin tuna plan the securing of European Fisheries Fund (EFF) financing may be an important reason.[61] The plan for European eel uses the word 'recovery' in its title. However, it contains no mention of Article 5 (or Article 6).

The plans for Baltic Sea cod, North Sea plaice and sole, and Western Channel sole each use the ambiguous term 'multiannual plan' in their titles and in their Article 1. For Baltic Sea cod, the plan is 'deemed' to be an Article 5 recovery plan '[d]uring the first three years of its application'. The North Sea plaice and sole plan is 'deemed' to be an Article 5 recovery plan 'during its first stage' and is 'deemed' an Article 6 management plan 'during its second stage'. For Western Channel sole, the plan is 'deemed' to be an Article 5 recovery plan '[d]uring the first stage in the years 2007, 2008 and 2009' and is 'deemed' an Article 6 management plan 'subsequently'. However, one purpose of these various deeming provisions seems to be to enable access to financing by the EFF.[62]

The plan for Bay of Biscay sole also uses the term 'multiannual plan' in its title and in Article 1. However, in contrast to the three plans mentioned above, it lacks a 'deeming' provision. Instead, its preamble contains the confusing statement that: 'Measures need . . . to be taken to establish a multiannual plan for the *management* of the sole stock in the Bay of Biscay in accordance with *Article 5* [of the Basic Regulation]' (emphasis added).[63] Thus the statement mixes a reference to Article 5 (which deals with recovery plans) with a reference to management. Despite the reference to Article 5, the text of the plan at no point uses the word 'recovery'.

The plan for southern hake and Norway lobster in the Cantabrian Sea and the western Iberian peninsula refers to 'recovery' in its title and in Article 1. Consistent with these references, the preamble states that: 'Measures should be taken to establish multi-annual plans for the recovery of these stocks in conformity with Article 5 [of the Basic Regulation]'.[64] The references to 'recovery' and 'Article 5' are internally consistent (in contrast to the plan for Bay of Biscay sole). The plan also contains references to replacing the recovery plan with a management plan under Article 6 once certain objectives have been met.[65]

The plan for northern hake likewise refers to 'recovery' in its title and in Article 1. The preamble states that '[m]easures need to be taken to establish a multiannual plan for the recovery of this stock',[66] but no reference is made to Article 5. However, the plan contains references to replacing the plan with a management

---

[60] Reg 2115/2005 (Greenland halibut), recital (7) (see also recital (4)); Reg 1559/2007 (bluefin tuna), recital (5).   [61] Reg 1559/2007, recital (7) and Art 29.
[62] Reg 1098/2007 (Baltic Sea cod), recital (12) and Art 28; Reg 676/2007 (North Sea plaice and sole), recital (15) and Art 19; Reg 509/2007 (Western Channel sole), recital (9) and Art 13.
[63] Reg 388/2006, recital (2).   [64] Reg 2166/2005, recital (2).
[65] Reg 2166/2005, recital (7) and Art 3(2).   [66] Reg 811/2004, recital (3).

plan under Article 6 once certain objectives have been met[67] (and a management plan for this stock was being discussed at the time of writing). The cod recovery plan takes a similar approach to the northern hake plan.[68] Thus neither plan contains an express reference to Article 5.

The plans vary as to whether targets are specified in terms of biomass (ie the minimum amount of fish to be achieved) or fishing mortality (ie the maximum amount of fish to be killed by fishing). In response to possible ecosystem alterations arising from climate change, there is a move towards specifying fishing mortality targets in preference to biomass targets, as indicated by the Commission's legislative proposal for amendments to the cod recovery plan.[69] Meanwhile, the existing cod recovery plan and the plans for bluefin tuna, Bay of Biscay sole, southern hake, Greenland halibut, and northern hake specify biomass targets,[70] while the plans for Baltic Sea cod and Western Channel sole specify fishing mortality targets.[71] The plan for North Sea plaice and sole specifies a combination of the two.[72]

Regarding use by the long-term plans of TACs as a management tool, the cod recovery plan and the plans adopted for Baltic sea cod, North Sea plaice and sole, Western Channel sole, Bay of Biscay sole, southern hake and Norway lobster, and northern hake all call for the setting of TACs on an annual basis as one of the principal means to achieve the desired aim for the stocks in question. The TACs are to be set on the basis of harvesting rules (see above).[73] In contrast to the above plans, the plans for bluefin tuna and Greenland halibut specify the actual TACs that are to apply for given years (albeit subject to amendment to reflect future developments within the relevant RFMOs).[74]

Process for setting TACs

TACs are set for particular stocks and are therefore set for particular sea areas. For that purpose the EC generally uses the subareas, divisions, and subdivisions adopted by the International Council for the Exploration of the Sea (ICES)[75] and,

---

[67] Reg 811/2004, recital (8) and Art 3.

[68] Reg 423/2004, recitals (3) and (8) and Arts 1 and 4.

[69] COM(2008) 162, explanatory memorandum (pp 2 and 6) and proposed recital (3).

[70] Reg 423/2004 (cod), Art 3; Reg 1559/2007 (bluefin tuna), Art 1; Reg 388/2006 (Bay of Biscay sole), Art 2; Reg 2166/2005 (southern hake), Art 2(a); Reg 2115/2005 (Greenland halibut), Art 1; Reg 811/2004 (northern hake), Art 2.

[71] Reg 1098/2007 (Baltic Sea cod), Art 4; Reg 509/2007 (Western Channel sole), Art 2.

[72] Reg 676/2007, Art 2.

[73] Reg 423/2004 (cod), Arts 5–7; Reg 1098/2007 (Baltic Sea cod), Arts 5–7; Reg 676/2007 (North Sea plaice and sole), Arts 6–8; Reg 509/2007 (Western Channel sole), Arts 3–4; Reg 388/2006 (Bay of Biscay sole), Arts 3–4; Reg 2166/2005 (southern hake and Norway lobster), Arts 4–7; Reg 811/2004 (northern hake), Arts 4–6.

[74] Reg 1559/2007 (bluefin tuna), Art 3; Reg 2115/2005 (Greenland halibut), Art 3.

[75] See Council Regulation (EEC) No 3880/91 of 17 December 1991 on the submission of nominal catch statistics by Member States fishing in the north-east Atlantic, OJ 1991 L365/1, as amended, Annexes II and III. See also proposal for a recast of this Regulation in COM(2007) 763, 29.11.2007, proposing Art 285(1) EC as the legal basis.

where necessary, the major fishing areas and subdivisions adopted by the Food and Agriculture Organization of the United Nations (FAO).[76]

In general terms, the process for setting TACs involves the following stages: (a) the provision of scientific advice to the Commission by the ICES (for those waters within the remit of the ICES); (b) the provision of advice, in the light of the ICES' advice, to the Commission by the STECF; (c) the issue of a proposed Regulation by the Commission, in the light of the advice it has received from the ICES and the STECF; and (d) the adoption by the Council of a Regulation setting out, *inter alia*, the TACs.

There are inevitable uncertainties involved in providing scientific advice on appropriate TACs, not helped by, *inter alia*, discarding and any unreported fishing. There is also inevitably a time lag between the collection of scientific data on fish stocks and the production of scientific advice, which may mean that TACs adopted in line with the advice do not always accurately represent the situation in the fishery in real time. Of course, subject to the constraining influence of any harvesting rules in long-terms plans and the general objectives of such plans, TACs may anyway end up not being adopted by the Council in line with scientific advice in those cases where the Council chooses to place weight on short- or medium-term social and economic goals (see further section 1 above).[77]

In almost all cases, TACs are fixed for target species; however, a few TACs are set for by-catch only, with the specification that there is to be no directed fishery for the stock in question.[78] TACs are nowadays set out in four separate series of Regulations. For certain deep-sea fish stocks, TACs are set out in a biennial Regulation. For the Baltic Sea, TACs are set out in an annual Regulation; the same applies for the Black Sea. For all other fish stocks for which TACs are set, the TACs are set out in a lengthy annual Regulation which will be referred to here as the 'principal annual Regulation' (sometimes abbreviated to 'PAR'). (TACs have not, to date, been set for Mediterranean Sea stocks, with the exception of stocks of some highly migratory species; TACs for the latter are fixed in the principal annual Regulation.) The three annual Regulations, ie those for the Baltic Sea and the Black Sea and the principal annual Regulation, will be referred to collectively as the 'annual fishing opportunities Regulations'.

---

[76] See Council Regulation (EC) No 2597/95 of 23 October 1995 on the submission of nominal catch statistics by Member States fishing in certain areas other than those of the North Atlantic, OJ 1995 L270/1, as amended, Annexes 1–3. See also proposal for a recast of this Regulation in COM(2007) 760, 29.11.2007, proposing Art 285(1) EC as the legal basis.

[77] A comparison (a) between ICES advice on TACs and Commission legislative proposals and (b) between Commission legislative proposals on TACs and Council decisions is available in: MRAG Ltd, *WWF Mid-Term Review of the EU Common Fisheries Policy* (Brussels: WWF, 2007), 13–19 (including Tables 2–5).

[78] See, for example, Council Regulation (EC) No 2015/2006 of 19 December 2006 fixing for 2007 and 2008 the fishing opportunities for Community fishing vessels for certain deep-sea fish stocks, OJ 2006 L384/28, as amended, Annex, Part 2, TACs for 'Deep Sea Sharks' in ICES areas V, VI, VII, VIII, and IX.

At the time of writing, the biennial Regulation for certain deep-sea stocks was Regulation 2015/2006, applying to 2007 and 2008,[79] while the annual fishing opportunities Regulations were as follows: the annual Regulation for the Baltic Sea was Regulation 1404/2007, applying to 2008;[80] the annual Regulation for the Black Sea was Regulation 1139/2008, applying to 2009; and the principal annual Regulation was Regulation 40/2008, applying to 2008.[81] It can immediately be seen that Regulation 1139/2008, on the Black Sea, is different to the other two annual Regulations in that it alone applies to 2009. This situation arises simply because the annual Regulation for the Baltic Sea for 2009 and the principal annual Regulation for 2009 had not, at the time of writing, been published in the *Official Journal*, in contrast to the annual Regulation for the Black Sea, and therefore could not be considered in this book.

References to the 'principal annual Regulation', the 'annual fishing opportunities Regulations', and the 'biennial Regulation setting TACs for certain deep-sea stocks' below should, unless otherwise stated, be regarded as generic in nature rather than as references to the specific Regulations 40/2008, 1404/2007, 1139/2008, and 2015/2006.

Until recently the principal annual Regulation addressed the Baltic Sea as well; however, the Baltic Sea has been treated separately since the 2006 fishing year (see further below). The content of Regulations 40/2008 (PAR) and 1404/2007 (Baltic Sea) is not restricted to TACs; both Regulations also address, *inter alia*, effort limits and transitional technical measures (on which, see subsections 2.2 and 2.3 below). Regulation 1139/2008 (Black Sea) establishes TACs and transitional technical measures, but does not address effort limits. Regulations 1404/2007 and 1139/2008 are covered in general terms in this section and in more detail in sections 3 and 5, respectively.

One potentially confusing feature of the annual fishing opportunities Regulations is that they sometimes, when setting out catch limits, fail to use the abbreviation 'TAC' to describe the catch limit applicable to the EC as a whole for the particular stock in question. Instead, the abbreviation 'EC' is used for that purpose. A 'TAC' figure may not be set at all, may be stated to be 'Not relevant', or may be set higher than the 'EC' figure. In the last of these cases, the reason is usually that the TAC is set at a bilateral or multilateral level and hence one or more third States also have a share of it. Sometimes the reason for the TAC being 'Not relevant' is

---

[79] By the end of November 2008, a successor to Reg 2015/2006 had been adopted by the Council but had not been published in the *Official Journal*. (The Commission's legislative proposal for this successor Regulation was issued as COM(2008) 595, 01.10.2008.)

[80] By the end of November 2008, a successor to Reg 1404/2007 had been adopted by the Council but had not been published in the *Official Journal*. (The Commission's legislative proposal for this successor Regulation was issued as COM(2008) 539, 08.09.2008.)

[81] By the end of November 2008, a successor to Reg 40/2008 had been neither adopted by the Council nor published in the *Official Journal*. (The Commission's legislative proposal for this successor Regulation was issued as COM(2008) 709, 07.11.2008.)

that the stock in question is located wholly in the waters of a third State, and thus, in the context of EC law, only the EC's allocation of the TAC for that stock is relevant. However, in other cases the reason for the practice summarized above is not clear.

Irrespective of the reasons for it, such practice leads to some inconsistencies in terminology. As is explained in more detail below, Regulation 847/96[82] requires the Council to specify, in relation to any TAC it fixes, whether that TAC is to be a 'precautionary TAC' or an 'analytical TAC' and whether or not certain provisions of Regulation 847/96 are to apply to the stock for which the TAC is being fixed. Regulation 847/96 is worded in terms of 'TACs'. The more variable terminology found in the annual fishing opportunities Regulations creates some inconsistencies. A clear example of this is provided in cases where such Regulations set out an 'EC' figure for a given stock (and either no 'TAC' figure is stated or the 'TAC' is stated to be 'Not relevant') and yet the accompanying information on the application of Regulation 847/96 refers to this figure as being an 'Analytical *TAC*' or a 'Precautionary *TAC*' (emphasis added).

Furthermore, in the case of Regulation 1404/2007 (Baltic Sea), Annex I states that '[t]he following tables set out *the TACs* and quotas . . . by stock' (emphasis added) and yet there are several cases where an 'EC' figure is provided and the 'TAC' is stated to be 'Not relevant'. The same point applies in respect of Regulation 1139/2008 (Black Sea). It should be added that in the case of Regulation 2015/2006 (deep-sea stocks), none of the entries on catch limits refer to 'TAC'; instead all provide an 'EC' figure. Adding further confusion, a provision in Regulation 2015/2006 on the application of Regulation 847/96 (see above) applies the latter Regulation to 'quotas'.[83] In this chapter, for the sake of simplicity, the term 'total allowable catch' or 'TAC' will be used to refer to any catch limit applicable to the EC as a whole, even though, as noted above, deviations from this straightforward terminology are found in the fishing opportunities Regulations themselves.

It should also be noted that the principal annual Regulation contains, for certain sea areas, a small number of catch limits for 'other species'. This has been the case since at least Regulation 2848/2000,[84] establishing fishing opportunities for 2001. In Regulation 40/2008, the principal annual Regulation at the time of writing, there are four entries for 'other species':[85] three such entries relate to catch limits in waters beyond Community waters, in respect of Community fishing vessels operating in the waters of Norway or the Faroe Islands, and the remaining entry

---

[82] Council Regulation (EC) No 847/96 of 6 May 1996 introducing additional conditions for year-to-year management of TACs and quotas, OJ 1996 L115/3.   [83] Reg 2015/2006, Art 5.

[84] Council Regulation (EC) No 2848/2000 of 15 December 2000 fixing for 2001 the fishing opportunities and associated conditions for certain fish stocks and groups of fish stocks, applicable in Community waters and, for Community vessels, in waters where limitations in catch are required, OJ 2000 L334/1, as amended.

[85] Reg 40/2008, Annex IA (last two entries) and Annex IB (penultimate two entries).

relates to catch limits in parts of Community waters, in respect of Norwegian and Faroese vessels fishing there.[86] There is correspondence between the four entries in question in Regulation 40/2008 and the 'agreed records' for the 2007 consultations between the EC and each of Norway and the Faroe Islands (on which, see above).[87] The term 'other species' is not defined, although various footnotes to the entries concerned provide some broad indications of what is or is not covered, as do the 'agreed records'. The concept of catch limits for 'other species' was discussed by the Court in its judgment in *Spain v Council*,[88] in the context of one of the predecessors to Regulation 40/2008. Amongst other things, the Court addressed the relationship between such catch limits and the existence of new fishing opportunities (see further below).

The principal annual Regulation has traditionally been adopted at the annual December meeting of the Agriculture and Fisheries Council. The Regulation is unusual in terms of its method of adoption. Taking Regulation 40/2008 as an example, the preamble does not refer to Article 37 EC or to the Council having had regard to the opinion of the European Parliament. That is because, as noted in Chapter 1, the Regulation is adopted by the Council having in effect delegated legislative power to itself acting on a proposal from the Commission, ie without any need to consult the European Parliament. (The same method of adoption is used for the other two annual fishing opportunities Regulations as well as for the biennial Regulation setting TACs for certain deep-sea stocks.)

In the case of the principal annual Regulation, the average interval between the date of issue of the Commission's legislative proposal and the adoption of the Regulation in question has tended to be only a few weeks. Dissatisfaction with this short interval, coupled with the intention in the Basic Regulation for there to be 'broad involvement of stakeholders at all stages of the policy from conception to implementation',[89] has led the Commission to initiate some reforms to the annual timetable for adoption of annual fishing opportunities.[90]

Some reforms were put into effect in 2005, since when fishing opportunities in the Baltic Sea have been proposed separately from those covered by the proposal for the principal annual Regulation. The 2005 proposal for the Baltic Sea, for the 2006

---

[86] In respect of Community fishing vessels operating in the waters of Norway and the Faroe Islands, see further Chapter 5. In respect of Norwegian and Faroese vessels fishing in Community waters, see further section 8 below and Chapter 5.

[87] Agreed Record of Conclusions of Fisheries Consultations between the European Community and Norway for 2008, Brussels, 26 November 2007, 30 (Table 3, see 'Others') and 32 (Table 4, see 'Others (by-catches)'); Agreed Record of the Fisheries Consultations between the European Community and the Faroe Islands for 2008, Brussels, 5 December 2007 (available on the website of the Faroe Islands Prime Minister's Office), 9 (Table 1.1, see 'Other species') and 10 (Table 1.2, see 'Other White Fish (by-catches only)'). [88] Case C-141/05 *Spain v Council* [2007] ECR I-9485.

[89] Reg 2371/2002, Art 2(2)(c).

[90] *Communication from the Commission to the Council and the European Parliament: Improving consultation on Community fisheries management*, COM(2006) 246, 24.5.2006.

fishing year, was issued in late November, ie still very late in the year. However the timing has since improved: the 2006, 2007, and 2008 proposals, for the 2007, 2008, and 2009 fishing years respectively, were issued in early September. The use of a separate proposal has been adopted from the outset for the Black Sea. Like the 2005 proposal for the Baltic Sea, the proposal for the first annual Regulation for the Black Sea was issued only in late November; however, the proposal for the second annual Regulation, 1139/2008, was issued in early October.

More significant reforms were implemented from 2006 onwards. In that year, for the first time, the Commission issued a policy statement regarding fishing opportunities for the following year.[91] However, the Commission accepted that its statement, issued in September, had been published 'too late in the year for an effective consultation process to take place before the December Council'.[92] Subsequent policy statements regarding the fishing opportunities for 2008 and 2009 were issued in June 2007 and May 2008 respectively.[93]

The purpose of the annual policy statement is for the Commission to set out its 'intentions with regard to the preparation of its proposals for total allowable catches . . . and fishing effort . . .'.[94] The idea is to give stakeholders an indication, well in advance of the legislative proposals themselves, of what principles and rules the Commission will be applying in preparing its proposals. Stakeholders' views on the policy statements are invited.

The 2006 policy statement, for the 2007 fishing year, classified stocks into six principal categories, for each of which actions for setting TACs were specified. In its 2007 policy statement, for the 2008 fishing year, the Commission stated that the principles and rules set out in the 2006 policy statement remained valid.[95] At the time of writing, the 2008 policy statement, for the 2009 fishing year, was the most recent in the series. It states that, where long-term plans are not yet in place, the rules provided in the 2006 and 2007 policy statements 'will continue, but with some changes as required by the latest scientific advice'.[96]

As a prelude to setting out the revised rules, the 2008 policy statement summarizes the situation regarding fisheries resources.[97] For example, of a total of ninety-six stocks under consideration for 2008 in one table in the policy statement, the 'state of the stock is unknown due to poor data' for fifty-five (57 per cent) of those stocks. Of the remainder, twenty-eight stocks are outside safe biological limits and thirteen stocks are inside safe biological limits.[98] Another table considers a total of thirty-three stocks for 2008 for which '[t]he rate of fishing on the stock is known compared to maximum sustainable yield rate'. Of these, twenty-nine

---

[91] *Communication from the Commission to the Council: Fishing Opportunities for 2007—Policy Statement from the European Commission*, COM(2006) 499, 15.9.2006.

[92] *Communication from the Commission to the Council: Fishing Opportunities for 2008—Policy Statement from the European Commission*, COM(2007) 295, 6.6.2007, section 1, p 3.

[93] COM(2007) 295; COM(2008) 331.   [94] COM(2008) 331, section 1, p 3.

[95] COM(2007) 295, section 3, p 8.   [96] COM(2008) 331, section 8, p 8.

[97] COM(2008) 331, section 2 and Annex I.   [98] COM(2008) 331, Annex I (Table 1).

(88 per cent) are 'overfished' and the remainder (four) are 'fished at the maximum sustainable yield rate'.[99] An accompanying Commission press release states succinctly that '88% of EU stocks are overfished, compared with 25% on average globally'.[100] However, it should be recalled that the 88 per cent figure is derived from (only) the thirty-three stocks for which the fishing rate is known compared to maximum sustainable yield rate.

The rules in the 2008 policy statement are set out in an annex.[101] Eleven categories of stock are identified; for each of these, the '[a]ction to take in setting TAC [sic]' is specified. There is a general preference for not increasing and/or decreasing TACs beyond a certain percentage of the previous year's TAC. The constraint on decreases, in particular, presumably reflects socio-economic considerations. However, constraints in either direction may in principle help provide stability to the fishing industry. In several cases, the percentage constraint is set at 15 per cent but, depending on the circumstances of the stock or the scientific advice relating to it, it is sometimes set at 20 per cent or 25 per cent. For example, in those cases where '[the] STECF advises a zero catch, a reduction to the lowest possible level or similar advice', the specified action to take in setting the TAC is as follows: 'The TAC should be reduced by at least 25%. Recovery measures should be implemented including effort reductions and introduction of more selective fishing gear.'[102] In cases where a stock is 'subject to long-term plan [sic] and scientists advise on the catch that corresponds to the plan', the TAC '*must* be set by following the relevant plan' (emphasis added).[103]

Of course, the suggested actions (merely) represent Commission policy. They are not legally binding on the Council, except to the extent that they represent what is anyway required by any long-term plans. As mentioned above, relatively few stocks are currently covered by such plans.

As noted above, both the ICES and the STECF provide advice to the Commission. The ICES is not mentioned at all in the Basic Regulation. However, the Regulation does make several references to the need for scientific advice to inform decision-making,[104] and such references may be taken to mean advice from, *inter alia*, the ICES. In addition, some of the EC's long-term plans make very specific reference to the need for advice from the ICES.[105] In practice, the EC has a cooperation agreement with the ICES[106] under which the ICES provides

---

[99] COM(2008) 331, Annex I (Table 2).

[100] IP/08/828, Brussels, 30 May 2008 (available on the website of the European Commission).

[101] COM(2008) 331, Annex II.   [102] COM(2008) 331, Annex II, 10th item in table.

[103] COM(2008) 331, Annex II, 4th item in table.

[104] Reg 2371/2002, Arts 2(2)(b), 4(2), 5(3), 1st para, and 6(3), 1st para.

[105] Eg Reg 423/2004 (cod), *inter alia*, Arts 5, 6, and 7.

[106] The current agreement, replacing a previous agreement of March 2004 and in force for three years from May 2007, is the *Agreement in the form of a Memorandum of Understanding between the European Community and the International Council for the Exploration of the Sea*, signed in Brussels on 16 May 2007 and available on the website of the ICES.

scientific advice to the Commission comprising, *inter alia*: (a) recurring (or 'standard') advice on the state and management of fisheries for particular species, generally on an annual basis; and (b) non-recurring advice on specific issues when requested.[107]

Whereas the ICES is an inter-governmental organization that is unrelated to the Commission other than by its agreement on cooperation (see further Chapter 5), the STECF is established by the Commission itself. The function, structure, and workings of the STECF are currently set out in Decision 2005/629 (see further Chapter 1).[108] The Basic Regulation requires that catch limits (and other management measures) are to be 'established taking into account available scientific, technical and economic advice and *in particular* of [sic] the reports drawn up by the [STECF] . . .' (emphasis added).[109] More specifically, the Commission is to 'take into account the advice from the STECF when presenting proposals on fisheries management under [the Basic Regulation]',[110] including, *inter alia*, proposals on TACs and quotas.

Regulation 847/96[111] requires the Council, when fixing TACs in accordance with Article 20 of the Basic Regulation, to decide 'which stocks are subject to a precautionary TAC and which stocks are subject to an analytical TAC, on the basis of scientific advice available on the stocks'.[112] The Regulation adds that: 'Precautionary TACs shall apply to stocks for which no scientifically-based evaluation of fishing possibilities is available specifically for the year in which the TACs are to be set; analytical TACs shall apply otherwise.'[113]

In practice, the obligation to state whether TACs are 'precautionary' or 'analytical' has been applied on a stock-by-stock basis in respect of most of the TACs contained in Regulations 40/2008 (PAR), 1404/2007 (Baltic Sea), and 1139/2008 (Black Sea).[114] Taking a different approach, Regulation 2015/2006 (deep-sea stocks) states that: 'For the purposes of Regulation [847/96], all quotas in the Annex to the present Regulation shall be considered "Analytic" [sic] quotas.'[115] The inconsistency in terminology between Regulation 847/96 being worded in terms of 'TACs' and the above provision in Regulation 2015/2006 referring to 'quotas' has already been noted above.

Regulation 847/96 also requires the Council, when fixing TACs, to decide the stocks to which: (a) 'Articles 3 or 4 *shall not* apply, on the basis of the biological status of the stocks and of commitments reached with third countries'; and (b) 'the

---

[107] EC/ICES MoU, May 2007, *inter alia*, para 5.

[108] Commission Decision 2005/629/EC of 26 August 2005 establishing a Scientific, Technical and Economic Committee for Fisheries, OJ 2005 L225/18, as corrected. See also Reg 2371/2002, Art 33(1).

[109] Reg 2371/2002, Art 4(2).   [110] Reg 2371/2002, Art 33(2).

[111] Council Regulation (EC) No 847/96 of 6 May 1996 introducing additional conditions for year-to-year management of TACs and quotas, OJ 1996 L115/3.   [112] Reg 847/96, Art 2, 1st indent.

[113] Reg 847/96, Art 1(1).

[114] See Annex I to each of Regs 40/2008, 1404/2007, and 1139/2008.

[115] Reg 2015/2006, Art 5, 1st para.

deductions envisaged in Article 5(2) *shall* apply, on the basis of their biological status' (emphasis added).[116] The content and application of Articles 3, 4, and 5(2) of Regulation 847/96 are discussed below, in relation to the administration of TACs and quotas.

Process for dividing TACs into quotas

Article 20(1) of the Basic Regulation states, *inter alia*, that the Council, having decided on catch limits, shall decide 'on the allocation of fishing opportunities among Member States'. It adds that: 'Fishing opportunities shall be distributed among Member States in such a way as to assure each Member State *relative stability* of fishing activities for each stock or fishery.' (Emphasis added.)

The term 'relative stability' is not defined in the Basic Regulation. However, some light is shed on its meaning by the Regulation's preamble. This states that ensuring relative stability of fishing activities is necessary '[i]n view of the precarious economic state of the fishing industry and the dependence of certain coastal communities on fishing'.[117] The principle 'should safeguard the particular needs of regions where local populations are especially dependent on fisheries and related activities as decided by the Council in [the Hague Preferences (see below)]' in view of 'the temporary biological situation of stocks'.[118] Relative stability is to be ensured 'by the allocation of fishing opportunities among the Member States, based upon a *predictable share of the stocks* for each Member State' (emphasis added).[119]

It can be seen that relative stability is, in effect, a tool to promote economic and social stability. There is some suggestion from the above extracts that it is a temporary solution, pending improvement in the status of the stocks and the industry. However, the Court has held that the reference to 'the *temporary* biological situation of stocks' (emphasis added) is merely a reference to natural fluctuations rather than implying scope for overall improvement.[120] In contrast, the 'precarious economic state of the fishing industry' is presumably subject to improvement, as confirmed by the Commission which has stated that: 'When the structural problems of the fisheries sector have been addressed and the economic and social situation within the sector has become more stable, it may be possible to reconsider the need to maintain the relative stability principle and the possibility of allowing market forces to operate in fisheries as in the rest of the EU economy.'[121] (See further subsection 9.6 below, regarding rights-based management.)

---

[116] Reg 847/96, Art 2, 2nd and 3rd indents.   [117] Reg 2371/2002, recital (16).

[118] Reg 2371/2002, recital (17).   [119] Reg 2371/2002, recital (16).

[120] Case C-4/96 *Northern Ireland Fish Producers' Organisation Ltd (NIFPO) and Northern Ireland Fishermen's Federation v Department of Agriculture for Northern Ireland* [1998] ECR I-681, paras 51 and 52.

[121] *Green Paper on the Future of the Common Fisheries Policy (Presented by the Commission)*, COM(2001) 135, 20.3.2001, section 5.1.4.1, p 24. See also *Communication from the Commission on the reform of the Common Fisheries Policy ('Roadmap')*, COM(2002) 181, 28.5.2002, section 3.8, p 23.

The Council allocated the fish stocks available in Community waters for the first time by means of Regulation 172/83 (see Chapter 1).[122] The preamble to that Regulation states that, in order to make a fair allocation of available resources, the Council simultaneously took particular account of three criteria, namely: (a) 'traditional fishing activities'; (b) 'the specific needs of areas particularly dependent on fishing and its dependent industries'; and (c) 'the loss of fishing potential in the waters of third countries' (caused by the increasing number of claims to 200 nm zones).[123]

Item '(a)' above was assessed 'on the basis of the average catches made by each Member State in the period 1973–1978'.[124] Item '(b)' was assessed 'on the basis of the values determined under the Hague Preference[s] in accordance with the parameters set out by the Commission in . . . 1980'.[125] The Court has clarified that recourse to the Hague Preferences for the purpose of item '(b)' is ongoing, rather than being limited in time.[126] Item '(c)' was calculated for the reference period 1973–76.[127] The results of applying the three criteria above in 1983 were so-called 'allocation keys'.

The principle of relative stability has been the subject of much litigation before the Court. That litigation has helped to make a number of points clear. First, relative stability constitutes a derogation from the general rule of equal conditions of access to fishery resources (see further subsection 2.5 below).[128] Secondly, the requirement in Article 20(1) of the Basic Regulation (see above) means, from year to year, 'maintenance of a fixed percentage for each Member State and not, therefore, the guarantee of a fixed quantity of fish'.[129] So changes in a TAC over the years do not affect the percentage shares allocated to the relevant Member States; an increase one year cannot justify the accommodation of an additional Member State in the allocation, since fish stocks fluctuate.[130] The use of percentages, rather than fixed tonnages, explains the use of the word 'relative'.[131]

---

[122] Eg Case 46/86 *Albert Romkes v Officier van Justitie for the District of Zwolle* [1987] ECR 2671, para 6.   [123] Reg 172/83, 4th recital.

[124] Case C-4/96 *NIFPO*, AG Opinion, para 18.

[125] Ibid. On the Hague Preferences, see Holden, M, *The Common Fisheries Policy* (Oxford: Fishing News Books, 1996), *inter alia*, 43, 44, 45, 46, 47, and 120; Churchill, RR, *EEC Fisheries Law* (Dordrecht: Martinus Nijhoff Publishers, 1987), 115. The areas currently covered by the Hague Preferences are Ireland, Scotland, Northern Ireland, the Isle of Man, and that part of England between the ports of Bridlington and Berwick (see Case C-4/96 *NIFPO*, AG Opinion, para 9 and footnotes (9) and (10)).   [126] Case C-4/96 *NIFPO*, paras 51 and 52.

[127] Case C-4/96 *NIFPO*, AG Opinion, para 18.

[128] Case C-216/87 *The Queen v Ministry of Agriculture, Fisheries and Food, ex parte Jaderow Ltd* [1989] ECR 4509, para 24.

[129] Eg Joined Cases C-63/90 and C-67/90 *Portugal and Spain v Council* [1992] ECR I-5073, para 28.

[130] Eg Case C-73/90 *Spain v Council* [1992] ECR I-5191, para 29.

[131] Joined Cases C-61/96, C-132/97, C-45/98, C-27/99, C-81/00, and C-22/01 *Spain v Council* [2002] ECR I-3439, para 40.

Thirdly, the allocation keys adopted in 1983 'will continue to apply as long as an amending regulation has not been adopted according to the procedure which was followed for Regulation No 170/83'.[132] Regulation 170/83 is the Regulation that established the first EC system of fisheries management (see Chapter 1) and which first made reference to quota allocations based on relative stability. The Court's statement itself is not entirely clear (although frequently repeated in the Court's judgments) but it presumably means, at least, that the 1983 allocation keys continue to apply unless amended by an act of the Council.

Fourthly, the allocation keys adopted in 1983, as well as any amendments to them and any additional allocation keys, are parts of the so-called '*acquis communautaire*' (ie the body of EC legislation existing at any given time).[133] The latter point is relevant to any newly acceding Member States. Such States may not therefore expect to be accommodated in pre-existing allocation keys unless that is provided for in the treaty of accession;[134] however, 'if and when the system is reviewed . . . those Member States may put forward their claims on the same footing as all the other Member States'.[135]

Fifthly, litigation before the Court has helped to clarify some points about the interaction between relative stability and fishermen. In that there is no guarantee of a fixed quantity of fish (see above), the principle of relative stability 'does not therefore confer on fishermen any guarantee that they can catch a fixed quantity of fish'.[136] Furthermore, because the principle of relative stability 'concerns only relations between Member States, it cannot confer individual rights upon private parties, the infringement of which would give rise to a right to compensation in accordance with the second paragraph of Article 288 EC'.[137]

Article 20(2) of the Basic Regulation states that: 'When the Community establishes *new* fishing opportunities the Council shall decide on the allocation for those opportunities, taking into account the interests of each Member State.' (Emphasis added.) The question of new fishing opportunities was addressed by the Court in *Spain v Council* (Case C-141/05, mentioned briefly above). The case concerned Regulation 27/2005,[138] one of the predecessors to Regulation 40/2008 (PAR). The judgment relates that Regulation 27/2005 was used to make

---

[132] Eg Joined Cases C-87/03 and C-100/03 *Spain v Council* [2006] ECR I-2915, para 27.

[133] Eg Joined Cases C-87/03 and C-100/03, para 29.

[134] Eg Joined Cases C-63/90 and C-67/90 *Portugal and Spain v Council*, para 49.

[135] Eg Joined Cases C-63/90 and C-67/90, para 37.

[136] Case T-415/03 *Cofradia de pescadores de 'San Pedro' de Bermeo and Others v Council* [2005] ECR II-4355, para 89.

[137] Case T-196/99 *Area Cova, SA and Others v Council and Commission* [2001] ECR II-3597, para 152. See also Case T-415/03 *Bermeo*, paras 55, 88, 92, 93, and 97.

[138] Council Regulation (EC) No 27/2005 of 22 December 2004 fixing for 2005 the fishing opportunities and associated conditions for certain fish stocks and groups of fish stocks, applicable in Community waters and, for Community vessels, in waters where catch limitations are required, OJ 2005 L12/1, as amended and corrected.

the first allocation of fishing opportunities for four stocks (all of them in Norwe-gian waters).[139] In respect of those stocks, a reference period of 1999 to 2003 for past catches had been used by the Council to determine the allocation between Member States,[140] which the Court considered to be 'a recent and sufficiently long period as not to be open to criticism'.[141]

For technical reasons, the Court in Spain v Council ultimately considered only one of the four stocks in question—anglerfish in ICES zone IV (Norwegian waters).[142] The case is particularly interesting because anglerfish in the said management area was, prior to Regulation 27/2005, covered by a TAC for 'other species' (on which, see above).[143] An allocation among the Member States of that 'other species' TAC had been made by, inter alia, the immediate predecessor to Regulation 27/2005.[144] Regulation 27/2005 in effect separated out anglerfish from the 'other species' TAC for the first time and gave it a TAC of its own for the management area in ques-tion.[145] In view of this, the Commission argued that the allocation by Regulation 27/2005 of the TAC among the Member States was not a new fishing opportunity for the purposes of Article 20(2) of the Basic Regulation.[146]

The Court rejected the Commission's argument, albeit for reasons that are not completely clear,[147] and held that the allocation of the anglerfish stock by Regu-lation 27/2005 was indeed a new fishing opportunity for the purposes of Article 20(2).[148] With regard to the requirement in Article 20(2) for Member States' interests to be taken into account, the Court held that '[t]he concept of "interests" may encompass the need to safeguard the relative stability of fishing activities, but is not limited to that need' (emphasis added).[149] Such a finding was, in principle, in Spain's favour. However, for various reasons, the Court ultimately ruled that the Council had not exceeded the limits of its discretion in not allocating any of the anglerfish TAC in question to Spain.[150]

A further example of new fishing opportunities, and their allocation, arises in the context of deep-sea stocks covered by Regulation 2340/2002 (a predecessor to Regulation 2015/2006).[151] Both the original version of Regulation 2340/2002 and an amending Regulation[152] fail to set out transparently the method of

---

[139] Case C-141/05 Spain v Council, paras 72 and 66.   [140] Case C-141/05, para 68.

[141] Case C-141/05, para 99.   [142] Case C-141/05, paras 73–77.

[143] Case C-141/05, para 70.

[144] Council Regulation (EC) No 2287/2003 of 19 December 2003 fixing for 2004 the fishing opportunities and associated conditions for certain fish stocks and groups of fish stocks, applicable in Community waters and, for Community vessels, in waters where catch limitations are required, OJ 2003 L344/1, as amended, Annex IB, penultimate entry.   [145] Reg 27/2005, Annex IB.

[146] Case C-141/05, paras 70 and 81; cf Council position at para 66.

[147] Case C-141/05, paras 88 and 89; cf para 97.   [148] Case C-141/05, para 90.

[149] Case C-141/05, para 87.   [150] Case C-141/05, paras 91–100.

[151] Council Regulation (EC) No 2340/2002 of 16 December 2002 fixing for 2003 and 2004 the fishing opportunities for deep-sea fish stocks, OJ 2002 L356/1, as amended, recital (4).

[152] Council Regulation (EC) No 2269/2004 of 20 December 2004 amending Regulations (EC) Nos 2340/2002 and 2347/2002 as concerns fishing opportunities for deep sea species for the new Member States which acceded in 2004, OJ 2004 L396/1.

allocating the new opportunities in question. The legislative proposal for the amending Regulation provides some clues,[153] but more clarity is given by a Commission report issued in 2007 which explains that the allocations were based on a reference period of 1990 to 1999 (or 1993 to 2002 for Member States acceding in 2004).[154]

The same report adds that the quotas for deep-sea stocks for the Member States joining in 2004 were simply added to those for existing Member States, thus increasing the TACs, and that '[t]he resulting overall allocation keys were used form [sic] the basis for setting the TACs amongst all Member States [for deep-sea stocks] in subsequent years'. The report notes that the allocation of quotas was contentious, 'because those [Member States] with established fisheries were allocated higher shares of the resources than those with aspirations to develop alternative fishing opportunities but little track record, at a time when the traditional fisheries centred on cod were becoming severely restricted'.[155]

As noted above, the effect of the principle of relative stability is to fix the percentages of TACs allocated to relevant Member States. However, some flexibility has been introduced on occasion by recourse to the Hague Preferences. As noted above, those preferences were anyway used to help determine the allocation key adopted in 1983. However, additional recourse to the preferences is not precluded. That was confirmed by the Court in the *NIFPO* case, which held that 'even if the special needs of [certain] fishing communities . . . were taken into account when the 1983 allocation keys were being applied, it does not follow that the Council is precluded from taking account of the Hague Preference system once again if a reduction in TACs affects the vital interests of those communities'.[156] However, the Commission has noted that supplementary application of the Hague Preferences 'has not been received favourably by all Member States and fishermen concerned'.[157]

One factor that may lead to changes to the allocation keys is climate change. It is generally acknowledged that climate change is altering the distribution of certain marine fish species.[158] As time goes by, there may be pressure from some Member States to acknowledge this fact by amending the allocation keys. However, any such amendments would presumably need to be subject to ongoing review as the climate, and hence fish distribution, continues to change. The Commission has noted that climate change 'means that new allocation *mechanisms* may need to be

---

[153] *Proposal for a Council Regulation amending Regulation (EC) No 2340/2002 and Regulation (EC) No 2347/2002 as concerns fishing opportunities for deep sea species for the Member States which acceded in 2004,* COM(2004) 685, 20.10.2004, explanatory memorandum, section entitled 'Quotas'.

[154] *Communication from the Commission to the Council and the European Parliament: Review of the management of deep-sea fish stocks,* COM(2007) 30, 29.1.2007, section 2, pp 3–4.

[155] COM(2007) 30, section 2, p 4.   [156] Case C-4/96 *NIFPO,* paras 53 and 54.

[157] COM(2001) 135, section 5.1.4.1, p 23.

[158] See, for example, regarding the North Sea, Perry, AL, Low, PJ, Ellis, JR and Reynolds, JD, 'Climate change and distribution shifts in marine fishes', *Science,* 24 June 2005, 1912–1915.

established as fish stocks change their distribution' (emphasis added).[159] Even if existing allocation keys are not changed, allocations may end up being introduced for any stocks that become newly-established in particular sea areas by virtue of climate change.

Administration of TACs and quotas

Once a TAC or quota has been set in a Council Regulation, that is not the end of the story. Instead, the TAC or quota may be subject to various acts that could loosely be called 'administration'. What follows will consider administration by Member States pursuant to Article 20(3) and (5) of the Basic Regulation and, at more length, administration by the Commission and the Council under Regulation 847/96 (introduced briefly above) and various other Regulations.

Article 20(3) of the Basic Regulation states that: 'Each Member State shall decide, for vessels flying its flag, on the method of allocating the fishing opportunities assigned to that Member State in accordance with Community law. It shall inform the Commission of the allocation method.' The discretion of the Member State in deciding its method of allocation was considered by the Court in the case of *Lootus v Council*,[160] which related to the biennial Regulation setting TACs for certain deep-sea stocks (in the form of two predecessors to Regulation 2015/2006). Having noted Article 20(3) of the Basic Regulation,[161] the Court observed that the biennial Regulations leave 'the Member States broad discretion as to how they manage fishing opportunities, since they do not lay down any specific system for the Member States to allocate fishing opportunities to individuals'. It continued: 'Member States are thus free to choose, for example, between a system for allocation of fishing opportunities according to the "first come, first served" rule, a system of equal distribution amongst all the undertakings concerned or an auction.'[162] This observation, although most directly about the biennial Regulations themselves, is a reflection of the discretion of the Member States under Article 20(3) of the Basic Regulation more generally. (See further subsection 9.6 below, regarding rights-based management.)

Article 20(5) states that: 'Member States may, after notifying the Commission, exchange all or part of the fishing opportunities allocated to them.' In that regard, the Court in *Lootus* noted that provisions on exchange of quotas 'allow Member States to exchange fishing quotas between themselves, which could lead to a situation where Member States availing themselves of that opportunity hold fishing quotas available for allocation to individuals which are very different from those originally allocated to them by the Council'.[163] There is not much

---

[159] House of Lords, 2008, HL Paper 146-II, p 196 (European Commission's evidence).

[160] Case T-127/05 *Lootus Teine Osaühing (Lootus) v Council*, Order of the Court of First Instance (Fourth Chamber) of 9 January 2007 (summary publication in [2007] ECR II-1; full text available on the website of the Court).   [161] Case T-127/05, para 42.

[162] Case T-127/05, para 43.   [163] Case T-127/05, para 44.

transparency regarding the amount of quota exchanged in any given year pursuant
to Article 20(5) of the Basic Regulation. Article 20(5) requires the Commission to
be notified, but the Commission itself does not appear to issue any public report
on the notifications it receives. To the authors' knowledge, no quota exchanges
between Member States directly, whether pursuant to Article 20(5) or the
equivalent provision in earlier basic Regulations, have been subject to challenge
before the Court.

Regulation 847/96 is an important legal basis for administration of TACs and
quotas. It introduces 'conditions for the pursuit of exploitation activities which
would improve the mechanisms at present available by the introduction of the
appropriate year-to-year flexibility in the management of [TACs] and quotas
which, within certain limits, is compatible with conservation policies'.[164] The
Regulation has survived unamended and in its original form for more than ten
years, although it has been subject to several derogations (on which, see below)
and an amendment was proposed in November 2008.[165] Some of its provisions
have already been mentioned above. The content of its Articles 3, 4, and 5 will be
described here.

The adoption by the Council of Regulation 847/96, at least in terms of the rules
on quota deductions that it establishes, represents a response by the Council to
Article 23(2) of Regulation 2847/93[166] (hereafter, 'the Control Regulation').[167]
In summary, Article 23(2) requires that 'the Council is to *adopt rules* for deducting
quantities fished in excess from the annual quotas. Those rules are to be established
in accordance with the objective and management strategies of the [CFP], taking
into account, as a matter of priority, the degree of overfishing and the biological
status of the resources concerned' (emphasis added).[168]

Article 5 of Regulation 847/96 is aimed at punishing overfishing by Member
States. It sets out two alternative rules in this respect, which are stated to be
'without prejudice' to Article 21(4) of the Control Regulation (on which, see
further below).[169] The first, and simplest, of the two rules is found in Article 5(1)
which requires that 'all landings in excess of the respective permitted landings shall
be deducted from the quotas of the same stock in the following year'. Thus Article
5(1) merely establishes a system of like-for-like deductions from Member States'

[164] Reg 847/96, 1st recital.
[165] *Proposal for a Council Regulation establishing a Community control system for ensuring compliance with the
rules of the Common Fisheries Policy*, COM(2008) 721, 14.11.2008, proposed Art 113(10).
[166] Council Regulation (EEC) No 2847/93 of 12 October 1993 establishing a control system
applicable to the common fisheries policy, OJ 1993 L261/1, as amended.
[167] Reg 847/96, preamble; and Council Regulation (EC) No 338/2008 of 14 April 2008 providing
for the adaptation of cod fishing quotas to be allocated to Poland in the Baltic Sea (Subdivisions 25–32,
EC Waters) from 2008 to 2011, OJ 2008 L107/1, recital (6).
[168] Reg 338/2008, recital (5); see also Reg 2847/93, Art 23(2) itself.
[169] Reg 847/96, Art 5(3).

quotas. Its deterrent value is low because the Member State in question still ends up with the same amount of quota over the long term.

In contrast, Article 5(2) provides for more punitive deductions. It requires that overfishing of permitted landings is to lead to weighted deductions from the corresponding quota in the following year. For the first 10 per cent overfished (or for any amount overfished if it is 100 tonnes or less), the proportion deducted is 100 per cent of the overfished amount. In other words, no weighing is applied. However, for 10–20 per cent overfished, 20–40 per cent overfished, and more than 40 per cent overfished, the proportion to be deducted is 110 per cent, 120 per cent, and 140 per cent respectively. A further 3 per cent of the overfished amount is to be deducted 'for each successive year in which permitted landings are overfished by more than 10%'. Clearly Article 5(2) is more potent than Article 5(1).

The relationship between Article 5(1) and (2) is established by Regulation 847/96 itself, albeit in a rather convoluted way. First, Article 5(1) applies '[e]xcept for the stocks referred to in [Article 5(2)]'.[170] Secondly, Article 5(2) applies to 'the stocks referred to in the third indent of Article 2'.[171] Thirdly, pursuant to Article 2, the Council, when fixing TACs, is to decide 'the stocks to which the deductions envisaged in Article 5(2) shall apply, on the basis of their biological status'.[172] In other words: (a) Article 5(1) is the default position: it applies to a stock unless the Council, when fixing TACs, specifies that Article 5(2) applies; and (b) a decision by the Council as to whether to apply Article 5(2) to a given stock depends on the 'biological status' of that stock.

Of the many TACs set out in Regulation 40/2008 (PAR), with the exception of TACs for highly migratory fish[173] and those in respect of the Commission for the Conservation of Antarctic Marine Living Resources[174] and the South East Atlantic Fisheries Organisation,[175] the statement that 'Article 5(2) . . . applies' accompanies virtually all of them.[176] Of the ten TACs set out in Regulation 1404/2007 (Baltic Sea), the statement that 'Article 5(2) . . . applies' accompanies all of them.[177] Only two TACs are set out in Regulation 1139/2008 (Black Sea); in both cases, there is an ambiguous statement that 'Article 5 . . . applies'.[178] On the basis that Article 5(1) applies by default, this is presumably a statement that Article 5(2) applies; however, it could be clearer.

In contrast to the widespread application of Article 5(2) in Regulations 40/2008, 1404/2007, and 1139/2008, Regulation 2015/2006 (deep-sea stocks) states that 'the measures provided for in Article 5(2) . . . shall *not* apply to [the listed] quotas' (emphasis added).[179] (See above regarding the inconsistency in terminology between Regulation 847/96 being worded in terms of 'TACs' and the above

---

[170] Reg 847/96, Art 5(1).   [171] Reg 847/96, Art 5(2), 1st para.
[172] Reg 847/96, Art 2, 3rd indent.   [173] Reg 40/2008, Annex ID.
[174] Reg 40/2008, Annex IE.   [175] Reg 40/2008, Annex IF.
[176] Reg 40/2008, Annex I.   [177] Reg 1404/2007, Annex I.
[178] Reg 1139/2008, Annex I.   [179] Reg 2015/2006, Art 5.

provision in Regulation 2015/2006 referring to 'quotas'.) It is unclear why Article 5(2) does not apply to the catch limits set out in Regulation 2015/2006. The biennial nature of the Regulation should not be an issue, since separate TACs (and hence quotas) are specified for each of the two years in question.

In addition to Article 5, Articles 3 and 4 of Regulation 847/96 are relevant to TAC and quota administration. Article 3 relates specifically to stocks for which a *precautionary* TAC (see above) has been set. Member States may request permission to increase the amount of fish available within any given year in two principal ways, both premised on the assertion that 'under certain conditions, precautionary TACs and quotas for certain stocks may be revised upwards during the year with negligible danger of undermining the principle of rational and responsible exploitation of marine resources'.[180]

First, under Article 3(1), when more than 75 per cent of the TAC has been utilized before 31 October of the year of its application, a Member State with a quota of that TAC may request the Commission for a specified increase in the TAC by submitting 'relevant supporting biological information'. If the Commission accepts the request, it may present a proposal to the Council for an amendment to the Regulation setting the TAC in question. Of course, the Council may either adopt or amend the proposal.

Secondly, under Article 3(3), when more than 75 per cent of a Member State's quota of a TAC has been utilized before 31 October, that Member State may request the Commission's permission to land a specified additional quantity of fish, not exceeding 10 per cent of the appropriate quota. The Commission is to decide on such a request by recourse to comitology procedure. Thus Article 3(1) relates to more than 75 per cent of the *TAC* having been utilized, whereas Article 3(3) relates to more than 75 per cent of the Member State's *quota* having been utilized. It is not clear whether a Member State could validly seek to invoke both Article 3(1) and Article 3(3) in combination.

A successful request for permission to access extra fish is not the only way to legitimately catch more fish: under Article 3(2), Member States with quotas of precautionary TACs are automatically allowed to take catches up to 5 per cent in excess of permitted landings. However, the corollary of increases under both Article 3(3) and Article 3(2) is that such increases are to be considered as 'exceeding permitted landings as regards the deductions envisaged in Article 5'.[181] In other words, any increase will be subject to a deduction from the following year's quota under Article 5. It is not specified whether Article 5(1) or 5(2) is to apply. However, because the maximum increases in question under Article 3(3) and 3(2) are 10 per cent and 5 per cent, respectively, of the quota, no weighting under Article 5(2) would anyway apply (see above).

---

[180] Reg 847/96, 5th recital.
[181] Reg 847/96, Art 3(2). Slightly different wording is used in Art 3(3).

Article 4 of Regulation 847/96 relates specifically to stocks for which an *analytical* TAC (see above) has been set. Article 4(1) applies Article 3(3) and (2) (but not Article 3(1)) to stocks subject to an analytical TAC. Article 4(2) enables a carry-over of unused quota to the following year. It states that: 'For stocks subject to analytical TAC, *except those referred to in Article 5(2)*, a Member State to which a relevant quota has been allocated may ask the Commission, before 31 October of the year of application of the quota, to withhold a maximum of 10% of its quota to be transferred to the following year.' (Emphasis added.) Thus, impliedly, any unused amount beyond 10 per cent of the quota may not be transferred in this way, and no transfer at all is available by this method for: (a) stocks subject to precautionary, rather than analytical, TACs; or (b) stocks with analytical TACs to which Article 5(2) applies. The Commission is to deal with transfers under Article 4(2) by means of comitology procedure.

The Council, when fixing TACs, is to decide the stocks to which Articles 3 and 4 shall *not* apply. It is to make that decision 'on the basis of the biological status of the stocks and of commitments reached with third countries'.[182] The implication is that Articles 3 and 4 apply by default to TACs fixed by the Council (Article 3 to precautionary TACs and Article 4 to analytical TACs) and that to be non-applicable they have to be expressly disapplied. In practice, and presumably in the interests of clarity, the Council's approach for the stocks covered by Regulations 40/2008 (PAR), 1404/2007 (Baltic Sea), and 1139/2008 (Black Sea) has generally been to state on a stock-by-stock basis not just when Articles 3 and 4 do *not* apply but also when they *do* apply.[183] In contrast, in the case of Regulation 2015/2006 (deep-sea stocks) the Council does not take this approach. The Regulation acknowledges that 'additional landings' may be allowed pursuant to Article 3 and that quantities may be withheld under Article 4,[184] but this is standard terminology for fishing opportunities Regulations.[185] As noted above, all the catch limits set out in Regulation 2015/2006 are 'analytical'. Analytical TACs are subject to Article 4, unless it is expressly disapplied. Regulation 2015/2006 does not disapply Article 4. Overall, therefore, the position would seem to be that Article 4 applies to the catch limits fixed in Regulation 2015/2006.

In the cases of Regulation 40/2008 (PAR) and Regulation 1404/2007 (Baltic Sea), some noteworthy derogations from the scheme foreseen in Regulation 847/96 are introduced. Thus Regulation 40/2008 states that: 'For the purpose of withholding quotas to be transferred to 2009, Article 4(2) of Regulation [847/96] shall apply, *by way of derogation* from that Regulation, to *all* stocks subject to ana-lytical TAC.'[186] (Emphasis added.) A derogation is invoked presumably because

---

[182] Reg 847/96, Art 2, 2nd indent.

[183] Regs 40/2008, 1404/2007, and 1139/2008; see Annex I to each Regulation.

[184] Reg 2015/2006, Art 4(c) and (d).

[185] Similar wording is used in Reg 40/2008, Art 7 and Reg 1404/2007, Art 5. See also Reg 1139/2008, Art 5.   [186] Reg 40/2008, Art 7(2).

normally Article 4(2) does not apply to the stocks to which Article 5(2) is applied (see above). Regulation 1404/2007 establishes a similar derogation, albeit using the wording 'may apply' instead of 'shall apply'.[187]

In general, the adjustments arising from the application of Regulation 847/96 are implemented on a routine basis by an annual Commission Regulation that is based on both Article 23(4) of the Basic Regulation (on which, see further below) and Regulation 847/96 itself. The latest such Regulation at the time of writing was Regulation 541/2008,[188] which was adopted mid-way through 2008 and increases or decreases certain quotas fixed in Regulations 2015/2006 (deep-sea stocks), 1404/2007 (Baltic Sea), and 40/2008 (PAR). The increases arise from Member States having requested part of certain quotas for 2007 to be transferred to 2008, presumably pursuant to Article 4(2) of Regulation 847/96.[189] Some of the decreases are stated to be pursuant to Article 5(1) and (2);[190] others arise from Member States having 'requested . . . permission to land additional quantities of fish of certain stocks in the year 2007',[191] presumably pursuant to Article 3(3), and/or Article 4(1), of Regulation 847/96.

A significant derogation from Regulation 847/96 occurred in the case of Regulation 338/2008. The latter was adopted by the Council in response to overfishing by Poland of its 2007 quota of cod in the eastern Baltic Sea (ie in 'Subdivisions 25-32, EC Waters'). The 2007 TACs for the Baltic Sea, including those for cod, were set out in Regulation 1941/2006,[192] the predecessor to Regulation 1404/2007 (Baltic Sea). Poland notified an overshooting of its quota by 8,000 tonnes.[193] The TAC for cod in the eastern Baltic Sea was stated in Regulation 1941/2006 to be subject to Article 5(2) of Regulation 847/96.[194]

Regulation 338/2008 provided for the 8,000 tonnes to be deducted from Poland's future quota of eastern Baltic Sea cod. However, two derogations from Article 5 were applied. First, despite the stated applicability of Article 5(2) in Regulation 1941/2006, the principles of Article 5(1) were in effect applied: the deductions amounted only to the amount overshot rather than anything more. Secondly, the deduction was levied over the period 2008–11, rather than just in 2008.[195] The preamble to Regulation 338/2008 seeks to justify these derogations on the basis of certain commitments given by Poland and 'given the high amount of overfishing and the resulting socio-economic consequences of its immediate pay-back'.[196]

---

[187] Reg 1404/2007, Art 5(2).
[188] Commission Regulation (EC) No 541/2008 of 16 June 2008 adapting certain fish quotas for 2008 pursuant to Council Regulation (EC) No 847/96 introducing additional conditions for year-to-year management of TACs and quotas, OJ 2008 L157/23.   [189] Reg 541/2008, recital (4).
[190] Reg 541/2008, recital (5).   [191] Reg 541/2008, recital (6).
[192] Council Regulation (EC) No 1941/2006 of 11 December 2006 fixing the fishing opportunities and associated conditions for certain fish stocks and groups of fish stocks applicable in the Baltic Sea for 2007, OJ 2006 L367/1, as amended.   [193] Reg 338/2008, recital (4).
[194] Reg 1941/2006, Annex I.   [195] Reg 338/2008, Art 2.
[196] Reg 338/2008, recital (9). See also recitals (8), (10), and (11).

It is notable that Regulation 338/2008 was adopted by the Council, rather than the Commission. The Regulation states that its legal basis is Article 23(2) of the Control Regulation.[197] Article 23(2) was introduced above: it is the legal basis for the rules on deductions that are set out in Regulation 847/96. The reason for the Council, rather than the Commission, adopting the Regulation presumably relates to the derogations from Regulation 847/96 that it provides for: Regulation 847/96 itself is a Council Regulation and neither it nor Regulation 1941/2006 (also a Council Regulation) gives the Commission power to derogate from it. Thus if derogations are to be made, they presumably need to be made by the Council. It should be added that once the derogations were established by the Council in Regulation 338/2008, the task of fixing the actual deductions, expressed in tonnes of fish, was left to the Commission, which specified the tonnage of the deductions in Regulation 635/2008[198] in accordance with Regulation 338/2008.

As noted above, the Commission's routine annual application of Regulation 847/96 occurs by means of a Regulation based on a combination of Regulation 847/96 itself and Article 23(4) of the Basic Regulation. Article 23(4) requires the Commission, when it has established 'that a Member State has exceeded the fishing opportunities which have been allocated to it', to 'operate deductions from the future fishing opportunities of that Member State'.[199] (The Commission has similar powers under Article 23(1) of the Control Regulation, which it used to adopt Regulation 635/2008 mentioned above.[200]) In addition to being used as a basis for the annual Regulations applying Regulation 847/96, Article 23(4) of the Basic Regulation has also been used as a basis for Regulation 147/2007,[201] which was adopted by the Commission in response to overfishing by Ireland of mackerel and by the UK of herring and mackerel. It is not entirely clear whether Regulation 147/2007 is an application of the rules set out in Article 5 of Regulation 847/96 or is something separate based directly on Article 23(4) since, in contrast to Regulation 541/2008, the preamble is largely silent about Regulation 847/96.

The duty of the Commission, under Article 23(4) of the Basic Regulation to make deductions from Member States' fishing opportunities in cases of overfishing is supplemented by a further duty, also set out in Article 23(4). This requires that if, as

[197] Reg 338/2008, preamble, including recitals (5) and (6).

[198] Commission Regulation (EC) No 635/2008 of 3 July 2008 adapting the cod fishing quotas to be allocated to Poland in the Baltic Sea (Subdivisions 25–32, EC Waters) from 2008 to 2011 pursuant to Council Regulation (EC) No 338/2008, OJ 2008 L176/8.

[199] Reg 2371/2002, Art 23(4), 1st para.

[200] The reason for the choice of Art 23(1) of the Control Regulation, rather than Art 23(4) of the Basic Regulation, as the legal basis for Reg 635/2008 may be that the latter implements Reg 338/2008 which was itself adopted on the basis of the Control Regulation.

[201] Commission Regulation (EC) No 147/2007 of 15 February 2007 adapting certain fish quotas from 2007 to 2012 pursuant to Article 23(4) of Council Regulation (EC) No 2371/2002 on the conservation and sustainable exploitation of fisheries resources under the Common Fisheries Policy, OJ 2007 L46/10.

'a direct result' of one Member State exceeding its fishing opportunities, another Member State has not been able to exhaust its own fishing opportunities, the second Member State may be reallocated fishing opportunities derived from those deducted from the first Member State, 'taking into account the interest to conserve resources, as well as the interest in compensation of both Member States concerned'.[202]

The Commission has similar powers under Article 21(4) of the Control Regulation. These were used to adopt Regulation 446/2008[203] in response to overfishing by France and Italy of their bluefin tuna quotas in 2007, the Commission having decided that it was appropriate 'to make deductions from the 2008 bluefin tuna quotas of France and Italy and to allocate the amounts deducted, as appropriate, to the Member States [Greece, Spain, Cyprus, Malta, and Portugal] whose fishing activities were halted before their quotas were exhausted'.[204] To the authors' knowledge, Regulation 446/2008 is the only use to date by the Commission of its powers to reallocate deducted quota among Member States in response to overfishing.

Another important element of administration of TACs and quotas is prohibition of any further fishing once a Member State's quota has been exhausted. Under Article 26(4) of the Basic Regulation, '[i]n the event of a Member State's quota, allocation or available share being deemed to be exhausted', the Commission 'may, on the basis of the information available, immediately stop fishing activities'. Similarly, under Article 21(3) of the Control Regulation, the Commission 'shall fix, on the basis of the information available, the date on which, for a stock or group of stocks, the catches subject to a TAC, quota or other quantitative limitation made by fishing vessels flying the flag of, or registered in, any Member State are deemed to have exhausted the quota, allocation or share available to that Member State or, as the case may be, to the Community'; this date must be notified to the Member States 'without delay'.[205] The Commission routinely exercises the above functions, by means of Regulations. Typically, any given Regulation will state that: (a) the quota for a named stock and Member State is deemed to be exhausted from a stated date; and (b) fishing for that stock, or retention on board, transhipment, or landing of such stock, by 'vessels flying the flag of or registered in the Member State' in question is prohibited from that date. Occasionally, the arrival of new information will lead to a closed fishery being reopened.[206]

---

[202] Reg 2371/2002, Art 23(4), 2nd para.

[203] Commission Regulation (EC) No 446/2008 of 22 May 2008 adapting certain bluefin tuna quotas in 2008 pursuant to Article 21(4) of Council Regulation (EEC) No 2847/93 establishing a control system applicable to the common fisheries policy, OJ 2008 L134/11.

[204] Reg 446/2008, recital (6).

[205] Reg 2847/93, Art 21(3), 1st para. See further Art 21(3), 2nd and 3rd paras and Art 21(2). Regarding Art 21, see also subsection 2.7 below.

[206] See, for example, Commission Regulation (EC) No 1132/2008 of 13 November 2008 reopening the fishery for industrial fish in Norwegian waters of IV by vessels flying the flag of Sweden, OJ 2008 L306/59.

It is noteworthy that the Commission Regulations referred to in the previous paragraph are often retrospective, in that the dates of their adoption and subsequent publication in the *Official Journal* are often several weeks later than the 'stop' date specified in the Regulation. The retrospective nature of the Commission Regulations is potentially problematic in terms of legal certainty.[207]

A challenge to the closure of a fishery by the Commission was made by Poland, in respect of Regulation 804/2007,[208] which closed a fishery for cod by Poland in the Baltic Sea. The application to the CFI by Poland alleges, *inter alia*, that the Commission made 'flagrant mistakes' in calculating the amount of cod landed by Polish fishing vessels and that the prohibition infringed the principle of proportionality.[209] The application to the CFI was made in October 2007. It preceded the adoption by the Council in April 2008 of Regulation 338/2008 dealing with Poland's overshooting of its 2007 quota allocation in the same fishery (see above). In September 2008 the case was removed from the CFI's register.[210]

In addition to the administration of TACs and quotas discussed above, the Commission or Council may, for other reasons, amend the TACs and quotas set out in the annual fishing opportunities Regulations. Amendments to Regulation 40/2008 (PAR) provide examples of the kinds of changes that may be made: they relate, *inter alia*, to TACs and quotas for sandeel (in the light of the harvest control rule for that species set out in Annex IID to Regulation 40/2008), for cod (in the light of 'a new scientific assessment' by the ICES), and for capelin and redfish (in the light of international negotiations).[211]

Links between the TAC and quota system and discarding

Discarding is a very contentious aspect of the CFP, and involves the throwing overboard of unwanted catch. In the case of most fish species, discarded individuals are usually dead or at least damaged by virtue of the catching process. A report published by the FAO in 2005 reviewed discarding in, *inter alia*, the North Sea. As well as considering some individual fisheries there, it stated that the 'total annual North Sea discards have been estimated to be between 500 000 tonnes . . . and 880 000 tonnes', citing papers published in 1995 and 2000.[212]

---

[207] See further Churchill, *EEC Fisheries Law*, 142; Craig, P and de Burca, G, *EU Law: Text, Cases, and Materials* (4th edn, Oxford: Oxford University Press, 2007), 551 *et seq*; and Hartley, TC, *The Foundations of European Community Law* (6th edn, Oxford: Oxford University Press, 2007), 146–8.

[208] Commission Regulation (EC) No 804/2007 of 9 July 2007 establishing a prohibition of fishing for cod in the Baltic Sea (Subdivisions 25–32, EC Waters) by vessels flying the flag of Poland, OJ 2007 L180/3.   [209] Case T-379/07 *Poland v Commission*, OJ 2007 C283/38.

[210] OJ 2008 C301/65.

[211] Reg 697/2008, OJ 2008 L195/9. Council Regulation (EC) No 718/2008 of 24 July 2008 amending Regulations (EC) No 2015/2006 and (EC) No 40/2008, as regards fishing opportunities and associated conditions for certain fish stocks, OJ 2008 L198/8, recitals (5) and (7)–(9) and Annex II.

[212] Kelleher, K, *Discards in the world's marine fisheries—An update*, FAO Fisheries Technical Paper No 470 (Rome: FAO, 2005), 24.

The catch that is discarded may be unwanted for regulatory or economic reasons (or both), and those reasons may vary depending on the fishery in question. Discarding for regulatory reasons stems principally from the quota system, the application of minimum landing sizes (especially where stocks are anyway overfished, because more individual fish from such stocks are likely to be near this size), and the application of catch composition rules (which set maximum or minimum percentages of certain species in the catch). Discarding for economic reasons arises in part because '[s]ome species of fish have no market value in the local area where they are landed' and '[f]or some species . . . the price available does not justify the handling costs involved in landing the fish'.[213] The most important economic reason is probably so-called 'highgrading', which the UK government has described as follows:[214]

. . . "highgrading" occurs when fishermen discard marketable fish which is both above [minimum landing size] and within quota, a practice which results from a combination of market reasons and quota limits. This arises with species such as cod for which quota limits are highly restrictive and for which there is a price premium for larger fish, creating an incentive for fishermen to discard marketable but lower price bracket fish in order to use their limited quota to land fish commanding the highest price.

Thus the quota system can lead to discarding both through highgrading and directly. The direct effect occurs because fish caught surplus to quota may not lawfully be landed (see above). The only option with surplus fish is therefore to discard them. In the case of mixed fisheries the direct effect of the quota system on discarding is exacerbated. This can be illustrated with an example, albeit one that will not consider highgrading (or effort limits—see subsection 2.2 below) in order to keep things more simple. Suppose a vessel is fishing in the North Sea. It has quota for species A and species B, and those two species are commonly found together. The vessel exhausts its quota for species A but it still has quota for species B. In continuing to fish for species B, the vessel also catches species A. The catch of species A is surplus to quota and must be discarded. In seeking to use its entire quota for species B, the vessel's discards of species A may potentially be very large. Furthermore, in fishing for species A and species B, the vessel may catch species C which is also subject to a TAC but for which the vessel has no quota. All of the vessel's catch of species C must therefore be discarded. In addition, in fishing for any non-quota species having exhausted its quotas for species A and B, the vessel may continue to catch species A, B, and C which will need to be discarded.

Discarding is clearly a very wasteful practice. It also leads to the loss of a great deal of data which would otherwise contribute to more accurate fisheries management. Although the TAC and quota system is undoubtedly responsible for a

---

[213] House of Lords, 2008, HL Paper 146-II, pp 283–4 (evidence of the UK government's Department for Environment, Food and Rural Affairs (Defra)).

[214] House of Lords, 2008, HL Paper 146-II, p 284 (Defra's evidence).

significant amount of discarding, it should be added that there are also potential links between effort control and discarding. If the TAC and quota system was ever to be abolished and replaced with effort control and technical measures (including a continuation of minimum landing sizes and catch composition rules), all of the above reasons for discarding, with the exception of those stemming from the effect of quotas, would potentially continue to apply. In 2007 the Commission issued an important Communication on discarding (see subsection 9.5 below).

2.2 Effort management

Introduction

Effort management is playing an increasingly important role in fisheries conservation in Community waters, although it does not yet apply to all stocks fished there. Whereas TACs and quotas limit the amount of fish that may be landed, effort management limits the amount of capacity and activity that may be put into catching fish. In order to help avoid high volumes of discards, particularly in mixed fisheries (see subsection 2.1 above), effort management potentially needs to be employed in parallel to TACs so that the amount of effort used in catching the TAC is proportional to the TAC itself.[215]

Effort management, as distinct from the use of catch limits, is not new within the CFP. It was a feature of Regulation 3760/92 (now repealed),[216] the predecessor to the current Basic Regulation. In the light of Regulation 3760/92, various Regulations addressing effort were adopted, including, inter alia, Regulations 685/95,[217] 2027/95,[218] and 779/97[219] (all now repealed) and Regulation 2347/2002 (on which, see below). Effort management is also an important feature of the current Basic Regulation and from 2003, or arguably 2002, onwards it has had a high profile role in respect of certain fisheries in the form of so-called 'days-at-sea'. The current legal framework for effort management is discussed below.

As with any other fisheries management measure, effort management has both advantages and disadvantages, and its suitability may depend on the nature of the

---

[215] See, for example, *Communication from the Commission to the Council and the European Parliament: A policy to reduce unwanted by-catches and eliminate discards in European fisheries*, COM(2007) 136, 28.3.2007, section 3, pp 4–5.

[216] Council Regulation (EEC) No 3760/92 of 20 December 1992 establishing a Community system for fisheries and aquaculture, OJ 1992 L389/1, as amended, *inter alia*, Arts 3(f), 8(1), and 8(4)(i).

[217] Council Regulation (EC) No 685/95 of 27 March 1995 on the management of the fishing effort relating to certain Community fishing areas and resources, OJ 1995 L71/5.

[218] Council Regulation (EC) No 2027/95 of 15 June 1995 establishing a system for the management of fishing effort relating to certain Community fishing areas and resources, OJ 1995 L199/1, as amended.

[219] Council Regulation (EC) No 779/97 of 24 April 1997 introducing arrangements for the management of fishing effort in the Baltic Sea, OJ 1997 L113/1, as corrected.

fishery in question. Its advantages include, *inter alia*, greater ease of enforcement compared to catch limits (subject to the number and complexity of derogations permitted) and its potential to reduce quota-based discarding by rendering effort proportional to the particular quota being fished. Its disadvantages include, *inter alia*, a difficulty in defining clearly the relationship between fishing effort and fishing mortality rate, a difficulty in allocating effort among Member States in a way that is compatible with relative stability (see further below), and the scope for so-called 'technical (or 'technological') creep'.

Technical creep arises from the fact that vessel operators may find ways to increase the efficiency of their vessels through technological progress while remaining inside the applicable effort limit. For example, if effort is defined in terms of engine size and time spent fishing (see below), a vessel operator may succeed in increasing the efficiency of the gear, thus increasing the efficacy of the fishing operation, whilst keeping within the required engine size and activity.[220] In contrast, despite their shortcomings, TACs represent a fixed quantity of fish. Technical creep is often cited as an important reason for not relying on effort control to the exclusion of TACs.

It is important to distinguish between 'effort' and 'capacity'. A report issued in 2007 by the Commission on improving indicators of effort and capacity defines fishing capacity in generic terms as 'the ability of a vessel or group of vessels to catch fish' and states that in the framework of the CFP 'fishing capacity has so far been quantified on the basis of vessel characteristics' (for example vessel tonnage, vessel engine power, or amount or size of fishing gear).[221]

Regulation of the capacity of the fleet of Community fishing vessels on a gross scale is described in subsection 2.8 below. However, the use of capacity limits for particular fisheries is discussed below regarding Regulation 2347/2002. Capacity limits are also provided for by the recovery plan for Bay of Biscay sole[222] and by Regulation 520/2007 (on highly migratory species),[223] but such limits are not discussed further here.

The Basic Regulation defines fishing effort as 'the product of *the capacity and the activity* of a fishing vessel; for a group of vessels it is the sum of the fishing effort of all vessels in the group' (emphasis added).[224] Thus the definition recognizes that capacity on its own does not catch fish. The capacity needs to be active for that to happen, and effort is then the product of capacity and activity. Activity is generally measured in terms of time (usually days, under the CFP). Where activity is measured in days and capacity is measured in kilowatts of engine power, the resulting

---

[220] See further *Communication from the Commission to the Council and the European Parliament on improving fishing capacity and effort indicators under the common fisheries policy*, COM(2007) 39, 5.2.2007, section 4, p 8.   [221] COM(2007) 39, section 2.1, p 3.

[222] Reg 388/2006, Art 5.

[223] Council Regulation (EC) No 520/2007 of 7 May 2007 laying down technical measures for the conservation of certain stocks of highly migratory species and repealing Regulation (EC) No 973/2001, OJ 2007 L123/3, as amended, Arts 12 and 18.   [224] Reg 2371/2002, Art 3(h).

unit of effort is the so-called 'kilowatt-day' (or 'kW-day'). Despite the above definition of effort in the Basic Regulation, the days-at-sea regime as used in several fisheries (see below), which addresses activity but not capacity, is none-theless widely referred to as an 'effort' management regime.

Legal basis for effort management

As with TACs and quotas, the principal current legal basis for the EC to undertake effort management is the Basic Regulation. Article 4 states that measures to be adopted by the Council for achieving the objectives of the CFP may, in particular, include 'measures for each stock or group of stocks to limit fishing mortality and the environmental impact of fishing activities by . . . [*inter alia*] . . . limiting fishing effort'.[225] Article 20(1) of the Regulation states, *inter alia*, that '[t]he Council, acting by qualified majority on a proposal from the Commission, shall decide on catch and/or *fishing effort limits* and on the allocation of fishing opportunities among Member States' (emphasis added).[226] As noted above, the Regulation defines fishing effort as the product of capacity and activity. Fishing effort limits along with catch limits are referred to collectively as 'fishing opportunities'.[227]

Article 20(1) of the Basic Regulation requires fishing opportunities, which include fishing effort limits, to be distributed among Member States 'in such a way as to assure each Member State *relative stability* of fishing activities for each stock or fishery' (emphasis added). The approach taken by the Council for that purpose in the context of TACs is described in subsection 2.1 above. However, the reference in Article 20(1) to fishing opportunities, rather than just catch limits specifically, being distributed in a way that assures relative stability raises the question of whether effort limits could ever become the principal way of assuring relative stability.

As noted in subsection 2.1 above, TACs are currently the 'carriers' of relative stability. Could 'total allowable effort' limits ever come to occupy that role instead? In *Azores v Council*, in the context of Regulation 1954/2003 (see below), the Commission was cited by the Court as stating that 'the principle of relative stability is, in any event, only relevant for the setting of TACs and not in the context of a limitation of fishing effort such as the one set out in [Regulation 1954/2003]'.[228] One problem is that allocations under relative stability are to be 'based upon a *predictable share of the stocks* for each Member State' (emphasis added; see subsection 2.1 above).[229] Given technical creep, it is questionable whether an allocation among Member States of, say, a 'total allowable effort' could ever, on its own, provide a 'predictable share' of the stocks. However, it is noteworthy that in *Azores v Council* the Council and/or the Commission (it is not clear which) asserted that, in the case

[225] Reg 2371/2002, Art 4(2)(f).
[226] See also Reg 2371/2002, Arts 4(2)(a), (b), and (e), 5(4), and 6(4).
[227] Reg 2371/2002, Art 3(q). See also Arts 11(1), 14(1), 20(1)–(5), and 23(4).
[228] Case T-37/04 R *Azores v Council* [2004] ECR II-2153, para 99.
[229] Reg 2371/2002, recital (16).

of Regulation 1954/2003 (see below), 'relative stability is . . . *preserved* given that the . . . Regulation caps effort on the basis of historical averages' (emphasis added).[230] New developments regarding effort management in the context of long-term plans (see below) are also potentially relevant in this regard.

Aside from Article 20(1) of the Basic Regulation, the principal instruments addressing effort limitation in Community waters are the following: (a) the long-term plans adopted pursuant to Article 5 and/or Article 6 of the Basic Regulation, as implemented by the annual fishing opportunities Regulations; (b) Regulations 1954/2003[231] and 1415/2004,[232] regarding so-called 'Western waters'; and (c) Regulation 2347/2002,[233] which introduces a capacity limit for certain deep-sea fisheries. These instruments are not necessarily limited in their scope to Community waters. Instead, the geographical scope depends on the instrument in question; the scope of Regulations 1954/2003 and 2347/2002 is mentioned below. Each of the above instruments will be addressed here. It should be added that the EC's effort management system is generally based on ICES and FAO zones, as defined in Regulations 3880/91 and 2597/95 (mentioned in subsection 2.1 above).

Long-term plans

The Basic Regulation, by virtue of its Articles 5 and 6, enables the use of effort limits as a tool within recovery plans and management plans (introduced in subsection 2.1 above).[234] Indeed, any recovery plan *must* include limitations on fishing effort 'unless this is not necessary to achieve the objective of the plan'.[235] In practice, the cod recovery plan[236] and the long-term plans for Baltic Sea cod,[237] North Sea plaice and sole,[238] and southern hake and Norway lobster[239] all call for the setting of effort limits on an annual basis, to complement TACs, as one of the tools to achieve the desired aim for the stocks in question. In the case of Western Channel sole, it is not clear whether the effort limits are to be set on an annual basis.[240] In some instances, there are back-up plans in case the Council fails to take a decision.[241]

---

[230] Case T-37/04 R, para 99.

[231] Council Regulation (EC) No 1954/2003 of 4 November 2003 on the management of the fishing effort relating to certain Community fishing areas and resources and modifying Regulation (EC) No 2847/93 and repealing Regulations (EC) No 685/95 and (EC) No 2027/95, OJ 2003 L289/1.

[232] Council Regulation (EC) No 1415/2004 of 19 July 2004 fixing the maximum annual fishing effort for certain fishing areas and fisheries, OJ 2004 L258/1.

[233] Council Regulation (EC) No 2347/2002 of 16 December 2002 establishing specific access requirements and associated conditions applicable to fishing for deep-sea stocks, OJ 2002 L351/6, as amended.   [234] Reg 2371/2002, Arts 5(4) and 6(4).

[235] Reg 2371/2002, Art 5(4).   [236] Reg 423/2004, Art 8.

[237] Reg 1098/2007, Art 8. See also Commission Regulation (EC) No 169/2008 of 25 February 2008 excluding ICES Subdivisions 27 and 28.2 from certain fishing effort limitations and recording obligations for 2008, pursuant to Council Regulation (EC) No 1098/2007 establishing a multiannual plan for the cod stocks in the Baltic Sea and the fisheries exploiting those stocks, OJ 2008 L51/3.

[238] Reg 676/2007, Art 9.   [239] Reg 2166/2005, Art 8.   [240] Reg 509/2007, Art 5.

[241] Reg 423/2004 (cod), Art 8(4); Reg 2166/2005 (southern hake and Norway lobster), Art 8(3), last sentence.

The long-term plan for Norway lobster, by means of an amendment to Regulation 850/98 (on which, see subsection 2.3 below), sets an ongoing effort ceiling in certain areas and periods.[242] The plan for northern hake[243] does not call for any effort limitation, presumably because that is 'not necessary to achieve the objective of the plan' (see above). As noted above, the plan for Bay of Biscay sole uses a system of capacity management; however, in some circumstances, it also permits an alternative system based on an ongoing effort ceiling.[244] In the case of the plan for bluefin tuna, there is only a vaguely worded provision on effort.[245] For European eel the plan is strongly focused on effort reduction.[246]

Where a long-term plan provides for effort limits to be set on an annual basis, they are set in the relevant annual fishing opportunities Regulation. With one exception, the vehicle for effort limits set under the long-term plans is Annex II to the principal annual Regulation, ie Regulation 40/2008 at the time of writing. The exception is the Baltic Sea cod plan, under which effort limits are set in the annual fishing opportunities Regulation for the Baltic Sea, ie Regulation 1404/2007 at the time of writing. The effort limits are expressed in a unit known colloquially as 'days-at-sea'. As noted above, days-at-sea are just a measure of activity rather than a combination of activity and capacity. However, that does not seem to deter the Commission, the Council, and others from referring to them as a measure of 'effort'. What follows is concerned with Annex II to Regulation 40/2008.

Within Regulation 40/2008, Annex II has three parts dealing with effort limits under the long-term plans: Annexes IIA, B, and C. Annex IIA is entitled 'Fishing effort for vessels in the context of the recovery of certain stocks in ICES zones IIIa, IV, VIa, VIIa, VIId and EC waters of ICES zone IIa'. A reader of that title would be forgiven for wondering what stocks constitute 'certain stocks'. Scrutiny of the Regulation's preamble, and a process of elimination taking into account the subject matter of Annexes IIB and C (see below), suggests that the term 'certain stocks' means those covered by the cod recovery plan (Regulation 423/2004) and the plan for North Sea plaice and sole (Regulation 676/2007).

The scope of Annexes IIB and C is clearer. Annex IIB is entitled 'Fishing effort for vessels in the context of the recovery of certain southern hake and Norway lobster stocks in ICES zones VIIIc and IXa excluding the Gulf of Cadiz'. It therefore covers the stocks covered by Regulation 2166/2005. Annex IIC is entitled 'Fishing effort for vessels in the context of the recovery of Western Channel sole stocks ICES zone VIIe [sic]' and therefore covers the stocks covered by Regulation 509/2007.

The approach used in each of Annexes IIA, B, and C is similar and may be summarized as follows. Each annex starts with some preliminary provisions including, *inter alia*: (a) a definition of the vessels covered by the annex; (b) a

---

[242] Reg 2166/2005, Art 15 (new Art 29b(5) and (6) of Reg 850/98).   [243] Reg 811/2004.
[244] Reg 388/2006, Arts 5 and 6.   [245] Reg 1559/2007, Art 4(1).
[246] Reg 1100/2007, *inter alia*, Arts 4(2), 5(4), and 8(1).

statement of the geographical area(s) covered by the annex (referred to here as the 'specified area(s)'); (c) a definition of the 2008 management period (ie 'the period from 1 February 2008 to 31 January 2009'[247]); (d) a definition of 'day present within an [or 'the'] area' (see below), which is the technical way of referring to 'day-at-sea'; and (e) a statement of the fishing gears covered by the annex, including those gears which fall into particular groupings (referred to here as the 'specified groupings').

Annexes IIA, B, and C only address vessels of length overall equal to or greater than 10 m.[248] A possible reason for that focus is revealed by the *Unitymark* case.[249] In that case, the validity of various limits on days-at-sea imposed on vessels of *at least* 10 m in length was in question. The applicants argued that rather than impose limits on the gear type used by their vessels, it would have sufficed to, *inter alia*, restrict the number of days-at-sea by vessels *under* 10 m in length.[250] The Court held that 'the particularly high number of those vessels [ie those under 10 m in length] was liable to make monitoring particularly difficult and was capable of justifying the choice made by the Community legislature to restrict the number of days spent at sea by fishermen using other types of vessel in order to help to preserve cod stocks'.[251]

A 'day present within an [or 'the'] area', ie the technical way of referring to 'day-at-sea', is defined as 'any continuous period of 24 hours (or part thereof) during which a vessel is present within the [specified area(s)] and absent from port. The time from which the continuous period is measured is at the discretion of the Member State whose flag is flown by the vessel concerned'.[252]

After the preliminary provisions in Annexes IIA, B, and C, there follow two broad general conditions. First, with some exceptions, a Member State is not to permit fishing by its vessels with a gear belonging to any of the specified groupings in the specified area(s) if the vessel does not have a record of such fishing activity in the area over one or more stated years, unless the Member State ensures that equivalent capacity is prevented from fishing in the area in question. Secondly, a Member State's vessel having no quotas in a specified area is not to be permitted to fish in that area with a gear belonging to any of the specified groupings unless the vessel is allocated a quota after a transfer in accordance with Article 20(5) of the Basic Regulation and is allocated days-at-sea according to the rules on transfer of days.[253]

For vessels covered by the annex that meet the above conditions, each Member State is to ensure that its vessels, when carrying on board any of the specified

---

[247] Reg 40/2008, Annex IIA, para 1, Annex IIB, para 1, and Annex IIC, para 1.1.

[248] Reg 40/2008, Annex IIA, para 1, Annex IIB, para 1, and Annex IIC, para 1.1.

[249] Case C-535/03 *The Queen, on the application of Unitymark Ltd and North Sea Fishermen's Organisation v Department for Environment, Food and Rural Affairs* [2006] ECR I-2689.

[250] Case C-535/03, para 39.   [251] Case C-535/03, para 75. See also para 47.

[252] Reg 40/2008, Annex IIA, para 3, Annex IIB, para 2, and Annex IIC, para 2.

[253] Reg 40/2008, Annex IIA, para 5, Annex IIB, para 4, and Annex IIC, para 4.

groupings of fishing gear, are present within the specified area(s) for no more than an allotted number of days-at-sea per year (except in certain emergency situations).[254] The latter are set according to a table, based on gear type and area and, in the case of Annexes IIA and B, some defined 'special conditions'. The tables in Annexes IIA and B set out maximum days for which a vessel may be present within the specified area(s) merely 'having carried on board' any of the specified groupings of gears; in contrast, the table in Annex IIC set out limits for 'having carried on board *and used*' (emphasis added) any of the specified groupings.[255]

In the case of Annex IIA, the table setting out the limits is very long, spanning four pages of the *Official Journal* and specifying maximum days-at-sea per specified area for a total of thirty-nine combinations of gear types and special conditions. The tables in Annexes IIB and C are much shorter, ie only two combinations of gear types and special conditions in each case. In the case of Annex IIA, some combinations have a limit on days-at-sea for some sea areas, but not for others. In the case of Annexes IIA and B, some gears that otherwise have days-at-sea limits have an unlimited number of days if certain special conditions are met. There are sometimes supplementary rules, eg on days-at-sea limits that apply to use of multiple areas and on the interaction between days limits set out in Annexes IIA and IIC.[256]

To take an example from the table in Annex IIA, the maximum number of days a vessel may be present in the 2008 management period within ICES area VIa with trawls or Danish seines on board with mesh size greater than or equal to 120 mm, and with no special conditions, is 70. That limit increases to 91 days or 103 days if the gear in question includes a 120 mm or 140 mm square mesh window, respectively, meeting certain conditions. The limit increases further if alternative special conditions, for example relating to the proportion of the catch comprising cod, are met.

The presence of thirty-nine combinations of gear types and special conditions within Annex IIA is an indication of how complicated the system of effort limits has become. The variety of gear categories and special conditions specified in the table in Annex IIA is a reflection of, *inter alia*, the variety of vessels and gears that may catch the stocks in question (including as by-catch) and the efforts of different parts of the catching sector to obtain derogations. The resulting complexity of the system does not facilitate control and enforcement.

To an outsider, and perhaps even to some insiders, there is also a lack of transparency within the effort control system pursuant to the long-term plans. It is not really clear how the effort limits, expressed as days-at-sea, correspond to the TACs that have been fixed for the stocks in question despite the requirement in several long-term plans that there should be such a correspondence. Indeed, the

---

[254] Reg 40/2008, Annex IIA, paras 6 and 7, Annex IIB, paras 5 and 6, and Annex IIC, paras 5 and 6.
[255] Reg 40/2008, Annex IIA, para 8.1, Annex IIB, para 7.1, and Annex IIC, para 7.1.
[256] Reg 40/2008, Annex IIA, paras 8.8–8.10 and Annex IIC, para 7.2.

relationship between catch limits and effort limits fixed under the cod recovery plan has been described as 'quasi-independent'.[257]

A Member State may, if it wishes, divide the maximum days-at-sea within the specified area(s) 'into management periods of durations of one or more calendar months', whereupon the number of days for which a vessel may be present within the area(s) during a management period is to be fixed at the discretion of the flag Member State. If a vessel uses up that number of days it is to remain in port or out of any the specified area(s) for the remainder of the management period unless using only gear not listed in the annex and complying with rules on use of such gear (Annex IIA) or gear for which days-at-sea limits have not been set (Annex IIC); Annex IIB is silent on that particular aspect.[258]

There are additional rules in Annexes IIA, B, and C on various other matters including, *inter alia*: (a) transfer of days-at-sea between fishing vessels flying the flag of the same Member State or of different Member States; (b) notification of fishing gear; (c) use of more than one grouping of fishing gear (Annex IIA only); (d) combined use of gear listed and not listed in the annex (Annexes IIA and IIB only); (e) carrying on board of fishing gear from more than one gear grouping (Annex IIA only); (f) non-fishing related activities (Annexes IIA and IIC only); (g) transit across a specified area; (h) monitoring of fishing activity; and (i) reporting of information by the Member State to the Commission.

Perhaps more significantly, Annexes IIA, B, and C contain incentive schemes whereby extra days-at-sea are potentially available: (a) to take into account permanent cessation of fishing activities that have taken place since a certain date;[259] (b) as a reward for 'enhanced observer coverage'; or (c) in the case of Annex IIA only, as a reward for signing up to 'a discard reduction plan' or participating in 'the cod avoidance reference fleet programme' (both these terms being explained in the Regulation). Furthermore, Annexes IIA, B, and C allow Member States to use a 'kilowatt-days' system as an alternative to the days-at-sea system. The kilowatt-days system and the rewards for involvement in discard reduction plans and in the cod avoidance reference fleet programme are discussed further below.

The concept of days-at-sea has not been free from litigation before the Court. In *Unitymark*,[260] referred to above, the claimants were a company fishing for flatfish using beam trawls and an organization representing fishermen.[261] In a reference for a preliminary ruling, they argued that various limits on days-at-sea imposed to protect certain cod stocks[262] were in breach of the general principles of

---

[257] House of Lords, European Union Committee, 21st Report of Session 2007–08, *The Progress of the Common Fisheries Policy*, Vol I, Report, HL Paper 146-I (London: The Stationery Office Ltd, 2008), para 60. [258] Reg 40/2008, Annex IIA, para 9, Annex IIB, para 8, and Annex IIC, para 8.
[259] See, for example, Commission Decision 2008/601/EC of 17 July 2008 on the allocation to the Netherlands of additional fishing days, for permanent cessation of fishing activities, within the Skagerrak, that part of ICES zone IIIa not covered by the Skagerrak and the Kattegat, ICES zone IV and EC waters of ICES zone IIa, OJ 2008 L193/18. [260] Case C-535/03.
[261] Case C-535/03, para 18. [262] Case C-535/03, para 3.

non–discrimination and proportionality in that, *inter alia*, they failed to distinguish adequately between: (a) the alleged lower catch of cod by beam trawls compared to gear specializing in cod or Norway lobster; and (b) two subcategories of beam trawls, one allegedly being less harmful to cod stocks than the other.[263] For a variety of reasons, the Court held that the contested measures were not manifestly inappropriate and were therefore valid.[264]

After several years of existence, the concept of effort management under the long-term plans by means of days-at-sea limits is being reviewed with an eye to reform. In its 2007 policy statement, the Commission stated that it 'will start a debate in 2007 to investigate . . . how to simplify, improve, and consolidate the existing effort regimes', beginning with its report on capacity and effort indicators (on which, see above).[265] One reason for initiating this debate was that, in the Commission's view, annual limitations on days-at-sea had 'not acted as a constraint on the fishing effort of the fleets which have used less that [sic] 75% of the allocated time'.[266]

Since then, ongoing failures in the effort management system have continued to vex the Commission. Commenting on the days-at-sea regime, the Commission stated in its 2008 policy statement that: 'The existing regime cannot deliver the necessary further reductions, because the current system allows offsetting the decrease in the days at sea [sic] by complex derogations. The system even allocates fishing rights to inactive vessels, which can be transferred to active vessels. Reducing days-at-sea has not been very effective in reducing the effort actually deployed. Consequently realistic effort reduction targets cannot be met only by reducing days-at-sea.'[267]

The weakness of the days-at-sea regime has led to discussion about an alternative effort regime that: (a) is based not just on activity (days) but also on engine size (kilowatts of engine power), ie a kilowatt-days regime that better reflects the definition of effort in the Basic Regulation (see above); and (b) involves effort limits expressed in kilowatt-days being allocated to each Member State which would then manage those limits itself. At the December 2007 Fisheries Council meeting, the Council and Commission agreed the following statement:[268]

The Council and the Commission agree that a kW-days approach would be better adapted to the management of fishing effort in the areas covered by the multi-annual regimes for cod, flatfish and southern hake. They endeavour to discuss during 2008 such an approach on the basis of the ideas advanced by the Commission in the context of the preparation of the 2008 TAC and Quota package. They shall aim at the implementation of such an approach in 2009.

---

[263] Case C-535/03, paras 32–37.   [264] Case C-535/03, paras 64, 67, 71, 74, 75, and 76.

[265] COM(2007) 295, section 3.4, p 11.

[266] IP/07/782, Brussels, 8 June 2007, penultimate paragraph (available on the website of the European Commission). See also COM(2007) 295, section 2.4, p 6–7.

[267] COM(2008) 331, section 4.2, p 6.   [268] COM(2008) 331, section 4.2, pp 6–7.

The kilowatt-days approach outlined above was included in the Commission's legislative proposal for an amendment to the cod recovery plan.[269] Adoption of such an approach in a revised cod recovery plan would, as currently, involve the setting of effort limits by the Council on an annual basis. However, rather than being in the form of days-at-sea, the limits would be in the form of kilowatt-days for each 'effort group'[270] per Member State. The limits would be fixed in the principal annual Regulation (ie in the successors to Regulation 40/2008).[271]

The 2008 policy statement notes that the Fisheries Council, at its December 2007 meeting, 'approved the early and voluntary use of the kW-day system to ease the transition to the fully-fledged kW-day system under the revised cod recovery plan in 2009'.[272] This 'voluntary' scheme is provided for in Annexes IIA, B, and C of Regulation 40/2008 (see above).[273] In short, it provides that during the 2008 management period a Member State may authorize a vessel to deviate from the prescribed days-at-sea limit for a given combination of gear type(s) and special condition(s) if the 'overall amounts of kilowatt days corresponding to such a combination is [sic] respected'.[274] The means for calculating the 'overall amounts of kilowatt days' is specified. A Member State may not benefit from the scheme unless the Commission authorizes its substantiated request.

In the case of Annex IIA specifically, the scheme is intended to lead to 'a more efficient use of fishing opportunities' or to 'stimulate fishing practices that lead to reduced discards and lower fishing mortality of both juvenile and adult fish'. Such practices 'may take the form of fishing plans designed in collaboration with the fishing industry including, as appropriate: (a) a specific target to reduce cod discards to below 10% of cod catch; (b) real-time closures for juveniles and for spawners; (c) Cod [sic] avoidance measures; (d) trying out new selective devices; (e) adequate monitoring by observers and (f) arrangements for follow-up and reporting'.[275]

It is not clear from Regulation 40/2008, or from the Commission's 2008 policy statement, how the voluntary kilowatt-days system and the reward system for involvement in discard reduction plans or the cod avoidance reference fleet programme, all provided for in Annex IIA, relate to each other. A version of the voluntary kilowatt-days system was present in the Commission's legislative proposal for what became Regulation 40/2008;[276] but that proposal contained no

---

[269] COM(2008) 162. See, regarding Reg 423/2004, inter alia, proposed new Arts 2, 2b, 8, and 8a–8e and Annex I. See also SEC(2008) 386, section 4.5.4, p 21.

[270] The term 'effort group' is defined by COM(2008) 162, proposed new Art 2(b) as 'a set of vessels flying the flag of a Member State which fish in one of the areas set out in [proposed new] Article 1 using fishing gear belonging to one of the groupings of gears set out in [proposed new] Annex I'.

[271] SEC(2008) 386, 2.4.2008, section 1.1, p 5.   [272] COM(2008) 331, section 4.2, p 7.

[273] Reg 40/2008, Annex IIA, paras 8.5–8.7, Annex IIB, paras 7.3–7.4, and Annex IIC, para 7.3–7.4.

[274] Reg 40/2008, Annex IIA, para 8.5. Slightly different wording is used in Annexes IIB and C.

[275] Reg 40/2008, Annex IIA, para 8.6.

[276] Proposal for a Council Regulation fixing for 2008 the fishing opportunities and associated conditions for certain fish stocks and groups of fish stocks, applicable in Community waters and, for Community vessels, in waters where catch limitations are required, COM(2007) 759, 28.11.2007, proposed Annexes IIA, paras 8.4–8.5, IIB, paras 7.3–7.4, and IIC, paras 7.3–7.4.

provisions on extra days–at–sea rewards regarding discard reduction plans or the cod avoidance reference fleet programme. The UK introduced cod avoidance measures (including, *inter alia*, real–time closures and more selective gears) in the course of 2008. These measures appear to have been part of a voluntary kilowatt-days system adopted by the UK pursuant to Annex IIA of Regulation 40/2008. [277] As noted above, Commission authorization is needed for a Member State to benefit from a kilowatt–days system under Regulation 40/2008. As at the end of November 2008, it was not clear to the authors whether such an authorization had been issued; no such authorization had been published in the *Official Journal* by that date.

It is noteworthy that the Commission's legislative proposal for a replacement for Regulation 850/98 on technical measures (on which, see subsection 2.3 below) contains a provision on national plans to reduce or eliminate discards. Assuming that this provision is adopted by the Council in due course, and assuming the successor to Regulation 40/2008 maintains the rewards scheme for participation in discard reduction plans, there would appear to be scope for potential linkages between these two initiatives.

Regulations 1954/2003 and 1415/2004

Regulation 1954/2003 'establishes the criteria and procedures for a system relating to the management of fishing effort in ICES areas V, VI, VII, VIII, IX and X and CECAF divisions 34.1.1, 34.1.2 and 34.2.0'.[278] Put briefly, the total area in question amounts to Atlantic waters off the western seaboard of the Member States plus some other waters in the eastern Atlantic; as noted above, the area is known colloquially as 'Western waters'. The Regulation uses virtually the same definition of 'fishing effort' as the Basic Regulation (see above).[279]

Regulation 1954/2003 deals separately with vessels 'equal to or more than 15 metres in length overall' and vessels 'equal to or less than 15 metres in length overall'. Vessels of 15 m in length overall fall into both categories, which potentially creates scope for confusion. The Regulation, in Article 11, provides for a daughter Regulation—subsequently adopted as Regulation 1415/2004.[280]

---

[277] For further information on the UK's cod avoidance measures for 2008, see, *inter alia, Draft Terms of Reference 30.10.2008*, STECF Plenary Meeting 3–7 November 2008, Brussels, section 3.4 entitled 'First evaluation of the UK cod avoidance measures introduced in 2008', pp 11–13 (available on the website of the STECF).

[278] Reg 1954/2003, Art 1. The abbreviation 'CECAF' means 'Fishery Committee for the Eastern Central Atlantic' (on which see further Chapter 5). For the location of CECAF divisions 34.1.1, 34.1.2, and 34.2.0, see Reg 2597/95.   [279] Reg 1954/2003, Art 2(b).

[280] Regs 1954/2003 and 1415/2004 have been the subject of litigation before the Court: see Case T-37/04 R *Azores v Council* [2004] ECR II-2153; Case T-37/04 *Azores v Council*, judgment of 1 July 2008 (an appeal against the judgment in that case was brought by the applicant on 8 October 2008); Case C-442/04 *Spain v Council*, judgment of 15 May 2008; and Case C-36/04 *Spain v Council* [2006] ECR I-2981.

For vessels 'equal to or more than 15 metres in length overall', the basic proposition is set out in Article 3 of Regulation 1954/2003. Article 3(1)(a) requires
Member States to assess the levels of fishing effort exerted by such vessels as an
annual average of the reference period 1998 to 2002 in each of the ICES areas and
CECAF divisions mentioned above, for certain categories of fisheries (see
below).[281] Article 3(1)(b) requires Member States to then allocate the assessed
levels of fishing effort.

In *Azores v Council*, the CFI held that the duty in Article 3(1)(b) to allocate the
assessed levels of fishing effort requires the Member States to limit the fishing effort
of their fleets in accordance with Article 3(1)(a), irrespective of when the daughter
Regulation provided for by Article 11 enters into force.[282] Thus the CFI appears
to interpret the regime established by Article 3 as being a free-standing means of
effort control that does not require a Regulation under Article 11 to become
effective. This interpretation will be discussed further below.

Regulation 1954/2003 recognizes that there may be some interaction between
Article 3(1) and any recovery plans that may be adopted by the Council. Thus the
effort regime laid down in Article 3(1) is stated to be without prejudice to the
regimes laid down in any such recovery plans.[283] Furthermore, recovery plans
involving effort management in all or part of the zones referred to in Article 3(1)
are to 'make any necessary adjustment' to Regulation 1954/2003.[284]

The three categories of fisheries in question in Article 3(1) are: (a) demersal
fisheries, excluding those 'covered by' Regulation 2347/2002; (b) fisheries for
scallops; and (c) fisheries for edible crab and spider crab. Of these three, category
'(a)' is the principal one. As can be seen, category '(a)' makes a link to Regulation
2347/2002. That Regulation relates to fishing effort for certain deep-sea stocks
and will be discussed below. However, the link between category '(a)' and
Regulation 2347/2002 is important and needs to be explored here.

In *Azores v Council*, the CFI seems to have interpreted the reference in category
'(a)' to demersal fisheries 'covered by' Regulation 2347/2002 as being a reference
to fisheries for those species listed in Annex I to that Regulation.[285] On that basis,
the demersal fisheries falling within the scope of category '(a)' in Article 3(1)

---

[281] The duty in Art 3(1)(a) does not apply to a particular sea area located off Ireland and defined in
Art 6(1); that area is subject to a separate regime (see below). In Case C-442/04 *Spain v Council*, the
Court found that the reference period 1998 to 2002 as used in Art 3(1), and also in Arts 4 and 6, was not
discriminatory against Spain; see paras 35–45. See also Case C-36/04 *Spain v Council*, AG Opinion,
paras 47–72.

[282] Case T-37/04 *Azores v Council*, para 73. See also Case T-37/04 R *Azores v Council*, para 172,
penultimate sentence.   [283] Reg 1954/2003, Art 3(2).

[284] Reg 1954/2003, Art 3(3).

[285] Case T-37/04 *Azores v Council*, paras 5 and 9. In the last sentence of para 5, the CFI defines the term
'deep-sea species' (as used later in the judgment) as the species listed in Annex I to Reg 2347/2002. In
turn, in para 9, the CFI summarizes Art 3(1) of Reg 1954/2003 in a way that interprets the reference in
Art 3(1) to demersal fisheries 'covered by' Reg 2347/2002 as meaning demersal fisheries for 'deep-sea
species', ie demersal fisheries for Annex I species.

of Regulation 1954/2003 include, *inter alia*, those for species listed in Annex II to Regulation 2347/2002 but exclude those for species listed in Annex I to that Regulation. As noted below, Annex I lists twenty-two species and two genera of deep-sea fish. Fisheries for a substantial number of deep-sea species are therefore outside the scope of Regulation 1954/2003.

The annex to Regulation 1954/2003 indicates that the assessment and allocation for each of the three categories '(a)', '(b)', and '(c)' above is to be done irrespective of gear type. Thus effort for, say, bottom trawling and longlining is to be lumped together with no distinction between those gears. The Member States' assessments are to be forwarded to the Commission.[286] The assessed levels of fishing effort have subsequently been used to inform the drafting of the daughter Regulation adopted under Article 11 (Regulation 1415/2004—see below).

Under Article 7 of Regulation 1954/2003, Member States are to establish a list of their fishing vessels 'authorised to carry out their fishing activities in the fisheries defined in [Article 3]'.[287] It is not entirely clear how the vessels are to be chosen, but the wording may refer to those vessels which have contributed over the period 1998 to 2002 to the effort levels assessed pursuant to Article 3.[288] Vessels entered on the list may subsequently be replaced by the Member State 'provided that the total fishing effort of vessels in any area and fishery defined in [Article 3] does not increase'.[289] Presumably the increase to be avoided is any increase in the effort that was being exerted prior to the replacement of the vessel in question. The Member States' lists are to be notified to the Commission.[290]

Article 8(1) requires Member States to 'take the necessary measures to regulate the fishing effort where the fishing effort corresponding to free access for fishing vessels entered on the lists of vessels referred to in Article 7 exceeds the allocated effort'. In *Azores v Council*, the CFI interpreted Article 8(1) as meaning that Member States are required to limit the fishing effort of vessels authorized to fish pursuant to Article 3.[291] Indeed, the CFI relied on that interpretation to reach its view (mentioned above) that Article 3 places obligations on the Member States to limit effort irrespective of the entry into force date of the daughter Regulation provided for by Article 11.

Article 8(2) requires Member States to regulate fishing effort 'by monitoring the activity of their fleet and by taking appropriate action if the level of the fishing effort authorised under Article 11 is about to be reached, to ensure that effort does not exceed the set limits'.[292] The reference to the effort level 'authorised under

---

[286] Reg 1954/2003, Art 10.   [287] Reg 1954/2003, Art 7(1).

[288] *Proposal for a Council Regulation on the management of the fishing effort relating to certain Community fishing areas and resources and modifying Regulation (EEC) 2847/93*, COM(2002) 739, 16.12.2002, explanatory memorandum, item A, p 3 and proposed Art 7(1).   [289] Reg 1954/2003, Art 7(2).

[290] Reg 1954/2003, Art 10. See also Commission Regulation (EC) No 2103/2004 of 9 December 2004 concerning the transmission of data on certain fisheries in the western waters and the Baltic Sea, OJ 2004 L365/12, Art 1.   [291] Case T-37/04 *Azores v Council*, para 74.

[292] See also Reg 2103/2004, Art 2.

Article 11' is a reference to the effort limits set subsequently by Regulation 1415/2004 (see below). Thus Article 8(2) relates expressly to the effort levels set by the daughter Regulation provided for by Article 11 whereas, according to the CFI in *Azores v Council*, Article 8(1) relates to the fishing effort of vessels authorized to fish pursuant to Article 3.

Regulation 1415/2004, adopted pursuant to Article 11 of Regulation 1954/2003, sets out, *inter alia*, 'the maximum annual fishing effort for each Member State and for each area and fishery defined in [Article 3 of Regulation 1954/2003]'.[293] It does so on the basis of information received by the Commission from the Member States regarding the assessments of fishing effort under Article 3(1).[294] Overall, the effect of the Regulation is to cap fishing effort for vessels of 15 m overall length or more for each of the three categories of fisheries concerned based on the average annual effort over the reference period 1998 to 2002.[295]

The explanatory memorandum to the Commission's proposal for what is now Regulation 1415/2004 sets out some specific criteria used for calculating the maximum effort levels from the Member States' assessments.[296] However, it is not entirely clear from the Commission's proposal or from Regulation 1415/2004 itself whether the effort levels in the Regulation are based exclusively on the Member States' assessments pursuant to Article 3 of Regulation 1954/2003 or are, alternatively, moderated to some extent by the Commission or the Council.

Some moderation by the Commission is suggested by the statement in the proposal that 'the Commission is now able to present effort ceilings that represent a *reasonable balance* between the previously established effort ceilings and the real fishing activity, during the reference period, of the vessels concerned in the areas covered by the new Western Waters regime' (emphasis added).[297] However, the CFI in *Azores v Council* states, *inter alia*, that:[298]

The aim of [the daughter Regulation provided for by Article 11] is not to establish a limit on the fishing effort which does not follow from other provisions of [Regulation 1954/2003], but to ensure, in accordance with recital 8 in the preamble to [Regulation 1954/2003] . . ., transparency and equity of management and monitoring procedures chosen by all Member States pursuant to their powers to adopt measures seeking to regulate the fishing effort of vessels flying the flag of those States.

This statement by the CFI is consistent with its interpretation, discussed above, of Article 3(1) and Article 8(1) of Regulation 1954/2003. However, it also implies that Regulation 1415/2004 simply codifies a system of effort control that exists anyway by virtue of Articles 3(1), 7, and 8(1). Such a straightforward role for

---

[293] Reg 1415/2004, Art 1.   [294] Reg 1415/2004, recitals (2)–(5).

[295] Reg 1415/2004, recital (5).

[296] *Proposal for a Council Regulation fixing the maximum annual fishing effort for certain fishing areas and fisheries*, COM(2004) 166, 12.3.2004, explanatory memorandum, pp 2–3.

[297] COM(2004) 166, explanatory memorandum, p 2.

[298] Case T-37/04 *Azores v Council*, para 76.

Regulation 1415/2004 leaves unexplained the express reference to what is now Regulation 1415/2004 in Article 8(2) of Regulation 1954/2003 but not in Article 8(1) (see above) and the apparent moderation role for the Commission referred to above.

The maximum effort levels set out in Regulation 1415/2004 are expressed in kilowatt-days, per ICES or CECAF zone, for each of the three fisheries categories in question and for each of nine Member States in total.[299] Regulation 1415/2004 also states that: 'Each Member State shall ensure that the utilisation of fishing effort allocations by area, as defined in [Article 3 of Regulation 1954/2003], will not result in *more time* spent fishing by comparison to fishing effort levels exerted during the reference period.'[300] (Emphasis added.) Thus there is a cap on activity, irrespective of any changes in capacity since the reference period. The effort levels fixed in the Regulation are 'without prejudice to fishing effort limitations fixed under recovery plans or any other management measure under Community law provided that the measure with the lower amount of fishing effort is complied with'.[301]

Article 12 of Regulation 1954/2003 focuses on the link between effort limits and TACs/quotas. It provides for the maximum effort levels set in Regulation 1415/2004 to be adjusted by the Commission in specified ways upon the substantiated request of a Member State, so 'allowing the Member State to take up fully its fishing possibilities, in the case of species subject to TACs, or to pursue fisheries not subject to such limitations'.[302] Furthermore, the effort levels set in Regulation 1415/2004 are to be 'adapted' by Member States in view of any quota exchanges under Article 20(5) of the Basic Regulation or any reallocations and/or deductions under Article 23(4) of the Basic Regulation or under various provisions of the Control Regulation, on the condition that the adaptations are to be notified to the Commission.[303]

The discussion so far has focused on effort limitation for vessels 'equal to or more than 15 metres in length overall'. As noted above, Regulation 1954/2003 also addresses effort management for vessels 'equal to or less than 15 metres in length overall'. Article 4 requires the Member States to: (a) assess fishing effort of such vessels 'globally for each fishery and area or division referred to in Article 3(1) during the [reference] period 1998 to 2002'; and (b) ensure that the fishing effort of the vessels in question is then limited to the assessed level of fishing effort.[304] Thus Article 4 in effect establishes a cap on effort for the smaller vessels operating in Western waters.

Regulation 1954/2003 also deals with effort in a large area 'to the South and West of Ireland [that] has been identified as an area of high concentration of juvenile hake'.[305] Articles 4, 6, 7, and 8 lay down special rules on effort to

[299] Reg 1415/2004, Art 2(1) and Annex I.   [300] Reg 1415/2004, Art 3(1).
[301] Reg 1415/2004, Art 5.   [302] Reg 1954/2003, Art 12(1).
[303] Reg 1954/2003, Art 12(2) and (3).   [304] Reg 1954/2003, Art 4(1) and (3).
[305] Reg 1954/2003, recital (7).

complement 'special restrictions on the use of demersal gear' in place in the area in question,[306] and Regulation 1415/2004 in turn sets out maximum effort levels for certain fisheries in the area.[307] In *Spain v Council*, Spain argued misuse of powers by the Council on the grounds that the real purpose of the area 'was not to protect juvenile hake but to maintain the discrimination against the Spanish fleet in that area'. The Court rejected that submission.[308]

Overall, it can be seen that Regulations 1954/2003 and 1415/2004 jointly serve to establish a fishing effort management regime for Western waters. However, there are some clear gaps in species or fisheries coverage, in that the Regulations only cover: (a) demersal fisheries, excluding those 'covered by' Regulation 2347/2002; (b) fisheries for scallops; and (c) fisheries for edible crab and spider crab. Obvious gaps are demersal fisheries 'covered by' Regulation 2347/2002 (on which, see below) and pelagic species. Furthermore, as noted above, the effort limits in place are irrespective of gear type. In comparison, the Commission's legislative proposal for what became Regulation 1954/2003 did address pelagic species and did provide for effort limits to be established by gear type.[309]

Regulation 2347/2002

Regulation 2347/2002 'applies to Community fishing vessels carrying out fishing activities in ICES . . . sub-areas I to XIV inclusive, and Community waters of CECAF areas 34.1.1, 34.1.2, 34.1.3 and 34.2 which lead to catches of species listed in Annex I' to the Regulation.[310] The area in question is huge, comprising in effect the entire north-east Atlantic (including, *inter alia*, the North Sea, Skagerrak, Kattegat, Channel, and Irish Sea) as well as some zones just to the south and the Baltic Sea.

Regulation 2347/2002 has three annexes. Annex III relates to an aspect of monitoring, control, and surveillance. Annexes I and II define the material scope of the Regulation. Annex I lists twenty-two species and two genera of deep-sea fish. The most significant provisions of the Regulation relate exclusively to Annex I. Annex II comprises twenty-two species, none in common with Annex I.

Article 4(1) requires each Member State to 'calculate the *aggregate power and the aggregate volume* of its vessels which, in any one of the years 1998, 1999 or 2000, have landed more than 10 tonnes of any mixture of the [species listed in Annex I]' (emphasis added), and to notify those values to the Commission. A slightly later reference period is used for those Member States acceding in 2004.[311] The terms 'power' and 'volume', as used in Article 4(1), are measures of vessel capacity,

---

[306] Reg 1954/2003, recital (7).   [307] Reg 1415/2004, Art 2(2) and Annex II.

[308] Case C-442/04 *Spain v Council*, paras 46–51. See also Case C 36/04 *Spain v Council*, AG Opinion, paras 73–81.

[309] COM(2002) 739. Regarding pelagic species, see explanatory memorandum, item C, p 4 and proposed Art 4(1). Regarding gear types, see proposed Annexes I and II.

[310] Reg 2347/2002, Art 1.   [311] Reg 2347/2002, Art 4(3).

rather than fishing effort. In turn, Article 4(2) permits each Member State to issue deep-sea fishing permits to its vessels only if the aggregate power and the aggregate volume of those vessels does not exceed the values calculated under Article 4(1).

Article 3 clarifies that a 'deep-sea fishing permit' is required for a vessel that catches and retains more than 10 tonnes of Annex I species per year to be able to catch and retain on board, tranship, or land any aggregate quantity of the Annex I species in excess of 100 kg in each sea trip.[312] Specific measures may be laid down to take account of 'seasonal or artisanal fisheries'.[313] Such measures have been adopted at the request of Denmark, to avoid discarding of 'unavoidable' by-catches of Annex I species in fisheries targeting other species.[314]

The combined effect of Article 4(1) and (2) is to establish a capacity limit per Member State for the fisheries in question, notwithstanding the title of Article 4 which reads 'Effort restriction' rather than, say, 'Capacity restriction'. The capacity limit has its weaknesses. For example, the reference to 'any one of the years' in the reference period widens the number of vessels to be included.[315] Furthermore, the limit includes vessels taking Annex I species merely as by-catch.[316] The Commission's assessment of the efficacy of the capacity limit is summarized below.

Regulation 2347/2002 also contains various provisions relating to monitoring, control, and surveillance.[317] Amongst these is an obligation on Member States to supply to the Commission (in addition to obligations under the Control Regulation), on a half-yearly basis, 'information about catches of [Annex I] species and fishing effort deployed . . . broken down by quarter of the year, by type of gear, by species, as well as information concerning those in Annex II and by ICES statistical rectangle or CECAF subdivision'.[318]

The capacity management regime for deep-sea fisheries established by Regulation 2347/2002 does not exist in isolation. First, an effort limit for certain deep-sea fisheries exists in the principal annual Regulation (ie Regulation 40/2008, at the time of writing, as well as its three immediate predecessors). This can be illustrated by reference to Regulation 40/2008. Article 8(4) requires Member States to ensure that for 2008 fishing effort by vessels holding deep-sea fishing permits does not exceed 75 per cent of the average effort deployed in 2003 'on trips when deep-sea fishing permits were held and/or deep-sea species, as listed in Annexes I and II to Regulation [2347/2002], were caught'.[319] It is noteworthy that the effort

---

[312] Reg 2347/2002, Art 3(1).   [313] Reg 2347/2002, Art 3(2).

[314] Commission Regulation (EC) No 876/2003 of 21 May 2003 defining specific measures pursuant to Council Regulation (EC) No 2347/2002 concerning catches and landings of deep-sea species for seasonal fisheries by Denmark in the Skagerrak and North Sea, OJ 2003 L126/22, recitals (3)–(5).

[315] COM(2007) 30, section 3.1.3, p 7.   [316] COM(2007) 30, section 3.1.3, pp 6–7.

[317] Reg 2347/2002, Arts 5, 6, 7, 8, and 9.   [318] Reg 2347/2002, Art 9.

[319] The provision adds that: 'This paragraph shall apply only to fishing trips on which more than 100 kg of deep sea species, other than greater silver smelt, were caught.'

limitation in Article 8(4) of Regulation 40/2008 refers to species of both Annexes I and II to Regulation 2347/2002, rather than just Annex I, being caught. The year 2003 was chosen as a reference because it was 'the year in which Regulation 2347/2002 came into force and therefore the first year for which reliable effort data are available'.[320]

Secondly, in addition to effort limitation in the principal annual Regulation, seventeen of the species and genera listed in Annex I to Regulation 2347/2002 are also covered by TACs set by Regulation 2015/2006 (see subsection 2.1 above), which additionally cover four species not found in Annex I. Thirdly, the species listed in Annex II (but not Annex I) to Regulation 2347/2002 fall within the scope of Regulation 1954/2003 (see above).

The Commission has provided a candid critique of management measures for deep-sea species in a report issued in January 2007.[321] In particular, in relation to Regulation 2347/2002, the Commission notes that the capacity ceiling provided for by Article 4 'was intended to limit the expansion of deep-sea fisheries, but in practice has probably had no effect'.[322] The Commission notes that this has in turn 'undermined the effectiveness' of the effort limitation established by the principal annual Regulations referred to above.[323]

2.3 Technical measures

Introduction

Technical measures, whether on their own or as a complement to TACs/quotas and effort limits, are an important means of fisheries conservation. The principal legal basis for their adoption is the Basic Regulation. In particular, Article 4 states that measures to be adopted by the Council for achieving the objectives of the CFP may, in particular, include 'measures for each stock or group of stocks to limit fishing mortality and the environmental impact of fishing activities by . . . [*inter alia*] . . . adopting technical measures'.[324] A list of potential technical measures is then provided, as follows:

(i) measures regarding the structure of fishing gear, the number and size of fishing gear on board, their methods of use and the composition of catches that may be retained on board when fishing with such gear;

(ii) zones and/or periods in which fishing activities are prohibited or restricted including for the protection of spawning and nursery areas;

(iii) minimum size of individuals that may be retained on board and/or landed;

---

[320] COM(2007) 30, section 3.1.3, p 7.   [321] COM(2007) 30.
[322] COM(2007) 30, section 3.1.3, p 6.   [323] COM(2007) 30, section 3.1.3, p 7.
[324] Reg 2371/2002, Art 4(2)(g).

(iv) specific measures to reduce the impact of fishing activities on marine eco-systems and non target species

The list above illustrates the types of measure regarded by the EC as 'technical measures'. It is not entirely clear whether the list is intended to be exhaustive, although subsequent practice by the EC suggests that it is not. It can be seen that Article 4 refers to adoption of technical measures both for fisheries conservation and to limit 'the environmental impact of fishing activities'.

The principal Regulations establishing long-term technical measures in Community waters are: (a) Regulation 850/98,[325] establishing a large number of measures; (b) Regulation 894/97,[326] regarding driftnets; (c) Regulation 1185/2003,[327] on finning of sharks; (d) Regulation 520/2007, regarding highly migratory species; (e) Regulation 812/2004,[328] on cetacean by-catch; (f) Regulation 2187/2005,[329] on the Baltic Sea; and (g) Regulation 1967/2006,[330] on the Mediterranean Sea. These instruments are not necessarily limited in their scope to Community waters. Instead, the geographical scope depends on the instrument in question, as referred to below.

Each of the above Regulations is addressed in this subsection, except Regulation 812/2004 (on cetacean by-catch; see section 6 below), Regulation 2187/2005 (on the Baltic Sea; see section 3 below), and Regulation 1967/2006 (on the Mediterranean Sea; see section 4 below). Some of the above Regulations are supplemented by other detailed or very specific Regulations which are not discussed here.[331] The annual fishing opportunities Regulations, and particularly the principal annual Regulation, are also important in the context of technical measures.

[325] Council Regulation (EC) No 850/98 of 30 March 1998 for the conservation of fishery resources through technical measures for the protection of juveniles of marine organisms, OJ 1998 L125/1, as amended and corrected.
[326] Council Regulation (EC) No 894/97 of 29 April 1997 laying down certain technical measures for the conservation of fishery resources, OJ 1997 L132/1, as amended and corrected.
[327] Council Regulation (EC) No 1185/2003 of 26 June 2003 on the removal of fins of sharks on board vessels, OJ 2003 L167/1.
[328] Council Regulation (EC) No 812/2004 of 26 April 2004 laying down measures concerning incidental catches of cetaceans in fisheries and amending Regulation (EC) No 88/98, OJ 2004 L150/12, as amended and corrected.
[329] Council Regulation (EC) No 2187/2005 of 21 December 2005 for the conservation of fishery resources through technical measures in the Baltic Sea, the Belts and the Sound, amending Regulation (EC) No 1434/98 and repealing Regulation (EC) No 88/98, OJ 2005 L349/1, as amended.
[330] Council Regulation (EC) No 1967/2006 of 21 December 2006 concerning management measures for the sustainable exploitation of fishery resources in the Mediterranean Sea, amending Regulation (EEC) No 2847/93 and repealing Regulation (EC) No 1626/94, OJ 2006 L409/11, as corrected (reissued as a corrected version in OJ 2007 L36/6).
[331] Eg Reg 517/2008, OJ 2008 L151/5; Reg 1922/99, OJ 1999 L238/8; Reg 1434/98, OJ 1998 L191/10, as amended; Reg 1638/87, OJ 1987 L153/7; Reg 954/87, OJ 1987 L90/27; Reg 1899/85, OJ 1985 L179/2; Reg 3440/84, OJ 1984 L318/23, as amended.

Regulation 40/2008 (the principal annual Regulation at the time of writing) will be mentioned in this subsection.

Long-term plans adopted under Articles 5 and 6 of the Basic Regulation may also contain technical measures.[332] In practice, only three such plans refer expressly to such measures, namely: (a) the plan for southern hake and Norway lobster (which, by means of an amendment to Regulation 850/98, establishes gear restrictions in certain locations and periods as well as limits on by-catch of Norway lobster);[333] (b) the plan for bluefin tuna (which establishes, *inter alia*, closed seasons, minimum sizes, and by-catch limits);[334] and (c) the plan for Baltic Sea cod (by means of, *inter alia*, closed seasons and closed areas).[335] Furthermore, some separate Regulations for cod and hake stocks covered by long-term plans establish technical measures for the stocks concerned.[336]

The emergency powers of the Commission under the Basic Regulation and Regulation 850/98, and the delegated powers of the Member States under those two Regulations, are also a basis for the adoption of technical measures in specific circumstances. The Member States' delegated powers are discussed in subsection 2.4 below. The emergency powers of the Commission will be addressed very briefly here. There are two sources of such powers, namely Article 7 of the Basic Regulation and Article 45(1) of Regulation 850/98. In both cases, the Commission has been delegated its powers by the Council. It is important to note that the Commission's emergency powers, despite being described in this subsection on technical measures, may potentially be used to adopt 'measures' in a sense broader than purely technical measures.

The powers under Article 7 of the Basic Regulation apply '[i]f there is evidence of a serious threat to the conservation of living aquatic resources, or to the marine eco-system resulting from fishing activities and requiring immediate action'. The Commission may use its powers at its own initiative or 'at the substantiated request' of a Member State. The adopted 'emergency measures' may last for six months, and may be extended for a further six months. A procedure is established for Member States making requests to the Commission, for the Commission itself, and for Member States unhappy with the Commission's decision. In practice, the emergency powers under Article 7 have been used only

---

[332] Reg 2371/2002, Arts 5(4) and 6(4).   [333] Reg 2166/2005, Art 15.

[334] Reg 1559/2007, *inter alia*, Arts 5, 7, and 9.

[335] Reg 1098/2007, Arts 8 and 9. See also Reg 169/2008.

[336] Council Regulation (EC) No 2549/2000 of 17 November 2000 establishing additional technical measures for the recovery of the stock of cod in the Irish Sea (ICES Division VIIa), OJ 2000 L292/5, as amended; Commission Regulation (EC) No 2056/2001 of 19 October 2001 establishing additional technical measures for the recovery of the stocks of cod in the North Sea and to the west of Scotland, OJ 2001 L277/13; Commission Regulation (EC) No 494/2002 of 19 March 2002 establishing additional technical measures for the recovery of the stock of hake in ICES sub-areas III, IV, V, VI and VII and ICES divisions VIII a, b, d, e, OJ 2002 L77/8.

a few times, namely in relation to Baltic Sea cod,[337] cold-water coral reefs,[338] anchovy,[339] and bluefin tuna.[340]

The powers under Article 45(1) of Regulation 850/98 apply '[w]here the conservation of stocks of marine organisms calls for immediate action'. In contrast to Article 7 of the Basic Regulation, Article 45(1) does not expressly allow for measures to protect the marine eco-system. It leaves unspecified the magnitude of the threat or damage required to trigger use of the powers and it specifies no maximum lifespan for the measures adopted. Measures under Article 45(1) are to be adopted using comitology procedure. The most recent Commission emergency Regulation citing Article 45(1) as its legal basis was adopted by the Commission in March 2002,[341] which pre-dates the adoption of the current Basic Regulation. However, the continuing relevance of Article 45(1), alongside Article 7 of the Basic Regulation, was acknowledged by the Court in July 2004 in the case of *Azores v Council*.[342] A legislative proposal issued in 2008 for a Regulation to replace Regulation 850/98 does not propose any emergency powers for the Commission to replace those in Article 45(1),[343] indicating the Commission's apparent intention to rely on Article 7 of the Basic Regulation for such purposes from the point at which Regulation 850/98 is replaced.

Regulation 850/98

Regulation 850/98 is the primary vehicle for technical measures adopted under the CFP. It does not only address 'the protection of juveniles of marine organisms', despite its title. The Regulation does not apply to all Community waters; for example it does not cover the Baltic Sea, Black Sea, or Mediterranean Sea.[344] The Regulation has been amended several times since its adoption.

The individual technical measures contained in Regulation 850/98 will not be described here because of their detailed nature and the fact that the Regulation is

---

[337] Commission Regulation (EC) No 677/2003 of 14 April 2003 establishing emergency measures for the recovery of the cod stock in the Baltic Sea, OJ 2003 L97/31.

[338] Commission Regulation (EC) No 1475/2003 of 20 August 2003 on the protection of deep-water coral reefs from the effects of trawling in an area north west of Scotland, OJ 2003 L211/14; and Commission Regulation (EC) No 263/2004 of 16 February 2004 extending for six months the application of Regulation (EC) No 1475/2003 on the protection of deep-water coral reefs from the effects of trawling in an area north-west of Scotland, OJ 2004 L46/11.

[339] Commission Regulation (EC) No 1037/2005 of 1 July 2005 establishing emergency measures for the protection and recovery of the anchovy stock in ICES Sub-area VIII, OJ 2005 L171/24; and Commission Regulation (EC) No 1539/2005 of 22 September 2005 extending the emergency measures for the protection and recovery of the anchovy stock in ICES sub-area VIII, OJ 2005 L247/9.

[340] Commission Regulation (EC) No 530/2008 of 12 June 2008 establishing emergency measures as regards purse seiners fishing for bluefin tuna in the Atlantic Ocean, east of longitude 45°W, and in the Mediterranean Sea, OJ 2008 L155/9.   [341] Reg 494/2002.

[342] Case T-37/04 R *Azores v Council*, para 158.

[343] *Proposal for a Council Regulation concerning the conservation of fisheries resources through technical measures*, COM(2008) 324, 4.6.2008.   [344] Reg 850/98, Arts 1 and 2.

due to be replaced (see below). Broadly speaking, its measures relate to gear type, minimum landing size, closed seasons, and closed areas. The Regulation also establishes some emergency powers for the Commission (in Article 45(1)—see above) and some delegated powers for the Member States (on which, see subsection 2.4 below).

A proposal for the replacement of Regulation 850/98 was issued by the Commission in June 2008.[345] The purpose of the new Regulation is to simplify the law and introduce an element of regionalization. The new Regulation will include 'all common permanent measures for all areas [within its scope], ie the guiding principles', whereas measures applicable to particular regions will be implemented through separate Commission Regulations.[346] Some delegated powers for the Member States, replacing those currently in Regulation 850/98 and supplementing those in the Basic Regulation, are proposed (see further subsection 2.4 below).[347]

The Commission, when proposing the new Regulation, noted that: 'The effectiveness of many of the provisions under [Regulation 850/98] has never been evaluated, and those measures have remained in force regardless of their value for conservation.'[348] Thus the proposed Regulation provides for a five-yearly review of the efficiency of technical measures.[349] The Commission also anticipates that 'when new and substantial measures are proposed (such as significant increases in mesh sizes)', it 'will carry out, if the data available allow it, a prior evaluation of their likely effects'.[350]

Regulation 894/97

Regulation 894/97, after several amendments, now deals exclusively with driftnets.[351] With the exception of waters covered by Regulation 2187/2005 (on which, see section 3 below), ie the Baltic Sea,[352] Regulation 894/97 'shall apply in all waters falling within the sovereignty of [sic] jurisdiction of the Member States and, outside those waters shall apply to all Community fishing vessels'.[353]

Article 11(2) states that: 'No vessel may keep on board, or use for fishing, one or more drift nets whose individual or total length is more than 2.5 kilometres.' More specifically, and irrespective of the length of the driftnet(s), Article 11a(1) states that '. . . no vessel may keep on board, or use for fishing, one or more drift-nets intended for the capture of species listed in Annex VIII' to the Regulation, and

---

[345] COM(2008) 324.   [346] COM(2008) 324, explanatory memorandum, p 3.

[347] COM(2008) 324, proposed Arts 16–18.

[348] COM(2008) 324, explanatory memorandum, p 4.

[349] COM(2008) 324, proposed Art 21.

[350] COM(2008) 324, explanatory memorandum, p 4.

[351] On the EC and driftnets, see also Caddell, R, 'The Prohibition of Driftnet Fishing in European Community Waters: Problems, Progress and Prospects' *Journal of International Maritime Law* 13 (2007) 265.   [352] Reg 2187/2005, Art 1 and Annex I.

[353] Reg 894/97, Art 11c.

Article 11a(2) states that '. . . it is prohibited to land species listed in Annex VIII which have been caught in drift-nets'. The Regulation also lays down conditions, including control measures, on the use of driftnets intended for the capture of Annex VIII species.

Annex VIII comprises albacore tuna, bluefin tuna, bigeye tuna, skipjack tuna, Atlantic bonito, yellowfin tuna, blackfin tuna, little tuna (*Euthynnus* spp), southern bluefin tuna, frigate tuna (*Auxis* spp), oceanic sea bream (*Brama rayi*), marlins (*Tetrapturus* spp and *Makaira* spp), sailfish (*Istiophorus* spp), swordfish, saury (*Scomberesox* spp and *Cololabis* spp), dolphinfish (*Coryphoena* spp), certain sharks (bluntnose sixgill shark, basking shark, Alopiidae, Carcharhinidae, Sphymidae, Isuridae, and Lamnidae), and all species of cephalopod. It shares some considerable similarities with the list of highly migratory species in Annex I to the United Nations Convention on the Law of the Sea (see Chapter 3) and with the list in Annex I to Regulation 520/2007 (see below).

Prior to 2007, Regulation 894/97 failed to define the term 'drift-net'. That omission has since been rectified by Regulation 809/2007[354] which introduces a definition as follows: '"Drift net" means: any gillnet held on the sea surface or at a certain distance below it by floating devices, drifting with the current, either independently or with the boat to which it may be attached. It may be equipped with devices aiming to stabilise the net or to limit its drift.'[355] The same definition is introduced by Regulation 809/2007 into Regulation 812/2004 (on cetacean by-catch; see section 6 below) and Regulation 2187/2005 (on the Baltic Sea; see section 3 below).[356] The preamble to Regulation 809/2007 asserts that: 'The establishment of a definition of drift nets does *not* expand the field of application of the restrictions and conditions on the use of drift nets implemented in Community law.'[357] (Emphasis added.)

The provisions on driftnets in Regulation 894/97, or those in its predecessors, have led to several cases before the Court. Two were direct actions by fishing entities and failed on admissibility.[358] Two others, *Mondiet* and *Pilato*, were references for a preliminary ruling, originating from proceedings in France between fishing entities.

In *Mondiet*[359] the Court found nothing to affect the validity of the restrictions on the use of driftnets in Regulation 345/92 (a predecessor to Regulation 894/97). In doing so, it held, *inter alia*, that the restrictions were adopted primarily for

---

[354] Council Regulation (EC) No 809/2007 of 28 June 2007 amending Regulations (EC) No 894/97, (EC) No 812/2004 and (EC) No 2187/2005 as concerns drift nets, OJ 2007 L182/1.

[355] Reg 809/2007, Art 1; Reg 894/97, Art 11(2).   [356] Reg 809/2007, Arts 2 and 3.

[357] Reg 809/2007, recital (5).

[358] Case C-131/92 *Thierry Arnaud and others v Council* [1993] ECR I-2573; Case T-138/98 *Armement Coopératif Artisanal Vendéen and others v Council* [2000] ECR II-341.

[359] Case C-405/92 *Etablissements Armand Mondiet SA v Armement Islais SARL* [1993] ECR I-6133.

fisheries conservation, as opposed to nature conservation, purposes.[360] In *Pilato*[361] the referred questions addressed the validity and interpretation of Article 11a(1) and (2) (see above). However, the Court decided that it was not competent to answer the questions because of the nature of the body in France that referred the questions.

Two further cases relate to France itself. In *France v Council* (not resolved at the time of writing) France 'disputes the definition of "drift net" adopted by the Council in Regulation No 809/2007 to the extent that it includes stabilised nets such as the "thonaille" (a tuna gillnet) among such drift nets', alleging failure by the Council to give reasons and breach of the principles of proportionality and non-discrimination.[362] France sought interim measures in that case, but failed.[363] In *Commission v France* (also not resolved at the time of writing) the Commission is seeking a declaration that France failed to fulfil its obligations regarding driftnets.[364]

Regulation 1185/2003

Regulation 1185/2003 seeks to address so-called 'shark finning', whereby 'the fins are removed from sharks, with the remainder of the shark being discarded at sea'.[365] Finning has arisen in response to high demand for shark fins, particularly for shark fin soup in Asia, in contrast to much lower demand for shark meat. It has the potential to 'contribute to the excessive mortality of sharks to such an extent that many stocks of sharks are depleted, and their future sustainability may be endangered'.[366]

The Commission seems to imply that Regulation 1185/2003 is a response to the duty to integrate environmental protection requirements into the CFP.[367] However, the Regulation is described here rather than below in section 6, on environmental protection, since sharks are increasingly a fisheries resource that is actively targeted rather than being a part of the wider environment that is by-caught. The Commission also considers the Regulation to form 'part of the development and implementation . . . of a more comprehensive [EC] management plan for the conservation and sustainable use of sharks, in line with the FAO Code of Conduct for Responsible Fisheries and the FAO International Plan of Action for sharks' (on which, see Chapter 3).[368]

---

[360] Case C-405/92, para 24.

[361] Case C-109/07 *Jonathan Pilato v Jean-Claude Bourgault*, Order of 14 May 2008.

[362] Case C-479/07 *France v Council*, OJ 2007 C297/32.

[363] Case C-479/07 R *France v Council*, Order of 28 February 2008 (not available in English).

[364] Case C-556/07 *Commission v France*, OJ 2008 C37/20.   [365] Reg 1185/2003, recital (5).

[366] Reg 1185/2003, recital (5).

[367] *Proposal for a Council Regulation on the removal of fins of sharks on board vessels*, COM(2002) 449, 05.08.2002, explanatory memorandum, last para.

[368] COM(2002) 449, explanatory memorandum, last para. In late 2007, the Commission issued a *Consultation on an EU Action Plan for Sharks*.

The Regulation applies to waters under the sovereignty or jurisdiction of the Member States and, in 'other maritime waters', to 'vessels flying the flag or registered in Member States'.[369] It entails: (a) a prohibition (subject to a derogation—see below) on the removal of shark fins on board vessels and on their retention on board, transhipment, or landing; and (b) a prohibition on the purchase, offer for sale, or sale of shark fins which have been removed on board, retained on board, transhipped, or landed in contravention of the Regulation.[370] The term 'shark' is defined as 'any fish of the taxon Elasmobranchii',[371] which, put briefly, means sharks, skates, and rays. However, the term 'shark fins' excludes raywings.[372]

As noted above, the prohibition on the removal and retention on board of shark fins, as well as on their transhipment or landing, is subject to a derogation.[373] The Commission justifies this derogation on the basis that 'for certain fisheries there could be a practical need to remove shark fins on board and for separate on-board processing of fins and bodies, even when the carcass is retained (e.g. for freezer vessels that stay for a long period at sea)',[374] although contrary views exist in this regard (see below).

Various conditions must be met for the derogation to apply. Amongst these are the requirements that: (a) '[t]he weight of the fins kept . . . shall never exceed the theoretical weight of the fins that would correspond to the remaining parts of the shark retained on board, transhipped or landed'; and (b) '[i]n no case shall the theoretical weight of the fins exceed 5% of the live weight of the shark catch'.[375] There has been much debate over whether the 5 per cent figure is too high or too low, depending on the particular standpoint of the protagonists (which include environmental NGOs on the one hand and fishing interests on the other).[376]

In a 2005 report on the implementation of the Regulation, the Commission concluded that 'the Regulation appears to be achieving its general objectives' and was content with the continued use of the 5 per cent figure. The report considered that no amendment was necessary at the time.[377] However, a Commission report issued a few days earlier had earmarked the Regulation as one of several on technical measures that needed 'to be simplified'.[378]

---

[369] Reg 1185/2003, Art 1.   [370] Reg 1185/2003, Art 3(1) and (2).

[371] Reg 1185/2003, Art 2(2).   [372] Reg 1185/2003, Art 2(1).

[373] Reg 1185/2003, Art 4.

[374] *Report from the Commission to the Council and the European Parliament on the operation of Council Regulation (EC) No 1185/2003 on the removal of fins of sharks on board vessels*, COM(2005) 700, 23.12.2005, section 1, p 3.   [375] Reg 1185/2003, Art 4(4) and (5).

[376] See, for example, Frentzel-Beyme, B, *El Anzuelo*, Vol 16, 2006, 8–9 (available on the website of the Institute for European Environmental Policy (IEEP)).

[377] COM(2005) 700, section 7, pp 9 and 10.

[378] *Communication from the Commission to the Council and the European Parliament: 2006–08 Action Plan for simplifying and improving the common fisheries policy*, COM(2005) 647, 8.12.2005, Annex, Sheet 2, p 11.

Regulation 520/2007

Regulation 520/2007 'lays down technical conservation measures applicable to the capture and landing of certain stocks of highly migratory species as referred to in Annex I [to the Regulation] and to the capture of by-catches'.[379]

The list in Annex I is the same as the list in Annex VIII to Regulation 894/97 (see above), except that: (a) regarding oceanic sea bream it refers to Bramidae in general rather than just *Brama rayi*; (b) regarding dolphinfish, it refers to 'Dolphinfish; common dolphinfish: *Coryphaena hippurus*; *Coryphaena equiselis*', rather than *Coryphoena* spp; (c) regarding sharks, it includes a specific reference to the whale shark; (d) it omits any reference to cephalopods; and (e) it includes the entry 'Cetaceans (whales and porpoises): *Physeteridae*; *Balenidae*; *Eschrichtiidae*; *Monodontidae*; *Ziphiidae*; *Delphinidae*'.

In general, the Regulation applies to Community fishing vessels.[380] Different parts of the Regulation apply to different numbered areas of the world's oceans. Areas 3 and 4 relate to parts of the Pacific Ocean and do not cover any Community waters. In contrast, Area 1 includes all waters of the Atlantic Ocean and adjacent seas as covered by the 1966 International Convention for the Conservation of Atlantic Tunas, and Area 2 covers all waters of the Indian Ocean as covered by the 1993 Agreement for the Establishment of the Indian Ocean Tuna Commission (hence encompassing the waters of Réunion, one of the outermost regions).[381] For each of Areas 1 and 2, the Regulation sets out a variety of technical measures, relating to target catch and/or by-catch.[382]

Regulation 40/2008

Regulation 40/2008 has already been described in subsections 2.1 and 2.2 above in respect of its provisions on fishing opportunities. However, the Regulation, in common with its recent predecessors, also contains some technical measures of a transitional nature. The large majority of those are set out in an annex entitled 'Transitional Technical and Control Measures'.[383] Some such measures are used in order to provide protection in the short-term, pending Council agreement on longer-term measures. An example of that approach is the restriction on the use of gillnets, entangling nets, and trammel nets in certain areas of the north-east Atlantic.[384] The corresponding recital in the preamble states, *inter alia*, that 'transitional measures to allow these fisheries to take place under certain conditions should be implemented until more permanent measures are adopted'.[385]

The Commission stated in June 2007 that '[t]he number of technical measures included in the annual "fishing opportunities" regulations will be reduced by

---

[379] Reg 520/2007, Art 1.   [380] Reg 520/2007, Art 2.

[381] Reg 520/2007, Art 4. On these two treaties, see further Chapter 5.

[382] See also Reg 520/2007, Art 29, which is general in application rather than being related to any of the Areas 1–4.   [383] Reg 40/2008, Arts 13 and 19 and Annex III.

[384] Reg 40/2008, Annex III, para 8.   [385] Reg 40/2008, recital (25).

moving measures to three other regulations', including, *inter alia*, the successor to Regulation 850/98 (on which, see above).[386] Subsequently the Commission stated that the use of Commission Regulations to be made under the successor to Regulation 850/98 'is intended to meet the concern of Member States to reduce or eliminate interim technical measures from the annual TAC and quota regulation, while taking account of the fact that the application of technical measures is very often a matter of urgency'.[387]

2.4 Member States' delegated powers

Introduction

As was explained in section 1 above, the EC has exclusive competence to make rules regarding fisheries conservation in Community waters. However, certain Council Regulations delegate powers back to the Member States to adopt fisheries conservation measures. (These are in addition to the powers provided to the Member States by Article 20(3) and (5) of the Basic Regulation to manage their fishing opportunities (on which, see subsection 2.1 above) and by Annex IIA to Regulation 40/2008 regarding the voluntary kilowatt-days system and the rewards for involvement in discard reduction plans and the cod avoidance reference fleet programme (on which, see subsection 2.2 above).)

The principal Regulations delegating powers to the Member States are the Basic Regulation, Regulation 850/98 (on technical measures) and, regarding the Baltic Sea and Mediterranean Sea respectively, Regulations 2187/2005 and 1967/2006. The powers provided vary depending on the Regulation in question. The powers delegated under the Basic Regulation and Regulation 850/98 are described below; those in Regulation 2187/2005 and 1967/2006 are described in sections 3 and 4 below, respectively.

Basic Regulation

In the Basic Regulation, the Member States' delegated powers are set out in Articles 8, 9, and 10. Under Article 10, 'Member States may take measures for the conservation and management of stocks in waters under their sovereignty or jurisdiction' in respect of: (a) fishing vessels flying the flag of the Member State concerned and registered in the Community; or (b) persons established in the Member State concerned (in the case of fishing activities which are not conducted by a fishing vessel). Such measures must be compatible with the objectives of the CFP and no less stringent than existing EC legislation.

The reference in Article 10 to 'waters under *their* sovereignty or jurisdiction' (emphasis added) is a little confusing. The term 'sovereignty or jurisdiction', as

---

[386] COM(2007) 295, section 4, p 11.
[387] COM(2008) 324, explanatory memorandum, p 4. See also COM(2008) 331, section 14, p 11.

applied to waters, means internal waters, territorial sea, and exclusive economic zone (EEZ) or exclusive fishing zone (EFZ) (and potentially the continental shelf too, subject to the meaning of 'waters'—see Chapter 2). The reference to Member States in the plural potentially leaves scope to argue that Article 10 could be used by a Member State to apply measures to its own-flag vessels irrespective of whether they are operating in its own waters or in the waters of other Member States. However, in *Pansard*, a similar formulation used in Regulation 3760/92 (the predecessor to the current Basic Regulation) was held by the Court to mean only the waters of the Member State adopting the measure.[388] That implies the same would be held in respect of Article 10 of the Basic Regulation.

Article 10 may be contrasted with Articles 8 and 9 of the Basic Regulation (see below) in two important respects. First, it may not be used to adopt measures applying to fishing vessels flying the flag of other Member States. Secondly, it does not expressly provide for measures to be taken for the purposes of protection of the marine ecosystem. The authors have been unable to ascertain whether the failure of Article 10 expressly to apply to marine ecosystems was an oversight on the part of those drafting the Regulation or was intentional.

Under Article 9 of the Basic Regulation, a Member State may take 'measures for the conservation and management of fisheries resources and to minimise the effect of fishing on the conservation of marine eco-systems' but only: (a) 'within 12 nautical miles of its baselines'; (b) if the measures are non-discriminatory; (c) if the EC 'has not adopted measures addressing conservation and management specifically for this area'; (d) if the measures are compatible with the objectives of the CFP; and (e) if the measures are no less stringent than existing EC legislation.[389]

The reference in Article 9 to 'within 12 nautical miles of its baselines' means that a Member State can use Article 9 to adopt the measures in question for fisheries resources and marine ecosystems in its internal waters, its territorial sea and, in cases where the territorial sea is less than 12 nm in breadth, that part of its EEZ or EFZ lying within 12 nm from the baseline.

Measures adopted under Article 9 may include those 'liable to affect the vessels of another Member State'.[390] However, such measures may be adopted 'only after the Commission, the Member State and the Regional Advisory Councils concerned have been consulted on a draft of the measures accompanied by an explanatory memorandum'[391] and are subject to the procedure laid down in Article 8(3)–(6) of the Basic Regulation.[392] The latter reads as follows:

3. The Member States and Regional Advisory Councils concerned may submit their written comments to the Commission within five working days of the date of notification.

---

[388] Case C-265/01 *Criminal Proceedings against Annie Pansard and others* [2003] ECR I-683, para 36.
[389] Reg 2371/2002, Art 9(1), 1st para.   [390] Reg 2371/2002 Art 9(1), 2nd para.
[391] Reg 2371/2002, Art 9(1), 2nd para.   [392] Reg 2371/2002, Art 9(2).

The Commission shall confirm, cancel or amend the measure within 15 working days of the date of notification.

4. The Commission decision shall be notified to the Member States concerned. It shall be published in the *Official Journal of the European Communities*.

5. The Member States concerned may refer the Commission decision to the Council within 10 working days of notification of the decision.

6. The Council, acting by qualified majority, may take a different decision within one month of the date of receipt of the referral.

Under Article 8 of the Basic Regulation, a Member State may take 'emergency measures': (a) '[i]f there is evidence of a serious and unforeseen threat to the conservation of living aquatic resources, or to the marine ecosystem resulting from fishing activities, in waters falling under the sovereignty or jurisdiction of [that] Member State'; and (b) 'where any undue delay would result in damage that would be difficult to repair'.[393] In principle, the measures may have a duration of up to three months.[394] The term 'sovereignty or jurisdiction' has the same meaning as explained above in relation to Article 10.

Measures under Article 8 may potentially apply to own-flagged vessels or vessels of another Member State. In both cases, the same procedure must be followed. First, 'Member States intending to take emergency measures shall notify their intention to the Commission, the other Member States and the Regional Advisory Councils concerned by sending a draft of those measures, together with an explanatory memorandum, before adopting them'.[395] Secondly, the procedure laid down in Article 8(3)–(6) must be followed (see above). The requirement to notify an 'intention' and the reference to 'sending a draft' in Article 8(1) suggest that the measure should not be allowed by the Member State to take effect until the Commission has reached its decision.

It is quite hard to ascertain how often the delegated powers referred to above have been used in practice. That is particularly the case regarding the powers under Articles 10 and 9 as applied to own-flag vessels, because use of those powers does not necessarily entail a Commission Decision. Regarding application of the powers under Articles 9 and 8 to foreign-flagged vessels, and the application of Article 8 powers to own-flag vessels, a Commission Decision is involved, pursuant to the procedure set out in Article 8(3)–(6). Under Article 8(4), any such Decision is to be published in the *Official Journal*. At the time of writing, the authors were aware of only two instances where the Commission had adopted a Decision pursuant to the procedure under Article 8(3)–(6).

The first relates to the UK. In January 2005, the UK consulted the Commission pursuant to Article 8(3) regarding a proposed measure under Article 9. The proposal concerned 'the extension of a domestic ban on pair trawling for bass within the 12 miles limit off the south-west coast of England to vessels of other Member

---

[393] Reg 2371/2002, Art 8(1).   [394] Reg 2371/2002, Art 8(1).

[395] Reg 2371/2002, Art 8(2).

States having fishing access to this area' for the purpose of reducing dolphin by-catch.[396] In its Decision, the Commission did not systematically consider whether the proposed measure was non-discriminatory, compatible with the objectives of the CFP, and no less stringent than existing EC legislation (all of which are conditions expressly set out in Article 9 itself).

Instead, the Commission focused on the scientific justification for the measure. In that regard, it concluded that: 'Although pursuant to Article 9 of [the Basic Regulation] a Member State may take measures in order to minimise the impact of fishing activities on marine ecosystems, according to the scientific information available the proposed measure is not likely to contribute to that objective.'[397] Thus the Commission considered that, on the basis of the available scientific information, the UK's proposed measure was not likely to contribute to the objective of minimizing dolphin mortality. That consideration seems to have been a significant factor in the Commission's ultimate decision to reject the proposal.

The second instance relates to the Netherlands. In February 2008 the Netherlands designated the Voordelta, a coastal area, as a 'special area of conservation' under the EC Habitats Directive (see further section 6 below). However, following the construction of the 'Massvlakte 2' harbour facilities in the Voordelta area, the Dutch government needed to adopt compensatory measures under Article 6(4) of the Habitats Directive. The compensatory measures necessitated the restriction of fishing activities, including the activities of vessels flagged to Member States other than the Netherlands. The Dutch government, in seeking to use Article 9 for the above purpose, applied to the Commission in May 2008 in respect of the measures affecting foreign-flagged vessels. The Commission confirmed the measures in question.[398] At the time of its confirmatory Decision, the Commission stated that: 'This is the *first time* a Member State has sought the Commission's assistance in protecting *marine habitats and species* within their own 12 nautical miles by using Article 9 of the Basic Regulation . . .'[399] (Emphasis added.) In fact, that statement is incorrect because the UK's request referred to above related to the use of Article 9 to protect marine species (dolphins in that case).

Regulation 850/98

In Regulation 850/98, the Member States' delegated powers are set out in Articles 45(2)–(3) and 46. As will be seen, these powers have similarities with those in

---

[396] Commission Decision 2005/322/EC of 26 February 2005 on the request presented by the United Kingdom pursuant to Article 9 of Council Regulation (EC) No 2371/2002 on the conservation and sustainable exploitation of fisheries resources under the Common Fisheries Policy, OJ 2005 L104/37, recital (1).   [397] Dec 2005/322, recital (6). See also recital (7).

[398] The Commission's Decision in this instance was adopted on 11 June 2008. However, the Decision had not been published in the *Official Journal* by the end of November 2008.

[399] Commission press release, 12 June 2008: 'Commission acts to protect precious habitat on the Dutch North Sea coast' (available on the website of DG Mare).

Articles 8 and 10, respectively, of the Basic Regulation. Despite that similarity, Articles 45 and 46 continue to be a valid source of delegated powers.

The legislative proposal for what became the Basic Regulation states that the Commission's intention was for Article 8 of the Basic Regulation to replace Article 45(2) of Regulation 850/98.[400] However, that replacement did not happen. Indeed, the ongoing validity of the power under Article 45 was confirmed by the Court in the interim measures case in *Azores v Council*, in which the President of the CFI noted the existence of the Member States' powers under Article 45.[401] Article 46 of Regulation 850/98 was 'redrafted to provide greater clarity with regard to its applicability', and hence in effect re-confirmed, in 2000.[402] Article 46 in its re-drafted form was referred to and relied upon by the Court in *Pansard*.[403]

A legislative proposal issued in 2008 for a Regulation to replace Regulation 850/98 proposes some delegated powers for the Member States, replacing those currently in Regulation 850/98 and supplementing those in the Basic Regulation. These would enable emergency conservation measures (albeit very short-lived) and, in respect of own-flag vessels, technical measures.[404] In 2006 the European Parliament urged the Commission to 'proceed cautiously' with any extension to the powers provided by Article 9 of the Basic Regulation when considering a successor to Regulation 850/98, so as to avoid 'the emergence of discriminatory conditions in the Member States concerned'.[405] There are some significant differences between the proposed powers and those already in the Basic Regulation, but these differences will not be discussed further here.

The geographical scope of Regulation 850/98 is more limited than that of the Basic Regulation, which may mean that the area in which its delegated powers can be exercised is correspondingly limited. Article 1 states that: 'This Regulation, laying down technical conservation measures, shall apply to the taking and landing of fishery resources occurring in the maritime waters under the sovereignty or jurisdiction of the Member States and situated in one of the regions specified in Article 2, except as otherwise provided in Articles 26 and 33.'

That wording is rather unclear in that Article 1 does not simply state '[t]his Regulation shall . . .'. Instead, it states '[t]his Regulation, *laying down technical*

---

[400] *Proposal for a Council Regulation on the conservation and sustainable exploitation of fisheries resources under the Common Fisheries Policy*, COM(2002) 185, 28.5.2002, OJ 2002 C203E/284, explanatory memorandum, p 4.   [401] Case T-37/04 R *Azores v Council*, paras 158, 159, and 183.

[402] Council Regulation (EC) No 1298/2000 of 8 June 2000 amending for the fifth time Regulation (EC) No 850/98 for the conservation of fishery resources through technical measures for the protection of juveniles of marine organisms, OJ 2000 L148/1, recital (3) and Art 1(3).

[403] Case C-265/01 *Pansard*, paras 12, 13, and 35.

[404] COM(2008) 324, proposed Arts 16 and 17. See also proposed Art 18.

[405] European Parliament resolution on the 2006–2008 Action Plan for simplifying and improving the Common Fisheries Policy (2006/2053(INI)), P6_TA(2006)0342, 6 September 2006, para 16. cf European Parliament resolution of 31 January 2008 on a policy to reduce unwanted by-catches and eliminate discards in European fisheries (2007/2112(INI)), P6_TA(2008)0034, para 37.

conservation measures, shall . . .' (emphasis added). Thus it could be argued that the limited geographical scope described in Article 1, which excludes the Baltic Sea, Black Sea, and Mediterranean Sea, is only applicable to the extent that Regulation 850/98 itself actually lays down technical measures and that otherwise the Regulation applies more generally.

On that basis, it would be arguable that the delegated powers set out in Articles 46 and 45 apply to the Baltic Sea, Black Sea, and Mediterranean Sea. However, that possibility is rendered less likely by the fact that Regulations pre-dating Regulation 850/98 relating to the Baltic Sea and Mediterranean Sea (Regulations 88/98 and 1626/94, respectively—both now repealed) themselves provided delegated powers to Member States that were left unaffected by Regulation 850/98,[406] thus suggesting that Regulation 850/98 was intended to provide delegated powers only in respect of geographical areas provided for in Article 1.

Under Article 46(1) of Regulation 850/98, 'Member States may take measures for the conservation and management of stocks' either (a) 'in the case of strictly local stocks which are of interest solely to the Member State concerned' or (b) 'in the form of conditions or detailed arrangements designed to limit catches by technical measures', so long as such measures supplement those laid down in CFP legislation or go beyond the minimum requirements in CFP legislation.

As with Article 10 of the Basic Regulation, the measures may only relate to: (a) fishing vessels flying the flag of the Member State concerned and registered in the Community; or (b) persons established in the Member State concerned (in the case of fishing activities which are not conducted by a fishing vessel). Thus Article 46(1) may not be used to adopt measures applying to fishing vessels flying the flag of other Member States. Also in common with Article 10, Article 46(1) does not expressly provide for measures to be taken for the purposes of protection of the marine ecosystem.

In one sense, Article 46(1) is broader than Article 10 of the Basic Regulation because it specifies no limit to its geographical scope for the adoption of technical measures. In *Pansard*,[407] the Court appeared to interpret Article 46(1), along with the predecessor to Article 10 of the Basic Regulation, as meaning that a Member State can only adopt fisheries conservation measures in respect of its own waters. However, that interpretation seems questionable in respect of Article 46(1). In another sense, Article 46(1) is narrower than Article 10 of the Basic Regulation in that it limits the measures that may be taken to technical measures or those relating to 'strictly local stocks which are of interest solely to the Member State concerned'.

---

[406] Council Regulation (EC) No 88/98 of 18 December 1997 laying down certain technical measures for the conservation of fishery resources in the waters of the Baltic Sea, the Belts and the Sound, OJ 1998 L9/1, as amended and corrected, Art 13 (equivalent in substance to Art 46 of Reg 850/98); Council Regulation (EC) No 1626/94 of 27 June 1994 laying down certain technical measures for the conservation of fishery resources in the Mediterranean, OJ 1994 L171/1, as amended, *inter alia*, Arts 1, 3(1) and (2), 4, and 5 (which provided broad delegated powers).

[407] Case C-265/01 *Pansard*, para 36.

The procedure for adoption of such measures is set out in Article 46(2)–(5). In particular, with regard to a Member State's 'plans to introduce or amend national technical measures', the Commission has the power to find that a planned measure does not comply with the provisions of Article 46(1) whereupon 'the Member State concerned may not bring it into force without making the necessary amendments thereto'.

Under Article 45(2) of Regulation 850/98, a Member State 'may take appropriate non-discriminatory conservation measures in respect of the waters under its jurisdiction' in cases '[w]here the conservation of certain species or fishing grounds is seriously threatened, and where any delay would result in damage which would be difficult to repair'. Thus Article 45(2) provides a power to adopt emergency measures. In contrast to Article 8 of the Basic Regulation, it contains no requirement for the threat to be 'unforeseen' but it does not expressly provide for measures to be taken for the purposes of protection of the marine ecosystem.

The procedure for adoption of emergency measures under Article 45(2) is set out in Article 45(3). Measures may be adopted without consultation with the Commission, but must be notified to the Commission immediately thereafter. Within ten working days of receipt of the notification, the Commission 'shall confirm such measures, or require their cancellation or amendment'. The Commission's decision may be referred to the Council by a Member State within ten working days of receiving notification of the decision, which may adopt a different decision within one month. Therefore, in practice, the duration of emergency measures adopted pursuant to Article 45(3) may potentially be rather short-lived, subject to the will of the Commission, one or more Member States, or the Council.

In 2008 the Commission issued a document entitled *Fisheries Measures for Marine Natura 2000 Sites* (see further section 6 below). Some criticism of this document is merited in respect of how it describes the delegated powers of the Member States. The document refers to Article 9 of the Basic Regulation as being relevant where a Natura 2000 site is located within 12 nm of the baseline. However, in respect of sites located beyond 12 nm (and indeed sites within 12 nm), it fails to mention Article 8 of the Basic Regulation and Article 26 of Regulation 2187/2005 (regarding the Baltic Sea—see section 3 below). Both Articles 8 and 26 do indeed have their shortcomings, but both expressly apply to protection of the marine ecosystem and should not have been ignored by the Commission in the context of its guidance on protection of Natura 2000 sites.

2.5 Access to fishing grounds

The access of fishing vessels to fishing grounds has been a major concern of the CFP since its inception. The very first CFP Regulation, Regulation 2141/70,[408]

---

[408] Council Regulation (EEC) No 2141/70 of 20 October 1970 laying down a common structural policy for the fishing industry, OJ S Ed 1970 (III), 703.

dealt with the matter, laying down what has become known as the 'equal access principle'. As formulated in Article 2(1) of Regulation 2141/70, the principle was as follows:

Rules applied by each Member State in respect of fishing in the maritime waters coming under its sovereignty or within its jurisdiction shall not lead to differences in treatment of other Member States.

Member States shall ensure in particular equal conditions of access to and use of the fishing grounds situated in the waters referred to in the preceding sub-paragraph for all fishing vessels flying the flag of a Member State and registered in Community territory.

The equal access principle is an application of, and underpinned by, one of the central principles of EC law, that there shall be no discrimination between nationals of EC Member States on the grounds of nationality.[409] As was seen in Chapter 1, the principle was very controversial in the early years of the CFP, especially at the time of the EC's first enlargement in 1973. In 1976 Regulation 2141/70 was repealed and replaced by Regulation 101/76,[410] Article 2(1) of which contained an identical provision to Article 2(1) of Regulation 2141/70. Regulation 101/76 was in turn repealed and partially replaced by the current Basic Regulation, which had the result that for the first time the equal access principle was included in a basic Regulation.

Article 17(1) of the Basic Regulation sets out the equal access principle in a somewhat different formulation to the earlier Regulations. It provides that 'Community fishing vessels shall have equal access to waters and resources in all Community waters other than those referred to in paragraph 2, subject to the measures adopted under Chapter II'. This last phrase embraces all the various conservation and management measures that the Council may adopt under that Chapter, including, *inter alia*, recovery plans, management plans, TACs (but not quotas), effort limitation measures, and technical conservation measures.

As just seen, Article 17(1) of the Basic Regulation stipulates that the equal access principle does not apply to the waters referred to in Article 17(2). The latter provides:

In the waters up to 12 nautical miles from baselines under their sovereignty or jurisdiction, Member States shall be authorised from 1 January 2003 to 31 December 2012 to restrict fishing to fishing vessels that traditionally fish in those waters from ports on the adjacent coast, without prejudice to the arrangements for Community fishing vessels flying the flag of other Member States under existing neighbourhood relations between Member States and the arrangements contained in Annex I, fixing for each Member State the geographical zones within the coastal bands of other Member States where fishing activities are pursued and the species concerned.

---

[409] Art 12 EC. For a detailed theoretical exploration of the equal access principle, see Churchill, *EEC Fisheries Law*, 122–33.

[410] Council Regulation (EEC) No 101/76 of 19 January 1976 laying down a common structural policy for the fishing industry, OJ 1976 L20/19.

A similar derogation to the equal access principle was originally introduced by Articles 100 and 101 of the 1972 Act of Accession to meet the concerns of the new Member States (Denmark, Ireland, and the UK) over the unbridled application of the equal access principle to their then 12 nm fishing zones. That derogation lasted ten years, until the end of 1982, when it was extended for a further ten-year period by the 1983 Basic Regulation,[411] and then extended again for ten years (until the end of 2002) by the 1992 Basic Regulation.[412]

Article 17(2) of the current Basic Regulation is not very clearly drafted. In particular, it is not obvious what is meant by the phrase 'fishing vessels that traditionally fish in those waters from ports on the adjacent coast', in relation to which fishing within 12 nm of the baselines is restricted. The equivalent phrase in the pre-2002 legislation was 'vessels which fish traditionally in those waters and which operate from ports in that geographical coastal area'.[413] The phrase 'that geographical coastal area' was criticized for its vagueness and uncertainty, in particular as to whether fishing in the waters referred to was reserved to *all* vessels from the Member State in which that 'geographical coastal area' was situated (as was argued by some Member States and commentators), or whether, in any particular locality, fishing was reserved to vessels *only* from that locality and not from other regions of that Member State.[414] Some observations by the Court in *Commission v United Kingdom* suggest that the second interpretation is correct,[415] and the formulation in Article 17(2) of the Basic Regulation also supports that view. Another matter of uncertainty is whether an 'adjacent coast' is limited to the coast of a single Member State, or whether it can stretch across the coasts of two (or more) Member States: for example, could the Dutch, German, and Danish coasts off which the Friesian Islands lie be considered as a single stretch of 'adjacent coast' for the purposes of Article 17(2)? Furthermore, what is meant by 'traditionally' in the phrase, 'fishing vessels that traditionally fish in those waters from ports on the adjacent coast'? How long does a vessel have to have fished in the waters concerned before it can be said to have done so 'traditionally'? Moreover, does an individual vessel have to show traditional fishing, or is it sufficient if a category of vessels to which an individual vessel belongs can point to traditional fishing? For example, would it be sufficient for a vessel from a Cornish port fishing for lobsters to show that lobster fishermen from Cornish ports have traditionally fished for lobsters within 12 nm of the baselines around Cornwall?

Apart from 'fishing vessels that traditionally fish in those waters from ports on the adjacent coast', Article 17(2) of the Basic Regulation provides that vessels from other Member States may also fish in the waters concerned if they have a right to do so under 'existing neighbourhood relations between Member States' or under

---

[411] Council Regulation (EEC) No 170/83 of 25 January 1983 establishing a Community system for the conservation and management of fishery resources, OJ 1983 L24/1, as amended and corrected, Art 6.   [412] Reg 3760/92, Art 6.

[413] 1972 Act of Accession, Art 100(1).   [414] See Churchill, *EEC Fisheries Law*, 135–6.

[415] Case C-146/89 *Commission v United Kingdom* [1991] ECR I-3533, para 42.

Annex I to the Basic Regulation. It is not clear what is covered by 'existing neighbourhood relations between Member States'. Presumably it refers to existing agreements or arrangements between two (or occasionally more) Member States under which fishermen from one State may fish in the waters of the other: it may, in particular, relate to fishing in border regions.[416] Annex I to the Basic Regulation sets out, by Member State, those stretches of its coastal waters where vessels from certain other Member States may fish and the species that may be taken. Those arrangements are based on, but are not always identical to, the historic rights that vessels of States parties to the 1964 European Fisheries Convention[417] were accorded in each other's then 12 nm fishing zones, as set out in bilateral treaties and national legislation implementing that Convention. In *Spain v Council* Spain challenged the validity of that part of Annex I setting out the rights to fish that it had been granted in France's coastal waters on the grounds, *inter alia*, that it had been discriminated against. The Court rejected that challenge, pointing out that the aim of Article 17(2) and Annex I to the Basic Regulation was to preserve traditional fishing activities.[418] No additions have been made to Annex I since the Basic Regulation was adopted, which means that any State that has become a member of the EC since 2002 has no rights of access to the waters within 12 nm of the baselines of other Member States and *vice versa*, unless there are rights of access under 'existing neighbourhood relations' or unless a Member State does not establish the access restrictions to which it is entitled under Article 17(2).

Member States are not obliged to establish the restrictions on access referred to in Article 17(2) of the Basic Regulation, but most have done so. One issue that has arisen in the practice of States relating to Article 17(2) and its forerunners is that of the baselines from which the 12 nm limit is measured. In *Commission v United Kingdom* the Court held that the baselines within 12 nm of which fishing was restricted under Article 100 of the Act of Accession, as continued by Article 6 of Regulation 170/83 (a forerunner of Article 17(2) of the current Basic Regulation, as mentioned above), were those that were operative at the time when Regulation 170/83 was adopted. If a Member State subsequently changed the baselines from which it measured the outer limits of its maritime zones (as the UK had done in 1987, adopting new baselines further seawards off part of its coast to reflect changes in international law), the 12 nm limit nevertheless continued to be measured from the baselines in force in 1983.[419] Since the Court gave its judgment, Regulation

---

[416] An example of such an agreement might be the 1958 Agreement between Denmark and the Federal Republic of Germany concerning Common Fishing in the Inner Flensborg Fjord, 684 UNTS 119. The authors have not been able to ascertain whether this Agreement is still in force. Flensborg Fjord forms the border between Denmark and Germany on their Baltic coasts.

[417] 581 UNTS 57.

[418] Case C-91/03 *Spain v Council* [2005] ECR I-2267, especially paras 50–56.

[419] Case C-146/89 *Commission v United Kingdom*, para 59. For an extended discussion of the case, see Katsoufros, T, *Questions de Droit International de Délimitation dans la Jurisprudence de la Cour de Justice des Communautés européennes* (Maastricht: Institut européen d'administration publique, 1994), especially ch 4.

170/83 has been repealed and replaced by Regulation 3760/92, which in turn has been repealed and replaced by the current Basic Regulation. The question today is whether the baselines referred to in Article 17(2) of the Basic Regulation are those that were operative in 2002 when that Regulation was adopted, or whether they remain those in force in 1983. There is much in the language of the Court's judgment, particularly its rejection of the notion of 'ambulatory baselines' (baselines that change from time to time as international law changes) and its view that the baselines existing in 1983 underpin the historic rights of access of non-coastal fishermen,[420] to suggest that the reference to baselines in Article 17(2) is to be construed as being to those baselines that were in force in 1983. If that is so, it raises the question of what the position is in the case of States that have become members of the EC after 1983. If one applies the Court's judgment by analogy but without introducing an element of retroactivity, it would seem that the baselines of those States, for the purposes of Article 17(2), are the baselines that were in force at the time when those States became members of the EC.

The second paragraph of Article 17(2) of the Basic Regulation provides that by the end of 2011, by which time the qualification on the application of the equal access principle to coastal waters will have been in place for almost 40 years, the Commission is to present a report on the arrangements in Article 17(2) to the European Parliament and the Council. The Council shall then decide before the end of 2012 on the provisions that will follow the current arrangements. As things stand at present, it seems likely that the Council will simply extend those arrangements for a further period as no Member State appears to wish to terminate or modify them.

The rationale for the restriction on access to coastal waters, according to the Commission, is the protection of fisheries resources as a result of 'reserving access to small-scale coastal fisheries activities which in general put less pressure on stocks in these zones which often harbour nurseries and to protect the traditional fishing activities of coastal communities, thus helping to maintain their economic and social fabric'.[421] That statement may be correct, but only if in practice the vessels that have access to the coastal waters covered by Article 17(2) of the Basic Regulation engage in 'small-scale' fisheries activities: it would not seem inevitable that that will always be the case.

Article 17 is located in Chapter IV of the Basic Regulation, which is entitled 'Rules on Access to Waters and Resources'. The only other substantive provision in Chapter IV apart from Article 17 and Article 20 (which deals with allocation of fishing opportunities and is discussed in subsection 2.1 above) is Article 18, which is concerned with fishing in an area known as the 'Shetland Box'. A similar provision to Article 18 was included in the two previous basic Regulations.[422]

---

[420] Case C-146/89 *Commission v United Kingdom*, paras 22–24, 28–30, and 34–37.

[421] COM(2001) 135, para 5.1.4.2, in respect of the waters between 6 and 12 nm from the baselines. That rationale is broadly repeated in recital (14) of the Basic Regulation, in respect of waters within 12 nm of the baselines.   [422] Reg 170/83, Art 7 and Annex II; and Reg 3760/92, Art 7 and Annex II.

The location of the current provision on the Shetland Box, in Chapter IV immediately following Article 17, and the close connection of its predecessors with the provisions on access restrictions to waters within 12 nm of the baselines in the earlier Basic Regulations, suggest that Article 18 is to be treated as a qualification to the equal access principle. In reality it is much the same kind of qualification as a Community effort management measure (discussed in subsection 2.2 above), and, were it not for its historic inclusion in the Basic Regulation, might be legislated for in the same way. Article 18 (together with Annex II) limits the number of vessels of 26 m or more in length that may fish for demersal species other than Norway pout and blue whiting in the 'Shetland Box', which covers not only the waters around the Shetland Islands but also an area around the north of Scotland and the Orkney Islands, extending in places beyond 12 nm from the baselines. The reasons for this arrangement are said to be because the species found in the Box are 'biologically sensitive by reason of their exploitation characteristics'.[423] However, the Box in fact appears to be a largely symbolic response to the UK's demands during the negotiation of the EC's fisheries management system in the late 1970s and early 1980s for preferential access to waters beyond 12 nm from its baselines. If the Box really was intended to protect 'biologically sensitive' fisheries, one might have expected both that there would have been some attempt made to limit and control the access of vessels under 26 m in length and that the number of vessels of 26 m or more in length permitted to fish in the Box when it was first introduced would have been less than the number actually fishing in that area before, whereas in fact the permitted number was greater;[424] nor has the number of permitted vessels subsequently been reduced even though the abundance of fish stocks in the Box has declined since its introduction.[425]

As was seen above, Article 17(1) provides that the equal access principle is 'subject to measures adopted under Chapter II', which include, *inter alia*, recovery plans, management plans, TACs, effort limitation measures, and technical conservation measures. In adopting measures under Chapter II the Council can and frequently does restrict access to particular areas either completely (for example, to protect spawning fish) or partially on the basis of the size of vessel, type of gear, and so on. Even though the equal access principle does not apply to those measures, when enacting them the Council is still bound by the non-discrimination provisions of Articles 12 and 34(2) EC.[426] The system of national quotas and the

---

[423] Reg 2371/2002, Art 18(1).

[424] House of Lords, Select Committee on the European Communities, 1st Report of Session 1984–85, *The Common Fisheries Policy*, HL Paper 39 (London: Her Majesty's Stationery Office, 1984), pp 171 and 177.

[425] *Communication from the Commission to the Council and the European Parliament: Review of certain access restrictions in the Common Fisheries Policy* (Shetland Box and Plaice Box), COM(2005) 422, 13.09.2005, pp 4–5.

[426] Art 12 prohibits discrimination on the grounds of nationality. Art 34(2) prohibits discrimination between producers or consumers. Note that differences in treatment that are objectively justified do not constitute discrimination. See, for example, Case 287/81 *Anklagemyndigheden v J Noble Kerr* [1982] ECR 4053.

allocation of other fishing opportunities do not fall under Chapter II but under Chapter IV (Article 20), and are therefore subject to the equal access principle. The consequence of that is that in any area of Community waters where a Member State has been allocated a quota or other form of fishing opportunity, the vessels of that Member State may fish for that quota or opportunity anywhere within the area concerned, regardless of the Member State(s) within whose maritime zones that area happens to fall, subject to any restrictions resulting from technical conservation or other measures and subject to any access restrictions under Articles 17(2) and 18 of the Basic Regulation. The same principle applies to fishing for any fish stocks not subject to catch or effort limitations.

Article 19 of the Basic Regulation provides that by the end of 2003 the Commission is to present a report to the European Parliament and Council on the rules concerning access other than those contained in Article 17(2), assessing the justification for those rules in terms of conservation and sustainable exploitation objectives. On the basis of that report, and having regard to the equal access principle, the Council is to decide by the end of 2004 on any necessary adjustments to those rules. The Commission did not publish any report concerning rules on access until September 2005.[427] That report dealt only with access to the Shetland Box and the so-called 'Plaice Box', a technical conservation measure adopted under Regulation 850/98 (see subsection 2.3 above). As regards the Shetland Box, the Commission concluded that while no clear conservation benefit from its existence could be shown, the Box should be maintained for a further three years from September 2005 while further evaluations of its effect were carried out.[428] No such evaluation had been published by the time of writing.

In the early years of the CFP the equal access principle was criticized by some, particularly those from States seeking to join the EC in the early 1970s, as a regime of free access.[429] There was some truth in that criticism, particularly in the period between 1977, when Member States extended their fishing limits to 200 nm, and 1983, when the EC's fisheries management system was adopted. During that period there were few restrictions on fishing in the waters between 12 and 200 nm from the baselines. However, nowadays fisheries in those waters are so highly regulated that such criticisms are no longer valid, and in fact the principle of equal access has lost much of its practical significance.

2.6 Community law and the nationality of fishing vessels

It was seen in Chapter 2 that the Basic Regulation stipulates that '[t]he Common Fisheries Policy shall cover conservation, management and exploitation of living

---

[427] COM(2005) 422.   [428] COM(2005) 422, pp 7–8. The Plaice Box is not considered here.
[429] Interestingly, in Case C-91/03 *Spain v Council* the Court referred to the equal access principle as 'the principle of free access': see paras 2 and 12.

aquatic resources . . . where such activities are practised [*inter alia*] . . . by Community fishing vessels'.[430] Much EC legislation relating to fisheries conservation and management applies to 'Community fishing vessels'. Such vessels are defined in Article 3(d) of the Basic Regulation as 'a fishing vessel flying the flag of a Member State and registered in the Community'. Thus to be a Community fishing vessel, a vessel must: (a) be a fishing vessel; (b) fly the flag of a Member State; and (c) be 'registered in the Community'. The first and third of these conditions were commented on extensively in Chapter 2, so there is no need to discuss them further here. As far as the phrase, 'flying the flag of a Member State', is concerned, a fishing vessel may fly the flag of a Member State if it is registered in that Member State. This raises the question of what rules govern the registration of fishing vessels by Member States, and thus the conferral by a Member State of the right to fly its flag, and therefore its nationality, on a vessel.

Such rules comprise a mixture of international, EC, and national law. National law will not be discussed here, as it varies from Member State to Member State. As far as international law is concerned, it seems that before 1958 States had complete discretion as to which ships they accorded their nationality,[431] and consequently national laws on the matter varied considerably. Article 5 of the 1958 Convention on the High Seas[432] sought to limit that discretion by introducing a requirement that there should be a 'genuine link' between a vessel and the State granting it its nationality, a requirement subsequently repeated in Article 91 of the 1982 UN Convention on the Law of the Sea.[433] However, neither Convention defines what is meant by a 'genuine link', and no consensus as to its meaning has subsequently emerged. As a result, the requirement of a genuine link has in practice made little or no difference to the broad discretion that States previously exercised when granting their nationality to ships.

As far as EC law is concerned, the conferral of nationality on fishing or other vessels remains within the competence of Member States.[434] Nevertheless, there are a number of provisions of general EC law (notably those relating to freedom of establishment and the free movement of workers) that potentially govern the way in which that competence is exercised. How those provisions do so in the case of fishing vessels has largely been determined by the Court in a series of cases decided in the late 1980s and early 1990s in the context of an issue known as 'quota hopping'. The latter refers to a situation where a fisherman or a fishing company having the nationality of one Member State takes advantage of the liberal conditions applying to the granting of nationality to fishing vessels in another Member State and re-registers

---

[430] Reg 2371/2002, Art 1(1).

[431] Churchill, RR and Lowe, AV, *The Law of the Sea* (3rd edn, Manchester: Manchester University Press, 1999), 257.   [432] 450 UNTS 11.

[433] 1833 UNTS 396.

[434] Case 223/86 *Pesca Valentia v The Minister for Fisheries and Forestry, Ireland and the Attorney General* [1988] ECR 83, especially at para 13.

his or its vessels in the latter State, thus obtaining that State's nationality for those vessels, or purchases second-hand vessels already having the nationality of that State. A fisherman or fishing company will have the incentive to do this if conditions for fishing are more liberal or economically advantageous in the new flag State than in the original flag State. The main practitioners of quota hopping have been Spanish and Dutch fishing enterprises. In the case of Spanish fishing vessel owners, the fishing opportunities available to them in Community waters were quite limited in the years immediately following Spain's accession to the EC (as was seen in Chapter 1). They therefore targeted the UK and Ireland for quota hopping because of the greater fishing opportunities for British and Irish vessels and the liberality of their laws relating to the acquisition of their nationality by vessels.[435] At the time of Spain's accession to the EC, British law provided that a vessel had British nationality if it was wholly owned by British subjects or wholly owned by companies incorporated and having their principal place of business in the UK.[436] There were no restrictions on foreigners setting up such companies. Irish legislation was similar.[437] It was therefore a fairly straightforward matter for a Spanish fishing concern to set up a company in the UK or Ireland and transfer the ownership of its vessels to that company, whereupon the vessels became British or Irish, or for the company (aided by EC rules on free movement of capital) to buy second-hand vessels that already had British or Irish nationality. In either case, those vessels could fish for the quotas allocated to the UK and Ireland. In reality such vessels remained Spanish: they were beneficially owned by Spanish nationals or companies, they were operated and crewed by Spaniards, and they landed their catches in Spain. Needless to say, the British and Irish authorities and fishing industries did not welcome this development as it reduced the quotas available for 'genuine' British and Irish fishing vessels.[438] Ex-Spanish vessels also counted as part of the British and Irish fishing fleets whose size had to be reduced under the Multi-Annual Guidance Programmes (discussed in subsection 2.8 below). From the mid-1980s both the UK and Ireland introduced a number of measures to try to counter quota hopping.

In 1985 the British government promulgated a set of conditions governing the issue of the licences required by all British vessels over 10 m in length fishing for UK quotas. Under those conditions, whose aim was to ensure that licensed vessels had a 'real economic link' with the UK, a vessel, to be eligible for a licence, had to: (a) be registered as a British fishing boat under the Merchant Shipping Act 1894; (b) normally operate from the UK, Channel Islands, or the Isle of Man, such

---

[435] For details of the limited amount of quota hopping outside the Spain–UK/Ireland context, see Long, RJ and Curran, PA, *Enforcing the Common Fisheries Policy* (Oxford: Fishing News Books, 2000), 216–17.   [436] Merchant Shipping Act 1894, s 1.

[437] Irish Mercantile Marine Act 1955, s 3.

[438] It has, however, been argued in a detailed study that the adverse economic impact of quota hopping in the UK has in fact been much less than is popularly supposed. See Hatcher, A, Frere, J, Pascoe, S, and Robinson, K, '"Quota-hopping" and the Foreign Ownership of UK Fishing Vessels' *Marine Policy* 26 (2002) 1.

operation being evidenced by regular landings or visits to ports in those territories; (c) have a crew at least 75 per cent of which were British or other EC nationals resident in the UK, Channel Islands, or the Isle of Man; and (d) have a crew which contributed to a national insurance scheme in the UK, Channel Islands, or the Isle of Man.[439] The issuing of those conditions prompted the Irish government to make regulations applying the same obligation as condition '(c)' above to British-flagged vessels fishing in Ireland's fishing zone, landing fish in Ireland, or tran-shipping fish within Ireland's fishing zone or an Irish port.[440] The motive for the Irish regulations was presumably to restrict activities in Irish waters by British-registered vessels that were the subject of quota hopping.

The UK's 1985 licensing conditions proved not to be very successful at halting quota hopping, partly because the third and fourth conditions were suspended not long after their adoption pending the outcome of a legal challenge (discussed below)[441] and partly because a number of former Spanish vessels were able to comply with the conditions and thus carried on fishing for UK quotas. In 1988 the UK therefore took a further step against quota hopping by amending the law governing the granting of its nationality to fishing vessels. The amendment, effected by the Merchant Shipping Act 1988, provided that in order for a fishing vessel owned by a company to obtain (or retain) British nationality, the company concerned had to be incorporated and have its principal place of business in the UK and at least 75 per cent of its shares had to be owned by, and at least 75 per cent of its directors had to be, British citizens resident and domiciled in the UK.[442] In addition, the vessel had to be managed and its operations directed and con-trolled from within the UK, and any charterer, manager or operator of the vessel had to be a British citizen resident and domiciled in the UK or a company fulfilling the conditions above.[443]

Most of the measures adopted by the UK and Ireland to combat quota hopping were challenged before the Court for their compatibility with EC law.[444] The

---

[439] Ministry of Agriculture, Fisheries and Food, press release of 6 December 1985. The conditions were not set out in legislation but were an administrative measure.

[440] Sea-Fishing Boats Regulations, 1986.

[441] Case C-3/87 *R v Ministry of Agriculture, Fisheries and Food ex p Agegate* [1989] ECR I-4459.

[442] Merchant Shipping Act 1988, s 14.   [443] Ibid.

[444] The resulting judgments have been the subject of considerable comment in the academic lit-erature: see, *inter alia*, Churchill, RR, 'European Community Law and the Nationality of Ships and Crews' *European Transport Law* 26 (1991) 591, especially at 595–602 and 610–12; Churchill, RR, 'Quota hopping: the Common Fisheries Policy Wrongfooted?' *CML Rev* 27 (1990), 209; Long and Curran, *Enforcing the Common Fisheries Policy*, 218–22; Morin, M, 'The Fisheries Resources in the European Union. The Distribution of TACs: Principle of Relative Stability and Quota-Hopping' *Marine Policy* 24 (2000), 265; Noirfalisse, C, 'The Community System of Fisheries Management and the *Factortame* Case' *Yearbook of European Law* 12 (1992), 325; and O'Reilly, J, 'Judicial Review and the Common Fisheries Policy in Community Law' in Curtin, D and O'Keefe, D (eds), *Constitutional Adjudication in European Community and National Law* (London: Butterworths, 1992), 51.

nationality requirements introduced by the UK in its 1988 legislation were the subject of two cases, one a preliminary ruling in response to a request from a British court,[445] the other an action brought by the Commission under what was then Article 169 (now 226) EC.[446] In its judgment in both cases the Court began by confirming that the competence to determine the conditions governing the nationality of vessels remained with the Member States, but emphasized that such competence had to be exercised in accordance with EC law.[447] The Court held that EC law required that where a fishing vessel 'constitutes an instrument for pursuing an economic activity which involves a fixed establishment in the Member State concerned, the registration of that vessel cannot be dissociated from the exercise of the freedom of establishment. It follows that the conditions laid down for the registration of vessels must not form an obstacle to freedom of establishment within the meaning of Article 52 et seq. of the [EC] Treaty'.[448] In this case the Court found that the provisions of the 1988 Merchant Shipping Act relating to the nationality of owners of fishing vessels were an obstacle to freedom of establishment because they discriminated, on grounds of nationality, against the nationals of other EC Member States (whether natural or legal persons) established in the UK who wished to carry out fishing operations from the UK, contrary to Article 52 EC (now Article 43 EC).[449] The Court did not discuss separately the position of directors, shareholders, charterers, managers, or operators (except to note that the nationality requirements for shareholders were contrary to Article 221 (now 294) EC[450]), but it would seem that the Court's pronouncement in relation to owners must also apply to all those other categories. As for the requirement that all such persons be resident and domiciled in the UK, the Court found that that, too, was discriminatory on grounds of nationality, contrary to Article 52 EC, because whereas most nationals of the UK would be resident and domiciled in the UK, nationals of other Member States would in most cases have to move their residence and domicile to the UK if they were to comply with the Act.[451] On the other hand, the Court found that the requirement in the Act for a fishing vessel to be managed and its operations directed and controlled from within the UK if it was to have British nationality was not contrary to EC law, as that requirement 'essentially coincides with the actual concept of establishment within the meaning of

---

[445] Case C-221/89 R v Secretary of State for Transport ex p Factortame [1991] ECR I-3905.

[446] Case C-246/89 Commission v United Kingdom [1991] ECR I-4585.

[447] Case C-221/89, paras 13–17; and Case C-246/89, paras 11–15.

[448] Case C-221/89, paras 22–23; and Case C-246/89, paras 23–24. Arts 52 et seq EC are now Arts 43 et seq EC. These Articles provide that a national of one Member State may move to another Member State and pursue activities there as a self-employed person or manage undertakings on the same conditions as nationals of the host Member State.

[449] Case C-221/89, paras 28–30; and Case C-246/89, paras 29–31.

[450] Case C-221/89, para 31; and Case C-246/89, para 33.   [451] Case C-221/89, para 32.

Article 52 *et seq*'.[452] The Court added, however, that in the case of a vessel owned by a person exercising a secondary right of establishment in a Member State, it would be contrary to EC law to prohibit the second establishment directing the vessel from acting on instructions from a decision-making centre located in the Member State of the principal establishment.[453]

In a number of later cases concerned with merchant shipping in general (rather than fishing vessels in particular), the Court has confirmed its finding that a Member State is in breach of EC law if, in the context of the freedom of establishment, free movement of workers or ownership of shares, it requires ships to be owned by its nationals in order to acquire its nationality.[454] Furthermore, in the case of a ship owned by a company exercising its right of establishment in an EC Member State, the Court has held that not only may the host Member State not limit share-ownership and directorships in such a company to its nationals as a requirement for the ship to have its nationality, it may not even limit share-ownership and direct-orships in the company to nationals of Member States in general or nationals of European Economic Area States.[455] Such a requirement, in the view of the Court, constitutes an impermissible obstacle to the exercise of freedom of establishment by the company because it is 'not apt to ensure the attainment of its objectives' (the exercise of effective control and jurisdiction over the ship(s) concerned by the flag State) and 'goes beyond what is necessary to attain them'.[456]

On a different aspect of nationality, the Court has held that where a fishing vessel is beneficially owned by EC nationals but has the nationality of a third State flag of convenience, it is not possible to go behind the vessel's nationality and claim that it is a Community fishing vessel.[457]

The UK's licensing conditions of 1985, as distinct from the nationality condi-tions of the 1988 Act, were the subject of three cases before the Court.[458] The overall purpose of those conditions, it will be recalled, was that licensed vessels should have a 'real economic link' with the UK. The Court held that such a purpose was justified by the aim of the quota system, provided that such a link 'concerns only the relations between the vessel's fishing operations and the

---

[452] Case C-221/89, para 34.

[453] Case C-221/89, para 35. A secondary right of establishment is where a company established in one Member State exercises its right of establishment in another Member State through a subsidiary in the latter State or even simply an office there: see further Morin, 'The Fisheries Resources', 268.

[454] See Case C-334/94 *Commission v France* [1996] ECR I-1307, especially paras 13–23; Case C-151/96 *Commission v Ireland* [1997] ECR I-3327, especially paras 12–15; and Case C-62/96 *Commission v Hellenic Republic* [1997] ECR I-6725, especially paras 18–20.

[455] Case C-299/02 *Commission v Netherlands* [2004] ECR I-9761, paras 19–22 and 32–38.

[456] Case C-299/02 *Commission v Netherlands*, para 21.

[457] Case C-286/90 *Anklagemyndigheden v Poulsen and Diva Navigation* [1992] ECR I-6019, paras 13–15.

[458] Case C-3/87 *R v Ministry of Agriculture, Fisheries and Food ex p Agegate*; Case C-216/87 *R v Ministry of Agriculture, Fisheries and Food ex p Jaderow* [1989] ECR I-4509; and Case C-279/89 *Commission v United Kingdom* [1992] ECR I-5785.

populations dependent on fisheries and related industries'.[459] Turning to the individual licensing conditions, in none of the cases was the first condition (that to be eligible for a licence a fishing vessel had to be registered as a British fishing boat under the Merchant Shipping Act 1894) challenged. As regards the second licensing condition, that a vessel must normally operate from a UK, Channel Islands, or Isle of Man port, the Court held that in principle a Member State could require its fishing vessels to operate from its ports because this was in accordance with the aim of the quota system, as long as it did not require a vessel to begin every voyage from one of its ports.[460] Furthermore, a Member State could stipulate that the landing of catches or calls at its ports were suitable evidence that a vessel was operating from one of its ports, provided that the Member State did not require a certain percentage of catches to be landed at its ports as the sole such evidence and that normal fishing operations were not hindered.[461]

As for the third licensing condition, requiring 75 per cent of the crew to be British or other EC nationals resident in the UK, Channel Islands, or the Isle of Man, the Court held that a Member State was entitled to require a certain proportion of the crew on its fishing vessels to be EC nationals, but it could not require them to be resident in its territory because such a 'residence requirement is not justified by the aim of the system of national quotas'.[462] It is difficult to follow the Court's reasoning here. It is not obvious why the question of residence should be assessed by reference to the aim of the quota system, which the Court defined as being 'to assure to each Member State a share of the Community's total allowable catch, determined essentially on the basis of the catches from which traditional fishing activities, the local populations dependent on fisheries and related industries of that Member State benefited before the quota system was established',[463] since that aim appears unrelated to where the crew of the fishing vessel resides. But if the legality of a requirement of residence is to be assessed in terms of the aim of the quota system, one might have thought that the requirement was justified by that aim since it would help to ensure that the benefits of the quota system went to 'local populations dependent on fisheries'.[464] Otherwise, given that the Court elsewhere in its judgment held that fishermen are workers for the purposes of EC law,[465] one might have

---

[459] Case C-216/87 *Jaderow*, para 27. For criticism of the Court's treatment of a 'real economic link', see Morin, 'The Fisheries Resources', 270–2.   [460] Case C-216/87 *Jaderow*, paras 28–29.

[461] Case C-216/87 *Jaderow* paras 31–32 and 34–41. The Advocate General suggested that a requirement to land catches at a port of the Member State licensing the vessel was equivalent to a quantitative restriction on exports and therefore a breach of Art 34 (now 29) EC. See AG Opinion, paras 30–47.   [462] Case C-3/87 *Agegate*, para 22.

[463] Case C-3/87 *Agegate*, para 24.

[464] That, in fact, was the view of the Advocate General: see AG Opinion, paras 81–82.

[465] Case C-3/87 *Agegate*, paras 32–37. But note that in a case decided shortly before *Agegate*, the Court held that a national of one Member State employed on a ship registered in another Member State would only be a 'worker' for the purposes of EC law relating to the free movement of workers if the legal relationship of employment was located within the territory of the Member State in which the ship was registered or retained a sufficiently close link with that State: see Case 9/88 *Lopes da Veiga v Staatsecretaries van Justitie* [1989] ECR 2989, paras 14–17.

expected the Court to have assessed the residence requirement in relation to the law relating to the free movement of workers.

As for the final licensing condition, which required the skipper and all the crew of a fishing vessel to contribute to a national insurance scheme in the UK, Channel Islands, or the Isle of Man, the Court held that this matter was governed by Regulation 1408/71,[466] which, by establishing a complete system of conflict rules relating to social security for migrant workers in the EC, had deprived Member States of the power to legislate for the application of social security conditions to migrant workers. However, the licensing condition at issue fell within Article 13 of Regulation 1408/71, which provides that a person employed on a ship flying the flag of a Member State is subject to the legislation of that Member State. Thus the licensing condition was in accordance with Community law provided that it respected Article 14 of Regulation 1408/71, which provides as an exception to Article 13 that in certain circumstances the legislation of a Member State other than the flag State applies to those employed on ships.[467]

Finally, legal challenges to various licensing conditions imposed by Ireland should be examined. Some of those conditions have already been noted above. In 1993 a new provision (section 222B(4)) was inserted in the Fisheries Consolidation Act 1979, stipulating that the Irish authorities would issue fishing licences only to vessels owned by an Irish citizen or by a company incorporated and having its principal place of business in Ireland and which was beneficially owned by and under the control of EC nationals. The Commission challenged that condition on the ground that by requiring nationals of other Member States to set up an Irish company in order to obtain a licence to fish, whereas Irish nationals did not need to set up a company in order to do so, Ireland had discriminated on grounds of nationality between Irish and other EC nationals in relation to the freedom of establishment and therefore was in breach of Article 52 (now 43) EC. The Court agreed.[468] The other Irish licensing conditions that were the subject of legal challenge were the Sea-Fishing Boats Regulations 1986, which, as noted above, required 75 per cent of the crew of *British* vessels fishing in Irish waters, landing fish in Irish ports or transhipping fish in Irish waters or ports to be resident in the UK. The Court found that that condition breached Article 2(1) of Regulation 101/76 (which provided that a Member State's rules governing fishing in its

---

[466] Council Regulation 1408/71 of 14 June 1971 on the application of social security schemes to employed persons, to self-employed persons and to members of their families moving within the Community, OJ S Ed 1971 (II), 416. A consolidated version of the Regulation, as amended, was published in OJ 1997 L28/1. Reg 1408/71 is due to be replaced by Reg 883/2004, OJ 2004 L166/1, when the latter becomes applicable, which it had not done at the time of writing.

[467] Case C-3/87 *Agegate*, para 22. See also Morin, 'The Fisheries Resources', 269–70.

[468] Case C-93/89 *Commission v Ireland* [1991] ECR I-4569, paras 10–15.

waters should not lead to differences on the ground of nationality in the treatment of other Member States) insofar as it related to fishing in Irish waters,[469]
and breached Article 30 (now 28) EC (which prohibits the imposition of
quantitative restrictions and measures having equivalent effect by one Member
State on imports from another Member State; see further Chapter 7) as it
related to the landing of catches in Irish ports.[470] By the time it was given, the
Court's judgment was largely academic, as Ireland had already repealed the
offending regulations.

The result of the Court's case law, which represents the triumph of general
EC law relating to the construction of the single market over the territoriality
represented by the quota system,[471] means that it is impossible for Member
States to prevent quota hopping, which has moved from being a matter of acute
controversy to being a fact of life in the CFP.[472] More pertinently for the
present discussion, the Court's case law also defines the way in which EC law
restricts a Member State's discretion under international law to determine
which fishing vessels are to have its nationality. According to the Court, a
Member State must permit natural and legal persons having the nationality of
another Member State who are established on its territory to register their
fishing vessels there and fly its flag if they wish to conduct fishing operations
from that territory. In the case of legal persons, share-ownership and directorships may not be limited to nationals of EC Member States or European Economic Area States. The host State must not impose on such natural and legal
persons conditions that amount to overt or covert discrimination on the
grounds of nationality. Conditions that are permissible include a requirement
that a vessel be managed and its operations directed and controlled from within
that State and an obligation that a vessel operate from that State's ports, provided that the vessel is not required to begin every fishing trip from such a port,
land a certain proportion of its catches there, or call so frequently at that State's
ports that normal fishing operations are hindered. Furthermore, a Member State
must permit the nationals of any other Member State who enjoy unrestricted
rights of free movement for workers to serve as crew on vessels having its
nationality[473] and cannot require such crew members to be resident on its
territory.

---

[469] Case C-280/89 *Commission v Ireland* [1992] ECR I-6185, paras 10–11.

[470] Case C-280/89 *Commission v Ireland*, para 14.

[471] Lequesne, C, 'Quota Hopping: The Common Fisheries Policy between States and Markets'
Journal of Common Market Studies 38 (2000) 779, at 780. A similar point is made by Morin: see Morin,
'The Fisheries Resources', 271.   [472] See Hatcher *et al*, '"Quota-hopping"'.

[473] Apart from Case C-3/87 *Agegate*, referred to above, see also, in a non-fisheries context, Case
167/73 *Commission v France* [1974] ECR 359; Case C-37/93 *Commission v Belgium* [1993] ECR I-6295;
and Case C-334/94 *Commission v France* [1996] ECR I-1307. See further Morin, 'The Fisheries
Resources', 268–9.

2.7 Enforcement[474]

Introduction

Even if one accepts, hypothetically, that EC conservation and management measures are adequate on paper, they will not be effective in practice unless they are (very largely) complied with. This subsection examines EC rules that are designed to secure such compliance. Those rules may be referred to for convenience as (and are popularly labelled) rules on enforcement: in EC terminology they are known as the 'Community Control and Enforcement System'[475] or sometimes as 'monitoring, control and surveillance' (MCS). The Community Control and Enforcement System applies to all aspects of the CFP, not simply fishing operations. Here the focus will be on the rules relating to fishing operations. The rules relating to compliance with other aspects of the CFP (such as marketing) will be dealt with at appropriate points in later chapters of this book.

In discussing enforcement, the framework of analysis will be to look at: (a) the different persons required to comply with EC rules (the addressees of compliance); (b) the EC measures with which they are required to comply; and (c) the mechanisms and persons through which compliance is sought (enforcers). As regards the addressees of compliance, there are three broad groups—individual fishing vessel operators and masters, fish buyers, and Member States. Each of those will be looked at in turn, examining the rules with which each has to comply and the relevant enforcer(s). EC law governing these matters is contained primarily in the Basic Regulation and the Control Regulation.[476] The current Basic Regulation is the first of its kind to contain substantive provisions on enforcement: its predecessors simply provided that the Council should establish a Community control and enforcement system. The reason for this change was to reinforce and clarify the existing provisions on enforcement in the Control Regulation.[477] To this end the main provisions of the latter are now included in the Basic Regulation. As a result, there is some duplication between them. There are also occasional inconsistencies. Where that is the case, it is unclear whether the Basic Regulation should prevail on the basis of the *lex posterior* principle or the Control Regulation on the basis of the *lex specialis* principle. Both the Control Regulation and the Basic Regulation apply to all Community waters (including therefore the Baltic, Black, and Mediterranean Seas), and to a considerable degree also to Community fishing vessels on the high seas and in the waters of third States: the application of the Regulations outside Community waters is discussed in Chapter 5. As well as the

---

[474] For comprehensive, although now somewhat dated, studies of this topic, see Long and Curran, *Enforcing the Common Fisheries Policy* and Berg, A, *Implementing and Enforcing European Fisheries Law* (The Hague: Kluwer, 1999). For a survey of more recent developments, see Johnson, C, 'Fisheries Enforcement in European Community Waters since 2002—Developments in Non-Flag Enforcement' *IJMCL* 23 (2008), 249.   [475] The title of Chapter V of the Basic Regulation.
[476] Reg 2847/93, introduced in subsection 2.1 above.   [477] Reg 2371/2002, recital (19).

Control and Basic Regulations, there is a considerable number of implementing and supplementary Regulations, often of considerable detail, some of which are referred to below. There are also some control measures contained in the annual fishing opportunities Regulations and in recovery and management plans (see subsection 2.1 above), but such measures are not considered further here or in subsection 2.1 above.

Recital (19) of the Basic Regulation appears to suggest that the Control Regulation will eventually be replaced. However, it was not until November 2008, following a public consultation on reform of the EC's control system, that the Commission published proposals for replacing the Control Regulation. Those proposals will be examined at the end of this subsection.

Enforcement against fishing vessel operators and masters

The EC rules with which fishing vessel operators (ie owners, charterers, and management companies) and masters have to comply have already been considered earlier in this chapter. They include, *inter alia*, technical measures (gear regulations, closed seasons and areas, by-catch rules etc), rules on access, and rules on days at sea and other effort limitation measures that apply directly to fishing vessels. Such rules may be labelled for convenience as 'primary rules'. As well as those rules, there is a set of rules addressed to operators and masters that is designed to secure their compliance with the primary rules. Those rules will be labelled 'secondary rules'. There is a considerable number of them. The main secondary rules include the following.

1. **Licences.** Since 1993/4 every Community fishing vessel has been required to have a licence, issued by its flag Member State.[478] In addition, every Community fishing vessel taking part in fisheries 'subject to Community measures in respect of the conditions of access to waters and resources adopted in accordance with' the Basic Regulation must have a separate authorization to fish, known as a special fishing permit.[479] Article 22(1)(a) of the Basic Regulation requires licences and, where applicable, authorizations, to be carried on board fishing vessels.

2. **Carriage of vessel monitoring system (VMS).** The obligation to carry a VMS has gradually been introduced for different groups of vessel since 1998. Currently all Community fishing vessels over 15 m in overall length must carry a VMS.[480] A VMS is a system that allows detection and identification of a vessel by remote monitoring systems.[481] It also enables a vessel to

---

[478] The original Regulations are no longer in force. Those currently governing the matter are Reg 2371/2002, Art 22 and Commission Regulation (EC) No 1281/2005 of 3 August 2005 on the management of fishing licences and the minimal [sic] information to be contained therein, OJ 2005 L203/3.
[479] Council Regulation (EC) No 1627/94 of 27 June 1994 laying down general provisions concerning special fishing permits, OJ 1994 L171/7, as amended, Art 1(1)(a).
[480] Reg 2371/2002, Art 22(1)(b).   [481] Ibid.

communicate by satellite to its flag State and the coastal State in whose waters it is fishing (if different) simultaneously. The vessel must communicate the information referred to in point 4 below to those States at specified times each day.[482]

3. **Log books**. The master of every Community fishing vessel of 10 m or more in length must keep a log book of its operations, detailing the quantities of each species caught and kept on board, the date and location of each catch, and the type of gear used.[483]

4. **Reporting obligations**. The master of every Community fishing vessel of 10 m or more in length must submit a declaration of the amounts of fish landed (and, in some cases, to be landed) and where it was caught to the competent authorities of the Member State where the landing takes place.[484] Masters fishing in areas subject to effort limitation measures must report to their flag State and the relevant coastal State(s) each time they enter and leave such an area and notify them of the amounts of fish caught there.[485]

5. **Transhipments**. Transhipments of catch from one vessel to another may only take place in Community waters or Member State ports where this has been authorized by the relevant coastal or port State. Masters of fishing vessels must comply with the conditions for transhipment laid down by that State.[486]

6. **Stowage of gear**. Nets on board vessels that are not used must be stowed so that they may not readily be used.[487] The purpose of this provision is to aid compliance with EC rules on mesh sizes (see subsection 2.3 above).

---

[482] Reg 2847/93, Art 3(6). More detailed provisions on VMS are contained in Commission Regulation (EC) No 2244/2003 of 18 December 2003 laying down detailed provisions regarding satellite-based Vessel Monitoring Systems, OJ 2003 L333/17. See also Long and Curran, *Enforcing the Common Fisheries Policy*, 314–26.

[483] Reg 2847/93, Arts 6(1) and (4) and 19e, and Reg 2371/2002, Art 20(3). More detailed provisions are contained in: (a) Commission Regulation (EEC) No 2807/83 of 22 September 1983 laying down detailed rules for recording information on Member States' catches of fish, OJ 1983 L276/1, as amended; (b) Council Regulation (EC) No 1966/2006 of 21 December 2006 on electronic recording and reporting of fishing activities and on means of remote sensing, OJ 2006 L409/1, as corrected; (c) Commission Regulation (EC) No 1303/2007 of 5 November 2007 laying down detailed rules for the implementation of Council Regulation (EC) No 1966/2006 on electronic recording and reporting of fishing activities and on means of remote sensing, OJ 2007 L290/3, as corrected; and (d) Commission Regulation (EC) No 1077/2008 of 3 November 2008 laying down detailed rules for the implementation of Council Regulation (EC) No 1966/2006 of 21 December 2006 on electronic recording and reporting of fishing activities and on means of remote sensing and repealing Regulation (EC) No 1566/2007, OJ 2008 L295/3, as corrected.

[484] Reg 2847/93, Arts 7, 8, and 12.

[485] Reg 2847/93, Art 19a, 19b, and 19c. More detailed provisions on this matter are contained in Regs 2807/83, 1966/2006, 1303/2007, and 1077/2008.

[486] Reg 2847/93, Art 11. More detailed provisions on this matter are contained in Regs 1966/2006, 1303/2007, and 1077/2008.   [487] Reg 2847/93, Art 20(1).

7. **Cooperation with inspectors**. The master of a Community fishing vessel
must accept inspectors on board and cooperate with them, as well as with
observers where an observer scheme applies.[488]

As well as having to comply with the secondary rules outlined above, it should not
be forgotten that fishing vessel operators and masters also have to observe rules
enacted by Member States in furtherance of the CFP. Such rules include, *inter alia*,
national measures relating to the utilization of quotas, measures implementing EC
rules on licensing and effort limitation, and measures adopted under the powers
delegated to Member States by, *inter alia*, the Basic Regulation (see, *inter alia*,
subsections 2.1, 2.2, and 2.4 above).

The responsibility for taking action to secure compliance by fishing vessel
operators and masters with the primary and secondary Community rules applicable
to them lies with the Member States, not the EC. That is because the latter lacks
the competence to take enforcement action against natural or legal persons in the
fisheries sector. Article 23 of the Basic Regulation and Article 2 of the Control
Regulation cast a general obligation on each Member State to ensure effective
control of the rules of the CFP: (a) on its territory (including therefore its ports);
(b) in the waters subject to its sovereignty and jurisdiction, regardless of the
nationality of the vessels involved; (c) in respect of vessels having its nationality
outside Community waters; and (d) in respect of its nationals outside Community
waters, albeit 'without prejudice to the primary responsibility of the flag State'.[489]
In the terminology of the international law of the sea, Member States have
enforcement responsibilities as port, coastal, and flag States. Member States must
'adopt the measures, allocate the financial and human resources and set up the
administrative and technical structure necessary for ensuring effective control,
inspection and enforcement . . .'.[490] In carrying out their enforcement responsibilities, Member States must act in such a way as to avoid undue interference with
normal fishing operations and must not discriminate on the basis of the sector or
vessels chosen for inspection.[491] Article 12 EC also requires Member States not to
discriminate on the ground of nationality. The types of inspection and enforcement measures that Member States must take include, *inter alia*, the inspection of
vessels at sea and in port, sightings of fishing vessels, and 'measures to prevent the
involvement of their nationals in fisheries activities that do not respect the
applicable conservation and management measures, without prejudice to the primary responsibility of the flag State'.[492] These last measures aim at preventing the
involvement of Member State nationals in illegal, unreported, and unregulated
(IUU) fishing, the nature of which was explained in the previous chapter.

Where a Member State, as a result of an inspection, suspects that a fishing vessel
operator or master has not complied with EC rules, it 'shall ensure that appropriate

[488] Reg 2371/2002, Art 22(1)(d).   [489] Reg 2371/2002, Art 23(2).
[490] Reg 2371/2002, Art 23(3).   [491] Reg 2847/93, Art 4.   [492] Reg 2371/2002, Art 24.

measures are taken, including administrative action or criminal proceedings in conformity with [its] national law', against that operator or master.[493] That provision reflects the different traditions of Member States, some of which (for example, the UK) deal with suspected breaches of fisheries regulations primarily through the criminal law, others through administrative proceedings, and yet others through a mixture of the two. Where a fishing vessel has been issued with a special fishing permit (see above), the flag Member State, 'in order to ensure compliance with' EC conservation measures, 'shall take the appropriate steps, including where necessary the modification or suspension, fully or in part,' of the permit that it has issued, and inform the Commission accordingly.[494]

Whatever form of proceedings is used, where a breach of EC law is established, sanctions must be imposed and may include, *inter alia*, depending on the gravity of the offence, a fine, confiscation of the gear, catch or vessel, and/or suspension or withdrawal of the licence.[495] In general, proceedings against offenders must be capable of 'effectively depriving those responsible of the economic benefit of the infringements and of producing results proportionate to the seriousness of such infringements, effectively discouraging further offences of the same kind'.[496] The Council has defined those breaches of EC rules that it considers to 'seriously infringe' the rules of the CFP, and requires Member States to report such breaches, and the action that they have taken in respect of them, to the Commission.[497] The Council is also empowered to establish the sanctions to be applied to such serious infringements,[498] which it did for the first time, at least to some degree, with the adoption of Regulation 1005/2008.[499] Article 44(2) of Regulation 1005/2008 provides that the maximum sanction shall be at least five times the value of the fishery products obtained as a result of committing a serious infringement (and at least eight times the value in the case of repeat offences within a five-year period). In applying those sanctions Member States 'shall also take into account the value of the prejudice to the fishing resources and the marine environment concerned'. Quite how this value is to be calculated is unclear. Article 44(3) goes on to add that Member States 'may also, or alternatively, use effective, proportionate and dissuasive criminal sanctions', while Article 45 provides that the sanctions referred to

---

[493] Reg 2371/2002, Art 25(1). Reg 2847/93, Art 31(1) is similar.   [494] Reg 1627/94, Art 7(4).

[495] Reg 2371/2002, Art 25(3). Reg 2847/93, Art 31(3) is similar.

[496] Reg 2371/2002, Art 25(2). Reg 2847/93, Art 31(2) is similar.

[497] Council Regulation (EC) No 1447/1999 of 24 June 1999 establishing a list of types of behaviour which seriously infringe the rules of the common fisheries policy, OJ 1999 L167/5. This Regulation will be repealed with effect from the beginning of 2010 by Art 56 of Council Regulation (EC) No 1005/2008 of 29 September 2008 establishing a Community system to prevent, deter and eliminate illegal, unreported and unregulated fishing, amending Regulations (EEC) No 2847/93, (EC) No 1936/2001 and (EC) No 601/2004 and repealing Regulations (EC) No 1093/94 and (EC) No 1447/1999, OJ 2008 L266/1. 'Serious infringements' will thenceforth be defined by Art 42 of Reg 1005/2008.

[498] Reg 2371/2002, Art 25(4).

[499] Reg 1005/2008 will apply as from 1 January 2010: see Art 57.

in Article 44 may be accompanied by other sanctions, including confiscation of the vessel, gear, and catch, the suspension or withdrawal of the authorization to fish, and a temporary or permanent ban on access to public funding. Member States are therefore left with a considerable degree of discretion as to what sanctions they impose. Nevertheless, Article 46 stipulates that the overall level of sanctions must be calculated so as to ensure that they 'effectively deprive those responsible of the economic benefits derived from their serious infringements without prejudice to the legitimate right to exercise a profession'. Article 47 provides that legal persons may be held liable for serious infringements committed for their benefit by a natural person or where commission of a serious infringement results from a lack of supervision or control of a natural person.

A Member State that finds a vessel or natural or legal person *in flagrante* committing a serious infringement must take immediate measures to prevent it from continuing.[500] Where a Member State has detected a breach of EC rules (of whatever degree of seriousness) and is not the flag State of the vessel concerned, it must report the details of that infringement and the follow-up action that it has taken to the flag State.[501] If the State detecting the infringement is the State where the catch was landed or in whose waters the catch was transhipped, it may transfer the prosecution to the flag State with the latter's agreement, provided that such transfer is more likely to deprive those responsible of the economic benefits of their alleged illegal fishing or of producing results proportionate to the seriousness of the infringement, effectively discouraging them from committing further offences of the same kind.[502] The flag State must then take action against the vessel concerned and notify the Commission of the action that it has taken.[503] Where a Community fishing vessel has seriously or repeatedly failed to comply with the secondary rules contained in the Control Regulation, its flag State may subject the vessel to 'additional control measures', in which case that State must notify the Commission and the other Member States of such measures.[504]

As mentioned above, sanctions for breaches of the CFP's rules must be of a kind to deprive offenders of the economic benefits of illegal fishing and to deter would-be offenders. At present that does not appear to be the case in many Member States. In 2006 the average fine for a 'serious' offence (within the meaning of Regulation 1447/1999) across all Member States was €1,548, and in some Member States the average fine for some kinds of serious offence was as little as €200 or less.[505] Clearly such low fines will not deter the commission of future offences. It is true that fines are not the only kind of penalty employed.

---

[500] Reg 2371/2002, Art 25(5). From the beginning of 2010 this obligation will be spelt out in more detail in Art 43 of Reg 1005/2008.   [501] Reg 2847/93, Art 33(1).

[502] Reg 2847/93, Art 31(4).   [503] Reg 2847/93, Art 33(2) and (3).

[504] Reg 2847/93, Art 22.

[505] *Communication from the Commission to the Council and the European Parliament: Reports from Member States on behaviours which seriously infringed the rules of the Common Fisheries Policy in 2006*, COM(2008) 670, 4.11.2008, pp 5 and 13.

Confiscation of the catch and/or gear and revocation or suspension of the licence may be used as additional or alternative penalties, but those penalties are used in only a minority of cases—confiscation in 26 per cent of all cases in 2006 and licence revocation/suspension in 10 per cent. Furthermore, eight Member States (including Spain, the EC's leading fishing Member State) did not use confiscation as a penalty in 2006, and twelve Member States (including five of those not using confiscation) did not use licence revocation/suspension.[506] In the Commission's view, 'the overall penalties imposed are not a sufficient deterrent, as they provide no real incentive to comply'[507] and it concluded that the 'inadequate level of the sanctions imposed' combined with the 'low probability of being caught . . . may convince the fisherman that the economic benefits that he can draw by breaching the rules outweigh the risk'.[508]

Enforcement of EC fisheries rules by Member States, particularly where it takes the form of inspection at sea, requires considerable expenditure. The burdens and costs of enforcement vary from Member State to Member State, depending on the extent of their maritime zones and the level and nature of fishing activity therein, the size of their fishing fleets, and the number and degree of use of their ports for landing catches. Enforcement, and the benefits that flow from effective enforcement, are in the interests of, and accrue to, the EC as a whole, rather than just the individual Member State carrying out enforcement. It has been recognized almost from the beginning of the CFP that it is appropriate for the EC to help defray the costs of enforcement, so that such costs, as well as the benefits of enforcement, are shared by all Member States, and also so that individual Member States' enforcement efforts should be improved. There has been a succession of Community legislative measures providing for EC aid towards those ends. The current measures are Council Regulation 861/2006[509] and Commission Regulation 391/2007,[510] the latter setting out detailed measures implementing Regulation 861/2006.

Regulation 861/2006 deals not only with financial aid to Member States to assist them in carrying out and improving their enforcement responsibilities, but also aid for a number of other purposes connected to the CFP.[511] Only the former are considered here: some of the other purposes are discussed in Chapter 8. The Regulation covers the period from the beginning of 2007 to the end of 2013,[512] and provides that during this period the EC will provide aid to Member States towards the costs of: (a) 'investments relating to control activities carried out by

---

[506] COM(2008) 670, pp 14–15.   [507] COM(2008) 670, p 7.   [508] COM(2008) 670, p 6.

[509] Council Regulation (EC) No 861/2006 of 22 May 2006 establishing Community financial measures for the implementation of the common fisheries policy and in the area of the Law of the Sea, OJ 2006 L160/1.

[510] Commission Regulation (EC) No 391/2007 of 11 April 2007 laying down detailed rules for the implementation of Council Regulation (EC) No 861/2006 as regards the expenditure incurred by Member States in implementing the monitoring and control systems applicable to the Common Fisheries Policy, OJ 2007 L97/30.   [511] Reg 861/2006, Art 2.

[512] Reg 861/2006, Art 33.

administrative bodies or by the private sector including implementation of new
control technologies and the purchase and modernisation of control means'; (b)
training and exchange of national officials responsible for monitoring, control, and
surveillance; (c) implementation of pilot inspection and observer schemes; (d)
cost/benefit analyses and assessment of audits performed and expenditure incurred
by national authorities in carrying out their enforcement activities; and (e) initiatives to raise awareness among fishermen, fisheries inspectors, public prosecutors,
judges, and others of the need to combat IUU fishing and implement CFP
rules.[513] Applications by Member States for aid must be accompanied by an annual
fisheries control programme that, *inter alia*, sets out the resources to be devoted to
enforcement, the overall expenditure to be devoted to projects for which aid is
sought, a schedule for the completion of each project, and a list of indicators that
will be used to assess the efficacy of the programme.[514] In 2008 nearly €15 million
worth of aid for enforcement was provided to Member States under Regulation
861/2006. Of that sum, the major share went on new technologies and IT networks (€4.7 million), electronic recording and reporting systems (€2.75 million),
and patrol vessels and aircraft (€2.16 million). The main Member States benefiting
from the aid were Greece (€2.5 million), Ireland (€2 million), and Italy (€1.8
million).[515]

It is, of course, possible for Member States to reduce their enforcement efforts
and costs by cooperating with each other. Such cooperation is strongly encouraged
by both the Basic Regulation and the Control Regulation.[516] Cooperation
between Member States should lead not only to more effective enforcement but
also to more uniformity in enforcement, thus reducing the likelihood of the CFP
being less rigorously enforced in one Member State's waters than another's, with
consequent distortion of competition.[517] Cooperation between Member States in
relation to fisheries control and inspection is to be coordinated by the Community
Fisheries Control Agency (hereafter, 'the Agency'), which was set up in 2005[518]
and came into operation at the beginning of 2007. Such coordination is to take
place through control and inspection programmes adopted by the Commission for
fisheries involving two or more Member States.[519] These programmes (also
known as 'specific monitoring programmes') are to be implemented operationally

---

[513] Reg 861/2006, Art 8.   [514] Reg 861/2006, Art 20.

[515] Commission Decision 2008/860/EC of 29 October 2008 on a Community financial contribution towards Member States' fisheries control, inspection and surveillance programmes for 2008, OJ
2008 L303/13.   [516] Reg 2371/2002, Art 28 and Reg 2847/93, Arts 34, 34a, 34b, and 34c.

[517] See recital (4) of Council Regulation (EC) No 768/2005 of 26 April 2005 establishing a
Community Fisheries Control Agency and amending Regulation (EEC) No 2847/93 establishing a
control system applicable to the common fisheries policy, OJ 2005 L128/1. For a further discussion of
this point, see *Communication from the Commission to the Council and the European Parliament: Towards
uniform and effective implementation of the Common Fisheries Policy*, COM(2003) 130, 21.3.2003, pp 7–18.

[518] By Reg 768/2005. The Agency is funded, at least in part, under Reg 861/2006: see Art 8(d).

[519] Reg 2847/93, Art 34c and Reg 768/2005, Art 9.

by joint deployment plans adopted by the Agency, through which the Member States concerned will pool their means of control and inspection.[520] Under a joint deployment plan a fisheries inspection vessel from one Member State may inspect Community fishing vessels of any nationality in the EEZ/EFZ of another Member State, although in practice it will normally carry an inspector from the latter Member State on board.[521] Arrest and prosecution of a vessel suspected of illegal fishing remain within the exclusive competence of the coastal State concerned.[522] Two or more Member States may also request the Agency to coordinate their control and inspection activities in relation to fisheries that are not subject to a specific monitoring programme.[523] The Agency has stated that initially it will concentrate on coordinating national control and inspection activities for those fish stocks 'covered by both recovery and multi-annual plans'.[524] In 2007 the Agency adopted its first joint deployment plan, which applied to the cod stocks of the North Sea and adjacent waters, and involved seven Member States.[525] In 2008 the Agency continued that plan, and adopted new joint deployment plans for the Baltic Sea cod stocks and the bluefin tuna fishery in the Mediterranean Sea and eastern Atlantic, as well as a further plan for the cod fisheries of Western waters to come into operation in 2009. (There are also joint deployment plans operational outside Community waters in the high seas areas of the north-east and north-west Atlantic.)[526] Apart from adopting and overseeing the operation of joint deployment plans, the Agency is tasked, *inter alia*, with: (a) providing training for national officials involved in fisheries monitoring, control, and inspection; (b) undertaking joint procurement of goods and services relating to control and inspection at the request of Member States; (c) elaborating joint operational procedures in relation to joint control and inspection; and (d) providing contractual services to Member States, if so requested, relating to control and inspection, including the chartering, operating, and staffing of control and inspection platforms and the provision of observers for joint operations.[527]

Article 28(3) of the Basic Regulation provides for inspections by a Member State outside its own waters not only under a specific monitoring programme but also in two other circumstances. First, 'without prejudice to the primary

---

[520] Reg 768/2005, Arts 2(c), 5(2), 9, and 13; and Reg 2847/93, Art 34c.

[521] Reg 2371/2002, Art 28(3) and information on the website of the Agency.

[522] Commission Regulation (EC) No 1042/2006 of 7 July 2006 laying down detailed rules for the implementation of Articles 28(3) and (4) of Council Regulation (EC) No 2371/2002 on the conservation and sustainable exploitation of fisheries resources under the Common Fisheries Policy, OJ 2006 L187/14, Art 8(1) and (2).   [523] Reg 768/2005, Art 15.

[524] See the Agency's Annual Work Programme for 2007, available on its website.

[525] For details see the website of the Agency.

[526] Community Fisheries Control Agency press release, 'The Community Fisheries Control Agency (CFCA) has adopted five Joint Deployment Plans for the year 2009', 10 October 2008, available on the website of the Agency. See also Commission press release, 'Commission launches major control campaign to clamp down on overfishing of bluefin tuna', 14 March 2008, available on the website of DG Mare.   [527] Reg 768/2005, especially Arts 3–9.

responsibility of the coastal State', Member States are authorized to inspect vessels flying their flag in 'all Community waters outside waters under the sovereignty of another Member State' (ie outside the internal waters or territorial sea of another Member State). Secondly, Member States are authorized to carry out inspections 'in accordance with the rules' of the CFP 'relating to fishing activities in all Community waters outside waters under their sovereignty on fishing vessels', if so authorized by the coastal Member State concerned. The reference to 'fishing activities' includes activities by vessels other than those flying the flag of the inspecting Member State.[528] Article 28(6) of the Basic Regulation provides that the powers given by Article 28(3) are not to be exercised until implementing rules have been laid down. Such rules did not come into being until the adoption of Regulation 1042/2006 in July 2006. Article 28(4) of the Basic Regulation provides that on the basis of appointments made by Member States, the Commission is to establish a list of Community inspectors to undertake inspections under Chapter V of the Basic Regulation, including therefore inspections referred to in Article 28(3). The first such list was adopted at the beginning of 2007, when some 450 Community inspectors were appointed.[529] Community inspectors have in principle the same powers as fisheries inspectors of the Member State in which the inspection takes place: however, they have 'no police and enforcement powers beyond the territory or outside the Community waters under the sovereignty or jurisdiction of their Member State of origin'.[530] When carrying out inspections, Community inspectors must submit a daily report on their activities to the coastal Member State concerned and submit a report on any detected infringements to that State.[531] The latter must consider and act on such a report in the same way as it would with a report from one of its own inspectors.[532] If so requested, a Community inspector shall give evidence in any infringement proceedings pursuant to his/her report.[533] That report is admissible evidence in judicial or administrative proceedings in any Member State.[534]

---

[528] Reg 1042/2006, Art 1.

[529] Commission Decision 2007/166/EC of 9 January 2007 adopting the list of Community inspectors and inspection means pursuant to Article 28(4) of Council Regulation (EC) No 2371/2002 on the conservation and sustainable exploitation of fisheries resources under the common fisheries policy, OJ 2007 L76/22, as amended. The number of Community inspectors was roughly doubled by Commission Decision 2008/201/EC of 28 February 2008 designating the Community Fisheries Control Agency as the body to carry out certain tasks under Regulation (EC) No 1042/2006 and amending Decision 2007/166/EC adopting the list of Community inspectors and inspection means, OJ 2008 L60/36.   [530] Reg 1042/2006, Art 8(1) and (2).

[531] Reg 1042/2006, Art 9(1) and (2).   [532] Reg 1042/2006, Art 10(1).

[533] Reg 1042/2006, Art 10(3).   [534] Reg 2371/2002, Art 28(5).

Enforcement in respect of fish buyers

As well as measures applying directly to fishing vessel operators and masters that are designed to secure their compliance with CFP rules, the EC has adopted measures that also aim to induce such compliance by regulating those who buy fish from fishing vessels (ie wholesalers). Such measures seek in particular to combat the possibility of black markets in fish developing, where illegally caught and/or unreported fish could be sold.

Article 22(2)(a) of the Basic Regulation provides that fisheries products may only be sold from a fishing vessel to a registered buyer or at a registered auction. To that end Article 22(2)(b) stipulates that buyers of fisheries products from a fishing vessel at first sale must be registered with the authorities of a Member State. Under Article 22(2)(c) such buyers must submit invoices or sales notes to the authorities unless sales take place through a registered auction that itself provides invoices or sales notes to the authorities.[535] Article 22(2)(d) of the Basic Regulation provides that all fisheries products landed in or imported into a Member State for which neither invoices nor sales notes have been submitted to the authorities and which are transported to a place other than that of landing or import must be accompanied by a document drawn up by the transporter until the first sale has taken place.[536] Article 22(2)(f) is designed to enforce EC rules on the minimum size of fish that may be landed (see subsection 2.3 above). It provides that where such minimum sizes have been fixed for particular species of fish, operators responsible for selling, stocking or transporting the fish species concerned must be able to prove the geographical origin of those species.[537]

As is the case with vessel operators and masters, responsibility for seeking to ensure compliance with the above rules rests primarily with Member States.[538] The Control Regulation promotes cooperation between Member States in this respect. Thus, Article 13(7) stipulates that Member States are to coordinate their control activities in order to ensure that inspection is as effective and economical as possible. To that end Member States must in particular exercise surveillance over the movement of fisheries products that may have been drawn to their attention as being subject to operations in breach of EC rules. Article 9(6) of the Control Regulation provides that where the first marketing of fisheries products does not take place in the Member State of landing, the Member State responsible for monitoring the first marketing shall ensure that a copy of the sales note is submitted to the authorities responsible for monitoring the landing of the product.

---

[535] Reg 2847/93, Art 9 is to similar effect but is more detailed, setting out, *inter alia*, the minimum information that must be contained in a sales note. Further provisions on this matter are contained in Regs 1966/2006, 1303/2007, and 1077/2008.

[536] Reg 2847/93, Art 13 is to similar effect but is more detailed, setting out, *inter alia*, the minimum information that must be contained in a transport document.

[537] Reg 2847/93, Art 28(2a) is similar.   [538] Reg 2371/2002, Art 23.

Enforcement against Member States

The rules of the CFP relating to fishing operations with which Member States have to comply are principally as follows: (a) the obligation not to exceed the fishing opportunities allocated to them; (b) the obligation to enforce the primary and secondary rules (outlined above) against fishing vessel operators and masters; and (c) various administrative obligations that are designed to promote the compliance of vessel operators and masters with EC rules or that underpin Member States' enforcement responsibilities. These last require each Member State, *inter alia*, to: (a) ensure that satellite-tracking devices are installed and operational on all vessels having its nationality that are required to carry a vessel monitoring system (VMS);[539] (b) establish and operate fisheries monitoring centres to monitor fishing activities and fishing effort;[540] (c) record details of certain catches landed at its ports;[541] (d) notify the Commission of certain landings each month and of its forecasts as to when 70 per cent of any of the quotas allocated to it will be taken;[542] (e) notify other Member States, when requested, of certain catches by their vessels landed at its ports or transhipped in its waters, such information also being notified to the Commission if the latter so requests;[543] (f) record the fishing effort deployed by its vessels in areas where there are EC effort limitation schemes in place;[544] (g) notify the Commission of such effort;[545] (h) assess in overall terms the fishing effort deployed by its vessels having a length of less than 15 m overall in such areas and of vessels of less than 10 m in the area to which Article 6 of Regulation 1954/2003 applies (ie a large 'biologically sensitive area' located to the south and west of Ireland);[546] (i) ensure that masters of its vessels comply with their reporting obligations in areas subject to fishing effort limitations;[547] (j) establish a validation system for checking and verifying all the data that it receives;[548] and (k) provisionally prohibit fishing for a particular stock once its quota is exhausted or its fishing effort level in Western waters is reached and notify the Commission of this.[549] Where certain kinds of fishing vessels are exempted from EC enforcement rules (for example, vessels below 10 m in length are exempted from keeping log books or reporting on the amounts of fish landed, see above), Member States are to carry out monitoring by sampling in order to ensure that those vessels 'respect' EC rules.[550] Member States are to transmit to the Commission a report on their enforcement activities each year,[551] and are to ensure that all data obtained in

---

[539] Reg 2847/93, Art 3(5).   [540] Reg 2847/93, Art 3(7).

[541] Reg 2847/93, Art 14. Not all landings will be by vessels having the port State's nationality since under EC law Community vessels have a right of equal access to any EC designated port: see Council Regulation (EC) No 104/2000 of 17 December 1999 on the common organisation of the markets in fishery and aquaculture products, OJ 2000 L17 /22, as amended and corrected, Art 33; and Reg 2847/93, Art 7.   [542] Reg 2847/93, Art 15.

[543] Reg 2847/93, Art 16.   [544] Reg 2847/93, Art 19g.   [545] Reg 2847/93, Art 19i.

[546] Reg 2847/93, Art 19h.   [547] Reg 2847/93, Arts 19b(3) and 19d.

[548] Reg 2847/93, Arts 19 and 19k.   [549] Reg 2847/93, Arts 21(2) and (3) and 21a.

[550] Reg 2847/93, Arts 6(6), 8(3), 14(4), and 19e(4).   [551] Reg 2847/93, Art 35(1).

carrying out their enforcement activities are treated in a confidential manner.[552] Member States may also adopt further control measures. Article 38 of the Control Regulation provides that the Regulation applies 'without prejudice to any national control measures which go beyond its minimum requirements, provided that they comply with Community law and are in conformity with' the CFP. Such measures must be notified to the Commission.[553]

The Commission is charged with ensuring that Member States comply with the above rules.[554] To this end it monitors Member States' enforcement activities and applies various forms of sanction to those Member States that it believes are not exercising their enforcement responsibilities adequately. As far as monitoring is concerned, the Commission carries out 'audits, inquiries, verifications and inspections' of Member States' enforcement activities.[555] It does so primarily through examining documentation provided by Member States and by conducting on-the-spot visits.[556] The latter are carried out by a small team of Commission inspectors (currently numbering twenty-five[557]), which has been in existence since 1983. *Commission* inspectors must be distinguished from *Community* inspectors, referred to earlier. Commission inspectors work for and report to the Commission, whereas Community inspectors are officials of Member States carrying out the monitoring and control activities described earlier. The role of Commission inspectors is primarily to observe the control and inspection activities carried out by national officials, both on land and at sea: to this end they may have access to all relevant documentation, premises, and vessels.[558] Where such observation suggests that 'irregularities could occur' in the application of the Control Regulation, the Commission may request the Member State concerned to notify it of the detailed inspection and control programme planned or adopted by that Member State. Commission inspectors may then, if necessary, carry out independent inspections to verify the implementation of that programme.[559] However, national officials are at all times responsible for the carrying out of that programme: Commission inspectors 'may not on their own initiative use the powers of inspection conferred on national agents', and they do not have access to vessels and premises unless accompanied by national agents.[560] The Basic Regulation introduced a power for Commission inspectors to carry out inspections on their own in relation to fisheries subject to a 'specific monitoring programme' adopted under Article 34c of the Control Regulation (see above), provided that the 'inspected party' does not object.[561] Nevertheless, a Commission inspector carrying out such an independent inspection has 'no police and enforcement powers'.[562] The findings of the inspector must be

---

[552] Reg 2847/93, Art 37(1).   [553] Reg 2847/93, Art 38.
[554] Reg 2371/2002, Art 26(1).   [555] Reg 2371/2002, Art 27(1).
[556] Reg 2847/93, Art 29(1).   [557] Information from the website of DG Mare.
[558] Reg 2847/93, Art 29(2). The operational expenditure of Commission inspectors is financed under Reg 861/2006, Art 8(c).   [559] Reg 2847/93, Art 29(3).
[560] Ibid.   [561] Reg 2371/2002, Art 27(1).   [562] Ibid.

notified to the Member State concerned, but the latter is not obliged to act against individuals on the basis of those findings.[563] Nevertheless, such reports and other reports drawn up following inspections by Commission inspectors are admissible evidence in judicial or administrative proceedings in any Member State.[564] In the period 2002–04 (the latest period for which figures were available at the time of writing) the Commission's inspectors carried out on average about 100 inspections a year.[565] Those inspections were targeted at vessels fishing for stocks subject to 'regional recovery and management measures' and '[h]orizontal control issues such as satellite monitoring, activity by third country vessels and marketing'.[566]

If the Commission's monitoring activities suggest that 'irregularities have occurred' in the implementation of the Control Regulation or that a Member State's 'existing monitoring powers and methods are not effective', the Commission shall inform the Member State concerned.[567] The latter must then conduct an administrative inquiry in which Commission officials may participate, although the inquiry is at all times conducted by the national authorities of the Member State concerned and Commission officials may not on their own initiative use the powers of inspection conferred on national officials: they do, however, have access to the same premises and documents as those officials.[568]

The Commission publishes quite a number of reports setting out the results of its monitoring and data collection activities. They include the triennial reports assessing the operation of the Control Regulation that are called for by Article 35(2) of that Regulation and Article 27(4) of the Basic Regulation; and annual reports on 'serious infringements' of the CFP that are called for by Article 2(2) of Regulation 1447/99.[569] In 2003 the Commission began publishing what was intended to be an annual 'compliance scoreboard', but after publishing three such 'scoreboards', the Commission appears to have abandoned this venture. From the scoreboards that it did publish and the reports mentioned above, it is clear that the level of compliance with the conservation and management rules of the CFP still left a good deal to be desired at the time (2006) to which the most recent of those reports relate. For example, the number of 'serious infringements' of CFP rules by individual vessel operators steadily increased following the adoption of Regulation 1447/99 (which introduced the concept of 'serious infringements') until 2005 (even allowing for the enlargement of the EC in 2004);[570] Member States continued to exceed the quotas allocated to them;[571] significant quantities of

---

[563] Reg 2371/2002, Art 27(2).   [564] Reg 2371/2002, Art 28(5).

[565] See the Commission's Compliance Scoreboards (referred to below).

[566] *Report from the Commission to the Council and the European Parliament on the Monitoring of the Member States' Implementation of the Common Fisheries Policy 2003–2005*, COM(2007) 167, 10.4.2007, p 2.

[567] Reg 2847/93, Art 30(2).   [568] Reg 2847/93, Art 30(2) and (3).

[569] These reports are published as COM documents.

[570] COM(2008) 670, p 5. The slight decrease in the number of infringements in 2006 is attributed by the Commission to a decrease in the number of active fishing vessels.

[571] *Third Edition of the Common Fisheries Policy Compliance Scoreboard* (2005), pp 1 and 11–16.

undersized fish were landed;[572] and few Member States complied fully with their catch reporting and fishing effort declaration obligations.[573] In its most recent triennial report on the operation of the Control Regulation, the Commission concluded that '[c]ompliance with key rules of the CFP remains poor in many fisheries'.[574]

The Commission has made it clear for many years that it considers the efforts of Member States to secure compliance by the owners and operators of Community fishing vessels with the rules of the CFP to be inadequate and unsatisfactory. In its 2001 *Green Paper on the Future of the Common Fisheries Policy* it said that Member States' monitoring and control activities 'are widely seen as insufficient and discriminatory',[575] and in a report on the situation in 2006 it expressed the view that there were still 'serious deficiencies in the control of and in the enforcement of sanctions against serious infringements, compromising the effectiveness' of the CFP.[576] There was also a lack of uniformity in sanctioning between Member States 'resulting in inequitable implementation at EC level'.[577] The Commission's most recent triennial report on the operation of the Control Regulation, covering the period 2003–05, identified a host of failings by Member States.[578] In the same vein the Third Compliance Scoreboard concluded that '[t]he effective implementation of conservation measures continues to be eroded by shortcomings in the enforcement, monitoring and control of CFP rules by a number of Member States. This, in turn, is undermining progress towards sustainable fisheries, and thus the future of the Community fishing industry itself.'[579] The Court of Auditors has been equally critical of Member States' enforcement efforts. In a report published in 2007 it criticized Member States in particular for numerous shortcomings in recording catches (with the consequence that data on catches, on which the monitoring of compliance with quotas turns, is unreliable); in carrying out inspections; and in taking proceedings against those found to have broken EC rules and imposing adequate penalties.[580]

There are a number of measures that the Commission can take against Member States that are not exercising their enforcement responsibilities adequately. Under Article 26(2) of the Basic Regulation, where poor enforcement 'may lead to a

---

[572] COM(2007) 167, p 10.

[573] *Third Edition of the Common Fisheries Policy Compliance Scoreboard* (2005), pp 1, 9–11, and 16–17.

[574] COM(2007) 167, p 9.   [575] COM(2001) 135, p 12.   [576] COM(2008) 670, p 7.

[577] Ibid.

[578] COM(2007) 167, pp 3–8. There is a similar catalogue of failings listed in *Communication from the Commission: Compliance with the Rules of the Common Fisheries Policy 'Compliance Work Plan and Scoreboard'*, COM(2003) 344, 11.06.2003, pp 3–5.

[579] *Third Edition of the Common Fisheries Policy Compliance Scoreboard* (2005), p 40.

[580] European Court of Auditors, *Special Report No 7/2007 (pursuant to Article 284(4) second paragraph, EC) on the control, inspection and sanction systems relating to the rules on conservation of Community fisheries resources together with the Commission's replies*, OJ 2007 C317/1, paras 18–43, 65-85, and 89–94.

serious threat to the conservation of living aquatic resources or the effective operation of the Community control and enforcement system necessitating urgent action', the Commission shall inform the Member State concerned and set it a deadline of not less than fifteen working days to demonstrate compliance and to give its comments. Such comments are to be taken into account in any action that the Commission may take under Article 26(3) of the Basic Regulation. Under that provision, 'if there is evidence of a risk that fishing activities carried out in a given geographical area could lead to a serious threat to the conservation of living aquatic resources', the Commission may take 'preventive measures'. The nature of such measures is not indicated other than that they must be 'proportionate to the risk of a serious threat' to conservation and must not last longer than six months.[581] There is a regrettable lack of clarity about the scope of the Commission's powers under Article 26(2) and (3), which were first introduced by the current Basic Regulation, and the relationship between those two paragraphs. The powers have not yet been used. The Commission has apparently been dissuaded from doing so because of the difficulty of gathering the necessary evidence and the need to observe the principle of proportionality.[582]

A second possible measure that the Commission can take is to penalize a Member State that has exceeded the fishing opportunities allocated to it by reducing its fishing opportunities in future years. The various ways open to the Commission to do this are discussed in subsection 2.1 above.

Another, and rather different, use of fishing opportunities deductions relates to the failure of a Member State to comply with its obligations relating to controlling the landing and transhipment of illegal catches. Where a Member State fails to take proceedings against a vessel not having its nationality that has landed illegally taken catches in one of its ports or transhipped such catches in its waters or does not transfer the prosecution to the flag State of the offending vessel, the quantities of illegally landed or transhipped fish may be set against the quotas allocated to the State of landing or transhipment.[583] Here the deduction does have a genuinely punitive character. However, this is not a power that the Commission appears yet to have used.

A final kind of sanction that can be used against a Member State that does not exercise its enforcement responsibilities adequately is for the Commission, as the guardian of the Community interest, to use its powers under Article 226 EC to bring that Member State before the Court. That is a power to which the Commission has increasingly resorted in more recent years. Whereas in the fifteen-year period from 1987 (when the first such case was brought before the Court) to 2001 the Commission brought nine cases involving alleged failures by Member States to

[581] Reg 2371/2002, Art 26(3).   [582] Court of Auditors, *Special Report No 7/2007*, para 101.
[583] Reg 2847/93, Art 32(2). The Court rejected a challenge to the equivalent provision in a predecessor of Reg 2847/93, based on the argument that it was a disproportionate penalty to impose on port States: see Case C-9/89 *Spain v Council* [1990] ECR I-1383, paras 26 and 30–31.

comply with their enforcement obligations to the Court, in the almost seven years from January 2002 to the end of November 2008 inclusive it brought a further eighteen cases.[584] As with other areas of EC law, the Commission commences far more proceedings under Article 226 EC than it ends up bringing before the Court. The majority of proceedings are discontinued either at the stage of the letter of formal notice or at the stage of the reasoned opinion, presumably because either the Commission is satisfied that there has been no breach or the Member State has taken action to comply or promises to take such action. Of the twenty-seven cases brought before the Court up to the end of November 2008, seven have been against France;[585] three each against Denmark,[586] the Netherlands,[587] and the UK;[588] two each against Ireland,[589] Italy,[590] and Spain;[591] and one each against Belgium, Finland, Greece, Portugal, and Sweden.[592] Judgment in four cases was pending at the time of writing, and therefore these cases are not discussed further here. In every case that has been decided the Court found the Member State concerned in breach of EC law.

The vast majority (seventeen) of the twenty-three decided cases were concerned with enforcement failures that led to the Member States concerned exceeding the quotas allocated to them. One case may sometimes cover several years of such failures. The cases against the Netherlands cover the years 1983–86; the UK 1985–88 and 1990–96; Denmark 1988, 1990–92 and 1994–97; France 1988 and 1990–96; Spain 1990–97; Belgium 1991–96; Portugal 1994–96; and Finland, Ireland, and

---

[584] These numbers do not include cases relating to failures of enforcement that occurred entirely outside Community waters. The handful of such cases is referred to in Chapter 5.

[585] Case C-64/88 *Commission v France* [1991] ECR I-2727; Case C-52/95 *Commission v France* [1995] ECR I-4443; Case C-333/99 *Commission v France* [2001] ECR I-1025; Joined Cases C-418/00 and C-419/00 *Commission v France* [2002] ECR I-3969; Case C-179/05 *Commission v France* [2006] ECR I-13; and Case C-556/07 *Commission v France*, OJ 2008 C37/20 (judgment pending).

[586] Joined Cases C-259/03, C-260/03, and C-343/03 *Commission v Denmark*, judgment of 14 July 2005 (unpublished). Unpublished judgments may be found on the website of the Court.

[587] Case 290/87 *Commission v Netherlands* [1989] ECR 3083; Case C-52/91 *Commission v Netherlands* [1993] ECR I-3069; and Case C-232/08 *Commission v Netherlands*, OJ 2008 C209/25 (judgment pending).

[588] Case C-454/99 *Commission v United Kingdom* [2002] ECR I-10323; Case C-140/00 *Commission v United Kingdom* [2002] ECR I-10379; and Case C-236/05 *Commission v United Kingdom* [2006] ECR I-10819.

[589] Case C-317/02 *Commission v Ireland*, judgment of 18 November 2004 (unpublished); and Case C-38/05 *Commission v Ireland*, judgment of 8 December 2005 (unpublished).

[590] Case C-161/05 *Commission v Italy* [2006] ECR I-125; and Case C-249/08 *Commission v Italy* OJ 2008 C209/30 (judgment pending).

[591] Case C-42/03 *Commission v Spain*, judgment of 2 December 2004 (unpublished); and Case C-189/07 *Commission v Spain*, OJ 2007 C129/10 (judgment pending).

[592] Case C-149/03 *Commission v Belgium*, judgment of 21 July 2005 (unpublished); Case C-43//02 *Commission v Finland*, judgment of 17 March 2005 (unpublished); Case C-22/04 *Commission v Greece*, judgment of 14 April 2005 (unpublished); Case C-332/03 *Commission v Portugal*, judgment of 26 May 2005 (unpublished); and Case C-271/02 *Commission v Sweden*, judgment of 16 December 2004 (unpublished).

Sweden all 1995–96. The only coastal EC Member State in the North Sea and north-east Atlantic that has not had a case brought against it relating to exceeding quotas (or, indeed, any other aspect of compliance with the conservation measures of the CFP) is Germany. In the cases against the other Member States, the Court did not as such find those Member States in breach of EC law for exceeding quotas. Most of the cases involved the breach of four distinct obligations. First, the Court invariably found Member States in breach of Article 20(3) of the Basic Regulation (or the equivalent provision in the previous basic Regulations) for failing to adopt a method for allocating quotas to their vessels. Secondly, the Court found Member States in breach of Article 2(1) of the Control Regulation (or the equivalent provisions of its predecessor Regulations) for failing to exercise their monitoring and inspection obligations satisfactorily. Those two provisions were usually taken together. The Court found Member States in breach of those provisions simply by reason of the fact that the Member State concerned had repeatedly exceeded its quotas by a significant margin.[593] The third obligation of which the Court invariably found a breach was the duty of a Member State under Article 21(2) of the Control Regulation (or its predecessors) provisionally to prohibit fishing once it is probable that it has exhausted its quota. That is an objective test in the sense that the position will be determined, not on the basis of what the Member State believed to be the size of the catch at the time that the prohibition on fishing should have been introduced, but on the actual size of the catch at that time.[594] Some reservations may be expressed about the use of such a test because in practice it will usually not be possible to determine the actual size of the catch until some time after the fishery should have been closed, when all the relevant figures for landings and transhipments have become available. Lastly, in most of the cases the Court found a Member State to be in breach of Article 31(1) of the Control Regulation (or its predecessors) for failing to prosecute those fishermen who continued to fish after a ban on fishing was eventually imposed. While a single failure to prosecute will not constitute a breach, a Member State that is unable to show a consistent pattern of administrative or criminal proceedings taken against alleged offenders will be in breach.[595] In such cases the Court takes a strict line with Member States. Pleas of an inability to know the size of the catch taken by its vessels because of the failure of the latter to report their catches accurately, or because of the failure of port States to pass on information about catches where vessels landed their catches in ports of States other than their flag State (as was frequently the case), or because of the malfunctioning of information technology systems, are all invariably and summarily rejected by the Court.

[593] See, for example, Case C-333/99 *Commission v France*, para 35 and Case C-454/99 *Commission v United Kingdom*, para 31. In Case C-317/02 *Commission v Ireland*, para 44, the Court suggested that any exceeding of a quota would be considered a breach of the provisions in question.

[594] See, for example, Case C-52/91 *Commission v Netherlands*, paras 35–39 and Case C-333/99 *Commission v France*, para 52.

[595] See Case C-149/03 *Commission v Belgium*, para 43; Case C-332/03 *Commission v Portugal*, paras 34–36; and Joined Cases C-259/03, C-260/03, and C-343/03 *Commission v Denmark*, paras 63–69.

To some extent the above cases have a symbolic rather than a practical value. In many of them the Court's judgment was given more than ten years after the year in which quotas were exceeded.[596] It is probably out of the question for a Member State to rectify its breaches—after ten years or more it is almost certainly impractical to contemplate proceedings against fishermen whose actions led to quotas being exceeded—or for the EC's institutions to make deductions from that Member State's future quotas. At most, the cases serve as a warning to Member States to improve their enforcement performance.

In that respect the remaining six of the twenty-three cases so far decided under Article 226 EC, which relate to matters other than exceeding quotas, are different, because in each of them there was corrective action that those States could take (and should have taken) following the Court's judgment. Four of the cases concerned the failure of the defendant Member States to supply the Commission with data on catches and/or fishing effort deployed as required by Articles 15(4), 18(1), and 19i of the Control Regulation.[597] In one of the earlier quota cases the same failure was also at issue: in that case the Court held that the obligation to supply data included a duty to ensure that the information was accurate.[598] The fifth case concerned the failure of Greece to ensure that its vessels complied with the obligation to carry a VMS by the specified deadlines.[599] The final case, Case C-64/88, concerned the failure by France during the mid-1980s adequately to monitor and inspect French vessels for compliance with EC rules on mesh sizes for nets, attachment to nets, and by-catches; to prohibit the sale of under-sized fish; and to take proceedings against those fishermen found to be in breach of EC rules.

A judgment by the Court under Article 226 EC is simply declaratory. However, since the entry into force of the 1992 Treaty on European Union the Commission has had the power, under Article 228 EC, to ask the Court to impose a lump sum or penalty payment on a Member State that has not complied with a judgment of the Court given under Article 226 EC. The purpose of that provision is to induce a Member State to comply with the Court's judgment.[600] Although Article 228 EC has been used several times in relation to other areas of EC law, it has so far been used only once in respect of failure to comply with a fisheries judgment. In 2005 the Court delivered a judgment in which it imposed on France a lump sum penalty of €20 million, as well as a penalty payment of €57.8 million for every six-month period thereafter that France continued in non-compliance, for its failure to comply with those parts of the judgment in Case C-64/88 (the last case mentioned above), given in 1991, concerning the sale of under-sized fish and the

---

[596] Seventeen years in the two most extreme cases, Case C-259/03 *Commission v Denmark* and Case C-454/99 *Commission v United Kingdom*.

[597] Case C-38/05 *Commission v Ireland*; Case C-161/05 *Commission v Italy*; Case C-179/05 *Commission v France*; and Case C-236/05 *Commission v United Kingdom*.

[598] Case C-454/99 *Commission v United Kingdom*, paras 47–49.

[599] Case C-22/04 *Commission v Greece*.

[600] Case C-304/02 *Commission v France* [2005] ECR I-6263, paras 80–81, 91, and 97.

failure to take proceedings against French fishermen breaching EC rules.[601] This is
the first time in any Article 228 EC case that the Court has imposed both a lump
sum and a penalty payment. Its action in doing so, and the size of both penalties
imposed, was prompted by the fact that France's failure concerned measures to
protect juvenile fish (the lack of such protection being characterized by the Court
as a 'serious threat to the maintenance of certain species' and as jeopardizing
'pursuit of the fundamental objective' of the CFP) and the duration of France's
non-compliance with the 1991 judgment.[602] By the end of the second six-month
period following the Court's 2005 judgment, the Commission considered that
France had taken sufficient action to be regarded as being in compliance with the
Court's original 1991 judgment.[603] According to the Court of Auditors, the
Court's 2005 judgment led to a rapid improvement in the enforcement of CFP
rules, not only in France but also in other Member States against which the
Commission had begun Article 228 EC proceedings.[604]

The Court of Auditors considers Article 226 EC to be an ineffective form of
sanction because of the length of time proceedings take, the extensive resources
that the Commission has to devote to such proceedings, and the fact that the
Court's judgment is only declaratory.[605] The Court of Auditors also regrets the
fact that the Commission has no power to suspend aid allocated to Member States
in cases of failure to apply the control rules, and is critical of the Commission's
failure to assess the extent to which Member States comply with their obligation to
recover aid granted under the fisheries structural funds from beneficiaries who
have violated CFP rules.[606]

Reform of the control system

As mentioned at the beginning of this subsection, the Commission published
proposals for reform of the Community control system in November 2008.[607] The
Commission introduced its proposals by recalling the criticisms of the current
control system already made by itself and the Court of Auditors, which have been
referred to above. In a nutshell, those criticisms are that the current system is
'inefficient, expensive, complex and it does not produce the desired results'.[608]
The Commission identified the 'drivers for non-compliance' as being the over-
capacity of EC fishing fleets (discussed in the following subsection of this chapter);

[601] Case C-304/02 *Commission v France.*   [602] Ibid, paras 104–105 and 114–115.
[603] Court of Auditors, *Special Report No 7/2007*, Commission's Reply, p 3.
[604] Court of Auditors, *Special Report No 7/2007*, para 100.
[605] Court of Auditors, *Special Report No 7/2007*, paras 96–98.
[606] Court of Auditors, *Special Report No 7/2007*, paras 103–104.
[607] *Communication from the Commission to the European Parliament and the Council on the proposal for a
Council Regulation establishing a Community control system for ensuring compliance with the rules of the Common
Fisheries Policy*, COM(2008) 718, 14.11.2008; and COM(2008) 721. See also the *Commission Staff
Working Document* accompanying the proposal, SEC(2008) 2760, 14.11.2008.
[608] COM(2008) 718, p 2.

the fact that the risk of infringement of CFP rules being detected is 'rather low'; lack of uniformity between Member States in control and inspection, which makes it difficult to follow up infringements in judicial and administrative systems systematically; lack of adequate sanctions where breaches of CFP rules are established; the complexity of the current control system; and the limited and ineffective powers of the Commission under the current system.[609] The costs of the shortcomings of the current control system are that catches by Community fishing vessels exceed prescribed levels, leading to a reduction in the size of fish stocks, lower catches, and reduced revenue for the fishing industry.[610]

The Commission's proposed reform of the control system is centred on the adoption of a new Regulation, running to some 116 Articles, that would replace the present Control Regulation, Regulation 1627/94, and the detailed provisions on control in the Basic Regulation (Articles 22–28), although much of the substance of those Regulations is reproduced in the proposed Regulation. The latter would apply to all fishing and fishing-related activities in Community waters, in the Member States, and to the activities of Community fishing vessels outside Community waters, and 'would encompass all control issues, from the net to the plate'.[611] The new Regulation would complement Regulations 1005/2008 (on IUU fishing) and 1006/2008[612] to 'form a new Control framework'.[613] The general objective of that new framework is to put in place 'a comprehensive integrated and uniform policy for the control of fishing activities in Community waters in order to ensure the effective implementation of the CFP. Overall, the new approach to control should be based on simplification, standardization, increased cost effectiveness and reduction of administrative burden.'[614]

According to the Commission, its proposed new control system has three broad features.[615] The first is a new, harmonized approach to control and inspection with the aim of ensuring uniformity in implementation. To that end there would be introduced a systematic risk analysis approach and a comprehensive traceability system. That would require data to be automated as far as possible and be subject to comprehensive and systematic cross-checking. In addition, there would be specific control measures for multi-annual plans, discards, marine protected areas, and real time closure of fisheries.[616] The second feature of the new control system is the promotion of a culture of compliance by simplifying and rationalizing the legal framework; introducing deterrent and harmonized sanctions (including the setting

---

[609] COM(2008) 718, p 4. See also SEC(2008) 2760, pp 8–12.   [610] COM(2008) 718, pp 4–5.
[611] COM(2008) 718, p 9.
[612] Council Regulation (EC) No 1006/2008 of 29 September 2008 concerning authorisations for fishing activities of Community fishing vessels outside Community waters and the access of third country vessels to Community waters, amending Regulations (EEC) No 2847/93 and (EC) No 1627/94 and repealing Regulation (EC) No 3317/94, OJ 2008 L286/33. This Regulation is discussed in section 8 below and in Chapter 5.   [613] COM(2008) 718, p 3.
[614] COM(2008) 718, p 5.   [615] COM(2008) 718, pp 5–8.
[616] Proposed Regulation, Arts 33–36 and 39–46.

of maximum and minimum levels of fines and the establishment of a penalty point system);[617] improving cooperation between Member States (including inspecting each other's vessels in all Community waters)[618] and cooperation between Member States and the Commission (especially in relation to exchange of data);[619] and extending the powers of the Community Fisheries Control Agency to cover audits and inspections of national control systems, organization of operational cooperation between Member States, assistance to Member States to improve their control systems, and the possibility of setting up emergency units of the Agency where a serious risk to the CFP could be identified which otherwise would not be tackled adequately.[620] Thirdly, the new control system would aim to ensure the effective application of CFP rules by strengthening the powers of the Commission and Commission inspectors. In particular, Commission inspectors would be given the same powers as national inspectors, and the Commission would be able to establish action plans for deficient Member States to improve their implementation of the CFP; close a fishery in wider circumstances than currently; impose financial measures against Member States whose control systems were inadequate; make deductions from future quotas or other fishing opportunities with a rather more punitive element than at present where a Member State had exceeded its past quotas or opportunities; and take various emergency measures where there were threats to the conservation of resources.[621]

The Commission's proposed Regulation is based on Article 37 EC. That means that it is to be adopted by the Council after it has received the European Parliament's opinion on the proposal. The Commission envisages that the European Economic and Social Committee, the Committee of the Regions, and the European Data Protection Supervisor will each also be asked for their opinions. It is thus likely to be some considerable time after its proposal by the Commission before the new Regulation is adopted, and in any case it is not intended to come into force until the beginning of 2010.[622] It remains to be seen how far the proposed Regulation will be amended during the process of its adoption, and whether the Commission's expectation that it will cure all the ills of the current control system and lead to Community vessels fishing profitably and sustainably[623] will be fulfilled.

2.8 Adjusting capacity

As explained in the introduction to subsection 2.2 above, 'capacity', in broad terms, refers to the potential of a vessel (or a group of vessels) to catch fish, and is usually expressed in terms of a vessel's characteristics, such as its tonnage and engine power, and/or the type and size of a vessel's fishing gear.[624] In Chapter 3 it

---

[617] Proposed Regulation, Arts 81–85.   [618] Proposed Regulation, Arts 71–73.
[619] Proposed Regulation, Arts 23–25 and 101–110.   [620] Proposed Regulation, Art 112.
[621] Proposed Regulation, Arts 27–28 and 87–101.   [622] Proposed Regulation, Art 116.
[623] COM(2008) 718, p 9. See also SEC(2008) 2760, pp ix and 37–46.
[624] For a detailed discussion of definitional issues relating to capacity, see COM(2007) 39, pp 3–8.

was pointed out that one of the major problems in world fisheries in recent years has been over-capacity in the fishing fleets of many States, in other words where the collective capacity of vessels in a particular fleet is greater than the optimum required to catch the quantities of fish (in the form of quotas) or other fishing opportunities (expressed, for example, in measures of effort) that may be available to them.[625] Over-capacity has two particular undesirable consequences. First, as pointed out in the last part of subsection 2.7 above, over-capacity is widely considered to be one of the major 'drivers for non-compliance' with fisheries regulations, and in particular as likely to lead to over-fishing.[626] Secondly, over-capacity often leads to fishing being well below the optimum economic level: in other words, the economic returns per vessel are lower than they would be with fewer vessels pursuing the same fishing opportunities.[627] As was seen in Chapter 3, one of the International Plans of Action adopted within the framework of the FAO Code of Conduct for Responsible Fisheries is aimed at reducing and eventually eliminating over-capacity in world fishing fleets.

It was pointed out in Chapter 1 that at the time of the extension of Member States' fisheries jurisdiction to 200 nm in the late 1970s and the first attempts to devise an EC system of fisheries management for those waters, there was considerable over-capacity in EC fishing fleets. The EC did not begin to try to address that problem and adjust capacity to catch potential until 1983, when it adopted the first of what became four 'multi-annual guidance programmes' (MAGPs).[628] The other three programmes were adopted in 1986,[629] 1992,[630] and 1997,[631] and covered the periods 1987–91, 1992–96, and 1997–2002, respectively. The

---

[625] Cf the Court of Auditors' definition of over-capacity as 'a fleet's excess catch capacity relative to the level of catch that would allow the resource to be sustainably exploited': Court of Auditors, *Special Report No 7/2007*, para 108.

[626] See further Court of Auditors, *Special Report No 7/2007*, paras 107 and 109–111; COM(2008) 718, p 3; and Brown, J, *Fishing Capacity Management in the EU post 2002 CFP Reform* (London: Institute for European Environmental Policy, 2006), 1.

[627] Sissenwine, M and Symes, D, *Reflections on the Common Fisheries Policy*, Report to the General Directorate for Fisheries and Maritime Affairs of the European Commission, July 2007, 19; and *Commission Working Document, Reflections on further reform of the Common Fisheries Policy* (2008), pp 1 and 5.

[628] Council Regulation (EEC) No 2908/83 of 4 October 1983 on a common measure for restructuring, modernizing and developing the fishing industry and for developing aquaculture, OJ 1983 L290/1, as amended.

[629] Council Regulation (EEC) No 4028/86 of 18 December 1986 on Community measures to improve and adapt structures in the fisheries and aquaculture sector, OJ 1986 L376/7, as amended.

[630] Commission Decisions 92/588/EC to 92/598/EC of 21 December 1992 on a multiannual guidance programme for the fishing fleet for the period 1993–1996 pursuant to Council Regulation (EEC) No 4028/86, OJ 1992 L401/3, as amended. Decisions on transitional programmes for 1992 were published in OJ 1992 L193/1–52.

[631] Council Decision 97/413/EC of 26 June 1997 concerning the objectives and detailed rules for restructuring the Community fisheries sector for the period from 1 January 1997 to 31 December 2001 with a view to achieving a balance on a sustainable basis between resources and their exploitation, OJ 1997 L175/27, as amended.

programmes required each Member State to adjust the size of its fishing fleet to a particular figure (designed to reflect the fishing opportunities available to that fleet) over the period of the programme concerned.

In its 2001 *Green Paper on the Future of the Common Fisheries Policy*,[632] the Commission argued that the MAGPs had not been a success. The programmes had been 'set by the Council at levels that were not ambitious enough to address the problem of excess capacity effectively and [had] often not been enforced. They were also complex to administer. Subsidies for construction/modernization and running costs may have aggravated the current situation.'[633] The fourth MAGP, in particular, had very weak objectives for capacity reduction and was 'very complex and costly to administer'.[634] Overall the Community fleet was 'much too large'.[635] Far from meeting the target of a 40 per cent reduction in capacity recommended by the 'Gulland' and 'Lassen' reports produced by two groups of independent experts in 1990 and 1996, respectively,[636] the overall reduction in capacity by 2001 was of the order of no more than 18 per cent in terms of tonnage and 12 per cent in terms of engine power.[637] The Commission therefore concluded that '[c]ontinuation of the current system would not only be unable to cut the excessive capacity of the fleet but would lead to an increased fishing effort in a situation where the state of the stocks cannot even support the present effort'.[638] Accordingly, it recommended the adoption of a different, more effective, more transparent, and simpler policy that could be more tightly enforced, and that would establish a balance between fleet capacity and exploitation rates that was consistent with long-term management objectives.[639]

Following the Commission's *Green Paper* and *Roadmap* with their proposals for change, the Council abandoned MAGPs in favour of a new approach to adjusting capacity to catch potential, set out in the current Basic Regulation. This is the first time that detailed, substantive provisions on capacity adjustment

---

[632] COM(2001) 135.

[633] COM(2001) 135, p 10. A similar view was expressed by the Court of Auditors in *Special Report No 7/2007*, para 112. Similar conclusions have been reached by commentators. See, for example, Hatcher, A, 'Subsidies for European Fishing Fleets: the European Community's Structural Policy for Fisheries 1971–1999' *Marine Policy* 24 (2000), 129, especially at 135–140; and Song, Y, 'The Common Fisheries Policy of the European Union: Restructuring of the Fishing Fleet and the Financial Instrument for Fisheries Guidance' *IJMCL* 13 (1998), 537, especially at 555–577.

[634] COM(2001) 135, p 11   [635] COM(2001) 135, p 10.

[636] *Report of an Independent Group of Experts on Guidelines for the Preparation of the Multiannual Guidance Programmes in relation to the Fishing Fleet for the Period 1992–1996*, Internal Document, European Commission, Brussels, 19.11.90 and *Report of the Group of Independent Experts to advise the Commission on the Fourth Generation of Multi-annual Guidance Programmes*, 26.4.96, XIV/298/96-EN, as cited in Hatcher, 'Subsidies for European Fishing Fleets', 140.   [637] COM(2001) 135, p 11.

[638] Ibid.

[639] COM(2001) 135, pp 26–27. See also pp 31–33, and *Communication from the Commission on the reform of the Common Fisheries Policy ('Roadmap')*, COM(2002) 181, 28.5.2002, pp 10–11.

have been included in a CFP basic Regulation. Those provisions are set out in Chapter III.[640]

The Chapter begins, in Article 11(1), with a general obligation on Member States to 'put in place measures to adjust the fishing capacity of their fleets in order to achieve a stable and enduring balance between such fishing capacity and their fishing opportunities'. The 'fishing opportunities' referred to are defined in Article 3(q) of the Basic Regulation as quantified entitlements to fish, 'expressed in terms of catches and/or fishing effort', and mean, *inter alia*, those opportunities allocated to Member States in the annual and biennial fishing opportunities Regulations (see subsection 2.1 above). 'Fishing capacity' is defined in general terms in Article 3(n) of the Basic Regulation as 'a vessel's tonnage in GT [ie gross tonnes] and its power in kW [ie kilowatts], as defined in Articles 4 and 5' of Regulation 2930/86.[641] Perhaps mindful of the Commission's criticism in its *Green Paper* that tonnage and power are an over-simplified way of measuring capacity and that there are 'many other factors that determine the fishing mortality generated by the fleet', such as fishing gear, fish finding equipment, and telecommunications,[642] Article 3(n) goes on to add that '[f]or certain types of fishing activity, capacity may be defined by the Council using for example the amount and/or the size of a vessel's fishing gear'.[643] The obligation in Article 11(1) on Member States to adjust fleet capacity so as to achieve a balance between such capacity and fishing opportunities is, fairly obviously, rather imprecise. It is an obligation that would be difficult to enforce through, for example, Article 226 EC proceedings because it is a difficult technical exercise to calculate the amount of capacity necessary to catch the fish available at the most efficient level, which is what Article 11(1) appears to require.[644] The obligation in Article 11(1) receives some reinforcement from the legislation governing the European Fisheries Fund (EFF).[645] That legislation provides that in order to receive funding from the EFF, each Member State must draw up a national strategic plan which, *inter alia*, sets out its strategy for 'the adjustment of fishing effort and

---

[640] Chapter III was partially amended in 2007 by Council Regulation (EC) No 865/2007 of 10 July 2007 amending Regulation (EC) No 2371/2002 on the conservation and sustainable exploitation of fisheries resources under the Common Fisheries Policy, OJ 2007 L192/1.

[641] Council Regulation (EEC) No 2930/86 of 22 September 1986 defining the characteristics of fishing vessels, OJ 1986 L274/1, as amended. See also Commission Decision 95/84/EC of 20 March 1995 concerning the implementation of the Annex to Council Regulation (EEC) No 2930/86 defining the characteristics of fishing vessels, OJ 1995 L67/33. For problems with the way engine power is defined in this legislation, see COM(2007) 39, pp 5 and 10–11.

[642] COM(2001) 135, pp 10–11. See also the Court of Auditors, *Special Report No 7/2007*, paras 115, 117, and 119.

[643] For the problems and possibilities of measuring capacity in this way, see COM(2007) 39, pp 6–7 and 10–11.

[644] Sissenwine and Symes, *Reflections on the Common Fisheries Policy*, 20. See also Brown, *Fishing Capacity Management*, 19.

[645] Council Regulation (EC) No 1198/2006 of 27 July 2006 on the European Fisheries Fund, OJ 2006 L223/1.

capacity', and an operational programme that, *inter alia*, takes into account the need to achieve 'a stable and enduring balance between fishing capacity and fishing opportunities' (see further Chapter 8).[646]

Following the general obligation to adjust fleet capacity to available fishing opportunities, Article 11 goes on, in paragraph 2, to stipulate more precisely that Member States must ensure that their fishing capacity does not exceed the 'reference levels' to be laid down by the Commission. Such reference levels relate to each Member State's fishing fleet as a whole, and not to particular segments of the fleet (such as beam trawlers or small-scale coastal vessels) as was the case under the fourth MAGP. For each Member State its reference level is the sum of the levels that were to be attained by each segment of that Member State's fleet by the end of the fourth MAGP.[647] As mentioned above, the Commission did not consider that the latter levels went far enough to eliminate excess capacity: this does not appear, therefore, to bode too well for the new system of capacity adjustment. However, reference levels are not immutable. Article 11(4) provides that where public aid is granted for the withdrawal of fishing capacity (a matter discussed further below) that goes beyond the reduction necessary to comply with the reference level established as described, the 'amount of the capacity' withdrawn (presumably that part over and above the amount necessary to comply with the reference level) is to be automatically deducted from the reference level, thus lowering the latter to a new level. The effect of that provision depends, of course, on how many vessels are withdrawn with public aid, but there has already been some decrease in reference levels: for example, the reference level for the thirteen pre-2004 flag Member States taken together[648] decreased by 5.72 per cent in terms of tonnage and about 5.91 per cent in terms of kW between the beginning of 2003 and the end of 2006.[649] A word of caution needs to be added about comparing tonnage levels between different years, both here and below. Prior to 2003 there was no uniform method used in the EC for calculating the tonnage of fishing vessels. In 1994 the EC introduced a harmonized system for calculating tonnage,[650] which was

---

[646] Reg 1198/2006, Arts 15(2)(a) and 19(a). See further Brown, *Fishing Capacity Management*, 10–15.

[647] Reg 2371/2002, Art 12(1). The actual reference levels are set out in Commission Regulation (EC) No 1438/2003 of 12 August 2003 laying down implementing rules on the Community Fleet Policy as defined in Chapter III of Council Regulation (EC) No 2371/2002, OJ 2003 L204/21, as amended. The validity of this Regulation was unsuccessfully challenged by Spain in Case T-219/04 *Spain v Commission* [2007] ECR II-1323.

[648] Austria and Luxembourg are not included because neither has a sea-fishing fleet.

[649] The authors' calculation is from the figures given: (a) for the beginning of 2003 in Reg 1438/2003, Annex I (as amended); and (b) for the end of 2006 in *Commission Staff Working Document, Annex I to the Annual Report from the Commission to the European Parliament and the Council on Member States' efforts during 2006 to achieve a sustainable balance between fishing capacity and fishing opportunities*, SEC(2007) 1703, 19.12.2007, p 9.

[650] See: (a) Council Regulation (EC) No 3259/94 of 22 December 1994 amending Regulation (EEC) No 2930/86 defining the characteristics of fishing vessels, OJ 1994 L339/11; and (b) Dec 95/84.

supposed to be fully operational by 2003: however, by the end of 2006 there were still a small number of vessels whose tonnage was not yet measured according to the EC's harmonized system.[651]

At the end of 2006, the most recent year for which figures were available at the time of writing, all thirteen pre-2004 flag Member States had complied with their obligation not to exceed reference levels, whether expressed in terms of tonnage or engine power—indeed, some Member States' fleets were very substantially below their reference levels: the lowest were the Portuguese and Spanish fleets, which were 57.81 and 65.65 per cent of their respective reference levels in terms of tonnage and 82.66 and 65.99 in terms of kW.[652] Collectively, the fleets of those thirteen Member States were at 76.15 per cent of reference levels in terms of tonnage and 82.23 per cent in terms of engine power.[653] Those figures are scarcely surprising in view of the fact that at the end of the fourth MAGP, virtually all Member States' fleets were well below target levels.[654]

The core of the new system of capacity adjustment, and the primary mechanism for meeting reference levels, is the so-called 'entry/exit scheme', which is set out in Article 13 of the Basic Regulation. That scheme provides that: (a) the addition of new capacity to a Member State's fishing fleet *without* public aid is only permitted where at least the same amount of capacity has previously been withdrawn from the fleet without public aid (the latter term is not defined but presumably covers both aid from the EC and aid from public bodies in Member States); (b) the addition of new vessel capacity *with* public aid is only permitted where at least the same amount of capacity (in the case of the entry of a new vessel equal to or less than 100 GT in size) or at least 1.35 times that amount of capacity (in the case of the entry of a new vessel over 100 GT) has previously been withdrawn without public aid;[655] and (c) a vessel, other than one engaged in 'small-scale coastal fishing', may only replace its engine with financial aid from the EFF where there is a reduction in engine power equal to 20 per cent of the power of the engine replaced: that reduction must be deducted from the reference level specified in engine power.[656] Regarding vessels engaged in 'small-scale coastal fishing',[657] Regulation 1198/2006 (the EFF Regulation) provides that the new engine may

---

[651] SEC(2007) 1703, p 5.   [652] SEC(2007) 1703, p 9.   [653] Ibid.

[654] *Annual Report from the Commission to the Council and the European Parliament on the results of the multiannual guidance programmes for the fishing fleets at the end of 2002*, COM(2003) 508, 21.08.2003, p 7.

[655] Note that no EC aid has been available for the construction of new fishing vessels since the beginning of 2007: see Reg 1198/2006, Art 25(2). Any public aid for the construction of new vessels would therefore have to come entirely from Member States (as explained below). The EFF is discussed further below and in Chapter 8; State aid is discussed in Chapter 8.

[656] Reg 2371/2002, Art 13. See also: (a) Reg 1198/2006, Arts 25(3)(b) and (c) and Art 25 generally; and (b) Commission Regulation (EC) No 498/2007 of 26 March 2007 laying down detailed rules for the implementation of Council Regulation (EC) No 1198/2006 on the European Fisheries Fund, OJ 2007 L120/1, Art 6.   [657] Such vessels are defined in Reg 1198/2006, Art 26(1).

have 'the same power as the old one or less'.[658] The consequence of the entry/exit scheme is that any renewal of a Member State's fishing fleet should not lead to an increase in its capacity, and in some cases will lead to a reduction in capacity. There is, however, a possible complication arising from the provisions of the EC Treaty on freedom of establishment. As was seen in subsection 2.6 above, a fisherman having the nationality of one Member State is entitled to move and establish himself in another Member State and re-register his fishing vessels under the flag of the latter State (the host State). Such action would have the result of adding new capacity to the fleet of the host State without there being any withdrawal of capacity, and therefore on the face of it would contravene Article 13. It would seem that such a conflict must be resolved in favour of the freedom of establishment, as that freedom derives from the Treaty, which, as a higher norm, will prevail over the provisions of a Regulation. In practice, this issue does not appear so far to have been of any great significance.

With the exception of engine replacement, Article 13 allows new capacity to be added to the fleet *only* where other capacity is withdrawn *without* public aid. Nevertheless, public aid is available for the withdrawal of capacity. The EFF Regulation provides that the EFF may contribute financial aid for the permanent withdrawal of a vessel from the fishing fleet provided that such withdrawal forms part of a so-called 'fishing effort adjustment plan', and is attained *only* by scrapping the vessel or reassigning it, under the flag of a Member State, to activities other than fishing (for example, as a supply vessel to the offshore oil and gas industry) or for the purpose of creating artificial reefs.[659] Furthermore, such permanent withdrawal of capacity must be 'programmed in the form of national decommissioning schemes which shall not exceed two years from the date of their entry into force'.[660] Where the EFF contributes to the costs of permanent withdrawal of a vessel, the flag Member State must also contribute to the costs.[661] Member States may also fund withdrawals entirely provided that they comply with EC rules on State aid.[662] Where the permanent withdrawal of a vessel from a Member State's fleet is publicly aided, that vessel's fishing licence (and, where relevant, fishing authorization) must be withdrawn and '[t]he capacity corresponding to the licence [and authorization] cannot be replaced'.[663] As mentioned above, Article 11(4) of the Basic Regulation provides that such publicly aided withdrawals result in a reduction in reference levels.

Under the entry/exit scheme new capacity may be added to a Member State's fleet only if accompanied by a withdrawal of the same amount of capacity, or in

[658] Reg 1198/2006, Art 25(3)(a).   [659] Reg 1198/2006, Art 23(1).

[660] Reg 1198/2006, Art 23(2). The Commission has set out what it considers should be the main elements of a national decommissioning scheme in its *EFF Vademecum*, available on the website of DG Mare (no document reference number in final published version), section 4.2.1.

[661] Reg 1198/2006, Art 53.

[662] Reg 1198/2006, Art 7. EC rules on State aid are discussed in Chapter 8.

[663] Reg 2371/2002, Art 11(3).

some cases greater capacity. There are, however, two limited exceptions to that principle. Under Article 11(5) and (6) of the Basic Regulation, in order to improve safety on board, working conditions, hygiene, and product quality: (a) a vessel aged five years or more may be modernized over the main deck, leading to an increase in tonnage of the vessel;[664] and (b) Member States may re-allocate to new or existing vessels 4 per cent of the tonnage withdrawn from the fleet with public aid, provided that in both cases that does 'not increase the ability of the vessels to catch fish'. Where there is an increase in tonnage as a result of the application of points '(a)' or '(b)', Article 11(5) and (6) provide that 'reference levels are to be adapted accordingly': presumably this means that reference levels increase in line with any added tonnage.

The policy for capacity adjustment contained in the Basic Regulation does not in principle require, or even encourage, a reduction in fleet capacity: it essentially obliges Member States not to increase the existing capacity of their fleets.[665] One qualification must be made to that statement. Under Article 11(2) of the Basic Regulation in its unamended form, between the beginning of 2003 and the end of 2004 each Member State that chose to enter into new public aid commitments for fleet renewal after the end of 2002 was obliged to achieve a reduction in the overall capacity of its fleet of 3 per cent 'for the whole period in comparison to the reference levels referred to in Article 12'. Although, apart from that time-limited exception, the Basic Regulation does not require a reduction in fleet capacity, some reduction has resulted and will continue to result from the operation of the entry/exit scheme. The EFF offers some encouragement to reducing capacity by providing funding for the permanent withdrawal of vessels, but there is no obligation on Member States to make use of this possibility (see further Chapter 8). The Commission regards EC limitations on effort (discussed in subsection 2.2 above) as an incentive for Member States to reduce capacity, but concludes that so far the impact of fishing effort measures on capacity reduction has been low.[666] Overall, therefore, it seems rather unlikely that EC measures have made or will make a significant impact on the problem of over-capacity that existed when the Basic Regulation was adopted.

Nevertheless, even though the Basic Regulation and other EC measures do not in general require a reduction in fleet capacity, such a reduction has in fact occurred since the adoption of the Basic Regulation. Between the beginning of 2003 and the end of 2006 (the most recent year for which figures were available at the time of writing), capacity for the thirteen pre-2004 flag Member States taken

---

[664] Such modernization is eligible for funding from the EFF: see Reg 1198/2006, Art 25(1) and (2).

[665] Court of Auditors, *Special Report No 7/2007*, para 114

[666] Court of Auditors, *Special Report No 7/2007*, para 115 and Commission's replies, pp 2, 13, and 14; and *Annual Report from the Commission to the European Parliament and the Council on Member States' efforts during 2006 to achieve a sustainable balance between fishing capacity and fishing opportunities*, COM (2007) 828, 19.12.2007, p 10.

together decreased in terms of tonnage by 8.9 per cent and in terms of engine power by 9.32 per cent.[667] The figures for tonnage reduction should be read subject to the caveat mentioned above about the problem of comparing tonnages from different years because of a lack of uniformity among Member States in the method for measuring tonnage. The figures also need to be read subject to the point about 'technical creep' made below. It does not follow, of course, that the reduction in capacity shown by these figures was due to the Basic Regulation and other EC measures. Market forces and reduced fishing opportunities may also have played some part. An interesting question is how fleet levels at the end of 2006 compared with those in the early 1990s when the Gulland Report recommended cuts of 40 per cent in capacity. At the end of 1991 the total capacity of the fishing fleets of the then eleven flag Member States was 2.051 million tonnes and 8.316 million kW,[668] whereas at the end of 2006 the equivalent figures were 1.639 million tonnes and 5.834 million kW,[669] representing reductions of 20.1 per cent and 29.8 per cent, respectively. Even allowing for the problem of comparing tonnages, the reduction in capacity is a long way short of the recommended 40 per cent. It also needs to be remembered that Gulland's figure was calculated in part according to the fishing opportunities available in the early 1990s: in general, the latter were greater than current fishing opportunities.

One of the weaknesses of the current capacity adjustment scheme is the lack of knowledge of the relationship between fishing capacity and available fishing opportunities. In 2007 the Commission set up a working group to draw up a harmonized method to assess the balance between fishing capacity and fishing opportunities.[670] The working group did not appear to have reported by the time of writing. A further factor that needs to be borne in mind in considering decreases in fishing capacity is that technological developments may lead to an increase in fish catching capacity even if the tonnage and engine power of a fishing fleet remain constant, a phenomenon known as technical (or technological) creep (see also subsection 2.2 above). The ICES estimates such increase to be of the order of 1 to 3 per cent per annum.[671] That means that the reductions in fleet tonnage and engine power achieved in recent years have largely been offset by developments in technology. The Court of Auditors' conclusion in 2007 was that there was still 'significant overcapacity' in Member States' fishing fleets.[672] That conclusion is broadly shared by the Commission, which in September 2008 stated that '[f]ishing fleets are still too large' and that there was 'still considerable overcapacity of fishing power in relation to the fish resources available'.[673] Given that the capacity of the EC fleet in

---

[667] SEC(2007) 1703, p 11.   [668] Hatcher, 'Subsidies for European Fishing Fleets', 136.

[669] SEC(2007) 1703, p 9.   [670] COM(2007) 828, p 10.

[671] Sissenwine and Symes, *Reflections on the Common Fisheries Policy*, 20.

[672] Court of Auditors, *Special Report No 7/2007*, para 120.

[673] *Commission Working Document, Reflections on further reform of the Common Fisheries Policy*, pp 1 and 4. See also WWF, *Mid-Term Review of the EU Common Fisheries Policy*, 59–60.

2006 was well below reference levels (see above), it is clear that reference levels are far too high and indeed are of little practical significance.

Because EC fleets are well within their reference levels, it would be possible for Member States not to comply with the entry/exit scheme while still remaining within reference levels. In fact, as at the end of 2006 all Member States were complying with the entry/exit scheme, apart from France and Spain, which had marginally exceeded the entry/exit ceiling in respect of tonnage (by 1.6 and 0.21 per cent, respectively), though not in respect of engine power.[674]

So far Member States have, with one or two minor exceptions, complied with current EC rules relating to the adjustment of capacity. Should they fail to do so in the future, Article 16 of the Basic Regulation provides for two relatively mild forms of sanction. First, financial aid from the EFF, other than for the scrapping of vessels, may be granted only if a Member State has, *inter alia*, not exceeded its reference level and has complied with the entry/exit scheme: where that is not the case, aid shall be suspended by the Commission.[675] Secondly, where the Commission deems that the capacity of the fleet of a Member State exceeds the capacity that would have resulted from compliance with, *inter alia*, its reference level and the entry/exit scheme, the Member State concerned 'shall immediately reduce its fishing effort to the level which would have existed' had there been such compliance and 'shall communicate its reduction plan to the Commission for verification'.[676] Articles 24, 25(1), and 27 of the Control Regulation require Member States to take appropriate control measures to verify that EC rules on capacity adjustment are complied with.[677] Article 25(2) of the Control Regulation provides that where a Member State has failed to adopt such measures, the Commission 'may make proposals to the Council for the adoption of appropriate general measures', without prejudice to its powers to institute proceedings against the Member State concerned under Article 226 EC. The latter powers are in any case available to the Commission to deal with non-compliance with reference levels and the entry/exit scheme.

In the case of those States joining the EC in 2004 and 2007, the system of reference levels in the Basic Regulation does not apply because they did not take part in the fourth MAGP.[678] They are, however, fully subject to the entry/exit

---

[674] SEC(2007) 1703, p 7.

[675] Art 16 of the Basic Regulation in fact refers to the predecessor Regulations of the EFF Regulation (Reg 1198/2006): Art 104(2) of the latter provides that references to the predecessor Regulations are to be construed as references to Reg 1198/2006.   [676] Reg 2371/2002, Art 16(2).

[677] For a detailed discussion of those provisions, see Long and Curran, *Enforcing the Common Fisheries Policy*, 175–80.

[678] Council Regulation (EC) No 1242/2004 of 28 June 2004 granting derogations to the new Member States from certain provisions of Regulation (EC) No 2371/2002 relating to reference levels of fishing fleets, OJ 2004 L236/1; and Council Regulation (EC) No 783/2007 of 25 June 2007 granting derogations to Bulgaria and Romania from certain provisions of Regulation (EC) No 2371/2002 relating to reference levels of fishing fleets, OJ 2007 L175/1. See also Commission Regulation (EC) No 916/2004 of 29 April 2004 amending Regulation (EC) No 1438/2003 laying down implementing rules on the Community Fleet Policy by reason of the Accession of the Czech Republic, Estonia, Cyprus, Latvia, Lithuania, Hungary, Malta, Poland, Slovenia and Slovakia to the European Union, OJ 2004 L163/81.

scheme, which means that the capacity of their fleets at the time of their accession to the EC should not increase: in fact, in the period between their accession in 2004 and the end of 2006, the capacity of the combined fleets of the seven new flag Member States decreased by 22.81 per cent in terms of tonnage and 22.73 per cent in terms of kW.[679]

Special provisions apply to fishing fleets registered in the EC's outermost regions.[680] Reference levels are set by fleet segment (as under the fourth MAGP), rather than for the fleet as a whole (as is the case with metropolitan fleets under the Basic Regulation). Transitional provisions allow some increases to the capacity of those fleets up to the end of 2011:[681] that arrangement is said to be justified by the 'relative importance of the fisheries sector' and the 'particular structural, social and economic situation' of the regions concerned.[682] From 2012 the entry/exit scheme of the Basic Regulation will apply fully to the outermost regions.[683] In addition, Article 3 of Regulation 639/2004 provides that any vessel transferred from an outermost region to the metropolitan fleet is to be treated as a new entry to the latter for the purposes of the entry/exit scheme. Where such a vessel was built or modernized with public aid, that aid must be reimbursed. In practice, with the exception of some fleet segments in the Azores and the French outermost regions, there was a significant decrease in the capacity of the fishing fleets of the outermost regions between the beginning of 2003 and the end of 2006.[684]

In the summer of 2008, when the price of oil soared to record levels, the Council adopted a package of measures to help the fishing industry cope with the resulting huge increase in the price of fishing vessel fuel.[685] The measures were designed to 'address both the immediate situation of economic and social hardship while tackling systemic overcapacity',[686] and have the potential to make a significant impact on the capacity of EC fishing fleets. Regulation 744/2008 provides, *inter alia*, for increased public aid to be granted up to the end of 2010 to

---

[679] SEC(2007) 1703, p 11.

[680] See: (a) Council Regulation (EC) No 639/2004 of 30 March 2004 on the management of fishing fleets registered in the Community outermost regions, OJ 2004 L102/9, as amended; and (b) Commission Regulation (EC) No 2104/2004 of 9 December 2004 laying down detailed implementing rules for Council Regulation (EC) No 639/2004 on the management of fishing fleets registered in the Community outermost regions, OJ 2004 L365/19, as amended. For the meaning of the term 'outermost region', see Chapter 2.   [681] Reg 639/2004, Art 2.

[682] Reg 639/2004, recital (3).   [683] Reg 639/2004, Art 2.

[684] COM(2007) 828, p 10 and SEC(2007) 1703, p 12.

[685] Council Regulation (EC) No 744/2008 of 24 July 2008 instituting a temporary specific action aiming to promote the restructuring of the European Community fishing fleets affected by the economic crisis, OJ 2008 L202/1. On the background to this measure, see *Communication from the Commission to the European Parliament and to the Council on promoting the adaptation of the European Union fishing fleets to the economic consequences of high fuel prices*, COM(2008) 453, 8.7.2008; and *Proposal for a Council Regulation instituting a temporary specific action aiming to promote the restructuring of the European Union fishing fleets affected by the economic crisis*, COM(2008) 454, 8.7.2008, pp 2–4.   [686] Reg 744/2008, recital (3).

those fishing fleets that are subject to a Fleet or Fleet Segment Adaptation Scheme.[687] Such Schemes, which are to be adopted and implemented by Member States, may be applied only to fleets or fleet segments whose energy costs represent on average at least 30 per cent of production costs and to vessels that carried out fishing activity of at least 120 days at sea during the two years preceding a Scheme's adoption.[688] A Scheme must result in a permanent reduction of at least 30 per cent of the fishing capacity of the fleet or fleet segment covered by the Scheme by the end of 2012 at the latest. The threshold of 30 per cent may be lowered to 20 per cent where: (a) a Scheme concerns a Member State whose fleet comprises less than 100 active vessels or less than 12,000 GT; or (b) where a Scheme covers only vessels of less than 12 m in length and a 30 per cent reduction 'would disproportionately affect the viability of the fisheries related activities depending on it'.[689] Schemes must by notified by Member States to the Commission by 30 June 2009 at the latest.[690] The increased public aid to be provided to vessels included in a Scheme covers, *inter alia*, the costs of permanent and temporary cessation of fishing activities, improvements in energy efficiency, and replacing an existing vessel by a vessel with less capacity and lower energy consumption (known as partial decommissioning).[691] By way of derogation from Article 11(3) and (4) of the Basic Regulation (which, as noted above, deal with the non-replacement of licences in the case of publicly funded withdrawals and the effect of such withdrawals on reference levels), Member States shall be entitled to reallocate up to a quarter of the capacity permanently withdrawn under a Scheme to new vessels resulting from partial decommissioning.[692] Such reallocation need not be taken into account in the operation of the entry/exit scheme under the Basic Regulation.[693] In Fleet Adaptation Schemes in which partial decommissioning is applied to more than one-third of initial fleet capacity, the total reduction in capacity under the Scheme must be at least 66 per cent.[694]

The widespread adoption of Fleet Adaptation Schemes by Member States would clearly have a major impact on reducing over-capacity in EC fishing fleets. At the time of writing, Member States still had more than six months in which to notify Schemes to the Commission, so it was not known how many Schemes might be adopted. Regulation 744/2008, and in particular its relationship to the EFF Regulation, is discussed further in Chapter 8.

As mentioned above, the Commission considers that there is still substantial over-capacity in EC fishing fleets. In its Working Document, *Reflections on further reform of the Common Fisheries Policy*, published in September 2008, the Commission argues that capacity could be further reduced by making more use of 'structural funds' (the Commission is presumably referring here primarily to the

---

[687] Reg 744/2008, Art 11.   [688] Reg 744/2008, Art 12(1), (3), and (5).
[689] Reg 744/2008, Art 12(4).   [690] Reg 744/2008, Art 12(6).
[691] Reg 744/2008, Arts 14–18.   [692] Reg 744/2008, Art 19(1).
[693] Reg 744/2008, Art 19(3).   [694] Reg 744/2008, Art 19(4).

EFF, even though it is not strictly speaking a structural fund in terms of the EC budget) and rights-based management approaches (discussed in subsection 9.6 below).[695]

Reducing the capacity of fishing fleets inevitably means some loss of jobs, which may have significant socio-economic implications in regions where alternative employment possibilities are limited.[696] To help those fishermen losing their jobs as a result of capacity adjustment, the EFF Regulation provides that the Fund 'may contribute to the financing of socio-economic measures proposed by Member States for fishers affected by developments in fishing which involve', *inter alia*, the payment of compensation to fishermen who have worked on board vessels withdrawn from the fleet, schemes for retraining fishermen for occupations outside fishing, and early retirement.[697]

3 EC fisheries management in the Baltic Sea

3.1 Introduction

The Baltic Sea, for the purposes of CFP Regulations, usually includes ICES divisions III b, c, and d but excludes the Skagerrak and the Kattegat. ICES divisions III b and c are defined in Regulation 3880/91.[698] The coastal States in the Baltic comprise eight Member States (Denmark, Estonia, Finland, Germany, Latvia, Lithuania, Poland, and Sweden) and Russia. The Russian territorial sea and EEZ constitute only a very small part of the Baltic Sea, most of which therefore comprises Community waters.

An agreement between the EC and Russia in respect of fisheries in the Baltic Sea was finalized in July 2006 and was subsequently initialled by both parties but at the time of writing it had not been formally approved by the Council (see further Chapter 5).[699] The legislative proposal for what became Regulation 1941/2006 (the predecessor to Regulation 1404/2007, on annual fishing opportunities in the Baltic Sea) stated that the EC and Russia 'have agreed to establish management measures for shared stocks already from 1 January 2007 based on a provisional application of

---

[695] *Commission Working Document, Reflections on further reform of the Common Fisheries Policy*, 6 and 8. For a critique of the Commission's approach to capacity management, see Brown, *Fishing Capacity Management*, 19–20.

[696] Further on this question, see *Communication from the Commission to the European Parliament and the Council: Action plan to counter the social, economic and regional consequences of the restructuring of the EU fishing industry*, COM(2002) 600, 6.11.2002.

[697] Reg 1198/2006, Art 27(1). See also Arts 43–45 and Reg 498/2007, Art 8.

[698] Reg 3880/91, Annex III.

[699] *Proposal for a Council Regulation on the conclusion of the Agreement between the European Community and the Government of the Russian Federation on co-operation in fisheries and the conservation of the living marine resources in the Baltic Sea*, COM(2006) 868, 22.12.2006.

the agreement'.[700] However, the legislative proposal for what is now Regulation 1404/2007, issued in September 2007, noted that: 'Joint management measures have *not* been established for the shared stocks at this stage.'[701] (Emphasis added.)

Two Decisions relating to Regional Advisory Councils (RACs) suggest that no Member State vessels other than those flagged to the eight coastal Member States mentioned above currently undertake fishing activities in the Baltic Sea. In Decision 2004/585, establishing RACs, the term 'Member State concerned' is defined as 'a Member State *having a fishing interest* in the area or fisheries covered by a [RAC]' (emphasis added),[702] thus potentially including flag States as well as coastal States. However, in turn, Decision 2006/191, making the Baltic Sea RAC operational, lists the Member States concerned for the Baltic as being only the eight EC coastal States,[703] thus implying that no other EC Member State has a 'fishing interest' in the Baltic Sea.

The CFP legislation surveyed in section 2 above applies to the Baltic Sea (except Russian waters) unless it is obvious from the terms of such legislation that it does not (for example, Regulations 1954/2003, on effort, and 850/98, on technical measures, on which, see subsections 2.2 and 2.3 above). However, there are some Regulations that apply specifically and exclusively to the Baltic Sea, of which the principal ones are: (a) Regulation 2187/2005, on technical measures; (b) the annual Regulation setting out fishing opportunities and associated conditions regarding the Baltic Sea (Regulation 1404/2007, at the time of writing); and (c) Regulation 1098/2007, establishing a long-term plan for Baltic Sea cod stocks. Regulations 2187/2005 and 1404/2007 will be addressed here; Regulation 1098/2007 has already been discussed in general terms in subsections 2.1 to 2.3 above and will not be considered further in this section except in passing. The above Regulations are supplemented by a few detailed or very specific Regulations which are not discussed here.

3.2 Regulation 2187/2005

Regulation 2187/2005 repealed and replaced its predecessor, Regulation 88/98. Article 1, on 'Subject matter and scope', states that: 'This Regulation lays down technical conservation measures in relation to the taking and landing of fishery

---

[700] *Proposal for a Council Regulation fixing the fishing opportunities and associated conditions for certain fish stocks and groups of fish stocks applicable in the Baltic Sea* for 2007, COM(2006) 485, 5.9.2006, explanatory memorandum, section 1, p 2.

[701] *Proposal for a Council Regulation fixing the fishing opportunities and associated conditions for certain fish stocks and groups of fish stocks applicable in the Baltic Sea* for 2008, COM(2007) 492, 3.9.2007, explanatory memorandum, p 2.

[702] Council Decision 2004/585/EC of 19 July 2004 establishing Regional Advisory Councils under the Common Fisheries Policy, OJ 2004 L256/17, as amended, Art 1(1).

[703] Commission Decision 2006/191/EC of 1 March 2006 declaring operational the Regional Advisory Council for the Baltic Sea under the common fisheries policy, OJ 2006 L66/50, recitals (4) and (3).

resources in the maritime waters under the sovereignty or jurisdiction of the Member States and situated in the geographical area specified in Annex I.' Annex I in turn lists and defines subdivisions 22–32 in the Baltic Sea, which jointly comprise ICES subdivisions III b, c, and d. The measures in Regulation 2187/2005 apply to Community fishing vessels in the waters referred to in Article 1 and, in principle, to Russian-flagged vessels when fishing in such waters.

As indicated by its Article 1, the focus of Regulation 2187/2005 is 'technical conservation measures'. That term is not defined, but the subsequent articles include specifications about, *inter alia*, minimum mesh sizes and other factors relating to mesh, minimum percentages of certain target species to be retained on board, gear types and adaptations, maximum lengths and maximum immersion time of certain passive gear, minimum landing size of fish, and closed areas, as well as some corresponding monitoring, control, and surveillance measures.

The technical measures on gear types address, *inter alia*, driftnets, reflecting the fact that Regulation 894/97 (see subsection 2.3 above) does not cover the Baltic Sea. In short, from the start of 2008 it is 'prohibited to keep on board, or use for fishing, driftnets'.[704] A definition of the term 'driftnet' has now been inserted in the Regulation by Regulation 809/2007 (see subsection 2.3 above). There are special measures regarding the Gulf of Riga, with its 'unique and rather sensitive marine ecosystem'.[705] The technical measures in Regulation 2187/2005 are supplemented by those in Regulation 1098/2007 (the Baltic Sea cod plan) and transitional technical measures in Regulation 1404/2007 (on fishing opportunities, on which, see subsection 3.3 below).

The technical measures set out in Regulation 2187/2005 relate to many more species than have TACs under Regulation 1404/2007. For example, required catch percentages are specified for up to twelve species as well as one family, and minimum landing sizes are fixed for eight species,[706] whereas TACs are set under Regulation 1404/2007 for only five species. That difference serves to illustrate that the Baltic Sea contains several commercially relevant species for which catch limits are currently non-existent (even taking into account those TACs set out in Regulation 40/2008 that cover Community waters in the Baltic Sea—see subsection 3.3 below).

Article 26 of Regulation 2187/2005 provides some delegated powers to the Member States, supplementing those in Articles 8–10 of the Basic Regulation. Thus Member States 'may, for the conservation and management of stocks or to reduce the effect of fishing on the marine eco-system, take technical measures designed to limit fishing opportunities which: (a) supplement measures set out in Community fisheries Regulations; or (b) go beyond minimum requirements set out in Community fisheries Regulations'.[707] Any such measures 'shall apply solely

---

[704] Reg 2187/2005, Art 9(1).   [705] Reg 2187/2005, Arts 20–22 and recitals (10) and (11).
[706] Reg 2187/2005, Annexes II, III, and IV.   [707] Reg 2187/2005, Art 26(1).

to the fishermen of the Member State concerned and shall be compatible with Community law'.[708]

A comparison with Article 10 of the Basic Regulation reveals some important differences between the two provisions. First, Article 26 relates only to technical measures, whereas Article 10 applies to measures more generally. Secondly, Article 26 does not refer to waters under Member State 'sovereignty or jurisdiction', whereas Article 10 does. Thirdly, Article 26 expressly permits measures 'to reduce the effect of fishing on the marine eco-system' whereas Article 10 does not. Fourthly, Article 10 does not specify any procedure while Article 26 does (not least an express power for the Commission to require withdrawal or modification of the measure if it does meet the requirements of Article 26).[709] Of note, Article 26 refers to 'fishermen' rather than 'fishing vessels', raising the question of whether a Member State could use the delegated power in respect of its nationals operating on fishing vessels flagged to other States.

3.3 Regulation 1404/2007

Prior to the 2006 fishing year, the annual fishing opportunities for the Baltic Sea were set out in the principal annual Regulation (see subsection 2.1 above). Now the Baltic Sea is dealt with in a separate Regulation, of which the latest at the time of writing was Regulation 1404/2007. The legal basis of the annual Regulation for the Baltic Sea is the same as that of the principal annual Regulation (see subsection 2.1 above). Notwithstanding the separate Regulation for the Baltic Sea, it should be noted that Regulation 40/2008 (the principal annual Regulation at the time of writing) also includes some TACs which cover Community waters in the Baltic Sea.[710] The reasons for this are not clear. The authors are unaware whether the species in question are found in commercial quantities in the Baltic Sea or whether, for example, the coverage of the Baltic Sea is intended (simply) to improve efficacy of control measures regarding catch of the species concerned taken in adjacent ICES area III a.

The process for the adoption of the annual Regulation for the Baltic Sea is similar to that for the principal annual Regulation, except that since 2006 the Commission's legislative proposal for Baltic Sea fishing opportunities has been issued in September each year. The Commission's annual policy statements, including the rules for TACs set out in Annex II to the 2008 policy statement (see subsection 2.1 above), apply to the Baltic Sea. Amongst other purposes,

---

[708] Reg 2187/2005, Art 26(2).   [709] Reg 2187/2005, Art 26(3)–(5).

[710] Reg 40/2008, Annex IA—see those TACs for, *inter alia*, common sole, haddock, hake, ling, and Norway lobster, referring to ICES area III a and EC waters of ICES areas III b, c, and d. See also TACs for mackerel and saithe.

Regulation 1404/2007 serves to implement the Baltic Sea cod plan (Regulation 1098/2007) for the year 2008.[711]

Article 2(1) of Regulation 1404/2007, on 'Scope', states that: 'This Regulation shall apply to Community fishing vessels . . . and fishing vessels flying the flag of, and registered in, third countries operating in the Baltic Sea.' The Baltic Sea is defined as ICES divisions III b, c, and d.[712] The reference to third country vessels is presumably a reference to Russian-flagged vessels if fishing in Community waters in the Baltic Sea (notably pursuant to the new EC-Russia fisheries agreement if it enters into force—see subsection 3.1 above).

As noted above, the catch limits set by Regulation 1404/2007 relate to only five species, namely herring, cod, plaice, Atlantic salmon, and sprat, in specified subdivisions of the Baltic Sea. When setting the catch limits, the Council has duly specified which TACs are analytical or precautionary and whether or not Articles 3, 4, and 5(2) of Regulation 847/96 apply (see further subsection 2.1 above).

In addition to TACs, Regulation 1404/2007 contains a short annex, Annex II, entitled 'Fishing effort limits',[713] which appears to be aimed at implementing the Baltic Sea cod plan specifically.[714] The Baltic Sea cod plan sets some periods in which fishing with certain gears is prohibited. Annex II to Regulation 1404/2007 sets the maximum number of 'days absent from port' for vessels using such gears outside those prohibited periods. It also makes some extra days available to take into account any permanent cessations of fishing activities using the gears in question.

Although Regulation 1404/2007 deals primarily with fishing opportunities, it also contains an annex on 'Transitional technical measures'.[715] As its title suggests, this annex contains some technical measures which are valid only for 2008, namely a prohibition on the retention on board of certain flatfish species in specified areas and periods, with some exceptions. The transitional technical measures in Regulation 1404/2007 may be contrasted with the longer-term technical measures in Regulation 2187/2005.

4 EC fisheries management in the Mediterranean Sea

4.1 Introduction

When seeking to adopt a system of fisheries management in the early 1980s, the EC concentrated its efforts on the north-east Atlantic and North Sea, and paid little or no attention to the Mediterranean Sea. There were various reasons for this. EC

---

[711] Reg 1404/2007, see references to Reg 1098/2007 in preamble and in Annex II.
[712] Reg 1404/2007, Art 3(b).   [713] Reg 1404/2007, Annex II.
[714] COM(2007) 492, explanatory memorandum, section 5, p 5.
[715] Reg 1404/2007, Annex III.

Member States' fishing industries in the Mediterranean were quite small, accounting for only around 10 per cent of the total Community catch.[716] Furthermore, most Mediterranean fisheries take place close to the coast and are undertaken from small vessels that generally confine their activities to their own waters.[717] Partly for that reason, few Mediterranean States had until very recently claimed EEZs or any other form of fisheries jurisdiction beyond the territorial sea.

In spite of its concentration on the north-east Atlantic and North Sea in the early years of the EC's fisheries management system, the EC has applied some elements of that system to the Mediterranean Sea since its inception. Those elements include the successive basic Regulations and the rules relating to access, capacity adjustment, and enforcement. What were notably not applied during the 1980s were the TAC and quota system and technical conservation measures.

By 1990 the EC's institutions were starting to show more interest in the Mediterranean Sea. In that year the Commission published a consultation paper in which it advocated EC measures to prevent the deterioration of stocks.[718] Four years later the Council responded by adopting Regulation 1626/94, which contained the EC's first fisheries measures applying specifically and exclusively to the Mediterranean Sea, namely a set of technical conservation measures to harmonize the legislation of Mediterranean Member States.[719] From 1996 the EC began adopting technical measures for highly migratory species in the Mediterranean Sea (which were not dealt with in the original version of Regulation 1626/94), and from 1998 onwards it adopted TACs and quotas for Community vessels fishing for bluefin tuna in the Mediterranean Sea. By 2001, the Commission was arguing that the EC should go much further and integrate the Mediterranean Sea fully into the CFP, but in a way that took account of the particular characteristics of Mediterranean fisheries.[720] In line with that thinking, the Commission published an Action Plan for the conservation and sustainable exploitation of Mediterranean fisheries in October 2002.[721] That Plan had the following principal elements: the concerted extension of Member States' fisheries jurisdiction in order to bring more fisheries under national and EC control, thus facilitating management; a reduction

---

[716] Lequesne, C., *The Politics of Fisheries in the European Union* (Manchester: Manchester University Press, 2004), 12–13.

[717] *Communication from the Commission to the Council and the European Parliament laying down a Community Action Plan for the conservation and sustainable exploitation of fisheries resources in the Mediterranean Sea under the Common Fisheries Policy*, COM(2002) 535, 09.10.2002, pp 5–6.

[718] *Outline of a Common Fisheries System in the Mediterranean*, SEC(90) 1136, 25 July 1990.

[719] Council Regulation (EC) No 1626/94 of 27 June 1994 laying down certain technical measures for the conservation of fishery resources in the Mediterranean, OJ 1994 L171/1, as amended. Those were, in fact, not quite the first EC technical measures applying to the Mediterranean. The initial EC legislation limiting the use of driftnets, adopted two years earlier, applied to the Mediterranean. see Council Regulation (EEC) No 345/92 of 27 January 1992 amending for the eleventh time Regulation (EEC) No 3094/86 laying down certain technical measures for the conservation of fishery resources, OJ 1992 L42/15. See also subsection 2.3 above.

[720] COM(2001) 135, p 38. See also COM(2002) 181, p 8.   [721] COM(2002) 535.

in capacity and fishing effort; changes to methods of fishing in order to conserve resources and protect the environment; and the improvement of control and enforcement. The Commission also argued that there was a need to improve scientific knowledge (the lack of which was an obstacle to effective management) and to involve stakeholders more in the consultation process.[722] Increased EC involvement in Mediterranean fisheries was also stimulated by the EC's accession to the General Fisheries Commission for the Mediterranean (GFCM) (the regional fisheries management organization with responsibility for the Mediterranean) in 1998 (see further Chapter 5); the deteriorating state of many Mediterranean stocks; the increasing realization that many Mediterranean stocks were shared or straddling;[723] and the prospect of three Mediterranean States (Cyprus, Malta, and Slovenia) becoming members of the EC in 2004.

As regards the first element in the Commission's Action Plan (the extension of fisheries jurisdiction), Spain had already claimed a 'fisheries protection zone' up to the equidistance line with neighbouring States in 1997 and one of the prospective Member States, Malta, had claimed a 25 nm EFZ in 1978. Since publication of the Commission's Action Plan, France, Italy, and Slovenia have all claimed 'ecological protection zones' and Cyprus (very unusually for a Mediterranean State) has claimed a 200 nm EEZ.[724] Thus, the only Mediterranean Member State that has not yet claimed any kind of zone in the waters beyond its territorial sea is Greece. It seems unlikely that it will do so, given the formidable delimitation problems with Turkey that would result if it did.

In October 2003 the Commission included some of the other elements of its Action Plan in a draft Regulation,[725] which would also repeal and replace Regulation 1626/94, which in the view of the Commission had been poorly implemented and enforced.[726] The Commission's draft, as amended, was eventually adopted by the Council in December 2006 as Regulation 1967/2006. The latter addresses six main issues, each of which will be examined in turn: (a) management plans; (b) technical measures; (c) Malta; (d) protected species and habitats; (e) control; and (f) leisure fisheries.

4.2 Management plans

Under Article 18 of Regulation 1967/2006 the Council 'may' adopt management plans for specific Mediterranean fisheries, in particular in areas totally or partially beyond the territorial sea (and therefore, of course, possibly including the high

---

[722] COM(2002) 535, pp 26–27.

[723] COM(2002) 535, pp 5 and 7–8. For the nature of shared and straddling stocks, see Chapter 3.

[724] See further Chapter 2.

[725] *Proposal for a Council Regulation concerning management measures for the sustainable exploitation of fishery resources in the Mediterranean Sea and amending Regulations (EC) No 2847/93 and (EC) No 973/2001*, COM(2003) 589, 9.10.2003.   [726] COM(2001) 135, p 20.

seas). Such plans may include, *inter alia*, fishing effort management measures; specific technical measures, including temporary derogations from other measures laid down by the Regulation (discussed below), provided that such derogations are necessary for the operation of the fisheries and that the sustainable exploitation of the resources concerned is ensured by the management plan; extension of vessel monitoring systems, which are already compulsory for vessels over 15 m (see subsection 2.7 above), to vessels between 10 and 15 m in length; and 'temporary or permanent restrictions to zones, reserved to certain gears or to vessels having undertaken obligations in the framework of the management plan'. As at the time of writing, the Council had not yet adopted any such plans, nor had the Commission put forward proposals for such plans.

Unlike the Council, which 'may' adopt management plans, each of the seven Mediterranean Member States 'must' adopt management plans for fisheries using certain kinds of gear within its territorial sea by the end of 2007.[727] Such plans may include measures that go beyond the provisions of Regulation 1967/2006 for the purpose of increasing the selectivity of fishing gear, reducing discards, and limiting fishing effort.[728] These national plans must be notified to the Commission.[729] If the Commission considers a plan insufficient to provide a 'high level of protection of resources and the environment', it may ask the Member State concerned to amend the plan in question or may propose to the Council 'appropriate measures for the protection of the resources and the environment'.[730] Where a plan is likely to affect the vessels of another Member State (and that is likely to be limited, by virtue of the effect of Article 17(2) of the Basic Regulation (see subsection 2.5 above)), the Member State proposing the plan may adopt it only after consulting the other Member State, the Commission, and the Regional Advisory Council in accordance with the procedure set out in Article 8(3) to (6) of the Basic Regulation (on which see subsection 2.4 above), which means that the Commission must confirm, cancel, or amend the proposed plan.[731] The authors have been unable to ascertain whether any national plans had been adopted by the 2007 deadline or subsequently by the time of writing.

4.3 Technical measures

The provisions of Regulation 1967/2006 on technical measures address 'fishing protected areas', restrictions regarding fishing gear, and the minimum sizes of marine organisms that may be caught. These measures are generally more restrictive and wider-ranging in scope than the measures contained in Regulation 1626/94 that they replace. Regarding 'fishing protected areas', Article 6 of

---

[727] Reg 1967/2006, Art 19(1).   [728] Reg 1967/2006, Art 19(4).
[729] Reg 1967/2006, Art 19(7).   [730] Reg 1967/2006, Art 19(9).
[731] Reg 1967/2006, Art 19(8).

Regulation 1967/2006 (which has no equivalent in Regulation 1626/94) provides that by the end of 2008 the Council is to designate fishing protected areas 'essentially beyond the territorial seas of Member States'. Such areas are defined as areas within which 'all or certain fishing activities are temporarily or permanently banned or restricted in order to improve the exploitation and conservation of living aquatic resources or the protection of marine ecosystems'.[732] A principal purpose of establishing such areas is to protect nursery and spawning grounds.[733] No such areas had been designated at the time of writing. In so far as any future such areas extend to the high seas, they will, of course, be binding only on Community fishing vessels. Under Article 7 Member States are also to designate fishing protected areas in their territorial seas by the end of 2008, additional to those that they may already have designated under Article 4 of Regulation 1626/94. The adoption of national fishing protected areas is subject to the same procedures as national management plans. The authors have been unable to ascertain whether any national fishing protected areas had been adopted by the time of writing. It would perhaps be sensible in most cases if both Community and national fishing protected areas were components of Community and national management plans, but no suggestion to this effect is explicitly made in Regulation 1967/2006.

Regarding restrictions on fishing gear, which are set out in Articles 8–14 of Regulation 1967/2006, certain types of gear (such as explosives, pneumatic hammers, or grabs) are prohibited completely, and restrictions are placed on the time, place, or manner in which other types of gear may be used. There are provisions on minimum mesh sizes, which are to be gradually increased (although not by as much as the Commission had proposed). These fishing gear regulations are designed in part to allow small-scale fishermen to operate close to the coast to the exclusion of larger vessels in order to protect nursery areas and sensitive habitats, and to 'enhance the social sustainability of Mediterranean fisheries'.[734] Articles 15 and 16 lay down the minimum permitted size of marine organisms that may be caught, retained, and sold. Article 25 requires the Council to adopt measures to protect juvenile swordfish by the end of 2007. As at the time of writing the only measure that the Council had adopted in this regard was a one-month long prohibition on the fishing of swordfish in the Mediterranean Sea during the autumn of 2008 '[i]n order to protect the swordfish, in particular small fish'.[735]

As well as the measure just mentioned, other technical measures for the Mediterranean Sea are found in the current principal annual Regulation. Article 29 of Regulation 40/2008 lays down a closed season for dolphinfish fisheries using fish aggregating devices, Article 30 deals with closed areas (and is further discussed in subsection 4.5 below), and Article 31 deals with the minimum mesh sizes of trawl nets used in certain fisheries.

---

[732] Reg 1967/2006, Art 2(2).   [733] Reg 1967/2006, Art 5.
[734] Reg 1967/2006, recital (18).   [735] Reg 40/2008, Art 81.

4.4 Malta

The provisions of Regulation 1967/2006 on Malta reflect an agreement reached in the 2003 Act of Accession that, following Malta's accession, restrictions would be introduced on the access of Community fishing vessels to the whole of Malta's 25 nm fishing zone (rather than just the inner 12 nm, to which access may in any case be restricted under Article 17(2) of the Basic Regulation).[736] Effect was initially given to that undertaking by an amendment to Regulation 1626/94,[737] and subsequently by Articles 26 and 27 of Regulation 1967/2006. Article 26(1) restricts the access of Community fishing vessels to Malta's 25 nm fishing limit to vessels of less than 12 m in length using other than towed gears: furthermore, the capacity of such vessels must not exceed specified limits, which correspond to the average level observed in 2000–01. Derogations to Article 26(1) are made for trawlers not exceeding 24 m in length up to specified capacity limits to fish in parts of the zone, as well as for vessels using purse seines or longlines and vessels fishing for dolphinfish.[738] Article 26(2)(d) provides that the specified capacity limits for trawlers authorized to fish in the zone are to be periodically re-evaluated. If, following such a re-evaluation, capacity limits are reduced, the Commission is to allocate the new level of fishing capacity between Member States according to the criteria set out in Article 26(5).

4.5 Protected species and habitats

Articles 3 and 4 of Regulation 1967/2006 deal with the impact of fishing on the marine environment. In part, they are designed to reinforce the EC Habitats Directive.[739] Thus, Article 3 prohibits, with some exceptions, the deliberate catching, retention, transhipment, or landing of marine species listed in Annex IV to the Directive. Article 4 prohibits fishing with certain fishing gears above seagrass beds, coralligenous habitats, maerl beds,[740] all Natura 2000 sites, and all specially protected areas designated under the 1995 Protocol concerning Specially Protected Areas and Biological Diversity to the Convention for the Protection of the Mediterranean Sea against Pollution,[741] subject to some limited exceptions. The use of towed dredges and trawls at depths below 1,000 m is also prohibited. The current principal annual Regulation is also relevant in this connection. Thus, Article 30 of Regulation 40/2008, which implements a recommendation of the

---

[736] Act of Accession, OJ 2003 L236/23, Art 21 and Annex III.

[737] Council Regulation (EC) No 813/2004 of 26 April 2004 amending Regulation (EC) No 1626/94 as regards certain conservation measures relating to waters around Malta, OJ 2004 L150/32 (reissued as a corrected version in OJ L185/13, which was itself then corrected).

[738] Reg 1967/2006, Art 26(2) and (6).

[739] Council Directive 92/43/EEC of 21 May 1992 on the conservation of natural habitats and of wild fauna and flora, OJ 1992 L206/7, as amended and corrected.

[740] These first three types of habitat are defined in Art 2(11)–(13) of Reg 1967/2006.

[741] OJ 1999 L322/3.

General Fisheries Commission for the Mediterranean (GFCM),[742] establishes three areas where fishing with towed dredges and bottom trawls is prohibited in order to protect deep sea sensitive habitats.

4.6 Control

The provisions of Regulation 1967/2006 on control, in Articles 20–24, supplement or amend the Control Regulation (on which see subsection 2.7 above). The most significant of those provisions are Articles 22 and 24. The former requires Member States to designate the ports at which catches taken by trawlers, purse seiners, surface longliners, and dredgers may be landed and marketed. Restricting the ports at which catches may be landed will make it easier for Member States to discover if the technical measures laid down by the Regulation are being complied with and to monitor the amounts of fish being caught because it will allow them to concentrate their monitoring and enforcement efforts in a limited number of ports rather than trying to control every possible landing point. Under Article 24, which is intended to implement a recommendation of the GFCM,[743] Community fishing vessels over 15 m in length may fish in the GFCM Agreement area only if so authorized by their flag Member State. Subject to some limited qualifications, a Member State shall not so authorize its vessels if they have engaged in IUU fishing, whether in the GFCM Agreement area or elsewhere.

---

[742] Rec GFCM/2006/3, available on the website of the GFCM.
[743] Rec GFCM/2005/2, available on the website of the GFCM. On EC implementation of GFCM measures, see Chapter 5.

4.7 Leisure fisheries

A considerable amount of non-commercial fishing (what Regulation 1967/2006 refers to as 'leisure fisheries') takes place in the Mediterranean Sea. Such fishing has the potential to impact on the sustainability of Mediterranean fisheries. Article 17 (2), therefore, requires Member States to ensure that leisure fisheries are conducted in a manner compatible with the objectives and rules of Regulation 1967/2006. In particular, Member States are to ensure that catches taken in leisure fisheries are not, subject to some exceptions, marketed.[744] In addition, the use of certain types of gear is prohibited in leisure fisheries.[745] Member States are to record data on catches taken in leisure fisheries of certain highly migratory species.[746]

4.8 Highly migratory species

The one type of Mediterranean fishery that Regulation 1967/2006 does not address to any significant degree is that for highly migratory species, whether within national jurisdiction or on the high seas. There is a separate body of EC legislation for such species, which largely implements measures adopted by RFMOs of which the EC is a member, including, *inter alia*, the International Commission for the Conservation of Atlantic Tunas (ICCAT), the RFMO with responsibility for the management of many of the highly migratory species in the Mediterranean Sea (see Chapter 5). EC legislation applying to Mediterranean highly migratory species includes, *inter alia*, technical measures,[747] a recovery plan for bluefin tuna,[748] annual quotas for bluefin tuna,[749] and enforcement measures.[750] In addition, the EC has restricted the use of driftnets, which in the Mediterranean Sea have been used largely for highly migratory species.[751]

4.9 Conclusion

The enactment of Regulation 1967/2006 is an important legislative step towards sustainable Community fisheries in the Mediterranean, but it is only a first step. It

---

[744] Reg 1967/2006, Art 17(3).   [745] Reg 1967/2006, Art 17(1) and (5).

[746] Reg 1967/2006, Art 17(4).

[747] Reg 520/2007. See also Reg 40/2008, Art 81 (mentioned above).   [748] Reg 1559/2007.

[749] See the principal annual Regulation. As noted in subsection 4.1 above, TACs and quotas for bluefin tuna in the Mediterranean Sea were first introduced in 1998. In 2002 the Commission foresaw more use of TACs and quotas for the management of highly migratory species in the Mediterranean Sea: see COM(2002) 535, p 16.

[750] Council Regulation (EC) No 1936/2001 of 27 September 2001 laying down control measures applicable to fishing for certain stocks of highly migratory fish, OJ 2001 L263/1, as amended.

[751] See further subsection 2.3 above and Chapter 5.

needs to be followed by the adoption of appropriate EC and national management plans and fishing protected areas. It is therefore of some concern that EC measures on these matters had not been adopted (or even proposed) at the time of writing. It is also essential that the Regulation is properly implemented and enforced, something that was not the case with the Regulation that it replaces, Regulation 1626/94.[752] Part of the reason for poor compliance with the latter is put down by the Commission to the fact that fishermen felt dissociated from the decision-making process,[753] hence the stress in its Action Plan on the need for consultation with stakeholders.[754] According to the Commission, there was considerable consultation over its draft of what became Regulation 1967/2006 and stakeholders had an important influence on its content.[755] It is therefore rather worrying that in May 2008 the Commission reported that 'Member States have accumulated considerable delays in implementing this Regulation [ie Regulation 1967/2006]. Serious shortcomings in compliance must be overcome urgently.'[756] One means of consultation with stakeholders, through the Regional Advisory Council (RAC) for the Mediterranean, was not available when Regulation 1967/2006 was being adopted because the Mediterranean RAC did not become operational until September 2008, some considerable time after the other RACs (see further section 7 below). It is to be hoped that now that the Mediterranean RAC is operational, there will be an improvement in the implementation of, and compliance with, Regulation 1967/2006.

5 EC fisheries management in the Black Sea

Since the accession of Bulgaria and Romania to the EC at the beginning of 2007, there have been Community waters in the Black Sea. Although Bulgaria and Romania have each claimed a 200 nm EEZ, Community waters represent a relatively small proportion of the total area of the Black Sea, as there are four other coastal States which are not members of the EC—Georgia, Russia, Turkey, and Ukraine—the length of whose combined coastlines considerably exceeds the combined length of the coastlines of Bulgaria and Romania. The CFP legislation surveyed in section 2 above applies to Community waters in the Black Sea unless it is obvious from the terms of such legislation that it does not (for example, Regulation 850/98, on technical measures, on which, see subsection 2.3 above, and Decision 2008/292, concerning the habitat of European eel[757]).

---

[752] COM(2001) 135, pp 19–20.   [753] Ibid.   [754] COM(2002) 535, pp 12, 14, and 21–22.
[755] COM(2003) 589, p 3.   [756] COM(2008) 331, p 10.
[757] Commission Decision 2008/292/EC of 4 April 2008 establishing that the Black Sea and the river systems connected to it do not constitute a natural habitat for European eel for the purposes of Council Regulation (EC) No 1100/2007, OJ 2008 L98/14.

In December 2007 the Council adopted the first EC fisheries legislation dealing specifically with the Black Sea, Regulation 1579/2007.[758] That Regulation fixed 'the fishing opportunities and conditions relating thereto for certain fish stocks' in the Black Sea for 2008. Regulation 1579/2007 was replaced by a very similar Regulation, Regulation 1139/2008, setting out fishing opportunities for 2009. Regulation 1139/2008 lays down catch limits for two stocks only, a 'precautionary TAC' for turbot and a 'precautionary TAC' for sprat.[759] The EC catch limit for turbot is divided equally between Bulgaria and Romania, whereas the EC catch limit for sprat is not divided but is available for fishing only by vessels from Bulgaria and Romania. Article 5 of Regulation 1139/2008 makes it explicit that the allocation of catch limits between Bulgaria and Romania (in practice only turbot at present) is subject to the provisions of EC law relating to quota exchanges and adjustments discussed in subsection 2.1 above.

Annex II to Regulation 1139/2008 sets out 'transitional technical measures' for the Black Sea. Those measures prescribe a closed season for turbot fishing, minimum mesh sizes for bottom-set nets used to catch turbot, and a minimum landing size for turbot. Recital (8) of Regulation 1139/2008 states that 'fishing opportunities should be used in accordance with Community legislation on the subject, in particular', *inter alia*, Regulation 850/98 (on technical measures). That is a rather odd provision because, as pointed out above, Regulation 850/98 does not include the Black Sea in the list of marine areas to which it applies.

As mentioned, Regulation 1139/2008 applies only to two stocks, turbot and sprat. In its proposal for what became Regulation 1579/2007, the Commission stated that '[i]n the future more stocks may be included in this management regime and more technical measures may be added' and that '[t]he proposal should be regarded as the first step in establishing conditions for long-term sustainable exploitation' in the Black Sea.[760] It is probable that some of the fish found in Community waters in the Black Sea belong to stocks that are shared with other Black Sea coastal States. The future management of such stocks might benefit from cooperation between the EC and those Black Sea States. Currently there are no fisheries agreements between the EC and other Black Sea States. In its proposal for Regulation 1579/2007 the Commission stated that it was 'promoting cooperation in fisheries management with third countries bordering the Black Sea. The possibility of establishing a Regional Fisheries Organisation is currently being explored.'[761] The Black Sea does, however, already fall within the area of application of the General Fisheries Commission for the Mediterranean (GFCM), and the GFCM, of

[758] Council Regulation (EC) No 1579/2007 of 20 December 2007 fixing the fishing opportunities and the conditions relating thereto for certain fish stocks and groups of fish stocks applicable to the Black Sea for 2008, OJ 2007 L346/1, as amended.

[759] See subsection 2.1 above for a discussion of the concept of 'precautionary TAC'.

[760] *Proposal for a Council Regulation fixing the fishing opportunities and associated conditions for certain fish stocks and groups of fish stocks applicable to the Black Sea for 2008*, COM(2007) 734, 20.11.2007, pp 2 and 3.

[761] COM(2007) 734, p 3.

which the EC is a member, has, in fact, adopted a number of fisheries management measures that apply to the Black Sea (and see further Chapter 5). It should be noted, however, that three coastal Black Sea States (Georgia, Russia, and Ukraine) are currently not members of the GFCM.

6 Environmental protection

Fishing activities obviously have an impact on the populations of the fish species that they target. However they may also have an impact on the wider marine environment, notably on non-target species and on habitats. Such impacts may be direct, for example because of by-catch, or indirect, such as by reducing populations of fish species relied on for prey by, say, seabirds. This section will consider the impact of fishing activities on the wider marine environment, with a particular focus on non-fish species and on habitats.[762] It will not address discarding specifically, which is already discussed in subsections 2.1 above and 9.5 below. In view of the scope of this chapter, it will also not address measures relating primarily or exclusively to non-Community waters. However, some such measures are mentioned in Chapter 5.

The legal basis for environmental protection measures under the CFP is provided by Article 6 EC, which states that '[e]nvironmental protection requirements must be integrated into the definition and implementation of', *inter alia*, the CFP, 'in particular with a view to promoting sustainable development'. Article 6 EC is in turn reflected in various provisions of the Basic Regulation. There is also the specific matter of the role of the CFP in helping Member States to meet their obligations under EC environmental legislation including, in particular, the Birds Directive,[763] the Habitats Directive,[764] and the Marine Strategy Directive (hereafter, 'the MSD').[765] These matters are discussed in this section.

At the policy level, the integration of environmental protection requirements into the CFP has been the subject of various Communications over the years from the Commission.[766] The most recent of these addressing the CFP specifically is a

---

[762] See Chapter 3 for a discussion of this subject in the context of international fisheries law.

[763] Council Directive 79/409/EEC of 2 April 1979 on the conservation of wild birds, OJ 1979 L103/1, as amended and corrected.   [764] Dir 92/43.

[765] Directive 2008/56/EC of the European Parliament and of the Council of 17 June 2008 establishing a framework for community [sic] action in the field of marine environmental policy (Marine Strategy Framework Directive), OJ 2008 L164/19.

[766] See, for example, *Communication from the Commission to the Council and the European Parliament: Fisheries management and nature conservation in the marine environment*, COM(1999) 363, 14.07.1999; *Communication from the Commission to the Council and the European Parliament: Biodiversity Action Plan for Fisheries*, COM(2001) 162, 27.3.2001; and *Communication from the Commission to the Council and the European Parliament: Elements of a Strategy for the Integration of Environmental Protection Requirements into the Common Fisheries Policy*, COM(2001) 143, 16.03.2001. See also Wolff, N, *Fisheries and the Environment* (Baden-Baden: Nomos Verlagsgesellschaft, 2002), especially ch 5.

Community Action Plan issued by the Commission in May 2002, several months before the adoption of the current Basic Regulation.[767] In January 2003 the Council welcomed the *Community Action Plan* and invited the Commission to present 'appropriate proposals' for its implementation 'within the new legal framework provided by' the then newly adopted Basic Regulation.[768] Since then, environmental integration has driven a number of legislative initiatives by the Commission (see further below). Arguably, such integration may now be seen as one component of the ecosystem approach, on which the Commission issued a Communication in April 2008 (see further subsection 9.3 below).

The Basic Regulation, in addition to its requirement in Article 2 for the EC to 'aim at a progressive implementation of an eco-system-based approach to fisheries management', contains various express or implied references to the environment beyond the target stock in question. Article 1, on scope of the CFP, states that the CFP 'shall provide for coherent measures concerning . . . [*inter alia*] . . . limitation of the environmental impact of fishing'.[769] Article 2, on CFP objectives, states that the CFP 'shall ensure exploitation of living aquatic resources that provides sustainable economic, *environmental* and social conditions' (emphasis added),[770] and goes on to refer to a role for the precautionary approach to, *inter alia*, 'minimise the impact of fishing activities on marine eco-systems'[771] and to the CFP being guided by 'consistence' with, *inter alia*, the EC's policy on environment.[772] Article 3 defines the terms 'sustainable exploitation' and 'precautionary approach to fisheries management' with reference to, *inter alia*, the wider environment.[773]

Article 4 of the Basic Regulation, on measures to achieve the CFP's objectives, refers to the role of such measures in reducing environmental impact.[774] Recovery plans and management plans, under Articles 5 and 6, may address the wider environment (although none yet do so; see further subsections 2.1 above and 9.3 below).[775] Certain delegated powers of the Commission and the Member States may be used for

---

[767] *Communication from the Commission setting out a Community Action Plan to integrate environmental protection requirements into the Common Fisheries Policy*, COM(2002) 186, 28.5.2002. The *Community Action Plan* referred to a possible review in or by 2005: see section 6, p 6 and section 9, p 6 (and also COM(2004) 394, section 3.7, p 25). However, to the authors' knowledge, no such review, at least in the public domain, has ever been conducted. On environmental integration and the CFP, see also *Communication from the Commission: Halting the loss of biodiversity by 2010—and beyond: Sustaining eco-system services for human well-being*, COM(2006) 216, 22.5.2006, section 4.2.4, p 8 and section 5.2.1.3, p 12, as well as accompanying SEC(2006) 621, Annex 1, Objective 3, A3.3–A3.7, p 5.

[768] Council of the European Union, 2481st Council meeting, Agriculture and Fisheries, 27–28 January 2003, press release, 5433/03 (Presse 13), VII–IX, para. 6.

[769] Reg 2371/2002, Art 1(2)(b).   [770] Reg 2371/2002, Art 2(1), 1st para.

[771] Reg 2371/2002, Art 2(1), 2nd para.   [772] Reg 2371/2002, Art 2(2)(d).

[773] Reg 2371/2002, Art 3(e) and (i).

[774] Reg 2371/2002, Art 4(2) *chapeau*, Art 4(2)(g)(iv), and Art 4(2)(h).

[775] Reg 2371/2002, Art 5(2) and (3) and Art 6(2) and (3).

environmental protection purposes.[776] Under Article 31 Regional Advisory Councils are to contribute to the achievement of the CFP's objectives (on which, see above) and under Article 33 the STECF is to be consulted on, *inter alia*, environmental considerations pertaining to resource conservation and management.[777]

Beyond the Basic Regulation, some other framework Regulations under the CFP also address environmental protection in relation to fishing. At the regional level, the framework Regulation for the Mediterranean Sea (Regulation 1967/2006; mentioned briefly below and more fully in section 4 above) is particularly notable in containing several references to the wider marine environment.[778] At the level of the CFP as a whole, two important framework instruments are the EFF Regulation and Council Regulation 199/2008 on data relating to the fisheries sector.[779] The EFF Regulation, including its provisions relevant to environmental protection, is dealt with at length in Chapter 8; however, its provisions relating to the Birds and Habitats Directives specifically will be mentioned below. Regulation 199/2008 is likewise discussed in general terms in Chapter 8, but its provisions on the wider environment will be described briefly here.

In summary, Regulation 199/2008, which entered into force in March 2008 and replaces a previous framework Regulation on data,[780] establishes a framework for the collection, management, and use of 'biological, technical, *environmental* and socio-economic data concerning the fisheries sector' (emphasis added).[781] Amongst other things, it requires Member States to establish 'multi-annual national sampling programmes'.[782] Such programmes are to include, *inter alia*, 'a sampling design for ecosystem data that allows the impact of the fisheries sector on the marine ecosystem to be estimated and that contributes to monitoring of the state of the marine ecosystem'.[783] Member States are also to 'carry out research surveys at sea to . . . [*inter alia*] . . . assess the impact of the fishing activity on the environment'.[784] There are accompanying provisions on the use of ecosystem impact data.[785] The inclusion of such data within the scope of the Regulation is justified on the basis that 'the ecosystem based approach to fisheries management should be progressively implemented'.[786] This reflects Article 2 of the Basic Regulation (see above).

---

[776] Reg 2371/2002, Arts 7(1), 8(1), and 9(1).

[777] Reg 2371/2002, Arts 31(1) and 33(1). On RACs, see further section 7 below.

[778] Reg 1967/2006, *inter alia*, Arts 2(2) (and Chapter III), 3, 4, 8, 9(7), 13 (including, *inter alia*, (5) and (11)), and 19(9).

[779] Council Regulation (EC) No 199/2008 of 25 February 2008 concerning the establishment of a Community framework for the collection, management and use of data in the fisheries sector and support for scientific advice regarding the Common Fisheries Policy, OJ 2008 L60/1. CFP framework Regulations aimed at ensuring compliance with fisheries management measures, where such measures relate to environmental protection, are also relevant; in this respect see the IUU Regulation and the Control Regulation, discussed in subsection 2.7 above.   [780] Reg 199/2008, Arts 29 and 28.

[781] Reg 199/2008, Art 1(1)(a) and (b).   [782] Reg 199/2008, Art 9(1).

[783] Reg 199/2008, Art 9(2)(b).   [784] Reg 199/2008, Art 12(1).

[785] Reg 199/2008, Art 15(1)(b)(iv) and Chapter IV generally.

[786] Reg 199/2008, recital (9); see also recital (6).

The practice of the Commission and the Council under the environmental provisions of the Basic Regulation is quite varied. Regarding Community waters, at the time of writing measures were in force regarding, *inter alia*, cold-water corals, seabirds, certain species and habitats of the Mediterranean Sea, cetaceans, and sharks. Regarding cold-water corals, the first EC measures were taken in respect of the Darwin Mounds site off Scotland.[787] Subsequently measures have also been adopted to protect cold-water corals around the Azores, the Canary Islands, and Madeira[788] as well as in specific sites located to the west of Ireland (see below).[789] Regarding seabirds, the principal annual Regulation is used to close certain parts of the North Sea to sandeel fishing in order to help maintain food supplies for seabirds.[790] Further measures for seabirds in Community waters may follow if the EC adopts an action plan on seabirds (on which, see Chapter 5). Measures regarding Mediterranean species and habitats are found in Articles 3 and 4 of Regulation 1967/2006 (see further section 4 above).

In relation to cetaceans, it should be noted at the outset that Article 12 of the Habitats Directive requires Member States to establish 'a system of strict protection' for this group (all species of cetacean being listed in Annex IV to the Directive).[791] In terms of legislation adopted under the CFP, the restriction on driftnets established by Regulation 894/97 (see subsection 2.3 above) and Regulation 2187/2005 (for the Baltic Sea; see section 3 above) is clearly relevant, although in the *Mondiet* case the Court held that restrictions on the use of driftnets in Regulation 345/92 (a predecessor to Regulation 894/97) were adopted primarily for fisheries conservation, as opposed to nature conservation, purposes.[792] In addition, Regulation 812/2004, as well as providing for the phasing out of driftnet use in the Baltic Sea,[793] seeks to reduce by-catch of small cetaceans by requiring use of 'active acoustic deterrent devices' and observers in certain sea areas within and beyond Community waters and in certain circumstances.[794] According

---

[787] Council Regulation (EC) No 602/2004 of 22 March 2004 amending Regulation (EC) No 850/98 as regards the protection of deepwater coral reefs from the effects of trawling in an area north west of Scotland, OJ 2004 L97/30 (preceded by Regs 1475/2003 and 263/2004, both adopted by the Commission using its emergency powers under Art 7 of Reg 2371/2002).

[788] Council Regulation (EC) No 1568/2005 of 20 September 2005 amending Regulation (EC) No 850/98 as regards the protection of deep-water coral reefs from the effects of fishing in certain areas of the Atlantic Ocean, OJ 2005 L252/2 (preceded by Reg 1811/2004, OJ 2004 L319/1 and Reg 27/2005, OJ 2005 L12/1, as amended and corrected, Annex III, para 16).

[789] Reg 40/2008, Annex III, paras 13.2–13.8.

[790] Reg 40/2008, Annex III, para 4; see also COM(2008) 187, section 5, p 8 (5th bullet point).

[791] The Court has held that the Habitats Directive applies to the EEZ: see Case C-6/04 *Commission v United Kingdom* [2005] ECR I-9017, para 117. Some limited derogations from Art 12 are provided for in Art 16. Two species of cetacean, bottlenose dolphin and harbour porpoise, are also listed in Annex I to the Directive, to which the site protection provisions of the Directive, in particular Arts 3, 4, and 6, relate.

[792] Case C-405/92, para 24. The finding in *Mondiet* may be contrasted with Reg 812/2004, recital (8).

[793] Reg 812/2004, Art 9. Art 9 amended Reg 88/98; see now Reg 2187/2005, which repealed and replaced Reg 88/98.   [794] Reg 812/2004, Arts 2–5 and Annexes I–III.

to its preamble, the Regulation is a response to, *inter alia*, Article 12 of the Habitats Directive.[795] In 2004 and 2005, the UK made certain requests to the Commission to act pursuant to concerns about by-catch of small cetaceans in a particular fishery. However, these requests were rejected because, *inter alia*, in the Commission's view 'according to the scientific information available' the measures proposed by the UK were 'not likely to contribute' to the objective of minimizing cetacean by-catch.[796] (See Chapter 5 for further discussion of cetaceans.)

Sharks are viewed in a somewhat mixed way under the CFP. In several respects, they are regarded as a fisheries resource. TACs are set by Regulation 2015/2006 for several deep-sea shark species (some for by-catch only)[797] and by Regulation 40/2008 for spurdog/dogfish (for by-catch only in the case of Member States' quotas), skates and rays, and porbeagle shark.[798] In other ways, sharks are nominally at least regarded as a part of the wider marine environment. For example, the Commission seems to imply that the EC's finning Regulation (Regulation 1185/2003; see subsection 2.3 above) is a response to the duty to integrate environmental protection requirements into the CFP.[799] In some cases it is not clear whether a particular measure regarding sharks is a fisheries conservation measure or an environmental integration measure, for example the prohibition on fishing for basking shark and great white shark by third State vessels in Community waters and by Community vessels.[800] More comprehensive measures regarding sharks may arise if the Commission adopts an EC action plan for this group.[801]

In some cases the principal annual Regulation on fishing opportunities has been used as a vehicle for technical measures designed to reduce the impact of fishing activities on the wider marine environment. An example is the measures to protect cold-water corals west of Ireland (see further below). However, that practice may well change if the Commission's legislative proposal[802] for a successor to Regulation 850/98 is adopted, since one intention behind that proposal is to reduce the use of the principal annual Regulation as a vehicle for technical measures (see further subsection 2.3 above).

As noted above, the CFP potentially has a role in assisting Member States to fulfil their obligations under the Birds Directive, Habitats Directive, and MSD. Regarding the Birds and Habitats Directives, obligations arise in relation to sites (special protection areas (SPAs), under the Birds Directive and special areas of

---

[795] Reg 812/2004, recital (2). As well as mentioning the general effect of Art 12, recital (2) also makes specific mention of the provisions of Arts 11 and 12(4) of the Habitats Directive.

[796] See Commission Decision of 24 August 2004 on the request presented by the United Kingdom pursuant to Article 7 of Regulation (EC) No 2371/2002—C(2004) 3229, referred to in Dec 2005/322, preamble, footnote (2); and Dec 2005/322, recital (6). On Dec 2005/322, see further subsection 2.4 above.   [797] Reg 2015/2006, Annex, Part 2, first three entries.

[798] Reg 40/2008, Annex IA.   [799] COM(2002) 449, explanatory memorandum, last para.

[800] Reg 40/2008, Arts 15 and 6.

[801] In late 2007, the Commission issued a *Consultation on an EU Action Plan for Sharks*.

[802] COM(2008) 324.

conservation (SACs), under the Habitats Directive, known collectively as 'Natura 2000' sites) and species.[803] Several Regulations under the CFP, already mentioned above, have been adopted with a view to protecting sites or species in Community waters that have some link to the Habitats or Birds Directive.[804] Regarding sites, some such Regulations have been adopted at the request of a given Member State in respect of a specific site or sites,[805] while others protect habitats covered by the Habitats Directive but are not aimed at specific sites.[806] In terms of financial support, the EFF Regulation provides for support for certain measures of 'common interest' relating to 'the protection and enhancement of the environment in the framework of [Natura] 2000 where its areas directly concern fishing activities, excluding operational costs'.[807]

In May 2007, the Commission issued *Guidelines for the establishment of the Natura 2000 network in the marine environment. Application of the Habitats and Birds Directives*, which include a section specifically on the CFP.[808] The following year the Commission issued a document entitled *Fisheries Measures for Marine Natura 2000 Sites* (hereafter, 'the 2008 guidance'),[809] providing guidance to Member States on how to approach any restrictions on fishing activities that become necessary in order to protect Natura 2000 sites. In summary, the 2008 guidance advocates use by Member States of their delegated powers under Article 9 of the Basic Regulation (on which, see subsection 2.4 above) in respect of Natura 2000 sites located within 12 nm of baselines and recourse to EC measures, via a 'formal request' by the Member State to DG Mare, in relation to other sites. Thus the guidance assumes that any restrictions required are necessarily a matter for regulation in the context of the CFP, although arguments may be made to the contrary.[810] For reasons of space it is not possible to provide any further critique of the 2008 guidance, except to note that neither of the abovementioned documents expressly addresses fishing restrictions that may be necessary under the species, as opposed to sites, protection provisions of the Birds and Habitats Directives.

---

[803] Regarding obligations relating to SACs and SPAs see Dir 92/43, Arts 6 and 7. Obligations also exist for certain categories of site that are precursors to SACs: see Dir 92/43, Arts 4(5) and 5(4). Sites which have not been classified as SPAs but which should have been so classified are subject to the first sentence of Art 4(4) of Dir 79/409: see Case C-374/98 *Commission v France* [2000] ECR I-10799 (also known as the 'Basses Corbières' case), para 47. In relation to species, see Dir 92/43, Arts 12 and 16 (in particular) and Dir 79/409, Arts 5 and 9 (in particular).

[804] See also the Commission's Decision regarding the Netherlands, referred to in subsection 2.4 above.

[805] Reg 602/2004 and its predecessors (requested by the UK); Reg 40/2008, Annex III, paras 13.2–13.8 (requested by Ireland).   [806] Reg 1568/2005 and its predecessors; Reg 1967/2006, Art 4.

[807] Reg 1198/2006, Art 38(2)(c) and Art 38 generally. See also Art 30(2)(d), (4)(d), and (5)(c).

[808] Section 6.

[809] Both documents are available on the websites of DG Mare and DG Environment.

[810] See, for example, Owen, D, *Interaction Between the EU Common Fisheries Policy and the Habitats and Birds Directives*, IEEP Policy Briefing (Brussels: IEEP, 2004), available on the website of the Institute for European Environmental Policy (IEEP).

Germany and Ireland provide two contrasting examples of how Member States have gone about seeking to protect suites of marine Natura 2000 sites from fishing activities. In both cases, their initiatives commenced before the Commission issued its 2008 guidance. In February 2006 the German government started a project, known as 'Environmentally Sound Fishery Management in Protected Areas' (EMPAS), with the ICES in order to identify fishery management measures for SPAs and candidate SACs in Germany's EEZ. In 2008, the ICES provided advice to the German government,[811] but it remains to be seen what steps Germany will take next.

In contrast, the Irish government turned directly to the Commission for assistance in protecting some offshore candidate SACs. The four sites in question were intended to protect cold-water corals west of Ireland. In 2006 the Irish authorities made a formal request to the Commission 'to bring forward proposals to ensure the protection' of the sites. In April 2007 the Commission sought advice on an urgent basis from the ICES, which reported later the same year.[812] In November 2007 the Commission included relevant protective measures in a legislative proposal for the principal annual Regulation on fishing opportunities.[813] Those proposals, albeit modified, were subsequently adopted by the Council in Regulation 40/2008.[814] It remains to be seen whether the measures will simply be repeated in the successor to Regulation 40/2008 or will be adopted on a more permanent basis. More significantly, it will be interesting to see how other coastal Member States go about fulfilling their site protection obligations under the Birds and Habitats Directives in relation to fishing activities, in the light of the 2008 guidance.

Turning now to the MSD, which entered into force in July 2008,[815] this Directive 'establishes a framework within which Member States shall take the necessary measures to achieve or maintain good environmental status in the marine environment by the year 2020 at the latest'.[816] The Directive recognizes the role of the CFP in the maintenance and restoration of the integrity, structure, and functioning of ecosystems and hence in achieving the Directive's objectives.[817] It does so by means of an important provision, Article 15, on the relationship between the Member States and the Commission.

[811] For further information see *Report of the Workshop on Fisheries Management in Marine Protected Areas (WKFMMPA)*, ICES CM 2008/MHC:11 (Copenhagen: ICES, 2008), available on the website of the ICES.
[812] For further information see *Report of the Ad hoc Group for Western Irish Natura Sites (AGWINS)*, ICES CM 2007/ACE:06 (Copenhagen: ICES, 2007), available on the website of the ICES.
[813] COM(2007) 759, proposed para 12.2 of Annex III. See also *Proposal for a Council Regulation amending Regulations (EC) No 2015/2006 and (EC) No 41/2007, as regards fishing opportunities and associated conditions for certain fish stocks*, COM(2007) 570, 5.10.2007, proposed new para 13.2 of Annex III to Reg 41/2007 (not adopted by the Council).
[814] Reg 40/2008, Annex III, para 13.2; see also paras 13.3–13.8.   [815] Dir 2008/56, Art 27.
[816] Dir 2008/56, Art 1(1).   [817] Dir 2008/56, recitals (39) and (40).

Article 15 requires that: 'Where a Member State identifies an issue which has an impact on the environmental status of its marine waters and which cannot be tackled by measures adopted at national level, or which is linked to another Community policy or international agreement, it shall inform the Commission accordingly and provide a justification to substantiate its view.' The Commission is to respond within six months. In turn, in cases '[w]here action by Community institutions is needed, Member States shall make appropriate recommendations to the Commission and the Council for measures' to address the issue in question. The Commission is to 'respond to any such recommendation within a period of six months and, as appropriate, reflect the recommendations when presenting related proposals to the European Parliament and to the Council' (unless 'otherwise specified in relevant Community legislation').

This broad wording is intended to cover, *inter alia*, situations where restrictions on the activities of fishing vessels are required and where, in the view of the Member State (and the Commission), the appropriate action should be taken by the EC under the CFP. Article 15 is important because it makes a clear connection between the ecosystem-related goals of the MSD and the role of the CFP and places duties on the Commission to act in response to relevant Member State requests. The need for such a connection is emphasized by Annex I to the Directive, which sets out 'Qualitative descriptors for determining good environmental status' and lists, *inter alia*, the following four such descriptors:

(1) Biological diversity is maintained. The quality and occurrence of habitats and the distribution and abundance of species are in line with prevailing physiographic, geographic and climatic conditions.
    [. . .]
(3) Populations of all commercially exploited fish and shellfish are within safe biological limits, exhibiting a population age and size distribution that is indicative of a healthy stock.
(4) All elements of the marine food webs, to the extent that they are known, occur at normal abundance and diversity and levels capable of ensuring the long-term abundance of the species and the retention of their full reproductive capacity.
    [. . .]
(6) Sea-floor integrity is at a level that ensures that the structure and functions of the ecosystems are safeguarded and benthic ecosystems, in particular, are not adversely affected.

Overall, it can be said that the duty on the Community under Article 6 EC to integrate environmental protection requirements into the definition and implementation of the CFP has been reflected in various CFP framework Regulations, including the Basic Regulation in particular, and has led to an array of legislative measures being adopted under the CFP in respect of a variety of species and habitats in Community waters. Full implementation of the Birds and Habitats

Directives in the marine environment, as well as implementation of the MSD, progressive implementation of an ecosystem approach, and various ad hoc developments, are likely to yield further legislative measures at EC level. Regarding the Birds, Habitats, and Marine Strategy Directives, in respect of which Member States potentially face a finding against them by the Court for any failure to meet their obligations, it remains to be seen whether the EC's actions to adopt measures to enable Member States to fulfil such obligations will be sufficient, both in terms of substance and timeliness.

7 Regional Advisory Councils and the Advisory Committee on Fisheries and Aquaculture

7.1 Introduction

Besides the Community institutions, the Member States, and various comitology committees, there are several bodies, or types of body, that are relevant to the functioning of the CFP. Some of these are provided for in EC law, namely the CFCA, producer organizations, the STECF, the Advisory Committee on Fisheries and Aquaculture (ACFA), and Regional Advisory Councils (RACs). One further body, the ICES, exists independently of EC law. Producer organizations, at least in terms of the role envisaged for them in EC legislation, are more relevant to the common organization of the markets in fishery products and so will be discussed in Chapter 6 rather than in the current chapter. The CFCA, the STECF, the ICES, the ACFA, and RACs were all introduced briefly in Chapter 1. The roles of the STECF and the ICES in relation to total allowable catches are considered in subsection 2.1 above and the CFCA is discussed in subsection 2.7 above. In the current section, it is RACs and the ACFA that will be addressed.

   The choice of this chapter as a 'home' for the discussion on RACs and the ACFA is based on their role in relation to fisheries management in Community waters. However, in the case of RACs, it should be noted that their role is not necessarily limited to fisheries management and that the geographical scope of each of the seven RACs extends beyond Community waters (and in one case relates entirely to *non*-Community waters). In the case of the ACFA, fisheries management in Community waters is clearly only a part of that body's role, as indicated by the titles of the ACFA's various working groups (see below). For the sake of convenience, RACs and the ACFA will be dealt with in this section in a general way rather than focusing specifically on their roles regarding fisheries management in Community waters. A significant amount of space has been devoted to these bodies because of their important role in involving stakeholders in the functioning of the CFP.

7.2 Regional Advisory Councils

RACs are an important innovation of the current Basic Regulation, and aim 'to enable the Common Fisheries Policy to benefit from the knowledge and experience of the fishermen concerned and of other stakeholders and to take into account the diverse conditions throughout Community waters'.[818] As a means of stakeholder involvement, they complement the ACFA (see subsection 7.3 below). In a review of the functioning of RACs issued in June 2008 (hereafter, 'the 2008 review'),[819] the Commission concludes that: 'It is too soon to pass any lasting judgement [sic] on the RACs, as each RAC is at a different stage of development and has to work in very different conditions. However, despite the difficulties encountered in the start-up phase, the RACs have already made a positive contribution to the development of the CFP.'[820]

The legal framework for RACs is provided by the Basic Regulation and Decision 2004/585 (hereafter, 'the 2004 Decision'). The Basic Regulation's principal provisions on RACs are Articles 31 and 32. The basic functions of RACs are stated in Article 31(1) as being 'to contribute to the achievement of the objectives of Article 2(1) [of the Basic Regulation] and *in particular* to advise the Commission on matters of fisheries management in respect of certain sea areas or fishing zones' (emphasis added; the 'objectives of Article 2(1)' are mentioned in Chapter 1). Article 31(2) and (3) addresses the composition of, and rights of participation in, RACs (see further below).

Article 31(4) and (5) of the Basic Regulation addresses the relationship between RACs and the Commission and Member States. RACs may (rather than must) be consulted by the Commission 'in respect of proposals for measures, such as multi-annual recovery or management plans, to be adopted on the basis of Article 37 of the [EC] Treaty that it intends to present *and* that relate specifically to fisheries in the area concerned' (emphasis added).[821] Thus this particular provision concerns only those proposals relating to fisheries in the area covered by the RAC in question.

RACs 'may also be consulted by the Commission and by the Member States in respect of other measures', albeit without prejudice to consultation of the STECF and the Committee for Fisheries and Aquaculture.[822] This provision clearly broadens the range of matters on which the Commission may consult an RAC. But it also allows Member States to consult RACs. For example, it provides scope for an RAC to be consulted by a Member State on any measures the latter may

[818] Reg 2371/2002, recital (27).

[819] *Communication from the Commission to the Council and the European Parliament: Review of the functioning of the Regional Advisory Councils*, COM(2008) 364, 17.6.2008. For an independent view on the role of RACs, see Sissenwine and Symes, *Reflections on the Common Fisheries Policy*, 66–8. See also House of Lords, 2008, HL Paper 146-I, paras 117–138.   [820] COM(2008) 364, section 4, p 11.

[821] Reg 2371/2002, Art 31(4).   [822] Reg 2371/2002, Art 31(4).

have in mind using its delegated powers (see subsection 2.4 above), although some such powers anyway call for consultation with RACs. The 2008 review notes that: 'Some Member States have made use of RAC meetings to discuss CFP issues, such as the designation of marine protected areas, with stakeholders.'[823]

RACs in turn have a broad power to 'conduct any . . . activities necessary to fulfil their functions'.[824] Two particular activities are identified in Article 31(5) of the Basic Regulation. One is a power to 'submit recommendations and suggestions . . . on matters relating to fisheries management to the Commission or the Member State concerned'.[825] That may be done of the RAC's own accord or at the request of the Commission or a Member State. The other is a power to 'inform the Commission or the Member State concerned of problems relating to the implementation of Community rules and submit recommendations and suggestions addressing such problems to the Commission or the Member State concerned'.[826]

Article 32 of the Basic Regulation requires the Council to 'decide on the establishment of a Regional Advisory Council'. The 2004 Decision in turn implements the framework provisions of Articles 31 and 32 of the Basic Regulation. It 'established' an RAC for each of 'the Baltic Sea', 'the Mediterranean Sea', 'the North Sea', 'north-western waters', 'south-western waters', 'pelagic stocks', and the 'high seas/long distance fleet'.[827] These seven RACs are intended to 'correspond to management units based on biological criteria'.[828] The act of establishing the seven RACs did not bring them into operation; instead the 2004 Decision establishes a procedure for that to happen (see below).

In its 2008 review, the Commission considers that 'the current geographical coverage [of the RACs] is satisfactory and . . . there is no need for additional RACs to be set up'.[829] It suggests that the Black Sea,[830] not referred to in the 2004 Decision, could be dealt with by the Mediterranean Sea RAC through a specific working group or by '[a]d hoc discussion forums between stakeholders from Romania, Bulgaria, relevant non-EU countries and the Commission'.[831] There has been concern expressed about the large size of some RACs' areas.[832] In response, the 2008 review states that full use should be made of the power provided by the 2004 Decision to 'create subdivisions to deal with issues that cover specific fisheries and biological regions'.[833]

Article 3 of the 2004 Decision sets out the procedure for making an individual RAC operational, to be initiated by a request from the relevant stakeholders.[834] The RACs established by the 2004 Decision were in turn rendered operational by

---

[823] COM(2008) 364, section 3.1, p 8.   [824] Reg 2371/2002, Art 31(5)(c).

[825] Reg 2371/2002, Art 31(5)(a).   [826] Reg 2371/2002, Art 31(5)(b).

[827] Dec 2004/585, Art 2 and Annex I.   [828] Dec 2004/585, recital (2).

[829] COM(2008) 364, section 2.1, p 4.   [830] The Black Sea is discussed in section 5 above.

[831] COM(2008) 364, section 2.1, p 4.

[832] House of Lords, 2008, HL Paper 146-II, inter alia, pp 72 and 288 (evidence of the Royal Society for the Protection of Birds (RSPB) and Defra, respectively).

[833] Dec 2004/585, Art 2(2). COM(2008) 364, section 2.1, p 4.   [834] Dec 2004/585, Art 3(1).

means of a series of Decisions adopted by the Commission over the period 2004–08.[835] The first RAC to become operational was the North Sea RAC (in November 2004); the most recent was the Mediterranean Sea RAC (in September 2008). In its 2008 review, the Commission implies that delays in establishing some of the RACs may be attributed to the lack of precedent for working through regional structures in those cases.[836] At the time of writing at least five RACs had established their own websites.[837] These websites provide a considerable insight into the practice of the RACs in question, although an analysis of such practice is beyond the scope of this book.

The Pelagic Stocks RAC and the High Seas/Long Distance Fleet RAC are somewhat anomalous, for different reasons. In contrast to the other six RACs, the scope of the Pelagic Stocks RAC is defined in terms of specific stocks rather than sea areas.[838] The High Seas/Long Distance Fleet RAC is stated to apply to 'All *non* EC-waters' (emphasis added),[839] and yet the Basic Regulation requires that any given RAC is to 'cover sea areas falling under the jurisdiction of at least two Member States'.[840] That said, the legal validity of the establishment and rendering operational of the High Seas/Long Distance Fleet RAC has not been challenged in the Court.

Articles 4, 5, 6, and 7 of the 2004 Decision relate to the structure, composition, and functioning of RACs, and as such elaborate on Article 31(2) and (3) of the Basic Regulation. Each RAC is intended to acquire legal personality,[841] and is to consist of a general assembly and an executive committee.[842] Membership of RACs is to comprise 'representatives from the fisheries sector and other interest

---

[835] Dec 2004/774, OJ 2004 L342/28 (North Sea RAC, operational as from 1 November 2004, 9 'Member States concerned', 32 members); Dec 2005/606, OJ 2005 L206/21 (Pelagic stocks RAC, operational as from 16 August 2005, 10 'Member States concerned', 60 members); Dec 2005/668, OJ 2005 L249/18 (North-Western Waters RAC, operational as from 26 September 2005, 6 'Member States concerned', 55 members); Dec 2006/191, OJ 2006 L66/50 (Baltic Sea RAC, operational as from 13 March 2006, 8 'Member States concerned', 42 members); Dec 2007/206, OJ 2007 L91/52 (High Seas/Long Distance Fleet RAC, operational as from 30 March 2007, 12 'Member States concerned', 72 members); Dec 2007/222, OJ 2007 L95/52 (South-Western Waters RAC, operational as from 9 April 2007, 5 'Member States concerned', 115 members); and Dec 2008/695, OJ 2008 L232/12 (Mediterranean Sea RAC, operational as from 15 September 2008, 7 'Member States concerned'). Regarding the first six RACs listed above, the number of 'Member States concerned' and members is provided by COM(2008) 364, Annex 1. See also recital (3) of each Decision. Regarding the North Sea RAC, Poland is included by COM(2008) 364 as one of the 'Member States concerned' yet is not listed in recital (3) of Dec 2004/774. Regarding the Mediterranean Sea RAC, Italy, included by COM(2008) 364 as one of the 'Member States concerned', is not listed in recital (3) of Dec 2008/695 but is mentioned earlier in the preamble.   [836] COM(2008) 364, section 3.1, p 9.

[837] North Sea RAC, Pelagic stocks RAC, North-Western Waters RAC, Baltic Sea RAC, and South-Western Waters RAC.

[838] Dec 2004/585, Annex I: blue whiting, mackerel, horse mackerel, and herring, in 'All areas (excluding the Baltic Sea and the Mediterranean Sea)'. See also Dec 2005/606, recital (2) and COM (2008) 364, section 2.1, p 4.   [839] Dec 2004/585, Annex I and Dec 2007/206, recital (2).

[840] Reg 2371/2002, Art 32.   [841] Dec 2004/585, Art 9(1).   [842] Dec 2004/585, Art 4(1).

groups affected by the Common Fisheries Policy'.[843] The term 'fisheries sector' is defined as 'the catching sub-sector, including shipowners, small-scale fishermen, employed fishermen, producer organisations as well as, amongst others, processors, traders and other market organisations and women's networks', while the term 'other interest groups' means 'amongst others, environmental organisations and groups, aquaculture producers, consumers and recreational or sport fishermen'.[844]

General assembly members are to be agreed on by the Member States concerned,[845] ie those Member States 'having a fishing interest in the area or fisheries covered by a [RAC]'.[846] The general assembly is then to appoint the executive committee.[847] In both bodies, two-thirds of the seats are to be allotted to fisheries sector representatives and one-third to representatives of the other interest groups.[848] This 'primacy of fishing interests' is justified by the Council 'given the effects on them of management decisions and policies'.[849] The Commission notes that, at least in the general assemblies, 'it is difficult to maintain this ratio'. For this and other reasons it states that the current composition rule should be 'adapted',[850] implying a forthcoming amendment to the 2004 Decision.

In its 2008 review, the Commission notes that the fishing subsector has been the most active in the fisheries sector and that in some RACs 'environmental and development NGOs have been active players despite some capacity problems and difficulties in resourcing all the working group meetings'. However, the Commission seeks more involvement from processors, traders, and other market organizations, as well as consumer organizations, aquaculture producers, and recreational and sports fishermen, and suggests broadening the agenda of RAC meetings, for example to cover 'eco-labelling and market trends', to help in this respect.[851] RACs are to adopt their own rules of procedure and, if appropriate, a secretariat and working groups,[852] and an 'annual strategic plan' is to be drawn up by the executive committee and approved by the general assembly.[853] At least five of the RACs have their own secretariat.

The principal products of the RACs are their recommendations, to be adopted by the executive committee and preferably by consensus.[854] The 2008 review indicates that, in approximate terms, the number of recommendations sent to the Commission by RACs tripled between 2005 (three RACs operational) and 2006

---

[843] Dec 2004/585, Art 5(1).

[844] Dec 2004/585, Art 1(2) and (3); cf definition of 'fisheries sector' in Reg 1198/2006, Art 3(a). There has been some litigation before the Court on whether or not, *inter alia*, an organization's membership of an RAC enables that organization to obtain standing under Art 230, fourth para, EC to challenge a Regulation adopted by the Council in relation to which the RAC has provided advice: see Cases T-91/07 and C-355/08 P, referred to in the footnotes to subsection 2.1 above.

[845] Dec 2004/585, Art 5(2).   [846] Dec 2004/585, Art 1(1).   [847] Dec 2004/585, Art 4(3).

[848] Dec 2004/585, Art 5(3).   [849] Dec 2004/585, recital (4).

[850] COM(2008) 364, section 2.2.3, p 6.

[851] COM(2008) 364, section 2.2.2, p 5 and section 2.2.3, p 6.   [852] Dec 2004/585, Art 7(1).

[853] Dec 2004/585, Art 4(2).   [854] Dec 2004/585, Arts 4(3), 7(2), 7(3), and 8.

(four RACs) and doubled between 2006 and 2007 (six RACs), with just over sixty recommendations being sent in 2007.[855] Upon receipt in writing of a recommendation from an RAC, 'the Commission and, where relevant, the Member States concerned shall reply precisely to them within a reasonable time period and, at the latest, within three months'.[856] However, the 2008 review provides no quantitative data on the extent to which the Commission follows RACs' recommendations. Instead, it sets out in broad terms how the Commission regards such advice and where it would like RACs to focus in the future.

The Commission states that its evaluation of RAC advice 'depends on whether that advice is compatible with CFP objectives and sustainable fisheries', rather than on whether or not the advice is based on consensus.[857] It considers that its consultation of RACs 'should *not* focus on short-term issues which have an immediate economic impact' (emphasis added), such as TACs for individual stocks. It would prefer to see RACs participating 'in the debate on long-term strategic issues, such as long-term management plans, discards or the ecosystem approach'.[858] The Commission intends to review its consultation of RACs, with a view to involving them in long-term issues, giving them more notice and clearer requests, and proposing 'benchmarks to improve the consistency of RAC advice with CFP objectives'.[859]

The Commission has the right to participate as an 'active observer' at any meeting of an RAC. The 'Member States concerned' may do likewise.[860] However, the Commission notes in its 2008 review that absence of its staff 'may sometimes facilitate more independent discussion'.[861] Other bodies or individuals may potentially participate in the work of RACs.[862] This includes invited scientists, a representative of the ACFA (see subsection 7.3 below), and invited representatives of third States. Scientists from the ICES play an important role regarding the RACs. This is provided for in the EC's cooperation agreement with the ICES.[863] ICES scientists 'often attend RAC meetings to explain advice . . . and comment on data'[864] and some of the RACs have started to have annual meetings with the ICES.[865] The Commission, in its 2008 review, considers that '[t]he definition of scientists in the [2004] Decision could be broadened to include other

---

[855] COM(2008) 364, Annex 2.   [856] Dec 2004/585, Art 7(3).

[857] COM(2008) 364, section 3.2, p 9.

[858] COM(2008) 364, section 3.3, p 10. See also: (a) House of Lords, 2008, HL Paper 146-II, *inter alia*, pp 37, 72, 92, 100, and 281/288 (evidence of Scottish Fishermen's Federation, RSPB, the UK government's Joint Nature Conservation Committee, the North-Western Waters RAC, and Defra, respectively); (b) Sissenwine and Symes, *Reflections on the Common Fisheries Policy*, 45.

[859] COM(2008) 364, section 3.3, pp 9–10 and section 4, p 11.   [860] Dec 2004/585, Art 6(2).

[861] COM(2008) 364, section 2.3, p 7.   [862] Dec 2004/585, Art 6(1), (3), and (4).

[863] *Agreement in the form of a Memorandum of Understanding between the European Community and the International Council for the Exploration of the Sea*, p 5.   [864] COM(2008) 364, section 2.3, p 7.

[865] House of Lords, 2008, HL Paper 146-II, pp 4 and 14 (evidence of the UK government's Centre for Environment, Fisheries & Aquaculture Science).

experts such as economists'[866] and anticipates cooperation between RACs and economists and social scientists from the STECF.[867] There is an emphasis on the need for transparency in the working of RACs.[868]

Article 8 of the 2004 Decision requires that if an issue is of common interest to two or more RACs, they are to 'coordinate their positions with a view to adopting joint recommendations on that issue'.[869] The RACs do undertake joint working in practice. For example, in December 2007, the 'Fifth RACs Coordination Meeting' took place.[870] In its 2008 review, the Commission reiterated the RACs' duty under Article 8 of the 2004 Decision and encouraged further inter-RAC meetings to enable 'secretariats and chairmen to plan the discussion of issues of common interest'.[871] More specifically, regarding deep-sea stocks, the Commission considered that joint working groups across relevant RACs 'should be set up to coordinate RAC advice on this subject and avoid duplication of workload'.[872]

Funding of RACs is provided for by the 2004 Decision and by Regulation 861/2006. In its original version, the 2004 Decision provided for decreasing Community financial aid over five years,[873] reflected in turn in Regulation 861/2006.[874] However, the funding of RACs has now been set on a firmer and more permanent footing by virtue of an amendment[875] to the 2004 Decision which allows RACs to 'apply for Community financial aid as a body pursuing an aim of *general European interest* [as defined]' (emphasis added).[876] In practice, under the amended regime, the maximum EC financial aid available for each RAC equates to €250,000 per year.[877]

Regarding interaction with the ACFA, the 2008 review notes that: 'Good co-ordination with ACFA is necessary to avoid duplication of work, but the division of responsibilities between RACs and ACFA is not always clear. It may be simplistic to divide the RAC and ACFA work into regional and horizontal matters respectively, as there may be legitimate "regional" dimensions to issues such as simplification, TACs and quotas, technical measures, etc. Likewise, advice from RACs can have implications across the board.'[878] The Commission adds that 'the co-operation between ACFA and the RACs and their respective roles' will be

---

[866] COM(2008) 364, section 2.3, p 7.   [867] COM(2008) 364, section 3.3, p 10.

[868] Dec 2004/585, Arts 6(5) and 7(2).   [869] Dec 2004/585, Art 8.

[870] Report available on the website of the North Sea RAC.

[871] COM(2008) 364, section 2.1, p 4.   [872] COM(2008) 364, section 2.1, p 4.

[873] Dec 2004/585 (original version), Art 9 and Annex II.   [874] Reg 861/2006, Art 12(c).

[875] Council Decision 2007/409/EC of 11 June 2007 amending Decision 2004/585/EC establishing Regional Advisory Councils under the Common Fisheries Policy, OJ 2007 L155/68.

[876] Dec 2004/585, Art 9(1). See also Art 9(2) and Annex II.

[877] See, for example, *Proposal for a Council Decision amending Decision 2004/585/EC establishing Regional Advisory Councils under the Common Fisheries Policy*, COM(2006) 732, 27.11.2006, section 5.2, pp 10–11 and section 8, pp 14–15.

[878] COM(2008) 364, section 2.3, p 8. See also House of Lords, 2008, HL Paper 146-II, *inter alia*, p 187 (Spain's evidence).

discussed in the light of its evaluation of the performance of the ACFA (on which see subsection 7.3 below).

In addition to Articles 31 and 32 of the Basic Regulation, the 2004 Decision, and Regulation 861/2006, RACs also feature in other CFP legislation. Within the Basic Regulation itself, Article 4(2) states that measures taken by the Council to achieve the objectives set out in Article 2(1) shall be established, *inter alia*, 'in the light of any advice received from [RACs] . . .'. RACs also have a consultative role under Article 7 (on Commission emergency measures) and under Articles 8 and 9 (on Member State delegated powers, on which see subsection 2.4 above). Amongst other CFP legislation mentioning RACs, Regulation 785/2005, on the Community Fisheries Control Agency (CFCA), is of particular significance. Article 31(1) states that the CFCA's Advisory Board, which is 'to advise the Executive Director [of the CFCA] and to ensure close cooperation with stake-holders',[879] is to be composed of representatives of the RACs. Outside the CFP, the Marine Strategy Directive requires Member States to 'ensure that all interested parties are given early and effective opportunities to participate in the implementation of this Directive, involving, where possible, [*inter alia*] . . . Regional Advisory Councils'.[880]

There has been some debate over whether or not RACs should move on from being merely advisory bodies to having a management role.[881] The 2008 review does not address this matter.[882] The Commission's 2008 Working Document on CFP reform does not expressly address the matter either, although the possibility of 'specific regional management solutions implemented by Member States whenever appropriate, subject to Community standards and control' is raised.[883] In general terms the Commission does foresee a more results-based approach to fisheries management whereby the result to be achieved is specified at the EC level and the solution is then found by industry.[884] In a written memorandum to an inquiry in 2008 on the CFP by the UK's Parliament, the Commission states that: 'It is . . . difficult to envisage at this early stage of their operation that the RACs should be transformed from being advisory bodies into bodies having some level of wider management responsibility *outside* a results-based management framework.'[885] (Emphasis added.) This statement, although somewhat ambiguous, may mean that the Commission potentially sees RACs taking on some degree of management responsibility *within* any future 'results-based management framework' that may be adopted pursuant to reform of the CFP. The possibility of a management role for RACs does, however, raise questions of accountability; these

[879] Reg 768/2005, recital (30); see also Art 31(3) and Art 31 generally.
[880] Dir 2008/56, Art 19(1).
[881] See, for example, House of Lords, 2008, HL Paper 146-I, paras 133–135 and 138.
[882] COM(2008) 364, section 1, p 3.
[883] *Reflections on further reform of the Common Fisheries Policy*, section 4, p 8.
[884] See, for example, *Reflections on further reform of the Common Fisheries Policy*, section 4, p 8.
[885] House of Lords, 2008, HL Paper 146-II, p 212.

would need to be addressed through the design of any management framework that was adopted.

7.3 Advisory Committee on Fisheries and Aquaculture

The ACFA has a longer pedigree than any of the RACs, having originally been established, albeit under a slightly different name, in 1971.[886] Its existence has most recently been renewed by Decision 1999/478 (hereafter, 'the 1999 Decision').[887] (The ACFA is distinct from the Committee for Fisheries and Aquaculture, which is a comitology committee established by the Basic Regulation.[888]) In essence, the ACFA is a means for the Commission to consult with stakeholders. Despite the advent of RACs, the non-regional nature of the ACFA means that it is potentially well-placed to continue to provide views on fisheries issues of general application across the EC. That said, the role of the ACFA was evaluated by consultants in 2008 at the request of the Commission (see below).

The 1999 Decision specifies that the ACFA is to comprise one plenary committee and four working groups.[889] The purpose of the working groups is to prepare the opinions of the ACFA,[890] and the four groups are to cover the following subjects: 'Access to fisheries resources and management of fishing activity'; 'Aquaculture: fish, shellfish and molluscs'; 'Markets and trade policy'; and 'General questions: economics and sectoral analysis'.[891] This rather prescriptive approach to the subject matter of working groups has not precluded the ACFA from establishing, in October 2008, a temporary ad hoc working group on CFP reform.[892] The ACFA also has a 'bureau' to 'prepare and organise the activities of the working groups . . .'.[893]

The 1999 Decision states that the ACFA is composed of representatives of the 'professional organisations representing the producer companies, the processing industry and traders in fishery and aquaculture products and non-professional organisations representing the interests of consumers, the environment and development'.[894] A highly prescriptive approach is taken to membership of the ACFA, the four working groups, and the bureau.

Having established that there are twenty-one members of the ACFA, the 1999 Decision identifies which interest groups are to be represented by eleven of these members. The remaining ten members are then identified as the chairman and

---

[886] Décision de la Commission 71/128/CEE, du 25 février 1971, portant création d'un comité consultatif de la pêche, JO 1971 L68/18, as amended (and subsequently repealed).

[887] Commission Decision 1999/478/EC of 14 July 1999 renewing the Advisory Committee on Fisheries and Aquaculture, OJ 1999 L187/70, as amended.   [888] Reg 2371/2002, Art 30.

[889] Dec 1999/478, Art 1(1).   [890] Dec 1999/478, Art 7, 1st para.

[891] Dec 1999/478, Art 7, 2nd para and Annex.

[892] Summary records of ACFA meetings are available on the website of DG Mare.

[893] Dec 1999/478, Art 5, 2nd and 3rd paras.   [894] Dec 1999/478, Art 1(2).

vice-chairman of each of the ACFA's four working groups and of the so-called 'Fisheries sectoral dialogue committee'.[895] Overall, the result is that of the twenty-one members of the ACFA, eighteen are derived from the fisheries sector while only three are derived from the consumer, environment, and development sectors. The chairman and vice-chairmen of the ACFA are to be elected.[896] The 1999 Decision sets out how the ACFA's members are to be appointed, as well as establishing some basic terms of service.[897]

Regarding the working groups, the 1999 Decision specifies which interest groups, and how many individuals per group, may have seats and which interest groups are to chair and vice-chair each working group.[898] In all cases, the chair and vice-chairs are drawn from the fisheries sector. Regarding the bureau, the membership is prescribed but the chairman is to be elected.[899] The membership of the ACFA for the period May 2007 to April 2010 is set out on the website of DG Mare.

The ACFA may be consulted by the Commission on 'questions concerning the rules of the [CFP] and in particular measures that the Commission may take in the framework of such rules as well as economic and social questions in the fisheries sector, apart from those which concern, as social partners, employers and workers'.[900] It may also take up such questions of its own initiative. It is under a duty to 'give an opinion on the proposals formulated by the Commission as well as on the subjects appearing in its work programme'.[901]

The ACFA is very much a body of the Commission. It is referred to as being set up 'within the Commission'.[902] The ACFA's members are appointed by the Commission, albeit on proposals from the organizations representing the relevant interest groups.[903] The participants in the working groups are to be chosen in agreement with the Commission,[904] and the Commission may designate additional experts for working group meetings.[905] The ACFA is to 'meet on notification by the Commission according to an annual work programme adopted in agreement with the Commission', and the bureau is to meet in agreement with the Commission.[906] The rules of procedure of the ACFA are to be drawn up in agreement with the Commission.[907] Representatives of the Commission are to take part in the meetings of the ACFA, the bureau, and the working groups,[908] and the Commission is to provide the Committee's secretariat.[909]

---

[895] Dec 1999/478, Art 3. On sectoral dialogue committees, see Commission Decision 98/500/EC of 20 May 1998 on the establishment of Sectoral Dialogue Committees promoting the Dialogue between the social partners at European level, OJ 1998 L225/27, as amended.

[896] Dec 1999/478, Art 5, 1st para.   [897] Dec 1999/478, Art 4.

[898] Dec 1999/478, Art 7, 2nd para and Annex.   [899] Dec 1999/478, Art 5, 2nd and 3rd paras.

[900] Dec 1999/478, Art 2.   [901] Dec 1999/478, Art 9, 1st para.

[902] Dec 1999/478, Art 1(1).   [903] Dec 1999/478, Art 4(1), 1st para.

[904] Dec 1999/478, Art 7, 3rd para.   [905] Dec 1999/478, Art 7, 3rd para and Annex.

[906] Dec 1999/478, Art 8(1).   [907] Dec 1999/478, Art 8(4).   [908] Dec 1999/478, Art 8(2).

[909] Dec 1999/478, Art 8(3).

Under Regulation 861/2006, EC financial assistance is made available to cover the 'travelling and accommodation costs of members of the European trade organisations required to travel in order to prepare meetings of the [ACFA]'[910] and so, in turn, 'improve the coordination of national organisations at European level and ensure greater industry cohesion on topics of Community interest'.[911] The reference in Regulation 861/2006 to 'European trade organisations' and 'industry cohesion' raises questions about whether the EC financial assistance under that Regulation is similarly available to those members of the ACFA from the consumer, environment, and development sectors.[912]

As noted above, the role of the ACFA was evaluated by consultants in 2008 at the request of the Commission. The consultants' final report is dated August 2008.[913] According to the minutes of the October 2008 plenary meeting of the ACFA, the main objective of the evaluation 'was to provide the Commission with the information needed to prepare the ground for reflection on the future of ACFA'.[914] The report is extensive and detailed. However, the Commission had not issued any formal feedback or proposals by the end of November 2008 and so the report will not be discussed further here, beyond noting that the report's recommendations address, *inter alia*, the role and objective of the ACFA, its membership, and its working methods.

The ACFA does not work in isolation from the RACs. The Commission's view, as provided in its 2008 review, on the relationship between the ACFA and the RACs has been set out in subsection 7.2 above. Some links between the ACFA and the RACs are made by CFP legislation. The 2004 Decision provides a right for a representative of the ACFA to participate at any RAC meeting as an 'active observer'.[915] Regulation 861/2006 in turn facilitates that participation, '[i]n order to ensure coordination of the work of the RACs with that of ACFA',[916] by providing that the cost of such participation is eligible for Community financial measures.[917] The 2004 Decision also requires each RAC to transmit its annual report to the ACFA.[918] The ACFA and some of the RACs had a joint meeting in November 2007 and in October 2008 to discuss the fishing opportunities for 2008 and 2009 respectively.[919]

---

[910] Reg 861/2006, Art 12(a). See also Art 18.   [911] Reg 861/2006, recital (16).

[912] See also *Summary Record of the Plenary Meeting of the Advisory Committee on Fisheries and Aquaculture, 5 July 2007*, section 8, p 10 (available on the website of DG Mare).

[913] COWI A/S (in collaboration with Framian and Nautilus Consultants), *Intermediate Evaluation of the Advisory Committee for Fisheries and Aquaculture (ACFA)*, Final report, August 2008 (available on the website of DG Mare).   [914] Section 2, p 2. Minutes available on the website of DG Mare.

[915] Dec 2004/585, Art 6(3).   [916] Reg 861/2006, recital (18).

[917] Reg 861/2006, Art 12(b). See also Art 18.   [918] Dec 2004/585, Art 10.

[919] Summary minutes of meetings available on the website of DG Mare. Further discussion of the interaction between the ACFA and RACs is provided in COWI A/S (in collaboration with Framian and Nautilus Consultants), 2008, *inter alia*, pp 64–7.

8 Fishing by third country vessels in Community waters[920]

Fishing in Community waters is largely reserved for Community fishing vessels. Nevertheless, for reasons explained in the next chapter, a limited number of vessels from a few third countries, currently Dominica, the Faroe Islands, Norway, and Venezuela, are permitted to fish in Community waters.[921] Such vessels are limited to fishing for quotas for particular species which are laid down by the Council in the principal annual Regulation (currently Regulation 40/2008).[922] The main rules governing such third country fishing are set out partly in that Regulation and partly in Regulation 1006/2008.[923] Third country vessels fishing in Community waters must: (a) have an authorization issued by the Commission;[924] (b) comply with specified EC conservation and control measures;[925] (c) keep a log book;[926] (d) transmit certain information to the Commission;[927] and (e) fish beyond the 12 nm limit (except for Norwegian vessels, which have historic rights to fish in the waters between 4 and 12 nm from the baselines off the coasts of Denmark and Sweden).[928] In addition, vessels over 15 m in length must have a vessel monitoring system approved by the Commission,[929] and vessels fishing in the waters off French Guiana must carry an observer if so requested by the Commission.[930] Once the fishing opportunities granted to a third country have been exhausted, all fishing for those opportunities by vessels from that country must cease.[931] Third country vessels may only land, tranship, or process their catches if so authorized by the Member State in whose waters such operations are to take place.[932] Furthermore, third country vessels must generally give advance

---

[920] For a more extended (if now rather dated) discussion of this topic than that which follows, see Long and Curran, *Enforcing the Common Fisheries Policy*, 84–91, 127–30, and 207–8.

[921] According to the Commission, some 250 third country vessels (the majority from Norway) fish in Community waters: see *Proposal for a Council Regulation concerning authorisations for fishing activities of Community fishing vessels outside Community waters and the access of third country vessels to Community waters*, COM(2007) 330, 18.6.2007, p 3.   [922] Reg 40/2008, Arts 14 and 18 and Annex I.

[923] Council Regulation (EC) No 1006/2008 of 29 September 2008 concerning authorisations for fishing activities of Community fishing vessels outside Community waters and the access of third country vessels to Community waters, amending Regulations (EEC) No 2847/93 and (EC) No 1627/94 and repealing Regulation (EC) No 3317/94, OJ 2008 L286/33. As the title of the Regulation indicates, it in part replaces earlier legislation.

[924] Reg 1006/2008, Arts 18 and 20. The conditions governing the issue of authorizations are set out in Art 21. An authorization is not to be granted to a third country vessel if, *inter alia*, it has engaged in IUU fishing. An authorization includes the issue of a licence and a special fishing permit (except for Norwegian vessels of less than 200 GT): see Reg 40/2008, Arts 22 and 23.

[925] Reg 40/2008, Arts 15, 19, and 27 and Annex III; and Reg 1006/2008, Art 22. The control obligations on masters and vessels set out in Art 22(1) of Reg 2371/2002 (on which see subsection 2.7 above) apply, *inter alia*, to all fishing in Community waters, and therefore apply to fishing by third country vessels in Community waters.   [926] Reg 40/2008, Arts 27(2) and 28(2).

[927] Reg 40/2008, Art 27(3); and Reg 1006/2008, Art 23.   [928] Reg 40/2008, Art 16.

[929] Reg 2371/2002, Art 22(1)(b).   [930] Reg 40/2008, Art 28(1).

[931] Reg 1006/2008, Art 24.   [932] Reg 1006/2008, Art 18(1)(b).

notice if they wish to use, or land their catches at, a Member State port and must provide the port authorities with a declaration of the amounts of fish landed.[933] That position will change at the beginning of 2010. Thenceforth, third country fishing vessels will only be allowed access to the ports of a Member State and to land their catches there if they meet certain conditions, including, *inter alia*, the use only of designated ports and advance notification by the master of a vessel of the intended use of a designated port and details of the catch to be landed: in addition, third country vessels will no longer be able to tranship catches at sea in Community waters but only in the designated ports of Member States.[934]

The above provisions are largely similar to those applying to Community vessels fishing in Community waters, although in some cases they are somewhat stricter (for example, in relation to the access and use of ports in Member States and transhipment).

It is primarily up to the Member States to monitor compliance with the relevant EC rules by third country vessels fishing in their waters, and to arrest and prosecute or deal administratively with those vessels infringing such rules.[935] In particular, where third country vessels use the ports of a Member State for landing or transhipping catches, the port State must inspect at least 5 per cent of such landing and transhipment operations each year, and must always do so in the case of vessels suspected of IUU fishing.[936] If the results of the inspection provide evidence of IUU fishing, the port State must refuse landing or transhipment of the catch and immediately notify the Commission and flag State.[937] As well as, or instead of, sanctions imposed by the authorities of Member States in administrative or judicial proceedings following inspection at sea or in port, the Commission may also impose a sanction on a third country vessel fishing contrary to EC rules. Under Article 25 of Regulation 1006/2008 Member States must immediately notify the Commission of any 'recorded infringement' of EC rules by a third country vessel, whereupon the Commission may suspend or withdraw the authorization of the vessel concerned.[938] There is a somewhat similar power in the principal annual Regulation under which the Commission may withdraw licences and special

[933] Reg 2847/93, Arts 28e and 28f. See also Council Regulation (EC) No 1093/94 of 6 May 1994 setting the terms under which fishing vessels of a third country may land directly and market their catches at Community ports, OJ 1994 L121/3. Note that Norwegian vessels (and Icelandic vessels if and when they obtain rights to fish in Community waters) enjoy somewhat less restrictive conditions on which to land their catches at Member State ports by virtue of Art 5 of Protocol 9 to the Agreement on the European Economic Area, OJ 1994 L1/160.
[934] Reg 1005/2008, Arts 4(2), 5(2), 6, and 7. Reg 1005/2008 will also repeal Arts 28e and 28f of Reg 2847/93 and Reg 1093/94: see Art 56.   [935] Reg 2847/93, especially Arts 1(3) and 2(1).
[936] Reg 1005/2008, Art 9.   [937] Reg 1005/2008, Art 11(2) and (3).
[938] More detailed rules for the application of Art 25 are contained in Commission Regulation (EC) No 2943/95 of 20 December 1995 setting out detailed rules for applying Council Regulation (EC) No 1627/94 laying down general provisions concerning special fishing permits, OJ 1995 L308/15. The references in Reg 2943/95 to the provisions of Reg 1627/94 that Reg 1006/2008 has replaced are to be read as references to the corresponding provisions of Reg 1006/2008: see Reg 1006/2008, Art 29(4).

permits if a third country vessel fails to fulfil the obligations laid down in that Regulation.[939] The term 'recorded infringement' in Article 25 of Regulation 1006/2008 is not defined. Some guidance as to its meaning is provided by Regulation 2943/95. Under Article 5 of that Regulation a Member State is to notify the Commission of 'any infringements detected' and provide 'details of any judicial, administrative or other action undertaken and any final decision in law concerning the infringement'. Under Article 6 the Commission is to assess the seriousness of each notified infringement, *inter alia*, 'in the light of judicial and administrative decisions by the competent authorities' of the Member State concerned. There is a degree of ambiguity about those provisions. It is clear from them that the term 'recorded infringement' includes a finding of a breach of EC law by a court. It also appears to include such a finding by a competent body where administrative proceedings are used as an alternative to criminal prosecutions. Whether it also includes a record of alleged infringement by a national fisheries inspector is more doubtful, although both the reference to 'other action undertaken' in Article 5 of Regulation 2943/95 and the factual situation in the case of *Fiskano* (discussed below) suggest that it might. The uncertainty over the term 'recorded infringement' and the vagueness of the provisions concerning the way in which the Commission is to exercise its powers under the principal annual Regulation (it is not clear, for example, if the provisions of Regulation 2943/95 apply in that situation) are somewhat unfortunate; and it is a pity that the 2008 reform of the law relating to third country fishing in Community waters did not take the opportunity to clarify the matter.

Withdrawal or suspension of a licence is a serious penalty that may threaten the livelihood of the fisherman concerned. It is therefore important, for a proper application of the rule of law, that it be clearly established that there has indeed been an infringement of EC fishery rules before the Commission withdraws or suspends a licence, and that such withdrawal or suspension is an appropriate sanction for the infringement committed. Because a Commission Decision to withdraw or suspend a licence is a legally reviewable act under Article 230 EC, it is possible for a third country fisherman who believes that the rule of law has been infringed by the Commission in withdrawing or suspending his licence to challenge the Commission's Decision before the Court of First Instance (the Court of Justice before 1993). This has happened on at least two occasions.

The first such case was *Fiskano v Commission*.[940] Before Sweden became a member of the EC in 1995, a number of Swedish vessels were licensed to fish in Community waters. A Swedish vessel, the *Lavoen*, was found to be fishing without a licence in Dutch waters by Dutch fisheries inspectors in December 1991. Although the *Lavoen* had been licensed to fish in Community waters earlier that year, it did not have a licence for December. The Commission informed the

---

[939] Reg 40/2008, Art 26.   [940] Case C-135/92 *Fiskano AB v Commission* [1994] ECR I-2885.

Swedish authorities that because of its unlicensed fishing the vessel would not be considered for a new licence for a period of twelve months. The owner of the *Lavoen*, Fiskano, challenged the Commission's Decision before the Court, arguing that by not giving it an opportunity to submit its observations before the Decision was adopted, the Commission had infringed a general principle of EC law, namely the right to be heard. The Court agreed. It held that 'observance of the right to be heard requires that any person on whom a penalty may be imposed must be placed in a position in which he can effectively make known his view of the matters on the basis of which the Commission imposes the penalty'.[941] In this case it was not disputed that the Commission had not given Fiskano any opportunity to submit observations before it adopted its Decision. One apparent consequence of this case was that a right to a hearing before suspension or withdrawal of the licence was included in Regulation 2943/95 (in Article 6), which was adopted some eighteen months after the Court's judgment.

The second case, *Kvitsjøen*,[942] concerned a Norwegian vessel licensed to fish in Community waters that was found by Dutch fishery inspectors to be fishing with a device by means of which the mesh in the net was obstructed and diminished, which was contrary to EC law. The vessel was taken to a Dutch port and its catch confiscated. In accordance with its powers outlined above, the Commission withdrew the vessel's licence for six months. The applicant did not deny that its vessel had infringed EC law, but argued that the Commission's Decision to withdraw its licence was invalid on the grounds that it had not been given the opportunity to comment on the allegations against it, that the Dutch authorities had failed to supply the Commission with the necessary information, and that the withdrawal of the licence was a disproportionate penalty. The Court rejected the applicant's first two arguments, finding that in fact the applicant had been given the opportunity to comment on the case against it (unlike Fiskano in the earlier case) and that the Dutch authorities had supplied the necessary information. In relation to the applicant's third argument, the Court held that withdrawal of the licence was not a disproportionate penalty because the offence which the applicant conceded that it had committed was considered in EC law to be a serious one and had a serious impact on fish stocks. Furthermore, no national sanction had been imposed on the applicant, who had also benefited financially from its infringement of EC law (the Court here seems to have overlooked the fact that the applicant's catch had been confiscated).

The above two cases go some way to suggesting that Article 230 EC provides an adequate remedy for a third country fisherman who believes his licence wrongfully to have been withdrawn or suspended. In those cases there was no dispute as to whether an infringement of EC rules had actually occurred, but it is quite possible that such a dispute could arise in some future case. If it did, it would seem that the Court could decide whether an infringement had in fact occurred. One of the

---

[941] Ibid, para 40.   [942] Case T-46/00 *Kvitsjøen AS v Commission* [2001] ECR II-3713.

grounds on which the Court can uphold a challenge to a Community act under Article 230 EC is lack of competence on the part of the EC institution that adopted the contested act (here the withdrawal or suspension of a licence). The Commission would lack such competence if no infringement had occurred. It would therefore seem that the Court could determine whether an infringement had occurred in order to decide whether the Commission had the competence to withdraw or suspend a licence. A further ground of challenge under Article 230 EC is breach of fundamental human rights. A licence to fish would appear, at least in some circumstances, to constitute a right to property under the European Convention on Human Rights,[943] which the Court strives to uphold. Under Article 1 of Protocol 1 to the Convention, a person cannot be deprived of her/his property except 'subject to the conditions provided for by law'. If there had been no infringement of EC rules, 'the conditions provided for by law' would not have been fulfilled and thus there might well be a breach of the applicant's property rights.

One potential drawback with Article 230 EC as a remedy to challenge alleged wrongful Decisions by the Commission is the fact that it normally takes two years or more before the Court gives judgment. By that time the applicant could have been deprived of many months of fishing and the consequent income. One way of reducing this delay would be for the applicant to seek suspension of the application of the Commission's Decision withdrawing or suspending the licence under Article 242 EC or other interim measures under Article 243 EC. If such remedies were not available, the applicant could instead seek to mitigate the adverse consequences of the time taken by the Court to reach its decision by claiming compensation for lost fishing opportunities from the Commission under Articles 235 and 288 EC. To succeed, the applicant would not only have to show that the Commission's suspension or withdrawal of the licence was unlawful, but also that the Commission was at fault in taking such action. If proceeding under Article 230 EC, one problem that in principle an aggrieved third country fisherman would not have to face, unlike many applicants under Article 230 EC, would be arguments as to whether he had the necessary standing to bring an action: a Commission Decision withdrawing or suspending a licence (even if formally addressed to the flag State) is, in principle, of direct and individual concern to the fisherman in question.

The discussion thus far has assumed that third country vessels fishing in Community waters fly the flags of countries with which the EC has agreements permitting such fishing, but it is of course always possible, and indeed it has happened on occasions, that vessels from other third countries fish in Community waters. Such fishing is clearly illegal, and Member States are not only empowered but required under the Control Regulation to prevent and punish such fishing.[944]

---

[943] See the judgment of the European Court of Human Rights in *Posti and Rakho v Finland* (2003) 37 EHRR 6, especially at para 76.   [944] Reg 2847/93, Arts 1(3), 3(1), and 31.

Unlike the situation with vessels fishing pursuant to an access agreement with a third country, the EC in this case has no power to sanction the vessels concerned. In order to try to reduce the chances of such illegal fishing occurring, EC law requires third country fishing vessels merely transiting Community waters to have their fishing gear stowed during such transit.[945]

9 Reform

9.1 Introduction

The CFP is constantly evolving. In terms of fisheries conservation in Community waters and in the context of the current Basic Regulation, there are several reforms in the pipeline that have not been discussed earlier in this chapter and that merit mention here. These relate to an ecosystem approach, maximum sustainable yield (hereafter, 'MSY'), discards, rights-based management (hereafter, 'RBM'), and consultation and simplification. The Commission's proposals on these matters are discussed below and some links between them will be identified where appropriate. Some of these proposals (namely those on MSY, discards, and RBM) are focused on Community waters, although the proposals on MSY and discards make mention of *non*-Community waters too. The others are more generic in nature. In any event, despite the scope of this chapter, the proposals will be discussed here without seeking to exclude elements relevant to non-Community waters.

In mentioning these individual areas of reform, it is of course also necessary to explain that a broader reform is also due to take place, colloquially referred to as 'the reform of the CFP'. Principally, before the end of 2012, there is to be a review by the Commission of 'the operation of the Common Fisheries Policy with respect to Chapters II and III' of the Basic Regulation.[946] Chapters II and III deal with 'conservation and sustainability' and 'adjustment of fishing capacity', respectively. A review of Chapter I, on 'scope and objectives', Chapter V, on the 'Community control and enforcement system', and Chapter VI, on 'decision-making and consultation', is not called for.[947] However, on Chapter IV, regarding 'rules on access to waters and resources', a specific review of the access restriction pursuant to Article 17(2) is to be completed by the Commission by the end of 2011.[948]

In practice, the Commission has already launched its review of Chapters II and III of the Basic Regulation, although the signs are that the review will not be

---

[945] Reg 40/2008, Art 17. On the legality (in international law) and practicalities of such a requirement, see Burke, WT, *The New International Law of Fisheries* (Oxford: Clarendon Press, 1994), 330–1.

[946] Reg 2371/2002, Art 35.

[947] On reform of the control system, see subsection 2.7 above. On review and reform of the common organization of the markets in fishery and aquaculture products, see Chapter 6.

[948] Reg 2371/2002, Art 17(2), 2nd para. On Art 17(2), see further subsection 2.5 above.

restricted to these two Chapters. At the time of writing, the website of DG Mare stated that: 'The review was launched at an informal [Fisheries] Council meeting on 29 September 2008 on the basis of a working paper by the Commission with an initial analysis and discussion of some options for reform.' The said paper, which is headed *Commission Working Document* and entitled *Reflections on further reform of the Common Fisheries Policy*,[949] is discussed in subsection 9.2 below. A press release on the website of the Commission states that at the meeting referred to above DG Mare 'received the broad support of the Member States to kick-start preparations immediately' for the review. In terms of next steps, the press release states that:

The debate . . . will continue in 2009 not only with the Member States, but through a broad-based consultation with the fisheries sector, other stakeholders and the wider public. The Commission intends to table a Green Paper early in 2009 which will provide the basis for a public debate. A summary of the consultation will be published in early 2010, and the Commission will aim to table reform proposals later in the same year, with a view to their coming into force in 2012.[950]

9.2 Commission's Working Document

The Commission's Working Document referred to above analyses, in broad terms, the effects of the CFP and then suggests some policy reforms. Such reforms are not exclusively relevant to Community waters and will be discussed here in a general sense despite the scope of this chapter. The paper acknowledges that: 'Fishing fleets are still too large, and as a result, it has not been possible to reduce overfishing to the extent necessary.'[951] Reflecting the mandate for review established by the Basic Regulation (see above), the paper focuses on conservation and fleet policy. However, it adds that it is necessary to consider how other elements of the CFP, 'especially the structural funds', can better support conservation and fleet policy and to address 'the external dimension of a reformed CFP'.[952] The need for early preparation for review is traced to, *inter alia*, the need to prepare for a possible move to the co-decision procedure for making secondary legislation (depending on the prospects for the Treaty of Lisbon), the existence of the 'new Integrated Maritime Policy' (see further below), and the need to start preparing for some 'major structural changes' to the CFP.[953]

The paper identifies several 'structural failings' of the CFP. The Commission is concerned that 'decisions on long-term principles and on implementation details are taken at the same level', the result being 'a short-term focus'. The CFP's

---

[949] Available on the website of DG Mare.
[950] 'Midday Express of 2008-09-30', MEX/08/0930, 30.09.2008.
[951] *Commission Working Document*, section 1, p 1. See also section 2, p 4.
[952] *Commission Working Document*, section 1, p 2.
[953] *Commission Working Document*, section 1, pp 1–2.

objectives mix 'long-term and short-term concerns and social, economic and environmental factors' and yet provide 'no clear order of priority'. Member States 'have not given the industry genuine responsibility for sustainable use of a public resource'. Relative stability has encouraged Member States to focus on their national interests 'rather than on the collective long-term benefit'. There is a reluctance among Member States to use the structural funds to adapt fleet size. There is 'no real willingness' to introduce RBM as a means of inducing 'long-lasting fleet adaptation'.[954]

The paper in turn provides some ideas on policy reform to address these structural failings. Most of these relate to the longer term. There should be 'a clear hierarchy in responsibilities for decision making between decisions on principles, community [sic] standards emerging from these principles and technical implementation decisions'. The CFP's objectives 'must be sufficiently specific to enable accountability and monitoring of performance' and 'long term *ecological* sustainability of fisheries must be the first priority' (emphasis added). The fishing industry 'must be made responsible and accountable for sustainable use of a public resource', perhaps by conditioning resource access rights on demonstration of responsible fishing and on payment of a fee. There could be a move to '[r]esults-based management, where the industry is made responsible for outcomes rather than means'. Relative stability will need 're-examining'. Means to reduce fleet capacity to match resources 'must be at the core' of the CFP, including 'a more effective use of structural funds and access rights which creates incentives for the fleet to tackle overcapacity'.[955]

It is noteworthy that the paper refers to the 'new Integrated Maritime Policy'. Presumably this is a reference to the Commission's Communication on an integrated maritime policy, issued in October 2007.[956] The paper states that the maritime policy 'provides an umbrella under which we can strengthen the coherence between the reformed CFP and other Community policies related to the sustainable development of seas, oceans and coastal areas'[957] and that it is 'necessary to consider . . . how the CFP should be integrated with policies regarding other maritime sectors in the Maritime Policy'.[958] On the theme of integration, the paper also states that the entry into force of the Marine Strategy Directive[959] (hereafter, 'MSD', on which see section 6 above) 'provides an important orientation in terms of the long-term goal on which we need to align the reformed CFP in a coherent manner'.[960] It will be interesting to see how the

---

[954] *Commission Working Document*, section 3, p 6.

[955] *Commission Working Document*, section 4.

[956] *Communication from the Commission to the European Parliament, the Council, the European Economic and Social Committee and the Committee of the Regions: An Integrated Maritime Policy for the European Union*, COM(2007) 575, 10.10.2007. [957] *Commission Working Document*, section 1, p 1.

[958] *Commission Working Document*, section 1, p 2. See also section 4, pp 7 and 9.

[959] Dir 2008/56. [960] *Commission Working Document*, section 4, p 8.

review of the CFP will take into account the integrated maritime policy and the MSD. In that regard, one commentator has stated that the CFP 'now faces the biggest challenge to its existence from the pressures of environmental integration and the incorporation of fisheries within the much broader concerns for maritime development and marine spatial planning'.[961]

9.3 Ecosystem approach

In April 2008 the Commission issued a Communication on the role of the CFP in implementing an ecosystem approach to marine management.[962] The justification for this document is traced by the Commission to Article 6 EC (on environmental integration), the Basic Regulation, which states that the EC 'shall aim at a progressive implementation of an eco-system-based approach to fisheries management',[963] and various international developments.[964] The 2008 Communication is not the first Commission document on this subject.[965] In addition it should be noted that the ICES, a key science adviser to the Commission, published an important report on the ecosystem approach in 2005[966] and has working groups on various ecosystem aspects.[967]

The Basic Regulation, despite referring to 'an eco-system-based approach to fisheries management', fails to define that term. Having looked at some of the definitions of an ecosystem approach arising from other fora, the Commission states that:[968]

the Commission's understanding is that an ecosystem approach to fisheries management is about ensuring goods and services from living aquatic resources for present and future generations within meaningful ecological boundaries. Such fisheries management will strive to ensure that benefits from living marine resources are high while the direct and indirect impacts of fishing operations on marine ecosystems are low and not detrimental to the future functioning, diversity and integrity of these ecosystems.

---

[961] Sissenwine and Symes, *Reflections on the Common Fisheries Policy*, 59 (Symes).

[962] *Communication from the Commission to the Council and the European Parliament: The role of the CFP in implementing an ecosystem approach to marine management*, COM(2008) 187, 11.4.2008. See also the associated *Commission Staff Working Document* SEC(2008) 449, 11.4.2008.

[963] Reg 2371/2002, Art 2(1), 2nd para.   [964] COM(2008) 187, p 2.

[965] See, in particular, *Commission Staff Working Paper: The Ecosystem-based Approach to Fisheries Management (EAFM): possibilities and priorities for international co-operation*, SEC(2001) 1696, 18.12.2001.

[966] Rice, J, Trujillo, V, Jennings, S, Hylland, K, Hagstrom, O, Astudillo, A, and Jensen, JN, *Guidance on the Application of the Ecosystem Approach to Management of Human Activities in the European Marine Environment*, ICES Cooperative Research Report No 273 (Copenhagen: ICES, 2005).

[967] For example the Working Group on Ecosystem Effects of Fishing Activities (WGECO).

[968] COM(2008) 187, section 1, p 3.

The title of the Commission's 2008 Communication refers to the role of the CFP in implementing an ecosystem approach to *marine management*. Furthermore, the Commission has stated elsewhere that, in view of the fact that '[a]n ecosystem approach cannot be implemented through one sector alone', its 2008 Communication 'does *not* deal with an ecosystem approach to fisheries management as such but how CFP measures can contribute to this cross-sectoral ecosystem approach' (emphasis added).[969] There are indeed several references in the document to the need for a cross-sectoral approach and links are made to the MSD which the Commission regards as 'the general basis for implementing an ecosystem approach to the marine environment'[970] (see further below). However, beyond these general statements and with the exception of a brief consideration of climate change,[971] the document focuses on the fisheries sector and does not address specific interactions with other economic sectors. In practice, overall, it is hard to see how the Communication differs from one that might have been written about an ecosystem approach to fisheries management specifically.

According to the Commission, the 'task of fisheries management within an ecosystem approach in a EU context' is twofold: (a) to 'keep direct and indirect impacts of fisheries on marine ecosystems within bounds in relation to healthy marine ecosystems and ecologically viable fish populations by including all the knowledge we have about the interactions between fisheries and marine ecosystems in decisions under the CFP'; and (b) to 'ensure that actions taken in fisheries are consistent with and supportive of actions taken under the cross-sectoral Marine Strategy [Directive] and Habitats Directive'.[972]

The Communication in turn identifies the following as being the main tasks of fisheries management, with a view to achieving an ecosystem approach: (a) reducing the overall fishing pressure to sustainable levels; (b) protecting sensitive habitats and species; and (c) preventing 'distortions in the food web' and ensuring that 'natural ecosystem processes are not disrupted'.[973] For the implementation of these tasks, the Communication places emphasis on the MSD and on long-term management plans.

Regarding the MSD, the Communication states that: 'The general boundaries of an overall ecosystem approach will be defined by identifying good environmental status through the implementation of the [MSD].'[974] It also states that '[t]he conditions of fish stocks and fish habitats will be important elements in the assessment of good environmental status . . .',[975] which may be a reference to the descriptors listed in Annex I to the MSD (see section 6 above). The

[969] House of Lords, 2008, HL Paper 146–II, p 209 (European Commission's evidence).
[970] COM(2008) 187, p 2.   [971] COM(2008) 187, section 3, p 6.
[972] COM(2008) 187, section 2, p 4.   [973] COM(2008) 187, section 3, pp 5–6.
[974] COM(2008) 187, section 4, p 7.
[975] COM(2008) 187, section 2, p 4; see also section 6, p 10.

Communication envisages that fisheries management measures taken under the CFP will contribute to achieving the MSD's goals.[976]

Regarding long-term management plans, the document states that: 'Specific objectives for fisheries [to implement an ecosystem approach] will be developed through long-term management plans based on the MSY concept, but will in the future also integrate considerations of ecosystem impacts of the specific fisheries concerned.'[977] In view of the fact that the MSD does not require good environmental status to be achieved until 2020 and in view of the currently small number of long-term management plans (see subsection 2.1 above), it looks like achieving an ecosystem approach to fisheries management by reference to good environmental status and by use of long-term plans is still some way off.

On the more practical side, the Commission acknowledges that '[p]rogress on the basis of existing knowledge and with present instruments can and must be achieved'.[978] It identifies various existing policies, legislation, and initiatives at the EC level that it considers 'will contribute to the objectives of integrated management of the seas based on an ecosystem approach',[979] some of which are discussed in section 6 above. In terms of next steps, the Communication lists various initiatives,[980] the first being that: 'In the short and medium term steps to reduce overall fishing pressure on marine ecosystems will continue, including implementation of the MSY approach through long-term management plans and in annual or multiannual proposals on catch limitations.' The MSY approach as proposed by the Commission is discussed in subsection 9.4 below.

Other 'next steps' include, *inter alia*, implementation of the new discard policy (on which, see subsection 9.5 below); publication of plans of action on sharks and seabirds; adoption of the proposed replacement for Regulation 850/98 (on technical measures; see subsection 2.3 above); adoption of measures to implement those MSD goals relating to fish populations and impacts of fisheries; adoption of a first set of indicators and collection of supporting data;[981] protection of Natura 2000 sites and other marine protected areas; research; and use of the EFF. It is surprising that, in its listing of existing initiatives and next steps, the Commission fails to emphasize the importance of broad stakeholder engagement through, in particular, the Regional Advisory Councils (RACs, on which, see section 7 above).[982] The Communication also makes surprisingly little of the need for so-called 'adaptive management',[983] particularly in the light of climate change.[984]

The Commission's proposals on the ecosystem approach do not relate exclusively to Community waters. Some are relevant to such waters specifically, by virtue of

---

[976] COM(2008) 187, section 2, p 4 and section 6, p 10.   [977] COM(2008) 187, section 4, p 7.
[978] COM(2008) 187, section 4, p 7.   [979] COM(2008) 187, section 5, pp 7–9.
[980] COM(2008) 187, section 6, pp 9–10.   [981] See further SEC(2008) 449.
[982] Cf a single reference to RACs at section 4, p 7.
[983] On adaptive management, see for example ICES Cooperative Research Report No 273, section 6.1, pp 8–9.   [984] Cf references at pp 7, 8, and 10.

the instruments being discussed (notably the MSD and the Habitats Directive). However, many have the potential to be more generic, reflecting the lack of geographical restriction on both the application of Article 6 EC and the Basic Regulation's reference to 'an eco-system-based approach'. The Communication notes at the outset that: 'Implementing an ecosystem approach through the CFP concerns not only Community waters, but all oceans worldwide. Community action will therefore unfold through the current CFP instruments for Community waters and via Community action in [RFMOs], through the UN and FAO process or, where appropriate, via bilateral agreements.'[985] This is further recognized in the 'next steps' listed by the Commission, in that the EC 'will support initiatives to promote an ecosystem approach in RFMOs, in the UN framework and other international fora and, where appropriate, in bilateral agreements'.[986]

Overall, the list of 'next steps' set out in the Communication has the feeling of an ad hoc amalgam of things that happen to fit with the ecosystem approach, rather than representing a strategic approach to the task in hand. The use of so-called 'fisheries ecosystem plans' has been suggested as a way for the Commission to 'formalize processes to demonstrate that it is applying an ecosystem approach',[987] but this is not proposed in the Communication, despite some EU-funded research on such plans[988] and a ministerial call in 2006 for such a plan to be developed for the North Sea.[989] The Commission states that an ecosystem approach 'will . . . be seen as *the* guiding principle for decisions under the CFP', albeit by means of 'an *incremental* approach' (emphasis added).[990] This fits with the Basic Regulation's aspiration to achieve 'a progressive implementation' of the ecosystem approach (see above). However, it does not suggest that anything very major will happen very fast. Perhaps the step-wise implementation of the MSD in the lead up to 2020 will be a more meaningful impetus than the loose wording in the Basic Regulation (subject to any revised wording arising from the review of the CFP).

In September 2008 the Council adopted conclusions on the Commission's Communication on the ecosystem approach.[991] It recognized that 'healthy

---

[985] COM(2008) 187, p 2. See also references to 'third countries' (in the context of ecosystems) at section 2, p 4 and shared stocks at section 5, p 9. [986] COM(2008) 187, section 6, p 10.

[987] Sissenwine and Symes, *Reflections on the Common Fisheries Policy*, 41. See also: House of Lords, 2008, HL Paper 146-II, pp 55 and 63 (RSPB's evidence); and Dunn, E, *El Anzuelo*, Vol 20, 2008, 10, available on the website of the Institute for European Environmental Policy (IEEP).

[988] European Fisheries Ecosystem Plan (EFEP) project, which used the North Sea as a case study. For more information see, for example, technical leaflet on EFEP available on the website of Profet Policy.

[989] Declaration, North Sea Ministerial Meeting on the Environmental Impact of Shipping and Fisheries, Göteborg, Sweden, 4 and 5 May 2006, Part II, para 2 (available on the website of the Dutch government's Ministry of Transport, Public Works and Water Management).

[990] COM(2008) 187, section 6, p 10.

[991] Council of the European Union, 2892nd meeting of the Council, Agriculture and Fisheries, 29–30 September 2008, press release, 13522/08 (Presse 274), 18 (and cross-reference to Council document 12769/08).

ecosystems are essential for the sustainable exploitation of marine resources'.[992] It wished 'to see the ecosystem approach continue to serve as a guide for the preparation of new initiatives under the [CFP], amongst other things in reducing discards and protecting vulnerable species and habitats, especially via action plans for the protection of sharks and seabirds and for specific fishery management measures under the Natura 2000 network'.[993] The Council called on the Commission 'to continue implementing and to develop the ecosystem approach to management of the marine environment'.[994]

9.4 Maximum sustainable yield

In July 2006 the Commission issued a Communication[995] responding to the commitment made at the 2002 World Summit on Sustainable Development to '[m]aintain or restore stocks to levels that can produce the [MSY] with the aim of achieving these goals for depleted stocks on an urgent basis and where possible not later than 2015'.[996] As noted in Chapter 3, the United Nations Convention on the Law of the Sea, to which the EC and all the Member States are parties, also uses the concept of MSY, albeit potentially qualified by various factors.

The Communication presents the Commission's 'policy approach to implementing a [MSY] based fisheries management in the Community'[997] and as such represents 'a new political orientation as regards fisheries management in the Community'.[998] The policy on MSY is relevant to the Commission's proposals on the ecosystem approach (see subsection 9.3 above).[999] The proposals focus on Community waters, although they also refer at one point to 'stocks jointly managed with third countries' (see further below). In December 2007 the Council provided a measured response to the Commission's proposals, but overall encouraged the Commission 'to work actively within the Community . . . in progressing towards MSY'.[1000]

The Commission considers that fishing at MSY levels will reduce the amount of effort, and hence costs, required per tonne of fish caught (because 'it would allow the development of larger fish stocks'[1001]), increase the competitiveness of the

[992] Council conclusions (12769/08), para 3.   [993] Council conclusions (12769/08), para 11.
[994] Council conclusions (12769/08), para 12.
[995] *Communication from the Commission to the Council and the European Parliament: Implementing sustainability in EU fisheries through maximum sustainable yield*, COM(2006) 360, 4.7.2006. See also accompanying SEC(2006) 868, 4.7.2006.
[996] Report of the World Summit on Sustainable Development, Chapter 1, Resolution 2, Plan of Implementation, para 31(a) (available on the website of the UN Department of Economic and Social Affairs, Division for Sustainable Development).   [997] COM(2006) 360, section 1, p 4.
[998] COM(2006) 360, section 1, p 3.   [999] See also COM(2006) 360, section 1, p 3.
[1000] Council of the European Union, 2841st Council meeting, Agriculture and Fisheries, 17–19 December 2007, press release, 16373/1/07 REV 1 (Presse 294), 59–60.
[1001] COM(2006) 360, section 2.1, p 4.

EC's fishing industry vis-à-vis imports of fishery products (because of, *inter alia*, competitive advantages arising from a stable domestic supply), and increase the proportion of large and high-value fish in the catch thus reducing discards.[1002] By virtue of the latter point, the Commission's policy on MSY is relevant to its proposals on discards (on which, see subsection 9.5 below).

Getting to stock sizes that produce MSY is potentially a painful process for the fishing industry, because catches of many stocks would initially need to be reduced in order to rebuild those stocks. The Commission foresees the use of long-term plans, albeit kept under review 'as ecosystems and environments change over time', to define the appropriate target rate of fishing and decide the rate at which annual adjustments to TACs and effort limits will be made to reach this target. Technical measures may be a necessary component of such plans, to control fishing for the species in question as well as to reduce collateral effects.[1003]

The Commission makes a distinction between defining a target rate of fishing and managing biomass levels; it prefers the former to the latter.[1004] Fishing at MSY levels may not be the objective in every case; exploitation at lighter levels may be desired 'in order to achieve some gain in productivity of other species'.[1005] Two contrasting approaches to achieve MSY are proposed: (a) 'reducing fishing capacity, investment and employment to no more than what is necessary to fish at the [MSY] rate'; or (b) 'maintaining the size of the fleet but reducing the efficiency of fishing'.[1006] The Commission states that it is up to the Member State to choose the economic strategy, eg '(a)' or '(b)' above; the Communication suggests that the Commission is in favour of decommissioning on the basis that it is 'the most easily controllable fisheries management measure'. Either way, the pace of change to enable stock sizes to reach MSY is clearly a crucial factor.[1007]

The Communication states that: 'Over the coming years the Commission will propose long-term plans with the aim of bringing all major fish stocks in Community waters to rates of fishing at which [MSYs] can be achieved. For stocks jointly managed with third countries, the Community will seek to develop joint management arrangements with the same objective.' The reference to jointly managed stocks is rather ambiguous; in principle, it could refer not only to stocks shared with neighbours (eg Norway) but also to any other stocks where management is somehow joint (eg stocks managed by RFMOs of which the EC is a member).

The long-term plans in question 'will be fishery-based, addressing groups of fish stocks that are caught together'. Some of the 'guiding principles' for their development include active consultation with RACs, including in relation to impact assessments, adoption of 'programmed reductions in fishing rates' (mainly through adjustments to TACs and effort limits) including mechanisms 'to assure a stable and

---

[1002] COM(2006) 360, sections 2.2–2.4, p 6.　　　[1003] COM(2006) 360, section 3.1, pp 6–7.
[1004] COM(2006) 360, section 3.3, p 8 (4th bullet point).
[1005] COM(2006) 360, section 3.3, p 8 (7th bullet point).
[1006] COM(2006) 360, section 4, p 9.　　　[1007] COM(2006) 360, section 4, pp 8–10.

smooth transition', five-yearly updating, and inclusion of 'milestones' to enable measurement of progress towards achieving MSY. Priority will be given to fisheries where a recommendation arises from an RAC and 'where the most rapid conservation and economic benefits can be gained by moving towards [MSY] fisheries'.[1008]

As noted above, the Communication was issued in July 2006. Between then and the end of November 2008, only four long-term plans were proposed by the Commission (aside from any that may have been proposed in negotiations between the EC and its neighbouring coastal States—see subsection 2.1 above).[1009] Three of those set MSY as their target,[1010] of which two are based on defining a target rate of fishing rather than a target biomass.[1011] The Commission acknowledges that '[p]utting a complete set of long-term plans in place to achieve the MSY target will take time', but meanwhile 'it will be necessary to ensure that the Community's annual management decisions take account of the 2015 objective, and at the very least do not make it more difficult to achieve'. The Commission states that the EC 'should, with effect from 2007, adopt management decisions that ensure that there is no increase in the fishing rate for any stock that is already overfished'.[1012]

Rather confusingly, the Commission adds that the process to achieve MSY 'will be without prejudice to other measures, such as recovery plans, taken in accordance with the precautionary approach to reduce risks of stock depletions in the short term'.[1013] Perhaps this is a reference to plans that had already been adopted or proposed prior to July 2006, rather than plans proposed subsequently.

9.5 Discards

Discarding has already been introduced in subsection 2.1 above. In March 2007[1014] the Commission proposed 'a progressive introduction of a discard ban— where all finfish and crustaceans caught will have to be landed',[1015] which it

---

[1008] COM(2006) 360, section 5, pp 10–11.

[1009] COM(2006) 411 (Baltic Sea cod); COM(2007) 169 (bluefin tuna); COM(2008) 162 (cod, amendment); and COM(2008) 240 (west of Scotland herring).

[1010] COM(2007) 169 (bluefin tuna), proposed Art 1; COM(2008) 162 (cod, amendment), proposed Art 1 (proposed Art 3(1) of revised Reg 423/2004); and COM(2008) 240 (west of Scotland herring), proposed Art 3(1).

[1011] COM(2008) 162 (cod, amendment); and COM(2008) 240 (west of Scotland herring).

[1012] COM(2006) 360, section 5, p 11.   [1013] COM(2006) 360, section 5, p 11.

[1014] *Communication from the Commission to the Council and the European Parliament. A policy to reduce unwanted by-catches and eliminate discards in European fisheries*, COM(2007) 136, 28.3.2007. See also the associated *Commission Staff Working Document* SEC(2007) 380, 28.3.2007; and *Communication from the Commission to the Council and the European Parliament: On a Community Action Plan to reduce discards of fish* COM(2002) 656, 26.11.2002.   [1015] COM(2007) 136, section 1, p 2.

acknowledges will be a 'long term project'.[1016] The Commission advocates a results-based approach, rather than an array of specific technical solutions. The approach would apply in Community waters; however, in addition, 'the Community will promote initiatives for elimination of discards in [RFMOs]'.[1017] In an initial reaction in June 2007, the Council gave a somewhat cautious welcome to the Commission's proposals.[1018] The proposals have obvious relevance to the Commission's policy on the ecosystem approach (see subsection 9.3 above, and see further below).

Regarding the results-based approach, the Commission states that: 'In this approach extensive micromanagement specifications of fishing gear and fishing practices are replaced by requirements for specific results (maximum acceptable by-catch) and the industry is then left free to choose those solutions which are most compatible with the practical and economic realities of the fisheries.'[1019] Thus the result to be achieved would be a specified 'maximum acceptable by-catch'. The onus would be on the fishermen to develop means to reduce discards and so make the most of their fishing opportunities and their operating costs. The possibility of using the EFF to support the required changes in technology and practices is raised.[1020]

It is not entirely clear from the Commission's Communication how use of a 'maximum acceptable by-catch' would work in conjunction with a 'discard ban'. However, the focus of the document is certainly on a discard *ban*, rather than on a reduction of discards to something other than zero. A non-paper issued by the Commission in April 2008 (hereafter, 'the non-paper'),[1021] over a year after the Communication's release, provides some further thinking. It defines the term 'maximum allowable by-catch limit' (hereafter, 'MABL') as follows:[1022]

Definition of MABL: the Maximum allowed by-catch limit refers to finfish and crustaceans caught in a fishing operation and not wanted by the vessel owner for whatever reason; it *may be discarded or brought ashore* and put to the uses to be defined in Community legislation, without generating an economic benefit for the vessel owner. Finfish and crustaceans caught in a fishing operation and not wanted by the vessel owner which exceeds the MABL *may not be discarded and have to be brought ashore* under the provisions defined in Community legislation. [Emphasis added.]

The above definition suggests that by-catch that is within the MABL may be either discarded or brought ashore whereas by-catch that is outside the MABL may not

---

[1016] COM(2007) 136, section 6, p 8.   [1017] COM(2007) 136, section 3, p 4.

[1018] Council of the European Union, 2806th Council meeting, Agriculture and Fisheries, 11–12 June 2007, press release, 10169/07 (Presse 123), 11 (and cross-reference to Council document 11063/07).

[1019] COM(2007) 136, section 3, p 5.   [1020] COM(2007) 136, section 5, p 7.

[1021] *Commission non-paper: On the implementation of the policy to reduce unwanted by-catch and eliminate discards in European fisheries* (available on the website of DG Mare).

[1022] Non-paper, p 5, footnote 4.

be discarded and hence has to be brought ashore. If that interpretation is correct, and assuming that a MABL were not set at zero, an amount of discarding (up to the MABL) would therefore be permissible. It is unclear from the Commission's non-paper whether MABLs would routinely be set at zero or at something above zero. However, two examples proposed in the non-paper use non-zero MABLs.[1023]

Furthermore, Commissioner Borg of DG Mare stated in May 2008 that: 'We are confident that, with the cooperation of all stakeholders, we can come up with workable solutions that will obviate the need for a total discard ban. This will, however, depend on developments in the fishery concerned. We may, however, as a measure of *last resort* move to introduce a total ban, albeit reluctantly, if such a step proves *absolutely necessary*. We are counting on cooperation from all concerned to ensure that such a *draconian step* can be avoided.'[1024] (Emphasis added.) Overall, in the light of the above, it appears that the Commission has softened its position somewhat since the issue of its Communication in March 2007.

It is not envisaged that MABLs would be imposed overnight in respect of any given fishery. The two example fisheries proposed in the non-paper both use a phased approach. For instance, in the case of bottom trawling targeting Norway lobster in ICES area VII (see further below), the Commission proposes a MABL of 10 per cent by weight of the total catch, but intends that this would be achieved only in Year 5, via a starting point of 50 per cent 'total discard rate' and then rates of 25 per cent, 20 per cent, and 15 per cent in Years 1–2, 3, and 4 respectively.[1025] There does seem to be some inconsistency over terminology. The 10 per cent figure mentioned above is cited as the MABL whereas, as can be seen, the other percentage figures are cited in terms of amount of discards. Perhaps the assumption being made is that MABL and the amount of discards are in practice synonymous, despite retention on board also being an option within the MABL (see definition above).

Equally, the Commission does not intend to adopt MABLs for all fisheries simultaneously. Instead, it proposes to introduce MABLs for only two fisheries in the first instance on a trial basis, with a view to expanding the policy to other fisheries in due course (see further below). One advantage of opting for a progressive fishery-by-fishery approach is that it will 'allow for margin to rectify if the proposed system is not working properly'.[1026]

The Commission's non-paper envisages that discard targets would 'apply to the total catches of all vessels of a Member State holding a special fishing permit for the fisheries concerned' and that 'Member States can apply the reduction targets to individual vessels or to groups of vessels'.[1027] That statement implies that discard reductions will be an area where discretion is given to Member States regarding

[1023] Non-paper, section 5, pp 5–7.
[1024] Speech by Commissioner Joe Borg at the Discards Workshop, Brussels, 27 May 2008, Opening speech, 3 (available on the website of DG Mare).   [1025] Non-paper, section 5.1, pp 5–6.
[1026] SEC(2007) 380, section 8, p 34.   [1027] Non-paper, section 6.1, p 7.

how to allocate the targets, in addition to the discretion on technical solutions arising from the results-based approach referred to above.

In its Communication, the Commission accepts that, in addition to the imposition of restrictions on discards, some further changes to existing regulatory approaches, as well as some new measures, would also be necessary—in particular to help avoid catches of unwanted fish in the first place. However, in respect of Community waters, the overall package of measures would be selected on a fishery-by-fishery basis.[1028] Examples of possible changes to existing regulatory approaches include, in respect of mixed fisheries, better use of effort control to avoid prolonged fishing on marginal amounts of remaining quota and development of mechanisms 'for some flexibility and transfer of quotas' and, more generally, introduction of 'minimum marketing sizes for human consumption' instead of the current minimum landing sizes.[1029] New measures could include, *inter alia*, real-time area closures to deal with large concentrations of juvenile fish arising suddenly.[1030] The Commission raises the possibility of introducing 'a preferential status such as preferential access to fisheries on the basis of track records of low by-catches',[1031] as well as other incentives.

In this vein, some proposed new technical measures to reduce discards, including 'Real time moving to another area when maximum by-catches are exceeded', are set out by the Commission in its proposal for a successor to Regulation 850/98 (on technical measures).[1032] The Commission's 2008 policy statement addresses discard reduction.[1033] More concretely, the beginnings of a results-based approach can be seen in Regulation 40/2008 (the principal annual Regulation on fishing opportunities). As noted in subsection 2.2 above, this Regulation makes the use of a kilowatt-days system of managing effort available on a voluntary basis to Member States. Annex IIA of the Regulation specifies that any use of this alternative system is to be made to, *inter alia*, 'stimulate fishing practices that lead to reduced discards and lower fishing mortality of both juvenile and adult fish' including by means of 'fishing plans designed *in collaboration with the fishing industry*' (emphasis added).[1034] Furthermore, again as noted in subsection 2.2 above, additional days-at-sea for fishermen are potentially available as a reward for signing up to 'a discard reduction plan'[1035] or for participating in 'the cod avoidance reference fleet programme' (which involves meeting cod discard targets).[1036]

The Commission, albeit referring to a 'requirement to land *all* fish' (emphasis added), accepts that an obligation to land by-catch would mean that 'occasionally

---

[1028] COM(2007) 136, section 3, p 4.

[1029] On the interaction between minimum marketing sizes and minimum landing sizes, see further Chapter 6.   [1030] COM(2007) 136, section 3, pp 4–5.

[1031] COM(2007) 136, section 5, p 7.

[1032] COM(2008) 324, proposed Arts 10 and 11. See also proposed Arts 18 and 22.

[1033] COM(2008) 331, section 10, pp 9–10.   [1034] Reg 40/2008, Annex IIA, paras 8.5–8.7.

[1035] Reg 40/2008, Annex IIA, paras 12.9 and 12.10.

[1036] Reg 40/2008, Annex IIA, paras 12.11–12.14.

fish above the quota or below minimum market size will be landed' and raises questions about how such fish should be treated (eg whether it should be counted against quotas and how it should be disposed of).[1037] It also readily acknowledges that enforcement, including use of at-sea observers, will be very relevant, since a temptation to discard for economic reasons will still arise.[1038] For example so-called 'highgrading' (see subsection 2.1 above) may well remain relevant in the face of limited hold space and the temptation to discard may arise if landed by-catches are counted against quotas or if preferential access arises from low by-catches.

In a press release dated January 2008,[1039] the Commission stated, *inter alia*, that: 'A list of six fisheries have been submitted to the . . . Scientific, Technical and Economic Committee on Fisheries (STECF) for their advice, which is expected shortly.' The relevant STECF subgroup, having met in December 2007, reported in due course. The STECF plenary meeting in April 2008 considered the subgroup's report and identified four 'case study fisheries' for further consideration by the subgroup.[1040] Also in April 2008, the Commission commenced a two-month consultation on the non-paper referred to above. The non-paper identified the bottom trawl fishery for Norway lobster in ICES area VII and the beam trawl fishery for flatfish in ICES areas IV and VIId as candidates for trialling the new policy in view of their high discard rates.[1041] The relevant STECF subgroup met again in June 2008, tasked with evaluating the approach in the Commission's non-paper and assessing the validity of MABLs as proposed by the Commission for the two fisheries in question. The subgroup's report was addressed by the STECF plenary meeting in July 2008.[1042] In August 2008, the Commission summarized the results of the consultation on the non-paper.[1043] In its January 2008 press release referred to above, the Commission had stated that, in the light of the STECF's advice, it would 'select certain fisheries as the subject of the first concrete discard bans' and at the same time 'draw up a roadmap, including a timetable, for applying this approach to all major European commercial fisheries'.[1044] However, by the end of November 2008, no legislative proposals and no roadmap had been issued by the Commission.

[1037] COM(2007) 136, section 3, pp 5–6.   [1038] COM(2007) 136, section 4, p 6.

[1039] IP/08/138, Brussels, 31 January 2008 (available on the website of the European Commission).

[1040] Draft *Commission Staff Working Document: . . . Evaluation of the STECF/SGMOS 07-04 Working Group on Discards, STECF Opinion expressed during the Plenary Meeting of 14–18 April 2008 in Hamburg*, 12 (available on the website of the STECF, as uncoded SEC document).

[1041] Non-paper, section 5, pp 5–7.

[1042] Draft *Commission Staff Working Document, Reduction of Dicarding [sic] Practices (SGMOS-08-01) . . . STECF Opinion expressed during the Plenary Meeting of 7–11 July [2008] in Helsinki* (available on the website of the STECF, as uncoded SEC document).

[1043] *Working document of [DG Mare]: Overview of the contributions received in answer to the consultation on the implementation of the policy to reduce unwanted by-catch and eliminate discards in European fisheries*, August 2008 (available on the website of DG Mare).   [1044] See also non-paper, section 2, p 2.

One significant omission from the Commission's Communication and non-paper is discussion in any detail of by-catch other than fish and crustaceans, such as cetaceans, seabirds, turtles, and invertebrates other than crustaceans.[1045] It is not clear whether MABLs would be set for such species or what sanctions would flow from breaching them. The Commission does note that exceptions from a discard ban 'may be made where high long-term survival of specific species discarded from specific fisheries has been clearly demonstrated'[1046] but does not emphasize the desirability of releasing some non-target species, such as sharks and turtles, that may well be able to survive if sufficient care is taken in their release. The failure to address these aspects in both its 2007 Communication and its 2008 non-paper suggests that the Commission needs to think more broadly in order to ensure consistency between its discards policy and an ecosystem approach (on which, see subsection 9.3 above).

9.6 Rights-based management

In February 2007 the Commission issued a Communication on RBM tools in fisheries.[1047] It defines RBM as 'a formalised system of allocating individual fishing rights to fishermen, fishing vessels, enterprises, cooperatives or fishing communities'.[1048] The Commission acknowledges that 'at this stage', in view of the principle of relative stability (on which, see subsection 2.1 above), 'there seems to be no possibility of moving to a Community-level RBM system, in which fishing rights would be freely tradable between Member States'.[1049] However, as noted in subsection 9.2 above, the Commission has stated subsequently that relative stability itself will need 're-examining' during the reform of the CFP (see further below).[1050]

In its Communication, the Commission focuses its attention on 'the tradability of fishing rights *within* the Member State' (emphasis added).[1051] It notes that 'markets in fishing rights *de facto* exist in most Member States' and that '[t]he economic value of these rights is at times substantial and can have a major effect on the development of the fisheries sector'.[1052] However, it is concerned about the impediments to economic efficiency arising from, *inter alia*, insufficient transparency and legal certainty in such markets.[1053] It seeks 'to open a discussion to share

---

[1045] House of Lords, 2008, HL Paper 146-II, p 58 (RSPB's evidence).

[1046] COM(2007) 136, section 3, p 4.

[1047] *Communication from the Commission on rights-based management tools in fisheries*, COM(2007) 73, 26.2.2007.   [1048] COM(2007) 73, section 1, p 3.

[1049] COM(2007) 73, section 5, p 6.

[1050] *Commission Working Document, Reflections on further reform of the Common Fisheries Policy*, section 4, p 8.   [1051] COM(2007) 73, section 5, p 6.

[1052] COM(2007) 73, section 2, p 4.

[1053] COM(2007) 73, section 2, p 4. See also section 3, p 4.

and improve knowledge in this field and to assess the need to act'.[1054] In addition the Commission seeks to investigate whether RBM can help achieve the objective of fisheries conservation,[1055] for example by reducing fishing pressure or by creating a vested interest by fishermen in sustainability.

The Communication touches on some of the barriers, legal or otherwise, to establishing a system of RBM, such as transferability of rights. These barriers, and possible solutions, are elaborated on in an accompanying working document.[1056] Regarding the constraints imposed by relative stability, the Commission notes that such constraints 'would not, of course, prevent a Member State from deciding that its own RBM system should allow for exchange in quotas with nationals of other Member States, as is already the case'.[1057] The Communication also accepts that some fundamental constraints exist to uniformity of RBM systems across the Member States, for example a reluctance in some Member States to grant 'access rights to a public resource to private interests, even temporarily'.[1058]

The Commission sets itself a target to report by February 2008,[1059] which it failed to meet. However, in a written memorandum to an inquiry in 2008 on the CFP by the UK's Parliament, the Commission stated that:

The European Commission will continue working on RBM over the coming months. A study to provide a knowledge basis of all RBM tools currently applied in the EU is on-going with results expected by the last quarter of 2008. The most likely follow up in the short term could be information documents or guidelines on RBM (including good/best practices) addressed to Member States. In the medium to long term, the European Commission will consider RBM in the context of the forthcoming CFP reform.[1060]

9.7 Simplification and consultation

The Commission has issued several Communications on simplifying the CFP,[1061] having concluded that 'the current rules have gradually become excessively

---

[1054] COM(2007) 73, section 2, p 4.   [1055] COM(2007) 73, section 3, p 4.

[1056] *Commission Staff Working Document Accompanying the Communication from the Commission to the Council and the European Parliament on Rights-based management tools in fisheries*, SEC(2007) 247, 26.2.2007.   [1057] COM(2007) 73, section 5, p 6.

[1058] COM(2007) 73, section 5, p 6.   [1059] COM(2007) 73, section 6, p 7.

[1060] House of Lords, 2008, HL Paper 146-II, p 213 (European Commission's evidence).

[1061] See in particular: *Communication from the Commission: Perspectives for simplifying and improving the regulatory environment of the Common Fisheries Policy*, COM(2004) 820, 15.12.2004; *Communication of the Commission to the European Parliament, the Council, the European Economic and Social Committee and the Committee of the Regions: Implementing the Community Lisbon programme: A strategy for the simplification of the regulatory environment*, COM(2005) 535, 25.10.2005; and *Communication from the Commission to the Council and the European Parliament: 2006–08 Action Plan for Simplifying and Improving the Common Fisheries Policy*, COM(2005) 647, 8.12.2005.

complex'. The drive for simplification arises from the so-called 'Lisbon strategy for achieving growth and jobs in Europe'. The latest Communication on simplification specific to the CFP was issued in December 2005. This is an *Action Plan for Simplifying and Improving the Common Fisheries Policy* over the period 2006–08 and identifies specific Regulations for simplification.[1062] Several of the proposals in the *Action Plan* have been progressed, such as a separate instrument on fishing opportunities in the Baltic Sea (see subsection 2.1 and section 3 above) and a legislative proposal for a new structure for technical measures legislation (see subsection 2.3 above).

The task of simplifying the CFP does not simply rest on repeal, codification, and recasting of existing legislation.[1063] It also relies on new approaches, including, *inter alia*, preliminary consultations with stakeholders.[1064] In May 2006 the Commission issued a Communication on improving consultation on EC fisheries management,[1065] which 'proposes a new working method for preparing Council decisions on annual fishing opportunities and associated conditions within the Community'.[1066] Some of the outcomes of that consultation have already been discussed in subsection 2.1 above.

9.8 Conclusion

In conclusion, it can be seen that reform of the CFP operates at two levels. First, as required by the Basic Regulation, there is the major review of Chapters II and III, plus the specific question of Article 17(2). As indicated by the Commission in its September 2008 Working Document,[1067] and in keeping with past practice, the above review is likely to lead to a legislative proposal for a new version of the Basic Regulation. Secondly, there are also a number of more specific reform initiatives that happen on an incremental basis. Whether these may be implemented under the existing Basic Regulation or whether they must await a new revised legal framework depends upon their content. The reforms relating to the ecosystem approach, MSY, discards, and consultation and simplification may well be achievable within the framework provided by the current Basic Regulation. However, any attempt to introduce RBM at the EC level will probably require a new version of the Basic Regulation.

Of the various specific reform initiatives mentioned in subsections 9.3–9.7 above, the ecosystem approach is potentially the most overarching. However, it is

---

[1062] COM(2005) 647, Annex, Sheets 1–7.

[1063] For the meanings of these terms see COM(2005) 535, section 3, pp 5–7.

[1064] COM(2004) 820, section 3, pp 5–7.

[1065] *Communication from the Commission to the Council and the European Parliament: Improving consultation on Community fisheries management,* COM(2006) 246, 24.5.2006.

[1066] COM(2006) 246, section 1, p 4.   [1067] *Commission Working Document,* section 5, p 9.

not entirely clear whether the Commission has in mind for the true potential of this overarching effect to be felt within the CFP, at least in the short term. The Commission's Communication on the ecosystem approach refers to, *inter alia*, implementation of the MSY approach and action on discards. In practice, it may be possible to achieve significant results sooner on discards than on the MSY approach, because the former can potentially be tackled without the painful effects for the fishing industry of getting to stock sizes that produce MSY. One means of getting to MSY is decommissioning. As noted in subsection 2.8 above, decommissioning has not been an easy process. It will be interesting to see whether or how the forthcoming reform of the CFP can add any new thinking on this task.

5

External aspects of fisheries management

1 Introduction

Chapter 4 looked at fisheries management in Community waters, where a large part of the total marine fish catch by Community fishing vessels is taken. However, a significant proportion of the total Community catch is taken outside Community waters. It is not possible to state exactly what that proportion is because fish catches are generally recorded by statistical areas of bodies such as the International Council for the Exploration of the Sea (ICES), rather than by States' maritime zones. Nevertheless, whatever its proportion (and the Commission has variously given figures of 25[1] and 40 per cent[2]), fishing outside Community waters has been, and continues to be, of considerable importance for the Common Fisheries Policy (CFP). First, it enables Community fishing vessels to catch species of fish that are not found, or are not so plentiful, in Community waters, either to satisfy consumer demand directly for fresh or frozen fish or to supply the raw material for fish processing plants in the EC (eg tuna for the canning industry). Secondly, it has enabled some of the excess capacity in the EC's fishing fleets to be deployed outside Community waters, thereby to some extent reducing the pressure on stocks in Community waters.

The non-Community waters where Community vessels fish comprise primarily the 200 nm zones of third States, the Faroe Islands, and Greenland, as well as the high seas. Access by Community fishing vessels to the waters of third States (which in this context may be regarded as including the Faroe Islands and Greenland, on the legal status of which, see Chapter 2) is normally by means of bilateral treaties (but see section 5 below on access to such waters by other means). Over the years the EC has concluded such treaties with around thirty States. Fishing on the high seas is in principle open to all States under the doctrine of the freedom of the high seas, but this is subject to a duty to cooperate. Such cooperation is generally through the medium of regional fisheries management organizations (RFMOs), as was explained in Chapter 3. The EC has become a member of most of the principal RFMOs.

---

[1] *Communication from the Commission to the Council and the European Parliament: fisheries agreements: current situation and perspectives*, COM(96) 488, 30.10.1996, p 7. It is not clear to which year the figure given refers.

[2] Commission, *European Distant Water Fishing Fleet* (2000), 9 (available on the website of DG Mare). The figure is the average annual catch for the period 1993–97.

The major part of this chapter is concerned with the EC's participation in the global instruments discussed in Chapter 3 that lay down the basic norms of current international fisheries law (section 3); EC access agreements with third States (section 4); and EC membership of RFMOs (section 6). Negotiating and concluding global fisheries instruments, bilateral access agreements, and membership of RFMOs obviously involve the exercise of treaty-making powers by the EC. The next section of this chapter therefore looks at the source and scope of the EC's competence to negotiate, and become a party to, treaties in the field of fisheries. The last part of the chapter (section 7) looks at EC involvement with some other international fisheries management issues.

2 The EC's treaty-making competence and treaty-making procedures

2.1 The EC's treaty-making competence in general

In order to understand the scope of the EC's competence to enter into treaties in the field of fisheries, it is first necessary to have some understanding of the general capacity of the EC to conclude treaties.[3] As an international organization with legal personality,[4] the EC clearly has the capacity in principle to make treaties. The extent and nature of that capacity are governed primarily by EC law rather than international law. Under EC law the EC's treaty-making powers are of two kinds. The first kind is those powers expressly conferred by the EC Treaty. Such express powers are confined to a limited number of areas, principally the common commercial policy (Article 133 EC), environmental matters (Article 174(4) EC), development cooperation (Article 181 EC), and association agreements (Article 310 EC). The second kind of treaty-making powers are those that may be implied from the provisions of the EC Treaty. Those implied powers are essentially the creation of the Court, beginning with its judgment in 1971 in *Commission v Council* (usually referred to as the *AETR* case after the French title of the treaty with which it was concerned).[5] In that case the Court held that the EC's treaty-making powers not only included the express powers referred to above:

but may equally flow from other provisions of the Treaty and from measures adopted, within the framework of these provisions, by the Community institutions.

---

[3] For detailed accounts of the EC's general treaty-making powers, see, *inter alia*, Dashwood, A and Hillion, C (eds), *The General Law of EC External Relations* (London: Sweet & Maxwell, 2000); Eeckhout, P, *External Relations of the European Union: Legal and Constitutional Foundations* (Oxford: Oxford University Press, 2004); Hartley, TC, *The Foundations of European Community Law* (6th edn, Oxford: Oxford University Press, 2007), ch 6; Koutrakos, P, *EU International Relations Law* (Oxford: Hart Publishing, 2007); and MacLeod, I, Hendry, ID, and Hyett, S, *The External Relations of the European Communities* (Oxford: Clarendon Press, 1996), especially chs 3 and 6.   [4] Art 281 EC.

[5] Case 22/70 *Commission v Council* [1971] ECR 263.

In particular, each time the Community, with a view to implementing a common policy envisaged by the Treaty, adopts provisions laying down common rules, whatever form these may take, the Member States no longer have the right, acting individually or even collectively, to undertake obligations with third countries which affect those rules.[6]

In the *AETR* case the Court suggested that the EC's implied treaty-making powers arose only where the EC had a power under the EC Treaty to legislate on the internal (ie Community) plane and such a power had actually been exercised. Subsequently, in *Opinion 1/76*,[7] the Court went further and held that the EC's powers were 'not limited to that eventuality'.[8] It was not essential that the EC should have adopted internal rules on a particular matter to obtain treaty-making powers in relation to that matter: it was enough that it had the power to adopt such rules and that its participation in a treaty related to that matter was necessary to attain a specific objective of the EC Treaty which could not be attained simply by means of EC internal measures.[9]

The Court has confirmed the principles that it enunciated in the *AETR* case and *Opinion 1/76* regarding the EC's implied treaty-making powers in a number of later cases.[10] Most recently it did so in *Opinion 1/03*.[11] As the Court put it there:

The competence of the Community to conclude international agreements may arise not only from an express conferment by the [EC] Treaty but may equally flow implicitly from other provisions of the Treaty and from measures adopted, within the framework of those provisions, by the Community institutions (see [*AETR* case], paragraph 16) . . . [In addition] whenever Community law create[s] for those institutions powers within its internal system for the purpose of attaining a specific objective, the Community ha[s] authority to undertake international commitments necessary for the attainment of that objective even in the absence of an express provision to that effect (Opinion 1/76, paragraph 3, and Opinion 2/91, paragraph 7).[12]

The EC's implied treaty-making powers may be either exclusive or shared with the Member States. Largely summarizing its previous case law, although not in the clearest of language, the Court in *Opinion 1/03* set out a number of situations in which the EC has exclusive competence. The first is one where 'internal

---

[6] Case 22/70, paras 16–17.

[7] *Opinion 1/76 (Re the Draft Agreement for a Laying-Up Fund for Inland Waterway Vessels)* [1977] ECR 741.   [8] *Opinion 1/76*, para 4.

[9] Ibid.

[10] See *Opinion 2/91 (Re ILO Convention 170)* [1993] ECR I-1061; *Opinion 1/94 (Re WTO Agreement)* [1994] ECR I-5267; *Opinion 2/92 (Re OECD National Treatment Instrument)* [1995] ECR I-521; and the so-called 'Open Skies' cases (eg Case C-476/98 *Commission v Germany* [2002] ECR I-9855). For a detailed and very useful discussion of these cases, see Eeckhout, *External Relations*, 69–100.

[11] *Opinion 1/03 (Re the Competence of the Community to conclude the new Lugano Convention on jurisdiction and the recognition of judgments in civil and commercial matters)* [2006] ECR I-1145.

[12] *Opinion 1/03*, para 114.

competence may be effectively exercised only at the same time as external competence . . . the conclusion of the international agreement being thus necessary in order to attain objectives of the Treaty that cannot be obtained by establishing autonomous rules'.[13] Secondly, 'where common rules have been adopted, the Member States no longer have the right, acting individually or even collectively, to undertake obligations with non-member countries which affect those rules'.[14] That principle also applies 'where rules have been adopted in areas falling outside common policies and, in particular, where there are harmonising measures'.[15] Lastly, and more generally, the EC has exclusive treaty-making competence 'where the conclusion of an agreement by the Member States is incompatible with the unity of the common market and the uniform application of Community law . . . or where, given the nature of existing Community provisions, such as legislative measures containing clauses relating to the treatment of nationals of non-member countries or to the complete harmonisation of a particular issue, any agreement in that area would necessarily affect the Community rules'.[16]

On the other hand, the EC's treaty-making competence is *not* exclusive 'where, because both Community provisions and those of an international convention la[y] down minimum standards, there [is] nothing to prevent the full application of Community law by the Member States'.[17] It is not clear what the Court means here, and its reference in this context to paragraph 18 of *Opinion 2/91* does not really shed any light on the matter. Secondly, the EC's competence is not exclusive where bilateral agreements concluded by the Member States might 'lead to distortions in the flow of services in the internal market' since there is nothing to prevent the EC institutions from arranging 'concerted action in relation to non-member countries or from prescribing the approach to be taken by the Member States in their external dealings'.[18] The Court emphasized that to determine whether the EC's implied treaty-making powers are exclusive or not, there needs to be 'a specific analysis of the relationship between the agreement envisaged and the Community law in force'.[19] Treaties where competence is shared are usually referred to as 'mixed agreements'.

The Court's case law on the EC's treaty-making powers has been largely codified in the Treaty of Lisbon. Were the Treaty to come into force, Article 216(1) of the Treaty on the Functioning of the European Union (as the EC Treaty would be renamed) would provide, in relation to the EC's treaty-making competence in general, that 'the Union may conclude an agreement with one or more third countries or international organisations where the Treaties so provide or where the conclusion of an agreement is necessary in order to achieve, within the framework of the Union's policies, one of the objectives referred to in the Treaties or is provided for in a legally binding Union act or is likely to affect

---

[13] *Opinion 1/03*, para 115.   [14] *Opinion 1/03*, para 116.   [15] *Opinion 1/03*, para 118.
[16] *Opinion 1/03*, para 122.   [17] *Opinion 1/03*, para 123.   [18] Ibid.
[19] *Opinion 1/03*, para 124.

common rules or alter their scope'. 'Treaties' in this context refers both to the Treaty on the Functioning of the European Union and the Treaty on European Union.[20] As regards the question of when the EC's treaty-making competence is exclusive, Article 3(2) of the Treaty on the Functioning of the European Union would provide that the Union shall have 'exclusive competence for an international agreement when its conclusion is provided for in a legislative act of the Union or is necessary to enable the Union to exercise its internal competence, or insofar as its conclusion may affect common rules or alter their scope'.

2.2 The application of the EC's general treaty-making powers to fisheries

This issue raises three interrelated questions: (a) does the EC have treaty-making powers in respect of fisheries; (b) if so, what is the material scope of those powers, in other words, in relation to which aspects of fisheries does the EC have treaty-making powers; and (c) how far are the powers that the EC does have exclusive? As to the first question, *express* treaty-making powers are of limited relevance to fisheries. Article 133 EC (on the common commercial policy) gives the EC the competence to enter into treaties with third States relating to trade in fishery products and is discussed briefly in Chapter 7, but it is not relevant to the kinds of treaty with which this chapter is concerned.[21] A question arises whether the EC's express treaty-making powers in relation to environmental matters could be used for the conclusion of fisheries agreements, but in practice that has not yet occurred, at least as regards treaties concerned directly and primarily with fisheries conservation and management.

However, the Court has held that the EC has *implied* treaty-making powers in relation to fisheries. This was first established in 1976 in the *Kramer* case.[22] The Court applied the principles that it had enunciated a few years earlier in the *AETR* case. It found that in the light of Articles 38–46 (now Articles 32–38) EC, the first two Regulations adopted thereunder (Regulations 2141/70 and 2142/70) and Article 102 of the 1972 Act of Accession, 'the Community has at its disposal, on the internal level, the power to take any measures for the conservation of the biological resources of the sea'.[23] It 'follows from the very duties and powers which Community law has established and assigned to the institutions of the Community on the internal level that the Community has authority to enter into

---

[20] Treaty on the Functioning of the European Union, Art 1(2).

[21] However, it should be noted that in the past some agreements on the access of Community fishing vessels to the waters of third States were based partly on Art 133: see MacLeod *et al*, *The External Relations*, 243.   [22] Joined Cases 3, 4, and 6/76 *Officier van Justitie v Kramer* [1976] ECR 1279.

[23] *Kramer*, para 30.

international commitments for the conservation of the resources of the sea'.[24] The Court has confirmed that ruling in a number of later cases.[25]

Having established that the EC has treaty-making powers in respect of fisheries, the next question is what the material scope of those powers is. In other words, what is meant more precisely by 'fisheries' in this context? To what aspects of fisheries do the EC's treaty-making powers relate? In *Kramer* and the other cases just referred to, the Court speaks of the EC's treaty-making powers being in relation to 'the conservation of the resources of the sea'. That may suggest that the EC's treaty-making powers are limited to fisheries conservation. Four comments may be made in response to that. First, as in its case law on EC competence in Community waters (discussed at the beginning of Chapter 4), the Court refers to the EC's treaty-making powers only in terms of 'conservation'. Secondly, the Court has never defined what it means by 'conservation', and it often uses the word quite loosely and more widely than some would use it. For example, in *Kramer* the Court included the allocation of quotas between Member States within the term 'conservation',[26] and in *Commission v Council* the Court found that most provisions of the Food and Agriculture Organization (FAO) Compliance Agreement,[27] including those relating to the duties of flag States (see further Chapter 3), lay within the treaty-making powers of the EC.[28] In both cases the matters concerned arguably do not fall within the concept of 'conservation', strictly defined. Thirdly, as will be seen below, the EC has entered into treaties with third States that contain provisions on, *inter alia*, fisheries research, promotion of joint ventures and enterprises, and financial assistance to developing States. It is hard to see such matters as being (purely) ones of 'conservation'. Fourthly, the *AETR* case and *Opinion 1/76* both assume that the material scope of the EC's treaty-making powers corresponds to the scope of the internal powers from which those treaty-making powers flow. In the case of fisheries, the EC's internal powers derive from Articles 32–38 EC. That suggests that the EC has treaty-making powers in relation to any matter for which Article 37 EC may serve as the legal base for the adoption of EC fisheries legislation. Such matters include, *inter alia*, any measure to give effect to the objectives of the CFP set out in Article 33(1) EC (on which see Chapter 2). Such objectives range considerably wider than 'conservation'. All this suggests that there is considerable uncertainty as to what the precise material scope of the EC's treaty-making powers is as regards fisheries, and that that scope may be wider than 'conservation' in a strict sense. Because of this uncertainty, and for

---

[24] *Kramer*, para 33.

[25] See, *inter alia*, Case C-258/89 *Commission v Spain* [1991] ECR. I-3977, para 9; and Case C-25/94 *Commission v Council* [1996] ECR I-1469, para 42.   [26] *Kramer*, para 30.

[27] Agreement to Promote Compliance with International Conservation and Management Measures by Fishing Vessels on the High Seas, 2221 UNTS 91.

[28] Case C-25/94 *Commission v Council*, paras 40–47.

convenience, in the discussion that follows the scope of the EC's treaty-making powers will simply be described as relating to 'fisheries'.

That leads on to the next question, which is how far the EC's treaty-making powers in relation to fisheries are *exclusive*. Applying the principles set out by the Court in *Opinion 1/03*, especially the principle set out in paragraph 116 that 'where common rules have been adopted, the Member States no longer have the right, acting individually or even collectively, to undertake obligations with non-member countries which affect those rules', it can be argued that, given that the EC has legislated extensively in relation to fisheries, the EC's treaty-making powers in relation to fisheries are exclusive in relation to those fisheries matters on which the EC has adopted 'common rules'. Up until the mid-1990s that was certainly the view taken by most writers[29] and the Commission.[30] That view also appears to have been shared by the Council.[31] In the *Kramer* case, where the Court was concerned only with 'conservation', it took the view that once the EC had acted to adopt conservation measures on the internal plane (which it had not done at the time that the case was decided), the EC's treaty-making powers in relation to 'conservation' were exclusive.[32] Community exclusivity is also reflected in the practice of the EC and its Member States during this period. Thus, the many agreements concluded on the access of Community fishing vessels to the waters of third States (which contained provisions on more than just 'conservation', such as the encouragement of joint ventures and enterprises) were entered into by the EC only, and not its Member States. The EC, to the exclusion of its Member States, became a member of a number of RFMOs—the Northwest Atlantic Fisheries Organization, the North-East Atlantic Fisheries Commission, the International Baltic Sea Fisheries Commission (now defunct), the North Atlantic Salmon Conservation Organization, and the International Commission for the Conservation of Atlantic Tunas. Those organizations were all concerned with more than just conservation matters strictly defined, including scientific research and various forms of enforcement measure. The one exception to exclusivity in RFMO membership during that period was the Commission for the Conservation of Antarctic Marine Living Resources (CCAMLR), of which both the EC and

---

[29] See, for example, Churchill, RR, *EEC Fisheries Law* (Dordrecht: Martinus Nijhoff Publishers, 1987), 171–4; Kaniel, M, *The Exclusive Treaty-Making Power of the European Community up to the Period of the Single European Act* (The Hague: Kluwer, 1996), 82–4; MacLeod *et al*, *The External Relations*, 56–5, 61 and 242–3; and Simmonds, KR, 'The European Economic Community and the New Law of the Sea' *Recueil des Cours* 218 (1989), 9 at 52.

[30] See, for example, its evidence to the House of Lords, Select Committee on the European Communities, *External Competence of the European Communities*, HL Paper (1984–85) 236, p 106.

[31] See its Hague Resolution of 3 November 1976, OJ 1981 C105/1.

[32] *Kramer*, paras 35–45. The same view was also expressed in passing in two cases that were not in fact concerned with fisheries: *Opinion 2/91*, para 8 and *Opinion 1/94*, para 85. In *Opinion 2/91* the Court supported its remarks by referring to its ruling in Case 804/79, *Commission v United Kingdom* [1981] 1045 that the EC has exclusive competence in relation to fisheries conservation in Community waters. See Chapters 1 and 4. See also Eeckhout, *External Relations*, 71.

some (but not all) of its Member States are members (and see further subsections 6.1 and 6.2 below). That was because the subject matter of the Convention establishing the CCAMLR includes matters that fall outside the EC's exclusive treaty-making competence: it is therefore a fairly typical example of a mixed agreement. Further support for Community exclusivity, as regards conservation, can be found in the declaration made by the EC when becoming a member of the FAO in 1991, in which it stated that it had 'exclusive competence in . . . all matters concerning fisheries which are aimed at protecting the fishing grounds and conserving the biological resources of the sea'.[33]

The prevailing orthodoxy as to which aspects of fisheries fall with the EC's exclusive treaty-making powers was challenged in the mid-1990s, when the issue of EC participation in the FAO Compliance Agreement, the UN Fish Stocks Agreement, and the UN Convention on the Law of the Sea (on all of which see Chapter 3) arose. Discussion by the EC institutions of such participation revealed a desire on the part of some Member States in the Council to narrow the scope of the exclusivity of the EC's treaty-making powers (and possibly also the scope of those powers where they were not exclusive but shared).

In the case of the Compliance Agreement, it was not clear whether it was the EC or its Member States that had the competence to participate in the Agreement. At the outset of the negotiations the emphasis was on conditions for the granting of nationality to fishing vessels, a matter that was generally considered to lie within the competence of the Member States.[34] Later, however, that matter was dropped and the emphasis shifted towards the authorization of vessels and the responsibilities of flag States. At the conclusion of the negotiations, the Commission appears to have considered that the Agreement fell within the EC's exclusive competence (even though its subject matter is arguably wider than 'conservation'), whereas the Council considered that competence was shared.[35] In 1994 the Commission sent the Council a proposal for the EC to accept (ie become a party to) the Agreement in which it argued that the Agreement in its entirety lay within the EC's exclusive competence.[36] Nearly two years later the Council decided that the EC should accept the Agreement,[37] and deposited an instrument of acceptance. It is not clear whether the Council agreed with the Commission about the

[33] FAO Doc 91/LIM/47, Annex B. The relevant part of the declaration is also reproduced in Heliskoski, J, 'Internal Struggle for International Presence: The Exercise of Voting Rights within the FAO' in Dashwood and Hillion (eds), *The General Law*, 79 at 83. See also the EC's declaration on *signature* of the UN Convention on the Law of the Sea, referred to below.

[34] Case C-25/94 *Commission v Council*, AG Opinion at 1494.   [35] Ibid, at 1478.

[36] *Proposal for a Council Decision on accession of the EC to the agreement to promote compliance with international conservation and management measures by vessels fishing on the high seas*, COM(94) 331, 22.07.1994.

[37] Council Decision 96/428/EC of 25 June 1996 on acceptance by the Community of the Agreement to promote compliance with international conservation and management measures by vessels fishing on the high seas, OJ 1996 L177/24.

question of competence, but there are several indications that it did. First, the text of the Council's decision is almost identical to the Commission's draft, both including a paragraph in their preamble to the effect that 'as regards maritime fishing, the Community has the authority to adopt fishery resource conservation and management measures and to conclude agreements in this field' with third States and international organizations. Secondly, no Member State has become a party to the Agreement.[38] Thirdly, Article X(4) of the Agreement provides that when accepting the Agreement, a regional economic integration organization shall, as appropriate, notify such modifications or clarifications to its original declaration of competence made when joining the FAO as may be necessary in the light of its acceptance of the Agreement. When accepting the Agreement, the EC gave no such notification. Thus, the matter is governed by the original declaration, quoted above, which refers to exclusive competence in the field of fisheries conservation.

At the same time as the Council was considering whether to accept the Compliance Agreement, the issue of EC participation in the UN Fish Stocks Agreement (hereafter, 'the FSA') arose. The Commission argued that the FSA in its entirety fell within the EC's exclusive competence.[39] That view was also shared by the Council's Legal Service,[40] but was contested by certain Member States, which argued that competence in respect of the FSA was shared.[41] The dispute over competence became rather protracted, but was eventually resolved when the Council decided that competence was shared and that the EC and the Member States should jointly sign the FSA.[42] When signing, the EC was required by Article 47(1) of the FSA to make a declaration indicating how competence was divided between it and its Member States. The brevity of this declaration,[43] which was repeated in identical wording on ratification of the FSA in December 2003,[44] belies its complexity. Although the declaration lists the division of competence between the EC and its Member States under two headings, exclusive competence and shared competence, in reality there are no less than five different categories of competence. Those categories comprise: (a) EC exclusive competence (which is stated to cover 'the conservation and management of marine living resources', including the regulatory competence granted under international law to the flag State); (b) competence shared between the EC and its Member States (relating to

---

[38] Note, however, that Cyprus and Sweden became parties to the Agreement before they joined the EC. According to the website of the FAO they were still parties to the Agreement as at November 2008. Arguably, they should have withdrawn from the Agreement on becoming members of the EC.

[39] *Communication from the Commission to the Council on the signature of the Agreement for the implementation of the provisions of the United Nations Convention on the law of the sea of 10th December 1982 relating to the conservation and management of straddling fish stocks and highly migratory fish stocks*, COM(95) 591, 22.11.1995, pp 2–3, 10, and 18–21.   [40] COM(95) 591, p 10.

[41] Yturriaga, JA de, *The International Regime of Fisheries* (The Hague: Martinus Nijhoff Publishers, 1997), 200 and 219–20.   [42] Bull EC, 1996, No 6, section 1.3.199.

[43] For the text of the declaration, see the website of the United Nations Division for Ocean Affairs and the Law of the Sea.   [44] Ibid.

the provisions of the FSA concerning the requirements of developing States, scientific research, port State measures, and measures adopted in respect of non-members of RFMOs and non-parties to the FSA); (c) 'provisions of the Agreement [which] apply both to the Community and to its Member States' (the general provisions of Articles 1, 4, and 34–50 and Part VIII on dispute settlement); (d) matters 'within the competence of the Member States in compliance with Community law' (primarily measures relating to enforcement); and (e) matters 'within the competence of the Member States in accordance with their national legislation' (matters concerning the masters and crew of fishing vessels).

Shortly after the EC signed the FSA, the Commission and Council were faced with the question of whether the EC should formally confirm its signature of, ie ratify, the UN Convention on the Law of the Sea (hereafter, 'the Convention'). That would also require a declaration to be made about the division of competence between the EC and its Member States in relation to matters covered by the Convention. The declaration made by the EC on signature of the Convention had stated, as far as fisheries were concerned, that 'its Member States have transferred competence to it with regard to the conservation and management of sea-fishing resources. Hence in the field of sea fishing it is for the Community to adopt the relevant rules and regulations (which are enforced by the Member States) and to enter into external undertakings with third States or competent international organisations'.[45] Following the Commission's proposal, the Council decided that the EC should confirm its signature of the Convention and that the declaration to be made about competence should be significantly different from that made on signature as far as fisheries were concerned.[46]

The new declaration[47] begins with the heading 'Matters for which the Community has exclusive competence'. That is followed by two sentences that are almost identical to those in the declaration on signature quoted above, except that in the second sentence the phrase about 'entering into external undertakings' is qualified by the phrase 'within its competence'. The declaration then continues, still under the same heading, as follows:

This competence applies to waters under national fisheries jurisdiction and to the high seas. Nevertheless, in respect of measures relating to the exercise of jurisdiction over vessels, flagging and registration of vessels and the enforcement of penal and administrative sanctions, competence rests with Member States whilst respecting Community law. Community law also provides for administrative sanctions.

---

[45] Ibid.

[46] Council Decision 98/392/EC of 23 March 1998 concerning the conclusion by the European Community of the UN Convention of 10 December 1982 on the Law of the Sea and the Agreement of 28 July 1994 relating to the Implementation of Part XI thereof, OJ 1998 L179/1.

[47] For the text of the declaration, see the website of the United Nations Division for Ocean Affairs and the Law of the Sea.

The next section of the declaration dealing with fisheries is under the heading 'Matters for which the Community shares competence with its Member States'. This section comprises the following statement:

> With regard to fisheries, for a certain number of matters that are not directly related to the conservation and management of sea fishing resources, for example research and techno-logical development and development co-operation, there is shared competence.

Whereas the declaration on signature of the Convention had suggested that the EC had exclusive competence across the whole field of fisheries conservation and management, the declaration on confirmation suggests that that is no longer the case, and that for some aspects competence is shared between the EC and its Member States. That change is probably explained by the debates that had been taking place within and between the EC institutions during the previous few years over the scope of EC competence in the context of signature and ratification of the Compliance Agreement and the FSA.

Where exactly the division of competence now lies between the EC and its Member States in relation to the conclusion of treaties concerning fisheries is not very clear. Treaties that are concerned solely with fisheries conservation *stricto sensu* fall without doubt within the EC's exclusive competence. It also seems quite clear that questions concerning the nationality of fishing vessels and the qualifications and certification of officers and crews fall within the exclusive competence of Member States, although such competence must be exercised in relation to any Community law that may be relevant, such as the prohibition of discrimination between EC nationals on grounds of nationality (see further Chapter 4). The declarations made by the EC on its ratification of the FSA and the Convention list various matters that fall within the shared competence of the EC and its Member States—the requirements of developing States, scientific research, port State mea-sures, and measures adopted in respect of non-members of RFMOs and non-par-ties to the FSA. However, those declarations are not consistent with either earlier or subsequent EC practice. As regards the *requirements of developing States*, several treaties that the EC has concluded, to the exclusion of its Member States, since it made the declarations referred to above contain provisions on special measures in favour of developing States that are similar to those found in the FSA.[48] Further-more, all the agreements on the access of Community fishing vessels to the waters of developing States (discussed in subsection 4.3 below) that the EC has concluded on an exclusive basis both before and since it became a party to the FSA contain extensive provisions to assist developing States. As regards *research*, most of the

---

[48] See, for example, the 2000 Convention on the Conservation and Management of Highly Migratory Fish Stocks in the Western and Central Pacific Ocean (hereafter, 'the WCPFC Convention'), OJ 2005 L32/3, Art 30; the 2001 Convention on the Conservation and Management of Fishery Resources in the South-East Atlantic Ocean (hereafter, 'the SEAFO Convention'), OJ 2002 L234/40, Art 21; and the 2003 Convention for the Strengthening of the Inter-American Tropical Tuna Com-mission (hereafter, 'the Antigua Convention'), OJ 2005 L15/10, Art XXIII.

agreements establishing RFMOs to which the EC became a party to the exclusion of its Member States before it became a party to the FSA contain provisions on cooperation in research not significantly different from those of the FSA, as do many of the bilateral access agreements and several of the RFMO agreements to which the EC has since become a party to the exclusion of its Member States.[49] Those RFMO agreements also contain provisions on *port State measures* that are similar to those in the FSA,[50] and a number of the RFMOs that the EC joined to the exclusion of its Member States before the mid-1990s have subsequently adopted provisions on port State control.[51] It may also be noted that the provisions on port State measures in the Compliance Agreement (which it was concluded above falls within the exclusive competence of the EC) are not so very different from those of the FSA. Furthermore, in 2008 the Council endorsed a proposal from the Commission that the latter should negotiate on behalf of the Community a proposed FAO legally binding instrument on port State measures to prevent, deter, and eliminate illegal, unreported, and unregulated fishing.[52] Lastly, several of the RFMO agreements to which the EC has become a party to the exclusion of its Member States in recent years have provisions on *non-members* that are similar to those of the FSA.[53]

The EC's declarations to the FSA and the Law of the Sea Convention state that measures relating to the exercise of jurisdiction by the flag State over its vessels on the high seas (including international cooperation in respect of enforcement) fall within the competence of the Member States. Again, that is not in conformity with EC practice either before or since. A number of the RFMOs that the EC joined to the exclusion of its Member States before the mid-1990s have provisions on the exercise of flag State jurisdiction on the high seas and have developed schemes of international inspection.[54] Likewise, several of the RFMO agreements

---

[49] For example, the WCPFC Convention, Arts 12 and 13; the SEAFO Convention, Arts 10 and 13; and the Antigua Convention, Arts XI and XIII.

[50] For example, the WCPFC Convention, Art 27; and the SEAFO Convention, Art 15.

[51] For example, the Northwest Atlantic Fisheries Organization and the North-East Atlantic Fisheries Commission. See further section 6 below.

[52] Council of the European Union, 23 June 2008, press release, 10590/08 (Presse 169), p 24. For the Commission's proposal, see *Recommendation from the Commission to the Council in order to authorise the Commission to conduct negotiations for the elaboration of an internationally legally-binding instrument on port State measures to prevent, deter and eliminate illegal, unreported and unregulated fishing*, COM(2008) 333, 28.5.2008. See also FAO, *Technical Consultation to draft a legally-binding instrument on port State measures to prevent, deter and eliminate illegal, unreported and unregulated fishing, Statement of Competence and Voting Rights submitted by the European Community (EC) and its Member States (MS)*, FAO Doc TC PSM/2008/Inf.5.

[53] For example, the WCPFC Convention, Art 32; the SEAFO Convention, Arts 6(5), 6(10), and 22; and the Antigua Convention, Art XXVI. There is a similar provision in Art XXII of the 1998 Agreement on the International Dolphin Conservation Programme, OJ 1999 L132/3, to which the EC is a party to the exclusion of its Member States (see subsection 7.1 below).

[54] For example, the Northwest Atlantic Fisheries Organization and the North-East Atlantic Fisheries Commission. See further section 6 below.

to which the EC has become a party to the exclusion of its Member States since the mid-1990s have provisions on the enforcement by flag States of their measures similar to, and indeed modelled on, the FSA.[55] The denial in the FSA declaration of EC competence in this area also appears to be contrary to the Court's judgment in *Opinion 2/91*, where it held that just as, for internal purposes, the EC may 'provide, in an area covered by Community rules, that national authorities are to be given certain supervisory powers . . . it may also, for external purposes, undertake commitments designed to ensure compliance with substantive provisions which fall within its competence and imply the attribution of certain supervisory powers to national authorities'.[56]

Apart from the FSA, there is one other treaty dealing solely with fisheries to which the EC has become a party that has been treated as a matter of shared competence. That is the Agreement establishing the General Fisheries Commission for the Mediterranean.[57] The declaration that the EC made on becoming a party, as subsequently amended, provides that the EC has exclusive competence as regards 'conservation and management of living marine resources'; that there is shared competence as regards statistics, aquaculture, research and development aid, cooperation with other organizations, and budgetary matters; and that the Member States have exclusive competence as regards organizational matters (legal and procedural issues).[58] That is out of line with the EC's practice in relation to other RFMOs, where the matters listed as shared or exclusive Member State competence in the declaration to the Mediterranean Agreement are treated as part of the EC's exclusive competence. It is not clear why the Mediterranean Agreement is different from other RFMO Agreements.

The above survey shows that the declarations on competence made by the EC on becoming a party to the FSA, the Law of the Sea Convention, and the Mediterranean Agreement are out of line with prevailing EC practice. Nevertheless, there is a common denominator to the EC's practice as a whole and to the Court's case law referred to earlier, namely that the EC has exclusive treaty-making competence as regards fisheries 'conservation'. Admittedly, there is some uncertainty about precisely what matters fall within the concept of 'conservation' (and see further Chapter 4). In any attempt to define what is meant by conservation (which will not be made here), Article 6 EC, which requires environmental protection requirements to be 'integrated into the definition and implementation of' EC policies, needs to be borne in mind (see further Chapter 4). As regards fisheries issues that fall outside the field of 'conservation', the position is unclear because of

---

[55] For example, the WCPFC Convention, Arts 23(5), 24–26, and 28; the SEAFO Convention, Arts 14 and 16; and the Antigua Convention, Arts XVIII and XX.   [56] *Opinion 2/91*, para 34.

[57] For the text of the Agreement, as amended, see OJ 2000 L197/37.

[58] Council Decision 2004/815/EC of 19 November 2004 amending the declaration by the European Community on the exercise of competence and voting rights submitted to the General Fisheries Commission for the Mediterranean, OJ 2004 L357/30.

the inconsistent practice. It could be argued, based on the predominant practice relating to fisheries access agreements and membership of RFMOs, that the EC has exclusive treaty-making competence not only as regards 'conservation', but also in relation to the requirements of developing States, scientific research, port State measures, flag State enforcement jurisdiction on the high seas, and measures adopted in respect of non-members of RFMOs. Such an argument would not be consistent with the Court's judgment in *Kramer* unless 'conservation' is given a very wide meaning. On the other hand, EC practice suggests that the nationality of fishing vessels and the qualification and certification of their officers and crews remain within the competence of the Member States. It would also seem to be the case, judging from the admittedly limited practice, that Member States concluding maritime boundary agreements with third States (a matter that is undoubtedly within the exclusive competence of the Member States) may include in such agreements matters relating to fisheries as an element of the boundary settlement without thereby needing to involve the EC as a party to the agreement.[59] Finally, it should be noted that even where the EC has exclusive treaty-making competence, Member States may become parties to treaties in respect of their overseas countries and territories listed in Annex II to the EC Treaty (hereafter, 'OCTs', on which see Chapter 2).[60] In practice, Member States have often done so in the case of fisheries treaties, as will be illustrated below.

2.3 Treaty-making procedure[61]

The procedure by which the EC negotiates and concludes treaties is laid down in Article 300 EC. It begins with the Commission requesting authorization from the Council to negotiate with the third State(s) or international organization concerned. Once it has received such authorization, the Commission begins negotiations, its room for manoeuvre generally being indicated in the negotiating directives contained in the authorization: the Commission must also consult with any committee appointed by the Council for this purpose. If the negotiations are successful, the Commission will forward the treaty to the Council. The latter, acting on the proposal of the Commission, then decides, by a qualified majority vote, whether to sign the treaty. If it does so decide, it will subsequently take a further decision, again acting by qualified majority vote on a proposal from the Commission, whether to conclude (ie ratify or accede to) the treaty on behalf of

---

[59] For an example of such practice, see the 1999 Agreement between the United Kingdom and Denmark (on behalf of the Faroe Islands) relating to the Maritime Delimitation in the Area between the Faroe Islands and the United Kingdom, UK Treaty Series No 76 (1999), Cm 4511. Although part of Denmark, the Faroe Islands are not part of the EC (see Chapter 2), and therefore are equivalent to a third State.

[60] This principle was recognized by the Court in *Opinion 1/78 (Re International Agreement on Natural Rubber)* [1979] ECR 2871, para 62.

[61] For a detailed account, see Eeckhout, *External Relations*, ch 6.

the EC. Before taking any such decision, the Council must consult the European Parliament. In certain circumstances, including where a treaty has 'important budgetary implications for the Community' (the only circumstance that is relevant to fisheries), the Council must go further and obtain the assent of the Parliament to the conclusion of the treaty.[62] The meaning of the quoted phrase was in issue in *Parliament v Council*.[63] In that case the European Parliament challenged the view of the Council that an agreement between the EC and Mauritania on the access of Community fishing vessels to Mauritanian waters did not have 'important budgetary implications for the Community'. The Court held that to determine whether a particular treaty had such implications, the amount to be expended under that treaty should be compared with the EC's total expenditure on the whole of its external relations operations.[64] As a subsidiary criterion, comparison could, 'in appropriate cases', also be made with total expenditure (on both internal and external matters) for the sector in question.[65] In the case of the agreement with Mauritania, the proportions of total external relations and CFP expenditure that the agreement represented were about 1 and 5 per cent, respectively.[66] The agreement did not, therefore, according to the Court, have 'important' budgetary implications.[67] In practice, very few fisheries agreements have been considered by the Council to have such implications. Once a decision has been taken to conclude a treaty, the EC will deposit an instrument of ratification or accession, and the treaty will then become legally binding on the EC.

In the case of a mixed agreement, negotiation of the agreement generally follows the same procedure as for pure Community agreements.[68] For its part, the EC will conclude the agreement by the process just described, while the Member States will follow the normal procedures for the ratification of treaties laid down by their own domestic laws. It has been argued that the EC and the Member States must ratify a mixed agreement simultaneously,[69] but in practice this does not often happen.[70]

If the Treaty of Lisbon were to come into force, it would make one, albeit significant, change of substance to the position described above. The consent of the European Parliament would thenceforth be required for the conclusion of all fisheries treaties, and not just those with important budgetary implications.[71]

---

[62] Art 300(3) EC.   [63] Case C-189/97 *Parliament v Council* [1999] ECR I-4741.
[64] Case C-189/97, para 31.   [65] Case C-189/97, para 32.   [66] Case C-189/97, para 33.
[67] Case C-189/97, para 35.   [68] Eeckhout, *External Relations*, 215–16.
[69] See Soons, AHA, 'The Position of the EC towards the LOS Convention', *Proceedings of the 84th Annual Meeting of the American Society of International Law* (1990), 278 at 280. On this question, see also Heliskoski, J, *Mixed Agreements as a Technique for Organising the International Relations of the European Community and its Member States* (The Hague: Kluwer, 2001), 92–5 and Eeckhout, *External Relations*, 218–19.
[70] For example, while the EC and its Member States all ratified the UN Fish Stocks Agreement at the same time, they ratified the UN Convention on the Law of the Sea separately over the space of several years. See further Heliskoski, *Mixed Agreements*, 94.
[71] Treaty on the Functioning of the European Union, Art 218(6)(a)(v).

It is also appropriate to mention here that the funding of the EC's fisheries access agreements, membership of RFMOs, and participation in UN bodies concerned with fisheries is provided for by Regulation 861/2006 (on which see further Chapter 8).[72]

2.4 The position of treaties within the EC's legal order[73]

When the Council concludes a treaty (whether a pure Community agreement or a mixed agreement) on behalf of the EC, the legal act by which it does so is a Decision or a Regulation, to which the treaty in question is annexed. It is not clear what factors determine the choice of instrument. In practice, most (but not all) treaties relating to RFMOs are concluded by means of a Decision (as were the FAO Compliance Agreement, the FSA, and the UN Convention on the Law of the Sea), whereas with fisheries access treaties there is no predominant use of one type of instrument rather than the other. Regardless of the instrument used, the treaty then becomes part of the Community legal order,[74] and so is binding on the EC's institutions and the Member States.[75]

For many years, the Court had held that individuals could invoke before national courts those provisions of treaties to which the EC was a party (both pure Community treaties and mixed agreements) that were sufficiently clear and precise (viewed in the light of the spirit, general scheme, and wording of the treaty in question), unless the treaty in question stipulated otherwise.[76] The Court, however, had always excluded the General Agreement on Tariffs and Trade (GATT) and other World Trade Organization (WTO) agreements from having such direct effect.[77] In 2008 the Court effectively extended that exception to embrace the UN Convention on the Law of the Sea. In the *Intertanko* case, a group of tanker owners sought to challenge before the British courts the validity of an EC Directive dealing with criminal liability for causing marine pollution on the basis, *inter alia*, that the Directive breached the Law of the Sea Convention. The matter was referred to the Court for a preliminary ruling under Article 234 EC. The Court held that

---

[72] Regulation (EC) No 861/2006 of 22 May 2006 establishing Community financial measures for the implementation of the common fisheries policy and in the area of the Law of the Sea, OJ 2006 L160/1, Arts 2(d), 3(f) and (g), and 13.

[73] For a detailed account, see Eeckhout, *External Relations*, ch 9.

[74] Case 13/00 *Commission v Ireland* [2002] ECR I-2943, para 14; Case 239/03 *Commission v France* [2004] ECR I-9325, para 25; and Case 459/03 *Commission v Ireland* [2006] ECR I-4635, paras 82–85.

[75] Art 300(7) EC.

[76] See, for example, Case 104/81 *Hauptzollamt Mainz v Kupferberg* [1982] ECR 3641, paras 9–27; and Case 213/03 *Syndicat professionnel coordination des pêcheurs de l'étang de Berre et de la région v Électricité de France* [2004] ECR I-7357, paras 39–47. See also Hartley, *The Foundations*, 222–4.

[77] See, for example, Joined Cases 21–24/72 *International Fruit Company v Produktschap voor Groenten en Fruit* [1972] ECR 1219; and Case C-149/96 *Portugal v Council* [1999] ECR I-8395.

individuals could not invoke a treaty before national courts to challenge the validity of EC legislation unless the treaty in question established 'rules intended to apply directly and immediately to individuals and to confer upon them rights or freedoms capable of being relied upon against States'.[78] The Court found that the Convention was not a treaty of that type.[79] For example, individuals did not have a direct right to freedom of navigation; they could only enjoy such a right by registering a ship with a State.[80] Many of the treaties considered in this chapter would appear to be of a similar quality to the UN Convention on the Law of the Sea in that they do not contain rules intended to apply directly to individuals. That means that such treaties could not be relied on by individuals before national courts, at least to challenge the validity of EC legislation.[81] On the other hand, the Court has in the recent past held that individuals may rely on treaties whose provisions are sufficiently clear and precise to challenge before national courts acts of Member States that are alleged to contravene mixed treaties to which both the EC and Member States are parties. That was the situation, for example, in a case where individual fishermen were held by the Court to be competent to rely on the protocol on land-based pollution to the Mediterranean Convention to challenge the pollution of a salt marsh by the French State-owned electricity company.[82] However, it is difficult to see that the protocol, any more than the Law of the Sea Convention, conferred rights directly on individuals. It would therefore seem, assuming that that case is still good law following *Intertanko*, that individuals wishing to invoke a treaty (whether a pure Community or mixed treaty) against the EC are in a markedly inferior position to individuals who wish to invoke a mixed treaty against a Member State. There seems no obvious reason for such differentiation.

3 EC participation in global fisheries instruments

3.1 Introduction

We now turn from matters of competence and procedure to the substance of EC external fisheries relations, beginning with the question of EC participation in the global instruments discussed in Chapter 3 that constitute the foundations of modern international fisheries law, namely the UN Convention on the Law of the Sea, the UN Fish Stocks Agreement, the FAO Compliance Agreement, the Code

---

[78] Case C-308/06 *The Queen on the application of International Association of Independent Tanker Owners (Intertanko) et al v Secretary of State for Transport*, judgment of 3 June 2008 (not yet reported), para 64.
[79] Ibid.   [80] Case C-308/06, para 59.
[81] For detailed comment on the implications of the *Intertanko* case, see Boelaert-Suominen, S, 'The European Community, the Court of Justice and the Law of the Sea' *IJMCL* 23 (2008), 643 at 699–711.
[82] Case 213/03 *Syndicat professionnel coordination des pêcheurs de l'étang de Berre*, paras 39–47.

of Conduct for Responsible Fisheries, the International Plans of Action, and the UN General Assembly resolutions on driftnet fishing and the protection of vulnerable marine ecosystems from the adverse impacts of bottom fishing. This section also briefly examines the degree to which the EC has implemented and complied with its obligations under those instruments.

3.2 EC participation in the UN Convention on the Law of the Sea[83]

The Convention provides for participation by international organizations to which their member States have transferred competence over matters governed by the Convention.[84] Article 2 of Annex IX provides that an international organization may sign the Convention when a majority of its member States have done so. In accordance therewith the EC signed the Convention on 7 December 1984. Article 3 of Annex IX provides that an international organization may formally confirm (ie ratify) the Convention when a majority of its member States have ratified. In the case of the EC, that condition was met when Sweden became the eighth of the then fifteen Member States to ratify the Convention on 25 June 1996. However, it was not until 1 April 1998, by which time twelve Member States had become parties to the Convention, that the EC deposited its instrument of formal confirmation and became a party to the Convention. Subsequently, all twenty-seven EC Member States have become parties to the Convention. Some Member States have also ratified the Convention in respect of their OCTs. Article 5(1) of Annex IX requires an international organization, when depositing an instrument of formal confirmation, to make a declaration about its competence. The declaration made by the EC on formal confirmation as it relates to fisheries was discussed in subsection 2.2 above.

In spite of, or perhaps because of, that declaration, there are real problems for other parties to the Convention in knowing where the division of competence between the EC and its Member States lies as regards responsibility for fisheries

---

[83] The discussion that follows deals with EC participation in the Convention only from the point of view of fisheries. For more general and fuller treatments of EC participation, see, from amongst a considerable literature, Ederer, M, *Die Europaische Wirtschaftsgemeinschaft und die Seerechtskonvention der Vereinten Nationen von 1982* (Munich: Verlag V Florentz, 1988); Gaja, G, 'The European Community's Participation in the UN Law of the Sea Convention: Some Incoherencies in a Compromise Solution' *Italian Yearbook of International Law* 5 (1983), 110; Garzon Clariana, G, 'L'Union européenne et la convention de 1982 sur le droit de la mer', *Revue Belge de Droit International* XXVIII (1995), 36; Heliskoski, *Mixed Agreements*, 15–21, 128–37, and 161–6; Nordmann, C, 'Regional Organisations: The European Community and the Law of the Sea Convention' in Vidas, D and Østreng, W (eds), *Order for the Oceans at the Turn of the Century* (The Hague: Kluwer, 1999), 355–63; Simmonds, 'The European Economic Community', 108–54; and Treves, T, 'The European Community and the Law of the Sea Convention: New Developments' in Cannizzaro, E (ed), *The European Union as an Actor in International Relations* (The Hague: Kluwer, 2002), 279.   [84] Art 305(1)(f) and Annex IX.

matters under the Convention. That is particularly the case as regards the 'certain number of matters that are not directly related to the conservation and management of sea fishing resources' in respect of which, according to the EC's declaration, competence is shared. In fact, the Convention does not envisage the possibility of shared competence. Arguably the EC is in breach of Annex IX in including matters of shared competence in its declaration without indicating which of itself or its Member States actually exercises competence in relation to those matters. That is because Annex IX requires declarations of competence to list the matters for which competence has actually been '*transferred*' to an organization: in the case of matters of shared competence no actual transfer appears to have taken place.[85] However, in *Commission v Ireland* the Court held that in areas where EC rules existed, a transfer of competence took place when the EC became a party to the Convention and merely by virtue of that fact. Where there were no EC rules, competence remained with the Member States.[86] While the Court's position is in accordance with the spirit of Annex IX, it hardly seems to reflect the text of the EC's declaration. The question of who has competence is important, because under Articles 4(3) and 6(1) of Annex IX the EC is responsible for non-compliance with the Convention in relation to matters for which it is competent, while the Member States are responsible for matters for which they are competent. Thus, a third State wishing to make diplomatic representations or invoke the Convention's dispute settlement procedures in respect of alleged non-compliance with a provision of the Convention needs to know whether it is the EC or its Member States that have competence in respect of that provision. If the third State is not sure, it may inquire of the EC and/or its Member States which of them has competence and responsibility for the provision in question.[87] Any answer given by the EC (through the Commission or Council) and/or EC Member States will not be authoritative as far as EC law is concerned, because only the Court can make an authoritative determination about competence.[88] Nevertheless, as far as international proceedings are concerned, a third State is entitled to rely on any answer given, even though that answer may not only not be authoritative as far as EC law is concerned, but may also turn out to be contrary to that law.

When becoming a party to the Convention, the EC did not adopt any specific measures to implement the Convention's fisheries provisions. Those provisions are part of the EC legal order for the reasons explained in subsection 2.4 above. However, the Convention requires more than that its fisheries provisions simply be made part of domestic law. Further steps must be taken to give practical effect

---

[85] See further Churchill, R and Scott, J, 'The MOX Plant Litigation: The First Half Life' *ICLQ* 53 (2004), 643 at 664–5.   [86] Case 459/03 *Commission v Ireland*, paras 105–108.

[87] Annex IX, Arts 5(5) and 6(2).

[88] See further Churchill and Scott, 'The MOX Plant Litigation', 662–3.

to them. As far as the exclusive economic zone (EEZ) is concerned, the Convention imposes four principal obligations on a coastal State: (a) to take such conservation and management measures as will ensure that fish stocks in its EEZ are not endangered by over-exploitation and that are designed to maintain or restore those fish stocks at or to levels that can produce the maximum sustainable yield as qualified by various environmental and economic factors;[89] (b) subject to that, to promote the optimum utilization of the living resources of its EEZ;[90] (c) to establish the allowable catch;[91] and (d) to permit foreign vessels to take that part of the allowable catch surplus to the harvesting capacity of its own fleet[92] (and see Chapter 3 for further discussion of these four obligations). Implementation of obligation '(d)' is considered in section 4 below. The EC has sought to fulfil the first three obligations with the adoption of the various conservation and management measures discussed in Chapter 4, even if the language of EC legislation does not always reflect the terminology of the Convention. However, it is doubtful whether in practice the EC has succeeded in fulfilling obligation '(a)'. In 2008 the Commission reported that largely because of inaccurate catch reports, the state of some 57 per cent of stocks in Community waters or for which Community vessels fished was unknown. Of the stocks where there was sufficient information, 68 per cent were at 'high risk of depletion' and only 32 per cent were fished sustainably. The demersal stocks of the North Sea currently produce only one-fifth of what was harvested from them twenty-five years ago (see further Chapter 4).[93]

Turning to the high seas, the main obligation imposed by the Convention on States is to cooperate over the conservation and management of the living resources of the high seas.[94] The EC has principally given effect to that obligation by becoming a member of almost all the RFMOs with management responsibility for the high seas areas where its vessels fish (as detailed in section 6 below) and by becoming a party to the UN Fish Stocks Agreement and the FAO Compliance Agreement. However, not all parties to the Law of the Sea Convention consider that the EC has fulfilled its obligations to cooperate over the conservation of the living resources of the high seas. In 2000 Chile instituted proceedings against the EC before the International Tribunal for the Law of the Sea, alleging that the EC had breached its obligations of cooperation under the Convention through the activities of Community vessels fishing for swordfish (a highly migratory species within the meaning of the Convention) on the high seas in the south-east Pacific adjacent to Chile's 200 nm EEZ. Proceedings were suspended shortly after the case

---

[89] Art 61(2) and (3).   [90] Art 62(1).   [91] Art 61(1).   [92] Art 62(2).

[93] *Communication from the Commission: Fishing Opportunities for 2009. Policy Statement from the European Commission*, COM(2008) 331, 30.5.2008, p 4.

[94] Arts 117–119. See also Arts 63(2) and 64. On these Articles, see further Chapter 3.

was brought as the parties had arrived at a provisional arrangement,[95] and have remained suspended ever since.[96]

3.3 EC participation in the UN Fish Stocks Agreement[97]

As was seen in subsection 2.2 above, when it came to consider possible signature of the Fish Stocks Agreement (hereafter in this subsection, 'the Agreement'), the Council decided that competence in respect of the matters covered by the Agreement was shared between the EC and the Member States. Article 47(1) of the Agreement provides that where an international organization does not have competence over all the matters governed by the Agreement, Annex IX of the Law of the Sea Convention applies *mutatis mutandis*, with the exception that prior participation by a majority of Member States is not required.

In June 1998 the Council decided to ratify the Agreement, stipulating that the EC and all its Member States should ratify the Agreement simultaneously 'in order to guarantee uniform application of the Agreement'.[98] It was inevitable that the process of ratification would move at the pace of the slowest Member State, so that it was not until December 2003, five and a half years after the Council's decision, that the EC and all its then fifteen Member States ratified the Agreement. All the Member States that have joined the EC since 2004 have also ratified the Agreement. Some Member States have also ratified the Agreement in respect of their OCTs.

When ratifying the Agreement, the EC made the declaration on competence discussed in subsection 2.2 above. The same objection to the inclusion in the declaration of matters in respect of which competence is said to be shared may be made as in the case of the declaration made on formal confirmation of the Law of the Sea Convention.

Like the Law of the Sea Convention, the Agreement is part of the EC legal order, although no specific legislation to implement its provisions was adopted

---

[95] *Case concerning the Conservation and Sustainable Utilisation of Swordfish Stocks in the South-Eastern Pacific Ocean (Chile/European Community)*, order of 15 March 2001, available on the website of the Tribunal. For discussion of the dispute, see McDorman, TL, 'The Chile v. EC Swordfish Case' *Yearbook of International Environmental Law* 11 (2000), 585; and Orellana, MA, 'The Swordfish Dispute between the EU and Chile at the ITLOS and the WTO' *Nordic Journal of International Law* 71 (2002), 55.

[96] For the most recent order at the time of writing continuing the suspension of proceedings, see *Case concerning the Conservation and Sustainable Utilisation of Swordfish Stocks in the South-Eastern Pacific Ocean (Chile/European Community)*, order of 30 November 2007, available on the website of the Tribunal.

[97] For a more detailed study, see Hedley, C, *The European Community and the United Nations Fish Stocks Agreement*, available on the International Fisheries Law website.

[98] Council Decision 98/414/EC of 8 June 1998 on the ratification by the European Community of the Agreement for the implementing [sic] of the provisions of the United Nations Convention on the Law of the Sea of 10 December 1982 relating to the conservation and management of straddling stocks [sic] and highly migratory fish stocks, OJ 1998 L189/14, Art 2(2).

when the EC became a party. However, many of the Agreement's provisions have been implemented by the EC in a rather piecemeal way through various EC legislative measures and some of its external fisheries relations practice. Because the Agreement contains a large number of quite detailed provisions (as seen in Chapter 3), it is not possible for reasons of space to do more here than sketch the action taken by the EC to implement some of the more significant of the Agreement's provisions.

The discussion will begin with the main obligations of the Agreement relating to action to be taken by coastal States. First, the Agreement requires coastal States to apply within their EEZs the principles of management set out in Articles 5 and 6 to straddling and highly migratory fish stocks. Broadly speaking, the EC endeavours to give effect to those principles through the various conservation and management measures that were discussed in Chapter 4, although it does not do so fully: for example, at present not only is there virtually no EC legislation aimed at minimizing discards but the way that the CFP operates actually encourages discards (see further Chapter 4). Under Article 7 of the Agreement a coastal State is to cooperate with high seas fishing States in order to try to achieve compatibility between its management measures for straddling and highly migratory fish stocks and the measures adopted by high seas fishing States (for example, through an RFMO). The EC has sought to give effect to that obligation by entering into arrangements for particular straddling stocks in the north-east Atlantic (including, *inter alia*, Norwegian spring-spawning herring and mackerel) with other States in the region and through its participation in the North-East Atlantic Fisheries Commission (on the Commission, see section 6 below).[99]

The majority of the Agreement's obligations relate to fishing on the high seas. A first set of obligations concerns participation in RFMOs and fishing in conformity with their measures.[100] The EC has sought to give effect to that set of obligations by becoming a member of almost all those RFMOs operating in areas where its vessels fish (see further section 6 below). A second set of obligations relates to the duties of flag States. In particular, a flag State must prohibit its vessels from fishing on the high seas unless it has authorized them to do so; and if it has so authorized them, it must ensure that its vessels comply with the conservation and management measures of RFMOs and do not engage in any activity that would undermine the effectiveness of such measures.[101] General measures seeking to give effect to those

---

[99] For further details of the arrangements referred to, see Churchill, RR, 'Managing Straddling Fish Stocks in the North-East Atlantic: A Multiplicity of Instruments and Regime Linkages but how Effective a Management?' in Stokke, OS (ed), *Governing High Seas Fisheries: The Interplay of Global and Regional Regimes* (Oxford: Oxford University Press, 2001), 235–72; and Henriksen, T, Hønneland, G, and Sydnes, A, *Law and Politics in Ocean Governance: the UN Fish Stocks Agreement and Regional Fisheries Management Regimes* (Leiden: Martinus Nijhoff, 2006), 119–20.

[100] Fish Stocks Agreement, Art 8. In this subsection the abbreviation 'RFMO' also includes the regional fisheries management *arrangements* to which the Agreement refers.

[101] Fish Stocks Agreement, Art 18.

provisions in EC law are found in, *inter alia*, the Basic Regulation,[102] Regulation 2847/93[103] (hereafter, 'the Control Regulation'), Regulation 1281/2005,[104] Regulation 1005/2008[105] (hereafter, 'the IUU Regulation', where 'IUU' fishing means illegal, unreported, and unregulated fishing), and Regulation 1006/2008.[106] In addition, specific measures have been adopted in respect of particular RFMOs.[107] The Agreement also requires a flag State to take legal proceedings where non-compliance with RFMO measures by its vessels is suspected and, where non-compliance is proved, impose sanctions adequate in severity to deter future violations and deprive offenders of the benefits of their illegal activities.[108] Effect is given to those obligations by Article 25 of the Basic Regulation and Article 31 of the Control Regulation, and, from the beginning of 2010, also by Articles 41–47 of the IUU Regulation. As well as flag States, port States are also subject to obligations under the Agreement. They have a duty to take action to promote the effectiveness of RFMO measures. To that end they may inspect vessels in their ports and may prohibit the landing of catches taken in a manner that undermines the effectiveness of RFMO measures.[109] As regards EC implementation, the Control Regulation obliges Member States to inspect vessels in their ports[110] and, under Article 28g, to prohibit the landing of catches by third States' vessels that have not been taken in compliance with RFMO measures.[111] There are also specific EC measures relating to particular RFMOs.[112] As from the beginning of 2010, Article 28g of the Control Regulation will be repealed by the

[102] Council Regulation (EC) No 2371/2002 of 20 December 2002 on the conservation and sustainable exploitation of fisheries resources under the Common Fisheries Policy, OJ 2002 L358/59, as amended and corrected, Art 23.
[103] Council Regulation (EEC) No 2847/93 of 12 October 1993 establishing a control system applicable to the common fisheries policy, OJ 1993 L261/1, as amended, Arts 2 and 24.
[104] Commission Regulation (EC) No 1281/2005 of 3 August 2005 on the management of fishing licences and the minimal [sic] information to be contained therein, OJ 2005 L203/3, Art 3.
[105] Council Regulation (EC) No 1005/2008 of 29 September 2008 establishing a Community system to prevent, deter and eliminate illegal, unreported and unregulated fishing, amending Regulations (EEC) No 2847/93, (EC) No 1936/2001 and (EC) No 601/2004 and repealing Regulations (EC) No 1093/94 and (EC) No 1447/1999, OJ 2008 L286/1, Art 37(1) and (2).
[106] Council Regulation (EC) No 1006/2008 of 29 September 2008 concerning authorisations for fishing activities of Community fishing vessels outside Community waters and the access of third country vessels to Community waters, amending Regulations (EEC) No 2847/93 and (EC) No 1627/94 and repealing Regulation (EC) No 3317/94, OJ 2008 L286/33, Arts 1(a), 3, 11, and 16.
[107] For some examples, see section 6 below.   [108] Fish Stocks Agreement, Art 19.
[109] Fish Stocks Agreement, Art 23.   [110] This is implicit in Art 2 of Reg 2847/93.
[111] Art 28g was added to Reg 2847/93 in 1998. EC Member States have, however, a poor record of complying with this obligation (at least in the fairly recent past): see *Report from the Commission to the Council and the European Parliament on the Monitoring of the Member States' Implementation of the Common Fisheries Policy 2003–2005*, COM(2007) 167, 10.4.2007, pp 5–6.
[112] For some examples, see section 6 below.

IUU Regulation, which contains more comprehensive port State control meas-ures.[113] Other obligations contained in the Agreement relate to actions to be taken by members of RFMOs collectively, for example to deter non-members of an RFMO from engaging in fishing in the area for which that RFMO is responsible unless complying with its conservation and management measures, and to adopt schemes providing for the inspection of fishing vessels on the high seas by other than their flag State. Most of the RFMOs of which the EC is a member have taken action to implement at least some of those obligations.[114]

3.4 EC participation in the FAO Compliance Agreement

As was indicated earlier, the EC is a party to the Compliance Agreement to the exclusion of its Member States. As with the Law of the Sea Convention and the Fish Stocks Agreement, the EC did not adopt any specific measures to implement the Agreement when it became a party. Subsequently the EC has adopted a number of measures to do so. Many of the Agreement's obligations are concerned with the duties of flag and port States and are similar to those of the Fish Stocks Agreement considered above, so nothing further need be said here about their implementation by the EC. The remaining principal obligation is for parties to the Agreement to send the FAO information about the vessels that they have authorized to fish on the high seas. There does not appear to be any EC legislation giving effect to that obligation. According to the publicly accessible part of the FAO's website dealing with this issue, which does not appear to be very up to date, all thirteen pre-2004 Member States with high seas fishing fleets and Cyprus have sent details of the vessels concerned to the FAO.

3.5 EC participation in the FAO Code of Conduct for Responsible Fisheries and International Plans of Action (IPOAs)

The Code of Conduct explicitly applies to the EC, Article 1(4) stating that 'in this Code, the term States includes the European Community in matters within its competence'. The IPOA on IUU fishing has a similar provision.[115] The other IPOAs are directed at 'States', which are defined as including members of the FAO: they appear, therefore, also to apply to the EC.

It will be recalled from Chapter 3 that the Code and the four IPOAs are not legally binding. Nevertheless, there is an expectation that FAO members will seek to comply with them. As far as the Code is concerned, the EC seeks, through the policy aspirations expressed in the Basic Regulation and the range of the

---

[113] Reg 1005/2008, Arts 4–11, 37(5) and (6), and 56.
[114] For some examples, see Henriksen *et al*, *Law and Politics in Ocean Governance*.   [115] Para 6(a).

conservation and management measures that it has adopted, to give effect to the principles of fisheries management set out in the Code.[116] However, it will be clear from Chapters 1 and 4, as well as subsections 3.2 and 3.3 above, that the EC has not yet succeeded in complying with key provisions of the Code, for example basing conservation on a long-term and sustainable approach (Art 7.1.1), eliminating excess capacity (Art 7.1.8), and minimizing discards (Art 7.2.2).

The EC also has its own code—the European Code of Sustainable and Responsible Fisheries Practices, which was adopted by the Advisory Committee for Fisheries and Aquaculture in 2003.[117] The European Code does not seek to implement the FAO Code. Instead, '[b]uilding on the framework' of the FAO Code, the European Code 'refers more relevantly to EU fishing activities and is fundamentally directed at fishing operators', not EC and Member State authorities.[118] The Code is 'intended to supplement international, European or national legislation in force on a voluntary basis and add to existing legislation with a view to contributing to a sustainable development of the fisheries sector'.[119] The Code lays down 'Guidelines' which 'European fishing operators will endeavour to respect'.[120] The Guidelines are arranged under the headings of 'Respect for fisheries resources and their environment', 'Maritime safety', 'Social aspects', 'Cooperation', 'Information and transparency', 'Marketing conditions', and 'Aquaculture'. Compared to the FAO Code, the European Code is quite short, with far less detail.

Turning to the IPOAs, the efforts of the EC to comply with the first IPOA, that on reducing the incidental catch of seabirds in longline fisheries, are detailed in section 7 below and show that the EC has yet to adopt the national plan of action for which the IPOA calls. As for the second IPOA, on the conservation and management of sharks, the Council adopted a Regulation in 2003 which establishes a qualified prohibition on the practice of shark finning in Community waters and by 'vessels flying the flag or registered in Member States' elsewhere (see further Chapter 4).[121] The Commission saw that Regulation as a first step towards the development of the comprehensive plan for the management of sharks for which the IPOA calls.[122] A further step towards the adoption of such a plan was taken in late 2007, when the Commission issued a *Consultation on an EU Action Plan for Sharks*. However, the EC is still some way from complying with the IPOA. Apart

---

[116] Those principles were summarized in Chapter 3. The provisions of the Code dealing with matters other than conservation and management are not considered here because the focus of this chapter is on fisheries management.   [117] The Code is available on the website of DG Mare.
[118] Code, p 5.   [119] Code, pp 5–6   [120] Code, p 8.
[121] Council Regulation (EC) No 1185/2003 of 26 June 2003 on the removal of fins of sharks on board vessels, OJ 2003 L167/1.
[122] *Proposal for a Council Regulation on the removal of fins of sharks on board vessels*, COM(2002) 449, 05.08.2002, p 3.

from the legislation on shark finning, the EC has adopted a number of other measures that aim to some extent at the conservation of sharks.[123]

The third IPOA deals with the management of fishing capacity. It exhorts FAO members, *inter alia*, to have a national plan for the management of fishing capacity and to reduce excess capacity. As was seen in Chapter 4, between 1983 and 2002 the EC had in place a series of multi-annual guidance programmes which were essentially equivalent to the national plan for which the IPOA calls, although those programmes did not succeed in eliminating excess capacity. Since 2002 the EC has not had anything equivalent to a national plan, not least because there is currently no official EC target as to what would constitute an appropriate level of capacity for EC fishing fleets. The entry-exit scheme is designed to prevent an increase in capacity, but it does not require a reduction in capacity, although in practice such a reduction has occurred (see further Chapter 4). On the other hand, the scheme has very largely removed subsidies that contribute to the build-up of excess capacity, which is another goal of the IPOA.[124]

The fourth IPOA addresses the issue of illegal, unreported, and unregulated (IUU) fishing. It exhorts FAO members, *inter alia*, to develop a national plan of action by 2004, to discourage their nationals and vessels from engaging in IUU fishing and punish those so engaged with sanctions of adequate severity, and to cooperate with other States to prevent, deter, and eliminate IUU fishing. The IPOA also sets out more specific measures to be taken by flag States, coastal States, and port States (many of which are similar to those in the Fish Stocks Agreement), as well as by RFMOs. In 2002 the Commission published an action plan of the kind called for in the IPOA.[125] In its introduction to the plan, the Commission observed that as 'Community rules in this area/on this matter are already relatively developed', the aim of its plan was not to 'draw up a list of resources available for controlling IUU fishing'.[126] Instead the Commission proposed a number of new measures or initiatives to be taken at: (a) the Community level; (b) within RFMOs; (c) at the global level; and (d) in collaboration with developing States. For reasons of space it is not possible to examine further the Commission's proposals or the degree to which they have been given effect.

Following publication of the Commission's action plan in 2002, the EC adopted a number of rather piecemeal provisions that address IUU fishing,

---

[123] For some examples, see Chapter 4. For a brief critique of EC action in respect of sharks, see Cator, J, 'European shark management, a long overdue plan, now a little closer' *El Anzuelo (European Newsletter on Fisheries and the Environment)* 20 (2008), 8 (available on the website of the Institute for European Environmental Policy).

[124] For a detailed study of how far the EC has complied with the IPOA on capacity management, see Brown, J, *Fishing Capacity Management in the EU post 2002 CFP Reform* (London: Institute for European Environmental Policy, 2006), 15–18 and Appendix 1.

[125] *Communication from the Commission: Community action plan for the eradication of illegal, unreported and unregulated fishing*, COM(2002) 180, 28.5.2002.   [126] COM(2002) 180, p 3.

most of which implement measures adopted by RFMOs (see further section 6 below).[127]

In 2008 the Council took a more comprehensive approach when it adopted the IUU Regulation, which establishes (with effect from the beginning of 2010) a general EC system to combat IUU fishing. The Regulation runs to fifty-seven Articles and deals, *inter alia*, with improving port State control of third States' fishing vessels, measures to halt the import into the EC of products stemming from IUU fishing, the identification of vessels engaged in IUU fishing and of 'non-cooperating' third States, measures to be taken against vessels and EC nationals involved in IUU activities and against 'non-cooperating' third States, and enforcement measures and sanctions. It is not possible to go into further detail here for reasons of space, but some of the Regulation's provisions are discussed more extensively elsewhere in this chapter (see especially section 6 below) and in Chapters 2, 4, and 7.

3.6 The EC and UN General Assembly Resolutions

It will be recalled from Chapter 3 that the UN General Assembly has adopted a significant series of resolutions on driftnet fishing and on the protection of vulnerable marine ecosystems from the adverse impacts of bottom fishing. Although the EC is not a member of the UN, and although the resolutions are not legally binding (although the moratorium on high seas driftnet fishing which the General Assembly called for may have become part of customary international law, as was suggested in Chapter 3), the EC has taken action to give effect to the resolutions concerned.

As far as driftnet fishing is concerned, the EC has not only implemented the moratorium for which the General Assembly called in respect of Community fishing vessels, but has gone further than that both beyond and within Community waters (see further Chapter 4).

Turning to the protection of vulnerable marine ecosystems (VMEs) from the adverse impacts of bottom fishing, it may be recalled from Chapter 3 that the UN General Assembly adopted a resolution, Resolution 61/105, on the matter in 2006. In that Resolution the General Assembly called on flag States, by the end of 2008, to prohibit their vessels from bottom fishing in the vicinity of VMEs in areas beyond national jurisdiction where there is no RFMO or regional fisheries

---

[127] For a brief overview of some of the measures taken by the EC, see *Commission Staff Working Document—Accompanying document to the Proposal for a Council Regulation establishing a Community system to prevent, deter and eliminate illegal, unreported and unregulated fishing—Impact Assessment,* SEC(2007) 1310, pp 11–13; and Committee on Fisheries of the European Parliament, *Report on the implementation of the EU action plan against illegal, unreported and unregulated fishing,* EP Document A6-0015/2007.

management arrangement with competence to regulate such fishing (or where there are no interim measures adopted by States negotiating to establish an RFMO or arrangement) unless conservation and management measures have been adopted to prevent such fishing having significant adverse impacts on VMEs.[128] The EC has a sizeable fleet conducting bottom fishing in the areas referred to in Resolution 61/105, especially in the south-west Atlantic (an area in respect of which there is currently no RFMO).[129] In July 2008 the EC adopted legislation (Regulation 734/2008) to give effect to Resolution 61/105 in respect of Community fishing vessels.[130] Although the EC was not legally required to implement Resolution 61/105, since the latter is not legally binding and the EC is in any case not a member of the UN, the Commission felt that the EC should do so, otherwise the EC's international credibility and its ability to play a leading role in enhancing international fisheries governance would be damaged.[131]

Regulation 734/2008 provides that in the areas referred to in Resolution 61/105, Community vessels may only fish with 'bottom gears' if they have a special fishing permit issued by their flag State in accordance with Regulation 1627/94[132] (on which see Chapter 4) and Regulation 734/2008 itself.[133] 'Bottom gears' are defined as 'gears deployed in the normal course of fishing operations in contact with the seabed, including bottom trawls, dredges, bottom-set gill nets, bottom-set longlines, pots and traps'.[134] In order to obtain a special fishing permit, the owner/operator of the vessel concerned must submit with the application for a permit a detailed fishing plan specifying the intended location of bottom fishing, the targeted species, the type of gear to be used and the depth at which it is to be deployed, and information on the 'configuration of the bathymetric profile of the seabed in the intended fishing grounds' which is not readily available to the authorities of the flag State.[135] Under Article 4(2)–(5) the flag State is then to carry out an assessment, based on the best scientific and technical information available and applying 'precautionary criteria', of the potential impact of the vessel's intended activities. In case of doubt as to whether the adverse impacts are significant or not, the flag State must 'consider that the likely adverse impacts resulting from the scientific advice provided are significant'.[136] A permit may only be issued where the flag State concludes that the intended fishing is 'not likely to have significant adverse impacts' on VMEs.[137] A VME is defined as 'any marine ecosystem whose integrity (ie ecosystem structure or

---

[128] Res 61/105, para 86.

[129] *Proposal for a Council Regulation on the protection of vulnerable marine ecosystems in the high seas from the adverse impacts of bottom fishing gears*, COM(2007) 605, 17.10.2007, p 2.

[130] Council Regulation (EC) No 734/2008 of 15 July 2008 on the protection of vulnerable marine ecosystems in the high seas from the adverse impacts of bottom fishing gears, OJ 2008 L201/8.

[131] COM(2007) 605, p 5.

[132] Council Regulation (EC) No 1627/94 of 27 June 1994 laying down general provisions concerning special fishing permits, OJ 1994 L171/7, as amended.   [133] Reg 734/2008, Art 3.

[134] Reg 734/2008, Art 2(d).   [135] Reg 734/2008, Art 4(1).

[136] Reg 734/2008, Art 4(5).   [137] Reg 734/2008, Art 4(2) and (6).

function) is, according to the best scientific information available and to the principle of precaution, threatened by significant adverse impacts resulting from physical contact with bottom gears in the normal course of fishing operations, including, inter alia, reefs, seamounts, hydrothermal vents, cold water corals or cold water sponge beds'.[138] 'Significant adverse impacts' are defined as 'impacts (evaluated individually, in combination or cumulatively) which compromise ecosystem integrity in a manner that impairs the ability of affected populations to replace themselves and that degrades the long-term natural productivity of habitats, or causes on more than a temporary basis significant loss of species richness, habitat or community types'.[139]

Under Article 6(1) fishing with bottom gears is prohibited in areas where 'no proper scientific assessment' has been carried out and made available. It is not clear whether the 'assessment' referred to in Article 6 is different from that required under Article 4. In addition, Article 8 requires Member States, in respect of their vessels, to close areas to fishing with bottom gears that they have identified '[o]n the basis of the best scientific information available on the occurrence or on the likelihood of occurrence of [VMEs] in the region where their fishing vessels operate'.[140] Again the relationship between that provision and Articles 4 and 6 is not clear. The Commission may also propose that the Council adopt measures to close certain areas to fishing with bottom gears, such proposals being based on information supplied by Member States or on the Commission's own initiative.[141] No such measures had been adopted at the time of writing. Where in the course of fishing operations, a vessel encounters a VME, it must immediately cease fishing and only resume operations when it has reached an alternative site not less than 5 nm from the site of the encounter, provided that the alternative site is within the area foreseen in its fishing plan.[142] A vessel must report each encounter with a VME to the authorities of its flag State.[143]

The provisions of the Control Regulation applicable to the high seas[144] will as a matter of course apply to the enforcement of Regulation 734/2008. However, the latter contains additional measures aimed at securing compliance with its provisions. First, under Article 5(1) a vessel must comply with the fishing plan that it has submitted with its application for a special fishing permit. Failure to do so constitutes a 'serious infringement' within the meaning of the EC's control system (see further Chapter 4), and will result in withdrawal of the permit, in the absence of circumstances beyond the control of the vessel operator.[145] Repeated instances of non-compliance with the provisions of Article 5 of Regulation 734/2008 prohibiting fishing in areas where no proper assessment has been carried out, the provisions of Article 7 on unforeseen encounters with VMEs, and the provisions of

---

[138] Reg 734/2008, Art 2(b).   [139] Reg 734/2008, Art 2(c).
[140] Reg 734/2008, Art 8(1).   [141] Reg 734/2008, Art 8(2).
[142] Reg 734/2008, Art 7(1).   [143] Reg 734/2008, Art 7(3).   [144] Reg 2847/93, Art 1(3).
[145] Reg 734/2008, Arts 5 and 10(1).

Article 9 on vessel monitoring systems (see below) also constitute 'serious infringements'. Secondly, every vessel fishing with bottom gears under a permit must carry an observer who shall, *inter alia*, record the vessel's catch, record any instances of alteration of the fishing plan, document any unforeseen encounters with VMEs, record the depths at which bottom gear is deployed, and report to the authorities of the Member State concerned and the Commission.[146] Thirdly, Member States must report to the Commission every six months on the catches made by their vessels, compliance with fishing plans and other provisions of Regulation 734/2008 by their vessels, the enforcement action that they have taken, and the assessments that they have made under Article 4 and the action that they have taken under Article 8.[147] The Commission is to transmit that information to the FAO and other relevant bodies.[148] The Basic Regulation requires all Community fishing vessels over 15 m in length to carry a vessel monitoring system (see Chapter 4).[149] Article 9 of Regulation 734/2008 adds that if that system malfunctions, the master of the vessel must report its location to the authorities of the flag State every two hours. The vessel must not be permitted to embark on further bottom-fishing trips until the device is functioning satisfactorily.[150]

The areas to which Regulation 734/2008 applies are by definition remote and ones where little is known about many of the target species of fishing with bottom gears or the nature and location of VMEs.[151] The most straightforward—and precautionary—approach would have been a ban on all fishing with bottom gears in the areas concerned. Article 2 of the Basic Regulation provides that the EC is to apply 'the precautionary approach in taking measures . . . to minimise the impact of fishing activities on marine eco-systems', as recital (4) of Regulation 734/2008 recalls and some provisions of the Regulation allude to (as seen above). However, the Commission, in proposing what became Regulation 734/2008, rejected a complete ban on high seas bottom fishing as this would have had 'significant economic and social negative impacts on the EU fleets'.[152] Instead, the EC has elected to adopt what is a fairly complex and bureaucratic system of regulation. In that respect it reflects the compromise embodied in Resolution 61/105 itself, of which the EC was, according to the Commission, one of the principal architects.[153] The success of the EC's system of regulation will depend largely on the quality of the assessments carried out by Member States under Articles 4, 6, and 8; the capacity and will of Member States to take the necessary action to ensure that their vessels comply with their fishing plans and other relevant provisions of Regulation 734/2008; and the way in which observers carry out their designated role.

---

[146] Reg 734/2008, Art 11.   [147] Reg 734/2008, Art 12(1) and (2).
[148] Reg 734/2008, Art 12(3).   [149] Reg 2371/2002, Art 22(1)(b).
[150] Reg 734/2008, Art 9(2).   [151] COM(2007) 605, p 2.   [152] COM(2007) 605, p 5.
[153] COM(2007) 605, pp 2–3.

4 Access agreements

4.1 Introduction

The introduction of the 200 nm EEZ (and exclusive fishing zone (EFZ)) into the law of the sea in the late 1970s had a major impact on those States, including many EC Member States, whose vessels had traditionally fished off the coasts of other States. Article 62(2) of the UN Convention on the Law of the Sea provides that a coastal State must give the vessels of other States access to that part of the allowable catch in its EEZ which its own vessels are not capable of harvesting (generally known as the surplus). In doing so, a coastal State has a broad discretion in determining which foreign vessels may be permitted to fish and on what terms.[154] In fact, the concept of surplus has played a very limited role in relation to the EC's practice in concluding fisheries access agreements. As will be seen below, the access of Community fishing vessels to third States' waters has either not been, or has not explicitly been, based on access to the surplus. As far as Community waters are concerned (with the exception of the waters off some of the outermost regions), Community vessels have been more than capable of taking the whole of the allowable catch since EC Member States extended their fisheries jurisdiction to 200 nm in the late 1970s, so there has been no surplus catch available for third States' vessels. Nevertheless, the EC has been interested in giving some access to Community waters for the vessels of those third States whose waters have traditionally been important for Community vessels, in return for the access of Community vessels to those third States' waters, in order to try to maintain as far as possible existing patterns of fishing (for example, in terms of species so as to satisfy consumer demand) and so to reduce the dislocation that would otherwise have been experienced by many Community vessels. Accordingly, the EC has concluded a number of agreements providing for such reciprocal access. With one exception (an agreement with Dominica, discussed in subsection 4.4 below), all those agreements have been with States in the North Atlantic (including the Baltic and North Seas). Those agreements are considered in subsection 4.2 below, along with one or two other agreements with North Atlantic States that are not based on reciprocity.

Outside the North Atlantic, there have been no third States with which the EC has wished to conclude *reciprocal* access agreements. Nevertheless, since the late 1970s the EC has been anxious to conclude some form of access agreements in order to provide fishing opportunities for its distant-water fleets so as to try to maintain fishing patterns that existed before the introduction of 200 nm limits for fisheries jurisdiction and to divert such fleets from fishing for stocks in Community waters that were and continue to be under considerable pressure as a result of the

---

[154] UN Convention on the Law of the Sea, Art 62(3) and (4). See further Chapter 3.

significant over-capacity in EC fishing fleets. A further reason for desiring such access agreements has been to obtain supplies of species not found in Community waters, thus reducing the need for imports since fish caught by Community vessels in the EEZs of third States are not classified as imports for trade purposes (see further Chapter 7). Over the years the EC has concluded access agreements with more than twenty States outside the North Atlantic, all of which are developing States. In the case of those agreements, which are discussed in subsection 4.3 below, access is based neither on the principle of reciprocity nor explicitly on the concept of surplus, but is determined by a number of other criteria.

Before examining the EC's fisheries access agreements according to the geo-political groupings of States with which they have been concluded, a few general observations that are applicable to all those agreements may be made. First, unlike the issue of EC participation in global fisheries instruments, which has been bedevilled by disputes and uncertainties about the scope of EC treaty-making competence, it has always been accepted without serious question that the EC is exclusively competent to negotiate and conclude fisheries access agreements with third States.

Secondly, all Community vessels fishing in the 200 nm zone of a third State must carry a licence issued by that State,[155] the general fishing licence that all Community vessels must carry wherever they fish,[156] and a fishing authorization issued by the third State concerned.[157] Community vessels are not eligible for such a fishing authorization, *inter alia*, if they are included on the EC list of vessels engaged in IUU fishing, or if, during the twelve months preceding their applica-tion for an authorization, they have been sanctioned for or suspected of a serious infringement, unless there has been a change of owner and the new owner pro-vides guarantees 'that the conditions [presumably of the authorization] will be fulfilled'.[158] Regulation 1006/2008 does not state as clearly as the principal annual Regulation has traditionally done that a Community vessel fishing in the 200 nm zone of a third State must carry a licence issued by that State. It remains to be seen whether, with the adoption of Regulation 1006/2008 in September 2008, the principal annual Regulation will continue to include a provision on carrying a licence from a third State when fishing in third States' waters.

[155] That requirement is contained in the principal annual Regulation: for the 2008 Regulation, see Council Regulation (EC) No 40/2008 of 16 January 2008 fixing for 2008 the fishing opportunities and associated conditions for certain fish stocks and groups of fish stocks, applicable in Community waters and, for Community vessels, in waters where catch limitations are required, OJ 2008 L19/1, as amended and corrected, Art 20.   [156] Reg 2371/2002, Art 22(1)(a) and Reg 1281/2005.
[157] Reg 1006/2008, Arts 1(a)(i), 3, 6, and 8.
[158] Reg 1006/2008, Art 5(1)(b) and (c) (and also Art 2(l) and (m)). See also Reg 1005/2008, Arts 27 (on establishment of the Community IUU vessel list) and 30 (on IUU vessel lists adopted by RFMOs).

Thirdly, the major legislative instruments of the EC's control and enforcement system,[159] discussed in Chapter 4, in general apply to Community vessels fishing in the waters of third States.[160] In addition, there are control measures that apply to fishing by Community vessels in the waters of third States, but not in Community waters. Regulation 500/2001 deals with the monitoring of catches taken in third States' waters,[161] while Regulation 1006/2008 addresses, *inter alia*, the reporting of catches, the closure of fisheries where fishing opportunities have been exhausted, and the suspension or withdrawal by the flag Member State of a fishing permit where a Community vessel has had its fishing authorization suspended or withdrawn by the third State concerned.[162] Under Article 36 of the IUU Regulation the Commission may, albeit 'without prejudice to the provisions set out in bilateral fishing agreements', prohibit Community vessels from fishing in the waters of a third State where the latter has adopted measures that undermine the conservation and management measures adopted by an RFMO. It may also be noted that the Community Fisheries Control Agency (on which, see Chapter 4) is authorized to cooperate with the competent authorities in third States over control and inspection within the framework of an access agreement.[163] A further point of interest is that in 2003 Denmark, Sweden, and Norway signed a memorandum of understanding on control which, *inter alia*, authorizes each party to inspect fishing vessels having its nationality in the EEZs of the other parties in the Skagerrak.[164]

Fourthly, a number of the EC's fisheries conservation measures apply to Community vessels fishing in third States' waters. Examples include, *inter alia*, measures relating to driftnets,[165] finning of sharks,[166] and the encircling of marine mammals with purse seine nets.[167] It is not entirely clear what happens should such EC measures be in conflict with the conservation measures of a third State in whose waters a Community vessel was fishing. Arguably, the third State's measures

---

[159] See, for example, Reg 2371/2002, Chapter V and Reg 2847/93. For further and more detailed examples, see section 5 below.   [160] Reg 2371/2002, Art 1 and Reg 2847/93, Art 1(3).

[161] Commission Regulation (EC) No 500/2001 of 14 March 2001 laying down detailed rules for the application of Council Regulation (EEC) No 2847/93 on the monitoring of catches taken by Community fishing vessels in third country waters and on the high seas, OJ 2001 L73/8.

[162] Reg 1006/2008, Arts 13–16.

[163] Council Regulation (EC) No 768/2005 of 26 April 2005 establishing a Community Fisheries Control Agency and amending Regulation (EEC) No 2847/93 of 12 October 1993 establishing a control system applicable to the common fisheries policy, OJ 2005 L128/1, Art 4(2).

[164] Norwegian Ministry of Fisheries, *Fiskerisamarbeidet med EU* (*Fisheries Cooperation with the EU*), available on the website of the Ministry.

[165] Council Regulation (EC) No 894/97 of 29 April 1997 laying down certain technical measures for the conservation of fishery resources, OJ 1997 L132/1, as amended, Art 11c.

[166] Reg 1185/2003.

[167] Council Regulation (EC) No 520/2007 of 7 May 2007 laying down technical measures for the conservation of certain stocks of highly migratory species and repealing Regulation (EC) No 973/2001, OJ 2007 123/3, as amended, Art 29.

would prevail. Under the EC's access agreements with third States Community vessels are required to comply with a third State's legislation. Agreements with third States are probably normatively superior to EC Regulations (which is the legislative form in which EC conservation measures are made).[168]

Finally, it should be noted that under the IUU Regulation the Commission is not to enter into negotiations to conclude a bilateral fisheries access agreement with any State that has been identified by the Commission under Article 31 of the Regulation as being a non-cooperating third country in fighting IUU fishing.[169] Furthermore, the Commission is to propose the denunciation of any existing agreement with such a State where that agreement provides for its termination in case of failure by that State to comply with undertakings that it has made to combat IUU fishing.[170]

4.2 The North Atlantic

The EC currently has access agreements with five States or territories in the North Atlantic—Norway, the Faroe Islands, Greenland, Iceland, and Russia. In the case of Norway, the Faroe Islands, and Russia, the basis of access is reciprocity; with Greenland and Iceland different criteria apply.

Norway

The Agreement with Norway, which was signed in 1980,[171] is by far the most important of those agreements, both because of the volume of fishing activity involved and also because the Agreement forms the basis for the cooperative management of the many important stocks of fish that Norway and the EC share in the North Sea and Skagerrak.

Under the Agreement each party gives vessels of the other access to its 200 nm zone (including, in a few places, parts of the territorial sea) to fish for such amounts as it determines each year, the aim being that such annual determinations should provide a 'mutually satisfactory balance in their reciprocal fisheries relations'.[172] The balance to be achieved is not in terms of the size of each party's catch, but of its value.[173] That is important because traditionally Norwegian vessels have caught predominantly relatively low value species, such as herring and mackerel, in Community waters, whereas EC catches in Norwegian waters have been mainly of higher value species such as cod and haddock. Thus, in order to achieve a 'mutually satisfactory balance', the amounts of fish that

---

[168] Hartley, *The Foundations*, 182–3.   [169] Reg 1005/2008, Art 38(9).

[170] Reg 1005/2008, Art 38(8).

[171] Agreement on Fisheries between the EEC and the Kingdom of Norway, OJ 1980 L226/48.

[172] Agreement, Art 2(1)(b) and Annex.

[173] Norwegian Parliamentary Paper St prp Nr 102 (1991–92), 2.

Community fishing vessels may catch in Norwegian waters are smaller than would have been the case had the balance to be achieved been a quantitative one. Vessels of one party granted access to fish in the waters of the other must obtain a licence from the other party and comply with the latter's legislation applicable to foreign vessels fishing in its waters.[174] Each party may enforce its legislation in its waters in respect of vessels of the other party 'in conformity with international law'.[175] The provisions of EC law relating to the exercise of jurisdiction over Norwegian (and other third State) vessels fishing in Community waters were examined in Chapter 4.

The amounts of fish that Norway determines are to be allocated to the EC each year are allocated to the EC as such and not to individual Member States. It is then up to the EC to decide how such amounts are to be allocated as quotas to individual Member States. In practice, the EC has allocated the amounts, originally in separate annual Regulations, more recently in the principal annual Regulation, in accordance with the same principle of 'relative stability' used to allocate most total allowable catches in Community waters (see further Chapter 4). The consequence of this practice for Portugal and Spain was that on their accession to the EC they were not granted any quotas to fish in Norway's EEZ as they had not had any rights to fish in Norwegian waters under access agreements with Norway of their own in the years immediately preceding their accession[176] (in contrast to Sweden, which did have an access agreement with Norway at the time of its accession and therefore was allocated quotas in Norwegian waters (see further Chapter 1)). Spain was extremely unhappy at the failure of the EC to allocate it any quotas in Norwegian waters, and from 1990 onwards began challenging before the Court the validity of the annual Council Regulations allocating quotas in Norwegian waters. Pointing out that it had fished in Norwegian waters in the past, Spain argued that the principle of relative stability should be modified to take account of the enlargement of the EC in 1986 and that failure to do so would constitute discrimination against it. In 1992 the Court gave judgment in the first of those challenges, finding for the Council and against Spain,[177] whereupon the outstanding cases brought by Spain were withdrawn. The Court strongly upheld the principle of relative stability, and emphasized that it had not been modified by the Iberian Act of Accession. It pointed out that Spain was in the same position as any other Member State that had not been given quotas in Norwegian waters, so that there was no question of discrimination.[178]

---

[174] Agreement, Arts 4 and 5.   [175] Agreement, Art 6(2).

[176] When Norway extended its fisheries jurisdiction to 200 nm in 1977, it concluded bilateral agreements with Portugal and Spain under which their vessels were allowed to fish in Norwegian waters until 1980. See Ulfstein, G, *Økonomiske soner—hva nå?* (Tromsø: Universitetsforlaget, 1982), 201.

[177] Case C-71/90 *Spain v Council* [1992] ECR I-5175.

[178] Case C-71/90, paras 15–21 and 29.

In 1992 a further dimension was introduced to the basis of EC access to Norwegian waters when the Agreement on the European Economic Area (EEA)[179] was signed between the EC, its Member States, and the then seven member States of the European Free Trade Association (EFTA). One of the principal aims of the EEA Agreement was to extend the EC's four fundamental freedoms (free movement of goods, persons, services, and capital) to the EFTA States. In spite of that, the EEA Agreement does not provide for completely free trade in fishery products between the EC and EFTA States, although it does remove or reduce many of the previously existing restrictions on trade.[180] In practice, that aspect of the EEA Agreement is of more benefit to the EFTA States than the EC, and the EC therefore insisted that in return for the trade concessions that it had made, its vessels should obtain increased access to EFTA waters. For political reasons, the provisions on such access were contained, not in the EEA Agreement itself, but in bilateral agreements with Sweden (now, of course, only of historical interest), Iceland (discussed below), and Norway.[181] The EC's bilateral agreement with Norway, which is in the form of an exchange of letters relating to the 1980 EC-Norway Fisheries Agreement,[182] provides that Norway will make increased amounts of cod available to Community fishing vessels in its waters north of 62°N, although this will be within the framework of balanced fishing opportunities under the 1980 Agreement and therefore will be offset by increased fishing opportunities for Norwegian vessels in Community waters. In addition, but outside the balance of the 1980 Agreement, Norway will continue to make available permanently a quota of 1500 tonnes of redfish that it introduced for Community vessels on the accession of Portugal and Spain to the EC in 1986. In reality the exchange of letters made only modest changes to arrangements under the 1980 EC-Norway Fisheries Agreement, although it did have the significant consequence that Portugal and Spain were given shares of the additional EC cod and redfish quotas in Norwegian waters.

EC Member States have not always observed the quotas that they have been allocated in Norwegian waters. The third 'Common Fisheries Policy Compliance Scoreboard' produced by the Commission shows that in the period 2002–04 several Member States exceeded their quotas, although in most cases by quite small amounts (5 per cent or less).[183] Earlier, however, Member States' failure to comply was on occasion on such a scale that the Commission instituted proceedings under Article 226 EC. A number of those proceedings resulted in the Court finding

---

[179] OJ 1994 L1/3.

[180] For further details, see Churchill, R R. and Ørebech, P, 'The European Economic Area and Fisheries' *IJMCL* 8 (1993), 453 at 454–7. See also Chapter 7.   [181] Ibid, 457–8.

[182] OJ 1993 L346/26.

[183] *Third Edition of the Common Fisheries Compliance Scoreboard* (2005), Tables 3a, 3b, and 3c, available on the website of DG Mare.

Member States to have exceeded their quotas in Norwegian waters.[184] The annual reports on its fisheries relations with other States published by the Norwegian Government[185] show that since 2002 the officially recorded catches for the EC as a whole have not generally exceeded EC quotas in Norwegian waters, except to a limited degree in the case of herring and mackerel. From the point of the management and well-being of stocks, it is the performance of the EC as a whole that is significant, not that of its individual Member States.

The extension of their fisheries jurisdiction to 200 nm by the EC and Norway in the late 1970s resulted in many of the commercially important fish stocks of the North Sea and Skagerrak becoming shared stocks. As mentioned earlier, the 1980 EC-Norway Fisheries Agreement provides for the cooperative management of those shared stocks.[186] In practice such management takes place through annual meetings between the parties, at which they determine total allowable catches (TACs) for each of their shared stocks for the following year, based on the recommendations of the ICES, and then allocate those TACs between them. The principle governing such allocation is that of 'zonal attachment', ie each party's share of the TAC should correspond to the proportion of the stock which is of catchable size found in its economic/fishing zone.[187] The parties also consult on the other conservation and management measures that they apply within their waters with a view to harmonizing such measures as far as possible.

These arrangements for the cooperative management of shared stocks have not always worked well. In the early years there were tensions, as the two parties had different management objectives.[188] Norway was also in favour of long-term management decisions, but found that it took some time and effort to persuade the EC of the value of such an approach. Nevertheless, the EC was eventually persuaded, and since 1999 there have been agreed long-term

---

[184] See, for example, Case C-244/89 *Commission v France* [1991] ECR I-163 (one quota in 1986); Case C-140/00 *Commission v United Kingdom* [2002] ECR I-10379 (various quotas in the period 1991–96); Case C-317/02 *Commission v Ireland*, judgment of 18 November 2004 (unpublished) (cod quotas in 1995 and 1996); Case C-271/02 *Commission v Sweden*, judgment of 16 December 2004 (unpublished) (various quotas in 1995 and 1996); and Case C-332/03 *Commission v Portugal*, judgment of 26 May 2005 (unpublished) (various quotas in 1995 and 1996). Unpublished judgments may be found on the website of the Court.

[185] The most recent such report at the time of writing was Norwegian Parliamentary Paper St meld Nr 34 (2007–2008) (available, in Norwegian, on the website of the Norwegian Ministry of Fisheries).

[186] Art 7. The main such stocks are cod, haddock, herring, mackerel, plaice, saithe, and whiting.

[187] Norwegian Government, *Markedsutvalgets Rapport Nr. XIV om De Europeiske Felleskap* (Oslo, 1980), 104.

[188] Holden, MJ, 'Management of Fisheries Resources: the Experience of the European Economic Community' in OECD, *Experiences in the Management of National Fishing Zones* (Paris: OECD, 1984), 113 at 115–16.

management strategies for shared stocks of cod, haddock, herring, mackerel, and saithe.[189] There have also been disagreements as to how TACs should be allocated between the parties, particularly as regards mackerel. The position with mackerel was complicated because the EC did not initially agree with Norway that mackerel was a shared stock, only conceding that it was so in the late 1980s. Due in part to changes in the migration patterns of mackerel, it is recognized that the stock is also shared with the Faroe Islands, with whom there has been joint management since 1999. The mackerel stock also migrates to the high seas, so that it is not only a shared stock but also a straddling stock and subject to management by the North-East Atlantic Fisheries Commission (on which, see section 6 below).[190] Finally, there is continuing friction between the parties over discards. Norway prohibits discards, whereas the CFP does not (and indeed in some respects encourages discarding). The EC is yet to address the discard problem satisfactorily (see further Chapter 4).

The practical results of joint management by the EC and Norway of their shared stocks have been rather mixed.[191] During much of the 1980s and 1990s there was considerable overfishing and, probably as a result, the spawning stock biomass of most of the stocks fell below safe biological limits. Since the late 1990s stricter management measures have been introduced. This, together with a number of good year classes for several of the stocks, has meant that the spawning stock biomass of the majority of stocks is now within safe biological limits. The exceptions are cod and herring. In the case of cod, the complete ban on directed fishing called for by the ICES every year since 2003 has not been followed, although the TAC is a now a small fraction of what it was a decade ago. The spawning stock biomass, perhaps partly as a result, remains well outside safe biological limits. In the case of herring, six poor year classes in succession since 2002, combined with TACs being set since 2001 at higher levels than those recommended by the ICES, have meant that there has been a drastic decrease in the spawning stock biomass since 2004.

Faroe Islands

The second agreement that the EC has in the North Atlantic is with the Faroe Islands. When Denmark joined the EC at the beginning of 1973, the Faroe Islands (which are part of the Kingdom of Denmark but have a high degree of autonomy) remained outside the EC and have continued to do so ever since (see further Chapter 2). Following the extension of fisheries jurisdiction to 200 nm by both EC

---

[189] For details of these strategies, see Norwegian Parliamentary Paper St meld Nr 45 (2003–2004), 49–51 (available, in Norwegian, on the website of the Norwegian Ministry of Fisheries). See also Chapter 4.

[190] See further Norwegian Parliamentary Paper St meld Nr 34 (2007–2008), 24 and 47–9.

[191] The information that follows in the remainder of this paragraph is taken from Norwegian Parliamentary Paper St meld Nr 34 (2007–2008), 45–53.

Member States and the Faroe Islands in the late 1970s, the EC negotiated and signed an access agreement with the government of Denmark and the home government of the Faroe Islands.[192] It is, of course, rather odd that the EC concludes, under its exclusive treaty-making powers, a bilateral treaty with one of its Member States. That situation results from the fact that the Faroe Islands are not part of the EC and that the Danish government is responsible for their international relations. The Agreement is based on the principle of reciprocal access of the vessels of the parties to each other's waters and is very similar in its content to the EC's Agreement with Norway. Like the latter, the Agreement also has provisions on the management of shared stocks, which function in a similar way to the EC-Norway Agreement. As in the case of Norway, EC quotas are allocated amongst the Member States according to the principle of relative stability, which (as happened in relation to the EC's practice concerning Norway) was the subject of an unsuccessful challenge by Spain.[193]

Greenland

Unlike the Faroe Islands, Greenland (which is also part of the Kingdom of Denmark) was included in the EC when Denmark became a member in 1973 (see further Chapter 2). When Greenland's fishing limits were extended to 200 nm in 1977, vessels from some other parts of the EC were allocated quotas within the new limits. In 1985, following the introduction of home rule in 1979, Greenland withdrew from the EC. Among the arrangements governing withdrawal was a fisheries agreement.[194] The Agreement, whose aim was to enable Community fishing vessels to continue to enjoy the access to Greenlandic waters that they would have had if Greenland had remained in the EC,[195] permitted Community vessels to fish under licence for specified tonnages of fish in return for the payment of 'financial compensation' and the admission to the EC of fishery exports from Greenland free of customs duties. The amount of fish that Community vessels could take and the level of financial compensation that the EC had to pay in return were fixed in periodic protocols to the Agreement. The EC's quotas in Greenlandic waters were distributed among the Member States in accordance with the principle of relative stability. As with the application of that principle to the EC's quotas in Norwegian and Faroese waters, that practice was the subject of an unsuccessful challenge by Spain (and Portugal).[196]

In 1994 the Agreement was amended so as to encourage the formation of joint ventures and joint enterprises between Community fishing vessel owners and

---

[192] Agreement on Fisheries between the European Economic Community, of the one part, and the Government of Denmark and the Home Government of the Faroe Islands, of the other part, 1977, OJ 1980 L226/12.   [193] Case C-70/90 *Spain v Council* [1992] ECR I-1519.

[194] Agreement on Fisheries between the EEC, on the one hand, and the Government of Denmark and the local Government of Greenland, on the other, 1985, OJ 1985 L29/9.

[195] MacLeod *et al*, *The External Relations*, 250.

[196] Joined Cases C-63/90 and C-67/90 *Portugal and Spain v Council* [1992] ECR I-5073.

Greenlandic enterprises.[197] A joint venture was defined as an association based on a contractual agreement between 'Community shipowners and physical or legal persons in Greenland' with the aim of jointly fishing for Greenlandic quotas by vessels flying the flag of an EC Member State and sharing the costs of doing so, with a view to priority supply of the EC market. A joint enterprise was defined as a company regulated by Greenlandic law comprising one or more Community shipowners and one or more partners in Greenland with the aim of fishing for Greenlandic quotas by a vessel flying the flag of Greenland with a view to priority supply of the EC market.[198] EC financial assistance was available for the formation of joint ventures and joint enterprises.[199]

In 2006 the 1985 Agreement was replaced by a fisheries partnership agreement.[200] The basis and conditions of access of Community fishing vessels to Greenlandic waters remain broadly the same as under the 1985 Agreement, and, as under the 1994 amendment to that Agreement, joint enterprises and joint ventures are encouraged. What is new (and presumably constitutes the 'partnership' element) is provision for a degree of EC involvement in the management of fisheries in Greenlandic waters. Greenland undertakes to 'continue the planning of a sectoral fisheries policy and manage its implementation through annual and multi-annual programmes in the light of objectives identified by common accord between the Parties. The Parties shall to that end continue the policy dialogue on the necessary reforms.'[201] The parties are also to monitor the evolution of resources in Greenland's EEZ. After consultation with the EC, Greenland is to adopt such conservation and management measures as it deems necessary to achieve the objectives of its fisheries policy.[202] Part of the EC's financial contribution for the access of its vessels to Greenland's waters is to be earmarked for 'improving and implementing a sectoral fisheries policy in Greenland with a view to securing continued responsible fishing in the Greenlandic EEZ': this contribution is to be managed by the Greenlandic authorities according to objectives agreed jointly by the parties.[203] The EC's fisheries partnership agreement with Greenland is similar to the fisheries partnership agreements that the EC has

[197] For the amendment, see OJ 1994 L351/16.

[198] These definitions were contained not in the amendment to the Agreement but in the Third Protocol to the Agreement, OJ 1994 L351/2, Art 3, adopted at the same time as the amendment. The definitions are repeated in the Fourth Protocol, OJ 2001 L209/2, Art 4.

[199] Third Protocol, Arts 5 and 6. Under the Fourth Protocol, Art 6, EC funding was available for joint enterprises, but not joint ventures.

[200] Fisheries Partnership Agreement between the European Community on the one hand, and the Government of Denmark and the Home Rule Government of Greenland, on the other hand, OJ 2007 L172/4.   [201] Fisheries Partnership Agreement, Art 3(2).

[202] Fisheries Partnership Agreement, Art 4.

[203] Protocol to the Fisheries Partnership Agreement, Art 4. See also the Fisheries Partnership Agreement, Art 7.

concluded in recent years with many developing States, which are discussed in subsection 4.3 below.

Iceland

The fourth country in the North Atlantic with which the EC has an access agreement is Iceland. When EC Member States extended their fishing limits to 200 nm in 1977, the EC sought to negotiate a reciprocal access agreement with Iceland. However, no doubt at least in part because of its then recent history of poor fisheries relations with the EC and various of its Member States, Iceland showed little interest in such an agreement.[204] Thereafter fisheries relations between Iceland and the EC remained moribund until the conclusion in 1992 of the Agreement on the European Economic Area (on which, see above). As with Norway, a separate bilateral agreement was concluded between the EC and Iceland at the same time as the EEA Agreement.[205]

The bilateral agreement provides that Iceland is to give the EC access to a quota of 3,000 tonnes of redfish to be fished in certain specified areas of its EEZ. In return, the EC is to make available for Icelandic vessels a 30,000 tonne capelin quota that it holds in Greenland's waters under its agreement with Greenland. Shortly after their EEA-related agreement was concluded, the EC and Iceland signed an Agreement on Fisheries and the Marine Environment.[206] This latter agreement is similar to the reciprocal access agreements with Norway and the Faroe Islands discussed earlier. On the parties' fishing opportunities in each other's waters, the Agreement simply states that the parties shall consult annually on 'the allocation of fishing possibilities for each Party with a view to obtaining a mutually satisfactory balance in their relations in the fisheries field'.[207] Each party is to grant access to the vessels of the other 'to fish for the allocations which may result' from their annual consultations.[208] Since the earlier bilateral agreement remains in force, the allocations provided for in that agreement continue to apply. The principal annual Regulations of recent years do not indicate any allocations of fishing opportunities made under Article 4 of the second agreement.

Russia

The final State in the North Atlantic with which the EC has an access agreement is Russia. Attempts to negotiate an agreement were originally made when the then Soviet Union and EC Member States extended their fisheries jurisdiction in 1977, but negotiations broke down over the Soviet Union's unwillingness to recognize the EC as a negotiating party.[209] Negotiations resumed in 1988 but for many years made no real progress. What appears finally to have been the spur to concluding an agreement was the enlargement of the EC in 2004, which resulted in nearly all of

---

[204] Churchill, *EEC Fisheries Law*, 181–2 and 263–4.
[205] Agreement concerning Fisheries, 1992, OJ 1993 L346/20.   [206] OJ 1993 L161/2.
[207] Agreement, Art 4(1).   [208] Agreement, Art 4(2).
[209] Churchill, *EEC Fisheries Law*, 181.

the Baltic Sea falling within the fisheries jurisdiction of EC Member States and the consequent withdrawal of the EC from the International Baltic Sea Fisheries Commission.[210] An agreement was initialled in the summer of 2006,[211] but as at the end of November 2008 had not been formally concluded by the Council on behalf of the EC. The Agreement,[212] which applies only to the Baltic Sea and replaces existing bilateral agreements between Russia and individual EC Member States,[213] deals with much more than just access. Its objective is to 'ensure a close co-operation between the Parties on the basis of the principle of equitable and mutual benefit for the purpose of conservation, sustainable exploitation and management of any straddling, associated and dependent stocks in the Baltic Sea'.[214] Confusingly, the Agreement uses the term 'straddling stock' not in the usual sense of a stock straddling the boundary between the EEZ and the high seas, but to mean 'any stock of fish that migrates regularly across the delimitations of Exclusive Economic Zones of the Parties in the Baltic Sea',[215] a concept to which the term 'shared stock' is usually applied. On access, the Agreement is surprisingly vague compared with the agreements discussed above. Article 5(1) provides that 'each Party may, on the basis of mutual benefit and in compliance with its own legislation, allow fishing vessels of the other Party to fish within the Exclusive Economic Zone of this Party in the Baltic Sea', while Article 5(2) goes on to state that 'the Parties may exchange quotas in the Baltic Sea on a reciprocal basis'. Where access is granted, the vessels of one party fishing in the EEZ of the other must be licensed by, and are subject to the legislative and enforcement jurisdiction of, the other party.[216] In relation to 'straddling stocks' (ie shared stocks in the particular case of this Agreement), the parties are to establish management measures through the adoption of, *inter alia*, TACs (which are to be allocated between the parties on the basis of the 'historical distribution of fishing possibilities'), long-term management plans, limitation of fishing effort, and technical measures.[217]

In 2008, the European Commission and Russia signed a memorandum of understanding on dialogue on fisheries,[218] albeit not specific to the Baltic.

Other North Atlantic States

Although the EC currently has access agreements with only five States or territories in the North Atlantic, it has in the past had agreements with a number of

---

[210] *Proposal for a Council Regulation on the conclusion of the Agreement between the European Community and the Government of the Russian Federation on co-operation in fisheries and the conservation of the living resources in the Baltic Sea*, COM(2006) 868, 22.12.2006, p 2.   [211] COM(2006) 868, p 2.

[212] Agreement between the European Community and the Government of the Russian Federation on co-operation in fisheries and the conservation of the living resources in the Baltic Sea, COM(2006) 868.   [213] Agreement, Arts 2 and 18(2).

[214] Agreement, Art 4(1).   [215] Agreement, Art 1(f).   [216] Agreement, Arts 7 and 8.

[217] Agreement, Art 5(3).

[218] European Commission press release, 25 April 2008: 'European Commission and Russia agree to strengthen dialogue on fisheries' (available on the website of DG Mare).

other States. They include Canada (to whose waters Community fishing vessels had access between 1979 and 1987) and the USA (to whose waters Community vessels had access between 1977 and 1989), as well as six Member States prior to their accession to the EC (Estonia, Finland, Latvia, Lithuania, Spain, and Sweden) with whom there was reciprocal access similar to that with Norway.[219] The agreements with Estonia, Latvia, and Lithuania differed to some degree from the usual reciprocal access agreements because in addition to reciprocal access, they stipulated that the EC was to provide the three States with funding for training and that the parties were to promote the establishment of joint venture arrangements (in the case of the 1992 agreements) or joint enterprise arrangements (in the case of the 1996 agreements) in the fisheries sector.

4.3 Developing States

The developing States with which the EC has concluded fisheries access agreements have changed and increased over time. Originally they were mainly West African States because it was largely in that region that distant-water fishing by vessels of the then nine EC Member States took place when the first agreements were being negotiated following the general extension of fisheries jurisdiction to 200 nm by coastal States in the late 1970s. Iberian accession in 1986 gave a new impetus to the negotiation of access agreements, as Portugal and Spain each had bilateral agreements with a number of African States with which the EC had not at that time concluded agreements. Under the 1985 Act of Accession the EC had undertaken to take over the management of those agreements and eventually to replace them with agreements between the EC and the third States concerned.[220] Furthermore, there was a view that additional fishing opportunities should be sought for Portuguese and Spanish vessels in the waters of developing States to offset Portuguese and Spanish unhappiness with the very restricted access of their vessels to the waters of other Member States that they had been given under the 1985 Act of Accession.[221] Over the following years access agreements with many more African States were concluded, as well as with one Latin American State and, from 2005, with some States in the Pacific Ocean, where Community vessels had begun to fish.

There have been three 'generations' of access agreements with developing States. The first generation agreements were concluded from the late 1970s

---

[219] For details of the agreements with Canada, the USA, Finland, Spain, and Sweden, see Churchill, *EEC Fisheries Law*, 177–8 and 181–4. For the agreements with the other three States, see EEC-Estonia Agreement on Fisheries Relations, 1992, OJ 1993 L56/2; EEC-Latvia Agreement on Fisheries Relations, 1992, OJ 1993 L56/6; and EEC-Lithuania Agreement on Fisheries Relations, 1992, OJ 1993 L56/10. In 1996 those agreements were replaced by three new agreements, OJ 1996 L332/2, 7, and 17.
[220] Act of Accession, OJ 1985 L302/1, Arts 167 and 354.
[221] On such restricted access, see Chapter 1.

onwards: the States with which they were concluded are listed below. As is explained later, nearly all of these agreements have been replaced or, if still formally in force, are no longer operational. The first generation agreements were essentially framework ones, with the details of EC fisheries access set out in protocols to the agreements. The protocols generally had a shorter duration than the agreements, typically of between two and five years. When a protocol expired, a new protocol was usually (but not invariably) concluded. Unless an agreement had a protocol that was in force, it was effectively non-operational. The main features of the various agreements and protocols were broadly similar, even if some of their details changed over time. They permitted limited access by Community fishing vessels to the waters of the States concerned, such limits being expressed in terms of the number, tonnage, and type of vessel. Sometimes catch limits were also stipulated. It is not clear how the number of vessels permitted access was calculated, or whether it was related to any surplus catch that might have been available in the EEZ of the developing State concerned. The Council allocated the total number of licences granted to Community fishing vessels under the relevant protocol among its Member States, the main criterion being past fishing performance by Member States' vessels in the waters of the third State in question. In return for the access of its vessels to the waters of those third States, the EC paid 'financial compensation', part of which was normally ear-marked to be used for particular projects to assist the third State concerned, such as fisheries research, enforcement, administrative support, training, the costs of membership of regional fisheries management organizations, and development of the local fishing industry. That part of the financial compensation not earmarked for specific projects could be spent by the third State concerned at its absolute discretion, and therefore may have been spent on matters quite unrelated to fisheries.

Community vessels given access to fish in the waters of a third State had to obtain a licence from that State, for which a fee had to be paid. The total amount paid in licence fees by Community vessel operators was normally about a quarter of the amount that the EC paid in financial compensation.[222] Thus, the cost of access for Community fishing vessels to the waters of developing States under the first generation agreements was borne primarily by the Community taxpayer, rather than by the fishing vessel owner (and, through the sale of the catch, ultimately the consumer). It was normally a condition of a licence that a Community vessel should employ one or more nationals from the third State concerned as crew, although that obligation could usually be avoided by paying an extra fee to that State. Where the obligation was observed, it meant that an access agreement not only provided a modest source of employment for the coastal State concerned but could also help to train local nationals in the use of more advanced technology. Under earlier protocols it was usually a further

---

[222] Court of Auditors, *Special Report No. 3/2001 concerning the Commission's Management of International Fisheries Agreements, together with the Commission's Replies*, OJ 2001 C210/1 at 26.

licence condition (although again one that could be avoided by paying an extra fee) that Community vessels should land part or all of their catches in the ports of the third State concerned, but that condition was abandoned in many of the later protocols to the first generation agreements. Such a requirement served a number of purposes—stimulating the domestic fish processing industry, providing food for the local population, and enabling catches to be more easily monitored. Many of the later protocols that did not contain a landing requirement nevertheless contained an exhortation to Community vessels to land part of their catches in the third State concerned. Other standard licence conditions included an obligation on Community vessels to observe the local coastal State's fisheries legislation and any relevant international regulations (such as those of the International Commission for the Conservation of Atlantic Tunas or the Indian Ocean Tuna Commission). All the agreements and/or protocols had provisions on monitoring and enforcement that were designed to secure the compliance of Community vessels with the conditions of their licences and local fisheries legislation. Such provisions, which were gradually tightened over time, included boarding and inspection at sea; reporting by vessels of their position and catch; the completion of log books; the employment of observers on board vessels to monitor their activities; and, in the case of those third States that had the necessary technological capacity, satellite monitoring of vessels. Finally, the agreements set up a joint committee to monitor their application.

The developing States with which the EC concluded first generation access agreements were Angola, Cape Verde, Comoros, Côte d'Ivoire, Equatorial Guinea, Gabon, Gambia, Guinea, Guinea-Bissau, Kiribati, Madagascar, Mauritania, Mauritius, Morocco, Mozambique, São Tomé and Príncipe, Senegal, Seychelles, Sierra Leone, and Tanzania. By November 2008 the majority of those agreements had been replaced by third generation agreements, as explained below, and the agreement with Angola had been denounced by the EC. The only first generation agreement still in force with an operational protocol was that with Guinea.[223] In addition, the first generation agreements with Equatorial Guinea,[224] Gambia,[225] Mauritius,[226] Senegal,[227] and Sierra Leone[228] formally remained in force, but most of them had not been operational for some years.[229] It may therefore be doubtful

[223] Agreement on Fishing off the Guinean Coast, 1983, OJ 1983 L111/2, as amended.

[224] Agreement on Fishing off the Coast of Equatorial Guinea, 1984, OJ 1984 L188/2.

[225] Agreement on Fishing off Gambia, 1987, OJ 1987 L146/3.

[226] Agreement on Fishing in Mauritian Waters, 1989, OJ 1989 L159/2, as amended.

[227] Agreement on Fisheries off the Coast of Senegal, 1979, OJ 1980 L226/18, as amended.

[228] Agreement on Fishing off Sierra Leone, 1990, OJ 1990 L125/28.

[229] The EC also concluded two first generation agreements with Tanzania, but neither appears ever to have come into force. See Agreement on Fishing off Tanzania, 1990, OJ 1990 L379/25, and the Agreement on Fishing in Tanzania's Fishing Zone, 2004, COM(2005) 693.

whether those agreements will eventually be replaced by third generation agreements.

Nearly all the developing States with which the EC concluded first generation access agreements are what are known as 'ACP States', that is to say they are parties to the Cotonou Agreement[230] and previously were parties to one or more of the four Lomé Conventions that preceded it.[231] This succession of agreements has been the EC's major vehicle for the conduct and promotion of its relations with developing States from Africa, the Caribbean, and the Pacific (ACP) concerning trade and economic and development cooperation. The Cotonou Agreement and three of the four preceding Lomé Conventions have provisions on fisheries cooperation.[232] Those provisions, *inter alia*, note the willingness of the ACP States to negotiate agreements providing for the access of Community fishing vessels to their waters on 'mutually satisfactory conditions'.[233] According to the Lomé Conventions, this last phrase is understood to include the payment of financial compensation by the EC:[234] there is, however, no equivalent understanding in the Cotonou Agreement. The provisions on fisheries access agreements that were first included in the second Lomé Convention reflected the already existing, if relatively limited, practice of the EC and developing States at that time.[235] Subsequently that practice and the corresponding provisions of the later Lomé Conventions and Cotonou Agreement have continued to evolve in tandem.

In 1991, in the course of its review of the CFP (on which, see Chapter 1), the Commission suggested the conclusion of a 'second generation' of fisheries access agreements with developing States.[236] It did not follow up that suggestion with a more detailed proposal until 1996, when it published a paper advocating such agreements.[237] Under that proposal access to the waters of third States would primarily be based on joint ventures and joint enterprises (of the kind described above in relation to Greenland) in order to achieve closer and more lasting cooperation with third States, particularly in terms of transfer of technology,

---

[230] [Cotonou] Partnership Agreement, 2000, OJ 2000 L317/3, as amended.

[231] First Lomé Convention, 1975, OJ 1976 L25/3; Second Lomé Convention, 1979, OJ 1980 L347/1; Third Lomé Convention, 1984, OJ 1986 L86/3; and Fourth Lomé Convention, 1990, OJ 1991 L229/3.

[232] Cotonou Agreement, Arts 23 and 53; Second Lomé Convention, Annex XVIII; Third Lomé Convention, Arts 50–59; Fourth Lomé Convention, Arts 58–68.

[233] See, for example, Cotonou Agreement, Art 53(1).

[234] See, for example, the Fourth Lomé Convention, Art 68.

[235] Second Lomé Convention, Annex XVIII, Arts 2–4.

[236] *Report 1991 from the Commission to the Council and the European Parliament on the Common Fisheries Policy*, SEC(91) 2288, pp 40 and 81–2.

[237] *Communication from the Commission to the Council and the European Parliament: fisheries agreements: current situation and perspectives*, COM(96) 488, 30.10.1996, pp 11–12.

supply of capital and equipment, vocational training, development of distribution networks, and the strengthening of scientific and technical cooperation. However, only one second generation agreement proper was concluded, an agreement with Argentina,[238] which was in force between 1994 and 1999. Some of the features of second generation agreements were found in the now defunct first generation agreements concluded with Mauritania and Morocco in 1996.[239] In general, however, developing States appear not to have been much interested in such agreements.

Having being compelled to abandon the idea of second generation agreements because of such lack of interest, the Commission in 2002 proposed that those first generation agreements still current should be replaced by fisheries partnership agreements (hereafter, 'FPAs').[240] While continuing to maintain the access of Community distant-water vessels to the waters of developing States, FPAs would strengthen cooperation between the EC and those States so as to ensure the 'implementation of a sustainable fisheries policy and a rational and responsible exploitation of the resources in the mutual interest of the Parties concerned'.[241] The Commission's proposals were endorsed by the Council in July 2004,[242] and the first FPAs signed in 2005. As of the end of November 2008 the EC had concluded FPAs with the following fourteen States: Cape Verde,[243] Comoros,[244] Côte d'Ivoire,[245] Gabon,[246] Guinea-Bissau,[247] Kiribati,[248] Madagascar,[249]

---

[238] Agreement on Relations in the Sea Fisheries Sector between the EEC and the Argentine Republic, OJ 1993 L318/1. For a detailed discussion of the Agreement, see Daverede, A, 'The 1993 Fishery Agreement between the European Community and the Argentine Republic' *Leiden Journal of International Law* 7 (1994), 5.

[239] OJ 1996 L334/20 (Mauritania) and OJ 1997 L30/5 (Morocco).

[240] *Communication from the Commission on an integrated framework for fisheries partnership agreements with third countries*, COM(2002) 637, 23.12.2002.   [241] COM(2002) 637, p 3.

[242] Council of the European Union, 2599th Council Meeting, Agriculture and Fisheries, 19 July 2004, press release, 11234/2/04 Rev 2 (Presse 221), 22–6.

[243] Fisheries Partnership Agreement between the European Community and the Republic of Cape Verde, with protocol, OJ 2006 L414/3.

[244] Partnership Agreement in the Fisheries Sector between the European Community and the Union of the Comoros, with protocol, OJ 2006 L290/7.

[245] Fisheries Partnership Agreement between the Republic of Côte d'Ivoire and the European Community, with protocol, OJ 2008 L48/41.

[246] Fisheries Partnership Agreement between the Gabonese Republic and the European Community, with protocol, OJ 2007 L109/3.

[247] Fisheries Partnership Agreement between the European Community and the Republic of Guinea-Bissau, with protocol, OJ 2007 L342/5.

[248] Fisheries Partnership Agreement between the European Community on the one hand, and the Republic of Kiribati, on the other, with protocol, OJ 2007 L205/3.

[249] Fisheries Partnership Agreement between the Republic of Madagascar and the European Community, with protocol, OJ 2007 L331/7.

Mauritania,[250] Micronesia,[251] Morocco,[252] Mozambique,[253] São Tomé e Prín-cipe,[254] Seychelles,[255] and Solomon Islands.[256] Except in the case of Micronesia and the Solomon Islands, those agreements all replace first generation agreements.[257]

While the FPAs differ from each other on points of detail, their basic structure is the same. Like the first generation agreements, much of the detail is contained in protocols to the agreements, rather than the agreements themselves, and, as with the earlier agreements, an FPA is operational only if there is an accompanying protocol in force. As with the first generation agreements, an FPA permits a lim-ited number of Community vessels to fish in the EEZ of the third State concerned under licence (for which the vessel owner pays a fee) in return for which the EC pays financial compensation. The ratio of the licence fee to the amount of the EC's financial compensation has not so far increased significantly, despite the Com-mission's view that it should.[258] The FPAs also contain similar provisions to the earlier agreements regarding the obligation of Community vessels to comply with the legislation of the third State concerned, enforcement, and the establishment of a joint committee to monitor implementation of the agreement. There is no obligation on Community vessels to land part of their catch in the third State, but if they do, the licence fee payable by the vessel owner is reduced. What is different between the first generation agreements and the FPAs (and what constitutes the 'partnership' element) is some of the objectives of the FPAs, and the means by which those objectives are to be achieved. Such objectives include the promotion of responsible and sustainable fishing in the waters of the third State concerned; the development of the third State's fishing industry; the establishment of a dialogue and prior consultations over the implementation of the third State's sectoral fish-eries policy and the potential impact of EC policies and measures on the third

[250] Fisheries Partnership Agreement between the European Community and the Islamic Republic of Mauritania, with protocol, OJ 2006 L343/4.

[251] Partnership Agreement between the European Community and the Federated States of Micro-nesia on fishing in the Federated States of Micronesia, with protocol, OJ 2006 L151/3.

[252] Fisheries Partnership Agreement between the European Community and the Kingdom of Morocco, with protocol, OJ 2006 L141/4.

[253] Fisheries Partnership Agreement between the European Community and the Republic of Mozambique, with protocol, OJ 2007 L331/35.

[254] Fisheries Partnership Agreement between the Democratic Republic of São Tomé and Príncipe and the European Community, with protocol, OJ 2007 L205/36.

[255] Fisheries Partnership Agreement between the European Community and the Republic of Sey-chelles, with protocol, OJ 2006 L290/2.

[256] Partnership Agreement between the European Community and Solomon Islands on Fishing off Solomon Islands, with protocol, OJ 2006 L105/34.

[257] For a detailed study of FPAs, see Walmsley, SF, Barnes, CT, Payne, IA, and Howard, CA, *Comparative Study of the Impact of Fisheries Partnership Agreements: Technical Report* (MRAG, CRE, & NRI, 2007), available on the website of the UK government's Department for Environment, Food and Rural Affairs (Defra). [258] COM(2002) 637, p 8.

State's fishing industry; and the promotion of partnerships between companies to develop, in the common interest, economic and related activities in the fisheries sector. To achieve those objectives a number of measures are to be taken. First, the parties are to cooperate to monitor the state of the fishery resources in the waters of the third State, to which end a joint scientific committee is to meet annually. Based on the conclusions of such meetings and the best scientific advice available, the parties are to consult and, where necessary and by mutual agreement, take measures to ensure the sustainable development of fishery resources. Secondly, part of the EC's financial compensation is to be allocated towards developing and implementing a national fisheries policy for the third State based on responsible and sustainable fishing and spent by the third State in accordance with jointly agreed objectives and guidelines. Thirdly, the parties are to endeavour to create conditions favourable to the promotion of cooperation between their enterprises by encouraging the establishment of an environment favourable to the development of business and investment and to promote the economic integration of EC operators into the third State's fishing industry.

The first generation access agreements with developing States were the subject of considerable criticism, not only from environmental and development NGOs (including an NGO specifically concerned with this issue, the Coalition for Fair Fisheries Arrangements)[259] and academics,[260] but also from within the EC itself, in particular from the Court of Auditors.[261] A major criticism was that the financial compensation paid under the EC's access agreements with developing States was effectively a form of subsidy: if the EC had not paid financial compensation, Community fishing vessel owners wishing to fish in the waters of those States would either not have been able to do so or would have had to pay a substantially higher licence fee. There were also other forms of subsidy related to access (although not funded by the fisheries access agreements themselves), such as the payment of compensation to fishing vessel owners no longer able to fish in the waters of a developing State because of the termination of the relevant access

---

[259] See, for example, Gorez, B, *Policy Study: EU-ACP Fisheries Agreements* (Brussels: Coalition for Fair Fisheries Arrangements, 2005); Johnstone, N, *The Economics of Fisheries Access Agreements: Perspectives on the EU-Senegal Case* (London: International Institute for Environment and Development, 1996); Sporrong, N, Coffey, C, and Bevins, K, *Fisheries Agreements with Third Countries—Is the EU moving towards Sustainable Development?* (London: Institute for European Environmental Policy, 2002); and WWF, *Fishing Madness* (Godalming: WWF, 2002). There are links to a considerable number of relevant NGO reports on the website of Agritrade.

[260] See, for example, Acheampong, A, *Coherence between EU Fisheries Agreements and EU Development Co-Operation: The Case of West Africa* (ECDPM Working Paper No 52 (1997)); and Kaczynski, VM and Fluharty, DL, 'European Policies in West Africa: Who benefits from Fisheries Agreements?' *Marine Policy* 26 (2002), 75.   [261] Court of Auditors, *Special Report No 3/2001.*

agreement with the EC[262] and, bizarrely and quite illogically (given the over-capacity in EC fishing fleets), the payment of grants to owners to build *new* vessels to fish in developing States' waters.[263] It was pointed out in Chapter 3 that one of the biggest problems currently facing world fisheries is over-capacity, a problem that is exacerbated by high levels of subsidy. By its practice in relation to first generation access agreements with developing States, the EC was contributing to this problem.

A second criticism of the first generation agreements was the failure of Community vessels frequently to observe third States' fisheries legislation (particularly in relation to the catching of immature fish, incomplete or incorrect log book entries, fishing in areas closed to them, and crewing requirements), as well as the EC's own control and enforcement regulations (especially in relation to incomplete and incorrect landing declarations).[264] It was also alleged that EC vessels discarded a significant amount of unwanted by-catches.[265] Those practices probably contributed to the overfishing of stocks in the waters of a number of developing States.

Thirdly, Community fishing vessels were frequently in competition with local fishermen to catch the same fish, often on unequal terms. This inequality arose because EC fleets were effectively subsidized (as explained), whereas local fleets usually were not, and because Community fishing vessels probably had more effective equipment for catching fish. Such competition led in some cases to local fishermen being put out of work and threats to the continued viability of some coastal communities dependent on fishing, as well as less fish for the nutritional needs of local communities.[266] The discarding by Community vessels of a substantial amount of their by-catch may also have deprived the local population of valuable food.

If they operate as intended, the FPAs should address some of the above criticisms, particularly that concerning overfishing in the waters of developing States. The FPAs do not, however, deal with the criticism that the EC is effectively

---

[262] For example, when the protocol to the EC's agreement with Angola lapsed in 2004 without being renewed, the EC paid compensation to the sixteen vessels affected: see *Proposal for a Council Regulation Denouncing the Agreement between the European Economic Community and the Government of the People's Republic of Angola on Fishing off Angola and derogating from Regulation (EC) No 2792/1999*, COM (2005) 677, 21.12.2005, p 2.

[263] For example, in the mid-1990s the EC provided co-financing for the construction of fifty-four new vessels to fish in Moroccan waters: see Court of Auditors, *Special Report No. 3/2001*, p 9.

[264] Court of Auditors, *Special Report No. 3/2001*, p 11; Gorez, *Policy Study*, 12–14; and Kaczynski and Fluharty, 'European Policies in West Africa', 78.

[265] Environmental Justice Foundation, *What's the Catch? Reducing By-Catch in EU Distant-Water Fisheries* (2005), 3, available on the website of the Foundation; Johnstone, *Economics of Fisheries Access Agreements*, 17; and Kaczynski and Fluharty, 'European Policies in West Africa', 83.

[266] Kaczynski and Fluharty, 'European Policies in West Africa', 82; and *The Courier (Africa–Caribbean–Pacific–European Community)*, No 156 (March–April 1996), 10–11 and No 163 (May–June 1997), 9–10 and 22.

subsidizing the export of its over-capacity to developing States' waters. It is true that vessel owners now pay a slightly higher proportion of the costs of access, but the EC taxpayer is still paying around two-thirds of the cost in most cases.[267] It is also the case that a larger proportion of the EC's financial compensation is spent on developing the third State's management capacity, but in a number of FPAs over half still goes to pay purely for access.[268] EC aid is also available under the European Fisheries Fund to adapt the Community fishing fleet in case of the non-renewal of a fisheries access agreement or 'a substantial cut in fishing opportunities under an international agreement or other arrangement'.[269] It is possible that the current position may eventually have to change as a result of developments at the WTO. For several years the WTO has been trying to negotiate a special regime to deal with fisheries subsidies, although no agreement is yet imminent.[270] Under some proposals that are being considered, payments for the access of distant-water fishing fleets to the waters of other States would be prohibited.[271]

One final comment that may be made about the EC's access agreements with developing States is that there is a certain irony in the fact that in the FPAs the EC undertakes to advise and assist developing States on how to manage the fisheries in their waters sustainably when it has so signally failed yet to do so in Community waters.

4.4 Outermost regions

There are separate arrangements relating to the access by vessels from third States to the maritime zones of the French overseas departments of French Guiana, Guadeloupe, and Martinique, which all fall within the scope of the CFP (see further Chapter 2). In the case of Guadeloupe and Martinique, an Agreement with Dominica, which was signed in 1993,[272] permits vessels from Dominica to fish in the 200 nm zones of Guadeloupe and Martinique and fishermen from the latter territories to fish in the 200 nm EEZ of Dominica.[273] The aim is that such access shall produce a 'mutually satisfactory balance' in the parties' fisheries relations.[274] There is thus, in this respect, considerable similarity between this Agreement and the reciprocal access Agreements that the EC has with Norway and the Faroe

---

[267] Walmsley et al, *Comparative Study*, 9.   [268] Walmsley et al, *Comparative Study*, 46–7.

[269] Council Regulation (EC) No 1198/2006 of 27 July 2006 on the European Fisheries Fund, OJ 2006 L223/1, Art 21(a)(iii).

[270] For a useful review of developments to the end of 2007, see Benitah, M, *Ongoing WTO Negotiations on Fisheries Subsidies* (ASIL Insights, 2004, with 2007 addendum, available on the website of the American Society of International Law). For subsequent developments, see the websites of Agritrade and the WTO. See also *El Anzuelo* 20 (2008), 4–5.   [271] Benitah, *Ongoing WTO Negotiations*.

[272] Agreement on Fisheries between the European Community and Dominica, 1993, OJ 1993 L299/2.   [273] Agreement, Arts 1 and 2.

[274] Agreement, Art 4(1).

Islands. However, the Agreement with Dominica has an additional element, reflecting the fact that Dominica is an ACP State. Article 5 provides that with a view to obtaining a 'satisfactory level of fishing possibilities' for the EC, the latter shall pay financial compensation as specified in the protocol to the Agreement 'in the event that there is an imbalance in catch possibilities'. Finally, the Agreement, like the EC's Agreements with Norway and the Faroe Islands, provides for the cooperative management of shared stocks.[275]

The situation is rather different in the case of French Guiana, whose 200 nm zone is probably the only area to which the CFP applies where there is a surplus of the total allowable catch available for foreign fishermen. For reasons that are not clear to the authors, the vessels of third States have been given access to fish under licence for that surplus since the late 1970s, not by means of bilateral agreements, but unilaterally under a succession of annual EC Regulations.[276] The third States concerned have varied somewhat over time. In 2008 only Venezuela was given access:[277] in the past vessels from Barbados, Brazil, Guyana, Japan, South Korea, Suriname, Trinidad and Tobago, and the USA have also been given access.

5 Access to third States' waters other than under EC fisheries access agreements

The EC's fisheries access agreements and fisheries partnership agreements (FPAs) with third States are not the only means for vessels flagged to Member States to fish in third States' waters. Another option is for the owner or operator of such a vessel to enter into a so-called 'private licence' with the third State in question, ie a licence granted by the third State directly to the owner or operator enabling the latter's vessel(s) to fish in the third State's waters. In practice, such licences are certainly granted but there is a significant lack of transparency regarding how many exist and the nature of their terms. Available information about them may improve in the light of Regulation 1006/2008 (see further below).[278]

Some examples of private arrangements involving fishing vessels flagged to EC Member States are provided in a report by Walmsley et al published in 2007.[279] The report refers, inter alia, to agreements between Mauritania and an Irish fishing company and between Madagascar and Spanish fishing associations.[280] It notes that 'a private fishing agreement for a number of EU tuna fishing vessels' has been concluded with Senegal.[281] It also refers to Mozambique's 'long-standing contracts

---

[275] Agreement, Art 3.

[276] In recent years these arrangements have been contained in the EC's principal annual Regulation, at the time of writing Reg 40/2008.   [277] Reg 40/2008, Art 14.

[278] Reg 1006/2008, Arts 11(2) and 17.   [279] Walmsley et al, Comparative Study.

[280] Walmsley et al, Comparative Study, section 2.1, p 3.

[281] Walmsley et al, Comparative Study, section 4.2.1, p 63. See also section 4.2.5, p 68.

with European tuna associations, Anabac and Opagac' under which 'EU vessels (mainly French) purchase private licenses outside of the EU fisheries agreements'.[282] The authors of this book are unaware whether the particular examples referred to above regarding Madagascar, Mauritania, and Mozambique have persisted in the light of the EC's FPAs with these third States.[283]

Private licences play a particular role in cases where no fisheries treaty has been made, or renewed, between the EC and a third State. In such cases, they provide a means for Member States' vessels to fish in the third State's waters. However, the use of such licences is not reserved for those occasions. Subject to any relevant EC law (see below), some owners or operators may still seek, and obtain, private licences despite the presence of a bilateral treaty between the EC and the third State if they are able to obtain more favourable terms that way or if the treaty does not provide for sufficient fishing opportunities. Some of the advantages and disadvantages of private arrangements from the point of view of both the third State and the operator are discussed in Walmsley *et al.*[284]

The scope for a bilateral fisheries treaty and private licences to exist in parallel has been a cause of concern to the Commission. This is because the use of private licences can reduce the take-up of fishing opportunities under a treaty and can potentially undermine its provisions on sustainability. In a policy document issued in 2002 on FPAs the Commission added that: 'In cases where private licenses are sold to operators, there is . . . no guarantee that the financial counterpart benefits the fisheries industry and their employees in the third country in the way that the Community targeted actions do.'[285] In 2004 the Council concluded 'that public agreements encompassing *all* fishing activities by Community fishermen operating in waters under the sovereignty and/or jurisdiction of third coastal States provide *the best means* of ensuring the sustainable exploitation of surpluses and a greater coherence between the political initiatives of the Community, notably with the cooperation and development policy' (emphasis added).[286]

Most FPAs now contain a provision stating that Community vessels may fish in the EEZ or EFZ of the third State in question 'only if they are in possession of a fishing licence issued under this Agreement' (or other similar formulations).[287]

---

[282] Walmsley *et al*, *Comparative Study*, section 4.5.3, p 82.

[283] For the FPAs in question, see OJ 2007 L331/7 (Madagascar); OJ 2006 L343/4 (Mauritania); and OJ 2007 L331/35 (Mozambique).   [284] See, for example, pp 82–4, 129–30, and 138–40.

[285] COM(2002) 637, section 2.1, p 5.

[286] Council Conclusions contained in Council document 11485/1/04 REV 1, Brussels, 15 July 2004, p 4.

[287] FPAs containing such a provision include, *inter alia*, those between the EC and the following third States: Cape Verde (OJ 2006 L414/3); Comoros (OJ 2006 L290/7); Côte d'Ivoire (OJ 2008 L48/41); Gabon (OJ 2007 L109/3); Greenland (OJ 2007 L172/4); Guinea-Bissau (OJ 2007 L342/5); Kiribati (OJ 2007 L205/3); Madagascar (OJ 2007 L331/7); Mauritania (OJ 2006 L343/4); Morocco (OJ 2006 L141/4); Mozambique (OJ 2007 L331/35); São Tomé and Príncipe (OJ 2007 L205/36); and Seychelles (OJ 2006 L290/2). In each case, see Art 6(1) of the FPA.

This provision (hereafter, 'the standard provision') is sometimes referred to as an 'exclusivity clause'. On its face, however, it is not clear why it should create exclusivity. It does not expressly prohibit the third State from granting a private licence to a Community vessel and nor does it expressly prohibit a Community vessel from fishing under such a licence. Instead, it merely prevents a Community vessel from fishing unless it has a fishing licence issued under the FPA in question which, on a literal interpretation, leaves room for the vessel to have a private licence *as well*.

It is perhaps arguable that the standard provision, despite not containing an express prohibition against private licences, *implies* that a Community vessel may not fish under a private licence with the third State in question. Indeed that may be the way in which it is interpreted by the Commission in practice. However, in that case, it is surprising that a more clearly worded provision was not negotiated and, ultimately, it may fall to the Court to interpret the extent to which the provision creates exclusivity.

The situation is complicated by an additional provision contained in the FPAs between the EC and each of Guinea-Bissau, Mauritania, and Morocco. Each of these agreements contains the standard provision but then adds that for 'fishing categories not covered by' the implementing protocol to the FPA and subject to a 'favourable opinion' from, *inter alia*, the EC, the third State may grant licences to Community vessels.[288] It is unclear whether any such licences would, in effect, be private licences, given the requirement for a 'favourable opinion'. However, the fact that they may relate to 'fishing categories not covered by' the relevant protocol suggests that they would indeed be private licences. If that is right, the fact that the additional provision is not stated to be 'without prejudice' to the standard provision suggests that the latter is *not* intended to create an effect of exclusivity, at least in respect of fishing categories not covered by the implementing protocol.

The standard provision applies only to 'Community vessels'. The term 'Community vessel' is defined as 'a fishing vessel flying the flag of a Member State of the Community and registered in the Community' or similar[289] (which is essentially the same wording as used in the Basic Regulation to define the term 'Community fishing vessel'[290]). Thus the reach of the standard provision is restricted to vessels flagged to the Member States and registered in the Community. No matter what its effect in relation to such vessels, the standard provision does not affect the right of the third State to grant fisheries access to, *inter alia*, fishing vessels

---

[288] In each case, see Art 6(2) of the FPA. The Mauritania and Morocco FPAs refer to 'licences' being granted by the third State, whereas the Guinea-Bissau FPA refers to 'fishing authorisations'. The Guinea-Bissau and Mauritania FPAs also allow for 'exploratory fishing' by the same mechanism. The Guinea-Bissau and Mauritania FPAs require the 'favourable opinion' to be from both the third State and the EC, whereas the Morocco FPA requires it to be from (just) the Commission. The Morocco FPA adds that: 'The procedure for obtaining a fishing licence for a vessel, the taxes applicable and the method of payment to be used by shipowners shall be laid down by mutual agreement.'

[289] In each case, see Art 2 of the FPA.   [290] Reg 2371/2002, Art 3(d). See further Chapter 2.

flagged to States other than Member States (including vessels in which nationals of
Member States may have some involvement) or fishing vessels that are flagged to
Member States but which are not 'registered in the Community' (on which, see
further Chapter 2).

It is important to emphasize that Community fishing vessels operating under
private licences are not wholly outside the scope of CFP measures regarding
fishing activities. Such a vessel will still need a fishing licence under Regulation
1281/2005.[291] At one point there were also plans for such vessels to be expressly
required to have authorizations to fish. Thus, in its legislative proposal for what
became Regulation 1006/2008,[292] the Commission proposed that 'Community
fishing vessels shall only be entitled to engage in fishing activities outside Community waters which are not covered by an [EC/third State fisheries agreement] if
they have been issued with an authorisation from their flag Member State in
accordance with national provisions'.[293] However, this proposal and some
important accompanying provisions on transparency and administrative sanctions[294] were not adopted by the Council.[295]

The result is that Regulation 1006/2008 contains no provisions expressly
requiring a Community fishing vessel to have an authorization from its flag
Member State before undertaking private licence fishing. The basic proposition in
Regulation 1006/2008 is that: 'Only Community fishing vessels for which a
fishing authorisation has been issued *in accordance with this Regulation* shall be entitled to engage in fishing activities outside Community waters.'[296] (Emphasis
added.) In the light of the Regulation making no express provision for authorizations for private licence fishing, the question arises whether the phrase 'in
accordance with this Regulation' has the effect of completely ruling out any private licence fishing by Community fishing vessels or, alternatively, allowing it.
Article 11(2) (see below) suggests that the latter is the case; otherwise, that Article
would presumably not be necessary. The same may be said of Article 38(6) of the
IUU Regulation (see below).

Either way, the absence of express provision on authorizations for private
licence fishing appears to be incompatible with: (a) the statement in the preamble
to Regulation 1006/2008 that 'it is necessary to introduce a general Community
system for the authorisation of *all* fishing activities of Community fishing vessels
outside Community waters' (emphasis added);[297] and (b) Article 1 which states
that the Regulation 'establishes provisions concerning . . . the authorisation for
Community fishing vessels to engage in . . . fishing activities . . . [*inter alia*] . . .

---

[291] Reg 1281/2005, Art 3. See also Reg 2371/2002, Art 22(1)(a).

[292] *Proposal for a Council Regulation concerning authorisations for fishing activities of Community fishing
vessels outside Community waters and the access of third country vessels to Community waters*, COM(2007) 330,
18.6.2007.   [293] COM(2007) 330, proposed Art 15(1).

[294] COM(2007) 330, proposed Art 15(3) and (2).

[295] Cf Reg 1006/2008, Art 11(1), which relates only to fishing on the high seas.

[296] Reg 1006/2008, Art 3.   [297] Reg 1006/2008, recital (2).

outside Community waters not falling under the scope of a fisheries agreement or a RFMO'.[298]

Despite Regulation 1006/2008 containing no provisions expressly requiring a Community fishing vessel to have an authorization from its flag Member State to undertake private licence fishing, Article 11(2), which falls within a section of the Regulation headed 'Fishing activities not falling within the scope of an agreement', does at least require Member States to 'endeavour to obtain information on any arrangements, between their nationals and a third country, which allow fishing vessels flying their flag to engage in fishing activities in waters under the jurisdiction or sovereignty of a third country' and to 'inform the Commission thereof by the electronic transmission of a list of the vessels concerned'. However, this obligation only applies to vessels exceeding 24 m in overall length.[299] It is also a significantly down-sized version of the obligation as originally proposed by the Commission, which: (a) required the Member States to obtain the information (rather than merely requiring them to 'endeavour' to obtain it); and (b) stated that where the vessels in question are 'targeting stocks that are deemed to be outside safe biological limits' (as defined) the Commission may request the Member State concerned to submit an evaluation of the stocks and may potentially 'impose restrictions on the fishing activities concerned'.[300]

It is noteworthy that Article 11(2), when mentioning Member States' fishing vessels, refers to 'fishing vessels flying their flag' rather than, more specifically, 'Community fishing vessels flying their flag'. This raises the question whether the scope of Article 11(2) includes *any* fishing vessel flying a Member State's flag, rather than just those which, in addition, are 'registered in the Community'.[301] The answer is not entirely clear. On the one hand, there are precedents in other Regulations for the use of the phrase 'Community fishing vessels flying their flag',[302] indicating that this term could readily have been used if those drafting Article 11(2) had so wished. On the other hand, the Basic Regulation states that beyond Community waters the CFP only applies to 'Community fishing vessels' (and nationals),[303] and Regulation 1006/2008 does not show any clear intention to go beyond this.

Regulation 1006/2008 also includes provisions on the theme of 'Reporting obligations and closure of fishing activities'. Of these, Article 12 provides for a so-called 'Community fishing authorisation information system', which appears to relate only to authorizations in the framework EC/third State fisheries agreements or RFMOs. On catch and effort reporting and on closure or suspension of fisheries, some provisions appear to relate only to fishing under an EC/third State

[298] Reg 1006/2008, Art 1(a)(iii).   [299] Reg 1006/2008, Art 11(3).

[300] COM(2007) 330, proposed Art 14(1) and (2).   [301] Cf Reg 2371/2002, Art 3(d).

[302] See, for example, Reg 2371/2002, Arts 23(2), 24, and 28(3); and Reg 520/2007, Art 5(2).

[303] Reg 2371/2002, Art 1(1). See further Chapter 2.

fisheries agreement,[304] whereas it is unclear whether or not the remaining provisions may have some application to private licence fishing.[305]

As well as the requirement for a fishing licence under Regulation 1281/2005 (see above), conservation measures that are of general application to Community fishing vessels outside Community waters will also apply,[306] such as the qualified prohibitions on: (a) the use of driftnets under Regulation 894/97;[307] (b) the finning of sharks under Regulation 1185/2003;[308] and (c) the encircling with purse seines of any school or group of marine mammals under Regulation 520/2007[309] (see Chapter 4). Certain measures on monitoring, control, and surveillance will also be applicable.[310] An example is Regulation 500/2001 on catch monitoring which expressly applies to catches taken by Member States' fishing vessels 'in waters subject to the sovereignty or jurisdiction of third countries'.[311] Other examples of applicable control measures include those on satellite-based vessel monitoring systems,[312] vessel marking,[313] and catch reporting.[314] If any CFP measures applicable to a Community fishing vessel were unacceptable to the third State in question, that State could of course decide to refuse a licence for that vessel.

Parts of the IUU Regulation have potential application to Community fishing vessels undertaking private licence fishing, just as they would to, say, Community fishing vessels fishing under EC/third State fisheries agreements. The Regulation also contains at least one provision of more specific application: Article 38(6) requires that, in respect of so-called 'non-cooperating third countries', 'private trade arrangements between nationals of a Member State and such countries in order for a fishing vessel flying the flag of that Member State to use the fishing possibilities of such countries shall be prohibited'. This would appear to relate to, *inter alia*, private licences, and uses the fact that, under Article 1(1) of the Basic Regulation, the CFP applies to 'nationals of Member States', albeit 'without

---

[304] Reg 1006/2008, Arts 14 and 16.   [305] Reg 1006/2008, Arts 13 and 15.

[306] See generally Reg 2371/2002, Art 22(1)(e).   [307] Reg 894/97, Art 11c.

[308] Reg 1185/2003, Art 1(2).   [309] Reg 520/2007, Art 29.

[310] See generally Reg 2371/2002, Art 23(1) and (2) and Reg 2847/93, Arts 1(3) and 2(2).

[311] Reg 500/2001, Art 1.

[312] Commission Regulation (EC) No 2244/2003 of 18 December 2003 laying down detailed provisions regarding satellite-based Vessel Monitoring Systems, OJ 2003 L333/17. See also Reg 2371/2002, Arts 22(1)(b) and 23(3) and Reg 2847/93, Art 3.

[313] Commission Regulation (EEC) No 1381/87 of 20 May 1987 establishing detailed rules concerning the marking and documentation of fishing vessels, OJ 1987 132/9. See also Reg 2371/2002, Art 22(1)(e).

[314] See, for example, Reg 2847/93, *inter alia*, Arts 17, 18, and 19 and Council Regulation (EC) No 1966/2006 of 21 December 2006 on electronic recording and reporting of fishing activities and on means of remote sensing, OJ 2006 409/1, as corrected (reissued as corrected version in OJ 2007 L36/3). (Art 18 of Reg 2847/93 was repealed by Reg 1006/2008, but continues to apply until a Regulation implementing Art 13 of Reg 1006/2008 has entered into force: see Reg 1006/2008, Arts 29(1) and 30(2).) See also Reg 2371/2002, Art 22(1)(c).

prejudice to the primary responsibility of the flag State'. The existence of Article 38(6), in a Regulation adopted on the same date as Regulation 1006/2008, indicates that, despite the uncertainty mentioned above, the continued existence of private licences was envisaged by the Council when it adopted Regulation 1006/2008.

It should be added that the use of private licences is not the only means by which Community fishing vessels or Member State nationals may gain opportunities to fish in the waters of third States other than under fisheries access agreements between the EC and such States. Other options include the establishment of joint ventures and joint enterprises. As seen in section 4 above, a small number of the EC's present and past fisheries access agreements with third States encourage(d) the formation of joint ventures and joint enterprises between Member State nationals and nationals of the third State concerned, such encouragement being made tangible by the provision of EC funding.

Those agreements generally define a joint venture as an association based on a contractual agreement between Community shipowners and nationals of the third State concerned with the aim of jointly fishing for stocks in the waters of that third State by vessels flying the flag of an EC Member State with a view to the priority supply of the EC market, and sharing the costs of such fishing. A joint enterprise is defined as a company set up by Community shipowners and nationals of the third State concerned under the law of that State and having its nationality. Fishing vessels acquired by the company are registered in the third State (and may formerly have been registered in an EC Member State) and fish in the waters of that third State with a view to the priority supply of the EC market.[315]

Access by Community fishing vessels by means of a joint venture to the waters of a third State would also seem to be possible outside the framework of a fisheries access agreement (subject to, in those cases where an FPA exists, the effect of the standard provision referred to above in the discussion on exclusivity). Indeed, in substance, a joint venture may differ little from access under a private licence, since a Community vessel fishing under a joint venture will presumably still require a licence of some kind from the third State and will be subject to CFP legislation applying outside Community waters. Although in the past the EC provided funding to support joint ventures outside of fisheries access agreements,[316] it no longer does so.

Turning to joint enterprises, it would seem to be possible for Community nationals to obtain opportunities to fish in the waters of a third State by setting up a

[315] Such definitions of joint ventures and joint enterprises may be found in, *inter alia,* the 1985 EC-Greenland Agreement, Third Protocol, Art 3; EC-Greenland Fisheries Partnership Agreement, Art 2(d) and (e); EC-Argentina Agreement, Art 2(e) and (f); and 1996 EC-Latvia Agreement, Art 5.

[316] For example, under Council Regulation (EEC) No 4028/86 of 18 December 1986 on Community measures to improve and adapt structures in the fisheries and aquaculture sector, OJ 1986 L376/7, as amended and corrected.

joint enterprise with nationals of that State. In this case Community nationals would either re-register their vessels (including those previously registered in a Member State) in the third State or purchase vessels already registered in that State. Either way, the vessel would not be registered in the Member State and so would not be a 'Community vessel' for the purposes of an FPA (see above). Prior to the operation of the European Fisheries Fund from 2007 onwards, the EC provided funding to encourage the creation of joint enterprises.[317]

A further way in which Community nationals may obtain rights to fish in the waters of a third State outside the framework of a fisheries agreement is under various trade and commercial agreements between the EC and developing countries that permit natural and legal persons having the nationality of an EC Member State to establish themselves in the third State concerned, subject to various conditions (notably reciprocity), and thereby gain access to that State's fishing industry. There appear to be two such agreements so far.

Under an agreement with Chile, a national of an EC Member State, whether a natural or legal person, established in Chile may own a majority share of the equity capital and control the management of new or existing fishing enterprises in Chile, and then apply for, register, and operate a vessel under the same conditions as legal entities whose majority shareholding is held by, and whose management is controlled by, Chilean nationals, provided that that EC Member State extends the same rights to Chilean nationals in its territory. A fishing enterprise that is majority-owned by a Member State national in this way may then apply for an authorization for industrial fishing in Chile's EEZ or receive authorizations that have been transferred to it, on the same conditions as Chilean companies in which the majority shareholding is owned by Chilean nationals.[318]

Secondly, under the Economic Partnership Agreement that the EC has concluded with the fifteen CARIFORUM States each party (ie the EC and its Member States, on the one side, and the CARIFORUM States, on the other) undertakes to accord nationals (whether natural or legal persons) of the other party the right to establish themselves on its territory for the purpose of carrying out activities in various economic sectors, including the fisheries sector, and be granted

---

[317] Most recently in Council Regulation (EC) No 2792/99 of 17 December 1999 laying down detailed rules and arrangements regarding Community structural assistance in the fisheries sector, OJ 1999 L337/10, as amended and corrected (and now repealed), Art 8. The Court of Auditors published a severe critique of a predecessor arrangement for such funding in *Special Report No. 18/98 concerning the Community measures to encourage the creation of joint enterprises in the fisheries sector accompanied by the replies of the Commission*, OJ 1998 C393/1.

[318] Agreement establishing an Association between the European Community and its Member States, of the one part, and the Republic of Chile, of the other part, OJ 2002 L352/3, Arts 130–135 and Annex X, B.

treatment no less favourable than that accorded to nationals.[319] Annex IVE to the Agreement lists a variety of quite wide-ranging limitations on this right that have been made by individual CARIFORUM States as far as the fishing industry is concerned. Subject to those limitations, the consequence of the Agreement is that an EC Member State national established in a CARIFORUM State would be able to fish in the waters of that State on the same conditions as that State's nationals. It is probable that similar provisions to those in the CARIFORUM Agreement will be included in other economic partnership agreements that the EC is currently in the process of concluding with developing States (see further Chapter 7).[320]

6 EC participation in regional fisheries management organizations

6.1 Introduction

This section focuses on the EC's participation in thirteen existing or prospective regional fisheries management organizations or arrangements, but ends with a short subsection on the EC's involvement with regional fishery bodies without management functions. Regional fisheries management organizations (RFMOs) have already been introduced in Chapter 3. As noted there, there are currently two principal categories: those dealing with straddling stocks (and sometimes, in addition, discrete high seas stocks) and those dealing with highly migratory stocks. An RFMO dealing with anadromous stocks will also be addressed in this section.

Of the eleven existing RFMOs described below, the EC is currently a member of all except two. Membership of RFMOs normally flows from becoming a party to the treaty establishing the RFMO; an exception is the Commission for the Conservation of Antarctic Marine Living Resources (CCAMLR), where being a party to the relevant treaty does not necessarily entail membership of the RFMO (see below). In all cases where the EC is a party to an RFMO treaty, with one exception (the NAFO Convention), the treaty in question expressly provides for so-called regional economic integration organizations (or the EC specifically) to be parties. The EC becomes a party to the RFMO treaty in question by virtue of a Council Decision (or, in one case, a Council Regulation) concluding the treaty on behalf of the EC.

---

[319] Economic Partnership Agreement between the CARIFORUM States, of the one part, and the European Community and its Member States, of the other part, OJ 2008 L289/1/3, Arts 65–69 and Annex IVE.

[320] With regard to nationals of EC Member States holding an interest in fishing vessels flagged to a third State, see Reg 1005/2008, Art 40(1). Regarding prospective reflagging of vessels from the flag of a Member State to that of a third State, see Reg 1005/2008, Art 40(4).

In some cases, both the EC and some of the Member States are members of the same RFMO. In most cases that arises because the Member States are participating on behalf of their OCTs, whether as flag States or coastal States or both. In the case of the CCAMLR, it also arises because the subject matter of the CCAMLR Convention relates to both fisheries conservation (in relation to which the EC has exclusive treaty-making competence) and broader environmental protection issues (where competence is shared by the EC and the Member States). In the case of the General Fisheries Commission for the Mediterranean, the reason for mixed membership by the EC and several Member States is not entirely clear (see further subsection 2.2 above).

As a member of any given RFMO, the EC is required to transpose that RFMO's binding measures into EC law (unless it has entered a reservation), and may choose to additionally transpose its non-binding measures. Transposition is done by means of Regulations, some of which are specific to one or more RFMOs. As well as Regulations adopted for the longer term (referred to in this section as 'standing' Regulations), the principal annual Regulation (currently Regulation 40/2008—on which, see Chapter 4) plays an important part in transposing RFMO measures. In addition to the various transposing Regulations mentioned below for the various RFMOs, the Control Regulation, Regulation 1185/2003 (on finning of sharks), and the IUU Regulation also serve to transpose RFMO measures. The role of the IUU Regulation is discussed in subsection 6.5 below in general terms, rather than being considered for each individual RFMO in turn. It should be added that this section, despite identifying the various Regulations by which the EC transposes RFMOs' measures, does not generally address whether EC law adequately transposes such measures.[321]

6.2 Regional fisheries management organizations concerned with straddling stocks and discrete high seas stocks

Commission for the Conservation of Antarctic Marine Living Resources (CCAMLR)

The CCAMLR was established by the 1980 Convention on the Conservation of Antarctic Marine Living Resources (hereafter, 'the CCAMLR Convention').[322] The CCAMLR Convention applies to 'Antarctic marine living resources' in two areas, namely: (a) the area south of 60°S latitude; and (b), in cases where such resources 'form part of the Antarctic marine ecosystem', the area between 60°S and the Antarctic Convergence.[323] The term 'Antarctic marine living resources'

---

[321] Each of the existing RFMOs discussed in this section has a website. RFMO materials (as distinct from EC materials) referred to in this section can be found on the website of the relevant RFMO.
[322] 1329 UNTS 47.   [323] CCAMLR Convention, Art I(1).

means the populations of all species of living organisms found south of the Ant-arctic Convergence.[324] The function of the CCAMLR is to give effect to the objective of the CCAMLR Convention, which is 'the conservation of Antarctic marine living resources', as well as to the Convention's conservation principles.[325] It is to do this by, *inter alia*, adopting conservation measures and implementing the system of observation and inspection established under the CCAMLR Convention.[326]

The EC has been a party to the CCAMLR Convention since 1981,[327] and a member of the CCAMLR since the Convention entered into force in 1982. Of the EC Member States, Belgium, France, Germany, Italy, Poland, Spain, Sweden, and the UK are members of the CCAMLR while Bulgaria, Finland, Greece, and the Netherlands are (merely) parties to the CCAMLR Convention.[328] France and the UK are parties not just because the CCAMLR Convention is a mixed agreement but also because both have OCTs in the Convention area. At the time of writing, the website of the CCAMLR indicated that, of the EC Member States, only Spain and the UK had 'vessels licensed to harvest in the Convention area in the 2008/09 intersessional period' (ie 1 December 2008 to 30 November 2009).

EC Regulations implementing measures adopted by the CCAMLR include the principal annual Regulation (40/2008),[329] as well as Regulations 1035/2001,[330] 600/2004,[331] and 601/2004.[332] Regulation 40/2008 establishes fishing opportunities,[333] prohibitions on some fisheries,[334] and restrictions on use of certain fishing gears.[335] It also has provisions on exploratory fisheries,[336] krill fisheries,[337] and the procedure for closure of fisheries.[338] Regulation 1035/2001 implements the CCAMLR's catch documentation scheme for toothfish, Regula-tion 600/2004 transposes various technical measures adopted by the CCAMLR

---

[324] CCAMLR Convention, Art I(2).   [325] CCAMLR Convention, Arts IX(1) and II.

[326] CCAMLR Convention, Art IX(1)(f) and (g).

[327] Council Decision 81/691/EEC of 4 September 1981 on the conclusion of the Convention on the conservation of Antarctic marine living resources, OJ 1981 L252/26, as corrected.

[328] See the website of the CCAMLR.

[329] Reg 40/2008, Arts 1, 41–56, and 85 and Annexes IE, IX, and X.

[330] Council Regulation (EC) No 1035/2001 of 22 May 2001 establishing a catch documentation scheme for *Dissostichus* spp., OJ 2001 L145/1, as amended.

[331] Council Regulation (EC) No 600/2004 of 22 March 2004 laying down certain technical measures applicable to fishing activities in the area covered by the Convention on the conservation of Antarctic marine living resources, OJ 2004 L97/1.

[332] Council Regulation (EC) No 601/2004 of 22 March 2004 laying down certain control measures applicable to fishing activities in the area covered by the Convention on the conservation of Antarctic marine living resources and repealing Regulations (EEC) No 3943/90, (EC) No 66/98 and (EC) No 1721/1999, OJ 2004 L97/16, as amended.   [333] Reg 40/2008, Art 1 and Annex IE.

[334] Reg 40/2008, Arts 41(1) and 85 and Annex IX.   [335] Reg 40/2008, Arts 54 and 55.

[336] Reg 40/2008, Arts 41(2), 42–49, and 53 and Annex X.

[337] Reg 40/2008, Arts 50–52 and Annex XI.   [338] Reg 40/2008, Art 56.

and the CCAMLR's scientific observer scheme, and Regulation 601/2004 transposes various CCAMLR control measures as well as some other measures.[339]

General Fisheries Commission for the Mediterranean (GFCM)

The GFCM was established by the 1949 Agreement for the Establishment of the General Fisheries Commission for the Mediterranean,[340] as amended (hereafter, 'the GFCM Agreement'), which entered into force in its original form in 1952. The GFCM Agreement is established under Article XIV of the FAO Constitution. The most recent amendments to the treaty were adopted in 1997, although some of these did not enter into force until 2004. The 1997 amendments provided, *inter alia*, for membership of the GFCM by the EC[341] and for an autonomous budget.[342] The GFCM addresses 'the Mediterranean and the Black Sea and connecting waters'.[343] Its purpose is to 'promote the development, conservation, rational management and best utilization of living marine resources, as well as the sustainable development of aquaculture' of that area,[344] by, *inter alia*, adopting conservation and management measures and corresponding control measures.[345]

The EC has been a party to the GFCM Agreement, and hence a member of the GFCM, since 1998.[346] Of the EC Member States, Bulgaria, Cyprus, France, Greece, Italy, Malta, Romania, Slovenia, and Spain are parties.[347] As noted above, the reason for mixed membership of the GFCM by the EC and several Member States is not entirely clear. For example, the Indian Ocean Tuna Commission (see below) also originates under Article XIV of the FAO Constitution and yet does not include any individual EC Member States other than in relation to their OCTs.

EC Regulations implementing measures adopted by the GFCM include the principal annual Regulation (40/2008) and Regulation 1967/2006.[348] Regulation 40/2008 transposes certain technical measures adopted by the GFCM in 2006 and 2007, pending adoption of an amendment to Regulation 1967/2006.[349] Regulation 1967/2006 transposes a GFCM control measure;[350] the degree to which it

---

[339] Reg 1005/2008, applicable from 1 January 2010, repeals Arts 26a, 28, 29, 30, and 31 of Reg 601/2004 (see Reg 1005/2008, Arts 56 and 57).　　　　[340] 126 UNTS 327.

[341] GFCM Agreement, Art I(2)(iii).　　　[342] GFCM Agreement, Art IX.

[343] GFCM Agreement, Art IV and 4th recital.　　　[344] GFCM Agreement, Art III(1).

[345] GFCM Agreement, Art III(1)(b).

[346] Council Decision 98/416/EC of 16 June 1998 on the accession of the European Community to the General Fisheries Commission for the Mediterranean, OJ 1998 L190/34. See also Dec 2000/487, OJ 2000 L197/35 and Dec 2004/815, OJ 2004 L357/30.　　　[347] See the website of the GFCM.

[348] Council Regulation (EC) No 1967/2006 of 21 December 2006 concerning management measures for the sustainable exploitation of fishery resources in the Mediterranean Sea, amending Regulation (EEC) No 2847/93 and repealing Regulation (EC) No 1626/94, OJ 2006 L409/11, as corrected (corrected version reissued as OJ 2007 L36/6).

[349] Reg 40/2008, recital (35), Arts 29–31, and Annex XIV. Arts 29, 30, and 31 implement Recommendations GFCM/30/2006/2, GFCM/30/2006/3, and GFCM/31/2007/1 respectively.

[350] Reg 1967/2006, Art 24 (implementing Recommendation GFCM/29/2005/2).

also transposes technical measures adopted by the GFCM prior to 2006 is not entirely clear.[351]

Northwest Atlantic Fisheries Organization (NAFO)

The NAFO was established by the 1978 Convention on Future Multilateral Cooperation in the Northwest Atlantic Fisheries (hereafter, 'the NAFO Convention').[352] The NAFO Convention has been amended several times since its adoption. In 2007 the NAFO adopted significant amendments to the Convention with a view to better reflecting the UN Fish Stocks Agreement (on which, see Chapter 3) and modern concepts of ocean governance. These amendments are yet to enter into force,[353] and the provisions of the Convention as they were prior to the 2007 amendments will be described here.

The objective of the NAFO is to 'contribute through consultation and cooperation to the optimum utilization, rational management and conservation of the fishery resources of the Convention Area'.[354] The term 'fishery resources' excludes 'salmon, tunas and marlins, cetacean stocks managed by the International Whaling Commission or any successor organization, and sedentary species of the Continental Shelf . . .'.[355] The NAFO consists of, *inter alia*, a Fisheries Commission.[356] This Commission is 'responsible for the management and conservation of the fishery resources of the Regulatory Area . . .',[357] meaning that part of the Convention's area lying beyond the areas in which coastal State parties exercise fisheries jurisdiction,[358] and may, *inter alia*, adopt fisheries conservation and control measures.[359]

The EC has been a party to the NAFO Convention since 1978,[360] and a member of the NAFO since the Convention entered into force in 1979. Its membership of the NAFO has been characterized for much of the time by a difficult relationship with Canada, which has been written about at length elsewhere.[361] Of the EC Member States, Denmark is a party in respect of the Faroe Islands and Greenland and

---

[351] Art 4(3) of Reg 1967/2006 appears to implement Recommendation GFCM/29/2005/1, Art 2. Art 31 of Reg 40/2008 implies that Arts 8(1)(h) and 9(3), point (2) of Reg 1967/2006 implement Recommendation GFCM/29/2005/1, Art 1.   [352] 1135 UNTS 369.

[353] See the website of the NAFO.   [354] NAFO Convention, Art II(1).

[355] NAFO Convention, Art I(4). On the International Whaling Commission, see subsection 7.1 below. On 'sedentary species', including as referred to elsewhere in this section, see Chapter 3.

[356] NAFO Convention, Art II(2)(c).   [357] NAFO Convention, Art XI(1).

[358] NAFO Convention, Art I(2) and (3).   [359] NAFO Convention, Art XI(2) and (5).

[360] Council Regulation (EEC) No 3179/78 of 28 December 1978 concerning the conclusion by the European Economic Community of the Convention on Future Multilateral Cooperation in the Northwest Atlantic Fisheries, OJ 1978 L378/1, as amended and corrected.

[361] See, for example: Applebaum, B, 'The Straddling Stocks Problem: The Northwest Atlantic Situation, International Law and Options for Coastal State Action' in Soons, AHA (ed), *Implementation of the Law of the Sea Convention through International Institutions* (Honolulu, Hawaii: Law of the Sea Institute, 1990), 282; Day, D, 'Tending the Achilles' Heel of NAFO' *Marine Policy* 19 (1995), 257; Freestone, D, 'Canada and the EU reach Agreement to Settle the *Estai* Dispute' *IJMCL* 10 (1995), 387; and Gazelius, SS, 'Limits to Externalisation: the EU NAFO Policy 1979–97' *Marine Policy* 23 (1998), 147.

France is a party in respect of Saint Pierre and Miquelon. The latest principal annual Regulation (Regulation 40/2008) indicates that Denmark, Estonia, Germany, Latvia, Lithuania, Poland, Portugal, and Spain all have fishing opportunities for 2008 arising from those 'adopted in the framework of NAFO'.[362]

EC Regulations implementing measures adopted by the NAFO include the principal annual Regulation (40/2008) as well as, *inter alia*, Regulations 2115/2005[363] and 1386/2007.[364] Regulation 40/2008 establishes fishing opportunities, based on TACs 'adopted in the framework of NAFO'.[365] It also transposes some measures adopted by the NAFO in 2007, notably some control measures regarding Greenland halibut and technical measures to protect cold-water corals.[366] Regulation 2115/2005, following on from some earlier provisional implementation, transposes a NAFO rebuilding plan for Greenland halibut adopted in 2003.[367] Regulation 1386/2007 transposes provisions of the NAFO's 'Conservation and Enforcement Measures' on technical measures and control and has been amended to take into account some changes to those provisions.

North-East Atlantic Fisheries Commission (NEAFC)

The NEAFC was established by the 1980 Convention on Future Multilateral Co-operation in North-East Atlantic Fisheries (hereafter, 'the NEAFC Convention').[368] The website of the NEAFC states that 'amendments to the [NEAFC Convention] have been adopted in 2004 and 2006 by the NEAFC Commission' and that 'contracting parties have agreed to use the "new" convention on a provisional basis, pending ratification'. The justification for these amendments is similar to that for the amendments made to the NAFO Convention (see above). Because of the agreement on provisional application, the amended Convention will be considered here.

The objective of the amended NEAFC Convention is to 'ensure the long-term conservation and optimum utilisation of the fishery resources in the Convention Area, providing sustainable economic, environmental and social benefits'.[369] The term 'fishery resources' means 'resources of fish, molluscs, crustaceans and including sedentary species, excluding, in so far as they are dealt with by other international agreements, highly migratory species listed in Annex I of the United Nations Convention on the Law of the Sea of 10 December 1982, and anadromous stocks'.[370] The NEAFC is to perform its functions in order to fulfil the

---

[362] Reg 40/2008, Annex IC.

[363] Council Regulation (EC) No 2115/2005 of 20 December 2005 establishing a recovery plan for Greenland halibut in the framework of the Northwest Atlantic Fisheries Organisation, OJ 2005 L340/3.

[364] Council Regulation (EC) No 1386/2007 of 22 October 2007 laying down conservation and enforcement measures applicable in the Regulatory Area of the Northwest Atlantic Fisheries Organisation, OJ 2007 L318/1, as amended. [365] Reg 40/2008, Arts 1 and 5(1) and Annex IC.

[366] Reg 40/2008, recital (11), Arts 32–34, and Annex VII.

[367] Reg 2115/2005, recitals (6) and (4). [368] 1285 UNTS 129.

[369] Amended NEAFC Convention, Art 2. [370] Amended NEAFC Convention, Art 1(b).

Convention's objective.[371] It may, *inter alia*, adopt fisheries conservation and control measures, principally in relation to 'fisheries conducted beyond the areas under jurisdiction of Contracting Parties'.[372]

The EC has been a party to the NEAFC Convention since 1981,[373] and a member of the NEAFC since the Convention entered into force in 1982. Of the EC Member States, Denmark is a party in respect of the Faroe Islands and Greenland. A particular characteristic of operation of the NEAFC is that each year, prior to the annual NEAFC meeting, the EC and other relevant coastal State parties negotiate catch limits and quotas for certain pelagic species.

EC Regulations implementing measures adopted by the NEAFC include the principal annual Regulation (40/2008) as well as, *inter alia*, Regulations 1899/85,[374] 1638/87,[375] 2791/99,[376] and 1085/2000.[377] Regulation 40/2008 establishes fishing opportunities and technical measures pursuant to those adopted by the NEAFC in 2007 or earlier.[378] It also transposes some measures in the NEAFC's 'Scheme of Control and Enforcement'.[379] It identifies the vessels on the NEAFC's IUU vessel list (which also includes those on the NAFO's IUU vessel list).[380] Regulation 2791/1999 transposes the NEAFC's control and enforcement measures and has been amended to take into account some changes to those measures. Regulation 1085/2000 lays down detailed rules for the application of Regulation 2791/1999. Regulations 1899/85 and 1638/87 establish minimum mesh sizes for capelin fishing and pelagic trawling for blue whiting respectively, transposing measures adopted by the NEAFC in 1984 and 1986.[381]

---

[371] Amended NEAFC Convention, Art 4(1).

[372] Amended NEAFC Convention, Arts 5(1) and 8(1).

[373] Council Decision 81/608/EEC of 13 July 1981 concerning the conclusion of the Convention on Future Multilateral Cooperation in the North-East Atlantic Fisheries, OJ 1981 L227/21.

[374] Council Regulation (EEC) No 1899/85 of 8 July 1985 establishing a minimum mesh size for nets used when fishing for capelin in that part of the zone of the Convention on future multilateral cooperation in the north-east Atlantic fisheries which extends beyond the maritime waters falling within the fisheries jurisdiction of Contracting Parties to the Convention, OJ 1985 L179/2.

[375] Council Regulation (EEC) No 1638/87 of 9 June 1987 fixing the minimum mesh size for pelagic trawls used in fishing for blue whiting in that part of the area covered by the Convention on Future Multilateral Cooperation in the North-East Atlantic Fisheries which extends beyond the maritime waters falling within the fisheries jurisdiction of Contracting Parties to the Convention, OJ 1987 L153/7.

[376] Council Regulation (EC) No 2791/1999 of 16 December 1999 laying down certain control measures applicable in the area covered by the Convention on future multilateral cooperation in the north-east Atlantic fisheries, OJ 1999 L337/1, as amended.

[377] Commission Regulation (EC) No 1085/2000 of 15 May 2000 laying down detailed rules for the application of control measures applicable in the area covered by the Convention on Future Multilateral Cooperation in the North-East Atlantic Fisheries, OJ 2000 L128/1.

[378] Reg 40/2008, Arts 1 and 5(1) and Annex IB and Art 13 and Annex III, paras 5, 8, 13, and 21.

[379] Reg 40/2008, recital (30), Arts 35–40 and Annex VIII, and Art 83 and Annex XIII.

[380] Reg 40/2008, Annex XIII, Appendix.

[381] Reg 1899/85, 3rd recital; and Reg 1638/87, 3rd recital.

South East Atlantic Fisheries Organisation (SEAFO)

The SEAFO was established by the 2001 Convention on the Conservation and Management of Fishery Resources in the South-East Atlantic Ocean (hereafter, 'the SEAFO Convention').[382] The objective of the SEAFO Convention is to 'ensure the long-term conservation and sustainable use of the fishery resources in the Convention area . . .'.[383] The term 'fishery resources' means 'resources of fish, molluscs, crustaceans and other sedentary species within the Convention area, excluding: (i) sedentary species subject to the fishery jurisdiction of coastal States pursuant to Article 77(4) of the [1982 United Nations Convention on the Law of the Sea], and (ii) highly migratory species listed in Annex I to the [1982 Convention]'.[384] The SEAFO consists of, *inter alia*, a Commission;[385] amongst other things, the Commission's functions are to 'formulate and adopt conservation and management measures' and 'adopt measures concerning control and enforcement . . . .'[386]

The EC has been a party to the SEAFO Convention since 2002,[387] and a member of the SEAFO since the Convention entered into force in 2003. The UK has OCTs within the Convention area but is not currently a party on behalf of these territories. Regarding the EC Member States, the latest report of the SEAFO Scientific Committee (from its October 2008 meeting) states that vessels flagged to Cyprus, Poland, Portugal, and Spain '[h]istorically . . . are known to have been fishing in the SEAFO Area'. The situation regarding the more recent past seems less clear. Regarding the EC, some landings data from Spanish and Portuguese vessels, for the periods 2001–07 and 2004–07 respectively, are summarized and it is noted that Cypriot vessels landed catch in Namibia in 2004. Generally there seems to be concern in the report at the inadequacy of fishing data overall.[388] At the time of writing, the SEAFO Record of Authorised Vessels listed forty-four vessels, of which only one was flagged to a non-EC Member State (Namibia) and the rest were flagged to Portugal (seven) and Spain (thirty-six).[389]

There is no standing EC Regulation implementing SEAFO measures. However, the principal annual Regulation (40/2008) establishes fishing opportunities pursuant to those adopted by the SEAFO in 2007.[390] The same Regulation transposes technical measures and control measures adopted by the SEAFO in

---

[382] 2221 UNTS 189.   [383] SEAFO Convention, Art 2.
[384] SEAFO Convention, Art 1(l).   [385] SEAFO Convention, Art 5(2)(i).
[386] SEAFO Convention, Art 6(3)(b) and (i).
[387] Council Decision 2002/738/EC of 22 July 2002 on the conclusion by the European Community of the Convention on the Conservation and Management of Fishery Resources in the South-East Atlantic Ocean, OJ 2002 L234/39.   [388] Report of SEAFO Scientific Committee 2008, pp 23–4.
[389] See the website of the SEAFO.
[390] Reg 40/2008, recital (36), Arts 1 and 5(1), and Annex IF.

2006 and 2007.[391] Although the preamble to Regulation 40/2008 refers to the need for 'detailed requirements regarding port state inspections' adopted by the SEAFO in 2007 to be incorporated into EC law,[392] the Regulation then fails to transpose those requirements (but see subsection 6.5 below regarding Regulation 1005/2008).

Meeting of the Parties of the Southern Indian Ocean Fisheries Agreement

The 2006 Southern Indian Ocean Fisheries Agreement (hereafter, 'the SIOFA'),[393] which has not yet entered into force, is, within the terminology of the UN Fish Stocks Agreement, a regional fisheries management *arrangement* rather than an RFMO. It provides for its parties to meet at regular intervals, as a 'Meeting of the Parties',[394] rather than as, say, a 'commission' or 'organization'.

The objectives of the SIOFA are to 'ensure the long-term conservation and sustainable use of the fishery resources in the [SIOFA] Area . . . and to promote the sustainable development of fisheries in the [SIOFA] Area . . .'.[395] The term 'fishery resources' is defined in the same way as under the SEAFO Convention (see above).[396] The purpose of the Meeting of the Parties to the SIOFA is, *inter alia*, to 'formulate and adopt conservation and management measures . . .' and 'develop rules and procedures for the monitoring, control and surveillance of fishing activities . . .'.[397]

The EC has been a party to the SIOFA since 2008.[398] Because the SIOFA is not yet in force, the Meeting of the Parties to the SIOFA has not yet been established and hence has not yet adopted any measures. However, the conference that adopted the SIOFA in July 2006 adopted a resolution on interim arrangements calling on the EC, amongst others, to implement the data collection measures set out in an earlier (2004) resolution and to undertake various other tasks relevant to management of fisheries covered by the SIOFA.[399]

South Pacific Regional Fisheries Management Organisation (SPRFMO)

The treaty providing for the establishment of the SPRFMO is still in draft form. In May 2007 the participants in negotiations to establish the SPRFMO adopted interim fisheries management measures. Although the measures are expressly non-binding, the EC chose to transpose some of them through the principal annual

---

[391] Reg 40/2008, recital (36), Arts 57–70, and Annex XII. See also, by way of comparison, Reg 41/2007 (the previous principal annual Regulation), OJ 2007 L15/1, as amended and corrected, recital (34), Arts 69–80, and Annex XVI.   [392] Reg 40/2008, recital (36).
[393] OJ 2006 L196/15.   [394] SIOFA, Art 5.   [395] SIOFA, Art 2.
[396] SIOFA, Art 1(f).   [397] SIOFA, Art 6(1)(d) and (h).
[398] Council Decision 2008/780/EC of 29 September 2008 on the conclusion, on behalf of the European Community, of the Southern Indian Ocean Fisheries Agreement, OJ 2008 L268/27.
[399] Final Act of the Conference on the Southern Indian Ocean Fisheries Agreement; Appendix 2.

Regulation (40/2008).[400] Further measures, regarding provision of data, have been adopted since May 2007 (in October 2008). However, it is unclear whether the relevant provision in the principal annual Regulation is intended to encompass these.[401]

6.3 Regional fisheries management organizations concerned with highly migratory stocks

Commission for the Conservation of Southern Bluefin Tuna (CCSBT)

The CCSBT was established by the 1993 Convention for the Conservation of Southern Bluefin Tuna (hereafter, 'the CCSBT Convention'),[402] which entered into force in 1994. The CCSBT Convention applies to southern bluefin tuna (hereafter, 'SBT'),[403] but contains no express description of its geographical scope. Its objective is to 'ensure, through appropriate management, the conservation and optimum utilisation of [SBT]'.[404] The CCSBT is to decide upon a TAC and its allocation and 'may, if necessary, decide upon other additional measures'.[405]

The EC is not a party to the CCSBT Convention, and so is not a member of the CCSBT or the so-called Extended Commission.[406] However, it has been a 'Co-operating Non-Member of the Extended Commission' (hereafter, 'CNM') since October 2006.[407] As a CNM, the EC has been allocated a cooperation quota of SBT by the Extended Commission. For 2009 this was 10 tonnes, despite a request by the EC for 20 tonnes.[408] At the 2008 meeting of the CCSBT, the EC advised that 'its SBT catch was a small "unavoidable" bycatch of its swordfish and shark fisheries and that it did not intend to allow an expansion of its SBT catch above the current level of by-catch or to develop an SBT fishery'.[409]

As a CNM, the EC is required to implement the CCSBT's conservation and management measures.[410] In practice, EC Regulations do not set out the EC's cooperation quota or transpose any of the CCSBT's conservation and

---

[400] Reg 40/2008, recital (38) and Arts 74–76.   [401] Reg 40/2008, Art 76.

[402] 1819 UNTS 360.   [403] CCSBT Convention, Art 1.

[404] CCSBT Convention, Art 3.   [405] CCSBT Convention, Art 8(3).

[406] See: Resolution to Establish an Extended Commission and an Extended Scientific Committee (adopted at CCSBT 7 (2001) and revised at CCSBT 10 (2003)).

[407] CCSBT 13 (2006) report, paras 91–93 and Attachment 6-1. See also Resolution to Establish the Status of Co-operating Non-Member of the Extended Commission and the Extended Scientific Committee (adopted at CCSBT 10 (2003)).

[408] CCSBT 15 (2008) report, paras 37–39 and Attachment 5-1 (cf CCSBT 14 (2007) report, para 132 and CCSBT 13 (2006) report, para 64).

[409] CCSBT 15 (2008) report, para 37; see also Attachment 5-1.

[410] Resolution to Establish the Status of Co-operating Non-Member of the Extended Commission and the Extended Scientific Committee; para 4.

management measures (including some that expressly apply to CNMs).[411] The report of the 2007 meeting of the CCSBT states that 'there were serious short-comings with the level of cooperation from the European Community'.[412] The report of the 2008 meeting states that: 'The Extended Commission was encouraged by the European Community's commitment to transpose the CCSBT's measures into Community law and therefore fully abide by the CCSBT's measures in the future.' On that basis, the CNM status of the EC was continued, although the EC was also encouraged to consider acceding to the CCBST Convention.[413]

Inter-American Tropical Tuna Commission (IATTC)

The IATTC was established by the 1949 Convention for the Establishment of an Inter-American Tropical Tuna Commission (hereafter, 'the IATTC Convention'),[414] which entered into force in 1950. A new treaty (the so-called 'Antigua Convention', adopted in 2003)[415] is set to replace the IATTC Convention but is not yet in force.

The EC is not a party to the IATTC Convention. Instead, in 1999 Spain was permitted by the EC to become a party 'on a temporary basis' in view of the fact that the Convention did not provide for accession by regional economic integration organizations (hereafter, 'REIOs').[416] That situation has persisted, and in 2005 the EC became a 'Cooperating Non Party' (hereafter, 'CNP') to the IATTC Convention.[417] However, in 2006 the EC approved the Antigua Convention,[418] which does provide for REIOs to become parties. Of the EC Member States aside from Spain, France is a party to the IATTC Convention and has also ratified the Antigua Convention (presumably in relation to its OCTs).

In view of the healthy rate of ratification of the Antigua Convention,[419] its provisions will be described here. The Convention covers a specified part of the eastern Pacific Ocean.[420] The objective of the Convention is to 'ensure the long-term conservation and sustainable use of the fish stocks covered by this

---

[411] See further: Owen, D, *Recommended Best Practices for Regional Fisheries Management Organizations: Technical Study No. 2* (London: Chatham House, 2007), 12–22.

[412] CCSBT 14 (2007) report, para 180; see also para 183.

[413] CCSBT 15 (2008) report, para 49; see also para 47 and Attachment 5-1.   [414] 80 UNTS 3.

[415] OJ 2005 L15/10.

[416] Council Decision 1999/405/EC of 10 June 1999 authorising the Kingdom of Spain to accede to the Convention establishing the Inter-American Tropical Tuna Commission on a temporary basis (IATTC), OJ 1999 L155/37.

[417] IATTC, *Minutes of the 73rd Meeting (Revised)*, p 5, item 10. See also Resolution C-04-02 on criteria for attaining the status of cooperating non-party or fishing entity in IATTC (now superseded by Resolution C-07-02).

[418] Council Decision 2006/539/EC of 22 May 2006 on the conclusion, on behalf of the European Community of the Convention for the Strengthening of the Inter-American Tropical Tuna Commission established by the 1949 Convention between the United States of America and the Republic of Costa Rica, OJ 2006 L224/22.   [419] See the website of the IATTC.

[420] Antigua Convention, Art III.

Convention . . .'.[421] The term 'fish stocks covered by this Convention' means 'stocks of tunas and tuna-like species and other species of fish taken by vessels fishing for tunas and tuna-like species in the Convention Area'.[422] The IATTC has broad fisheries management powers.[423]

At the time of writing, Spain had 126 vessels flying its flag on the IATTC's Regional Vessel Register; France had fourteen.[424] Parties to the IATTC Convention are required to implement the IATTC's conservation and management measures. However, as a CNP, the EC has in principle had to 'confirm its commitment to respect the [IATTC's] conservation and management measures'.[425] In practice, it is not entirely clear how the EC and Spain between them share the responsibility to transpose the IATTC's measures (pending entry into force of the Antigua Convention). Only EC Regulations, rather than any Spanish regulations, transposing IATTC measures will be considered here.

The standing EC Regulation on technical measures for highly migratory species, Regulation 520/2007, states that the EC, as a CNP of the IATTC Convention, 'has *decided to* apply the technical measures adopted by the IATTC' which 'should therefore be incorporated in Community law' (emphasis added).[426] That wording suggests a more relaxed approach to transposition of the IATTC's measures than CNP status requires (see above). The Regulation then transposes a capacity limit for seiners and some other measures.[427]

In the principal annual Regulation (40/2008), the EC notes that the IATTC 'failed to adopt catch limitations for yellowfin tuna, bigeye tuna and skipjack tuna at its Annual Meeting in 2007, and although the Community is not a member of the IATTC, it is necessary to adopt measures to ensure sustainable management of the resource under the jurisdiction of that Organisation'.[428] In turn, the Regulation continues the application in 2008 of some technical measures (closed seasons) for the said three tuna species that were originally intended to apply only in 2007,[429] as well as transposing some other measures.[430]

The standing EC Regulation on control measures for highly migratory species is Regulation 1936/2001,[431] which in respect of the IATTC merely requires each Member State to 'take the action necessary in order that vessels flying its flag respect the IATTC measures transposed into Community law'.[432] The phrase 'the

---

[421] Antigua Convention, Art II.   [422] Antigua Convention, Art I(1).

[423] Antigua Convention, Art VII.   [424] See the website of the IATTC.

[425] IATTC Resolution C-04-02 (now replaced by Resolution C-07-02); para 4a. See further: Owen, *Recommended Best Practices*, 23–36.   [426] Reg 520/2007, recital (9).

[427] Reg 520/2007, Arts 22 and 21, 26, and 27. (Arts 23–25 relate to the International Dolphin Conservation Program, on which, see subsection 7.1 below.)   [428] Reg 40/2008, recital (33).

[429] Reg 40/2008, Art 13 and Annex III, para 18.

[430] Reg 40/2008, Art 13 and Annex III, paras 19 and 20.

[431] Council Regulation (EC) No 1936/2001 of 27 September 2001 laying down control measures applicable to fishing for certain stocks of highly migratory fish, OJ 2001 L263/1, as amended.

[432] Reg 1936/2001, Art 22; see also recitals (8) and (10).

IATTC measures transposed into Community law' may be a reference to the measures mentioned above. In any event, the IATTC has adopted several detailed measures on control, some of which are expressly applicable to CNPs by virtue of their wording; such measures do not appear to have been transposed into EC law (but see subsection 6.5 below regarding Regulation 1005/2008).

International Commission for the Conservation of Atlantic Tunas (ICCAT)

The ICCAT was established by the 1966 International Convention for the Conservation of Atlantic Tunas (hereafter, 'the ICCAT Convention'),[433] which entered into force in 1969. Amendments to the Convention were adopted in 1984 and 1992, which entered into force in 1997 and 2005 respectively. The first of these amendments made it possible for REIOs to become parties.

The ICCAT Convention covers 'all waters of the Atlantic Ocean, including the adjacent Seas'[434] (which include, inter alia, the Mediterranean Sea) and 'the populations of tuna and tuna-like fishes' found there.[435] The objective of the Convention is to maintain 'the populations of these fishes at levels which will permit the maximum sustainable catch for food and other purposes'.[436] The ICCAT may, inter alia, make recommendations designed to achieve that objective; furthermore, the parties agree to 'take all action necessary to ensure the enforcement' of the Convention.[437]

The EC has been a party to the ICCAT Convention, and a member of the ICCAT, since 1997 (when the amendment allowing REIOs to be parties entered into force).[438] Of the EC Member States, France (in respect of Saint Pierre and Miquelon) and the UK (in respect of several of its OCTs) are also parties. The Netherlands, on behalf of its OCTs, is not a party; however, the Netherland Antilles is a cooperating non-party. EC involvement in the ICCAT fishery can be illustrated by, for example, considering those flag EC Member States with vessels on the ICCAT's record of fishing vessels larger than 24 m authorized to fish for tuna and tuna-like species in the Convention Area: at the time of writing, there were ten such Member States, with the number of authorized vessels per Member State ranging from less than five up to more than 500.[439]

---

[433] 673 UNTS 63.   [434] ICCAT Convention, Art I.
[435] ICCAT Convention, preamble.   [436] ICCAT Convention, preamble.
[437] ICCAT Convention, Arts VIII(1)(a) and IX(1).
[438] See the website of the ICCAT. See also Council Decision 86/238/EEC of 9 June 1986 on the accession of the Community to the International Convention for the Conservation of Atlantic Tunas, as amended by the Protocol annexed to the Final Act of the Conference of Plenipotentiaries of the States Parties to the Convention signed in Paris on 10 July 1984, OJ 1986 L162/33.
[439] See the website of the ICCAT. For other indices of EC involvement see, for example, the other Records on the website of the ICCAT as well as Reg 40/2008, Annex ID.

Four standing EC Regulations are used to transpose the ICCAT's measures, namely Regulations 520/2007,[440] 1936/2001,[441] and 1984/2003[442] (which also apply to some other tuna RFMOs), and Regulation 1559/2007 (regarding an ICCAT recovery plan for bluefin tuna in the eastern Atlantic and the Mediterranean).[443] The ICCAT's trade-related measures against certain named States are implemented by Regulation 827/2004.[444] The principal annual Regulation (40/2008) transposes the fishing opportunities and most of the technical measures adopted by the ICCAT in 2007.[445]

Indian Ocean Tuna Commission (IOTC)

The IOTC was established by the 1993 Agreement for the Establishment of the Indian Ocean Tuna Commission (hereafter, 'the IOTC Agreement').[446] The IOTC Agreement is established under Article XIV of the FAO Constitution, but has an autonomous budget.[447]

The Agreement covers various tuna and tuna-like species.[448] In addition to the Indian Ocean, it covers 'adjacent seas, north of the Antarctic Convergence, insofar as it is necessary to cover such seas for the purpose of conserving and managing stocks that migrate into or out of the Indian Ocean'.[449] The IOTC is to 'promote cooperation among its Members with a view to ensuring, through appropriate management, the conservation and optimum utilization of stocks covered by this Agreement and encouraging sustainable development of fisheries based on such stocks'.[450] To achieve these objectives, the IOTC is to, *inter alia*, adopt conservation and management measures and 'carry out such other activities as may be necessary . . . .'[451]

The EC has been a party to the IOTC Agreement since 1995,[452] and a member of the IOTC since the Agreement entered into force in 1996. Of the EC Member States, France and the UK are parties (presumably in relation to their OCTs). EC

---

[440] Reg 520/2007, Arts 5–17.

[441] Reg 1936/2001, Arts 4–19c (but Reg 1005/2008, applicable from 1 January 2010, repeals Arts 8, 19a, 19b, and 19c—see Reg 1005/2008, Arts 56 and 57).

[442] Council Regulation (EC) No 1984/2003 of 8 April 2003 introducing a system for the statistical monitoring of trade in bluefin tuna, swordfish and bigeye tuna within the Community, OJ 2003 L295/1.

[443] Council Regulation (EC) No 1559/2007 of 17 December 2007 establishing a multi-annual recovery plan for bluefin tuna in the Eastern Atlantic and Mediterranean and amending Regulation (EC) No 520/2007, OJ 2007 L340/8.

[444] Council Regulation (EC) No 827/2004 of 26 April 2004 prohibiting imports of Atlantic bigeye tuna (*Thunnus obesus*) originating in Bolivia, Cambodia, Equatorial Guinea, Georgia and Sierra Leone and repealing Regulation (EC) No 1036/2001, OJ 2004 L127/21, as amended.

[445] Reg 40/2008, recital (39), Arts 1 and 5(1) and Annex ID, and Arts 80–82. See also, in respect of bluefin tuna, Arts 82a–82c.　　　　　　　　　　　　　　　　　　　　　　[446] 1927 UNTS 329.

[447] IOTC Agreement, Art XIII.　　　　[448] IOTC Agreement, Art III and Annex B.

[449] IOTC Agreement, Art II.　　　　[450] IOTC Agreement, Art V(1).

[451] IOTC Agreement, Art V(2)(c) and (h).

[452] Council Decision 95/399/EC of 18 September 1995 on the accession of the Community to the Agreement for the establishment of the Indian Ocean Tuna Commission, OJ 1995 L236/24.

involvement in the IOTC fishery can be illustrated by, for example, considering those flag EC Member States with vessels on the IOTC Record of fishing vessels authorized to fish for tuna and tuna-like species in the IOTC Area: at the time of writing, there were five such Member States, with the number of authorized vessels per Member State ranging from one up to 295.[453]

Three standing EC Regulations are used to transpose the IOTC's measures, namely Regulations 520/2007,[454] 1936/2001,[455] and 1984/2003 (which also apply to some other tuna RFMOs). The principal annual Regulation (40/2008) transposes some of the measures adopted by the IOTC in 2006 and 2007.[456]

Western and Central Pacific Fisheries Commission (WCPFC)

The WCPFC, also known as the Commission for the Conservation and Management of Highly Migratory Fish Stocks in the Western and Central Pacific Ocean, was established by the 2000 Convention on the Conservation and Management of Highly Migratory Fish Stocks in the Western and Central Pacific Ocean (hereafter, 'the WCPFC Convention')[457] which entered into force in 2004.

The Convention applies to 'all stocks of highly migratory fish within the Convention Area except sauries'.[458] The term 'highly migratory fish stocks' is defined as 'all fish stocks of the species listed in Annex 1 of the [1982 United Nations Convention on the Law of the Sea] occurring in the Convention Area, and such other species of fish as the Commission may determine'.[459] The Convention's objective is to 'ensure . . . the long-term conservation and sustainable use of highly migratory fish stocks in the western and central Pacific Ocean . . .'.[460] The WCPFC has broad fisheries management powers.[461]

The EC has been a party to the WCPFC Convention since 2004,[462] and a member of the WCPFC since 2005.[463] Of the EC Member States, France is a party (presumably in relation to its OCTs). Some of France's OCTs are also 'participating territories'. The UK has an OCT within the Convention Area but is not currently a party on its behalf. EC involvement in the WCPFC fishery can be illustrated by, for example, considering the 'European Union' vessels on the WCPFC Record of Fishing Vessels: the Record, at the time of writing, listed a

---

[453] See the website of the IOTC.   [454] Reg 520/2007, Arts 18–20.
[455] Reg 1936/2001, Arts 20–21c (but Reg 1005/2008, applicable from 1 January 2010, repeals Arts 21, 21b, and 21c—see Reg 1005/2008, Arts 56 and 57).
[456] Reg 40/2008, recital (37) and Arts 71–73.   [457] 2275 UNTS 43.
[458] WCPFC Convention, Art 3(3).   [459] WCPFC Convention, Art 1(f).
[460] WCPFC Convention, Art 2.   [461] WCPFC Convention, Art 10.
[462] Council Decision 2005/75/EC of 26 April 2004 on the accession of the Community to the Convention on the Conservation and Management of Highly Migratory Fish Stocks in the Western and Central Pacific Ocean, OJ 2005 L32/1.   [463] Reg 40/2008, recital (34).

total of 121 such vessels, although it did not identify the individual flag EC Member States comprising that fleet.[464]

Regarding transposition of the WCPFC's measures into EC law, Regulation 520/2007 contains a loosely worded provision on 'Waste reduction'[465] while the principal annual Regulation (40/2008) contains some more specific provisions that transpose some of the measures adopted by the WCPFC in 2006[466] and some (non-binding) WCPFC measures adopted in 2005.[467]

6.4 Regional fisheries management organizations concerned with anadromous stocks

North Atlantic Salmon Conservation Organization (NASCO)

The NASCO was established by the 1982 Convention for the Conservation of Salmon in the North Atlantic Ocean (hereafter, 'the NASCO Convention').[468] The Convention applies to 'the salmon stocks which migrate beyond areas of fisheries jurisdiction of coastal States of the Atlantic Ocean north of 36°N latitude throughout their migratory range'.[469] The objective of the NASCO is to 'contribute through consultation and cooperation to the conservation, restoration, enhancement and rational management of salmon stocks subject to this Convention . . .'.[470] In practice, the only NASCO regulatory measures currently in force relate to the Faroese salmon fishery and the West Greenland salmon fishery.[471] Article 2 of the Convention itself establishes some important prohibitions on salmon fishing: (a) '[f]ishing of salmon is prohibited beyond areas of fisheries jurisdiction of coastal States';[472] and (b), with certain exceptions regarding West Greenland and the Faroe Islands, '[w]ithin areas of fisheries jurisdiction of coastal States, fishing of salmon is prohibited beyond 12 nautical miles from the baselines'.[473]

The EC has been a party to the NASCO Convention since 1982,[474] and a member of the NASCO since the Convention entered into force in 1983. Of the three regional Commissions established by the Convention,[475] the EC is a member of two, namely the West Greenland Commission and the North-East Atlantic Commission.[476] Of the EC Member States, Denmark is a party to the Convention

---

[464] See the website of the WCPFC.   [465] Reg 520/2007, Art 28.
[466] Reg 40/2008, recital (34) and Arts 77–79.
[467] Reg 40/2008, Art 13 and Annex III, paras 19 and 20.   [468] 1338 UNTS 33.
[469] NASCO Convention, Art 1(1).   [470] NASCO Convention, Art 3(2).
[471] See the website of the NASCO.   [472] NASCO Convention, Art 2(1).
[473] NASCO Convention, Art 2(2).
[474] Council Decision 82/886/EEC of 13 December 1982 concerning the conclusion of the Convention for the Conservation of Salmon in the North Atlantic Ocean, OJ 1982 L378/24.
[475] NASCO Convention, Arts 3(3) and (4) and 7–8.
[476] NASCO Convention, Art 10. See also Art 11(2).

in respect of the Faroe Islands and Greenland. France is not a party in respect of St Pierre and Miquelon, although cooperation has been sought with France in that regard.[477]

The NASCO is currently undertaking a 'Next Steps Strategy' process to assist implementation of its main work areas (fishery management, habitat protection and restoration, and aquaculture and associated activities). The process involves 'the Parties and relevant jurisdictions' preparing so-called Implementation Plans. The report of the 25th annual meeting of the NASCO Council, held in June 2008, states that, of the EC Member States, such plans have been prepared by Denmark, Finland, France, Germany, Ireland, Sweden, and the UK; however, concern was expressed at the failure by Portugal and Spain to submit plans.[478]

The prohibitions in Article 2 of the NASCO Convention (see above) are transposed by Regulations 850/98[479] and 2187/2005.[480] In general, under these two Regulations, fishing for Atlantic salmon is permitted only within 6 nm or less from the baseline of coastal Member States; such fisheries therefore lend themselves to regulation by the Member States using their delegated powers (see Chapter 4). No EC fisheries legislation appears to have been used to transpose the regulatory measures adopted by the NASCO, perhaps because Community fishing vessels do not fish for salmon in the waters covered by those measures. However, at the EC level, the EC Habitats Directive[481] and the EC Water Framework Directive[482] are both relevant to the conservation of the Atlantic salmon.

6.5 The IUU Regulation

The IUU Regulation entered into force in October 2008 and is applicable from the beginning of January 2010.[483] The Regulation 'establishes a Community system to prevent, deter and eliminate' IUU fishing (see further subsection 3.5

---

[477] NASCO Resolutions CNL(00)59 (and note 10th recital) and CNL(02)47.

[478] NASCO 25 Council report, p 4 and Annex 11.

[479] Council Regulation (EC) No 850/98 of 30 March 1998 for the conservation of fishery resources through technical measures for the protection of juveniles of marine organisms, OJ 1998 L125/1, as amended and corrected, Arts 26 and 36.

[480] Council Regulation (EC) No 2187/2005 of 21 December 2005 for the conservation of fishery resources through technical measures in the Baltic Sea, the Belts and the Sound, amending Regulation (EC) No 1434/98 and repealing Regulation (EC) No 88/98, OJ 2005 L349/1, as amended, Art 17. By virtue of the wording of Art 17 of Reg 2187/2005, the EC's transposition of Art 2(2) of the NASCO Convention appears to be only partial regarding the Baltic Sea.

[481] Council Directive 92/43/EEC of 21 May 1992 on the conservation of natural habitats and of wild fauna and flora, OJ 1992 L206/7, as amended and corrected.

[482] Directive 2000/60/EC of the European Parliament and of the Council of 23 October 2000 establishing a framework for Community action in the field of water policy, OJ 2000 L327/1, as amended.   [483] Reg 1005/2008, Art 57.

above).[484] As such, it focuses on improving compliance with, *inter alia*, the conservation and management measures of RFMOs.[485] RFMOs have adopted an array of measures to help ensure compliance with their conservation and management measures. Depending on the RFMO in question, these may relate to, *inter alia*, sightings of IUU-implicated vessels, port State control and transhipment, catch certification, vessel registers, IUU vessel lists and accompanying measures, trade-related measures against named countries, and measures in relation to nationals. (Measures regarding nationals are motivated by the fact that nationals, whether natural or legal persons, may support or engage in IUU fishing other than directly through the flag vessels of an RFMO's members.)

The Commission has provided several justifications for the IUU Regulation with regard to RFMOs. One of these relates to simplification of the EC legal framework. The Commission has noted that in the system existing prior to the IUU Regulation, ie as described in subsections 6.2–6.4 above, RFMOs' measures 'are transposed into EC law by the Council on a case-by-case basis, via regular amendments to existing regulations specific for each RFMO or each type of RFMOs [sic]' which 'results in a proliferation of different regulations and a very complex and changing regulatory environment, where rules differ for Community operators depending on its [sic] location'.[486] In seeking to address this problem, the IUU Regulation is clearly very relevant to the transposition by the EC of RFMOs' compliance measures. Another justification for the IUU Regulation is the Commission's objective of 'harmonizing and generalizing the application of the most far-reaching measures adopted within one RFMO to all Community operators present in RFMOs areas',[487] in other words taking the most progressive RFMO measures and applying them generally.

The IUU Regulation establishes (sometimes overlapping) regimes relating to port State control and transhipment;[488] catch certification;[489] a 'Community alert system';[490] a 'Community IUU vessel list';[491] non-cooperating third countries;[492] nationals involved in IUU fishing;[493] sanctions for 'serious infringements';[494] and

---

[484] Reg 1005/2008, Art 1(1).
[485] See, for example, Reg 1005/2008, Art 2(2)(b) and (c), (3)(b), and (4)(a).
[486] *Commission Staff Working Document, Accompanying document to the Proposal for a Council Regulation establishing a Community system to prevent, deter and eliminate illegal, unreported and unregulated fishing: Impact Assessment*, SEC(2007) 1336, 17.10.2007, section 4.6, p 70. See also: (a) *Commission Staff Working Document, Accompanying document to the Proposal for a Council Regulation establishing a Community system to prevent, deter and eliminate illegal, unreported and unregulated fishing*, SEC(2007) 1310, 17.10.2007, Annex I, Proposal No 4, pp 4–5; and (b) *Proposal for a Council Regulation establishing a Community system to prevent, deter and eliminate illegal, unreported and unregulated fishing*, COM(2007) 602, 17.10.2007, explanatory memorandum, pp 8–9.
[487] SEC(2007) 1336, section 4.6, p 70. See also: (a) SEC(2007) 1310, Annex I, Proposal No 4, pp 4–5; and (b) COM(2007) 602, explanatory memorandum, pp 8–9.   [488] Reg 1005/2008, Arts 4–11.
[489] Reg 1005/2008, Arts 12–22.   [490] Reg 1005/2008, Arts 23–24.
[491] Reg 1005/2008, Arts 25–30 and 37.   [492] Reg 1005/2008, Arts 31–36 and 38.
[493] Reg 1005/2008, Arts 39–40.   [494] Reg 1005/2008, Arts 41–47.

sightings of IUU-implicated vessels.[495] Reflecting the justifications mentioned above, the Regulation does not transpose any given RFMO's compliance measures specifically. Instead, its regimes are generic in nature. Through being generic, they capture elements of a given RFMO's own regimes to varying degrees. It is beyond the scope of this work to analyse systematically whether or not a given RFMO's compliance measures on a particular theme, such as, for example, port State control, are totally encompassed by the IUU Regulation's regime on that theme. If they are not totally covered by the IUU Regulation, or other EC legislation, and yet they are binding on the EC, full transposition would require either an amendment to the IUU Regulation or some other change to the EC legal framework (see further below). In contrast, if a given RFMO's measures did not go as far as those set out in the IUU Regulation, the IUU Regulation would, in effect, be supplementing that RFMO's measures.

This can be illustrated using the IUU Regulation's approach to IUU vessel lists. The IUU Regulation provides for the establishment of a 'Community IUU vessel list'.[496] Under Article 30 of the IUU Regulation, this list is to include 'fishing vessels included in the IUU vessel lists adopted by regional fisheries management organisations'.[497] Such vessels are to be added to the Community IUU vessel list through comitology procedure.[498] Thus Article 30 of the IUU Regulation has the effect of (indirectly) transposing the RFMOs' IUU vessel lists into Community law as from the point in time that such lists are incorporated within the Community IUU vessel list.[499]

Article 37 of the IUU Regulation sets out various measures to apply in respect of fishing vessels included in the Community IUU vessel list. RFMOs that maintain their own IUU vessel lists have also adopted measures to apply to the vessels on their lists. Without further research, it cannot readily be said whether the various measures set out in Article 37 encompass all the kinds of measures that have so far been adopted by RFMOs. However, it can at least be said that, to the extent that any given RFMO's measures regarding listed IUU vessels are included in Article 37, the IUU Regulation therefore transposes such measures. Reflecting the general point made above, further transposition into EC law would be required for any binding RFMO measures not encompassed by Article 37 whereas, in contrast, the IUU Regulation would be supplementing an RFMO's measures where the latter did not go as far as those set out in Article 37.

The IUU Regulation's approach to RFMOs' IUU vessel lists, whereby it provides for the incorporation of such lists into the Community IUU vessel list, may be contrasted with the Regulation's approach to non-cooperating third countries. Article 33 of the IUU Regulation provides for the establishment of a list of such countries; Article 38 sets out the measures, including trade-related

---

[495] Reg 1005/2008, Arts 48–50.   [496] Reg 1005/2008, Arts 25–30.
[497] Reg 1005/2008, Art 30(1).   [498] Reg 1005/2008, Art 30(1).
[499] See further Reg 1005/2008, Art 30(2) and (3).

measures, that are to apply to the countries concerned. Some RFMOs have like-wise adopted provisions that enable them to identify non-cooperating countries and to adopt trade-related measures against such countries. However, the relevant provisions of the IUU Regulation do not expressly provide for countries identified by RFMOs to be incorporated into the EC's list of non-cooperating third coun-tries. There are several possible reasons for this. One may be that, in contrast to IUU vessel lists, the instances of RFMOs identifying non-cooperating countries are very few. Indeed, the only RFMO to have actually identified any such countries and to have employed trade-related measures against them is the ICCAT. Therefore, the EC may have decided that the more appropriate legislative response to any RFMO lists of countries is to transpose such measures separately. The ICCAT's measures are transposed by Regulation 827/2004 (see subsection 6.3 above), and the latter Regulation is not repealed by the IUU Regulation.

Where the IUU Regulation establishes a particular compliance regime at the EC level, it varies in how it describes the relationship between its own measures and those of any RFMOs. In two cases, the IUU Regulation states expressly that its own measures are 'without prejudice' to stricter measures adopted by RFMOs. The first case relates to port inspections. Article 9 of the IUU Regulation estab-lishes a minimum percentage of landings and transhipments by third State fishing vessels to be inspected. However, it adds that the stated percentage is 'without prejudice to the higher thresholds adopted by regional fisheries management organisations'.[500] The second case relates to fishing vessel sightings, which are dealt with in a chapter of the Regulation entitled 'Implementation of provisions adopted within certain regional fisheries management organisations pertaining to fishing vessel sightings'. Article 48, which takes a generic approach to transposing such provisions, adds that: 'This Article shall apply without prejudice to stricter provisions adopted by regional fisheries management organisations to which the Community is a contracting party.'[501]

A deference to certain RFMO measures can also be implied from Articles 13, 27, and 50 of the IUU Regulation. Article 13(2) states that Article 13, which establishes a certain role for catch documents under catch documentation schemes adopted by RFMOs, applies 'without prejudice to the specific regulations in force whereby such catch documentation schemes are implemented into Community law'. Article 27(8) states that Community fishing vessels are not to be included in the Community IUU vessel list in certain specific circumstances but adds that this exception is 'without prejudice to the action taken by regional fisheries manage-ment organisations'. Article 50(5) states that Article 50, on investigations by Member States of sighted IUU-implicated vessels, 'shall apply without prejudice . . . [inter alia] . . . to the provisions adopted by regional fisheries management organisations to which the Community is a contracting party'.

---

[500] Reg 1005/2008, Art 9(1).   [501] Reg 1005/2008, Art 48(6).

However, beyond the five instances cited above, the IUU Regulation is silent about whether or not its provisions are without prejudice to measures adopted by RFMOs. This variation in practice within the IUU Regulation, whereby some of its provisions expressly establish the relationship between the Regulation's provisions and RFMOs' measures and some do not, is potentially confusing. For example, no such relationship is stated in respect of Article 37 (which sets out measures to apply in respect of vessels on the Community IUU vessel list), Article 38 (which establishes measures to apply to non-cooperating third countries), or Article 39 (which relates to nationals). The question arises whether such provisions are intended to be without prejudice to any stricter or more specific measures adopted by RFMOs.

Notwithstanding the uncertainties raised above, the fact remains that the generic approach taken in the IUU Regulation does in principle reduce the need for year-on-year transposition of individual RFMOs' compliance measures into EC law. Indeed, the Regulation repeals some provisions of EC law that were specific to particular RFMOs but which the EC presumably regards as no longer being necessary in view of the new generic regimes:[502] it repeals parts of Regulation 1936/2001 that sought to transpose certain compliance measures adopted by the ICCAT and the IOTC and parts of Regulation 601/2004 that sought to transpose certain compliance measures adopted by the CCAMLR.

However, it is important to emphasize that the need for year-on-year transposition of RFMOs' compliance measures is not removed entirely. First, the IUU Regulation does not establish generic regimes for all types of compliance measures adopted by RFMOs, vessel registers being a principal example.[503] Secondly, in the wake of the annual meeting of any given RFMO, it will remain necessary for the Commission to scrutinize any compliance measures that have been adopted by that RFMO and consider whether or not they go further than the measures already contained in the IUU Regulation. As noted above, if they do go further, and if they are binding on the EC, they will need to be transposed into EC law, whether through a timely amendment to the IUU Regulation or some other change to the EC legal framework.

6.6 Other fisheries bodies

The bodies examined in subsections 6.1 to 6.4 above are all regulatory in nature. There also exist a number of other bodies that have an advisory and/or recommendatory, rather than regulatory, function of which the EC is a member or with which it is associated. Such bodies include the FAO, various FAO regional committees and commissions, and the ICES.

---

[502] Reg 1005/2008, Art 56.
[503] Regarding its treatment of vessel registers, see Reg 1005/2008, Arts 4(4), 25(1)(b)(iii), and 31(2).

The FAO is the UN's specialized agency with responsibility for food, agriculture, and fisheries. Some indication of its role and work in relation to fisheries was given in Chapter 3. Originally only States could be members of the FAO. In 1991 the constitution of the FAO was amended to open membership to any REIO to which the member States of that REIO had transferred competence over matters within the field of the FAO's activities, provided that a majority of the member States of that REIO were also members of the FAO. As a result of, and shortly after the adoption of, that amendment, the EC became a member of the FAO. In accordance with Article II(10) of the Constitution of the FAO, which provides for a system of alternate exercise of membership rights as between an REIO and its member States, the EC exercises membership rights (including voting rights) in respect of matters for which it is competent (including therefore fisheries conservation), while the Member States do so in relation to matters that fall within their competence.[504] The EC is also a member of the Committee on Fisheries, which is the FAO's principal body dealing with fisheries issues.

The FAO has established a number of regional bodies that provide advice on fisheries, as well as in some cases making recommendations (although such recommendations are not binding), for the region concerned. The EC is a member of three such bodies—the Fishery Committee for the Eastern Central Atlantic, the Western Central Atlantic Fishery Commission, and the European Inland Fisheries Advisory Commission.[505] Because these bodies are no more than advisory or recommendatory, there has been no question of the EC having to take any implementing action in respect of management measures, unlike the case with RFMOs (see subsections 6.2–6.4 above)

The ICES promotes and coordinates research relating to fisheries and pollution in the north-east Atlantic, North Sea, and Baltic Sea. As was seen in Chapter 4, the ICES provides the EC with advice on the state of fish stocks in Community waters and on possible management measures. That advice forms part of the scientific basis for most of the fisheries opportunities Regulations adopted by the Council, even if the Council often does not fully follow the advice of the ICES. The treaty establishing the ICES[506] is open to participation only by States. Thus, the EC is not a member of the ICES, although all its Member States bordering the north-east Atlantic, North Sea, and Baltic Sea are. The EC has concluded a succession of agreements with the ICES setting out arrangements for the provision of advice by the latter: the most recent was concluded in 2007.[507]

---

[504] Further on EC membership of the FAO, see MacLeod et al, *The External Relations*, 176–9 and literature cited there; and Fried, R, *The Relations between the EC and International Organizations—Legal Theory and Practice* (The Hague: Kluwer, 1995), 243–79.

[505] Information on the membership, functions, and work of these bodies can be found on the FAO's website.

[506] Convention on the International Council for the Exploration of the Sea, 1964, 652 UNTS 237.

[507] Agreement in the form of a Memorandum of Understanding between the European Community and the International Council for the Exploration of the Sea, available on the website of the ICES.

7 The EC and some other international fisheries management issues

7.1 Cetaceans

Cetaceans are an order of marine mammals that includes whales, dolphins, and porpoises. Even though cetaceans are not fish, they are not unconnected to the CFP. First, as seen in Chapter 2, some cetacean products fall within the material scope of the CFP. However, there has long been political disagreement as to whether cetaceans as a whole fall within the scope of the CFP, and over how far the EC has competence in respect of cetaceans under the CFP, in particular the competence to enter into agreements concerning their conservation and management. The division of opinion lies between the Commission and some Member States. The latter take the view that such agreements fall outside the scope of the CFP, whereas the Commission, which strongly reasserted its position in 2007, takes the view that they do not.[508] The issue appears to remain unresolved. In practice this does not matter greatly because even if the EC should lack competence under the CFP to enter into agreements concerning cetaceans, it has the competence to do so under the environmental policy (in particular under Article 174(4) EC).[509] The second reason why cetaceans are of some relevance to the CFP is because, as will be seen, the conservation of some cetaceans (particularly dolphins and porpoises) is threatened by various kinds of fishing practice, including practices undertaken in Community waters or by Community fishing vessels elsewhere (see further Chapter 4). It should be noted, however, that there is no directed hunting or killing of cetaceans in Community waters or by Community fishing vessels.[510]

This subsection looks at five treaties concerning cetaceans to which the EC and/or its Member States are parties. The first of those is the International Convention for the Regulation of Whaling,[511] adopted in 1946, which established the International Whaling Commission (IWC). As currently drafted, the Convention permits only States to become parties to it, so the EC is not and cannot become a party to it and thus a member of the IWC. In both 1979 and 1992 the Commission proposed that EC Member States should try to secure amendment of the

---

[508] *Proposal for a Council Decision establishing the position to be adopted on behalf of the European Community with regard to proposals for amendments to the Schedule of the International Convention on* [sic] *the Regulation of Whaling,* COM(2007) 821, 19.12.2007, pp 2–4; and *Communication from the European Commission to the European Parliament and to the Council on Community action in relation to whaling,* COM (2007) 823, 19.12.2007, p 7. For earlier expressions of the Commission's views, see *Recommendation for a Council Decision authorising the Commission to negotiate on behalf of the Community for the establishment of a new International Convention on Whaling,* COM(79) 364, 30.08.1979, pp 2–4 and *Communication from the Commission to the Council concerning the conservation of whales within the framework of the IWC,* COM(92) 316, 29.07.1992.   [509] COM(2007) 821, pp 2 and 4.
[510] COM(2007) 823, pp 6–7.   [511] 161 UNTS 72.

Convention so as to permit the EC to become a party to it,[512] but there was no agreement in the Council to do so.[513] As of 30 November 2008 twenty-two EC Member States were parties to the Convention and thus members of the IWC. The five Member States that were not members of the IWC were Bulgaria, Estonia, Latvia, Malta, and Poland.[514] A year earlier the Commission had called on those EC Member States that were not members of the IWC to become members.[515]

In 1982 the IWC adopted a moratorium on all commercial whaling. Although some pro-whaling States (such as Japan and Norway) have sought in recent years (so far unsuccessfully) to have the moratorium lifted or relaxed, this has been opposed by many members of the IWC, including EC Member States.[516] That position is reflected in Community law. The Habitats Directive requires Member States to prohibit the deliberate capture or killing of all species of cetacean in Community waters,[517] while Regulations 348/81 and 338/97 prohibit the commercial importation into the EC of all cetaceans and cetacean products.[518] In 2007 the Commission proposed that the Council should adopt a Decision that would require the Member States to adopt a common Community position at future meetings of the IWC.[519] The Council adopted a Decision based on the proposal in June 2008.[520] In 2008 the Commission followed up its 2007 proposal with a proposal for a Council Decision with a longer-term approach to the adoption of a common position.[521] Under that approach the common position to be adopted by Member States at future meetings of the IWC should be in accordance with the following policy objectives: (a) support to maintain the moratorium on commercial whaling; (b) oppose proposals regarding new types of whaling that could undermine the moratorium unless such proposals would guarantee a significant improvement in the long-term conservation status of whales and bring all whaling operations by IWC members under IWC control; (c) support proposals for the

---

[512] COM(79) 364 and COM(92) 316.   [513] See COM(2007) 821, p 3.

[514] Information about membership of the IWC may be found on its website.

[515] COM(2007) 821, p 4.   [516] See reports of meetings of the IWC on its website.

[517] Dir 92/43, Art 12. The Court has held that the Directive applies to the EEZ: see Case C-6/04 *Commission v United Kingdom* [2005] ECR I-9017, para 117 (see also Chapters 2 and 4). Some limited derogations to the prohibition in Art 12 are provided for in Art 16.

[518] Council Regulation (EEC) No 348/81 of 20 January 1981 on common rules for imports of whales and other cetacean products, OJ 1981 L39/1, as amended and corrected; and Council Regulation (EC) No 338/97 of 9 December 1996 on the protection of species of wild fauna and flora by regulating trade therein, OJ 1997 L61/1, as amended and corrected.

[519] COM(2007) 821, pp 4–8.

[520] Council of the European Union, 2874th Council meeting, Environment, 5 June 2008, press release, 9959/08 (Presse 149), 15. The Council's Decision does not appear to have been published in the *Official Journal*.

[521] *Proposal for a Council Decision establishing the position to be adopted on behalf of the European Community with regard to proposals for amendments to the International Convention on* [sic] *the Regulation of Whaling and its Schedule*, COM(2008) 711, 6.11.2008. See also Chapter 2.

creation of whale sanctuaries; (d) support proposals for the management of aboriginal subsistence whaling, provided that the conservation of stocks was not compromised; (e) support proposals to end 'scientific whaling' outside IWC control; and (f) oppose any proposals to amend the IWC's rules of procedure to broaden the scope of secret ballots.[522] As at the time of writing the Council did not appear to have adopted the Commission's proposal.

The second treaty to be considered is the 1979 Convention on the Conservation of Migratory Species of Wild Animals (hereafter, 'the CMS Convention').[523] Unlike the International Convention for the Regulation of Whaling, the CMS Convention permits REIOs to become parties to it. Availing itself of this possibility, the EC became a party to the Convention in 1983.[524] In addition, all EC Member States are parties.[525] The Convention is thus a mixed agreement (as to which see section 2 above). The Convention is concerned with the conservation of migratory species both on land and at sea. In relation to 'endangered' migratory species, which are listed in Appendix I and at the time of writing included twelve species of cetacean, the Convention provides that its parties shall take a variety of protective measures set out in Article III. Some of the cetacean species listed in Appendix I are found in Community waters. For such species, the Habitats Directive at least partially implements Article III. Appendix II lists migratory species with an 'unfavourable conservation status' and at the time of writing included forty-two species of cetacean. Article IV(3) provides that parties to the Convention that are range States[526] of the species listed in Appendix II 'shall endeavour to conclude AGREEMENTS [sic] where these would benefit the species'. Article IV(4) encourages parties to the Convention to conclude 'agreements for any population . . . of any species . . . members of which periodically cross one or more national jurisdictional boundaries'. Such species, it would seem, are not limited to those listed in Appendix II. There is further flexibility when concluding agreements under Article IV(4) because such agreements do not need to contain the information required by Article V for AGREEMENTS concluded under Article IV(3), nor are there any guidelines of which Article IV(4) agreements need to take account, unlike Article IV(3) AGREEMENTS.

Two agreements relating to cetaceans have been concluded under Article IV(4) that are of particular interest to the EC and its Member States—the Agreement on the Conservation of Small Cetaceans of the Baltic and North Seas (ASCOBANS) in 1992,[527] and the Agreement on the Conservation of Cetaceans of the Black Sea, Mediterranean Sea and Contiguous Atlantic Area (ACCOBAMS) in 1996.[528] The

[522] COM(2008) 711, p 9.
[523] 1651 UNTS 333. The CMS Convention is also discussed in subsection 7.3 below.
[524] Council Decision 82/461/EEC of 24 June 1982 on the conclusion of the Convention on the conservation of migratory species of wild animals, OJ 1982 L210/10.
[525] Information on parties to the CMS Convention may be found on its website.
[526] A term explained below.   [527] 1772 UNTS 217.   [528] 2183 UNTS 303.

ASCOBANS is concerned with the conservation of all small cetaceans (primarily dolphins and porpoises) found in the area to which it applies.[529] That area was originally the Baltic and North Seas,[530] but under an amendment to the Agreement that came into force in 2008, the area of application of the ASCOBANS has been extended to the seas off Ireland, France, and the Iberian peninsula, so that it meets up with the area to which the ACCOBAMS applies (see below).[531] As a result, the ASCOBANS has been retitled the 'Agreement on the Conservation of Small Cetaceans of the Baltic, North East Atlantic, Irish and North Seas'. The ASCOBANS is open to participation by any 'range State' (defined as any State that exercises jurisdiction over any part of the migratory range of a species to which the ASCOBANS applies or a State whose vessels engage in operations adversely affecting small cetaceans in areas beyond national jurisdiction but within the ASCOBANS area[532]) and any REIO. So far ten range States, all of which are EC Member States, have become parties to the ASCOBANS. The EC itself has signed, but not (yet) ratified, the ASCOBANS.[533]

The main threats to the conservation of cetaceans in the ASCOBANS area have been identified as being the incidental by-catch of cetaceans in various kinds of fishing gear, particularly driftnets, bottom-set gill nets, and large pelagic trawls; pollution of the marine environment; and disturbance of their habitat: of these, the first is the most significant.[534] The ASCOBANS, through the Conservation and Management Plan attached to the Agreement and the triennial Meetings of the Parties, has addressed several recommendations to its members to address those threats.[535] The Meetings of the Parties, in adopting measures to mitigate by-catch of cetaceans in fisheries, need of course to bear in mind the competence of the EC regarding such measures, as well as those measures that the EC has already adopted in that regard.[536] The latter measures include a restriction on driftnets, a prohibition on the use of certain types of fishing gear in waters covered by the ASCOBANS unless fitted with acoustic deterrent devices, and a scheme for monitoring incidental catches of cetaceans (see further Chapter 4). It has been suggested that the fact that by-catch mitigation measures fall within the scope of the CFP and the fact that all the parties to the ASCOBANS are members of the EC has discouraged

---

[529] ASCOBANS, Art 1.1.   [530] ASCOBANS, Art 1.2(b).

[531] Information on the website of the ASCOBANS.   [532] ASCOBANS, Art 1.2(f).

[533] Information on parties to the ASCOBANS may be found on its website.

[534] Churchill, RR, 'The Agreement on the Conservation of Small Cetaceans of the Baltic and North Seas' in Burns, WCG and Gillespie, A (eds), *The Future of Cetaceans in a Changing World* (Ardsley, NY: Transnational Publishers, 2003), 283 at 284–5.

[535] The recommendations adopted by the Meetings of the Parties can be found in the reports of the Meetings on the website of the ASCOBANS.

[536] See further Churchill, 'The Agreement', 291–2, 296–301, and 309; and Owen, D, *The interaction between the ASCOBANS MOP and the IWC, NAMMCO and EC*, paper presented at the 13th meeting of the Advisory Committee of ASCOBANS (available on the website of the ASCOBANS), 40–1 and 44–9.

the ASCOBANS in recent years from pursuing a more active by-catch mitigation strategy of its own.[537] In adopting its own measures, the EC appears to have been little influenced by the ASCOBANS.[538]

The ACCOBAMS is concerned with the conservation of all cetaceans (not just small cetaceans), unlike the ASCOBANS, found in the area to which it applies.[539] The latter comprises the Black Sea, the Mediterranean Sea, and the immediately contiguous area of the Atlantic.[540] Like the ASCOBANS, the ACCOBAMS is open to participation by any 'range State' and any REIO. At the time of writing twenty-one range States (including ten EC Member States) were parties to the ACCOBAMS. The EC, on the other hand, had neither signed nor ratified the ACCOBAMS.[541] The Commission has not (yet) proposed that the EC should become a party to either the ACCOBAMS or the ASCOBANS. That is rather surprising, given that in a Communication on Community action in relation to whaling, published in December 2007, the Commission called for 'coherent international action by the Community aimed to ensure . . . an effective international regulatory framework for the protections of whales'.[542] This document fails to make any mention of the ACCOBAMS or the ASCOBANS, let alone suggest Community participation in those bodies, whereas it contains extensive discussion of the IWC and the EC's role in relation thereto.

Cetaceans in the ACCOBAMS area face similar threats to those in the ASCOBANS area. As far as responses to those threats are concerned, the ACCOBAMS has been less affected by the discouraging effect that it was suggested above the existence of the EC's fisheries competence appears to have had on the ASCOBANS, probably because EC Member States constitute a much smaller proportion of the membership of the ACCOBAMS. The ACCOBAMS, through its Meetings of the Parties, has therefore succeeded in adopting a number of cetacean by-catch mitigation measures,[543] including, *inter alia*, a total ban on the use of driftnets.[544] The ACCOBAMS measures are couched in rather more prescriptive language than those of the ASCOBANS, although whether they are legally binding is uncertain. The ACCOBAMS speaks of its Meetings of the Parties adopting 'recommendations',[545] but does not elaborate on their legal nature.

---

[537] Caddell, R, 'Biodiversity Loss and the Prospects for International Co-Operation: EU Law and the Conservation of Migratory Species of Wild Animals' *Yearbook of European Environmental Law* 8 (2008) 218 at 247 and 249–50.   [538] Caddell, R, 'Biodiversity Loss', 247.

[539] ACCOBAMS, Art I.2.   [540] ACCOBAMS, Art I.1(a).

[541] Information on parties to the ACCOBAMS may be found on its website.

[542] COM(2007) 823, p 7.   [543] See further Caddell, 'Biodiversity Loss', 251–4.

[544] Amendment/Resolution 3.1: Amendment to Annex 2 to ACCOBAMS related to the use of driftnets, *Report of the Third Meeting of the Contracting Parties to ACCOBAMS*, 2007, 331, available on the website of the ACCOBAMS. See also Resolution 3.12 on By-Catch, Competitive Interactions and Acoustic Devices, ibid, 226.   [545] ACCOBAMS, Art III(8)(c) .

The final agreement to be considered in this section is the Agreement on the International Dolphin Conservation Program (AIDCP).[546] The AIDCP, which was adopted in 1998 and operates under the auspices of the IATTC (see subsection 6.3 above), is aimed at reducing incidental dolphin mortality in the Eastern Pacific tuna fishery. Dolphins tend to shoal with tuna, especially in tropical waters, and when tuna are fished with conventional purse-seine nets, many dolphins are also caught and die. To try to reduce those deaths, the AIDCP requires its parties to adopt a number of measures (including the use of selective fishing gear) that will result in the annual catch of dolphins in the Eastern Pacific being no greater than 0.1 per cent of their minimum estimated abundance.[547] The AIDCP is open to participation by REIOs.[548] The EC has availed itself of this possibility and became a party provisionally in 1999[549] and definitively in 2006.[550] In 1999 the parties to the AIDCP adopted a system to track and verify tuna caught in the AIDCP area by their vessels in order to enable tuna caught by dolphin-safe methods to be distinguished from non-dolphin-safe tuna. That system was not implemented into EC law until 2003.[551] The delay led to the USA imposing an embargo on imports of tuna from Spain (the only EC Member State whose vessels fished in the AIDCP area) in 2000.[552] The authors assume that the embargo was subsequently lifted, at least by the time that the EC adopted implementing measures.

7.2 CITES

This subsection discusses the 1973 Convention on International Trade in Endangered Species of Wild Fauna and Flora (CITES),[553] which entered into force in 1975. The CITES establishes regimes for international trade in specimens of particular species. The strictness of those regimes depends on whether the species

---

[546] Text in OJ 2005 L348/28. [547] AIDCP, Art V and Annex III.

[548] AIDCP, Arts XXIV–XXVI.

[549] Council Decision 1999/386/EC of 7 June 1999 on the provisional application of the Agreement on the International Dolphin Conservation Programme [sic], OJ 1999 L147/23.

[550] Council Decision 2005/938/EC of 8 December 2005 on the approval on behalf of the European Community of the Agreement on the International Dolphin Conservation Programme [sic], OJ 2005 L348/26. The provisions of the AIDCP were originally implemented into EC law by Council Regulation (EC) No 2723/1999 of 17 December 1999 amending Regulation (EC) No 850/98 for the conservation of fishery resources through technical measures for the protection of juveniles of marine organisms, OJ 1999 L328/9 and Council Regulation (EC) No 973/2001 of 14 May 2001 laying down technical measures for the conservation of certain stocks of highly migratory species, OJ 2001 L137/1, as amended. The latter was replaced in 2007 by Reg 520/2007.

[551] Council Regulation (EC) No 882/2003 of 19 May 2003 establishing a tuna tracking and verification system, OJ 2003 L127/1.

[552] Commission, Joint Answer to Written Questions E-3205/00 and P-3325/00, OJ 2001 L151E/95 and Answer to Written Question E-2846/01, OJ 2002 L115E/173. [553] 993 UNTS 243.

concerned is listed in the treaty's Appendix I, II, or III.[554] Parties remain entitled to take stricter domestic measures in relation to listed species as well as measures in relation to unlisted ones.[555] The treaty also contains provisions on trade with non-parties.[556] The term 'trade' in the CITES is defined in terms of processes ('export, re-export, import and introduction from the sea'[557]) rather than in terms of the purpose of such trade, although, as noted below, the purpose of trade is highly relevant at various points in the treaty.

For a species to be included in Appendix I, it must be 'threatened with extinction' and, actually or potentially, be 'affected by trade'.[558] Not surprisingly the corresponding trade regime is very strict.[559] Of particular note, import (and 'introduction from the sea') may not occur unless the receiving State 'is satisfied that the specimen is *not* to be used for primarily commercial purposes' (emphasis added).[560] Appendix I does include some commercially exploited aquatic species, including, *inter alia*, two sturgeon species, coelacanths, and all marine turtle species.[561] Appendix II applies principally to species 'which although not necessarily now threatened with extinction may become so unless trade in specimens of such species is subject to strict regulation in order to avoid utilization incompatible with their survival'.[562] The regime corresponding to Appendix II is less strict than that for Appendix I and use of specimens for primarily commercial purposes is acceptable.[563]

The rest of this subsection will consider the listing of commercially exploited aquatic species on Appendix II of the CITES and the role of the EC in relation to that process. Listing of such species on Appendix I is also of interest, but the fact that trade in specimens for primarily commercial purposes is not acceptable under the Appendix I regime means that, in principle, there is likely to be great reluctance by certain States, notably fishing States, to list in that Appendix species for which fisheries, and international trade in the products of such fisheries, are conducted. In contrast, in respect of such species, the regime corresponding to

---

[554] Appendix III will not be considered further here. It relates to 'species which any Party identifies as being subject to regulation within its jurisdiction for the purpose of preventing or restricting exploitation, and as needing the co-operation of other Parties in the control of trade' (CITES, Art II(3); see also Arts V and, *inter alia*, VII).

[555] CITES, Art XIV(1). See also CITES CoP Resolution 6.7. The abbreviation 'CoP' as used in this subsection means 'conference of the parties'. CITES CoP Resolutions and Decisions, and other CITES materials referred to in this subsection, are available on the website of the CITES.

[556] CITES, Art X. See also CITES CoP Resolution 9.5, as amended.   [557] CITES, Art I(c).

[558] CITES, Art II(1). See also CITES CoP Resolution 9.24, as amended.

[559] CITES, Arts III and, *inter alia*, VII.

[560] CITES, Art III(3)(c) and (5)(c). See also CITES CoP Resolution 5.10.

[561] Some States have reservations in respect of the listing in Appendix I of certain marine turtle species.

[562] CITES, Art II(2)(a). See also Art II(2)(b) and CITES CoP Resolution 9.24, as amended.

[563] CITES, Arts IV and, *inter alia*, VII.

Appendix II offers scope for a balance to be struck between a continuation of trading for primarily commercial purposes and regulation of such trade.

Over the past few meetings of the conference of the parties (hereafter, 'CoP') to the CITES, there has been a slow but steady procession of proposals for Appendix II listing of commercially exploited aquatic species. Such species currently listed in Appendix II include, *inter alia*, the basking shark, the great white shark, the whale shark, some sturgeon species, the European eel (from March 2009), the humphead wrasse, seahorses, giant clams, the queen conch, and the Mediterranean date mussel.[564]

Some proposals to list commercially exploited aquatic species in Appendix II have failed or been withdrawn. For example, attempts to list the porbeagle shark[565] and the spiny dogfish[566] were unsuccessful (see further below) and a proposal to list the Patagonian toothfish and the Antarctic toothfish[567] was withdrawn. Some commercially exploited aquatic species, whether listed in the CITES appendices or not, have also been the subject of various Resolutions and Decisions of the CITES CoP as well as the subject of discussion by its subsidiary bodies. Examples include sharks[568] and the Patagonian toothfish and Antarctic toothfish.[569] (Certain cetacean species are listed in Appendices I and II of the CITES, but these listings will not be addressed here.)

The path to inclusion of commercially exploited aquatic species in Appendix II of the CITES has not been a smooth one. In particular, the FAO has taken a strong interest in the listing, or proposed listing, of such species and in the marine application of the CITES in general.[570] There is a memorandum of understanding between the FAO and the CITES secretariat under which the two bodies 'will work together to ensure adequate consultations in the scientific and technical evaluation of proposals for including, transferring or deleting commercially exploited aquatic species in the CITES Apendices [sic]' and 'should also cooperate in addressing technical and legal issues involved with the listing of such species and the implementation of those listings'.[571] Furthermore a body called the 'FAO Ad Hoc Expert Advisory Panel for the Assessment of Proposals to Amend Appendices I and II of CITES Concerning Commercially-exploited Aquatic Species' convenes and reports prior to CITES CoP meetings.[572] Of course, the CITES CoP is not bound to follow the Panel's assessment.

---

[564] Some States have reservations in respect of the listing in Appendix II of some of these species.

[565] CITES CoP 14, Proposal 15.   [566] CITES CoP 14, Proposal 16.

[567] CITES CoP 12, Proposal 39.

[568] See, *inter alia*: (a) CITES CoP Resolution 12.6; (b) Decisions 14.101–14.117; and (c) *Summary Record of the Twenty-third meeting of the Animals Committee, April 2008*, section 15, pp 27–9.

[569] See CITES CoP Resolution 12.4.

[570] See, *inter alia*, FAO Fisheries Reports 667 (2002), 741 (2004), 746 (2004), 748 (2004), and 833 (2007) (available on the website of the Fisheries and Aquaculture Department of the FAO).

[571] CITES CoP 14, document 'CoP14 Doc. 18.1', para 7 and see paras 4–7 generally.

[572] FAO Fisheries Reports 748 and 833.

All twenty-seven EC Member States are parties to the CITES. However, because of the terms of the treaty, the EC itself is currently unable to become a party. That situation may change in the future if an amendment to the CITES known as the 'Gaborone amendment', adopted in 1983 and providing for regional economic integration organizations to become parties, is accepted by sufficient parties to the treaty.[573] Despite not being a party to the CITES, the EC has become significantly involved in the Member States' implementation of the treaty. The Commission's justification for this involvement derives from the EC's exclusive competence regarding external trade rules, the absence of systematic border controls between Member States as a result of the customs union, and the shared competence regarding environmental protection.[574] The CITES is currently implemented across the EC by means of: (a) Council Regulation 338/97, whose legal basis is provided by the Environment Title of the EC Treaty; (b) Commission Regulation 865/2006;[575] (c) Commission Regulation 811/2008;[576] and (d) Commission Recommendation 2007/425.[577]

In addition, prior to each CITES CoP meeting, the Commission issues a proposal for the EC's negotiating position.[578] The Commission justifies the need for an EC position in view of the scope for CoP Resolutions, and amendments to the appendices of the CITES, to affect the implementation of Regulation 338/97.[579] Because of time constraints, an EC position on certain issues can sometimes only be established during the CoP meeting itself.[580] The Commission attends CoP meetings because it represents the EC as an observer (pending the EC being able to become a party to CITES). Whilst at those meetings, it also performs an important coordination role amongst the Member States, which are expected to represent the EC position by 'acting jointly in the Community interest'.[581]

---

[573] For further information on the Gaborone amendment, see the website of the CITES and the website of DG Environment.

[574] European Commission, *Gaborone Amendment to the Convention: Information pack for Parties*, March 2007, available on the website of DG Environment, 15.

[575] Commission Regulation (EC) No 865/2006 of 4 May 2006 laying down detailed rules concerning the implementation of Council Regulation (EC) No 338/97 on the protection of species of wild fauna and flora by regulating trade therein, OJ 2006 L166/1, as amended.

[576] Commission Regulation (EC) No 811/2008 of 13 August 2008 suspending the introduction into the Community of specimens of certain species of wild fauna and flora, OJ 2008 L219/17.

[577] Commission Recommendation 2007/425/EC of 13 June 2007 identifying a set of actions for the enforcement of Council Regulation (EC) No 338/97 on the protection of species of wild fauna and flora by regulating trade therein, OJ 2007 L159/45.

[578] See, for example, *Proposal for a Council Decision on the Community position to be adopted on certain proposals submitted to the 13th meeting of the Conference of the Parties to the Convention on International Trade in Endangered Species of Wild Fauna and Flora (CITES), Bangkok, Thailand, 2–14 October 2004*, COM(2004) 529, 29.7.2004.

[579] COM(2004) 529, explanatory memorandum, para 3 and proposed recital (2).

[580] COM(2004) 529, explanatory memorandum, para 6 and proposed Art 2.

[581] COM(2004) 529, proposed recital (5) and proposed Art 1.

The EC, through its Member States, has played an active role in proposing the inclusion of commercially exploited aquatic species in Appendix II of the CITES. At CoP 12 (in 2002), the UK, on behalf of the EC Member States, proposed inclusion of the basking shark on Appendix II,[582] the main threat to that species being targeted fisheries and by-catch.[583] Liver oil, fins, cartilage, and meat of the basking shark 'are known to enter the international trade in significant (albeit largely unrecorded) quantities'.[584] The proposal emphasizes the demand for fins in international trade and states that this 'maintains the viability of targeted fisheries . . . and encourages incidental take in non-target fisheries'.[585] The proposal was accepted by the CITES CoP, although five non-EC States have a reservation on the listing.

At CoP 13 (in 2004), Ireland, on behalf of the EC Member States, in conjunction with two other parties, proposed the humphead wrasse for inclusion in Appendix II.[586] The proposal stated that '[t]he most serious threat to this species is overfishing for international trade'.[587] The FAO's Ad Hoc Expert Advisory Panel (see above) concluded that 'the available evidence supports the inclusion of humphead wrasse on CITES Appendix II . . .' and that 'regulation of trade as a result of CITES listing could make a significant contribution to the conservation of this species'.[588] The proposal was accepted, and there are no reservations. Also at CoP 13, Italy and Slovenia, on behalf of the EC Member States, proposed the Mediterranean date mussel for inclusion on Appendix II.[589] The FAO's Ad Hoc Expert Advisory Panel appeared not to be in favour of the listing.[590] The proposal was accepted nonetheless, and there are no reservations.

At CoP 14 (in 2007), Germany, on behalf of the EC Member States 'acting in the interest of the European Community',[591] proposed the listing of the European eel in Appendix II.[592] According to the proposal, 'one of the major threat [sic] to this species is over-exploitation by some types of fisheries targeting the various life stages'[593] and '[t]he international trade of [the relevant genus] is high'.[594] The FAO's Ad Hoc Expert Advisory Panel concluded that 'the available evidence did support the proposal to include [the European eel] in Appendix II of CITES . . .' and that 'a substantial fraction of the production of [the European eel] is in

[582]   CITES CoP 12, Proposal 36.
[583]   CITES CoP 12, document 'Prop. 12.36', section 2.7, p 8.
[584]   CITES CoP 12, document 'Prop. 12.36', section 3.2, p 9.
[585]   CITES CoP 12, document 'Prop. 12.36', Annex 7, p 35.
[586]   CITES CoP 13, Proposal 33.
[587]   CITES CoP 13, document 'CoP13 Prop. 33', section 2.7, p 8.
[588]   FAO Fisheries Report 748, Appendix F, p 29.
[589]   CITES CoP 13, Proposal 35. See document 'CoP13 Prop. 35'.
[590]   FAO Fisheries Report 748, Appendix G.
[591]   CITES CoP 14, document 'CoP14 Prop.18', section B, p 2.
[592]   CITES CoP 14, Proposal 18.
[593]   CITES CoP 14, document 'CoP14 Prop. 18', section 5, p 9.
[594]   CITES CoP 14, document 'CoP14 Prop. 18', section 6, p 11.

international trade'.[595] The proposal was accepted, with no reservations, but will only enter into force in March 2009.

Proposals at CoP 14 by Germany, on behalf of the EC Member States, to list two shark species, the porbeagle and the spiny dogfish, on Appendix II failed. Regarding the porbeagle shark,[596] the proposal stated that the principal threat to the species worldwide is 'over-exploitation, in target and bycatch fisheries, with many products entering international trade'.[597] The proposal for the spiny dog-fish[598] stated that the species 'is subjected to unsustainable fisheries in several other parts of its range, because of international trade demand for its high-value meat'.[599] In both cases, the CITES Secretariat recommended adoption of the proposals.[600] In contrast, for both species, the FAO's Ad Hoc Expert Advisory Panel concluded that the available evidence did not support inclusion in Appendix II,[601] although this assessment was contested by Germany 'on behalf of the European Community and its Member States'.[602] The proposals were not accepted by the CITES CoP.

Overall, six marine species, ie the basking shark, the humphead wrasse, the European eel, the Mediterranean date mussel, the porbeagle shark, and the spiny dogfish, have been proposed on behalf of the EC Member States for Appendix II listing from CoP 12 onwards. However, none of these species is the subject of a fishery of major economic importance in Community waters or by Community fishing vessels. It remains to be seen whether the EC Member States would be prepared to propose listing in Appendix II of a species that was the subject of such a fishery.

7.3 Seabirds

Fisheries have the potential to affect seabirds both directly, by taking them as by-catch or disturbing them, and indirectly, by taking their prey or otherwise affecting habitats that are important to them. Currently, the principal issue of global concern regarding the interaction between fisheries and seabirds is the by-catch of alba-trosses and petrels in longline fisheries. At the international level, the impact of fisheries on seabirds specifically, as distinct from the marine environment more generally, has been acknowledged in several fora, including the FAO and various RFMOs as well as the institutional frameworks of the CMS Convention and the Agreement on the Conservation of Albatrosses and Petrels. This subsection dis-cusses these international developments and the EC's response to them. For the

---

[595] FAO Fisheries Report 833, Appendix H, p 81.   [596] CITES CoP 14, Proposal 15.
[597] CITES CoP 14, document 'CoP14 Prop. 15', section 5, p 9.
[598] CITES CoP 14, Proposal 16.
[599] CITES CoP 14, document 'CoP14 Prop. 16', section A, p 1.
[600] CITES CoP 14, document 'CoP14 Doc. 68', pp 34 and 36.
[601] FAO Fisheries Report 833, Appendices E and F.
[602] CITES CoP 14, document 'CoP14 Inf. 48'.

sake of convenience, it considers the EC's response not just beyond Community waters but also within such waters.

The FAO's International Plan of Action for Reducing Incidental Catch of Seabirds in Longline Fisheries (hereafter, 'IPOA-Seabirds'), adopted in 1999 and endorsed by the FAO Council the same year, has already been summarized in Chapter 3 and referred to briefly in subsection 3.5 above. It applies: (a) to States 'in the waters of which longline fisheries are being conducted by their own or foreign vessels'; and (b) to States 'that conduct longline fisheries on the high seas and in the [EEZ] of other States'.[603] It calls on States with longline fisheries to adopt a National Plan of Action (hereafter, 'NPOA-Seabirds') for reducing seabird by-catch, if a prior assessment shows that a problem exists.[604] However, the response of FAO members in drawing up NPOAs has so far been poor. An FAO report published in September 2008 states that: 'In the nine year period following unanimous adoption of the IPOA-Seabirds . . . *only ten* NPOA-Seabirds were developed including Brazil, Canada, Chile, Japan, New Zealand, Uruguay, Namibia, South Africa, United States of America and Australia. Others are in draft stage or awaiting government implementation.' (Emphasis added.)[605]

In 2007, the FAO's Committee on Fisheries (COFI) agreed that 'depending on cost and related considerations, best practice technical guidelines to support the elaboration of National Plans of Action . . . for seabirds would be developed through continuing joint work between FAO and relevant bodies and organiza-tions or an expert consultation'.[606] The same meeting of the COFI also agreed that 'FAO should, in cooperation with relevant bodies, develop best practice guidelines to assist countries and RFMOs in implementation of the IPOA-Seabirds and that the best practice guidelines should be extended to other relevant fishing gears'.[607] In response, an expert consultation, held in September 2008, adopted draft guidelines covering not just longline fisheries but also trawl and gillnet fisheries.[608]

The EC is amongst the large majority of longline fishing States that have so far failed to adopt an NPOA-Seabirds. That is despite concerns about the impact on seabirds of longlining both in Community waters and by Community fishing vessels in other parts of the world.[609] The Commission's response to the IPOA-Seabirds actually began fairly promptly after the IPOA's endorsement in 1999. Following a questionnaire to EC Member States, the Commission presented 'a

---

[603] IPOA-Seabirds, para 9.   [604] IPOA-Seabirds, para 12.

[605] *Report of the Expert Consultation on Best Practice Technical Guidelines for IPOA/NPOA-Seabirds, Bergen, Norway, 2–5 September 2008*, FAO Fisheries and Aquaculture Report No 880, Appendix E, para 5.

[606] *Report of the twenty-seventh session of the Committee on Fisheries, Rome, 5–9 March 2007*, FAO Fisheries Report No 830, para ii, p ix and para 14, p 2.

[607] FAO Fisheries Report No 830, para vi, p xiii and para 80, p 13.

[608] FAO Fisheries and Aquaculture Report No 880; see Appendix E for draft guidelines.

[609] See, for example, Commission Answer (10 August 2007) to Written Question E-3455/07, available on the website of the European Parliament.

preliminary plan of action' to the February 2001 meeting of the COFI 'in which the need for a better assessment of the incidental catch of seabirds in longline fisheries is underlined'.[610]

Early in 2002, in a written answer to a question posed by a member of the European Parliament, the Commission reported that 'the Community is preparing a Community action plan [on seabirds] to be presented at the next Committee for Fisheries (COFI, February 2003)'.[611] A few months later, the Commission used a COM document to set out its intention to propose legislation before the end of 2003 to implement such a plan.[612] In practice, no EC action plan on seabirds was presented to the COFI in 2003. Nor was one presented to the COFI at its meetings in 2005 and 2007.[613] In July 2007, the Commission wrote to the ICES 'to explore the possibilities' for advice from the ICES on the interactions between fisheries and seabirds 'in EU waters', citing an intention to complete an NPOA-Seabirds by 2009.[614] In its letter, the Commission's explanation for the lack of progress since 2001 was that it had instead 'given priority to work on other areas of environmental concern'. The ICES responded to the Commission's request.[615] It remains to be seen whether the Commission will, as intended, adopt an NPOA-Seabirds in 2009.

In any event, based on the Commission's request to the ICES, it appears that any such NPOA-Seabirds will only address Community waters. This is a surprising result in view of the IPOA applying to States in their capacity as both coastal States and flag States (see above). The Commission appears to justify its geographically limited approach by stating that the EC tackles the seabird by-catch problem in waters beyond Community waters by promoting the adoption of relevant measures to RFMOs of which the EC is a member and then implementing such measures in EC law.[616] However, it is arguable that more coherent results across RFMOs could potentially be achieved if the Commission were to extend its NPOA-Seabirds to non-Community waters. Furthermore, the combined approach of tackling Community waters through the NPOA-Seabirds and tackling non-Community waters solely through RFMOs of which the EC is a member means that several categories of fisheries beyond Community waters in which

---

[610] Commission Answer (27 February 2002) to Written Question P-0233/02, OJ 2002 C172E/166.

[611] Ibid.

[612] *Communication from the Commission setting out a Community Action Plan to integrate environmental protection requirements into the Common Fisheries Policy*, COM(2002) 186, 28.5.2002, annex.

[613] Further information on the EC's response to the IPOA-Seabirds can be found in Dunn, E, *The case for a Community Plan of Action for reducing incidental catch of seabirds in longline fisheries* (Cambridge: BirdLife International, 2007), available on the website of BirdLife International.

[614] Letter from Commission to ICES, 9 July 2007, available on the website of the ICES. See also Commission Answer to Written Question E-3455/07. Regarding the 2009 deadline, see subsequently *Communication from the Commission to the Council and the European Parliament: The role of the CFP in implementing an ecosystem approach to marine management*, COM(2008) 187, 11.4.2008, section 6, p 9.

[615] See the website of the ICES for more information.

[616] See, for example, Commission Answer to Written Question E-3455/07.

Community fishing vessels actually or potentially participate are not covered, namely high seas fisheries beyond the mandate of any RFMO, high sea fisheries governed by an RFMO of which the EC is not a member (see further section 6 above), and fisheries in third States' waters.

The halting progress of the Commission in adopting an NPOA-Seabirds contrasts sharply with its rapid adoption of an action plan to address illegal, unreported, and unregulated fishing[617] only one year after the endorsement by the FAO Council of an International Plan of Action on the same subject.[618] Furthermore, the restricted geographical scope of the Commission's prospective NPOA-Seabirds contrasts with the Commission's approach regarding a draft EU Action Plan for Sharks in order to implement the FAO's International Plan of Action for the Conservation and Management of Sharks ('IPOA-Sharks'), the latter endorsed by the FAO Council in 1999 (see further Chapter 3). The Commission consulted on its draft Action Plan for Sharks in February 2007, and stated that the plan would apply both inside and outside Community waters.[619] The reason for this difference in geographical scope, depending on whether the Commission is implementing the IPOA-Seabirds or the IPOA-Sharks, is not clear.

As indicated above, the EC is a member of various RFMOs which have adopted measures to reduce by-catch of seabirds. Such RFMOs having adopted binding measures include the CCAMLR,[620] the ICCAT,[621] the IOTC,[622] the SEAFO,[623] and the WCPFC.[624] (Some RFMOs of which the EC is a member have in addition, or alternatively, adopted non-binding measures.) It is beyond the scope of this subsection to address whether or not existing EC Regulations adequately transpose the current RFMO binding measures on seabird by-catch mitigation. However, in general terms, it may be noted that the EC seeks to implement RFMOs' binding measures through a combination of long-term Regulations and the principal annual Regulation (currently Regulation 40/2008) for the year in question. The broader issue of the EC's participation in RFMOs is discussed in section 6 above.

The FAO's IPOA-Seabirds and RFMO measures on seabird by-catch mitigation are not the only tools adopted at the international level to reduce the impact of fishing activities on seabirds. The EC is also a party to the CMS Convention (see subsection 7.1 above), as are all the EC Member States. The CMS Convention establishes a qualified prohibition on the 'taking' of species listed in its

---

[617] COM(2002) 180. See further subsection 3.5 above.

[618] FAO's International Plan of Action to Prevent, Deter and Eliminate Illegal, Unreported and Unregulated Fishing, endorsed by the FAO Council in 2001; see further Chapter 3.

[619] For more details, see the website of DG Mare.

[620] CCAMLR Conservation Measures 25-02 (2008), 24-02 (2008), and 25-03 (2003).

[621] ICCAT Recommendation 07-07.   [622] IOTC Resolution 08/03.

[623] SEAFO Conservation Measure 05/06.

[624] WCPFC Conservation Measure CMM-2007-04.

Appendix I, as well as some positive conservation duties for these species.[625] Appendix I includes nine species of albatrosses and petrels. Some of those are, or have historically been, taken as by-catch in longline fisheries, for example the Balearic shearwater (see below), the Short-tailed albatross, and the Amsterdam albatross.[626]

The conference of the parties to the CMS Convention (hereafter, 'CMS CoP') has adopted some measures on seabird by-catch, the most recent of which is Resolution 8.14 adopted in November 2005, which supplements Resolution 6.2 and Recommendation 7.2 adopted in 1999 and 2002 respectively. Resolution 8.14 calls on parties to the CMS Convention to, *inter alia*, implement the FAO's IPOA-Seabirds and develop corresponding NPOAs, 'require the implementation of proven by-catch solutions' regarding seabirds, and 'work within [RFMOs] to reduce [seabird] by-catch . . . through *inter alia* the development of by-catch action plans, independent observer schemes, assessments of the scale of the problem, awareness raising, and promoting technical mitigation'.[627] However, Resolution 8.14, in common with Resolution 6.2 and Recommendation 7.2, refrains from setting out any specific mitigation measures.

Furthermore, the Balearic shearwater, an Appendix I species that is subject to by-catch at least in Community waters,[628] was designated for 'concerted action' by the CMS CoP in 2005.[629] The concept of 'concerted action' was established in 1991 by Resolution 3.2, which requires, *inter alia*, a formal review process at each meeting of the CMS CoP for the selected species 'with a view to recommending initiatives to benefit those species'.[630] Thus the Balearic shearwater was due to be subject to a review process at the next CMS CoP meeting in December 2008. In practice, notwithstanding CMS CoP Resolutions 6.2 and 8.14 and the obligations in the CMS itself, the EC's specific response to date to seabird by-catch problems has been limited to implementing relevant RFMO measures.

The CMS also encourages the development of separate agreements on species of conservation concern (see subsection 7.1 above).[631] There is one such agreement relating to seabirds, the 2001 Agreement on the Conservation of Albatrosses and Petrels (ACAP),[632] which entered into force in 2004 and currently covers nineteen species of albatross and seven species of petrel.[633] Although the ACAP allows for regional economic integration organizations to be parties,[634] the EC is not yet a party. However, three EC Member States are parties, namely France, Spain, and

---

[625] CMS Convention, Art III(4) and (5).

[626] See the website of BirdLife International ('Data Zone').

[627] CMS CoP Resolution 8.14, para 2(a)–(c); see also paras 3–5.

[628] Dunn, E, *The case for a Community Plan of Action for reducing incidental catch of seabirds in longline fisheries*; see, *inter alia*, section 5.3.1, p 14.   [629] CMS CoP Resolution 8.29.

[630] CMS CoP Resolution 3.21, para 1.   [631] CMS Convention, Art IV(3) and (4).

[632] 2258 UNTS 257. ACAP is an AGREEMENT within the meaning of Art IV(3) of the CMS— see ACAP, Art I(5).   [633] ACAP, Art I(1) and Annex 1.

[634] ACAP, Art XV.

the UK. The objective of the ACAP is to 'achieve and maintain a favourable conservation status for albatrosses and petrels',[635] for which purpose the parties are to implement a specified Action Plan.[636] The latter includes a section specifically on incidental mortality in fisheries.[637] The ACAP expressly requires the parties to support the implementation of the FAO's IPOA-Seabirds.[638] It remains to be seen whether the EC will become a party to the ACAP, or whether it will hold off doing so as with two other marine agreements made under the auspices of the CMS, namely the ASCOBANS and the ACCOBAMS (on which, see subsection 7.1 above).

8 Conclusions

The EC has wide-ranging powers to become a party to treaties concerning fisheries. It has the competence to conclude treaties relating to fisheries 'conservation' to the exclusion of its Member States. There is some uncertainty as to how far the EC has the competence to conclude treaties on fisheries concerning matters that do not fall within the concept of 'conservation', and as to how far any such competence is exclusive. However, this uncertainty has caused problems and controversy on only a handful of occasions. In practice, the EC has made extensive use of its treaty-making powers, and has become a party to a large number of treaties dealing wholly or partly with fisheries. It has exercised its exclusive treaty-making powers to conclude bilateral fisheries access agreements with more than twenty States, mainly neighbouring States in the North Atlantic and developing States along the Atlantic and Indian Ocean seaboards of Africa; to become a member of seven RFMOs; and to become a party to the FAO Compliance Agreement. In addition, it has become a party, along with some or all of its Member States, to the UN Fish Stocks Agreement, the UN Convention on the Law of the Sea, and two RFMOs, as well as some of the treaties incidental to fishing discussed in section 7 above.

This extensive exercise of treaty-making powers, together with the wide geographical range of the areas to which those treaties apply, mean that the EC is without doubt a leading actor in international fisheries relations. That brings not only rights for the EC but also responsibilities—in particular the responsibility to set a good example, notably by only entering into treaties that promote sustainable fishing and by complying with its international obligations. On paper the new generation of fisheries partnership agreements with developing States and most of the RFMOs of which the EC is a member (especially those established, or whose constituent treaties have been amended, since the adoption of the Fish Stocks

---

[635] ACAP, Art II(1).   [636] ACAP, Art III(6) and Annex 2.
[637] ACAP, Annex 2, paras 3.2.1–3.2.4.
[638] ACAP, Art III(1)(h). See also Art XI(1) and 15th recital.

Agreement) aim to promote sustainable fishing, although whether they will actually do so in practice remains in many cases still to be seen. There may also be some question as to how far what is effectively the subsidized access of Community fishing vessels to the waters of developing States under the fisheries partnership agreements is in conformity with the spirit of sustainability. Where the picture is certainly less positive is in relation to the question of compliance by the EC with its treaty obligations. Although it has not been possible for the authors to carry out an exhaustive analysis of this matter in this chapter, several examples have been given at various points of less than complete compliance by the EC with its obligations. However, and regrettably, the EC's record here is probably no worse than that of many States.

Part III

Other issues

6

The common organization of the markets in fishery products

1 Introduction

This chapter addresses the common organization of the markets in fishery products. After an introduction to its legal basis and objectives, the chapter considers the subject matter of the common organization of the markets. It then proceeds through the various areas covered by the common organization, including common marketing standards, consumer information, producer organizations, interbranch organizations, and prices and intervention, and ends with a section on enforcement and some conclusions. The trade aspects of the common organization of the markets are dealt with separately, in Chapter 7.

2 Legal basis and objectives

A common organization of the markets in fishery products is required by the EC Treaty. Article 34(1) EC states that 'a common organisation of agricultural markets' is to be established '[i]n order to attain the objectives set out in Article 33 [EC]'. By virtue of the definition of the term 'agricultural products' in the EC Treaty (see Chapters 1 and 2), agricultural markets include markets for fishery products. Of course, the reference to the Article 33 objectives (on which see Chapter 2) should now be read as also including the duty to integrate environmental protection requirements pursuant to Article 6 EC.[1]

According to the Commission, the common organization of the markets in fishery products 'was created to achieve the objectives laid down in Article 33 of the [EC] Treaty in the fishery sector, *in particular* to provide *market stability* and to guarantee a *fair income* for producers' (emphasis added),[2] ie objectives '(c)' and '(b)' in Article 33(1) EC. However, the Commission considers that the common organization as set out in the current basic Regulation on markets 'now lays more emphasis on *sustainability-supportive* fishing and marketing activities' (emphasis added),[3] implying increasing relevance of objectives '(a)' and '(d)' in Article 33(1).

---

[1] See, by analogy, Case C-440/05 *Commission v Council* [2007] ECR I-9097, para 60.
[2] *Report from the Commission to the Council and the European Parliament on the implementation of Council Regulation (EC) No 104/2000 on the common organisation of the markets in fishery and aquaculture products,* COM(2006) 558, 29.9.2006, section 1, p 2.   [3] Ibid.

A common organization is also relevant to ensuring that supplies reach consumers at reasonable prices, ie objective '(e)' in Article 33(1).

Stability of the market in fishery products is presumably an issue not least because of the fluctuations in fish stocks that can occur from year to year and also within any given fishing year. In the preamble to the original basic Regulation on markets, ie Regulation 2142/70, the need for market stability is emphasized in the context of fishermen in 'certain coastal regions of the Community' where 'the fishing industry is of special importance to the agricultural economy'.[4] That emphasis is retained in the current basic Regulation on markets (see below),[5] subject to some small changes in wording, suggesting that one particular and unchanging role of the common organization of the markets in fishery products is to help look after the interests of fishermen in fishing-dependent regions.

In principle, there is some choice over the form taken by the common organization. Article 34(1) EC states that: 'This organisation shall take one of the following forms, depending on the product concerned: (a) common rules on competition; (b) compulsory coordination of the various national market organisations; (c) a European market organisation.' In practice, the third of those has been adopted for the common organization of the markets in fishery products. However, as will be seen, the EC market organization does not currently extend to all fishery products covered by the Common Fisheries Policy (CFP).

Article 34(2) EC sets out a non-exhaustive list of the kind of measure that may be included within the common organization in order to attain the Article 33 EC objectives. Thus the measures may comprise 'in particular regulation of prices, aids for the production and marketing of the various products, storage and carryover arrangements and common machinery for stabilising imports or exports'. Any common price policy is to be based on 'common criteria and uniform methods of calculation'.

The EC Treaty is clear that the common organization 'shall be limited to pursuit of the objectives set out in Article 33'.[6] The implication is that any use of the common organization for pursuit of any other objectives would be unlawful, although that should of course be subject to Article 6 EC. The Treaty adds that any discrimination between producers or consumers within the EC is unlawful;[7] that is a specific manifestation of the EC law general principle of equal treatment.

Regulation 2371/2002[8] confirms that marketing of fishery and aquaculture products is indeed a part of the CFP, where that activity is 'practised on the territory

---

[4] Regulation (EEC) No 2142/70 of the Council of 20 October 1970 on the common organisation of the market in fishery products, JO 1970 L236/5, as amended and corrected, 2nd recital.

[5] Council Regulation (EC) No 104/2000 of 17 December 1999 on the common organisation of the markets in fishery and aquaculture products, OJ 2000 L17/22, as amended and corrected, recital (4).

[6] EC Treaty, Art 34(2), 2nd para.   [7] EC Treaty, Art 34(2), 2nd para.

[8] Council Regulation (EC) No 2371/2002 of 20 December 2002 on the conservation and sustainable exploitation of fisheries resources under the Common Fisheries Policy, OJ 2002 L358/59, as amended and corrected.

of Member States or in Community waters or by Community fishing vessels or, without prejudice to the primary responsibility of the flag State, nationals of Member States'.[9] The same Regulation also confirms that the CFP 'shall provide for coherent measures concerning . . . [*inter alia*] . . . common organisation of the markets'.[10]

In common with other CFP measures, the legal basis for Regulations implementing the common organization of the markets in fishery products is Article 37 EC. As noted in Chapter 1 and above, the first Regulation on the subject was Regulation 2142/70. The current basic Regulation on markets is Regulation 104/2000 (hereafter, 'the Markets Regulation'), which is the latest in a line of successors to Regulation 2142/70.[11] The Markets Regulation (re-)establishes a common organization of the markets in fishery products 'comprising a price and trading system and common rules on competition'.[12]

The Markets Regulation's preamble introduces the various components of the common organization of the markets that are then elaborated in the various Articles that follow. However, before doing this, the preamble makes two general points. The first emphasizes the particular need for market stability in the context of fishermen in fishing-dependent regions (see above).[13] As noted above, this point was also made in the first basic Regulation on markets. The second general point is that 'the production and marketing of fishery products should take account of *the need to support sustainable fishing*' (emphasis added).[14] To this end, the common organization 'should . . . comprise such measures as will ensure that supply is better matched to demand . . . and increase the return on products'. Such means are also acknowledged as being equally relevant to a more traditional goal, namely 'to improve the income of producers by ensuring stability of market prices'.[15] The role for the common organization of the markets in helping to achieve sustainable fisheries is considered further in section 10 below.

The Markets Regulation is divided into six titles, addressing marketing standards and consumer information; producer organizations; interbranch organizations and agreements; prices and intervention; trade with third States; and some general

[9] Reg 2371/2002, Art 1(1).   [10] Reg 2371/2002, Art 1(2)(g).

[11] (a) Council Regulation (EEC) No 100/76 of 19 January 1976 on the common organization of the market in fishery products, OJ 1976 L20/1, as amended; (b) Council Regulation (EEC) No 3796/81 of 29 December 1981 on the common organization of the market in fishery products, OJ 1981 L379/1, as amended and corrected; (c) Council Regulation (EEC) No 3687/91 of 28 November 1991 on the common organization of the market in fishery products, OJ 1991 L354/1; and (d) Council Regulation (EEC) No 3759/92 of 17 December 1992 on the common organization of the market in fishery and aquaculture products, OJ 1992 L388/1, as amended. All of these Regulations, in their titles, refer to 'the market' (singular). In contrast, Reg 104/2000 refers to 'the markets' (plural). It is not clear to the authors whether this difference in terminology has any significance.

[12] Reg 104/2000, Art 1, 1st para.   [13] Reg 104/2000, recital (4).

[14] Reg 104/2000, recital (5). See also recital (14).   [15] Reg 104/2000, recital (5).

provisions. This chapter will address the above matters, with the exception of trade with third States which is covered by Chapter 7.

Of the general provisions of the Markets Regulation, comprising Articles 31–43, some will be mentioned in this section.[16] Article 31 requires the Council to 'take the necessary measures to remedy the situation' in cases '[w]here price increases and supply problems are recorded on the Community market for one or more of the products [covered by the Markets Regulation] such that the attainment of some of the objectives of Article 33 of the [EC] Treaty might be jeopardised, and where this situation is likely to persist'. The necessary measures are to be adopted 'by qualified majority on a proposal from the Commission'; the implication is that, exceptionally,[17] the European Parliament need not be consulted, in the interests of rapid action. The corresponding recital in the preamble refers to experience having shown that 'it may prove necessary to take measures very rapidly, in order to ensure the supply of the community [sic] market and to ensure that the Community's international undertakings are complied with'.[18] The authors are not aware of any occasion where the Council has adopted a measure under Article 31.

Article 33 states that: 'Without prejudice to other community [sic] provisions, the Member States shall take the necessary steps to ensure that all fishing vessels flying the flag of one of the Member States enjoy equal access to ports and first-stage marketing installations together with all associated equipment and technical installations.' This provision has no corresponding recital in the preamble; however an almost identical provision is also found in the original basic Regulation on markets.[19] The reference to equal access being '[w]ithout prejudice to other community [sic] provisions' is presumably a reference to, *inter alia*, relevant provisions on enforcement of the fisheries conservation regime, such as those on the use of designated ports (see Chapter 4).

The Markets Regulation contains some important substantive provisions itself, many of which are explained below. However, it also enables or requires, as appropriate, the Commission or the Council to adopt further Regulations on specified matters. The adoption of such Regulations by the Commission is to be through the 'Management Committee for Fishery Products', established by Article 38 of the Markets Regulation.[20] This is a committee composed of representatives of the Member States and chaired by a representative of the Commission. Article 41 requires the Commission to send 'an evaluation report on the results of implementing this Regulation' to the Council and the European Parliament by the end of December 2005 at the latest. The Commission fulfilled this duty a little

---

[16] Arts 35 and 36 are referred to in subsection 6.5 and section 9 below. Art 32 is referred to in Chapter 8.　　　　[17] Cf EC Treaty, Art 37(2), 3rd para and Reg 2371/2002, Art 29.
[18] Reg 104/2000, recital (36).　　　　[19] Reg 2142/70, Art 23(2).
[20] See also Reg 104/2000, *inter alia*, Arts 37 and 39.

belatedly in March 2006. Its report will be referred to in this chapter as 'the Commission's 2006 report'.[21]

3 Subject matter

As noted above, the Markets Regulation (re-)establishes a common organization of the markets in fishery products, 'comprising a price and trading system and common rules on competition'.[22] Article 1 defines the term 'fishery products' as 'products caught at sea or in inland waters and the products of aquaculture listed below'. The list in Article 1 in turn comprises various codes from the so-called 'Combined Nomenclature' (CN codes; see Chapter 2) and corresponding descriptions of goods. The descriptions are the same as those in Annex I to Regulation 2658/87 (see Chapter 2).[23] The list is set out in Table 6.1.

As can be seen, the list in Article 1 comprehensively covers Chapter 3 of the CN (comprising CN headings 0301 to 0307), and also covers parts of other chapters (ie parts of Chapters 5, 16, 19, and 23 of the CN). However, it omits some CN chapters or headings containing products potentially covered by the CFP (see Chapter 2). For example, the list does not cover: (a) CN Chapter 1 ('Live animals'); (b) CN headings 0208 and 0210, which relate, *inter alia*, to some marine mammal groups; (c) CN heading 1504 ('Fats and oils and their fractions, of fish or marine mammals, whether or not refined, but not chemically modified'); (d) CN heading 1603 ('Extracts and juices of meat, fish or crustaceans, molluscs or other aquatic invertebrates'); or (e) CN heading 2309 ('Preparations of a kind used in animal feeding').

4 Common marketing standards

4.1 Introduction

The framework for the adoption of common marketing standards is provided by Article 2 of the Markets Regulation. The standards themselves are contained principally in Regulation 2406/96 (hereafter, 'the CMS Regulation').[24] Detailed rules for applying these standards are found in Regulation 3703/85.[25] Further,

---

[21] COM(2006) 558.   [22] Reg 104/2000, Art 1, 1st para.

[23] Council Regulation (EEC) No 2658/87 of 23 July 1987 on the tariff and statistical nomenclature and on the Common Customs Tariff, OJ 1987 L256/1, as amended and corrected.

[24] Council Regulation (EC) No 2406/96 of 26 November 1996 laying down common marketing standards for certain fishery products, OJ 1996 L334/1, as amended.

[25] Commission Regulation (EEC) No 3703/85 of 23 December 1985 laying down detailed rules for applying the common marketing standards for certain fresh or chilled fish, OJ 1985 L351/63, as amended.

Table 6.1 List in Article 1 of Regulation 104/2000

CN code	Description of goods
(a) 0301	Live fish
0302	Fish, fresh or chilled, excluding fish fillets and other fish meat of heading No 0304
0303	Fish, frozen excluding fish fillets and other fish meat of heading No 0304
0304	Fish fillets and other fish meat (whether or not minced), fresh, chilled or frozen
(b) 0305	Fish, dried, salted or in brine; smoked fish, whether or not cooked before or during the smoking process; flours, meals and pellets of fish, fit for human consumption
(c) 0306	Crustaceans, whether in shell or not, live, fresh, chilled, frozen, dried, salted or in brine; crustaceans, in shell, cooked by steaming or by boiling in water, whether or not chilled, frozen, dried, salted or in brine; flours, meals and pellets of fish [sic*], fit for human consumption
0307	Molluscs, whether in shell or not, live, fresh, chilled, frozen, dried, salted or in brine; aquatic invertebrates other than crustaceans and molluscs, live, fresh, chilled, frozen, dried, salted or in brine; flours, meals and pellets of aquatic invertebrates other than crustaceans, fit for human consumption
(d)	Animal products not elsewhere specified or included; dead animals of Chapter 1 or 3, unfit for human consumption: — Other: — — Products of fish or crustaceans, molluscs or other aquatic invertebrates; dead animals of Chapter 3:
0511 91 10	— — — Fish waste
0511 91 90	— — — Other
(e) 1604	Prepared or preserved fish; caviar and caviar substitutes prepared from fish eggs
(f) 1605	Crustaceans, molluscs and other aquatic invertebrates, prepared or preserved
(g)	Pasta, whether or not cooked or stuffed (with meat or other substances) or otherwise prepared, such as spaghetti, macaroni, noodles, lasagne, gnocchi, ravioli, cannelloni; couscous, whether or not prepared: — Uncooked pasta, not stuffed or otherwise prepared:
1902 20	— Stuffed pasta, whether or not cooked or otherwise prepared:
1902 20 10	— — Containing more than 20% by weight of fish, crustaceans, molluscs or other aquatic invertebrates
(h)	Flours, meals and pellets, of meat or of meat offal, of fish or of crustaceans, molluscs or other aquatic invertebrates, unfit for human consumption; greaves:
2301 20 00	— Flours, meals and pellets, of fish or of crustaceans, molluscs or other aquatic invertebrates

* Regulation 2658/87, regarding CN code 0306, refers to '. . . flours, meals and pellets of *crustaceans* . . . ' (emphasis added). So the reference to 'fish' in this item in the list in Article 1 of Regulation 104/2000, as reproduced above, is presumably a drafting error.

more specific, common marketing standards are to be found in Regulation 2136/89 (regarding preserved sardines)[26] and Regulation 1536/92 (regarding preserved tuna and bonito).[27]

The term 'marketing' is defined by the CMS Regulation as 'the first offer for sale and/or the first sale, on Community territory, for human consumption'.[28] On that basis, sales, or offers for sale, subsequent to the first are not 'marketing', and first sales or first offers for sale for purposes other than human consumption are also not 'marketing'. The Commission's 2006 report states that: 'The first sale is organised through mandatory auctions in 8 Member States and direct sales to buyers in 12 Member States. There are non-mandatory auctions in 2 Member States and a mixed system involving auctions and direct sales in 6 Member States.'[29]

The preamble to the Markets Regulation states that applying common marketing standards 'should tend to keep products of unsatisfactory quality off the market and facilitate commerce based on fair competition, thus helping to improve the profitability of production'.[30] The Commission's 2006 report adds that the common marketing standards 'are essential for the proper functioning of the internal market and the intervention mechanisms'.[31]

The CMS Regulation states that the standards serve principally to 'improve products [sic] quality and thus make marketing easier to the benefit of both producers and consumers'.[32] It adds that supplementary purposes are '[to define] uniform trade characteristics for the products in question across the entire Community market in order to prevent distortions of competition and . . . to enable the market organization price arrangements to be applied uniformly'.[33]

The Markets Regulation states that the standards, and their scope, may be determined for the products listed in its Article 1 or groups of those products.[34] The contents of the list in Article 1 have already been set out in Table 6.1 above. As already noted, common marketing standards currently exist in the CMS Regulation itself as well as in Regulations 2136/89 and 1536/92.

Regulation 1536/92 adopts standards for preserved tuna and bonito and Regulation 2136/89 adopts standards for preserved sardines. Preserved fish fall within the CN code 1604 ('Prepared or preserved fish . . . '). Thus the subject matter of Regulations 1536/92 and 2136/89 is compatible with the list in Article 1 of the Markets Regulation, which includes CN code 1604.

---

[26] Council Regulation (EEC) No 2136/89 of 21 June 1989 laying down common marketing standards for preserved sardines and trade descriptions for preserved sardines and sardine-type products, OJ 1989 L212/79, as amended.
[27] Council Regulation (EEC) No 1536/92 of 9 June 1992 laying down common marketing standards for preserved tuna and bonito, OJ 1992 L163/1.   [28] Reg 2406/96, Art 1(2)(a).
[29] COM(2006) 558, section 2, pp 2–3.   [30] Reg 104/2000, recital (6).
[31] COM(2006) 558, section 2, p 2. On 'the intervention mechanisms', see section 8 below.
[32] Reg 2406/96, 2nd recital.   [33] Reg 2406/96, 4th recital.
[34] Reg 104/2000, Art 2(1).

The CMS Regulation adopts standards for the following four groups set out in its Article 3: (a) various named species or genera of 'Saltwater fish falling under CN code 0302'; (b) four named species of 'Crustaceans falling under CN code 0306 whether presented live, fresh or chilled, or cooked by steaming or by boiling in water'; (c) two named species of 'Cephalopods falling under the code CN 0307'; and (d) two named species (both molluscs) of 'Common scallop and other aquatic invertebrates falling within code NC [sic] 0307'.

The four groups covered by the CMS Regulation are compatible with the list in Article 1 of the Markets Regulation. However, it is also clear that no use is made by the CMS Regulation of the opportunity provided by the Markets Regulation to adopt common standards for, *inter alia*, frozen fish (CN code 0303) or fish fillets (CN code 0304). Furthermore, despite the broadness of CN code 0307, it can be seen that common standards have been adopted for only four species of mollusc.

The Markets Regulation sets out a non-exhaustive list of characteristics which common marketing standards may cover, namely 'quality, size or weight, packing, presentation and labelling'.[35] Of those, the characteristics pursued under the CMS Regulation are freshness (presumably a reflection of 'quality') and size (usually expressed as weight). The nature of those standards is discussed in subsections 4.2 and 4.3 below.

Article 2(2) of the Markets Regulation states that: 'Where marketing standards have been issued, the products to which they apply may *not* be displayed for sale, offered for sale, sold or otherwise marketed *unless* they conform to these standards, subject to special rules which may be adopted for trade with third countries.' (Emphasis added.) Member States are to undertake inspections to ensure conformity with the standards, and to enforce the standards as necessary (see further section 9 below).[36]

As can be seen, the general prohibition established by Article 2(2) of the Markets Regulation relates to products being 'displayed for sale, offered for sale, sold or otherwise marketed'. The Markets Regulation does *not* define the term 'marketing' and so the scope of its general prohibition is not entirely clear. However, some clarity is provided by the CMS Regulation. As noted above, that Regulation *does* define the term 'marketing'. Its Article 2(1) then states that: 'Fishery products, as specified in Article 3, of Community origin or from third countries, may be marketed only if they meet the requirements of this Regulation.' Article 2(2) adds, however, that the CMS Regulation 'shall not . . . apply to small quantities of products disposed of directly to retailers or consumers by inshore fishermen'.

4.2 Common freshness standards under the CMS Regulation

In short, the CMS Regulation establishes common standards on freshness as follows: (a) for particular groups of organisms, it specifies the categories of freshness

---

[35] Reg 104/2000, Art 2(1).   [36] Reg 104/2000, Art 3.

into which products may be classified; and (b) for those same groups of organisms, it specifies how a particular freshness category is to be determined. The basic unit upon which the CMS Regulation operates is the so-called 'lot', which is defined as 'a quantity of fishery products of a given species which has been subjected to the same treatment and may have come from the same fishing grounds and the same vessel'.[37] Each lot, other than small lots, 'must contain products of the same degree of freshness'.[38]

The categories of freshness into which products may be classified vary depending on the group of organisms in question. Article 4(2) states that '. . . products as specified in Article 3 shall be classified by lot in one of the following freshness categories' and then lists categories Extra, A, or B for fish, selachii, cephalopods, and Norway lobster and categories Extra or A in the case of 'shrimps'. It adds that 'live Norway lobsters shall be classified in category E[xtra]'. Thus freshness category B is not available for 'shrimps' and freshness categories A and B are not available for live Norway lobster.

One important consequence of this approach is that, pursuant to Article 2(1) of the CMS Regulation (see above), there will be a prohibition on marketing a particular lot of a product in cases where: (a) the CMS Regulation has established common standards on freshness for the product in question by reference to one or more of the above categories; and (b) the lot of that product does not, on account of its lack of freshness, fall into one of the freshness categories available for that product. Thus, for example, any lot of cephalopods that does not fall into categories Extra, A, or B (those categories being available for cephalopods) may not be marketed. For some products, this consequence is reinforced by a 'Not admitted' column (see further below).

Furthermore, under Article 6(1) of the CMS Regulation, any lots of fish, selachii, cephalopods, or Norway lobster falling into freshness category B are ineligible for financial assistance granted in respect of permanent withdrawal or carry-over as provided for in Articles 21, 23, and 24 of the Markets Regulation (on which see further section 8 below).[39] Regarding Article 6(1), the Commission's 2006 report states that: 'The [common marketing] standards have . . . contributed to increase [sic] the quality of products . . . A Commission staff working paper on the application of [Article 6(1)] confirmed that the improvement of product quality was mainly related to the decrease in landings of category B products.'[40] However, the working paper referred to by the Commission dates from 2001.[41]

The freshness category of a given lot is to be determined on the basis of: (a) 'the freshness of the product'; and (b) 'a number of additional requirements'.[42]

---

[37] Reg 2406/96, Art 1(2)(b).   [38] Reg 2406/96, Art 5(1).
[39] References in Art 6(1) of Reg 2406/96 to Reg 3759/92 are now to be construed as references to Reg 104/2000 (see Reg 104/2000, Art 42(2)).   [40] COM(2006) 558, section 2, p 2.
[41] *Commission Staff Working Paper on the results of the application of Article 6(1) of Council Regulation (EC) No 2406/96 laying down common marketing standards for certain fishery products*, SEC(2001) 1764, 7.11.2001.   [42] Reg 2406/96, Art 4(1), 1st para.

Freshness is to be defined by reference to 'the special ratings for different types of products set out in Annex I' to the Regulation.[43] Annex I relates to five categories of organism: 'Whitefish' (24 listed common names); 'Bluefish' (10 listed common names); 'Selachii' ('Dogfish, skate'); 'Cephalopods' ('Cuttlefish'); and 'Crustaceans' ('Shrimps', Norway lobster). The species, genera, or groups listed in the five categories of organism covered by Annex I correspond broadly to those listed in Article 3. However, making comparisons between the two lists is somewhat hampered by the list in Annex I not using Latin names; a few of the species listed in Article 3 are not listed in Annex I (but are listed in Annex II—see subsection 4.3 below).

Annex I comprises five tables (for each of whitefish, bluefish, selachii, cephalopods, and crustaceans). In each table, the available freshness categories are specified along the top and correspond to those specified in Article 4(2) (see above). For example, the table for whitefish specifies three freshness categories: Extra, A, and B. Criteria for judging freshness are arranged down the side of each table. For each criterion and freshness category, there is then a description. For example, the whitefish table lists seven criteria for judging freshness. One of them is 'Skin mucus': mucus that is 'Aqueous, transparent' corresponds to freshness category Extra, while mucus that is 'Milky' corresponds to freshness category B.

The Commission, in its 2006 report, concluded that: 'The grading for freshness is relatively simple, easy to use and adapted to major groups of species.'[44] That assertion seems somewhat questionable in view of a system using up to seven basic criteria to judge freshness, where the descriptions often leave scope for interpretation. Furthermore, it is not clear from the wording of the CMS Regulation whether a particular freshness category is to be allocated based on the lot in question having attained that category in respect of all the criteria or only some of them.

The tables for whitefish, bluefish, and selachii also include a column, in addition to the freshness categories, entitled 'Not admitted'. For each of the freshness criteria in those tables, the 'Not admitted' column contains a description. For example, the description corresponding to 'Skin mucus' for whitefish is 'Yellowish grey, opaque mucus'. Annex I states that the 'Not admitted' category 'will apply only until a Commission Decision is taken establishing criteria for fish which is unfit for human consumption, pursuant to Council Directive 91/493/EEC'. Meanwhile, the 'Not admitted' category itself sets out the criteria for fish which is unfit for human consumption.[45] It is not entirely clear what purpose the descriptions in the said category serve, other than to help indicate at what point the lower limits to freshness category B have been exceeded. The category is not present in the tables for cephalopods and crustaceans. The Directive referred to above, Directive 91/493, laid down 'the health conditions for the production and the

---

[43] Reg 2406/96, Art 4(1), 2nd para.   [44] COM(2006) 558, section 2, p 3.
[45] Reg 2406/96, Art 1(3)(b).

placing on the market of fishery products for human consumption'.[46] It was subsequently repealed,[47] in view of a new legal regime on health conditions. The authors are not aware of any Commission Decision of the type referred to above, including under the new health conditions regime; this would explain the persistence of the 'Not admitted' category in the CMS Regulation to date.

As noted above, the freshness category of a given lot is to be determined not just by recourse to 'the freshness of the product' but also on the basis of 'a number of additional requirements'. Those additional requirements are found in Article 6 of the CMS Regulation. In summary, they work by making the application of a particular freshness category (Extra, A, or B) conditional on supplementary things like absence of blemishes or bad discoloration.

Under the CMS Regulation, the grading of fishery products for freshness is to be undertaken by the fishing industry 'in collaboration with experts designated for that purpose by the trade organizations concerned'.[48] The Member States are to carry out controls to ensure compliance with that duty, and may otherwise undertake the necessary grading themselves.[49] (See further section 9 below.) The names of the designated experts and the trade organizations concerned are to be notified to the Commission and to all Member States.[50] The provisions of the CMS Regulation on freshness are stated to be without prejudice to the requirements of Directive 91/493 (on which see above).[51]

4.3 Common size standards under the CMS Regulation

The CMS Regulation establishes common standards on size for all the species and genera listed in Article 3. The standards are set out in Annex II to the Regulation, which specifies, for any given species or genus, a number of size categories. The number of categories varies from just one in the case of 'Pandalid shrimps . . . fresh or chilled' up to eleven for herring. Most species or genera have between three and five categories. There is no maximum size in the largest category, but there is a minimum size in the smallest category (hereafter, 'the minimum marketing size'). In some cases, the smallest category is reserved exclusively for the Mediterranean. With some exceptions, size is specified in terms of weight, whether as weight of individual fish or number of fish per kilogram or both. The

---

[46] Council Directive 91/493/EEC of 22 July 1991 laying down the health conditions for the production and the placing on the market of fishery products, OJ 1991 L268/15, as amended and corrected, Art 1.

[47] Directive 2004/41/EC of the European Parliament and of the Council of 21 April 2004 repealing certain Directives concerning food hygiene and health conditions for the production and placing on the market of certain products of animal origin intended for human consumption and amending Council Directives 89/662/EEC and 92/118/EEC and Council Decision 95/408/EC, OJ 2004 L157/33, as corrected, Art 2(10). [48] Reg 2406/96, Art 12(1).

[49] Reg 2406/96, Art 12(1) and (2). [50] Reg 2406/96, Art 13.

[51] Reg 2406/96, Art 1(3)(a).

exceptions are for shrimps, edible crab, common scallop, and common whelk, where size is specified as shell width.[52]

The size categories set out in Annex II are to be applied to individual lots.[53] Each lot, other than small ones, must contain products of the same size category; a small lot that is not of one single size category is to be 'placed in the lowest size category represented therein'.[54] One result of this approach is that, pursuant to Article 2(1) of the CMS Regulation (see above), there will be a prohibition on marketing a particular lot of a product in cases where: (a) the CMS Regulation has established common size standards for the product in question; and (b) the size of the product comprising the lot is below the minimum marketing size specified for that product. However, exemptions from the minimum marketing sizes specified in Annex II may be adopted '[i]n order to ensure local or regional supplies of shrimps and crabs for certain coastal zones of the Community', such zones to be determined by means of comitology procedure.[55]

As with freshness, the CMS Regulation requires the grading of fishery products for size to be undertaken by the fishing industry 'in collaboration with experts designated for that purpose by the trade organizations concerned'.[56] The corresponding duties on the Member States are the same as for freshness (see subsection 4.2 above).[57]

The minimum marketing sizes set out in the CMS Regulation are stated to apply without prejudice to the minimum lengths required under three fisheries conservation Regulations (Regulations 1866/86, 3094/86, and 1626/94).[58] By way of clarification, the Regulation adds that: 'For the purposes of control by the competent authorities, the species covered by marketing standards shall respect the minimum biological sizes as laid down. . . .',[59]

In practice, Regulations 1866/86, 3094/86, and 1626/94 have all since been repealed and replaced. Their current equivalents are Regulations 2187/2005,[60] 850/98,[61] and 1967/2006,[62] respectively (see Chapter 4). The current Regulations all provide for references to their predecessors to be construed as references to

---

[52] Reg 2406/96, Art 7(1) and Annex II.   [53] Reg 2406/96, Art 8(1).
[54] Reg 2406/96, Art 8(2).   [55] Reg 2406/96, Art 10.   [56] Reg 2406/96, Art 12(1).
[57] Reg 2406/96, Art 12(1) and (2).   [58] Reg 2406/96, Art 7(2), 1st para.
[59] Reg 2406/96, Art 7(2), 2nd para.
[60] Council Regulation (EC) No 2187/2005 of 21 December 2005 for the conservation of fishery resources through technical measures in the Baltic Sea, the Belts and the Sound, amending Regulation (EC) No 1434/98 and repealing Regulation (EC) No 88/98, OJ 2005 L349/1, as amended. See Arts 14, 15, and 24(2)(a) and Annex IV.
[61] Council Regulation (EC) No 850/98 of 30 March 1998 for the conservation of fishery resources through technical measures for the protection of juveniles of marine organisms, OJ 1998 L125/1, as amended and corrected. See Arts 17–19 and Annexes XII and XIII.
[62] Council Regulation (EC) No 1967/2006 of 21 December 2006 concerning management measures for the sustainable exploitation of fishery resources in the Mediterranean Sea, amending Regulation (EEC) No 2847/93 and repealing Regulation (EC) No 1626/94, OJ 2006 L409/11, as corrected (reissued as a corrected version in OJ 2007 L36/6). See Arts 15 and 16 and Annexes III and IV.

themselves.[63] Therefore any conflict between, on the one hand, a size category under the CMS Regulation that seemingly permits a certain size of fish to be marketed and, on the other hand, a minimum size established by Regulation 2187/2005, 850/98, or 1967/2006 is to be resolved in favour of the latter.

The Commission, in a discussion document[64] issued soon after the adoption of the CMS Regulation, noted the potential for conflict between minimum marketing sizes and minimum biological sizes but explained that the CMS Regulation sought to address that by setting out 'to establish the primacy of minimum biological sizes over minimum marketing sizes'.[65] However, the Commission acknowledged that problems could still remain and that consistency between the two types of minimum size would be desirable.

For example, it stated that it will be 'examining the idea that, for each species, the minimum sizes expressed by weight for the categories that can be marketed should also be expressed by length and should constitute the biological size'.[66] Subsequently, in its 2006 report, the Commission acknowledged complications in that respect because '[i]n certain species, a given length may correspond to different weights . . . due to seasonal variations in weight'. It conceded that 'the relationship between marketing standards and minimum biological sizes is an issue which may need to be revisited'.[67]

The authors are not aware of the Commission having taken matters further regarding the relationship between the two types of minimum size. However, the relationship may become particularly topical in the context of the Commission's new policy on discards (see Chapter 4). In that regard, the Commission has stated that: 'If a requirement to land all fish is introduced, juvenile fish should be protected against targeted fisheries by making the marketing rather than the landing of such fish illegal by introducing minimum marketing sizes for human consumption instead.'[68] As explained above, minimum marketing sizes already exist in many cases so the reference to 'introducing' such sizes is rather confusing. The Commission's statement may mean that, as well as discontinuing the concept of minimum landing sizes and instead allowing minimum marketing sizes to prevail, it has in mind to introduce: (a) minimum marketing sizes that are different to the current ones; and/or (b) minimum marketing sizes for species that have hitherto not been landed and hence not exposed to markets.

---

[63] Reg 2187/2005, Art 31 (and, prior to that, Reg 88/98, Art 15); Reg 850/98, Art 49 (and, prior to that, Reg 894/97, Art 19); Reg 1967/2006, Art 31.

[64] *Communication from the Commission to the Council and to the European Parliament: The Future for the Market in Fisheries Products in the European Union: Responsibility, Partnership and Competitiveness*, COM (1997) 719, 16.12.1997.   [65] COM(1997) 719, p 6.

[66] COM(1997) 719, p 6.   [67] COM(2006) 558, section 2, p 3.

[68] *Communication from the Commission to the Council and the European Parliament: A policy to reduce unwanted by-catches and eliminate discards in European fisheries*, COM(2007) 136, 28.3.2007, section 3, p 5.

5 Consumer information

Article 4 of the Markets Regulation aims to improve the information provided to the final consumers of certain fishery products. In its legislative proposal for what became the Markets Regulation, the Commission stated that the purpose of Article 4 was to 'prevent the increasing danger of consumers being misled because of the diversity of supply on the market' as well as to 'facilitate verification of compliance with technical measures, particularly regarding minimum sizes, which sometimes vary for the same species depending on the catch zone'.[69]

Article 4 works by placing a general prohibition on the offer 'for retail sale to the final consumer' of certain categories of fishery product unless appropriate marking or labelling indicates three things, namely 'the commercial designation of the species', 'the production method (caught at sea or in inland waters or farmed)', and 'the catch area'.[70] Regulation 2065/2001[71] in turn specifies the information to be used for indicating the production method and catch area (see further below).

The categories of fishery product in question are those referred to in sections '(a)', '(b)', and '(c)' of the list in Article 1 of the Markets Regulation, ie products falling within CN codes 0301 to 0307 (see section 3 and Table 6.1 above). The prohibition is stated to be without prejudice to Directive 79/112,[72] on labelling, and does not apply to 'small quantities of products disposed of directly to consumers by either fishermen or aquaculture producers'.[73] Directive 79/112 has been repealed and replaced by Directive 2000/13.[74] The latter provides for references to Directive 79/112 to be construed as references to itself.[75] In January 2008, the Commission issued a legislative proposal for a Regulation repealing and replacing Directive 2000/13.[76]

The phrase 'commercial designation of the species' means the accepted name used in the territory of a Member State for trading in the product in question.[77] Member States are, not later than 1 January 2002, to 'draw up and publish a list of the commercial designations accepted in their territory, for at least all the species

---

[69] Proposal for a Council Regulation (EC) on the common organisation of the markets in fishery and aquaculture products, COM(1999) 55, 16.02.1999, explanatory memorandum, section 2, p 4. See also COM(1997) 719, p 11.   [70] Reg 104/2000, Art 4(1).
[71] Commission Regulation (EC) No 2065/2001 of 22 October 2001 laying down detailed rules for the application of Council Regulation (EC) No 104/2000 as regards informing consumers about fishery and aquaculture products, OJ 2001 L278/6, as amended and corrected.
[72] Council Directive 79/112/EEC of 18 December 1978 on the approximation of the laws of the Member States relating to the labelling, presentation and advertising of foodstuffs for sale to the ultimate consumer, OJ 1979 L33/1, as amended.   [73] Reg 104/2000, Art 4(1).
[74] Directive 2000/13/EC of the European Parliament and of the Council of 20 March 2000 on the approximation of the laws of the Member States relating to the labelling, presentation and advertising of foodstuffs, OJ 2000 L109/29, as amended and corrected.   [75] Dir 2000/13, Art 26(2).
[76] Proposal for a Regulation of the European Parliament and of the Council on the provision of food information to consumers, COM(2008) 40, 30.1.2008.   [77] Reg 104/2000, recital (8).

listed in Annexes I to IV to this Regulation'[78] (which cover various products falling within CN codes 0302, 0303, 0304, 0306, and 0307). Member States are required to 'recognise designations listed by other Member States for the same species in the same language'.[79]

Detailed rules for implementing Article 4 are to be drawn up where necessary.[80] In turn, the Commission has adopted Regulation 2065/2001, which specifies, *inter alia*: (a) the means for Member States to change their lists of commercial designations;[81] (b) optional additional information that may be provided to the final consumer (notably the scientific name of the species concerned and more precision on the catch area);[82] (c) the information to be used for indicating the production method and the catch area;[83] and (d) a maximum threshold purchase value for the 'small quantities' exception (see above).[84]

The information to be used for indicating the production method is 'caught', 'caught in fresh water', or 'farmed' (or 'cultivated').[85] For indicating catch area, the approach depends on the production method.[86] For products caught at sea, one of twelve large sea areas or oceans must be specified (eg 'North-East Atlantic', 'Baltic Sea', 'Pacific Ocean'). For products caught in fresh water, the country of origin must be specified. For farmed products, the country 'in which the product undergoes the final development stage' must generally be specified.

On traceability, Regulation 2065/2001 states that the information required about commercial designation, production method, and catch area 'shall be available at each stage of marketing of the species concerned'. For those purposes, the information is to be supplemented by the scientific name of the species concerned and is to be provided 'by means of the labelling or packaging of the product, or by means of a commercial document accompanying the goods . . . '.[87] Member States are to establish arrangements for checking the application of those requirements.[88]

In its 2006 report, the Commission concludes that Regulation 2065/2001 'has generally enhanced the consumer awareness about fishery products although with differences between Member States'. It continues: 'The main issues of interest in some Member States are the origin of fish and the method of production. In other Member States, consumers are more concerned about other aspects such as quality, price and whether fish was caught in a sustainable manner.'[89] For a consumer interested in discriminating in favour of products from sustainable fisheries or sustainable aquaculture, the information required under the Markets Regulation and Regulation 2065/2001 is unlikely to be of much assistance on its own. The question of labelling to indicate sustainability will be considered next.

[78] Reg 104/2000, Art 4(2).　　[79] Reg 104/2000, Art 4(3).
[80] Reg 104/2000, Art 4(4).　　[81] Reg 2065/2001, Art 2.
[82] Reg 2065/2001, Arts 3 and 5(2).　　[83] Reg 2065/2001, Arts 4 and 5.
[84] Reg 2065/2001, Art 7.　　[85] Reg 2065/2001, Art 4.　　[86] Reg 2065/2001, Art 5.
[87] Reg 2065/2001, Art 8.　　[88] Reg 2065/2001, Art 9(1).
[89] COM(2006) 558, section 3, p 4.

As early as 1997 a discussion document prepared by the Commission recognized that: 'By making it possible for consumers to know that the product they are being offered has been taken or produced using a responsible fishing or aquaculture method, certification allows demand to become the arbiter and, therefore, to penalise conduct that is unsatisfactory in terms of stock conservation and environmental protection'.[90] A requirement to provide information on sustainability did not make it into the Markets Regulation or Regulation 2065/2001. However, in 2005 the Commission launched a debate 'on a Community approach towards eco-labelling schemes for fisheries products'.[91]

In its Communication on the subject, the Commission took the view that 'a coherent Community policy on eco-labelling for fish and fisheries products should be developed to address the consequences of the emergence of disparate sets of eco-labels'.[92] It put forward three options: (a) no action; (b) creation of a single EC scheme; and (c) establishment of minimum requirements for voluntary demand-led eco-labelling schemes.[93] The Commission considered that the third of these options 'would be the most appropriate one at this juncture' and indicated that it 'may come forward with appropriate legislative proposals' in the light of the debate.[94]

Since the issue of the Communication in 2005, the European Economic and Social Committee has provided an opinion[95] and the European Parliament has adopted a resolution. The European Parliament was disappointed with the Commission's 'lack of ambition' and requested a further Communication within six months 'detailing the minimum requirements and guidelines with which a Community eco-labelling scheme for fisheries products must comply'.[96] The Commission did not produce a further Communication in response to this request.

In the first half of 2007, the Council held an exchange of views in which 'most delegations indicated that they were in favour of establishing minimum requirements for voluntary eco-labelling schemes'. The minutes concluded that: 'After a final report on the issue, the Commission may present a legislative proposal on the eco-labelling scheme accompanied by a full impact assessment.'[97] As at the end of November 2008 no legislative proposal specific to fishery products had been issued.

However, in July 2008 the Commission issued a legislative proposal on a 'Community Ecolabel scheme', based on Article 175(1) of the EC Treaty, which

---

[90] COM(1997) 719, p 11.

[91] *Communication from the Commission to the Council, the European Parliament and the European Economic and Social Committee: Launching a debate on a Community approach towards eco-labelling schemes for fisheries products*, COM(2005) 275, 29.06.2005.   [92] COM(2005) 275, section 4, p 5.

[93] COM(2005) 275, section 5, pp 6–9.   [94] COM(2005) 275, section 6, p 10.

[95] OJ 2006 C88/27.   [96] P6_TA(2006)0347, paras 6 and 14.

[97] Council of the European Union, 2793rd Council meeting, Agriculture and Fisheries, Luxembourg, 16 April 2007, press release, 8297/07 (Presse 76), 13.

expressly covers, *inter alia*, 'products of fishing and aquaculture'.[98] The proposal, if adopted, is intended to replace Regulation 1980/2000.[99] Furthermore, in January 2008, the Commission issued a proposal for a Regulation on the provision of food information to consumers, based on Article 95 EC.[100] As at the end of November 2008 both proposals were with the Council and the European Parliament; they are not discussed further here.

A further issue of relevance to consumer information, as well as to common marketing standards, is organic production and labelling of organic products. Regulation 834/2007,[101] which has Article 37 EC as its legal basis and applies from 1 January 2009,[102] 'establishes common objectives and principles to underpin the rules set out under this Regulation concerning: (a) all stages of production, preparation and distribution of organic products and their control; (b) the use of indications referring to organic production in labelling and advertising'.[103] The Regulation states that '[t]he products of . . . fishing of wild animals shall *not* be considered *as* organic production' (emphasis added).[104] However, products of fisheries may be used *in* organic production, for example as feed materials, if certain conditions are met.[105]

The Regulation establishes specific production rules for aquaculture animals and for seaweed.[106] The rules for aquaculture animals and farming of seaweed are considered briefly in Chapter 9. On collection of wild seaweed, the Regulation states that, subject to certain conditions being met, '[t]he collection of wild seaweeds and parts thereof, growing naturally in the sea, *is* considered as an organic production method' (emphasis added).[107] The Regulation envisages the adoption of specific measures to implement its production rules for aquaculture animals and for seaweed,[108] but to the authors' knowledge no such measures had been adopted as at the end of November 2008. However, other detailed rules have been adopted, and these are to apply, *mutatis mutandis*, to, *inter alia*, products originating from

---

[98] *Proposal for a Regulation of the European Parliament and of the Council on a Community Ecolabel scheme*, COM(2008) 401, 16.7.2008, proposed Art 2, 2nd para. Cf *Summary Record of the Meeting of Working Group 3 (Markets and Trade Policy) of the Advisory Committee on Fisheries and Aquaculture*, 12.06.08, section 5 (available on the website of DG Mare).

[99] Regulation (EC) No 1980/2000 of the European Parliament and of the Council of 17 July 2000 on a revised Community eco-label award scheme, OJ 2000 L237/1.   [100] COM(2008) 40.

[101] Council Regulation (EC) No 834/2007 of 28 June 2007 on organic production and labelling of organic products and repealing Regulation (EEC) No 2092/91, OJ 2007 L189/1, as amended.

[102] Reg 834/2007, Art 42, 3rd para. (Art 24(1)(b) and (c) applies from 1 July 2010.)

[103] Reg 834/2007, Art 1(1), 2nd para.

[104] Reg 834/2007, Art 1(2), 2nd para; cf Art 23(4)(c)(i).

[105] Reg 834/2007, *inter alia*, Arts 16 and 14(1)(d)(iv). See further Commission Regulation (EC) No 889/2008 of 5 September 2008 laying down detailed rules for the implementation of Council Regulation (EC) No 834/2007 on organic production and labelling of organic products with regard to organic production, labelling and control, OJ 2008 L250/1, *inter alia*, Art 22(3) and Annex V.

[106] Reg 834/2007, Arts 15 and 13 respectively.   [107] Reg 834/2007, Art 13(1)(a) and (b).

[108] Reg 834/2007, Arts 15(2) and 13(3) respectively.

aquaculture and to seaweeds 'until detailed production rules for those products are laid down . . . '.[109] The application of those detailed rules, as well as that of Regulation 834/2007's own objectives, principles, and rules, is not considered here for reasons of space.

6 Producer organizations

6.1 Introduction

Producer organizations are a key instrument of the common organization of the markets in fishery products. This is because of their fundamental role regarding the system of prices and intervention (see section 8 below) as well as in helping to match supply to demand and improve product quality (see subsection 6.4 below). The organizations are prohibited from holding a dominant position on a given market unless that is necessary under the objectives set out in Article 33 EC.[110] Sissenwine and Symes note that in some Member States 'the role of the [producer organization] has evolved to include the collective management of the member vessels [sic] quotas';[111] however, this aspect of their activity is not addressed in this book.

In short, producer organizations are groups of fishermen or fish farmers, associating freely, that become formally recognized and have rights and obligations regarding the markets in fishery products. The Markets Regulation defines the term 'producer organisation' for its purposes, and hence impliedly for the purposes of the common organization of the markets in fishery products, by means of five elements, defining the term 'producer' as 'physical or legal persons using means of production to produce fishery products with a view to first-stage marketing of them'.[112] The five elements are considered next.

First,[113] a producer organization must be a legal entity 'set up on the own initiative of a group of producers of one or more of the products referred to in Article 1(a), (b) and (c) in so far, in the case of frozen, treated or processed products, as the operations in question have been carried out on board fishing vessels'. The products referred to in Article 1(a), (b), and (c) are those falling within CN codes 0301 to 0307 (see Table 6.1 above). Where those products are 'frozen, treated or processed', the producers in question must have done that freezing, treating, or processing on board fishing vessels (as opposed to, say, on land).

Secondly,[114] the producer organization must have been established 'for the purpose, *in particular*, of ensuring that fishing is carried out along rational lines and

---

[109] Reg 889/2008, Art 1(2).   [110] Reg 104/2000, Art 5(3). See also Art 32.
[111] Sissenwine, M and Symes, D, *Reflections on the Common Fisheries Policy*, Report to the General Directorate for Fisheries and Maritime Affairs of the European Commission, July 2007, 69.
[112] Reg 104/2000, Art 1, 2nd para.   [113] Reg 104/2000, Art 5(1)(a).
[114] Reg 104/2000, Art 5(1)(b).

that conditions for the sale of their members' products are improved' (emphasis added) by 'taking such measures as will: 1. encourage the planning of production and its adjustment to demand, in terms of both quantity [sic], in particular by implementing catch plans; 2. promote the concentration of supply; 3. stabilise prices; 4. encourage fishing methods which support sustainable fishing'.

Thirdly,[115] a producer organization's rules of association must require its producer members to, *inter alia*: (a) apply the organization's rules to fishing, production, and marketing, as well as any measures adopted in response to the Member State concerned having 'decided that some or all of its catch quota or quotas and/or application of fishing effort measures are to be managed by producer organisations'; (b) dispose of their total output of products in respect of which they are members through the producer organization (although that requirement can be waived by the organization in certain circumstances); (c) pay the financial contributions for the intervention fund (see subsection 8.3 below); and (d) remain members of the organization for at least three years after its recognition and to give at least one year's notice if they wish to leave.

Fourthly,[116] its rules of association must provide for, *inter alia*: (a) procedures for determining, adopting, and amending the organization's rules relating to fishing, production, and marketing; (b) the exclusion of all forms of discrimination among members; (c) the levying on members of the financial contributions needed to finance the organization; and (d) penalties for infringement of obligations under the rules of association and the rules of the organization.

Lastly,[117] the producer organization must have been recognized by the Member State concerned. A Member State is under an obligation to recognize as producer organizations all producer groups which meet the above requirements and which, *inter alia*, have their official headquarters in its territory, are 'sufficiently active economically' in its territory, and apply for recognition.[118] The Markets Regulation sets out further provisions on recognition of producer organizations, or associations of producer organizations, by Member States.[119] The Commission has a role in recognition in that it may request a Member State to withdraw recognition in specified circumstances.[120] Detailed rules on recognition have been implemented subsequently (see below).

6.2 Recognition

Supplementing the provisions on recognition in the Markets Regulation (see above), Commission Regulations lay down detailed rules regarding recognition by

[115] Reg 104/2000, Art 5(1)(c).   [116] Reg 104/2000, Art 5(1)(d).
[117] Reg 104/2000, Art 5(1)(e).   [118] Reg 104/2000, Art 5(2).
[119] Reg 104/2000, Arts 5(2) and 6(1)–(4).   [120] Reg 104/2000, Art 6(5).

Member States of producer organizations.[121] In particular, Regulation 2318/2001 establishes, *inter alia*: (a) criteria for judging whether a producer organization is 'sufficiently active economically' for the purposes of the Markets Regulation;[122] (b) the conditions for granting recognition to an association of producer organizations, including where the associating producer organizations are recognized in different Member States;[123] and (c) various procedural rules regarding recognition of producer organizations.[124]

Regulation 1924/2000[125] contains detailed rules for the grant of so-called 'specific recognition'. This is a form of recognition granted to producer organizations which market the products covered by the common marketing standards laid down in the CMS Regulation (see section 4 above), or products from aquaculture, 'when they have submitted a plan to improve the quality of such products that has been approved by the competent national authorities'.[126] Such plans are discussed further in subsection 6.4 below. Financial support for the implementation of such plans is potentially available under the European Fisheries Fund to those producer organizations that have been granted specific recognition (see subsection 6.5 below).

The *List of the recognised producers' organisations in the fishery and aquaculture sector* published in 2008[127] reveals a total of 202 recognized producer organizations and nine recognized associations of producer organizations in a total of sixteen Member States as follows: Belgium (1 producer organization, zero associations of producer organizations); Denmark (4, zero); Estonia (3, zero); France (31, 4); Germany (19, 2); Greece (3, zero); Ireland (5, zero); Italy (32, 2); Latvia (2, zero); Lithuania (2, zero); Netherlands (11, zero); Poland (6, zero); Portugal (14, zero); Spain (43, 1); Sweden (6, zero); and the UK (20, zero).

6.3 Extension of rules to non-members

A producer organization's rules are applicable to its own members. However, in some circumstances, its rules may become applicable to non-members too, 'in

---

[121] (a) Commission Regulation (EC) No 2318/2001 of 29 November 2001 laying down detailed rules for the application of Council Regulation (EC) No 104/2000 as regards the recognition of producer organisations and associations of producer organisations in the fishery and aquaculture sector, OJ 2001 L313/9, as amended; and (b) Commission Regulation (EC) No 80/2001 of 16 January 2001 laying down detailed rules for the application of Council Regulation (EC) No 104/2000 as regards notifications concerning recognition of producer organisations, the fixing of prices and intervention within the scope of the common organisation of the market in fishery and aquaculture products, OJ 2001 L13/3, as amended.   [122] Reg 2318/2001, Art 1.

[123] Reg 2318/2001, Art 2.   [124] Reg 2318/2001, Arts 4–7.

[125] Commission Regulation (EC) No 1924/2000 of 11 September 2000 laying down detailed rules for the application of Council Regulation (EC) No 104/2000 as regards the grant of specific recognition to producers' organisations in the fisheries sector in order to improve the quality of their products, OJ 2000 L230/5.   [126] Reg 104/2000, Art 12(1).

[127] OJ 2008 C163/9.

order to support the activity of producer organisations and facilitate greater market stability'[128] or, put another way, to help avoid the possibility that market regulation measures adopted by producer organizations 'will be undermined by the behaviour of non-members'.[129] The Markets Regulation sets out the basic conditions for the application of rules to non-members, and Regulation 696/2008[130] contains detailed rules in that regard.

Under the Markets Regulation, the extension of rules becomes a possibility where the producer organization in question 'is considered to be *representative of production and marketing* in one or more landing places of a Member State' (emphasis added). In those circumstances, any extension would be addressed to 'producers who are not members of the organisation and who market any of the products referred to in Article 1 [of the Markets Regulation] within the area of which the producer organisation is representative'.[131]

However, the organization must make an application to the competent national authorities to extend the rules, and only these authorities may require the extension.[132] There are two categories of rules that may be extended: (a) production and marketing rules introduced by the organization to attain objectives relating to rational fishing and improvement of conditions for sale of products; and (b) rules on 'market withdrawal and carry-over' (see section 8 below) for the fresh and chilled products falling within CN codes 0301, 0302, 0303, 0304, 0306, and 0307.[133]

For products listed in Annex I to the Markets Regulation, ie various products falling within CN codes 0302, 0306, and 0307, the rules may be extended only in so far as the price applied by the producer organization is, subject to certain tolerance limits, 'the withdrawal price or the Community selling price' (see section 8 below).[134] Furthermore, the Member State concerned may decide to apply the rules in question in respect of only some categories of sale.[135] In any event, the extended rules may apply only: (a) up to the first-stage sale of the products on the market; (b) for a period not longer than twelve months; and (c) for a regionally limited area.[136] The Member State concerned is to take all the necessary measures to ensure compliance with the extended rules.[137]

The Markets Regulation sets out the role of the Commission regarding the extension of rules.[138] In particular, the Commission may declare the extension null

[128] Reg 104/2000, recital (11).

[129] European Commission, *The common organisation of the markets in fishery and aquaculture products* (Luxembourg: Office for Official Publications of the European Communities, 2002), section 6, p 15.

[130] Commission Regulation (EC) No 696/2008 of 23 July 2008 laying down detailed rules for the application of Council Regulation (EC) No 104/2000 as regards the extension to non-members of certain rules adopted by producers' organisations in the fisheries sector, OJ 2008 L195/6.

[131] Reg 104/2000, Art 7(1), 1st para.   [132] Reg 104/2000, Art 7(1), 1st para.
[133] Reg 104/2000, Art 7(1), 1st para, (a) and (b).   [134] Reg 104/2000, Art 7(1), 2nd para.
[135] Reg 104/2000, Art 7(1), 3rd para.   [136] Reg 104/2000, Art 7(2).
[137] Reg 104/2000, Art 7(7).   [138] Reg 104/2000, Art 7(3)–(7).

and void in certain circumstances (for example if it finds that the extension jeopardizes free trade).[139] The Regulation also explains the consequences for non-members beyond merely the duty to abide by the extended rules. First, the Member State concerned may decide that non-members bound by the rules are liable to the producer organization for relevant administrative costs.[140] Secondly, it must also ensure the withdrawal of non-members' products that do not, for example, satisfy the relevant marketing rules.[141]

Thirdly, presumably as a sweetener to the non-members to whom rules are extended, a Member State may grant compensation to those non-members (if they are established in the EC) in respect of products which: (a) cannot be marketed under the extended rules; or (b) have been withdrawn from the market under extended rules on market withdrawal for the fresh and chilled products falling within CN codes 0301, 0302, 0303, 0304, 0306, and 0307. However, quantitative limits are placed on the amount of compensation that may be granted. Furthermore, the expenditure arising from granting any such compensation is to be 'borne by the Member State concerned';[142] this presumably means that the Member State will not, in turn, be compensated by the EC.

As noted above, Regulation 696/2008 contains detailed rules on the extension of rules to non-members. It establishes, *inter alia*: (a) quantitative criteria for judging whether the production and marketing activities of a producer organization are 'considered to be sufficiently representative in the area within which it is proposed to extend the rules' for the purposes of the Markets Regulation;[143] (b) more detail on the content of the production and marketing rules that may be extended;[144] and (c) a minimum period for application of extended rules (ninety days).[145]

The Commission's 2006 report provides information on the extension of rules. It states that:[146]

Four Member States applied the extension of [producer organizations'] rules to non-member producers. 2 applications were accepted in Belgium, 2 in Spain, 7 in France and one in Italy. The extensions affected 12 species in Belgium, 3 in Spain, 3 in France and one in Italy. The percentage of non-members affected varied from less than 10% in Belgium to 53% in France. The duration ranged between 3 and 12 months. No extension was granted to aquaculture products.

The measures most frequently extended were catch restriction [sic] as well as ban [sic] on landings and first sale. The observance of certain withdrawal prices was also applied in Belgium and Italy. Non-members were made liable for fees related to extension of rules only in Belgium. On the other hand, despite an extension of withdrawal rules, no Member State granted compensation to non-members for products which could not be marketed.

---

[139] Reg 104/2000, Art 7(3)–(5).   [140] Reg 104/2000, Art 7(8).
[141] Reg 104/2000, Art 7(9).   [142] Reg 104/2000, Art 8.
[143] Reg 696/2008, Art 1.   [144] Reg 696/2008, Art 2.   [145] Reg 696/2008, Art 3.
[146] COM(2006) 558, section 4.2, pp 5–6.

6.4 Production, marketing, and quality planning

Operational programmes

With a time-limited exception for newly established producer organizations,[147] the Markets Regulation requires each producer organization to draw up a so-called 'operational programme' at the beginning of each fishing year and send it to the relevant Member State's competent authorities.[148] The programme is to cover the species listed in Annexes I, IV, and V to the Regulation, ie various products falling within CN codes 0301, 0302, 0304, 0306, and 0307.[149] (Just to be clear, it should be noted that the operational programmes required under the Markets Regulation are *not* the same as those required under the European Fisheries Fund, on which see Chapter 8.)

Operational programmes are '*strategies for balancing supply and demand* by requiring producer organisations to plan in advance deliveries from their members for particular species and to examine ways of improving financial returns once a catch has been landed' (emphasis added).[150] Put another way, they are intended as a means for producer organizations to 'guide the production of their members towards meeting market requirements and foster conditions that will ensure that their members obtain the best possible returns on their catches . . . '.[151]

The programmes are stated by the Commission to be a tool to help ensure that 'market operators make a much greater contribution to the responsible management of resources'.[152] Examples provided in a Commission brochure published in 2002 (see below) suggest the contribution of operational programmes to responsible management is to be through maximizing the value of the catch (including avoiding waste).

The operational programme is to comprise five elements, namely (in brief): (a) a marketing strategy 'to match the quantity and quality of supply to market requirements'; (b) a catch plan (for certain species, in particular those covered by catch quotas); (c) a production plan (for certain species); (d) so-called 'special anticipatory measures' (for adjusting the supply of species 'which habitually present marketing difficulties'); and (e) penalties (for members infringing implementing decisions).[153]

The information to be included in the programme, particularly the marketing strategy, is elaborated in Regulation 2508/2000.[154] Stemming from that, a Commission brochure published in 2002 provides a helpful illustration of what

---

[147] Reg 104/2000, Art 9(1), 3rd para.   [148] Reg 104/2000, Art 9(1), 1st para.

[149] Reg 104/2000, Art 9(1), 1st para.   [150] European Commission, 2002, section 3, p 7.

[151] Reg 104/2000, recital (14).

[152] European Commission, 2002, section 3, p 7. See also Reg 104/2000, recital (14).

[153] Reg 104/2000, Art 9(1), 1st para.

[154] Commission Regulation (EC) No 2508/2000 of 15 November 2000 laying down the detailed rules for the application of Council Regulation (EC) No 104/2000 as regards operational programmes in the fisheries sector, OJ 2000 L289/8.

each of the five elements may entail.[155] For example, it states that the marketing strategy is to include 'specific measures to maximise the value of the catch' such as 'redirecting products towards different market outlets, raising their quality, introducing voluntary labelling initiatives or developing other promotional activities' or 'concentrating fishery production in periods of higher prices'.[156]

The operational programme is subject to Member State approval.[157] The Member State is to check to ensure that the programme has been drawn up and submitted as required.[158] Failure to meet the requirements, and failure to implement the programme, is to be penalized by means of the Member State not providing all or part of the financial assistance for the various intervention operations that are discussed in section 8 below.[159] Aid to producer organizations in relation to their operational programmes is addressed in subsection 6.5 below.

Regulation 2508/2000 contains detailed rules regarding operational programmes. As well as establishing the information to be included in the programme (see above), it sets out, *inter alia*: (a) procedures for submission of the programme by the producer organization, approval by the Member State, and granting of compensation by the Member State;[160] (b) a duty on the producer organization to 'immediately implement' the programme after its submission to the Member State;[161] (c) rules for working out compensation;[162] and (d) a duty, seemingly unrelated to the operational programme, for the producer organization to 'take all the necessary steps to try to remedy the situation where . . . serious market difficulties arise'.[163]

The Commission's 2006 report concludes that operational programmes 'have contributed to improve [sic] the organisation of [producer organizations'] activities and their financial returns' and 'have been working in a satisfactory manner'. However, the report also acknowledges the influence of factors outside the control of producer organizations ('i.e. climatic and biological fluctuations, conservation measures') and the difficulties in matching supply with demand caused by the unpredictability of fishing activities. The report recommends that, for better effect, the programmes 'should focus more on measures to spread out supplies throughout the fishing year and the establishment of links between producers and downstream stages of the marketing chain' (on which see so-called 'interbranch organizations', discussed in section 7 below).[164]

Quality improvement plans

In addition to the mandatory operational programmes, producer organizations have the option to submit a plan to improve the quality of products covered by the common marketing standards laid down in the CMS Regulation (see section 4

---

[155] European Commission, 2002, section 3, pp 7–9.
[156] European Commission, 2002, section 3, pp 7–8.   [157] Reg 104/2000, Art 9(2).
[158] Reg 104/2000, Art 9(3), 1st para.   [159] Reg 104/2000, Art 9(3).
[160] Reg 2508/2000, Arts 9 and 10.   [161] Reg 2508/2000, Art 9(2).
[162] Reg 2508/2000, Art 11.   [163] Reg 2508/2000, Art 6.
[164] COM(2006) 558, section 4.3, p 6.

above) or products from aquaculture.[165] Member States may choose to reward the submission of such a plan, once approved, with so-called 'specific recognition'[166] which in turn is a condition of eligibility for European Fisheries Fund support for implementation of quality improvement plans (see subsection 6.2 above and subsection 6.5 below).[167] However, the Commission's 2006 report states that only three Member States granted specific recognition to producer organizations submitting quality improvement plans, namely France (to one organization), Italy (one), and Spain (two),[168] indicating that specific recognition was very rare at the time that the Commission was compiling its figures.

The quality improvement plans should, in principle, include all stages of production and marketing.[169] The Markets Regulation sets out a non-exhaustive list of matters to be covered by the plans, including: (a) 'a substantial improvement in the quality of products while held on board vessels or while being farmed'; (b) 'optimal maintenance of quality during, as appropriate, catching, unloading, extraction, handling, transport and marketing of the products'; (c) 'the application of appropriate techniques and know-how to attain the above objectives'; and (d) 'a description of the planned measures, including preparatory studies, training and investments'.[170]

A Commission brochure published in 2002 lists the following as '[e]xamples of methods used to improve quality across the [European] Union' and hence, by implication, examples of methods that could be included within a quality improvement plan: 'shorter periods at sea, fewer fish in boxes, better use of ice packaging and less handling throughout the production chain'.[171] In contrast to operational programmes, a quality improvement plan may not be approved by the Member State until the Commission has had an opportunity to scrutinize it.[172]

Regulation 1924/2000 contains detailed rules regarding quality improvement plans and specific recognition. It identifies, *inter alia*: (a) the aquaculture products for which improvement plans may be prepared;[173] (b) information to be included in the plans and, more generally, in an application for specific recognition;[174] (c) the procedure for approval or rejection of the plans;[175] and (d) the procedure and conditions for grant, withdrawal, or refusal of specific recognition.[176]

6.5 Financial aid

Introduction

The legal framework regarding aid to producer organizations comprises, in particular, the Regulations relating to the European Fisheries Fund (namely Regulation

---

[165] Reg 104/2000, Art 12(1).   [166] Reg 104/2000, Art 12(1).
[167] Reg 104/2000, Art 12(4).   [168] COM(2006) 558, section 4.4, p 6.
[169] Reg 104/2000, Art 12(2).   [170] Reg 104/2000, Art 12(2).
[171] European Commission, 2002, section 4, p 10.   [172] Reg 104/2000, Art 12(3).
[173] Reg 1924/2000, Art 1.   [174] Reg 1924/2000, Art 2.
[175] Reg 1924/2000, Art 3.   [176] Reg 1924/2000, Arts 3 and 4.

1198/2006,[177] Regulation 498/2007,[178] and Regulation 744/2008[179]) and the Markets Regulation. The European Fisheries Fund (EFF) is the successor to the Financial Instrument for Fisheries Guidance (FIFG). The detailed framework for EC assistance under the FIFG was provided by Regulation 2792/99.[180] With effect from 1 January 2007, Regulation 1198/2006 establishing the EFF (hereafter, 'the EFF Regulation') repealed Regulation 2792/99.[181] The EFF Regulation states that references to Regulation 2792/99 'shall be construed as references to this Regulation'.[182] However, it provides no correlation table which in turn creates some uncertainty about how references to particular Articles of Regulation 2792/99 are to be construed (see further below).

Regulations relating to the EFF

The general functioning of the EFF, including the prerequisites for accessing the funding, is discussed in Chapter 8. The text that follows deals specifically with the EFF's funding of producer organizations, with reference to the EFF Regulation and Regulation 498/2007. The effects of Regulation 744/2008, which is also discussed in general terms in Chapter 8, will be dealt with separately below in the context of the Markets Regulation.

Article 37 of the EFF Regulation, located within priority axis 3 on 'measures of common interest' and entitled 'Collective actions', states that the EFF 'may support measures of common interest which are implemented with the active support of operators themselves or by organisations acting on behalf of producers or other organisations recognised by the Member State' and then sets out a non-exhaustive list of aims for such measures. One of the listed aims is to '(n) create producer organisations recognised under [the Markets Regulation], their restructuring and the implementation of their plans to improve quality'.

Thus EFF funding is available for measures which aim to create producer organizations, restructure them, or implement their 'plans to improve quality'.

---

[177] Council Regulation (EC) No 1198/2006 of 27 July 2006 on the European Fisheries Fund, OJ 2006 L223/1.

[178] Commission Regulation (EC) No 498/2007 of 26 March 2007 laying down detailed rules for the implementation of Council Regulation (EC) No 1198/2006 on the European Fisheries Fund, OJ 2007 L120/1.

[179] Council Regulation (EC) No 744/2008 of 24 July 2008 instituting a temporary specific action aiming to promote the restructuring of the European Community fishing fleets affected by the economic crisis, OJ 2008 L202/1.

[180] Council Regulation (EC) No 2792/1999 of 17 December 1999 laying down the detailed rules and arrangements regarding Community structural assistance in the fisheries sector, OJ 1999 L337/10, as amended and corrected.   [181] Reg 1198/2006, Art 104(1).

[182] Reg 1198/2006, Art 104(2).

Article 37(n) is implemented by Regulation 498/2007, which, in Article 15(2), states that the support provided for in Article 37(n) may be granted for:

(a) the creation of producer organisations in order to facilitate the setting up and administrative operation of producer's organisation [sic] recognised under [the Markets Regulation] after 1 January 2007;

(b) the implementation of plans of producer organisations that have been specifically recognised under Article 12 of [the Markets Regulation] in order to facilitate the implementation of their plans to improve the quality of their products; or

(c) the restructuring of producers' organisations [sic] in order to increase their efficiency in line with market requirements.

Item '(a)' above, although slightly ambiguous and potentially circular, appears to be restricted to those producer organizations recognized by the relevant Member State after 1 January 2007. Item '(b)', although again potentially circular, relates to implementation of quality improvement plans of those producer organizations that enjoy so-called 'specific recognition' (see subsection 6.4 above). It is consistent with Article 12(4) of the Markets Regulation which states, in effect, that specific recognition of producer organizations is a condition for eligibility for aid to facilitate implementation of quality improvement plans. Item '(c)' relates to 'restructuring' in order to increase an organization's efficiency 'in line with market requirements'. The Commission's guidelines on implementation of the EFF state that the term 'restructuring', as used in item '(c)', 'covers cases where a producer organisation undergoes significant changes such as membership, product's [sic] covered, volume of production etc., but these changes do not lead to the creation of a new producer organisation and its recognition under [the Markets Regulation]'.[183]

The EFF Regulation makes it clear that EFF support for producer organizations under Article 37(n) is not perpetual. Thus Article 37 states that such aid 'shall be granted for a maximum of three years following the date of recognition or following the date of the decision on restructuring of the producer organisation and shall be degressive over these three years'.[184] That provision, by its references to 'recognition' and 'restructuring', limits the duration of aid under items '(a)' and '(c)' in Article 15(2) of Regulation 498/2007. Article 15(3) of Regulation 498/2007 in turn clarifies that the same limitation applies in respect of item '(b)', with time running from the date of specific recognition. The Commission's guidelines add that: 'The level of support for the creation or restructuring of producer organisations, or the implementation of their plans (Article 37(n) of the EFF [Regulation]) and the degressivity of this support shall be fixed by the Member State.'[185] This

---

[183] *EFF Vademecum*, available on the website of DG Mare (no document reference number in final published version), section 6.2.2.   [184] Reg 1198/2006, Art 37, 2nd para.

[185] *EFF Vademecum*, section 6.2.2.

approach contrasts with the more prescriptive approach that was used in Article 15(1)(a) and (b) of Regulation 2792/99 (see below) in respect of the FIFG.

Whilst Article 37(n) is clearly aimed at producer organizations, including in relation to fundamental matters such as their creation and restructuring, it is not necessarily the only source of funding under the EFF for such organizations. As noted above, the *chapeau* of Article 37 refers to measures implemented 'with the active support of operators themselves or by organisations acting on behalf of producers or other organisations recognised by the Member State'. That this phrase includes, *inter alia*, producer organizations is clearly implied by Article 37(n). However, the inclusion of producer organizations means in turn that EFF funding is potentially available to producer organizations in respect of any of the aims listed in Article 37.

The list in Article 37 comprises fifteen aims in total including the aim in item '(n)' but also, *inter alia*, to 'contribute sustainably to better management or conservation of resources';[186] to 'promote selective fishing methods or gears and reduction of by-catches';[187] to 'contribute to the transparency of markets in fisheries and aquaculture products including traceability';[188] to 'improve quality and food safety';[189] to make 'investments concerning production, processing or marketing equipment and infrastructure . . . ';[190] and to 'improve management and control of access conditions to fishing areas . . . '.[191] It is beyond the scope of this book to consider systematically whether any provisions of the EFF Regulation other than Article 37 potentially enable funding for producer organizations in respect of particular aims or activities. However, one possibility is Article 40, entitled 'Development of new markets and promotional campaigns' (see further below).

Having looked at the EFF's role in relation to the funding of producer organizations, some mention should also be made here of Regulation 1985/2006.[192] This Regulation relates specifically to aid to producer organizations. It repeals and replaces its predecessor, Regulation 908/2000[193] (which was also repealed, for a second time, by Regulation 498/2007).[194] It was adopted in December 2006, ie several months *after* the EFF Regulation was adopted, and it entered into force in January 2007.[195] However, despite this timing, Regulation 1985/2006 does not relate to the EFF. Instead it relates to the EFF's predecessor, the FIFG (see above), under which financial assistance was still possible for a limited period after the advent of the EFF by virtue of, *inter alia*, transitional provisions under the EFF

[186] Reg 1198/2006, Art 37(a).   [187] Reg 1198/2006, Art 37(b).
[188] Reg 1198/2006, Art 37(e).   [189] Reg 1198/2006, Art 37(f).
[190] Reg 1198/2006, Art 37(h).   [191] Reg 1198/2006, Art 37(m).
[192] Commission Regulation (EC) No 1985/2006 of 22 December 2006 laying down detailed rules for calculating aid granted by Member States to producer organisations in the fisheries and aquaculture sector, OJ 2006 L387/13, as corrected (reissued as a corrected version in OJ 2007 L34/11).
[193] Commission Regulation (EC) No 908/2000 of 2 May 2000 laying down detailed rules for calculating aid granted by Member States to producer organisations in the fisheries and aquaculture sector, OJ 2000 L105/15, as amended.   [194] Reg 1985/2006, Art 7.
[195] Reg 1985/2006, Art 8.

Regulation.[196] The temporal application of Regulation 1985/2006 is therefore restricted to any residual application of the FIFG.[197] The Regulation relates to a part of one of the FIFG Regulations, Regulation 2792/99: it lays down 'detailed rules on granting aid to producer organisations in fisheries and aquaculture under Article 15(1)(a) and (b) of Regulation [2792/99]'.[198]

A brief description of Article 15(1)(a) and (b) of Regulation 2792/99 is provided here because these provisions are also relevant below. Article 15(1)(a) allowed the Member States to 'encourage the creation and facilitate the operation of [recognized] producer organisations' by granting aid over three years following the date of recognition, such aid for the first, second, and third years being within 3, 2, and 1 per cent respectively of 'the value of the products marketed' by the producer organization and within 60, 40, and 20 per cent respectively of 'the administrative costs' of the organization. Regulation 1985/2006 sets out rules for establishing 'the value of the products marketed' and 'the administrative costs'.[199]

Article 15(1)(b) of Regulation 2792/99, stated as being without prejudice to the aid referred to in Article 15(1)(a), allowed the Member States to grant aid to those producer organizations enjoying specific recognition (see subsection 6.4 above), in order to facilitate the implementation of their quality improvement plans. The aid was to be granted over three years following the date of specific recognition, such aid for the first, second, and third years not to exceed 60, 50, and 40 per cent respectively of 'the costs incurred' by the organization in implementing the plan. Regulation 1985/2006 sets out rules for establishing 'the costs incurred'.[200]

The Markets Regulation

In addition to providing for aid or compensation to producer organizations under the system of financial intervention discussed in section 8 below, the Markets Regulation also provides for support to such organizations in other respects, under its Articles 10 and 11. Article 10 states that: 'Without prejudice to aid which might be granted to encourage the creation and facilitate the operation of producer organisations under Article 15(1)(b) of Regulation [2792/99], Member States may grant producer organisations compensation for a limited period *to offset the costs arising from the obligations imposed on them under Article 9.*'[201] (Emphasis added.) The Article 9 obligations relate to operational programmes (see subsection 6.4 above). Article 10 provides rules for working out such compensation.[202] Detailed rules on the granting of compensation are provided in Regulation 2508/2000.[203]

Until the adoption of Regulation 744/2008, the compensation for the purpose set out in Article 10 was time-limited as follows: (a) producer organizations recognized before 1 January 2001 could receive the compensation for five years

---

[196] Reg 1198/2006, Arts 104 and 103(1).   [197] See also Reg 2792/99, Art 15(1)(c).
[198] Reg 1985/2006, Art 1.   [199] Reg 1985/2006, Arts 2, 3, and 4.
[200] Reg 1985/2006, Art 5.   [201] Reg 104/2000, Art 10(1), 1st para.
[202] Reg 104/2000, Art 10(2).   [203] Reg 2508/2000, Arts 10 and 11.

from that date; and (b) producer organizations recognized subsequently could receive the compensation for five years following the year in which they were granted recognition.[204] The expenditure incurred by the Member States within those time limits is funded by the European Agricultural Guarantee Fund (EAGF). This arises by virtue of Article 35(1) of the Markets Regulation (on which see further subsection 8.1 below).

The situation has changed temporarily with the adoption of Regulation 744/2008. This now provides that 'to offset the costs arising from the obligations imposed on [producer organizations] under Article 9 [of the Markets Regulation]', ie for exactly the same purpose as set out in Article 10 of the Markets Regulation, the EFF may assist *beyond* the time limits specified in Article 10.[205] Thus Regulation 744/2008 has two effects. First, it enables EC funding to offset Article 9 costs for longer than is available under Article 10. Secondly, in doing so, it specifies that the additional EC funding is to come from the EFF rather than from the EAGF. However, such assistance by the EFF is itself time-limited: it is to apply 'only to public aid which has been the subject of an administrative decision by the relevant national authorities by 31 December 2010'.[206]

As can be seen, Article 10 of the Markets Regulation refers to a provision of the now repealed Regulation 2792/99. The provision in question is Article 15(1)(b), which was described above. As noted above, the EFF Regulation requires that references to Regulation 2792/99 'shall be construed as references to this Regulation'. The equivalent of Article 15(1)(b) of Regulation 2792/99 is presumably Article 37(n) of the EFF Regulation and, more specifically, Article 15(2)(b) of Regulation 498/2007. Article 15(2)(b) relates to support for implementation of quality improvement plans by specifically recognized producer organizations (see above). On that basis, any support granted under Article 10 of the Markets Regulation in relation to operational programmes is without prejudice to any support granted under Article 15(2)(b) of Regulation 498/2007 for implementation of quality improvement plans (as well as, of course, any support under Article 15(1)(b) of Regulation 2792/99 arising from any residual application of the FIFG).

Article 11 of the Markets Regulation allows Member States to grant 'additional aids' to producer organizations 'which, *within the framework of operational programmes mentioned in Article 9(1)* develop measures for improving the organisation and the functioning of the marketing of fish as well as measures allowing for a better balance of supply and demand, in accordance with [Regulation 2792/99], and in particular, its Articles 14 and 15' (emphasis added). Article 11 refers to, in particular, Articles 14 and 15 of Regulation 2792/99. The closest contemporary equivalents of those provisions are presumably Articles 40 and 37 of the EFF Regulation. However, as can be seen, the additional aids available under Article 11

---

[204] Reg 104/2000, Art 10(1), 2nd and 3rd paras.   [205] Reg 744/2008, Art 9(3).
[206] Reg 744/2008, Art 2; see also Art 5.

are for measures 'within the framework of operational programmes mentioned in Article 9(1)' of the Markets Regulation, rather than more widely.

Article 11 provides for Member States to grant the additional aids in question. Its reference to Regulation 2792/99, now to be construed as a reference to the EFF Regulation, suggests that the EFF may contribute to the financing of such additional aids. However, this is not entirely clear. If the EFF may indeed contribute, it is still not completely clear to the authors what purpose Article 11 serves beyond that already served by the EFF Regulation. In view of the restriction of Article 11's scope to measures within the framework of producer organizations' operational programmes, and in view of the EFF Regulation (and Regulation 498/2007) not referring expressly to such programmes at any point, it may be that the current purpose of Article 11 is to clarify that the additional aids in question do fall within the scope of the EFF Regulation including, *inter alia*, Articles 40 and 37 thereof.

7 Interbranch organizations

7.1 Introduction

In short, an interbranch organization is a group of organizations or associations involved in two or more parts of the supply chain. A 'branch' means, in effect, a part of the supply chain. Thus an interbranch organization differs from a producer organization in that the former is not restricted to just the production part of the supply chain. Interbranch organizations are intended to help overcome 'divisions between various branches of the fishing sector [which] have weakened the industry'[207] and 'generally help to attain the goals of the [CFP] and Article 39 [now 33] of the EC Treaty'.[208]

The active association of various branches of the supply chain, with a view to adopting agreements, decisions, or concerted practices, raises the possibility of a breach of EC competition law. Therefore, to reconcile the requirements of competition law with the potential benefits of interbranch organizations, the Markets Regulation grants a derogation from Article 81(1) EC so long as certain conditions are met.[209]

The Markets Regulation defines the term 'interbranch organisation' for its purposes, and hence impliedly for the purposes of the common organization of the markets in fishery products, by means of several elements as set out below.[210]

An interbranch organization must be a legal person established on the territory of the Member State concerned and comprising 'representatives of activities linked to the production of and/or trade in and/or processing of the products referred to

---

[207] European Commission, 2002, section 6, p 15.
[208] COM(1999) 55, explanatory memorandum, section 2, p 5.   [209] Reg 104/2000, Art 14.
[210] Reg 104/2000, Art 13(1).

in Article 1' of the Markets Regulation (on which see section 3 above).[211] Thus the potential branches in question are production, trade, and processing. The organization, in contrast to its constituent organizations or associations or their members, must not itself be 'engaged in activities relating to the production, processing or marketing of fishery products or products processed from fishery products'.[212]

The organization must have been established at the initiative of all or some of the constituting organizations or associations (rather than, say, at the initiative of the Commission).[213] It must 'represent a significant share of the production of and trade in and/or processing of fishery products and products processed from fishery products in the region or regions in question'.[214] Where more than one region is involved, the organization must be able to demonstrate a minimum level of representativeness in each region for each of the branches that it covers.[215]

The organization must carry out two or more specified measures 'in one or more regions of the Community, under conditions that are compatible with Community rules, particularly as regards competition, taking account of the interest of consumers, and provided [it does] not hinder the sound operation of the market organisation'.[216] Most of the specified measures referred to are facilitatory or procedural in nature, for example 'improving knowledge of and the transparency of production and the market'; 'helping to coordinate better the way fishery products are placed on the market . . . '; 'study and develop techniques to optimise the operation of the market . . . '; and 'drawing up standard contracts . . . '. However, a few are more substantive, for example 'laying down rules on the catching and marketing of fishery products which are stricter than Community or national rules'.[217]

7.2 Recognition

The Markets Regulation enables Member States to formally recognize those interbranch organizations that meet the criteria described in subsection 7.1 above and that make 'an appropriate application'.[218] Whereas the Markets Regulation states that Member States 'shall' recognize producer organizations if certain conditions are met (see subsections 6.1 and 6.2 above),[219] it states that Member States 'may' recognize interbranch organizations, thus implying that Member States still have discretion under EC law not to recognize such an organization even if the relevant criteria are met and the application is 'appropriate'. The Markets Regulation sets out several provisions on recognition of interbranch organizations.[220]

[211] Reg 104/2000, Art 13(1).   [212] Reg 104/2000, Art 13(1)(c).
[213] Reg 104/2000, Art 13(1)(a).   [214] Reg 104/2000, Art 13(1)(b).
[215] Reg 104/2000, Art 13(1)(b).   [216] Reg 104/2000, Art 13(1)(d).
[217] Reg 104/2000, Art 13(1)(d).   [218] Reg 104/2000, Art 13(1).
[219] Reg 104/2000, Art 5(2).   [220] Reg 104/2000, Art 13(2)–(5).

In particular, the Commission may object to recognition or may request a Member State to withdraw recognition in specified circumstances.[221]

Detailed rules on recognition have been adopted. Regulation 1813/2001[222] establishes, *inter alia*: (a) quantitative criteria for judging whether an interbranch organization is 'representative at a regional level' for the purposes of the Markets Regulation;[223] and (b) the information to be included in an application for recognition of an interbranch organization.[224]

The *List of recognised interbranch organisations in the fisheries and aquaculture sector* published in 2007[225] reveals a total of only four recognized interbranch organizations (one in France, one in Italy, and two in Spain). The Commission's 2006 report records the same number of organizations. It states that: 'The reasons for this low number are not entirely clear and may be due to poor co-operation between the different sub-sectors of the value chain.'[226] It concludes that: 'The introduction of inter-branch organisations was no success.'[227]

7.3 Extension of rules to non-members

The Markets Regulation allows a Member State to make some of the rules ('agreements, decisions or concerted practices') of an interbranch organization binding for a limited period on non-member operators in the same region or regions in question in cases where: (a) that organization 'is considered to be representative of the production of and/or trade in and/or processing of a given product'; and (b) the organization requests the extension.[228]

The Regulation sets out a quantitative criterion for judging whether the organization is sufficiently 'representative' for its rules to be extended.[229] It also requires that the rules to be extended must have been in force for at least one year and may be made binding on non-members for no more than three marketing years.[230] The extended rules must not cause any harm to operators established in other regions.[231] They must concern one of the following: 'information about production and the market'; 'stricter production rules than any laid down in Community or national rules'; 'drawing up standard contracts which are compatible with Community rules'; or 'rules on marketing'.[232]

---

[221] Reg 104/2000, Art 13(2) and (4).
[222] Commission Regulation (EC) No 1813/2001 of 14 September 2001 laying down the detailed rules for the application of Council Regulation (EC) No 104/2000 as regards the conditions for, the grant of and the withdrawal of recognition of interbranch organisations, OJ 2001 L246/7.
[223] Reg 1813/2001, Art 1.   [224] Reg 1813/2001, Art 2.   [225] OJ 2007 C85/22.
[226] COM(2006) 558, section 5, p 7. The reference to 'the different sub-sectors of the value chain' presumably means the different parts of the supply chain.
[227] COM(2006) 558, section 8, p 11.   [228] Reg 104/2000, Art 15(1).
[229] Reg 104/2000, Art 15(2).   [230] Reg 104/2000, Art 15(3)(b) and (c).
[231] Reg 104/2000, Art 15(3)(d).   [232] Reg 104/2000, Art 15(3)(a).

The Commission may decide, on specified grounds, that a Member State is not authorized to extend the rules or may decide, on the same grounds, that an existing extension is null and void.[233] The Markets Regulation also lays down the conditions in which a Member State may decide to require non-members to pay contributions to an interbranch organization.[234] The Commission's 2006 report states that the extension of rules of interbranch organizations to non-members 'has not been applied yet'.[235]

7.4 Financial aid

As noted in subsection 6.5 above, the EFF Regulation and Regulation 498/2007 refer expressly to producer organizations. In particular, Article 37(n) of the EFF Regulation provides for the EFF to support measures aiming to, *inter alia*, create such organizations. In contrast, neither Regulation at any point refers expressly to interbranch organizations. The Markets Regulation likewise fails to provide expressly for any funding of interbranch organizations. However, Article 37 of the EFF Regulation does state that the EFF 'may support measures of common interest which are implemented with the active support of operators themselves or by organisations acting on behalf of producers or other organisations recognised by the Member State . . . '. To the extent that interbranch organizations are organizations acting on behalf of (*inter alia*) producers or, alternatively, fall within 'other organisations recognised by the Member State', funding is available under Article 37 of the EFF Regulation for those of their measures having aims covered by that Article. As with producer organizations, it is beyond the scope of this book to consider systematically whether any other provisions of the EFF Regulation potentially enable funding for interbranch organizations but one possibility is Article 40, entitled 'Development of new markets and promotional campaigns'.

8 Prices and intervention

8.1 Introduction

Central to the common organization of the markets in fishery products is a system of financial intervention. The system revolves around producer organizations: in broad terms, these organizations receive aid or compensation in certain circumstances from the Member States, which in turn are reimbursed by the EC. The justification for intervention is that it is relevant to achieving certain

---

[233] Reg 104/2000, Art 16(1) and (2).   [234] Reg 104/2000, Art 16(4).
[235] COM(2006) 558, section 5, p 7.

objectives of the CFP, in particular ensuring a fair standard of living for fishermen and stabilizing markets.[236]

There are four different types of process that can lead to the payment of aid or compensation: (a) permanent withdrawal, whereby products are permanently withdrawn from the market; (b) 'carry-over', in which products are taken off the market, stabilized or preserved, and then reintroduced to the market later; (c) 'private storage', whereby frozen products are taken off the market, stored and reintroduced later; and (d) the 'compensatory allowance' for tuna producers.

The expenditure incurred by the Member States under the intervention system is funded by the EAGF. This arises by virtue of Article 35(1) of the Markets Regulation. Article 35(1) has been amended by Regulation 1759/2006.[237] In its amended form, Article 35(1) states that expenditure incurred by the Member States in accordance with Articles 21, 23, 24, 25, and 27 (and also Article 10—see subsection 6.5 above) of the Markets Regulation 'shall be deemed' to be expenditure referred to in Article 3(2)(f) of Regulation 1290/2005. Articles 21, 23, 24, 25, and 27 relate to the various forms of intervention mentioned above.

Regulation 1290/2005, as referred to by Article 35(1), deals with the financing of the Common Agricultural Policy.[238] Amongst other things, it establishes the EAGF. Its Article 3(2)(f) states that: 'The EAGF shall finance the following expenditure in a centralised manner and in accordance with Community legislation: . . . (f) expenditure relating to fisheries markets.' Thus the effect of the deeming provision in Article 35(1) of the Markets Regulation is that expenditure incurred by the Member States under the intervention system is funded by the EAGF.[239] In the interests of fisheries conservation, the Markets Regulation clarifies that any such EC financing shall be granted 'in respect of products from a stock or group of stocks only up to the limit of any quantities allocated to the Member State in question from the total volume of allowable catches for the stock or group of stocks in question'.[240]

The financial support relates to various products listed in Annexes I to IV to the Markets Regulation. In summary: Annex I relates mainly to fresh or chilled products; Annex II relates exclusively to frozen products; Annex III relates only to tuna; and Annex IV relates exclusively to fresh or chilled products. Permanent withdrawal relates to certain Annex I products. Carry-over relates to all Annex I

[236] Art 33(1) EC, paras (b) and (c).

[237] Council Regulation (EC) No 1759/2006 of 28 November 2006 amending Regulation (EC) No 104/2000 on the common organisation of the markets in fishery and aquaculture products, OJ 2006 L335/3.

[238] Council Regulation (EC) No 1290/2005 of 21 June 2005 on the financing of the common agricultural policy, OJ 2005 L209/1, as amended and corrected.

[239] See also Commission Regulation (EC) No 2003/2006 of 21 December 2006 laying down detailed rules for the financing by the European Agricultural Guarantee Fund (EAGF) of expenditure relating to the common organisation of the markets in fishery and aquaculture products, OJ 2006 L379/49.

[240] Reg 104/2000, Art 35(2).

products. Permanent withdrawal and carry-over also relate to Annex IV products in certain circumstances. Private storage relates to Annex II products. The compensatory allowance for tuna producers relates to Annex III products.

In more detail, Annex I comprises three parts. Part A relates to 'Fresh or chilled products of [CN] heading Nos 0302 and 0307'. It lists various finfish species (14) and genera (6) as well as two cuttlefish species, each with their corresponding CN codes. Part B relates to 'Live, fresh or chilled products or products cooked by steaming or by boiling in water'. It lists 'Shrimps of the species *Crangon crangon* and deepwater prawn (*Pandalus borealis*)' and relevant CN codes. Part C relates to 'Live, fresh or chilled products or products cooked by steaming or by boiling in water'. It lists sole, edible crab, and Norway lobster and their corresponding CN codes.

Annex II addresses frozen products of various species falling under CN headings 0303, 0304, 0306, and 0307. Annex III relates to tuna, notably skipjack tuna and species of the genera *Thunnus* and *Euthynnus*. Annex IV relates to fresh or chilled products of various finfish species and genera as well as two shellfish species; there is no duplication in species or genera between Annex IV and Annex I.

The provisions of the Markets Regulation on prices and intervention are supplemented by an array of implementing Regulations, many of which are discussed in the subsections that follow. Certain numerical values in the overall scheme (for example guide prices and Community withdrawal prices) are set on an annual basis. Most of the Regulations setting such values for the 2008 fishing year are mentioned below, on the basis that they serve to illustrate the current approach for setting annual values.

The Commission's 2006 report, in an annex,[241] shows a significant reduction in the expenses used by the EC to fund the market intervention mechanisms under the CFP. In the period 1992–97, across fourteen Member States, the average annual expense was €28,465,500, whereas in the period 1998–2004, the average annual expense was €10,312,428. The Commission concludes that the common organization of the markets 'has largely reduced the overall level of intervention'.[242] However, the report provides no clear evidence that it was the common organization of the markets, rather than any extrinsic factors, that was responsible for the observed reduction in intervention.

The rest of this section will explain the various processes comprising the system of intervention under the common organization of the markets in fishery products. First, the concepts of guide prices, Community withdrawal prices, and Community selling prices will be considered. Then permanent withdrawal, carry-over,

---

[241] *Commission Staff Working Document: Accompanying document to the Report from the Commission to the Council and the European Parliament on the implementation of Council Regulation (EC) No 104/2000 on the common organisation of the markets in fishery and aquaculture products*, SEC(2006) 1218, 29.9.2006, Annex 6, entitled 'Total intervention expenses 1992–2004'. The authors have assumed for the purposes of this chapter that the figures in the said annex relate to expenses by the EC to fund the market intervention mechanisms under the CFP.   [242] COM(2006) 558, section 6.2, p 7.

private storage, and the compensatory allowance for tuna producers will each be explained in turn.

8.2 Guide prices, Community withdrawal prices, and Community selling prices

Guide prices

The guide price is fixed at EC level by the Council, on a proposal from the Commission.[243] The guide price is used in determining both the Community withdrawal price and the Community selling price. In turn, the Community withdrawal price is relevant to permanent withdrawal and to carry-over for certain products, and the Community selling price is relevant to carry-over for certain (other) products and to private storage. Thus it can be seen that the guide price has a central role in the system of intervention.[244]

The guide price is to be fixed before the beginning of each fishing year for the following products listed in the annexes to the Markets Regulation: (a) the products listed in Parts A and B of Annex I (for the purposes of permanent withdrawal and carry-over); (b) the products listed in Part C of Annex I (for the purposes of carry-over); and (c) the products listed in Annex II (for the purposes of private storage).[245] The guide price is to be based on various factors, including 'the average of prices recorded for a significant proportion of Community output on wholesale markets or in ports during the three fishing years immediately preceding the year for which the price is fixed'.[246]

The Commission's 2006 report states that guide prices 'should broadly follow market trends while remaining *below* the market prices with the necessary safety margin to take account of price fluctuations' (emphasis added).[247] An annex to the report sets out guide prices and market prices for the years 2001–04.[248] In the case of products listed in Parts A and B of Annex I, for 2004, the guide price was indeed lower than the market price with the exception of saithe and deepwater prawn. With one exception, market price exceeded guide price by a factor of 1.04 to 1.92; the exception was for mackerel where the factor was 4.8. Overall, the guide prices 'are intended to reflect the market situation for relevant species'.[249]

The guide prices for the 2008 fishing year are fixed by Regulation 1447/2007.[250] Guide prices, sometimes for more than one 'commercial presentation' of a particular

---

[243] Reg 104/2000, Art 18(3).   [244] See also, for example, Reg 104/2000, recital (19).
[245] Reg 104/2000, Art 18(1).   [246] Reg 104/2000, Art 18(2).
[247] COM(2006) 558, section 6.1, p 7.   [248] SEC(2006) 1218, Annex 4.
[249] COM(2006) 558, section 6.1, p 7.
[250] Council Regulation (EC) No 1447/2007 of 4 December 2007 fixing for the 2008 fishing year the guide prices and Community producer prices for certain fishery products pursuant to Regulation (EC) No 104/2000, OJ 2007 L323/1.

product, are set for each of the products listed in Parts A and B of Annex I to the Markets Regulation, and also for products listed in Part C of Annex I and in Annex II to that Regulation. The result is a total of forty-three guide prices, ranging from €277 per tonne for 'Whole fish' of herring (a species listed in Part A of Annex I) to €7,819 per tonne for 'Frozen, in original packages containing the same products' of certain prawn species of the family Penaeidae (a family listed in Annex II).

Community withdrawal prices

The Community withdrawal price is fixed by the Commission. In broad terms, it applies to the products listed in Parts A and B of Annex I to the Markets Regulation and is a trigger for the provision of compensation or aid to producer organizations undertaking permanent withdrawals or certain carry-over operations. The price is to be fixed on the basis of the freshness, size or weight, and presentation of the product by applying a conversion factor to the guide price, yielding an amount that is not to exceed 90 per cent of the guide price.[251] (Some concessions are made for species 'in landing areas which are very distant from the main centres of consumption'; see further below.)

The Community withdrawal prices for the 2008 fishing year are fixed by Regulation 1570/2007.[252] This Regulation fixes conversion factors (in its Annex I) and corresponding withdrawal prices (in its Annex II). Any given withdrawal price in Annex II is derived by multiplying the corresponding conversion factor in Annex I by the relevant guide price in Regulation 1447/2007 (see above). However, it is not clear from Regulation 1570/2007 (or from the Markets Regulation) how the conversion factors themselves are derived.

The conversion factors are fixed for each of the products listed in Parts A and B of Annex I to the Markets Regulation. They are provided for various presentations, for each size category defined in the CMS Regulation (except the 'Mediterranean' size category) and for the freshness categories Extra and A. The absence of a conversion factor for freshness category B is deliberate. That is because the CMS Regulation provides that any lots of fish, selachii, cephalopods, or Norway lobster falling into freshness category B are ineligible for financial assistance granted in respect of permanent withdrawal or carry-over (see subsection 4.2 above). In some cases, the conversion factor is set at zero.

In Annex II to Regulation 1570/2007, a withdrawal price (expressed in euros per tonne) is set for every presentation, size category, and freshness category for which a conversation factor is fixed in Annex I. In those cases where the conversion factor has been set at zero, the corresponding withdrawal price is therefore

---

[251] Reg 104/2000, Art 20(1).

[252] Commission Regulation (EC) No 1570/2007 of 21 December 2007 fixing the Community withdrawal and selling prices for the fishery products listed in Annex I to Council Regulation (EC) No 104/2000 for the 2008 fishing year, OJ 2007 L340/69.

likewise set at zero. The latter applies only in the case of the 'Gutted fish, with head' presentation of some shoaling pelagic species (herring, sardine, mackerel, Spanish mackerel, and anchovy), redfish, and cuttlefishes; perhaps such species are not sold in this presentation.

Annex III to Regulation 1570/2007 fixes adjusted withdrawal prices for certain species 'in landing areas which are very distant from the main centres of consumption'.[253] Such areas include specified parts of Ireland, mainland Portugal, and the UK, as well as some of the outermost regions (namely the Azores, the Canary Islands, and Madeira).[254] In all cases, the withdrawal prices fixed in Annex III are lower than the equivalent withdrawal prices fixed in Annex II. (Further assistance in respect of the outermost regions is provided by Regulation 791/2007.[255])

Community selling prices

There are two types of Community selling price, which is rather confusing. One type relates to carry-over for certain products, while the other relates to private storage. In respect of private storage, the Community selling price is to be fixed for each of the products listed in Annex II to the Markets Regulation before the beginning of the fishing year, at a level between 70 per cent and 90 per cent of the guide price.[256] The Community selling prices in question for the 2008 fishing year for Annex II products are fixed in Regulation 1571/2007.[257]

In respect of carry-over, the Community selling price is to be fixed for each of the products listed in Part C of Annex I to the Markets Regulation on the same terms as those laid down for fixing Community withdrawal prices.[258] So, in short, it is be to fixed by the Commission on the basis of the freshness, size or weight, and presentation of the product by applying a conversion factor to the guide price, yielding an amount that is not to exceed 90 per cent of the guide price (see above). The Community selling prices in question, and the corresponding conversion factors, for the 2008 fishing year are set out in Regulation 1570/2007 (which also contains the Community withdrawal prices—see above).

8.3 Permanent withdrawal

It is necessary to start with a point of terminology. In relation to fishery products, the Markets Regulation uses the term 'withdrawal' or 'withdrawn' in two

---

[253] See also Reg 104/2000, Art 20(2) and Reg 1570/2007, Art 3.

[254] On the meaning of the term 'outermost region', see Chapter 2.

[255] Council Regulation (EC) No 791/2007 of 21 May 2007 introducing a scheme to compensate for the additional costs incurred in the marketing of certain fishery products from the outermost regions the Azores, Madeira, the Canary Islands, French Guiana and Réunion, OJ 2007 L176/1.

[256] Reg 104/2000, Art 25(1).

[257] Commission Regulation (EC) No 1571/2007 of 21 December 2007 fixing the Community selling prices for the fishery products listed in Annex II to Council Regulation (EC) No 104/2000 for the 2008 fishing year, OJ 2007 L340/77.   [258] Reg 104/2000, Art 22.

contexts. The first is permanent withdrawal, whereby products are withdrawn from the market and then disposed of in prescribed ways. The second context is carry-over, whereby products are withdrawn from the market but not permanently so; instead they are stabilized or preserved and then reintroduced to the market later. In this subsection, the focus is on *permanent* withdrawal and so the term 'withdrawal' or 'withdrawn' is used here in that specific context.

The EC's system of financial support for withdrawal of products is based on producer organizations having in place a system of withdrawal of their own. The rights and obligations of producer organizations in respect of their own withdrawal systems are set out in Article 17 of the Markets Regulation. Under Article 17, the underlying principle is that a producer organization may, but is not required to, fix a so-called 'withdrawal price' for any of the products listed in Article 1 of the Markets Regulation (see section 3 above), below which it will not sell such a product supplied by its members.[259] Once the market price falls below any withdrawal price that has been fixed, the product in question is withdrawn from the market by the producer organization which in some cases must, and in all other cases may, then grant an indemnity to its members.[260]

An indemnity is *required* to be granted in respect of withdrawn products listed in Annex I (Parts A and B only) and Annex IV to the Markets Regulation, so long as those products conform to the common marketing standards adopted under that Regulation (see section 4 above).[261] Some obligations on the level of that indemnity are established by Article 21 of the Markets Regulation (see below).[262] The producer organization also has *discretion* to grant an indemnity in respect of any other withdrawn products covered by Article 1 of the Markets Regulation (see section 3 above).[263] The real-time granting of indemnities is to be financed from an 'intervention fund' that is established by the producer organization and funded by contributions from members 'assessed on quantities offered for sale'.[264] As an alternative to an intervention fund, the producer organization may apply something called an 'equalisation system',[265] although there is no indication in the Markets Regulation of what that term means.

The above distinction between mandatory and discretionary indemnity is related to the system of financial support under the Markets Regulation. In the case of the *mandatory* indemnity, the producer organization has recourse to compensation. For the products listed in Parts A and B of Annex I to the Markets Regulation, the system of compensation is discussed in this subsection; for the products listed in Annex IV, the system is discussed in subsection 8.5 below. In respect of the *discretionary* indemnity, ie that for any other products covered by Article 1 of the Markets Regulation, the producer organization does not have recourse to

---

[259] Reg 104/2000, Art 17(1), 1st para.   [260] Reg 104/2000, Art 17(1), 2nd para.
[261] Reg 104/2000, Art 17(1), 2nd para, 1st indent.   [262] Reg 104/2000, Art 21(6).
[263] Reg 104/2000, Art 17(1), 2nd para, 2nd indent.
[264] Reg 104/2000, Art 17(3); see also Art 5(1)(c)(6).   [265] Reg 104/2000, Art 17(3).

compensation under the Markets Regulation. Any products withdrawn under Article 17 must be disposed of in prescribed ways (see further below).

The system of compensation for products in respect of which there is a mandatory indemnity works by compensation being provided to the producer organization by the relevant Member State and the Member State in turn receiving compensation from the EC. The framework of the system is set out in Article 21 of the Markets Regulation. Member States are under a duty to grant financial compensation to producer organizations 'carrying out withdrawals under Article 17 in respect of the products listed in Annex I, Parts A and B',[266] but only if certain requirements in addition to those of Article 17 are met.

In particular: (a) the withdrawal price applied by the producer organizations must be the Community withdrawal price, give or take 10 per cent 'to take account in particular of seasonal fluctuations in market prices';[267] (b) the Community withdrawal price must be applied by the producer organizations throughout the fishing year for each product category concerned (with one exception),[268] 'to ensure [the withdrawal arrangements] have the intended stabilising effect';[269] (c) the products withdrawn must meet the common marketing standards adopted under Article 2 of the Markets Regulation (see section 4 above);[270] and (d) the products withdrawn must be disposed of in certain ways. It can be seen that Article 21 duplicates the requirement from Article 17 about common marketing standards and that both Articles have a requirement about disposal of withdrawn products (see further below).

The amount of compensation to be provided by the Member State does not simply correspond to the Community withdrawal price. As a starting point, the compensation is to be equal to 85 per cent of the withdrawal price applied by the producer organization, so long as the quantities withdrawn do not exceed 4 per cent of the quantities of the product concerned put up for sale each year.[271] At the other end of the scale, no compensation at all is to be granted in respect of quantities withdrawn exceeding 10 per cent for pelagic species, and 8 per cent for other species, of the quantities of the product concerned put up for sale annually.[272]

In cases where the quantities withdrawn *exceed* 4 per cent of the quantities put up for sale each year but do *not* exceed 10 per cent (for pelagic species) or 8 per cent (for other species) of the quantities put up for sale each year, it is not clear what percentage reduction is to be applied to the withdrawal price by the Member State. For this category, the Markets Regulation contains a transitional rule for the years 2001, 2002, and 2003 but does not explain what happens after 2003.[273] For 2003, the compensation payable by the Member State for this category was 55 per cent of the producer organization's withdrawal price.

[266] Reg 104/2000, Art 21(1).   [267] Reg 104/2000, Art 21(1)(a).
[268] Reg 104/2000, Art 21(1)(c).   [269] European Commission, 2002, section 5.1, p 12.
[270] Reg 104/2000, Art 21(1)(b).   [271] Reg 104/2000, Art 21(3)(a)(i).
[272] Reg 104/2000, Art 21(3)(b).   [273] Reg 104/2000, Art 21(3)(a)(ii).

The above rules mean that producer organizations 'run the risk that withdrawing large quantities will increase their financial burden', which in turn 'makes it in their interests to persuade members to plan fishing efforts according to the market's capacity to absorb their catches'.[274] The rules may be adjusted by Commission measures, lasting for periods of no more than six months, '[i]n the event of serious market disturbance'.[275]

As a general rule, the indemnity granted by a producer organization to its members in respect of withdrawal of products listed in Parts A and B of Annex I is to be at least equal to the sum of the financial compensation calculated under the above rules, plus an amount equal to 10 per cent of the withdrawal price applied by the producer organization.[276] However, the organization has discretion, 'under a system of internal penalties', to grant its members lower indemnity, 'provided the difference is placed in a reserve fund exclusively called on for subsequent intervention operations'.[277] It is not clear whether or how that 'reserve fund' relates to a producer organization's intervention fund (see above).

Detailed rules may be adopted regarding financial compensation for withdrawals.[278] In turn, Regulation 2509/2000[279] fills out the Markets Regulation's framework in some significant ways. It sets out, *inter alia*, rules for the application of the 10 per cent margin of tolerance[280] and rules for the payment by Member States of financial compensation.[281] It also states that financial compensation is only available for quantities withdrawn if they: (a) were caught by a member of a producer organization; (b) were put up for sale through the producer organization or by a member in accordance with the organization's common rules; (c) failed to find a buyer at the Community withdrawal price (plus or minus 10 per cent); and (d) were not subject to carry-over aid (on which see subsection 8.4 below) or a request for such aid.[282]

Regarding common freshness standards, Regulation 2509/2000 has two requirements. First, it goes beyond the requirements of Articles 21 and 17 of the Markets Regulation by stating that the grant of financial compensation for quantities eligible as above 'shall be subject to the condition that, for the product or group of products concerned, *all* the quantities put up for sale by the producer organisation or its members during the fishing year must have been classified previously in accordance with the [the applicable common marketing standards]' (emphasis added).[283] Thus compensation is contingent not just on those products withdrawn meeting the relevant common marketing standards (see above), but on

---

[274] European Commission, 2002, section 5.1, p 12.   [275] Reg 104/2000, Art 21(7).
[276] Reg 104/2000, Art 21(6), 1st para.   [277] Reg 104/2000, Art 21(6), 2nd para.
[278] Reg 104/2000, Art 21(8).
[279] Commission Regulation (EC) No 2509/2000 of 15 November 2000 laying down detailed rules for the application of Council Regulation (EC) No 104/2000 as regards granting financial compensation for withdrawals of certain fishery products, OJ 2000 L289/11.
[280] Reg 2509/2000, Arts 2 and 3.   [281] Reg 2509/2000, Arts 5 and 6 and Annex I.
[282] Reg 2509/2000, Art 4.   [283] Reg 2509/2000, Art 4(2).

all the quantities of that product put up for sale over the fishing year meeting the relevant standards. This requirement appears to reflect, but arguably goes beyond, the judgment of the Court in the *Intervention Board* case in 1990.[284] Secondly, in line with the CMS Regulation (see section 4 above), Regulation 2509/2000 requires that quantities of products falling into freshness category B are not to be used in the calculation of quantities of product eligible for financial compensation.[285]

The Commission's 2006 report, in an annex,[286] shows that for 2004 the figure for 'Community withdrawals and carry-over expenses' was €8,768,000 (across fourteen Member States). That figure represents just under 85 per cent of the EC's total market intervention expenses under the CFP for 2004.[287] The annexes to the report do not contain expenses figures for withdrawals separately from carry-over operations. However a graph entitled 'Community withdrawals and carry-over expenses 2000–2005', which depicts expenses for carry-over and (presumably permanent) withdrawals separately, indicates that in 2004 expenses for withdrawals were between €5 million and €6 million while expenses for carry-over operations were between €3 million and €4 million.[288]

Another annex to the report, entitled 'Production and withdrawals 2001–2004',[289] shows figures for quantities withdrawn against quantities produced. It is not clear whether 'withdrawals' in this context means permanent withdrawal or, in addition, withdrawal prior to carry-over operations. The annex shows that in the period 2001–04, the quantities withdrawn accounted for between 1.34 and 2.04 per cent of the production of pelagic species and between 0.62 and 1.46 per cent of the production of whitefish. In the case of pelagic species, there is no clear trend in the per cent figures over the four years in question. In the case of whitefish, the figures increased (albeit only from 0.62 per cent to 1.46 per cent) over the period 2001–03 but then decreased to 0.82 per cent in 2004.

The Commission's 2006 report states that the common organization of the markets 'has decreased the compensation for fish withdrawn from the market' and that '[t]he expenses derived from withdrawals have decreased in accordance with the objectives of [the Markets Regulation]'.[290] However, it is not clear what period is being referred to. The only annex to the report that depicts EC expenses for withdrawals separately from those for carry-over operations is a graph covering the period 2000–05.[291] The graph does not depict a steady decline in withdrawals expenses over the period, although there is a net decline of approximately 50 per cent.

---

[284] Case C-301/88 *The Queen and Intervention Board for Agricultural Produce, ex parte The Fish Producers' Organization Ltd and The Grimsby Fish Producers' Organization Ltd* [1990] ECR I-3803, para 15. See also Reg 2509/2000's predecessor, Reg 3902/92 (now repealed), Art 4(2).
[285] Reg 2509/2000, Art 1. [286] SEC(2006) 1218, Annex 7.
[287] SEC(2006) 1218, Annex 6, which shows the total intervention expenses for 2004 to be €10,350,000. There is a separate annex, Annex 9, on 'expenses' for flat-rate aid.
[288] SEC(2006) 1218, Annex 8. [289] SEC(2006) 1218, Annex 12.
[290] COM(2006) 558, section 6.2.1, p 8 and section 8, p 10. [291] SEC(2006) 1218, Annex 8.

The report expresses some concern about withdrawals of 'species subject to conservation measures'. It states that the withdrawal of such species 'can be questioned, in particular if the fish taken off the market is destined to destruction [sic]'.[292] In practice, almost all of the species for which financial compensation for withdrawals is available can be said to be 'subject to conservation measures' of one form or another. Perhaps the Commission had in mind species subject to recovery plans (on which see Chapter 4).

Disposal of withdrawn products

Under the Markets Regulation, the means of disposal of products withdrawn from the market is to be determined by producer organizations 'in such a way as not to interfere with normal marketing of the products in question'.[293] The duty on Member States to grant financial compensation to producer organizations for withdrawal of products likewise only applies if the products withdrawn are 'disposed of for purposes other than human consumption or in such a way as not to interfere with normal marketing of other products'.[294]

Regulation 2493/2001[295] in turn deals with the disposal of products withdrawn. It notes that '[m]arket stabilisation measures can be fully effective only if the withdrawn products are not reintroduced into the usual distribution network for those products' and concludes that '[a]ny use which could, by substitution, influence the consumption of products which have not been the subject of market stabilisation measures must therefore be ruled out'.[296]

The Regulation sets out the permitted ways of disposing of products withdrawn by producer organizations 'and not intended to be eligible for . . . carry-over aid . . . ' (on which see subsection 8.4 below). The Regulation refers to 'products withdrawn . . . in accordance with Article 17' of the Markets Regulation.[297] That implies that the Regulation applies to any (permanent) withdrawal by a producer organization, irrespective of whether that withdrawal is in turn eligible for compensation under Article 21.

The disposal options are as follows: (a) distribution, so long as it is under the responsibility of the Member States, 'free of charge in the natural state for their own consumption to philanthropic or charitable institutions established in the Community or to persons who are recognised by the national legislation of the Member State concerned as being entitled to public assistance'; (b) 'used in the fresh or preserved state for animal feed'; (c) 'used, after processing into meal, for animal feed'; (d) 'used as bait'; and (e) 'used for non-food purposes'.[298] Additional

[292] COM(2006) 558, section 6.2.1, p 8.   [293] Reg 104/2000, Art 17(2).
[294] Reg 104/2000, Art 21(2).
[295] Commission Regulation (EC) No 2493/2001 of 19 December 2001 on the disposal of certain fishery products which have been withdrawn from the market, OJ 2001 L337/20.
[296] Reg 2493/2001, recital (2).   [297] Reg 2493/2001, Art 1(1).
[298] Reg 2493/2001, Art 1(1)(a)–(e).

options 'may be authorised by the Commission on an ad hoc basis at the request of a Member State'.[299]

In the case of options '(b)'–'(e)' above, the products are to be 'rendered unfit for human consumption immediately after their withdrawal from the market' and 'offered for sale open to any interested operators in accordance with customary regional and local practice'.[300] Sales are to be evidenced by paper work to be sent to the Member State.[301] If the products have not found a purchaser since their offer for sale, and the producer organizations satisfy the Member State concerned of this, the products must then 'be rendered unusable by the producer organisations under the control of the Member State'.[302]

Under the Markets Regulation, there is a link between the financial compensation for withdrawal of products listed in Parts A and B of Annex I and the disposal of the products so withdrawn. Thus the financial compensation paid by the Member State is to be reduced 'by the value, set at a standard amount, of products intended for purposes other than human consumption or any net revenue from the disposal of products for human consumption . . . '.[303] The latter part of that provision does not fit entirely comfortably with Regulation 2493/2001, since the latter envisages that products destined for human consumption must only be offered free of charge (see above).

The standard amount referred to in the preceding paragraph is to be set at the beginning of each fishing year, albeit with scope for adjustment in certain circumstances.[304] Regulation 1575/2007[305] adopts the standard amounts (referred to as 'standard values') for the 2008 fishing year in respect of products withdrawn that are intended for purposes other than human consumption. The values are expressed in euros per tonne. For the same product and intended use, the values sometimes vary across different Member States. For some uses, the standard amount is zero euros per tonne.

8.4 Carry-over

With a view to reducing the amount of product that is permanently withdrawn from the market, the EC has created a system of aid to finance 'carry-over' operations that stabilize or preserve the products withdrawn so that they can be reintroduced to the market later. It is not entirely clear from the wording of the Markets Regulation whether the Member States have an obligation to grant carry-

---

[299] Reg 2493/2001, Art 1(2).   [300] Reg 2493/2001, Art 2(1).
[301] Reg 2493/2001, Art 2(2).   [302] Reg 2493/2001, Art 2(3)
[303] Reg 104/2000, Art 21(5).   [304] Reg 104/2000, Art 21(5).
[305] Commission Regulation (EC) No 1575/2007 of 21 December 2007 fixing the standard values to be used in calculating the financial compensation and the advance pertaining thereto in respect of fishery products withdrawn from the market during the 2008 fishing year, OJ 2007 L340/86.

over aid or whether they (merely) have discretion to do so.[306] The processing methods eligible for Member State aid are freezing, salting, drying, marinating, and boiling and pasteurization (as well as filleting, cutting-up, and heading where accompanied by one of the above processes).[307] Regulation 2814/2000 adds that the storage of live edible crabs in certain conditions 'shall qualify as preservation for payment of the carry-over aid'.[308]

Carry-over aid is available for two categories of product. The first category consists of those products listed in Parts A and B of Annex I to the Markets Regulation which are withdrawn from the market at the Community withdrawal price, give or take 10 per cent 'to take account in particular of seasonal fluctuations in market prices'.[309] As noted in subsection 8.3 above, the use of the Community withdrawal price is also a condition for compensation for permanent withdrawal of Part A and B products under Article 21.[310] Following withdrawal from the market, products for which carry-over aid is sought must then be subject to one of the processing methods mentioned above; in contrast, products being permanently withdrawn must be disposed of as described in the previous subsection.

The second category for which carry-over aid is available is products listed in Part C of Annex I to the Markets Regulation 'which have been put up for sale but for which it can be shown that a buyer has not been found at the *Community selling price* . . . ' (emphasis added), give or take 10 per cent 'to take account in particular of seasonal fluctuations in market prices'.[311] Part C products are not subject to any mandatory indemnities under Article 17 or therefore to any financial compensation for permanent withdrawal under Article 21. To fix a Community *withdrawal* price for such products would therefore be confusing and potentially misleading. Instead, for Part C products, a 'Community selling price' is fixed albeit, as noted in subsection 8.2 above, 'on the same terms' as are laid down for fixing Community withdrawal prices.[312]

The Markets Regulation clarifies that, to be eligible for carry-over aid, the quantities in question must have been supplied by a member of a producer organization.[313] They must also 'meet certain quality, size and presentation requirements' and be stabilized or preserved 'in accordance with conditions and for a period to be determined' (see below).[314]

There is an upper limit on the amount of product to which carry-over aid may apply. For any given product, that limit is 18 per cent of the quantities put up for sale each year, less the percentage of quantities for which financial compensation

[306] Reg 104/2000, Art 23(1) and (2); cf Art 23(3).   [307] Reg 104/2000, Art 23(4).

[308] Commission Regulation (EC) No 2814/2000 of 21 December 2000 laying down the detailed rules for the application of Council Regulation (EC) No 104/2000 as regards the grant of carry-over aid for certain fishery products, OJ 2000 L326/34, Art 3(3).

[309] Reg 104/2000, Art 23(1), 1st para, (i) and 2nd para.   [310] Reg 104/2000, Art 21(1)(a).

[311] Reg 104/2000, Art 23(1), 1st para, (ii) and 2nd para.   [312] Reg 104/2000, Art 22.

[313] Reg 104/2000, Art 23(2)(a).   [314] Reg 104/2000, Art 23(2)(b) and (c).

for permanent withdrawal has been paid.[315] The amount of aid is not to exceed the amount of 'the technical and financial costs associated with the operations which are essential for stabilisation and storage'.[316]

Regulation 2814/2000 contains detailed rules regarding carry-over aid. It sets out, *inter alia*: (a) the scope of the costs that are eligible for aid, including the costs that are to be considered as 'technical costs';[317] (b) rules for the application of the 10 per cent margin of tolerance (by reference to Regulation 2509/2000—see subsection 8.3 above);[318] (c) eligibility requirements (some by reference, again, to Regulation 2509/2000), including detailed processing and storage requirements;[319] and (d) rules for the payment by Member States of aid (similar to those in Regulation 2813/2000—see subsection 8.6 below).[320]

Regarding common freshness standards, Regulation 2814/2000 has several requirements. It states that the requirement in Article 23 of the Markets Regulation for eligible quantities to 'meet certain quality, size and presentation requirements' (see above) is fulfilled when the products in question are classified under the common marketing standards 'set out' in Article 2 of the Markets Regulation.[321] In practice, no such standards are set out in Article 2 itself, so the wording above is presumably intended to be a reference to standards made under Article 2, notably those in the CMS Regulation (see section 4 above). In line with the CMS Regulation, Regulation 2814/2000 requires that quantities of products falling into freshness category B are not to be used in the calculation of quantities of product eligible for carry-over aid.[322]

Regulation 2814/2000 then goes further than Article 23 of the Markets Regulation by stating that the payment of carry-over aid for eligible quantities of products 'shall be subject to the condition that, for the product or group of products concerned, *all* the quantities put up for sale by the producers [sic] organisation or its members during the fishing year have been classified previously in accordance with the [applicable common marketing standards]' (emphasis added).[323] This is the same approach as taken in Regulation 2509/2000 regarding permanent withdrawals (see subsection 8.3 above). It appears that Regulation 2814/2000 has taken the finding of the Court in *Intervention Board* (see subsection 8.3 above) in respect of compensation for permanent withdrawals, and applied it to carry-over aid.[324]

Regulation 2814/2000 also requires the level of carry-over aid to be fixed before the beginning of each fishing year.[325] In turn, for the 2008 fishing year,

---

[315] Reg 104/2000, Art 23(3), 1st para.   [316] Reg 104/2000, Art 23(3), 2nd para.
[317] Reg 2814/2000, Art 5(2), (3), and (4).   [318] Reg 2814/2000, Art 5(6).
[319] Reg 2814/2000, Arts 2(2), 3, 4, and 5(6).
[320] Reg 2814/2000, Arts 7 and 8 and Annex.   [321] Reg 2814/2000, Art 2(3).
[322] Reg 2814/2000, Art 1.   [323] Reg 2814/2000, Art 2(2).
[324] See also Reg 2814/2000's predecessor, Reg 3901/92 (now repealed), Art 2(4).
[325] Reg 2814/2000, Art 5(1).

Regulation 1573/2007[326] fixes the amount of carry-over aid for products listed in Parts A, B, and C of Annex I to the Markets Regulation for the 2008 fishing year. The amounts are expressed in euros per tonne and are specific to the various processing methods permitted by the Markets Regulation (see above).

The Commission's 2006 report states that the common organization of the markets 'has substantially increased the aid for processing and storage of products with a view to their reintroduction into the market' and that '[a] steady shift from wasteful withdrawals to carry-over operations can be observed'.[327] The only annex to the report which gives separate treatment to carry-over operations and (presumably permanent) withdrawals is a graph depicting changes in 'Community withdrawals and carry-over expenses' over the period 2000–05.[328] It is questionable whether a 'steady shift' can be identified, although carry-over expenses do exceed withdrawals expenses for the first time in that period in 2005.

The report notes that '[t]he procedures for granting the aid [for carry-over operations] are more complex than those concerning withdrawals' and that '[t]he grant of advances . . . is not linked to the value of the stored product'. As a result, the Commission concedes that: 'In certain circumstances, the possibility to withdraw fish permanently from the market could be more attractive to [producer organizations] than the processing and storage of products.'[329] Presumably that is a result that the Commission would wish to guard against.

8.5 Flat-rate aid

For some species, 'the regional variations in prices . . . are such that those species cannot yet be covered by the scheme to grant financial compensation to producer organisations'.[330] Put another way: 'Certain fishery products, while accounting for a significant proportion of producers' incomes regionally or locally, cannot be covered by the EU's intervention mechanisms because of substantial price differences in a single national market or between one region and another and because the overall scale of their production throughout the Union is too low.'[331]

For those species, 'in order to foster greater market stability for the products concerned',[332] the Markets Regulation establishes a system of aid, known as flat-rate aid, addressing both permanent withdrawal and carry-over.[333] The wording of the Regulation implies that Member States are required to grant the flat-rate aid, whether for permanent withdrawals or carry-over, rather than merely having a

---

[326] Commission Regulation (EC) No 1573/2007 of 21 December 2007 fixing the amount of the carry-over aid and the flat-rate aid for certain fishery products for the 2008 fishing year, OJ 2007 L340/83.

[327] COM(2006) 558, section 6.2.2, p 8 and section 8, p 10.

[328] SEC(2006) 1218, Annex 8.   [329] COM(2006) 558, section 6.2.2, p 8.

[330] Reg 104/2000, recital (27).   [331] European Commission, 2002, section 5.3, p 13.

[332] Reg 104/2000, recital (27).   [333] Reg 104/2000, Art 24.

power to do so.[334] The species concerned are those listed in Annex IV to the Regulation (see subsection 8.1 above).[335]

The system works by avoiding the use of centralized Community guide prices, withdrawal prices, and selling prices, thereby allowing for regional differences. To be eligible for flat-rate aid from a Member State, a producer organization must 'practise intervention in accordance with Article 17'. As noted in subsection 8.3 above, Article 17 provides that a producer organization may, but is not required to, fix a withdrawal price; if such a price is fixed, and products are then withdrawn permanently, an indemnity is required to be granted to the members concerned in respect of withdrawn products listed in, *inter alia*, Annex IV to the Markets Regulation; and the real-time granting of indemnities is to be financed from an intervention fund or an 'equalisation system'.

To be eligible for flat-rate aid, the withdrawal price set by the producer organization must be an 'autonomous withdrawal price'. This must be set before the beginning of each fishing year and must be applied throughout the year (give or take 10 per cent).[336] The autonomous withdrawal price 'may not . . . exceed 80% of the weighted average price recorded for the product categories in question in the area of activity of the producer organisations concerned during the previous three fishing years'.[337] The products withdrawn must meet the common marketing standards adopted under Article 2 of the Markets Regulation.[338]

Where products are withdrawn permanently, the indemnity granted to producers must be equal to the autonomous withdrawal price.[339] The amount of flat-rate aid paid to producer organizations is to be 75 per cent of the autonomous withdrawal price and the quantities eligible for such aid may not exceed 5 per cent 'of the annual quantities of the products concerned put up for sale in accordance with Article 5(1)'. The reference to Article 5(1) is not very specific, since this provision contains what is, in effect, the Markets Regulation's lengthy definition of the term 'producer organization' (see subsection 6.1 above). As with compensation for withdrawal under Article 21, flat-rate aid may be reduced 'by the value, fixed at a standard amount, of the product which is disposed of . . . '.[340] Furthermore, there is a somewhat ambiguous requirement that: 'The flat-rate aid shall be granted for quantities withdrawn from the market which have been put up for sale *in accordance with Article 5(1)* and which are disposed of in a way that does not affect the *normal disposal of production.*' (Emphasis added.) Where products are withdrawn but are then to be subject to carry-over operations, the amount of flat-rate aid is not to exceed 'the amount of the technical and financial costs associated with the operations which are essential for stabilisation and storage' of the products withdrawn.[341] The quantities eligible for flat-rate aid for permanent withdrawal and for

---

[334] Reg 104/2000, Art 24(1)–(4).   [335] Reg 104/2000, Art 24(1).
[336] Reg 104/2000, Art 24(1)(a).   [337] Reg 104/2000, Art 24(1)(a).
[338] Reg 104/2000, Art 24(1)(b).   [339] Reg 104/2000, Art 24(1)(c).
[340] Reg 104/2000, Art 24(3).   [341] Reg 104/2000, Art 24(4).

carry-over, taken together, may not exceed 10 per cent of the annual quantities put up for sale 'in accordance with Article 5(1)' of the Markets Regulation.[342]

Detailed rules may be adopted regarding flat-rate aid.[343] These are contained in Regulation 939/2001,[344] which relies in large part on cross-references to Regulations 2509/2000 and 2814/2000, on permanent withdrawal and carry-over respectively.

For flat-rate aid for permanent withdrawal, Regulation 939/2001 sets out, *inter alia*: (a) eligibility requirements;[345] (b) rules for the application of the 10 per cent margin of tolerance;[346] and (c) rules on how the 'standard amount' fixing the value of products disposed of is to be calculated.[347] The eligibility requirements include, *inter alia*, the provisions in Regulation 2509/2000 on common marketing standards (see subsection 8.3 above). For flat-rate aid for carry-over, Regulation 939/2001 sets out, *inter alia*: (a) the scope of the costs that are eligible for aid, including the costs that are to be considered as 'technical costs';[348] and (b) eligibility requirements.[349] The eligibility requirements do *not* include the provisions in Regulation 2814/2000 on common marketing standards (see subsection 8.4 above). For both categories of aid, the Regulation also specifies rules for the payment of such aid by Member States.[350]

Regulation 939/2001 also requires that the amount of flat-rate aid for carry-over operations is to be fixed before the beginning of each fishing year.[351] In turn, for the 2008 fishing year, Regulation 1573/2007 (see subsection 8.4 above) fixes the amount of such aid, expressed in euros per tonne, for products listed in Annex IV to the Markets Regulation.

The Commission's 2006 report, in an annex,[352] shows that in 2004 €1,533,000 (across fourteen Member States) of flat-rate aid were used to fund withdrawals and carry-over operations. That figure represents just under 15 per cent of the EC's total market intervention expenses under the CFP for 2004.[353]

8.6 Private storage

The EC has created a system of aid to finance private storage of frozen products listed in Annex II to the Markets Regulation.[354] To be eligible, the products 'must

---

[342] Reg 104/2000, Art 24(5).   [343] Reg 104/2000, Art 24(8).

[344] Commission Regulation (EC) No 939/2001 of 14 May 2001 laying down detailed rules for the application of Council Regulation (EC) No 104/2000 as regards the grant of flat-raid aid for certain fishery products, OJ 2001 L132/10.   [345] Reg 939/2001, Art 3.

[346] Reg 939/2001, Art 3.   [347] Reg 939/2001, Art 4.

[348] Reg 939/2001, Art 5(2), (3), and (4).   [349] Reg 939/2001, Art 6.

[350] Reg 939/2001, Arts 2, 7, and 8.   [351] Reg 939/2001, Art 5(1).

[352] SEC(2006) 1218, Annex 9.

[353] SEC(2006) 1218, Annex 6, which shows the total intervention expenses for 2004 to be €10,350,000.   [354] Reg 104/2000, Art 25.

have been fished, frozen on board and land [sic—presumably 'landed'] in the Community by a member of a producer organisation' and 'must be stored for a minimum period and then placed on the Community market again'.[355] The restriction of the scheme to products frozen on board means that the aid 'may not be claimed by the freezing industry'.[356]

For producer organizations that, throughout the fishing year, apply the Community selling price set for Annex II products (see subsection 8.2 above), give or take 10 per cent 'to take account in particular of seasonal fluctuations in market prices', private storage aid 'may' be granted.[357] For Annex II products 'which have been put up for sale but for which it can be shown that a buyer has not been found at the Community selling price . . . ', private storage aid 'shall' be granted.[358] It is not clear from the wording of the Markets Regulation whether that distinction between a power and a duty is intended and, if so, what it means.

There is an upper limit on the amount of product to which private storage aid may apply. For the products concerned, that limit is 15 per cent of the quantities of the products concerned put up for sale annually by the producer organization.[359] The amount of private storage aid may not exceed 'the sum of technical costs and interest for a maximum period of three months'; the amount is to diminish over time.[360] Regulation 2813/2000 (see below) adds that: 'The amount of the aid shall be calculated on the basis of the real technical costs and financial costs of operations indispensable for storing the products in question as recorded in the Community during the previous fishing year'.[361]

Detailed rules may be adopted regarding private storage aid.[362] In turn, Regulation 2813/2000 sets out, *inter alia*: (a) the scope of the costs that are eligible for aid, including the costs that are to be considered as 'technical costs';[363] (b) a minimum storage period (fifteen days) and a maximum storage temperature;[364] (c) rules for the application of the 10 per cent margin of tolerance (by reference to Regulation 2509/2000—see subsection 8.3 above);[365] and (d) rules for the payment by Member States of financial compensation (including the requirement that applications for aid be submitted by the producer organization to the Member State concerned within four months of the end of the relevant fishing year, unless a security has been lodged in which case a monthly advance must be granted).[366]

Regulation 2813/2000 also requires the level of private storage aid to be fixed before the beginning of each fishing year.[367] In turn, for the 2008 fishing year,

---

[355] Reg 104/2000, Art 25(4).   [356] European Commission, 2002, section 5.4, p 14.
[357] Reg 104/2000, Art 25(2).   [358] Reg 104/2000, Art 25(3).
[359] Reg 104/2000, Art 25(4).   [360] Reg 104/2000, Art 25(5).
[361] Commission Regulation (EC) No 2813/2000 of 21 December 2000 laying down detailed rules for the application of Council Regulation (EC) No 104/2000 as regards the grant of private storage aid for certain fishery products, OJ 2000 L326/30, Art 1(2).   [362] Reg 104/2000, Art 25(6).
[363] Reg 2813/2000, Art 1(2), (3), and (4).   [364] Reg 2813/2000, Art 2(1) and (2).
[365] Reg 2813/2000, Art 3.   [366] Reg 2813/2000, Arts 5 and 6 and Annex.
[367] Reg 2813/2000, Art 1(1).

Regulation 1574/2007[368] fixes the amount of private storage aid. There is aid for the first month (€210 per tonne, irrespective of the product in question) and no aid for subsequent months.[369] The use of a single instalment is to 'discourage long-term storage . . . shorten payment times and . . . reduce the burden of controls'.[370]

The Commission's 2006 report, in an annex,[371] shows that in 2004 €49,000 (across 14 Member States) were used to fund private storage operations of the type described in this subsection. That figure represents 0.5 per cent of the EC's total market intervention expenses under the CFP for 2004.[372] Assuming the data are complete, the annex also indicates that in the period 1993–2004 only Spain used the system for private storage aid.

8.7 Compensatory allowance for tuna producers

The Markets Regulation provides for a system of direct aid to tuna producers, known as the 'compensatory allowance'.[373] The Commission states that the system 'was introduced to compensate tuna fishermen for the absence of tariff protection on imports for the tuna processing industry'. The allowance 'is designed to provide tuna fishermen with some shelter from world market fluctuations . . . [and] . . . is therefore granted only if it can be shown that the adverse marketing conditions are due to the level of world prices and not to an abnormal increase in the quantities caught inside the Union'.[374]

Article 27(1) of the Markets Regulation, in its first sentence, states that: 'An allowance may be granted to the producer organisations for the quantities of products listed in Annex III caught by their members, then sold and delivered to processing industries established within the customs territory of the Community and intended for the industrial manufacture of products falling within CN code 1604.' Thus the allowance is to be granted to producer organizations (for onward distribution to their members—see below); it is not available to producers outside such organizations. It relates only to the products listed in Annex III to the Markets Regulation (see subsection 8.1 above). The products must have been: (a) caught by the members of the producer organizations in question; (b) sold and delivered to processors within the EC's customs territory; and (c) intended for industrial manufacture of products within CN code 1604, ie 'Prepared or preserved fish; caviar and caviar substitutes prepared from fish eggs' (for example canned tuna).

---

[368] Commission Regulation (EC) No 1574/2007 of 21 December 2007 fixing the amount of private storage aid for certain fishery products in the 2008 fishing year, OJ 2007 L340/85.

[369] Reg 1574/2007, Art 1.   [370] Reg 1574/2007, recital (2).

[371] SEC(2006) 1218, Annex 10.

[372] SEC(2006) 1218, Annex 6, which shows the total intervention expenses for 2004 to be €10,350,000.   [373] Reg 104/2000, Arts 26 and 27.

[374] European Commission, 2002, section 5.5, p 14. See also Reg 104/2000, recitals (29) and (31).

The wording in the above extract from Article 27(1) of the Markets Regulation, which states that '[a]n allowance *may* be granted' (emphasis added),[375] suggests that the Member State has a power to grant the compensatory allowance to the producer organization concerned, but is not required to do so. However, other wording in Article 27(1),[376] and also in Regulation 2183/2001 (see below),[377] suggests that the payment of the allowance is mandatory.

The allowance is only to be granted when specified market conditions arise. The requirements are set out in the second sentence of Article 27(1). The key factor is a so-called 'triggering threshold' set at 87 per cent of the 'Community producer price' for the tuna product in question. The allowance is to be granted when, for a given calendar quarter, 'the average selling price recorded on the Community market' and the 'import price referred to in Article 29(3)(d)' are *both* less than the triggering threshold.

Thus the 'Community producer price', the 'average selling price recorded on the Community market', and the 'import price referred to in Article 29(3)(d)' are all relevant to determining when the allowance should be granted. Those three concepts are introduced briefly in the following paragraphs.

The 'Community producer price' is to be fixed by the Council, acting by qualified majority on a proposal from the Commission, for each of the products concerned before the start of the fishing year.[378] The prices are to be established on the basis of various factors including, *inter alia*, some of those used to establish the guide price (see subsection 8.2 above), namely 'the average of prices recorded for a significant proportion of Community output on wholesale markets or in ports during the three fishing years immediately preceding the year for which the price is fixed' and 'taking into account trends in production and demand'.[379]

The Commission's 2006 report states that the Community producer price is 'intended to reflect market realities and to contribute to prevent [sic] excessive price variations'.[380] It can be seen that the lower the triggering threshold, expressed as a percentage of the Community producer price, the less favourable the system becomes to tuna producers. The 2006 report states that the common organization of the markets 'has reduced the level at which the mechanism is activated'.[381] This is presumably a reference to the triggering threshold in the Markets Regulation being 87 per cent of the Community producer price compared to 91 per cent in the preceding basic Regulation.[382]

---

[375] Reg 104/2000, Art 27(1), 1st para, 1st sentence.
[376] Reg 104/2000, Art 27(1), 1st para, 2nd sentence.
[377] Commission Regulation (EC) No 2183/2001 of 9 November 2001 laying down detailed rules for the application of Council Regulation (EC) No 104/2000 as regards granting the compensatory allowance for tuna intended for the processing industry, OJ 2001 L293/11, Arts 3(1), 5, and 9(1).
[378] Reg 104/2000, Art 26(1).   [379] Reg 104/2000, Arts 26(1) and 18(2), 1st para.
[380] COM(2006) 558, section 6.3, p 9.   [381] COM(2006) 558, section 6.3, p 9.
[382] Reg 3759/92, Art 18(1).

Regulation 1447/2007 (see subsection 8.2 above) claims to set out Community producer prices for the 2008 fishing year in its Annex II.[383] In practice, the only producer price contained therein is for 'Whole' yellowfin tuna 'weighing more than 10 kg each'. However, the preamble states that it is appropriate to calculate the producer price for other tuna species 'by means of the conversion factors established by Commission Regulation [802/2006]'.[384] Regulation 802/2006[385] does indeed set out conversion factors as promised, but it is not stated how those are to be used to calculate producer prices. Presumably they are to be applied to the one producer price that is contained in Annex II to Regulation 1447/2007.

The 'average selling price recorded on the Community market' is elaborated in Regulation 2183/2001. It is to be 'determined by the Commission on the basis of the monthly average prices notified by the Member States calculated on the basis of the value of the quantities sold and delivered to industry pursuant to Article 6 of [Regulation 80/2001]'.[386] Regulation 2183/2001 also sets out how Member States are to determine the said monthly average prices.[387]

An explanation of the 'import price referred to in Article 29(3)(d)' of the Markets Regulation requires a brief look at that Article. Article 29(3)(d), in Title V on trade with third countries, states that: 'Reference prices adopted . . . for other products [ie products other than those in Annexes I or II], shall be fixed, in particular, on the basis of the weighted average of customs values recorded on the import markets or in the ports of import in the Member States during the three years immediately preceding the date on which the reference price is fixed, taking account of the need to ensure that prices reflect the market situation'. Thus the 'import price', as in the 'import price referred to in Article 29(3)(d)', is presumably the reference price referred to in, and set according to, Article 29(3)(d).

The system of allowances operates retrospectively. Once a calendar quarter has been identified as one in which, for a given tuna product, the average selling price and the import price fell below the triggering threshold, it is necessary for the Commission to determine the maximum amount of the allowance and allocate it among the producer organizations concerned. Regulation 2183/2001 specifies that the Commission is to adopt a Regulation for those purposes.[388] The method for determining the allowance and allocating it is complex, and has been the subject of litigation before the CFI in OPTUC v Commission.[389]

First, Article 27(2) of the Markets Regulation specifies that the amount of the allowance (expressed in euros per tonne) for the particular tuna product in question may not in any case exceed either: (a) the difference between the triggering

---

[383] Reg 1447/2007, Art 2.   [384] Reg 1447/2007, recital (4).

[385] Commission Regulation (EC) No 802/2006 of 30 May 2006 fixing the conversion factors applicable to fish of the genera *Thunnus* and *Euthynnus*, OJ 2006 L144/15.

[386] Reg 2183/2001, Art 4(1), 1st para.   [387] Reg 2183/2001, Art 4(1), 2nd para.

[388] Reg 2183/2001, Art 2.

[389] Joined Cases T-142/01 and T-283/01 *Organización de Productores de Túnidos Congelados (OPTUC) v Commission* [2004] ECR II-329.

threshold and the average selling price on the Community market; or (b) a flat-rate amount equivalent to 12 per cent of the triggering threshold. That maximum amount applies irrespective of the number of producer organizations concerned.

Secondly, Article 27(3) specifies that, in respect of the quarter concerned: 'The maximum total quantity of each of the products eligible for the allowance shall be limited to an amount equal to the average of the quantities sold and delivered, under the terms set out in [the first paragraph of Article 27(1)], during the equivalent quarter in the three fishing years preceding the quarter for which the allowance is paid.' That maximum total quantity is expressed in tonnes.

Thirdly, Article 27(4), in its first paragraph, establishes a system for working out the amount of the allowance to be granted to each producer organization, under which some of a producer organization's tuna is compensated at the ceiling set out in Article 27(2) and the rest is to be compensated at a lesser amount.

The first indent of Article 27(4) specifies that where the quantities of the product in question do not exceed 'the average of the quantities sold and delivered under the same conditions by the [producer organization's] members in the equivalent quarter in the three fishing years preceding the quarter for which the allowance is paid', the amount of allowance to be granted to that producer organization is equal to the ceiling laid down in Article 27(2).

The second indent addresses those quantities that 'exceed the quantities referred to in the first indent and which are equal to the surplus of the quantities resulting from allocating the quantities eligible under [Article 27(3)] among the producer organisations'. For such quantities, the amount of allowance to be granted to each producer organization is equal to 50 per cent of the ceiling laid down in Article 27(2).

Under the second paragraph of Article 27(4), the allocation is to be 'made proportionately between the producer organisations in question on the basis of their respective average production in the equivalent quarter in the three fishing years preceding the quarter for which the allowance is paid'.

In *OPTUC v Commission* the CFI held that, 'in order to determine the allowance due to a [producer organization] for a given quarter, in accordance with [what is now Article 27(4) of the Markets Regulation] it is necessary to allocate to it the average previous production of all producers who, in that quarter, are members of the [organization]'.[390] Otherwise, 'unjustified and unfair distortions would arise for the real beneficiaries of the compensatory allowances, that is the producers, whose level of income which the allowances are intended to protect would be likely to be seriously affected by changes of membership of the [producer organizations]'.[391]

Lastly, under Article 27(5), the organizations are to 'allocate the allowance granted to their members proportionately on the basis of the quantities produced by them and sold and delivered in accordance with [Article 27(1)]'.

[390] Joined Cases T-142/01 and T-283/01 *OPTUC v Commission*, para 89.
[391] Joined Cases T-142/01 and T-283/01 *OPTUC v Commission*, para 90.

Detailed rules may be adopted regarding the compensatory allowance.[392] In turn, Regulation 2183/2001 sets out, *inter alia*: (a) rules for determining the average selling price recorded on the Community market (see above);[393] (b) rules governing the submission of applications for payment of the allowance;[394] and (c) rules for the payment by Member States of the allowance and for onward payment by the producer organization to its members.[395]

In practice, as at the end of November 2008, the payment of a compensatory allowance was last triggered by market conditions arising in the first quarter of 2007, leading to Regulation 1537/2007.[396] This Regulation related to albacore tuna. The Regulation set: (a) the maximum amount of compensation (expressed in euros per tonne) pursuant to Article 27(2); (b) the total quantity of product on which the allowance was payable (expressed as tonnes) pursuant to Article 27(3); and (c) the allocation of the total quantity between the producer organizations concerned pursuant to Article 27(4).

8.8 Penalties

Regulation 150/2001[397] establishes penalties for producer organizations arising from irregularities in the implementation of the provisions of the Markets Regulation on financial compensation for permanent withdrawal, carry-over aid, flat-rate aid, private storage aid, and the compensatory allowance for tuna producers.[398]

In short, the Regulation requires that where an irregularity involves amounts of (a) less than 5 per cent, (b) between 5 and 10 per cent, or (c) more than 10 per cent of the annual aid received by the producer organization under the particular intervention mechanism in question, the Member State is to retain an amount (a) up to 20 per cent, (b) of between 30 and 50 per cent, or (c) of between 60 and 80 per cent, respectively, 'of the intervention price applicable to the quantities of product concerned depending on the seriousness in financial terms of the infringement'.[399]

However, where there has been an intentional irregularity or one caused by serious negligence, the Member State is to retain 'all the aid for which the pro-

---

[392] Reg 104/2000, Art 27(6).   [393] Reg 2183/2001, Art 4.

[394] Reg 2183/2001, Arts 7 and 8.   [395] Reg 2183/2001, Art 9.

[396] Commission Regulation (EC) No 1537/2007 of 20 December 2007 providing for compensation to producer organisations for tuna delivered to the processing industry between 1 January and 31 March 2007, OJ 2007 L337/46.

[397] Commission Regulation (EC) No 150/2001 of 25 January 2001 laying down detailed rules for the application of Council Regulation (EC) No 104/2000 as regards the penalties to be applied to producer organisations in the fisheries sector for irregularity of the intervention mechanism and amending Regulation 142/98, OJ 2001 L24/10.   [398] Reg 150/2001, Art 1.

[399] Reg 150/2001, Art 3(1), (2), and (3).

ducer organisation is eligible under that mechanism for the fishing year concerned'. Furthermore, in the case of an intentional irregularity, the Member State
is not to grant the aid under that mechanism for the following year either.[400]

The various sanctions provided for in the Regulation are not to be regarded as
criminal penalties.[401] Where aid is to be retained by a Member State, the amount
in question is to be 'either refunded to the Member State, taken from the security
left by the producer organisation or deducted from the aid to be received for the
next fishing year'.[402] In turn, the amounts retained by or refunded to the Member
State are to be credited to the European Agricultural Guarantee Fund (on which
see subsection 8.1 above).[403]

The Commission's 2006 report states that:[404]

Only one Member State detected irregularities of the intervention mechanisms, in particular
withdrawals. The Commission performed audits of intervention expenditures in 3 Member
States in 2003, 2004 and 2005. The administration and control of the intervention in Ireland
was deficient in 2002–2003. Main findings are related to insufficient monitoring over
[producer organizations] to ensure that they take every measure to avoid intervention and
improper control over the destination of fish withdrawn from the market. There have been
instances where fishing operations were carried out for the sole purpose of benefiting from
intervention.

9 Enforcement

Article 36 of the Markets Regulation requires Member States to 'adopt appropriate
measures to ensure compliance with this Regulation and to forestall and bring to
an end any fraud'. As can be seen, this duty has two components. The first is
general in nature: it relates to compliance with the Markets Regulation. The
second component is specific to addressing fraud, and exists because of the financial assistance that is an inherent part of the common organization of the markets,
as discussed in particular in section 8 above. In that regard, the Markets Regulation
requires Member States to 'regularly carry out checks on the beneficiaries of
financial assistance' and, if checks are carried out by sampling, to ensure that the
checks are appropriate and adequate.[405]

Article 36 of the Markets Regulation is supplemented by various specific provisions on enforcement[406] and by Regulation 2847/1993 (hereafter, 'the Control Regulation').[407] Various general provisions of Title I of the Control

---

[400] Reg 150/2001, Art 3(4).   [401] Reg 150/2001, Art 3(5).
[402] Reg 150/2001, Art 4(1).   [403] Reg 150/2001, Art 4(2).
[404] COM(2006) 558, section 6.2, p 8.   [405] Reg 104/2000, Art 36, 1st and 2nd indents.
[406] See, for example, Reg 104/2000, Arts 3 and 7(7) and Reg 2406/96, Art 12.
[407] Council Regulation (EEC) No 2847/93 of 12 October 1993 establishing a control system
applicable to the common fisheries policy, OJ 1993 L261/1, as amended.

Regulation are relevant to, *inter alia*, the common organization of the markets. In particular, Article 1(1) states that: 'In order to ensure compliance with the rules of the common fisheries policy, a Community system is hereby established including in particular provisions for the technical monitoring of: . . . [*inter alia*] measure [sic] concerning *the common organization of the market*, as well as certain provisions relating to the effectiveness of sanctions to be applied in cases where the above-mentioned measures are not observed.' (Emphasis added.)

However, the Control Regulation also contains a provision, Article 28, that is specific to inspection and control regarding the common organization of the markets in fishery products. Article 28 refers to ensuring compliance with 'the technical aspects' of Regulation 3759/92, which is the immediate predecessor to the Markets Regulation. The latter states that references to Regulation 3759/92 are to be construed as referring to the Markets Regulation.[408] Therefore, Article 28 now relates to the Markets Regulation. It requires each Member State to 'organize on its own territory regular checks of all persons involved in the application of the measures'.[409]

Such checks are to 'concern the technical aspects of applying: (a) the marketing standards, and in particular minimum marketing sizes; (b) the price arrangements, in particular . . . withdrawal of products from the market for purposes other than human consumption . . . [and] . . . storage and/or processing of products withdrawn from the market'.[410] The Control Regulation is careful to emphasize that its role is control of 'the technical aspects' of the measures, rather than the financial aspects.[411] Other aspects of control, beyond those relating directly to the common organization of the markets, are dealt with in Chapter 4.

10 Conclusions

As noted in section 1 above, the provision of market stability and the guarantee of a fair income for producers are important objectives of the common organization of the markets in fishery products. However, as stated in Regulation 2371/2002, the objective of the CFP is to 'ensure exploitation of living aquatic resources that provides sustainable economic, environmental and social conditions'.[412] Thus economic and social sustainability is not the whole picture, and it is relevant to ask what contribution the common organization of the markets currently makes, and could make, to ecological sustainability, from the point of view of both the productivity of fish stocks and the health of the wider marine environment.

Avoiding incompatibility with the EC's fisheries conservation legislation is clearly one contribution that the common organization can make to achieving

---

[408] Reg 104/2000, Art 42(2).   [409] Reg 2847/93, Art 28(1).
[410] Reg 2847/93, Art 28(2), 1st para.   [411] See also Reg 2847/93, 27th recital.
[412] Reg 2371/2002, Art 2(1), 1st para.

ecological sustainability. Steps have been taken in this regard by the Markets Regulation and the CMS Regulation. As noted in subsection 4.3 above, the CMS Regulation requires the minimum marketing size to apply without prejudice to the minimum biological size. Furthermore, as noted in subsection 8.1 above, the Markets Regulation requires EC financing for, *inter alia*, permanent withdrawals, carry-over, private storage, and the compensatory allowance for tuna producers to be compatible with Member States' quotas as derived from total allowable catches.

However, arguably, the common organization of the markets should be going a lot further than merely avoiding incompatibility with EC's fisheries conservation legislation and should seek to use the power of the markets to help achieve ecological sustainability. To some extent, the common organization does indeed move in this direction. The Markets Regulation places an emphasis on matching supply to demand and on trying to ensure that maximum value is obtained for fish caught. This is manifested in particular through the requirement for producer organizations to draw up operational programmes and the option for such organizations to submit quality improvement plans (see subsection 6.4 above) as well as aid for processes, particularly carry-over, that avoid wasteful permanent withdrawals of fish from the market.

In principle, assuming that a surplus of fish would otherwise be caught, matching supply to demand should help to avoid fish being wasted. However, it would be interesting to know the extent to which any systematic attempts by producer organizations to match supply to demand through their operational programmes, or otherwise, have indeed led to a reduction in the amount of fish wasted, and how any such reduction compares with the waste of fish arising from discarding. It should also be borne in mind that matching supply to demand, in terms of quantity, in cases where demand is high may promote over-fishing.

It is arguable that seeking to maximize value is relevant to ecological sustainability by helping to reduce the quantities of fish taken and hence reduce the pressure on stocks and damage to the wider environment. However, the Commission's 2006 report indicates that the use of quality improvement plans, one of the means for maximizing value, has not proved popular with producer organizations. Furthermore, if the Markets Regulation's mechanisms for maximizing value were to be successful in systematically maximizing catch value, care would presumably be needed to avoid that situation itself leading to pressure on stocks.

Beyond avoiding incompatibilities with the EC's fisheries conservation legislation, seeking to avoid waste by matching supply to demand, and seeking to reduce pressure on stocks by maximizing the value of catches, what else could be done by the common organization of the markets to help conserve fish stocks? Being lawyers, the authors are not in the best position to answer this question. That said, one rather obvious area for consideration is eco-labelling. As noted in section 5 above, a requirement to provide information on sustainability did not make it into the Markets Regulation. A policy document on fisheries eco-labelling issued by the Commission in 2005 had not, as at the end of November 2008, led to a legislative proposal in that regard, although a broader legislative proposal, based on Article 175(1) EC, was issued in July 2008.

Overall, it seems that further consideration is needed by the Commission and others about how the power of the markets could be used to help achieve ecological sustainability. In fact, a review of the common organization of the markets is currently underway. The review is general in nature, rather than looking at the contribution of the market organization to ecological sustainability specifically. In autumn 2008, an external consultant completed an evaluation for the Commission of the 'financial and non-financial instruments' of the common organization of the markets.[413] A second study, on supply and marketing of fishery and aquaculture products in the EC, was commissioned in 2008 with the report due in 2009.[414]

In October 2008, the Commission anticipated that, in the light of, *inter alia*, the above-mentioned reports, it would adopt a legislative proposal on reform of the common organization of the markets in fishery and aquaculture products in the second half of 2009.[415] In view of the early onset of the review of other aspects of the CFP (see Chapter 4), it will be interesting to see how much the two review initiatives now become integrated. Any such integration may help to ensure that full use is made of the potential for the common organization of the markets, including the producer organizations and perhaps also the largely unused concept of interbranch organizations, to assist in achieving sustainable fisheries.

---

[413] *Summary Record of the Meeting of Working Group 3 (Markets and Trade Policy) of the Advisory Committee on Fisheries and Aquaculture*, 20.10.08, section 5, p 5 (available on the website of DG Mare).

[414] *Summary Record of the Plenary Meeting of the Advisory Committee on Fisheries and Aquaculture*, 02.10.08, Annex 3 (available on the website of DG Mare).

[415] *Summary Record of the Plenary Meeting of the Advisory Committee on Fisheries and Aquaculture*, 02.10.08, section 5, p 5 (available on the website of DG Mare).

7

Trade in fishery products

1 Introduction

The EC is a major player in global trade in fishery products.[1] During the period 2004–06 inclusive the now twenty-seven EC Member States collectively imported on average each year fishery products to the value of US$ 18.6 billion from third States, which represented 27.7 per cent of total global imports (excluding imports in intra-EC trade), making the EC the largest importer of fishery products in the world, ahead of Japan (21.3 per cent) and the USA (18.5 per cent).[2] The EC was also a modest exporter, exporting on average some US$ 3.2 billion worth of fishery products a year to third States, making it the world's sixth largest exporter of such products.[3] Overall, however, the EC is, and for many years has been, a large net importer of fishery products. During the period 2004–06 the EC was the largest net importer in the world, just ahead of Japan.[4] Imports from third States account for about 60 per cent of consumption of fishery products in the EC.[5]

Apart from trade between the EC and third States, there is also a considerable volume of intra-EC trade in fishery products, facilitated by the fact that under EC law fishing vessels registered in one Member State have the right to land their catches in the ports of any other Member State.[6] Over the period 2004–06 such trade represented around US$13.9 billion a year on average.[7]

In spite of its economic importance, trade in fishery products is the most obscure and least written about aspect of the Common Fisheries Policy (CFP). Indeed, it is questionable whether such trade falls within the scope of the CFP.

---

[1] The term 'fishery products' is used in this chapter to refer to the fish and other aquatic organisms covered by the CFP, whether processed or unprocessed. The term includes the products of marine fisheries, inland fisheries, and aquaculture. However, it should also be noted that Reg 104/2000 (Art 1) and Reg 1005/2008 (Art 2(8); see also Art 12(5)), both introduced below, each have their own, more limited, definitions of the term 'fishery products'. See further Chapters 2 and 6.

[2] Food and Agriculture Organization of the United Nations (FAO), *Yearbook of Fishery Statistics Summary Tables 2006* (available on the website of the Fisheries and Aquaculture Department of the FAO), Table A-3 and Appendix III, Table 1-1-1.   [3] Ibid.

[4] This conclusion follows from the figures given in FAO, *Yearbook of Fishery Statistics Summary Tables 2006*, Table A-3 and Appendix III, Table 1-1-1.

[5] *Commission Working Document, Reflections on further reform of the Common Fisheries Policy* (2008), available on the website of DG Mare.

[6] Council Regulation (EC) No 104/2000 of 17 December 1999 on the common organisation of the markets in fishery and aquaculture products, OJ 2000 L17/22, as amended and corrected, Art 33.

[7] FAO, *Yearbook of Fishery Statistics Summary Tables 2006*, Appendix III, Table 1-1-1.

That scope is defined in Article 1 of Regulation 2371/2002 (hereafter, 'the Basic Regulation').[8] There is no specific reference there to trade. The nearest that Article 1 of the Regulation comes to referring to trade is when it states that the CFP 'shall cover . . . the processing and marketing of fishery and aquaculture products' and 'shall provide for coherent measures concerning . . . (g) common organisation of the markets, and (h) international relations'. As will be seen below, the basic Regulation on the common organization of the markets in fishery products[9] has provisions dealing with some, though not all, aspects of trade with third States. This suggests that such aspects fall within the concepts of 'marketing' and the 'common organisation of the markets'. The phrase 'international relations' is arguably broad enough to include all aspects of trade with third states. While intra-EC trade in fishery products appears to fall outside the scope of the CFP, it would give an incomplete picture were it not dealt with in this chapter.

Accordingly, the next section of this chapter considers EC law relating to trade between Member States, while the following section deals with the legal regime governing trade in fishery products between the EC and third States. The EC is a customs union.[10] That means that not only are there in principle no barriers to trade between EC Member States but also that, as far as trade with third States is concerned, the EC is to be considered as a single unit. It would seem to follow from the latter proposition that external trade relations, at least as far as trade in goods is concerned, ought to fall within the EC's exclusive competence (under the common commercial policy): that is implied in Article 133 EC and has been confirmed to be so by the Court.[11]

2 The legal regulation of intra-EC trade

2.1 Introduction

The EC is not only a customs union, as mentioned above, but also constitutes an internal market.[12] The latter is defined by Article 14(2) EC as 'an area without internal frontiers in which the free movement of goods, persons, services and capital is ensured'. In the same vein, Article 3 EC, which sets out a list of the 'activities of the Community', describes an internal market as 'characterised by the

---

[8] Council Regulation (EC) No 2371/2002 of 20 December 2002 on the conservation and sustainable exploitation of fisheries resources under the Common Fisheries Policy, OJ 2002 L358/59, as amended and corrected.   [9] Reg 104/2000.

[10] Art 23(1) EC.

[11] *Opinion 1/75 (re Understanding on a Local Cost Standard)* [1975] ECR 1355. See further Eeckhout, P, *External Relations of the European Union: Legal and Constitutional Foundations* (Oxford: Oxford University Press, 2004), ch 2 and Barnard, C, *The Substantive Law of the EU* (2nd edn, Oxford: Oxford University Press, 2007), 211–20.   [12] Art 14(1) EC.

abolition, as between Member States, of obstacles to the free movement of goods, persons, services and capital'. It follows from those provisions that there is in principle complete freedom of trade in goods between EC Member States (although when new Member States accede to the EC, there may be some temporary restrictions on free trade between those Member States and the old Member States), which is governed by the provisions of the EC Treaty dealing with free movement of goods, as interpreted and applied by the Court. The term 'goods' is, surprisingly (given its importance), nowhere defined in the EC Treaty or secondary legislation. That omission has been cured by the Court, which has defined 'goods' as 'products which can be valued in money and which are capable, as such, of forming the subject of commercial transactions'.[13] Clearly fishery products fall within that definition. This means that trade in fishery products between EC Member States is governed by the provisions of the EC Treaty dealing with the free movement of goods.[14] By trade in fishery products between EC Member States is meant where such products are imported by one Member State from another Member State (or, from the perspective of the latter Member State, where goods are exported from that Member State to the importing Member State). A fishery product is imported where it originates in one Member State (a concept whose meaning is explained below) and enters another Member State, either by being landed at a port in that Member State or by entering the territory of that Member State by road, rail, air or some other form of transport. The Treaty provisions on free movement of goods, in broad outline, prohibit, in intra-EC trade, customs duties and charges having equivalent effect, discriminatory taxation, and quantitative restrictions and measures having equivalent effect. Before exploring how those three sets of prohibitions apply to trade in fishery products, it is necessary to consider more precisely the circumstances in which the EC Treaty's provisions on free movement of goods are applicable.

Article 23(2) EC states that the provisions of the Treaty on free movement of goods apply to 'products originating in Member States' and to 'products coming from third countries which are in free circulation in Member States'. As regards the latter, according to Article 24 EC, 'products coming from a third country shall be considered to be in free circulation in a Member State if the import formalities have been complied with and any customs duties or charges having equivalent effect which are payable have been levied in that Member State'. That category of (fishery) product is therefore relatively straightforward. The position is less clear-cut in relation to 'products originating in Member States', particularly in relation to fishery products. That is because many fishery products originate from fish caught at sea: in the latter situation it may be questioned whether they do, in fact, originate in a Member State.

---

[13] Case 7/68 *Commission v Italy* [1968] ECR 423 at 428–429.
[14] This was confirmed by the Court in Joined Cases 3, 4, and 6/76 *Officier van Justitie v Kramer* [1976] ECR 1279, paras 53–54; and in Case C-228/91 *Commission v Italy* [1993] ECR I-2701, para 11.

Rather curiously, perhaps, neither the EC Treaty nor secondary legislation directly defines the phrase 'products originating in Member States'. That origin of goods is defined for the purposes of trade between the EC and third States by the Community Customs Code,[15] and that definition may be applied by analogy to intra-EC trade, as was implicitly done by the Advocate General in *Pansard*.[16] Article 23(1) of the Code provides that goods originate in a country if they are 'wholly obtained in that country'. Article 23(2) goes on to provide that the expression 'goods wholly obtained in a country' includes, *inter alia*, '(e) products of hunting or fishing carried on therein' and '(f) products of sea-fishing and other products taken from the sea outside a country's territorial sea by vessels registered or recorded in the country concerned and flying the flag of that country'. Article 23(3) provides that for the purposes of Article 23(2) 'country' includes 'that country's territorial sea'. There is a degree of ambiguity about the first use of the word 'country' in Article 23(2)(f). Does 'a country's territorial sea' refer to the territorial sea of any country or only to the territorial sea of the country where the vessel is registered and whose flag it flies?

In *Pansard*, which concerned a request for a preliminary ruling from a French court as to whether scallops caught by a French vessel in the territorial sea of Jersey (one of the Channel Islands) and landed in France were to be regarded as imports from another Member State,[17] the French government (supported by the Dutch government) argued that 'a country' in the phrase 'a country's territorial sea' in Article 23(2)(f) referred to the country where the vessel concerned was registered. The Advocate General disagreed. In his view 'a country' referred to any country.[18] The Court found that it was not necessary to consider this question. If the Advocate General's view is correct, fish originate in a Member State for the purposes of the free movement of goods if they are caught within the territorial sea of that Member State, if they are caught by a vessel registered in that Member State in the exclusive economic zone (EEZ) or exclusive fishing zone (EFZ) of another Member State or a third State, or if they are caught on the high seas, but not if they are caught within the territorial sea of another Member State or of a third State. That interpretation of Article 23(2)(f) produces some rather odd consequences. Take the situation where a vessel registered in Member State A takes part of its catch in Member State B's EEZ and part in Member State B's territorial sea

---

[15] Council Regulation (EEC) No 2913/92 of 12 October 1992 establishing the Community Customs Code, OJ 1992 L302/1, as amended and corrected. Reg 2913/92 has been repealed and will gradually be replaced by Regulation (EC) No 450/2008 of the European Parliament and the Council of 23 April 2008 laying down the Community Customs Code (Modernized Customs Code), OJ 2008 L145/1. The provisions of Reg 450/2008 that correspond to the provisions of Reg 2913/92 that are discussed below will not come into force until 24 June 2009 at the earliest: see Reg 450/2008, Art 188.

[16] Case C-265/01 *Criminal proceedings against Annie Pansard and Others* [2003] ECR I-683, AG Opinion, paras 29–30.

[17] The Channel Islands are within the EC's customs territory: see Art 3(1) of the Community Customs Code. See also Chapter 2.   [18] *Pansard*, AG Opinion, paras 30–35.

(something that is quite possible under EC rules on access to fishing grounds, discussed in Chapter 4) and then lands its catch in Member State A. That part of the catch taken in State B's EEZ will not be an import into State A because it originates in State A. However, that part of the catch taken in State B's territorial sea will be an import into State A from another Member State and therefore subject to EC rules on the free movement of goods. Likewise, where a vessel registered in an EC Member State takes part of its catch in a third State's EEZ and part in that State's territorial sea (something that is possible in practice under at least one of the EC's agreements on the access of Community vessels to the waters of third States, discussed in Chapter 5) and then lands its catch in its home Member State, that part of the catch taken in the third State's EEZ will not be an import, whereas that part taken in the territorial sea will be an import and subject to Community rules on trade with third States. It is doubtful whether in practice the national authorities at the port of landing distinguish catches in that way or whether indeed it is practicable for them to do so. The position just described would be avoided if the French government's interpretation of Article 23(2)(f) were adopted, an interpretation that seems a more natural reading of at least the English version of Article 23, whereby the term 'the country concerned' in Article 23(2)(f) would refer back to 'a country' earlier in the sentence. That interpretation also accords with the way that the original version of the Community Customs Code was drafted.[19] It is also supported by the Commission Regulation implementing Regulation 2913/92, namely Regulation 2454/93.[20] The latter contains two provisions that govern the origin of goods for the purposes of certain trade regimes. Article 68(1) provides that '[t]he following shall be considered as wholly obtained in a beneficiary country or in the Community . . . (f) products of sea fishing and other products taken from the sea outside *its* territorial waters by *its* vessels' (emphasis added). The natural reading of this provision is that, as regards the Community, 'its' refers to the territorial waters of, and vessels registered in, EC Member States. Article 99(1) is identically worded except that in subparagraph (f) the phrase '*the* territorial waters' appears, rather than '*its* territorial waters' (emphasis added). The phrase '*the* territorial waters' in Article 99(1)(f) is ambiguous and could be taken as referring to the territorial waters of any State, with the consequence that Article 99(1)(f) would not cover fish caught in the territorial sea of a third State. However, '*the* territorial waters' appears to be a drafting error, as the Danish, French, German, and Italian versions of Article 99(1)(f) are identical to Article 68(1)(f), although, compared with the English version, all use 'their' rather than 'its' ('their territorial waters', 'their vessels'): other language versions have not been consulted.

[19] Council Regulation (EEC) No 802/68 of 27 June 1968 on the Common Definition of the Concept of the Origin of Goods, OJ S Ed 1968 (I), 165, as amended (and now repealed), Art 4.

[20] Commission Regulation (EEC) No 2454/93 of 2 July 1993 laying down provisions for the implementation of Council Regulation (EEC) No 2913/92 establishing the Community Customs Code, OJ 1993 L253/1, as amended and corrected.

The Advocate General in *Pansard* supports his view by reference to the purpose of the Code, which is to raise income for the EC in the form of customs duties. He presumably considers that such income would be reduced if fish caught in the territorial sea of a third State by Community vessels were not considered to be imports. That overlooks the fact that under Article 188 of the Code customs duties are not levied on such fish (see further subsection 3.2 below). The Advocate General also appears to overlook the practical difficulties of determining the origin of fish according to the maritime zone in which the catch was taken. Those difficulties would be avoided if the origin of the catch were determined by the nationality of the vessel making the catch rather than its location, which would follow from the French government's interpretation. Nevertheless, whatever problems there may be with the Advocate General's interpretation of Article 23 of the Customs Code, that interpretation is supported by Article 188 of the Code, which, as mentioned, exempts fish caught by a Community vessel in a third State's territorial sea from customs duties: that provision must presuppose that such fish would otherwise be subject to duties, ie that they do not originate in a Member State. The Advocate General's interpretation is also supported by the rules of origin applying to exports from third States to the EC (discussed in subsection 3.2 below) and Article 325 of Commission Regulation 2454/93, which lays down a system of documentation for fish to be considered as originating in the EC: that system applies to 'the products of sea-fishing caught by a Community fishing vessel, in waters other than the territorial waters of a country or territory outside the customs territory of the Community'. The Advocate General's position also reflects the fact that under international law the territorial sea is considered to be part of the territory of a State,[21] as is indeed implicitly recognized in Article 23(3) of the Customs Code (referred to above).

As mentioned above, Regulation 2913/92 is gradually being replaced by Regulation 450/2008. The provision of Regulation 450/2008 that is said by the latter to correspond to Article 23 of Regulation 2913/92 is Article 36.[22] The latter only corresponds to Article 23(1) of Regulation 2913/92, however. There is nothing in Article 36 (or elsewhere in Regulation 450/2008) that corresponds to Article 23(2) and (3) of Regulation 2913/92. Article 4(18) of Regulation 450/2008 defines 'Community goods' as 'goods wholly obtained in the customs territory of the Community', and the latter territory includes, according to Article 3(1), the territorial sea of that territory. Article 133 of Regulation 450/2008 corresponds to Article 188 of Regulation 2913/92 (dealing with fish caught by Community vessels in the territorial sea of third States). Thus, there is no provision in Regulation 450/2008 that deals with the customs status of fish caught by Community vessels outside the territorial sea of a Member State or of a third State. In its proposal for what became Regulation 450/2008, the Commission explained that

---

[21] United Nations Convention on the Law of the Sea, 1833 UNTS 396, Art 2(1). See further Chapter 3.   [22] Reg 450/2008, Annex, Correlation Tables.

no provisions on rules of origin were included in the draft regulation because international harmonization work under the World Trade Organization (WTO) Agreement on Rules of Origin had not been completed at that time: such provisions would subsequently be included in legislation implementing Regulation 450/2008.[23] Until such legislation is adopted, Regulation 2454/93 will govern the situation, in particular Articles 68, 99, and 325 (discussed above).

The question as to the origin of fish for trade purposes has also arisen in the context of the, presumably rather unusual, situation where fish are caught by a vessel registered in a third State and the nets with the catch still in them are then transferred to a Community vessel. In *Commission v United Kingdom* the Court held that in such circumstances the catch does not originate in a Member State but in the third State concerned.[24] The same reasoning would appear to be applicable to the rather more common situation of transhipment, a matter that is not addressed by the Community Customs Code and its implementing legislation. If so, fish caught by a vessel registered in a third State and transhipped to a Community vessel would not be of Community origin. That would be so regardless of where the transhipment took place; otherwise by transhipping to a Community vessel in the territorial sea or port of a Member State, a third State vessel would easily be able to avoid the custom duties that would otherwise be payable. While the Community Customs Code does not deal with the issue of transhipment, it does cover the situation where catches are transferred from the vessel making the catch to another vessel for processing. Article 23(2)(g) of Regulation 2913/92 (and Articles 68(1)(g) and 99(1)(g) of Regulation 2454/93) provide that where goods are produced on board a factory ship registered in a Member State from fish caught by a Community vessel, they will be of Community origin: if either the factory ship or the catching vessel is not registered in a Member State, the processed goods will not be of Community origin.

To sum up: fishery products *will* 'originate' in a Member State for the purposes of EC law on the free movement of goods, if: (a) they are wholly produced on the territory of that Member State (for example, from aquaculture, inland fishing, or the processing of fish either originating in that Member State or, if imported from a third State, in free circulation in that Member State); (b) they are caught by Community fishing vessels registered in that Member State in (i) the internal waters or territorial sea of that Member State, (ii) the EEZ or EFZ of that or any other Member State, (iii) on the high seas or (iv) the EEZ or EFZ of a third State; or (c) they are produced on board a factory ship registered in that Member State from fish caught by a Community fishing vessel registered in the same Member State. Fishery products will *not* originate in a Member State if transhipped to a vessel registered in that Member State from a vessel registered in another Member

---

[23] *Implementing the Community Lisbon Programme. Proposal for a Regulation of the European Parliament and the Council laying down the Community Customs Code (Modernized Customs Code)*, COM(2005) 608, 30.11.2005, p 9.

[24] Case 100/84 *Commission v United Kingdom* [1985] ECR 1169, paras 19–22.

State or a third State. There is uncertainty as to the status of origin of fish caught by Community fishing vessels registered in a Member State in the territorial sea of another Member State or a third State.

2.2 Customs duties and charges of equivalent effect

As mentioned above, the free movement of goods provisions of the EC Treaty contain three sets of prohibitions designed to achieve free trade between Member States. First, Article 25 EC prohibits customs duties on imports and exports between Member States and 'charges having equivalent effect'. While the concept of customs duties is well known and straightforward, that of 'charges having equivalent effect' is much less so. There are a number of significant terms relating to the free movement of goods used in the EC Treaty (including 'charges having equivalent effect') for which no definition is provided either in the Treaty or secondary legislation. In all those cases the Court has provided definitions that it has applied consistently over many years. In the case of 'charges having equivalent effect', the term has been defined by the Court to mean 'any pecuniary charge, however small and whatever its designation and mode of application, which is imposed unilaterally on domestic goods by virtue of the fact that they cross a frontier, and which is not a customs duty in the strict sense . . . even if it is not imposed for the benefit of the State, is not discriminatory or protective in effect and if the product on which the charge is imposed is not in competition with the domestic product'.[25] There are, however, two types of charge that may be levied by a Member State on imports or exports that will not be regarded as 'charges having equivalent effect' to customs duties and so will not fall foul of Article 25. The first is a charge for a service that is of direct benefit to the trader and that represents no more than the cost of that service.[26] The second is a charge for the inspection of goods crossing a frontier that is required by EC law, provided that the fee for such an inspection does not exceed its actual cost, that the inspection is mandatory and uniform for all the products concerned in the EC and is prescribed by EC law in the general interest, and that such inspection promotes the free movement of goods, in particular by neutralizing obstacles to trade that could arise from unilateral inspections.[27] As far as fishery products are concerned, there is EC legislation that requires the inspection of some such products.[28]

---

[25] Case 24/68 *Commission v Italy* [1969] ECR 193, para 9.

[26] See, for example, Case 170/88 *Ford España v Spain* [1990] ECR 2305.

[27] Case 18/87 *Commission v Germany* [1988] ECR 5427, para 8. For further discussion of these two types of charge, see Barnard, *The Substantive Law of the EU*, 41–4.

[28] The main such legislation is Council Directive 2002/99/EC of 16 December 2002 laying down animal health rules governing the production, processing, distribution and introduction of products of animal origin for human consumption, OJ 2003 L18/11; and Regulation (EC) No 854/2004 of the European Parliament and of the Council of 29 April 2004 laying down specific rules for the organisation of official controls on products of animal origin intended for human consumption, OJ 2004 L226/83, as amended and corrected.

Only two cases concerning Article 25 EC that relate to fishery products appear to have come before the Court. In *United Foods*[29] the Court considered that Belgian legislation imposing a levy to cover the cost of health checks on imported fish was contrary to Article 25 because that levy lacked 'objective justification, in accordance with particular criteria concerning the nature or condition of the goods, which [were] not comparable to the criteria used in fixing pecuniary charges on domestic products of the same kind'.[30] In *Koornstra*[31] a Dutch regulation imposed a levy on Dutch vessels transporting shrimp in order to finance the purchase and operation by the Fish Marketing Board of shrimp sieves and peelers. The levy was payable whether the shrimp were landed in the Netherlands or another Member State. In a request for a preliminary ruling the Court was asked whether the levy constituted either a charge of equivalent effect to a customs duty, contrary to Article 25 EC, or discriminatory taxation, contrary to Article 90 EC (discussed in subsection 2.3 below). Having noted that the levy imposed a heavier burden on vessels landing shrimp in another Member State (ie for export) than in the Netherlands because they received no benefit from the equipment financed by the levy, the Court held that it was for the national court to determine whether the levy fell within Article 25 or Article 90 in the light of all the circumstances. If 'the advantages stemming from the use of the revenue' from the levy 'fully offset the burden borne' by vessels landing shrimp in the Netherlands (the 'advantages' to which the Court refers are presumably the benefits to such vessels of the equipment purchased out of the levy), the levy would be a charge equivalent to a duty on exports, contrary to Article 25 EC. If, on the other hand, the advantages referred to 'offset only partially the burden borne' by vessels landing shrimp in the Netherlands, the levy would constitute discriminatory taxation contrary to Article 90 EC (presumably because while both those landing shrimp in the Netherlands and those landing elsewhere would bear a financial burden, that burden would fall less heavily on those landing shrimp in the Netherlands).[32]

2.3 Discriminatory taxation

The second set of prohibitions designed to ensure free movement of goods is that concerned with discriminatory taxation. If imported goods are taxed more heavily than domestic goods, the latter will gain a competitive advantage, thus undermining the idea of the EC as a single market. Article 90 EC aims to prevent that. Article 90(1) provides that 'no Member State shall impose, directly or indirectly, on the products of other Member States any internal taxation of any kind in excess

---

[29] Case 132/80 *NV United Foods and Van den Abeele v Belgian State* [1981] ECR 995.
[30] Case 132/80, para 43.
[31] Case C-517/04 *Visserijbedrijf D J Koornstra & Zn vof v Productschap Vis* [2006] ECR I-5015.
[32] Case C-517/04, para 26. See also para 28.

of that imposed directly or indirectly on similar domestic products'. That provision thus prohibits both directly and indirectly discriminatory taxation. There is direct discrimination if a tax is levied only on imported goods and not on 'similar domestic products'. According to the Court, products are similar if they have similar characteristics and meet the same needs of consumers;[33] or, put another way, if they can be substituted interchangeably. There is indirect discrimination if a tax, although applicable to all goods of a particular kind, falls in practice more heavily on imported goods than domestic products. However, indirectly discriminatory tax will not be contrary to Article 90(1) if based on objective criteria that are designed to achieve economic policy objectives that are compatible with EC law and applied so as to avoid discrimination.[34] Article 90(2) prohibits the taxation of imported goods which, even if not 'similar' to domestic goods, are in some degree of competition with them, if such a tax is of 'such a nature as to afford indirect protection' to domestic goods.[35] The only case concerning Article 90 and fishery products appears to be *Koornstra* (discussed above).

2.4 Quantitative restrictions and measures of equivalent effect

The final set of provisions of the EC Treaty designed to ensure free movement of goods between Member States deals with quantitative restrictions and measures of equivalent effect. Article 28 provides that '[q]uantitative restrictions on imports and all measures having equivalent effect shall be prohibited between Member States', while Article 29 contains a similar prohibition in respect of exports. The Court has defined quantitative restrictions as 'measures which amount to a total or partial restraint of . . . imports, exports or goods in transit'.[36] 'Measures having equivalent effect' to quantitative restrictions have been defined by the Court, in what is known as the *Dassonville* formula, as 'all trading rules enacted by Member States which are capable of hindering, directly or indirectly, actually or potentially, intra-Community trade'.[37] That formula is extremely wide and is capable of catching a large number of national measures relating to trade, production, and marketing. It includes not only overtly protective measures or measures that apply solely to imports or exports (which are known as distinctly applicable measures), but also measures that apply equally to imported (or exported) and domestic products alike, often for apparently beneficial purposes (such as regulating

---

[33] Case 106/84 *Commission v Denmark* [1986] ECR 833 (especially para 12).
[34] Case 140/79 *Chemial Farmaceutici v DAF* [1981] ECR 1.
[35] Case 184/85 *Commission v Italy* [1987] ECR 2013. For further discussion of the scope of Art 90, see Barnard, *The Substantive Law of the EU*, 45–63.
[36] Case 2/73 *Geddo v Ente Nazionale Risi* [1973] ECR 865, para 7.
[37] Case 8/74 *Procureur du Roi v Dassonville* [1974] ECR 837, para 5.

the quality of goods), but which may nevertheless have a restraining effect on intra-Community trade. The latter kinds of measures are known as indistinctly applicable measures.[38]

There are two exceptions to the prohibition in Article 28. The first, which also applies to Article 29, is contained in Article 30, and reads as follows:

> The provisions of Articles 28 and 29 shall not preclude prohibitions or restrictions on imports, exports or goods in transit justified on grounds of public morality, public policy or public security; the protection of health and life of humans, animals or plants; the protection of national treasures possessing artistic, historic or archaeological value; or the protection of industrial and commercial property. Such prohibitions or restrictions shall not, however, constitute a means of arbitrary discrimination or a disguised restriction on trade between Member States.

The Court has added that for a measure to be justified under Article 30 it must be necessary to achieve the objective desired (in terms of the grounds listed in Article 30) and it must not be possible to achieve that objective by means that are less restrictive of intra-EC trade (the principle of proportionality).[39] Furthermore, the matter with which the national measure is concerned must not be governed by specific EC legislation intended to harmonize the area in question, at least where harmonization is total.[40]

Of the various grounds listed in Article 30, the one that in practice is likely to be most relevant to trade in fishery products is the protection of the health and life of humans and animals. However, as indicated, that ground cannot be invoked if EC legislation totally harmonizing national laws in that field already exists. In the case of fishery products, there is, in fact, a considerable body of legislation on public health. (There is some discussion of that legislation in subsection 3.2 below, but it is beyond the scope of this book to attempt a comprehensive discussion.) Where there is no comprehensive EC legislation in existence, a Member State may invoke the public health exception in Article 30, but the Court has held that to do so, the Member State must be able to produce convincing scientific evidence of the threat to health that the measure in question seeks to counter and to demonstrate that the measure meets a real need.[41]

The second exception to the prohibition on measures having equivalent effect to quantitative restrictions on imports is the so-called 'rule of reason' developed by

---

[38] However, the Court has held that the *Dassonville* formula does not apply to indistinctly applicable measures relating to selling arrangements: see Joined Cases C-267/91 and C-268/91 *Keck and Mithouard* [1993] ECR I-6097 and Case C-405/98 *Gourmet International* [2001] ECR I-1795.

[39] Case C-131/93 *Commission v Germany* [1994] ECR I-3303, para 18; and Case C-24/00 *Commission v France* [2004] ECR I-1277, para 52.

[40] Case C-169/89 *Van den Burg* [1990] ECR I-2143, para 8; and Case C-350/97 *Monsees* [1999] ECR I-2921, para 24. See further Barnard, *The Substantive Law of the EU*, 88–90.

[41] Case C-228/91 *Commission v Italy*, para 28; and Case C-24/00 *Commission v France*, para 53.

the Court in the *Cassis de Dijon* case, so known because of the eponymous liqueur at the centre of the case. The Court held that:

In the absence of common rules . . . [o]bstacles to movement within the Community resulting from disparities between the national laws relating to the marketing of the products in question must be accepted in so far as those provisions may be recognized as being necessary in order to satisfy mandatory requirements relating in particular to fiscal super-vision, the protection of public health, the fairness of commercial transactions and the defence of the consumer.[42]

Thus, for a trading measure to satisfy the rule of reason it must relate to a 'mandatory requirement', be 'necessary', and not relate to a matter covered by a Community harmonization measure ('the absence of common rules'). A national measure that satisfies those requirements will not contravene Article 28, even though it appears to fall within the *Dassonville* formula. The Court has added to the (non-exhaustive) list of mandatory requirements set out in *Cassis de Dijon* in a number of later cases, notably by including protection of the environment.[43]

At first sight there appears to be a substantial degree of overlap between Article 30 and the rule of reason. One of the most frequently invoked grounds under Article 30 (protection of public health) is the same as one of the mandatory requirements of the rule of reason, and both Article 30 and the rule of reason require national trading measures to be necessary and not relate to a matter totally covered by an EC measure. However, in practice the two serve different purposes. Article 30 is used in practice by the Court to test the lawfulness of a distinctly applicable measure (ie a measure applying solely to imports or exports) that falls within the *Dassonville* formula of being equivalent to a quantitative restriction, whereas the rule of reason is used by the Court to judge the lawfulness of an indistinctly applicable measure (ie one applying equally to imported and domestic products alike): if such a measure satisfies the rule of reason it will not contravene Article 28.[44]

About a dozen cases concerning fishery products and the prohibition on quantitative restrictions and measures of equivalent effect have come before the Court. Three cases concern catch quotas. In those cases it was argued that such quotas breach Article 29 by restricting the amount of fish that may be exported. The Court has consistently rejected such arguments, taking the view that catch quotas introduced for reasons of fisheries conservation fall outside the scope of Article 29 because they are concerned with production, whereas the prohibition on quantitative restrictions and equivalent measures is concerned with a different stage of the economic process, namely marketing: in any case, quotas are designed to increase supplies to consumers by restricting production in the short term in

---

[42] Case 120/78 *Rewe-Zentrale AG v Bundesmonopolverwaltung für Branntwein* [1979] ECR 649, para 8.

[43] Case 302/86 *Commission v Denmark* [1988] ECR 4607.

[44] Steiner, J, Woods, L, and Twigg-Flesner, C, *EU Law* (9th edn, Oxford: Oxford University Press, 2006), 378. Note that Art 29 EC does not apply to indistinctly applicable measures: ibid, 390–1.

order to lead to a sustainable optimum yield in the long run.[45] The Court's consistent approach in those cases is obviously to be welcomed.

The remaining cases all involve what were fairly obviously breaches of Article 28, with the question in most of the cases being whether those breaches were saved by the exception in Article 30. A first group concerns bans or restrictions on the landing of catches. In *Commission v Ireland* the Court found a complete prohibition imposed by Ireland on the landing in Ireland of catches by British vessels unless 75 per cent of the crew were EC nationals and ordinarily resident in the UK (which was designed to address the problem of quota hopping, discussed in Chapter 4) was contrary to Article 28.[46] Ireland did not attempt to justify the measure under Article 30. *Pansard* (discussed above) concerned a prohibition on the landing of scallops in France (wherever caught) that was designed to reinforce a ban on scallop fishing in France's territorial sea during the summer months. Pansard was prosecuted for landing scallops caught in Jersey's territorial sea during the prohibited period but argued in her defence that the landing ban was contrary to EC law. While the Court discussed the issue purely in terms of the scope of the competence of the Member States to adopt fisheries conservation measures (see Chapter 4), the Advocate General also discussed the matter from the point of view of free movement of goods. He concluded that the prohibition on landings breached Article 28. Although the prohibition was for the protection of the health and life of animals within the meaning of Article 30, it was not justified by that Article because it was disproportionate as it applied to scallops wherever caught, whereas the ban on catching scallops applied only to France's territorial sea.[47] The third case of the group concerned with landing bans is *Commission v United Kingdom*.[48] That case related to the validity in EC law of a number of national measures adopted by the UK, one of which was a restriction on the number of ports at which Irish fishermen could land herring caught in British waters. The Commission argued that that restriction was a breach of Article 28. The Court did not find it necessary to discuss that point, but the Advocate General appeared to favour the Commission's argument.[49] The question of whether a Member State may restrict the number of ports at which catches may be landed for the purpose of facilitating the enforcement of fisheries conservation measures (which was the motive for the UK's measure at issue in *Commission v United Kingdom*) has since been clarified by the Community legislature. Regulation 2847/93 (hereafter, 'the Control Regulation') (discussed extensively in Chapter 4) recognizes that as part of its powers to

---

[45] Joined Cases 3, 4, and 6/76 *Officier van Justitie v Kramer*, paras 55–60; Case 46/86 *Albert Romkes v Officier van Justitie for the District of Zwolle* [1987] ECR 2671, para 24; and Case C-535/03 *R ex p Unitymark Ltd and North Sea Fishermen's Organisation v Department for Environment, Food and Rural Affairs* [2006] ECR I-2689, paras 50–51.

[46] Case C-280/89 *Commission v Ireland* [1992] ECR I-6185, para 14.

[47] *Pansard*, AG Opinion, paras 41–64.

[48] Case 32/79 *Commission v United Kingdom* [1980] ECR 2403.

[49] Case 32/79, AG Opinion, at 2473–2474.

adopt national measures going beyond the requirements of that Regulation, a Member State may designate (and hence restrict the number of) ports at which catches must be landed, subject to the right of the Commission to adopt limited and temporary exceptions.[50]

A second group of fisheries cases where there was clearly a breach of Article 28 all concerned bans imposed on imported fish for health reasons, and turned on whether such bans were justified under Article 30. In *Hahn*, a preliminary ruling, the Court held that a ban by Austria on imports of smoked salmon from Denmark because such imports contained listeria was saved by Article 30 because it was scientifically justified and proportionate.[51] On the other hand, in *Commission v Italy* the Court held that a ban on the import of fish with dead or devitalized nematode larvae as a result of prior treatment was not justified under Article 30 because Italy had failed to prove that the fish were a threat to health.[52] In *Commission v Germany* a prohibition imposed by Germany on imported live crayfish (except where licensed) because of the risk of spreading disease to native crayfish, of which hardly any were left in the wild, was found to be disproportionate, and therefore not justified by Article 30, because the same objective (to prevent the spread of disease) could have been achieved with less restrictive measures.[53] In *Motte*, a preliminary ruling, the Court left it to the national court to determine whether Belgian legislation prohibiting the addition of colourants to potted roe met the requirements of Article 30 in terms of scientific justification and proportionality.[54]

A final group of cases concerns inspections of imported fish on health grounds. Such inspections breach Article 28 unless authorized under EC legislation, but are in principle justifiable under Article 30. In *United Foods* (one aspect of which was discussed above), the Court, in response to a request for a preliminary ruling, considered that Belgian inspections of imported fish for health control purposes appeared to constitute a disguised restriction on trade, contrary to Article 30, because of the length of notice that the importer had to give of import, the fact that inspections could take place only at certain locations and times, and the fact that the fish had to undergo inspection even if they had already been inspected in their State of origin. A definitive determination was, however, a matter for the national court.[55] In the other case in this group, *Commission v Italy*, the Italian authorities prohibited imports of fish from other Member States that contained nematode larvae (as mentioned above) and inspected consignments of fish to reinforce that prohibition. The Court found that such inspections were in principle permitted

---

[50] Council Regulation (EEC) No 2847/93 of 12 October 1993 establishing a control system applicable to the common fisheries policy, OJ 1993 L261/1, as amended, Arts 7 and 38.

[51] Case C-121/00 *Walter Hahn* [2002] ECR I-9193.

[52] Case C-228/91 *Commission v Italy*, para 28. [53] Case C-131/93 *Commission v Germany*.

[54] Case 247/84 *Motte* [1985] ECR 3887.

[55] Case 132/80 *NV United Foods and Van den Abeele v Belgian State*, paras 19–31.

under Article 30, but insofar as Italy had carried out systematic checks on imported fish that were accompanied by a health certificate from the exporting State to the effect that the fish were free of nematode larvae, its actions were not justified under Article 30. Such systematic checks were disproportionate; spot checks would have been sufficient.[56]

Finally, it is worth moving briefly from decided cases to the realms of speculation. If a Member State were to seek to ban imports of fish from another Member State on the ground that such fish had been taken in contravention of applicable EC measures to conserve fish stocks or, pursuant to Article 6 EC, to minimize the impact of fishing on the wider marine environment (hereafter, in this subsection, 'EC measures'), would that be contrary to EC law? The Court has held that measures adopted for reasons of fisheries conservation (whether at national level or at EC level) do *not* constitute measures having an effect equivalent to quantitative restrictions because such measures aim to ensure a sustainable yield from fishing in the long term (see case law cited at footnote 45). It is arguable that the same should be said of actions, including import bans, intended to *enforce* fisheries conservation measures. That said, any import ban adopted at the national level for that purpose would presumably have a greater degree of protection from a challenge based on trade restriction arguments if it were to have been adopted pursuant to a power or duty established by EC legislation. Therefore, the following analysis will consider briefly EC legislation adopted under the CFP that requires or allows import bans on fishery products in the context of intra-EC trade.

A Member State is not explicitly authorized by EC legislation as currently applicable to ban the landing in its ports of catches taken by the vessels of another Member State. However, it is implicitly authorized to do so by the Control Regulation. Under Articles 31(1)–(3) and 32(1) of that Regulation a Member State must take 'appropriate' measures, including by administrative action or criminal proceedings, where the rules of the CFP have not been 'respected': the sanctions 'arising from [such] proceedings' may include the seizure of prohibited catches. (Those provisions also apply in respect of the importing Member State's own vessels, so what is being considered here is in fact an indistinctly applicable measure.) It would seem to follow from Articles 31 and 32 of the Control Regulation that a Member State may temporarily hold a catch that the vessel of another Member State wishes to land where the first Member State (the port Member State) suspects that the catch has been taken in breach of EC measures (for example, because some of the fish are undersized or of a species for which the flag Member State does not hold a quota) until the port Member State's suspicions are confirmed in administrative or criminal proceedings or proceedings are transferred to the flag Member State. Where the port Member State's suspicions are confirmed, the catch may be confiscated. There will be some reinforcement of the above provisions of the Control Regulation from the beginning of 2010, when

---

[56] Case C-228/91 *Commission v Italy*, paras 17–26.

Regulation 1005/2008 (hereafter, 'the IUU Regulation'), which is aimed at combating illegal, unreported, and unregulated (IUU) fishing, takes effect.[57] Under Article 37(5) of that Regulation a Community vessel on the Community IUU vessel list may not enter the port of another Member State except for reasons of *force majeure* or distress; and if it does so, its catch must be confiscated. Alternatively a Member State may authorize the entry of such a vessel into its ports on the condition that catches on board are confiscated. Under Article 43(1), where a Member State suspects a natural person of having committed, or finds her/him in the act of committing, a 'serious infringement' (defined as including, *inter alia*, activities that constitute IUU fishing within the meaning of Article 3 of the Regulation[58]), or suspects a legal person of being liable for such an infringement, that State must start a full investigation of the infringement and take immediate enforcement measures such as seizure of the catch and fishery products. Articles 37(5) and 43(1) require (or in the case of Article 43(1), at least allows) a Member State, in effect, to ban the landing of catches by vessels of another Member State in the circumstances there specified.

The previous paragraph has considered EC legislation adopted under the CFP that requires or allows, explicitly or otherwise, a Member State to ban the landing in its ports of catches taken by the vessels of another Member State. It is also necessary to consider the situation whereby fishery products from one Member State are imported into another Member State by some means other than being landed in the latter's ports (eg by air, rail or road). There is currently no EC law that authorizes a Member State to refuse such imports where the fish from which they have been produced have been caught in contravention of EC rules. The IUU Regulation, when it comes into operation, will not in principle change that position, since, aside from the landing of catches in port, it will regulate 'importation', a term defined in Article 2(11) of the Regulation as meaning 'the introduction of fishery products into the territory of the Community'. The authors take this phrase to refer to the introduction of fishery products from outside the EC, as opposed to products that originate in the EC. It may be recalled from the discussion in subsection 2.1 above that, broadly speaking, fishery products originate in the EC if they have been caught by a Community fishing vessel anywhere, with the possible exception of the territorial sea of third States. Consequently 'importation' covers only products from third States (including products caught by third State vessels and landed directly in a Member State port) and possibly the relatively small amount of fishery products caught by Community vessels in the territorial sea of third States.

Despite the exclusion from the scope of the IUU Regulation of imports from Member States (other than in the form of catches landed by a vessel registered in

---

[57] Council Regulation (EC) No 1005/2008 of 29 September 2008 establishing a Community system to prevent, deter and eliminate illegal, unreported and unregulated fishing, amending Regulations (EEC) No 2847/93, (EC) No 1936/2001 and (EC) No 601/2004 and repealing Regulations (EC) No 1093/94 and (EC) No 1447/1999, OJ 2008 L266/1.   [58] Reg 1005/2008, Art 42(1)(a).

one Member State in the ports of another), there are two provisions of the IUU Regulation that somewhat obliquely, and in certain circumstances, might permit a Member State to prohibit imports from another Member State. The first is Article 39, which provides that nationals of Member States shall not 'support' IUU fishing and that Member States must take 'appropriate action' with regard to such nationals. One could argue that 'supporting' IUU fishing could include exporting the products of IUU fishing, and that 'appropriate action' could include banning the import of such products. However, the examples of 'support' given in Article 39(1) suggest that that term is not intended to cover support in the form of selling and trading fishery products. The second provision that might permit a Member State to prohibit imports from another Member State is Article 43(1), which, as noted above, requires a Member State to take immediate enforcement measures (which may include seizure of the catch) in cases of the suspected or actual commission of a 'serious infringement'. The latter term includes, *inter alia*, 'the conduct of business directly connected to IUU fishing, including the trade in/or the importation of fishery products'.[59] It is not altogether clear that the reference to 'trade' includes intra-EC trade, since as seen, 'importation' has, at best, very limited application to imports from Member States.

It is difficult to see how, in practice, a Member State could prohibit imports of fishery products derived from fish caught in breach of EC rules from other Member States (other than when landed by Community fishing vessels in its ports) without some form of catch documentation scheme. However, any attempt by a Member State unilaterally to introduce such a scheme for imports from other Member States is likely to be condemned by the Court as disproportionate (since under the Control Regulation the Member State of export should have prevented the landing in its ports of catches taken in breach of EC rules[60]) and perhaps also as amounting to arbitrary discrimination and a disguised restriction on trade. Given that fishing that breaches EC rules falls within the definition of IUU fishing in the IUU Regulation[61] and that recital (5) of the Regulation states that the EC 'should substantially enhance its action against IUU fishing and adopt new regulatory measures designed to cover *all* facets of the phenomenon' (emphasis added), it is perhaps a matter of regret that the catch certification scheme that the IUU Regulation introduces for imports from third States into the EC (discussed in subsection 3.2 below) does not apply to intra-EC trade. Recital (9) justifies that position by pointing out that the provisions of the Control Regulation, especially on the monitoring of catches, establish a 'comprehensive system designed to monitor the legality of catches from Community fishing vessels'. That justification would have

---

[59] Reg 1005/2008, Art 42(1)(b).

[60] Where the fishery product to be exported from the Member State of export had been imported from a third State or processed from such imports, its import would be subject to compliance with the catch certification scheme introduced by the IUU Regulation (see subsection 3.2 below).

[61] See Art 2(2). See also Arts 3, 41, and 42.

some force if the Control Regulation was strictly applied by all Member States, but, as was seen in Chapter 4, that appears still to be some way from being the case.

So far the discussion has concerned the possibility for one Member State to ban imports of fishery products from another Member State where such products have been taken in breach of *EC* measures. Under Articles 8 and 9 of the Basic Regulation a Member State may, in certain circumstances, adopt *national* measures applicable to the vessels of other Member States (on which, see Chapter 4). These measures may apply to conservation of fish stocks or protection of the wider environment from fishing activities. May a Member State ban imports of fishery products from another Member State where such products have been taken in breach of national measures adopted by the first Member State? Arguably, the points made above in the context of *EC* measures—about the scope for applying the case law cited at footnote 45 to enforcement actions—are equally applicable in the context of *national* measures (cf the Advocate General's approach in *Pansard*—see above). Where the imports took the form of fishery products being landed directly in port, it is arguable that the points made above regarding Article 31(1)–(3) of the Control Regulation in the context of EC measures should apply likewise to national measures adopted under the CFP. However, where the act of import was by another means, the same kind of considerations would apply as in the case of a Member State attempting to prohibit imports of fishery products taken in breach of EC measures, as discussed above.

3 The regulation of trade between the EC and third States

3.1 Introduction

The legal framework regulating trade in fishery products between the EC and third States has a number of components. First, there is the basic Regulation on the common organization of the markets in fishery products (hereafter, 'the Markets Regulation')[62] and measures adopted thereunder. As was explained in Chapter 6, there has been a succession of such Regulations since 1970. Each has contained a title dealing with trade with third States (Title V in the current Regulation). Over time the provisions in that title have gradually decreased in number and become less complex. That development is largely due to the need to comply with various agreements concluded in 1974 within the framework of the WTO (of which the EC and all its Member States are members). Article 40 of the Markets Regulation provides that it is to be applied so that it takes account at the same time of the objectives both of the CFP and of the common commercial policy (the objectives

---

[62] Reg 104/2000.

of the latter being set out in Article 131 EC). The second component of the legal framework regulating trade in fishery products between the EC and third States is the general body of EC trade law, particularly that concerned with customs duties, dumping, and subsidies, which applies as much to trade in fishery products as any other kinds of goods. The third component is a number of trade and commercial agreements between the EC and individual third States or groupings of third States (such as the African, Caribbean, and Pacific (ACP) States) that contain provisions on trade in fishery products. The fourth component is the general body of international trade law, particularly that stemming from the WTO, which provides an overarching framework within which EC trade with third States must operate. For the reasons explained in Chapter 5, trade and commercial agreements with third States and agreements concluded within the framework of the WTO are part of EC law. However, as also explained in Chapter 5, the provisions of those agreements cannot be invoked by natural or legal persons in proceedings before national courts to challenge the validity of acts of the EC institutions. A further component of the legal framework regulating trade in fishery products between the EC and third States is the Convention on International Trade in Endangered Species of Wild Fauna and Flora,[63] which regulates trade in, *inter alia*, a number of commercially exploited aquatic species. That Convention and its implementation by the EC are discussed in Chapter 5, and therefore are not considered further in this chapter.

The law regulating the import of fishery products from third States into the EC is quite different from that regulating the export of such products from the EC to third States. Each is therefore considered separately.

3.2 The regulation of imports

Since its inception the EC has never been self-sufficient in fish and therefore has always been a net importer of fishery products.[64] It is thus obviously not in the interests of consumers for the EC to discourage the import of fish, provided that it is of good quality: to the latter end, there is EC legislation (discussed below) that imposes health and quality controls on imported fish. Processors also require a liberal import regime for many kinds of fish used as the raw material in fish processing. While the unrestricted import of fish may be in the interests of consumers and many processors, it is not necessarily in the interests of EC fishermen. The EC uses a number of forms of regulation—customs duties, reference prices, anti-dumping and countervailing duties, and safeguard measures—that influence the price and/or volume of imported fish in order to prevent excessive

---

[63] 993 UNTS 243.

[64] Lequesne, C, *The Politics of Fisheries in the European Union* (Manchester: Manchester University Press, 2004), 14–15 and 131.

damage to EC fishermen by competition from imports. It is also worth recalling here a non-trade measure to aid EC fishermen, the compensatory allowance for tuna producers, discussed in Chapter 6, which is designed to provide some protection to EC tuna fishermen from fluctuating prices due to conditions on the world market.

It is EC policy to give products caught by EC fishermen priority on the EC market by means of the forms of regulation just mentioned.[65] The Court has, however, emphasized that such Community preference is a matter of policy, not a legal requirement: EC law does not prevent the adoption of tariff measures that increase competition for EC producers.[66] Import regulation for a rather different objective has developed in recent years with the EC seeking to encourage sustainable fishing by prohibiting the import of fishery products into the EC that are the product of IUU fishing.

In this section each of these different forms of regulating imports is examined in turn, beginning with measures to provide some protection to EC fishermen from imports. At the outset it should be borne in mind that, just as with intra-EC trade, import from a third State into the EC may be by means not only of carriage by road, rail, sea, or air, but also of a third State vessel directly landing its catch at a designated port of an EC Member State, provided that certain conditions are observed.[67] A new set of conditions will have to be met from the beginning of 2010 when the IUU Regulation takes effect.[68] Under that Regulation a third State fishing vessel wishing to access the port of a Member State (and only designated ports may be accessed) will be required, *inter alia*, to notify the Member State whose port it wishes to use at least three days before its estimated time of arrival, to carry a catch certificate validated by its flag State to the effect that its catches carried on board have been made in accordance with all applicable laws and regulations, and to submit a declaration indicating the amount of fish to be landed and when and where it was caught.[69] Further measures applying to third State vessels under the IUU Regulation are discussed below.

Customs duties

A first means of protecting EC fishermen is to impose customs duties on imported fish, thereby increasing its price and reducing the possibility of EC fishermen being undercut by cheaper imports. As the EC is a customs union, only the EC,

---

[65] Commission, *Reform of the Common Organisation of the Markets in fishery and aquaculture products*, Information Notes, 22.12.1999, 2, available on the website of DG Mare.

[66] Case C-342/03 *Spain v Council* [2005] ECR I-1975, paras 18–19 and 24.

[67] Council Regulation (EC) No 1093/94 of 6 May 1994 setting out the terms under which fishing vessels of a third country may land directly and market their catches at Community ports, OJ 1994 L121/3.   [68] Reg 1005/2008, Arts 56 and 57. Art 57 repeals Reg 1093/94.

[69] Reg 1005/2008, Arts 4(2) and 5–8. See also the Regulation's provisions on port inspections of third State vessels, in Arts 9–11. The catch certification scheme referred to is discussed below.

and not its individual Member States, may impose customs duties on imports. Nor may Member States impose charges of equivalent effect to customs duties on imports.[70] The products subject to such duties and the level of duties—the common customs tariff (CCT)—are laid down for all products (including fish) in Part Two of Annex I to Regulation 2658/87.[71] Since the CCT is frequently revised, an amended version of Annex I is adopted each year. In general customs duties are higher on processed fishery products than on unprocessed fish, thus reflecting the interests of EC fish processors in particular. The CCT applies to goods of non-Community origin. As was seen in subsection 2.1 above, Article 23 of the Community Customs Code provides that fishery products will be of non-Community origin if they were caught by a non-Community vessel outside the territorial sea of an EC Member State or produced on a non-Community factory ship. Where a Community vessel lands its catch in a third State for processing and such processing 'result[s] in the manufacture of a new product or represent[s] an important stage of manufacture', any such processed fish that is subsequently exported to the EC will also be of non-Community origin.[72] According to the Advocate General's interpretation of Article 23 of the Community Customs Code in *Pansard* (see subsection 2.1 above), fish will also be of non-Community origin if they are caught by a Community vessel in the territorial sea of a third State (although as pointed out in subsection 2.1 above, there are counter-arguments to that interpretation). As mentioned in subsection 2.1, the current Community Customs Code is in the process of being replaced.

There are, however, many cases where the customs duties set out in the CCT do not apply. First, because the EC is not self-sufficient in fish, duties are frequently reduced or suspended autonomously by the EC, for longer or shorter periods, in order to encourage increased supplies of fish for consumers and especially processors. By an 'autonomous' reduction or suspension is meant one that is not required as a consequence of a treaty to which the EC is a party. Autonomous reductions and suspensions are provided for by Article 28 of the Markets Regulation. The latter reduces or suspends duties on various kinds of fish (listed in Annex VI to the Markets Regulation) indefinitely in order to ensure an adequate supply of raw material for EC processors. In order not to jeopardize the various intervention measures applicable to EC fishermen (discussed in the previous chapter), imports of the fish listed in Annex VI must comply with the relevant reference price (explained below) if they are to benefit from the reduced or suspended duties. If, despite such compliance, there is a 'serious market disturbance', the Council, acting on a proposal from the Commission, may reinstate the full customs duty due under the CCT for the product

---

[70] Case C-125/94 *Aprile* [1995] ECR I-2919, paras 34–37.
[71] Council Regulation (EEC) No 2658/87 of 23 July 1987 on the tariff and statistical nomenclature and on the Common Customs Tariff, OJ 1987 L256/1, as amended and corrected.
[72] Reg 2913/92, Art 24.

concerned.[73] In addition to reductions and suspensions of customs duties under Article 28 of the Markets Regulation, there are further autonomous reductions or suspensions by the Council from time to time for specified quotas[74] of particular products (usually those in more direct competition with EC fishermen) for certain periods of time, provided that the declared customs value of the products is at least equal to the reference price.[75] Once the quota is exhausted, the full duty becomes payable. In a report on the implementation of the Markets Regulation published in 2006, the Commission observed that the arrangements just described appeared insufficient to meet the needs of processors, but that it would be inappropriate to change the system until the then ongoing WTO negotiations on market access were concluded.[76] At the time of writing such negotiations had still not been concluded.

A second reason why the full customs duties under the CCT are not payable on many imports of fishery products is because of provisions in various trade agreements between the EC and third States. Such agreements include bilateral trade agreements with a number of developing States, such as Algeria,[77] Chile,[78] Mexico,[79] Morocco,[80]

---

[73] Reg 104/2000, Art 29(3).

[74] The term 'quotas' as used in this subsection refers to tariff quotas, ie amounts of fishery product subject to particular tariff arrangements. Such quotas are to be distinguished from catch quotas referred to in, *inter alia*, Chapters 3–5.

[75] For examples of such measures, see Council Regulation (EC) No 975/2003 of 5 June 2003 opening and providing for the administration of a tariff quota for imports of canned tuna covered by CN codes 1604 14 11, 1604 14 18 and 1604 20 70, OJ 2003 L141/1; and Council Regulation (EC) No 824/2007 of 10 July 2007 opening and providing for the management of autonomous Community tariff quotas for certain fishery products for the period 2007 to 2009, OJ 2007 L184/1. Reg 975/2003, which resulted from WTO mediation of a dispute between Thailand and the Philippines on one side and the EC on the other (see recital (1) of the Regulation), was the object of an unsuccessful challenge by Spain in Case C-342/03 *Spain v Council*. For a brief account of the WTO mediation, see Van den Bossche, P, *The Law and Policy of the World Trade Organization* (2nd edn, Cambridge: Cambridge University Press, 2008), 177–8.

[76] *Report from the Commission to the Council and the European Parliament on the implementation of Council Regulation (EC) No 104/2000 on the common organisation of the markets in fishery and aquaculture products*, COM(2006) 558, 29.9.2006, p 10.

[77] Euro-Mediterranean Agreement establishing an Association between the European Community and its Member States, of the one part, and the People's Democratic Republic of Algeria, of the other part, OJ 2005 L265/2, Arts 14 and 18, and Protocol 3.

[78] Agreement establishing an Association between the European Community and its Member States, of the one part, and the Republic of Chile, of the other part, OJ 2002 L352/3, Arts 60 and 68.

[79] Economic Partnership, Political Coordination and Cooperation Agreement between the European Community and its Member States, of the one part, and the United Mexican States, of the other part, OJ 2000 L276/45, Art 5; and Decision No 2/2000 of the EC-Mexico Joint Council of 23 March 2000, OJ 2000 L157/10, Arts 7–10.

[80] Euro-Mediterranean Agreement establishing an Association between the European Community and its Member States, of the one part, and the Kingdom of Morocco, of the other part, OJ 2000 L70/2, Arts 15–18 and Protocol 2.

South Africa,[81] and Tunisia,[82] under which imports of fishery products from those States enter the EC at nil or reduced duty (although in some cases a quota is set for the amount of imports that enjoy such tariff concessions); the Agreement on the European Economic Area (EEA),[83] under which customs duties are reduced or abolished for many (but by no means all) fishery products from Iceland, Liechtenstein, and Norway; an agreement with the Faroe Islands under which duties on nearly all imports of fishery products from the Faroe Islands are abolished;[84] and a protocol concerning Greenland under which duties on all fishery imports from Greenland are abolished.[85]

The Cotonou Agreement, between the seventy-nine ACP States and the EC,[86] likewise provides for a departure from the customs duties applicable under the CCT. Article 36(3) and Annex V, which continue the position applying under the predecessor Lomé Conventions, provide that fishery products from the ACP States may enter the EC duty-free. However, the Cotonou Agreement requires its parties 'gradually' to replace its original trading arrangements, including those in Article 36(3) and Annex V, by 'WTO compatible trading arrangements', in the form of economic partnership agreements (EPAs), by the end of 2007.[87] It was determined that EPAs should be concluded primarily with different groups of ACP States that were engaged in a regional economic integration process, rather

[81] Agreement on Trade, Development and Co-Operation between the European Community and its Member States, of the one part, and the Republic of South Africa, of the other part, OJ 1999 L311/3, Arts 13 and 14 and Annex V. The latter provides that tariff concessions shall not begin to operate until the fisheries agreement provided for in Art 62 has entered into force. Art 62 provides that the parties shall conclude a 'mutually beneficial' fisheries agreement providing for cooperation in promoting sustainable management and use of fishery resources. As no such agreement has yet been concluded, tariff concessions have not begun to operate. Although South Africa is a party to the Cotonou Agreement (discussed below), the provisions of its bilateral Agreement with the EC take precedence over the Cotonou Agreement: see Protocol 3 to the latter Agreement.

[82] Euro-Mediterranean Agreement establishing an Association between the European Community and its Member States, of the one part, and the Republic of Tunisia, of the other part, OJ 1998 L97/2, Arts 15–18 and Protocol 2.

[83] Agreement on the European Economic Area, OJ 1994 L1/3, Arts 8(3) and 20, and Protocol 9. Reduction in customs duties is coupled with increased access for Community fishing vessels to the maritime zones of Iceland and Norway: see further Chapter 5. For discussion of the trade provisions of the Agreement, see Churchill, RR and Ørebech, P, 'The European Economic Area and Fisheries', *IJMCL* 8 (1993), 453 at 454–7.

[84] Agreement between the European Community, of the one part, and the Government of Denmark and the Home Government of the Faroe Islands, of the other part, OJ 1997 L53/2, Protocol 1, as replaced by Decision No 1/1999 of the EC/Denmark–Faroe Islands Joint Committee, OJ 1999 L178/58, as amended.

[85] Protocol No 15 to the EC Treaty on Special Arrangements for Greenland, OJ 2006 C321E/254, Art 1. Abolition is conditional on 'the possibilities for access to Greenland fishing zones granted to the Community' being 'satisfactory to the Community' and on compliance with 'the mechanisms of the common market organisation'. See further Chapter 2.

[86] [Cotonou] Partnership Agreement, 2000, OJ 2000 L317/3, as amended.

[87] Cotonou Agreement, Arts 36(1) and (2) and 37.

than with individual ACP States.[88] Of the various ways in which trade arrangements with ACP States might be made WTO-compatible, it was decided to follow
the rules of the General Agreement on Tariffs and Trade (GATT) on free trade
areas.[89] That would allow the EC to continue to admit goods (including fishery
products) from the ACP States free of customs duties, but it would require the ACP
States to do likewise for imports from the EC.[90] The negotiation of EPAs has,
however, proved tough, complex, and protracted, and the 2007 deadline was not
met. By the time of writing (the end of November 2008), only one EPA had been
signed, namely an Agreement with fifteen Caribbean ACP States members of
CARIFORUM, which was signed in October 2008.[91] That agreement, in line with
the policy position just referred to, provides for the duty-free access of fishery
products from the CARIFORUM States to the EC.[92] Seven interim EPAs had also
been initialled (in November and December 2007).[93] In order to provide temporary
arrangements for trade with ACP States after the 2007 deadline, pending the conclusion and entry into force of EPAs, the EC adopted Regulation 1528/2007.[94]

[88] *Communication from the Commission to the European Parliament and the Council. Economic Partnership
Agreements*, COM(2007) 635, 23.10.2007, p 3.

[89] COM(2007) 635, p 4. The rules of the GATT on free trade areas are contained in Art XXIV. The
text of the GATT is available on the website of the WTO.   [90] COM(2007) 635, p 4.

[91] Economic Partnership Agreement between the CARIFORUM States, of the one part, and the
European Community and its Member States, of the other part, OJ 2008 L289/I/3.

[92] CARIFORUM-EC EPA, Art 15.

[93] Most of those agreements had been published in the COM series at the time of writing, as follows:
*Proposal for a Council Decision on the signature and provisional application of the stepping stone Economic Part-
nership Agreement between the European Community and its Member States, of the one part, and Côte d'Ivoire, of
the other part*, COM(2008) 438, 10.7.2008; *Proposal for a Council Decision on the signature and provisional
application of the stepping stone Economic Partnership Agreement between the European Community and its
Member States, of the one part, and Ghana, of the other part*, COM(2008) 440, 10.7.2008; *Proposal for a
Council Decision on the signature and provisional application of the stepping stone Economic Partnership Agreement
between the European Community and its Member States, of the one part, and Central Africa, of the other part*,
COM(2008) 445, 10.7.2008; *Proposal for a Council Decision on the signature and provisional application of the
agreement establishing a framework for an Economic Partnership Agreement between the European Community and
its Member States, of the one part, and the East African Community Partner States, of the other part*, COM
(2008) 521, 30.9.2008; and *Proposal for a Council Decision on the signature and provisional application of the
Interim Economic Partnership Agreement between the European Community and its Member States, of the one
part, and the SADC EPA States, of the other part*, COM(2008) 562, 18.9.2008. Two further agreements
had not been published in the COM series at the time of writing but are referred to on the website of
the European Commission's Directorate General for Trade. Those agreements are the Interim Partnership Agreement between the European Community and its Member States, of the one part, and the
Pacific States, of the other part; and the Interim Agreement establishing a framework for an Economic
Partnership Agreement between Eastern and Southern Africa States on one part and the European
Community and its Member States on the other part. Because the above seven agreements are nearly all
interim ones and have been no more than initialled, they are not discussed further in this chapter.

[94] Council Regulation (EC) No 1528/2007 of 20 December 2007 applying the arrangements for
products originating in certain states which are part of the African, Caribbean and Pacific (ACP) Group
of States provided for in agreements establishing, or leading to the establishment of, Economic
Partnership Agreements, OJ 2007 L348/1, as amended.

Under that Regulation fishery products originating from the thirty-six ACP States listed in Annex I to the Regulation with which the EC has conducted negotiations 'establishing or leading to the establishment of' EPAs may be imported into the EC free of customs duties,[95] thus continuing the position under the Cotonou Agreement and anticipating the position under the EPAs as far as fishery products are concerned. Those ACP States to which Regulation 1528/2007 does not apply comprise least-developed States enjoying tariff concessions under the system of generalized preferences (see below), States that have no significant exports to the EC, and South Africa, which has its own agreement with the EC (as seen above).

To benefit from the reduction or abolition of customs duties provided for in the agreements surveyed above, imports from the third States concerned must satisfy the rules of origin contained in those agreements.[96] Under those rules, which are all very similar, goods must be wholly obtained in the third State concerned. In the case of fishery products, that means that they must be caught in the territory (including the territorial sea) of the third State concerned, or caught by a vessel having the nationality of that State outside the territorial sea, or processed on a factory ship having the nationality of that State from fish caught by a vessel having the same nationality. Furthermore, fishing vessels and factory ships must not only have the nationality of the third State concerned, they must also be owned to the extent of at least 50 per cent by natural persons who are nationals of that State or by a company with its head office in that State, of which a majority of the members of the board and a majority of the shareholders are nationals of that State. In addition, at least 75 per cent (50 per cent in the case of the Cotonou Agreement) of the crew (including the master and officers) must also be nationals of the third State concerned. The purpose of those provisions, at least in part, is to prevent the EC's tariff concessions being taken advantage of by flags of convenience or by vessels having the nationality of States not party to the agreement in question which land their catches in, or have their catches processed on factory ships of, the third State concerned. As the Court put it in a case involving the interpretation of various aspects of the rules of origin in earlier arrangements relating to the Faroe Islands, the purpose of the provisions relating to the ownership and crew of fishing vessels is to ensure that vessels of the third State have a 'genuine economic link' with that State.[97] The

---

[95] Reg 1528/2007, Arts 1, 2(1), and 3(1).

[96] EC-Algeria Agreement, Protocol 6, Arts 2 and 6; EC-Chile Agreement, Annex III, Arts 2 and 4; Decision No 2/2000 of the EC-Mexico Joint Council of 23 March 2000, Annex III, OJ 2000 L245/953, Art 4; EC-Morocco Agreement, Protocol 4, Arts 2 and 6; EC-South Africa Agreement, Protocol I, Arts 2 and 4; EC-Tunisia Agreement, Protocol 4, Arts 2 and 6; EEA Agreement, Protocol 4, Art 3; EC-Faroe Islands Agreement, Protocol 3 (as amended), OJ 2006 L110/1, Arts 2 and 5; and Cotonou Agreement, Protocol 1 to Annex V, Arts 2–3. The Protocol with Greenland does not contain any rules of origin. That means, according to Art 188 EC, that the rules of origin applying to the OCTs (discussed below) apply to Greenland.

[97] Joined Cases C-153/94 and C-204/94 *The Queen v Commissioners of Customs & Excise, ex parte Faroe Seafood Co Ltd, Føroya Fiskasøla L/F* and *The Queen v Commissioners of Customs & Excise, ex parte Smith* [1996] ECR I-2465, para 44.

requirements of the rules of origin relating to the ownership and crew of fishing vessels have caused some unhappiness among ACP States[98] because the structure of the fishery sector in many of those States is based on vessel-chartering arrangements, joint ventures, and so on, which makes it impossible for many of the catches landed in those States to comply with the rules of origin and thus benefit from tariff concessions.[99] In 2005 the Commission proposed some relaxation to the rules of origin in relation to vessel requirements.[100] Some such relaxation is now starting to take place. Thus, Regulation 1528/2007, applying interim arrangements for trade with certain ACP States from the beginning of 2008, lays down rules of origin under which a vessel must be registered in and fly the flag of an ACP State, and be owned to at least 50 per cent by natural persons who are nationals of that ACP State or by a company having its head office and main place of business in that State and which is at least 50 per cent owned by public authorities or nationals of that State: there is no longer a crewing requirement.[101] Furthermore, fishery products will also originate in an ACP State if caught by a vessel chartered or leased by that State to undertake fisheries activities in its EEZ provided that that State offered the EC the opportunity to negotiate a fisheries agreement which the EC declined and that the charter or lease contract has been accepted by the Commission as providing adequate opportunities for the development of the capacity of that State to fish on its own account and as conferring on that State responsibility for the nautical and commercial management of the vessel.[102] Similar provisions are found in the first EPA that the EC has signed, that with the CARIFORUM States.[103] There are, however, indications that there is not complete satisfaction with the rules of origin contained in the CARIFORUM Agreement. In a Joint Declaration attached to that Agreement,[104] the parties agree that those rules 'have to be examined in order to determine what possible changes may have to be made in the light of the first paragraph', in which the EC 'acknowledges the right of the coastal CARIFORUM States to the development and rational exploitation of the fishery resources in all waters within their jurisdiction'. The Declaration goes on to state that, 'conscious of their respective concerns and interests', the parties 'agree to continue examining the problem posed by the entry, onto EC Party markets, of the fishery products from

[98] Expressed, *inter alia*, in Declaration XXXIX attached to the Cotonou Agreement.

[99] Coalition for Fair Fisheries Arrangements, *Comparing EU free trade agreements: Fisheries*, In Brief No 6J (2006), 7 and ibid, *ACP-EU Economic Partnership Agreements: Fisheries*, Discussion Paper No 69 (2005), 12, both available on the website of the European Centre for Development Policy Management.

[100] *Communication from the Commission to the Council, the European Parliament and the European Economic and Social Committee. The rules of origin in preferential trade arrangements. Orientations for the future*, COM (2005) 100, 16.3.2005, pp 8–9. See also COM(2007) 635, pp 5–6.

[101] Reg 1528/2007, Annex II, Art 3.

[102] Ibid. See further Campling, L, 'Rules of Origin for Fish in Interim EPAs' *Trade Negotiations Insights* 7 (2008), 7.   [103] CARIFORUM-EC EPA, Protocol I, Art 6.

[104] Joint Declaration relating to Protocol I on the Origin of Fishery Products, OJ 2008 L289/II/1954.

catches made in zones within the national jurisdiction of the CARIFORUM states, with a view to arriving at a solution satisfactory to both sides'.

A third means whereby customs duties on fishery products laid down by the CCT are not fully applied results from the EC's system of generalized preferences for imports from developing States, which has been in place since 1971.[105] Under that system the EC has autonomously reduced customs duties for fishery products by 3.5 percentage points in general.[106] For some fourteen States included in the special incentive arrangement for sustainable development and good governance and for some fifty least-developed States, duties on fisheries products are suspended entirely.[107] To benefit from those concessions, the States and territories concerned must comply with rules of origin that are very similar to those of the agreements with Algeria etc discussed above.[108] Interestingly and importantly, the tariff concessions made by the EC may be withdrawn if the State or territory concerned has engaged in 'serious and systematic infringements of the objectives' of regional fisheries management organizations (RFMOs) of which the EC is a member relating to the conservation and management of fishery resources.[109]

Fourthly, fishery products from the overseas countries and territories listed in Annex II to the EC Treaty (hereafter, 'OCTs', on which see Chapter 2) may be imported into the EC free of customs duties, provided that they comply with the rules of origin.[110] The latter are similar to those applicable under the Cotonou Agreement, with the added proviso that fishery products will also originate in an OCT if caught by a vessel chartered or leased by that OCT to undertake fisheries activities in its EEZ provided that: (a) that OCT offered the EC the opportunity to negotiate a fisheries agreement which the EC declined; (b) at least 50 per cent of the crew of the vessel are OCT, Member State, or ACP nationals; and (c) the charter or lease contract has been accepted by the Commission as providing adequate opportunities for the development of the capacity of that OCT to fish on its own account and as conferring on that OCT responsibility for the nautical and commercial management of the vessel.[111]

Lastly, under Article 188 of the Community Customs Code fish caught by a Community vessel in a third State's territorial sea are exempted from the CCT

---

[105] The current legislation governing the matter is Council Regulation (EC) No 980/2005 of 27 June 2005 applying a system of generalised tariff preferences, OJ 2005 L169/1, as amended. The Regulation lays down arrangements until the end of 2008.

[106] Reg 980/2005, Art 7(2) and Annex II.   [107] Reg 980/2005, Arts 8 and 12.

[108] Reg 980/2005, Art 5(2) and Reg 2454/93, Art 68.   [109] Reg 980/2005, Art 16(e).

[110] Arts 184(1) and 185 EC; and Council Decision 2001/822/EC of 27 November 2001 on the association of the overseas countries and territories with the European Community, OJ 2001 L314/1, as amended and corrected, Art 35. On Dec 2001/822, see further Chapter 2.

[111] Dec 2001/822/EC, Annex III, Art 3. Art 37 provides for the possibility of derogations from the rules of origin: see, regarding fishery products, Commission Decs 2007/767, OJ 2007 L310/19; 2007/167, OJ 2007 L76/32; 2005/578, OJ 2005 L197/31; 2003/673, OJ 2003 L243/106; 2002/644, OJ 2002 L211/16; and 2001/936, OJ 2001 L345/91.

(see also subsection 2.1 above).[112] That position will not change when the new Customs Code comes into effect.[113]

The result of all the exceptions just described is that around two-thirds of imported fishery products are not subject to the CCT.[114]

Reference prices

Article 29 of the Markets Regulation provides for a system under which certain tariff concessions are withdrawn where they result in the price of imported fish falling below the reference price. Article 29(1) provides that reference prices may be fixed for three different types of imported fishery product: (a) those products that are subject to 'tariff reduction or suspension arrangements, where the rules binding them in the WTO provide for compliance with a reference price'; (b) those products subject to the autonomous reduction or suspension of customs duties under Article 28(1) of the Markets Regulation (discussed above); and (c) those products that are subject to other arrangements that provide for compliance with a reference price and are in line with the EC's international obligations. Reference prices are fixed by the Commission each year by means of a Regulation, and in most cases relate to the various prices set under the Markets Regulation for intervention in the market that are discussed in the previous chapter. Thus, for the products listed in Parts A and B of Annex I to the Markets Regulation, which include fresh and chilled products of various finfish species (fourteen) and genera (six) and two cuttlefish species as well as certain products of two shrimp species, reference prices are the same as the Community withdrawal prices fixed for those products; and for the products listed in Part C of Annex I (which include certain products of sole, edible crab, and Norway lobster) and the frozen products listed in Annex II, they are the same as the Community selling prices for those products. For other kinds of products covered by the Markets Regulation, the reference price is to be fixed, in particular, on the basis of the weighted average of customs values recorded on import markets or ports of import in the Member States during the preceding three years, 'taking account of the need to ensure that [reference] prices reflect the market situation'.[115]

Reference prices operate as follows. Where the 'declared customs value' of an imported product is lower than the reference price for that product, the 'quantities concerned shall not qualify for the tariff arrangements in question',[116] ie for the arrangements listed in Article 29(1), whereupon customs duties under the CCT will then apply fully to such imports. This will presumably lead to an increase in the price of such imports.

---

[112] Further provision for this category of goods is made by Reg 2454/93, Art 856a.

[113] See Reg 450/2008, Art 133.

[114] Lequesne, *The Politics of Fisheries*, 132. It is not clear to which year(s) Lequesne's statement relates.   [115] Reg 104/2000, Art 29(3)(d).

[116] Reg 104/2000, Art 29(2).

The current system of reference prices is much more straightforward than the system of references prices found in the predecessors to the Markets Regulations.[117] That is due to the need to comply with WTO obligations.[118]

Anti-dumping and countervailing duties

Where EC producers are facing competition from imports that is considered to be unfair either because imported fishery products are being dumped on the EC market (ie sold at artificially low prices) or subsidized, it is possible for the EC to step in and provide protection under the commercial defence instruments of general EC trade law. Where products are dumped, the EC may impose an anti-dumping duty on the products concerned under Regulation 348/96.[119] In the case of subsidized imports, the EC may impose a countervailing duty under Regulation 2026/97,[120] which is designed to offset the subsidy granted to the import concerned. Both Regulations implement the WTO agreements dealing with those matters.[121]

As far as fishery products are concerned, the main use of anti-dumping and countervailing duties has been in respect of Norwegian farmed salmon, in what has become quite a saga of legislation and litigation. In response to complaints from Scottish salmon farmers, the Council from 1997 onwards adopted a succession of Regulations imposing anti-dumping or countervailing duties on imports of Norwegian farmed salmon. The most recent Regulation, Regulation 85/2006,[122] was challenged both before the CFI by individual Norwegian salmon farmers[123] and under the WTO's Dispute Settlement Understanding by the Norwegian government. In addition, an Estonian court requested a preliminary ruling on the meaning of certain provisions of the Regulation.[124] In the WTO case a panel found, in a report adopted by the WTO Dispute Settlement Body in January 2008, that the EC had acted inconsistently with a number of provisions of the WTO's Anti-Dumping Agreement.[125] The EC accepted the panel's ruling and repealed

---

[117] As to which, see Churchill, RR, *EEC Fisheries Law* (Dordrecht: Martinus Nijhoff, 1987), 264–7.

[118] *Proposal for a Council Regulation (EC) on the common organisation of the markets in fishery and aquaculture products*, COM(1999) 55, 16.02.1999, p 6.

[119] Council Regulation (EC) No 384/96 of 22 December 1995 on protection against dumped imports from countries not members of the European Community, OJ 1996 L56/1, as amended.

[120] Council Regulation (EC) No 2026/97 of 6 October 1997 on protection against subsidized imports from countries not members of the European Community, OJ 1997 L288/1, as amended.

[121] See further Barnard, *The Substantive Law of the EU*, 236–7.

[122] Council Regulation (EC) No 85/2006 of 17 January 2006 imposing a definitive anti-dumping duty and collecting definitively the provisional duty imposed on imports of farmed salmon originating in Norway, OJ 2006 L15/1.

[123] Case T-113/06 *Fjord Seafood Norway and Others v Council*, OJ 2006 C131/47; and Case T-115/06 *Fiskeri og Havbruksnæringens Landsforening and Others v Council*, OJ 2006 C143/32.

[124] Case C-56/08 *Pärlitigu*, judgment pending, OJ 2008 C92/19.

[125] WTO, *European Communities—Anti-Dumping Measure on Farmed Salmon from Norway*, Report of the Panel, WT/DS337/R, 16 November 2007, available on the website of the WTO.

the anti-dumping duty imposed by Regulation 85/2006.[126] That action was also the outcome of an internal EC review of Regulation 85/2006, initiated in April 2007 at the request of several Member States which argued that Norwegian farmed salmon was no longer being dumped on the EC market.[127] However, Regulation 85/2006 as a whole was not repealed in order to allow the market situation to continue to be monitored until the end of the period provided for by that Regulation, namely the end of 2011.[128] The two cases brought by Norwegian salmon farmers, which seek the annulment of Regulation 85/2006, were still pending before the CFI at the time of writing, as was the request for a preliminary ruling from the Estonian court. The way in which earlier anti-dumping Regulations were applied to individual salmon farmers has also been the subject of litigation before the CFI.[129]

Safeguard measures

Under the EC's body of general trade law, various safeguard measures may be taken where a product is imported into the EC in such greatly increased quantities and/or such conditions and terms as to threaten or cause serious injury to EC producers.[130] This general power is particularized for fishery products in Article 30 of the Markets Regulation, which provides that 'where, by reason of imports or exports', the EC market for one or more fishery products is 'affected by, or is threatened with, serious disturbance likely to jeopardise the achievement of the objectives set out in Article 33 of the [EC] Treaty, appropriate measures may be applied in trade with third countries until such disturbance or threat of disturbance has ceased'. There has been little use of safeguard measures in relation to fishery products under the current Markets Regulation to date, although equivalent powers under predecessors to the Markets Regulation were used on a number of occasions.[131] The main use under the current Markets Regulation has been in respect of farmed salmon. Following complaints from Ireland and the UK in 2004 over the rapid increase in imports of farmed salmon, the Commission adopted provisional safeguard measures in August 2004. Those measures lapsed in December 2004. In February 2005 the Commission imposed definitive safeguard measures, which included the imposition of quotas for the amount of farmed salmon that could be imported from Chile, the Faroe Islands, and Norway and a

---

[126] Council Regulation (EC) No 685/2008 of 17 July 2008 repealing the anti-dumping duties imposed by Regulation (EC) No 85/2006 on imports of farmed salmon originating in Norway, OJ 2008 L192/5.   [127] Reg 685/2008, recitals (2)–(5).

[128] Reg 685/2008, recitals (104)–(106).

[129] Case T-178/98 *Fresh Marine Company AS v Commission* [2000] ECR II-3331, appealed as Case C-472/00P *Commission v Fresh Marine Company AS* [2003] ECR I-7541; and Case T-340/99 *Arne Mathisen AS v Commission* [2002] ECR II-2905.

[130] Council Regulation (EC) No 3285/94 of 22 December 1994 on common rules for imports and repealing Regulation (EC) No 518/94, OJ 1994 L349/53, as amended, Title V. The latter is based on the WTO Agreement on Safeguards.

[131] Berg, A, *Implementing and Enforcing European Fisheries Law* (The Hague: Kluwer, 1999), 57–8.

minimum import price.[132] Almost immediately Chile and Norway initiated proceedings under the WTO's Dispute Settlement Understanding, arguing that the
EC's measure was contrary to the WTO Safeguards Agreement.[133] Possibly as a
consequence, the Commission revoked the safeguard measures[134] and replaced
them with a provisional anti-dumping duty on Norwegian farmed salmon.[135]
Chile then terminated proceedings against the EC. Norway did not do so, but
proceedings in that case have been dormant. Subsequently, the form of the EC's
anti-dumping measure was changed to a minimum import price and applied until
January 2006,[136] at which point the measure was replaced by Regulation 85/2006
imposing a definitive anti-dumping duty (discussed above).

In general terms safeguard measures are seen as less effective than anti-dumping
measures and in any case are intended to be used only in exceptional situations.[137]

Health and quality controls

We turn now from controls on imports primarily designed to protect the interests
of EC fishermen and processors to those that serve other purposes, beginning with
controls in the interests of consumers. There is a considerable volume of EC
legislation that is designed to ensure that fishery products imported from third
States do not pose a health risk to EC consumers.[138] The basic principle of that
legislation is that the EC applies the same food safety and hygiene standards to
imported fishery products as it applies to fishery products originating and traded
within the EC.[139] In order to export fishery products to the EC, a third State
must be approved by the EC.[140] To be so approved, the third State must have a

---

[132] Commission Regulation (EC) No 206/2005 of 4 February 2005 imposing definitive safeguard
measures against imports of farmed salmon, OJ 2005 L33/8, as amended. Pursuant to Art 30 of the
Markets Regulation, Reg 206/2005 was adopted under Reg 3285/94.

[133] WTO, *European Communities—Definitive Safeguard Measure on Salmon*, Disputes DS326 and
DS328.

[134] Commission Regulation (EC) No 627/2005 of 22 April 2005 revoking Regulation (EC) No
206/2005 imposing definitive safeguard measures against imports of farmed salmon, OJ 2005 L104/4.

[135] Commission Regulation (EC) No 628/2005 of 22 April 2005 imposing a provisional anti-
dumping duty on imports of farmed salmon originating in Norway, OJ 2005 L104/5, as amended.

[136] Commission Regulation (EC) No 1010/2005 of 30 June 2005 amending Commission Regulation (EC) No 628/2005 of 22 April 2005 imposing a provisional anti-dumping duty on imports of
farmed salmon originating in Norway, OJ 2005 L170/32, as corrected.

[137] Barnard, *The Substantive Law of the EU*, 235–6.

[138] For a helpful overview of such legislation, see European Commission, Directorate-General for
Health and Consumer Protection, *Guidance Document: Key questions related to import requirements and the
new rules on food hygiene and official controls* (Brussels, 2006).

[139] Regulation (EC) No 178/2002 of the European Parliament and of the Council of 28 January
2002 laying down the general principles and requirements of food law, establishing the European Food
Safety Authority and laying down procedures in matters of food safety, OJ 2002 L31/1, Art 11.

[140] Regulation (EC) No 854/2004 of the European Parliament and of the Council of 29 April 2004
laying down specific rules for the organisation of official controls on products of animal origin intended
for human consumption, OJ 2004 L226/83, as amended and corrected, Art 11(1).

competent authority responsible for official health controls throughout the production chain in that State, which has been duly recognized by the Commission.
To check whether such a competent authority exercises its responsibilities effectively, the Commission may visit the third State concerned and inspect the
authority's activities.[141] Where a third State has been duly approved, exports to the
EC are permitted only from those establishments and vessels of that State that have
been approved by its competent authority as meeting EC standards.[142] Furthermore, imports of fishery products from third States must enter the EC through an
approved Border Inspection Post where each consignment is subject to a systematic
documentary check, identity check, and, where appropriate, physical check.[143]
The above provisions do not apply to fresh fish landed at an EC port directly from a
vessel registered in a third State. Such landings are subject only to the same hygiene
controls as Community vessels landing their catches in EC ports.[144]

Developing States, particularly ACP States, have complained that the EC's food
safety and hygiene controls on imported fishery products are unnecessarily strict
and constitute a significant obstacle to their ability to export fishery products to the
EC, which is their most important export market.[145] The point has also been made
that the EC's system of controls penalizes well-managed seafood companies in
States that do not have the resources or capacity to set up an effective competent
authority recognized by the Commission because it prohibits such companies from
exporting their products to the EC.[146] As far as the authors have been able to
discover, no complaint has (yet) been made to the WTO about the EC's health
controls on imported fishery products.

---

[141] Reg 854/2004, Art 11(2)–(5). For examples of unsuccessful challenges by EC importers of
fishery products to Commission decisions withholding approval from third States, see Case C-183/95
Affish BV v Rijksdienst voor de keuring van Vee en Vlees [1997] ECR I-4315; and Case T-155/99 *Dieckmann
& Hansen GmbH v Commission* [2001] ECR II-3143. An appeal in the latter case, as Case C-492/01, was
dismissed, OJ 2003 C135/7.

[142] Reg 854/2004, Arts 12 and 15. Specific provisions relating to the import of aquaculture products,
similar to the system laid down in Reg 854/2004, are contained in Council Directive 2006/88/EC of
24 October 2006 on animal health requirements for aquaculture animals and products thereof, and on
the prevention and control of certain diseases in aquatic animals, OJ 2006 L328/14, as amended and
corrected, Chapter IV and Art 58(2).

[143] Council Directive 97/78/EC of 18 December 1997 laying down the principles governing the
organisation of veterinary checks on products entering the Community from third countries, OJ 1998
L24/9, as amended; and Regulation (EC) No 882/2004 of the European Parliament and of the Council
of 29 April 2004 on official controls performed to ensure the verification of compliance with feed and
food law, animal health and animal welfare rules, OJ 2004 L191/1, as amended, Chapter V.

[144] Reg 854/2004, Art 15(1) and Annex III.

[145] Coalition for Fair Fisheries Arrangements, *ACP-EU Economic Partnership Agreements: Fisheries*
(Maastricht: European Centre for Development Policy Management, Discussion Paper No 69, 2005),
11 and 21. It should also be noted that the EC provides financial aid to help ACP States meet the EC's
health standards: see *Fishing for the truth: is Europe really destroying African fisheries' industry?*, 25 July 2008,
p 2 (available on the website of the European Commission's Directorate General for Trade).

[146] FAO, *The State of World Fisheries and Aquaculture 2006* (Rome: FAO, 2007), 137.

The common marketing standards and labelling requirements that the EC has adopted for fishery products that are marketed for human consumption, discussed in the previous chapter, apply to imported products.[147] In their application to imports, such standards and requirements are subject to international trade rules since they constitute potential obstacles to trade. In a case brought by Peru against the EC under the WTO's Dispute Settlement Understanding, the Appellate Body upheld a panel finding that the EC's then marketing standards for preserved sardines did not comply with Article 2.4 of the Agreement on Technical Barriers to Trade because they permitted too narrow a range of species to be marketed as 'preserved sardines'.[148] In response, the EC accepted the Appellate Body's ruling,[149] and amended the relevant Regulation accordingly.[150] In an earlier WTO case, Canada brought a complaint against the EC that a French order relating to the labelling of scallops violated Articles I and III of the GATT and Article 2 of the Agreement on Technical Barriers to Trade.[151] Peru and Chile subsequently made similar complaints.[152] A single panel was constituted and completed its substantive work, but did not give a ruling as the parties had in the meantime reached a mutually agreed solution that involved France amending the offending order.[153] The cases appear to have been brought against the EC rather than France because Canada had been unable to settle the dispute with France, despite efforts to do so, whereas subsequent consultations with the EC enabled a temporary solution to be identified.[154] The offending French order does not appear to have been intended to implement any EC measure.

Measures to combat IUU fishing

EC fisheries trade policy with third States also has a dimension that goes beyond traditional measures to regulate trade. In recent years trade measures have become increasingly used as a means of trying to combat IUU fishing. As was seen in

---

[147] Reg 104/2000, Art 2(2); Council Regulation (EC) No 2406/96 of 26 November 1996 laying down common marketing standards for certain fishery products, OJ 1996 L334/1, as amended, Art 2(1); and Commission Regulation (EC) No 2065/2001 of 22 October 2001 laying down detailed rules for the application of Council Regulation (EC) No 104/2000 as regards informing consumers about fishery and aquaculture products, OJ 2001 L278/6, as amended and corrected, Art 1.

[148] *European Communities—Trade Description of Sardines*, Report of the Appellate Body, WT/DS231/AB/R (2002). For discussion of the case, see Tarasofsky, RG, *Regional Fisheries Organizations and the World Trade Organization: Compatibility or Conflict?* (Cambridge: TRAFFIC International, 2003), 13–14.

[149] WTO Doc WT/DS231/18, 29 July 2003.

[150] Commission Regulation (EC) No 1181/2003 of 2 July 2003 amending Council Regulation (EEC) No 2136/89 laying down common marketing standards for preserved sardines, OJ 2003 L165/17.

[151] *European Communities—Trade Description of Scallops*, Dispute DS7.

[152] *European Communities—Trade Description of Scallops*, Disputes DS12 and DS14.

[153] *European Communities—Trade Description of Scallops*, WTO Docs WT/DS7/R and WT/DS7/12, both of 19 July 1996.

[154] *European Communities—Trade Description of Scallops*, WTO Docs WT/DS7/1, 24 May 1995.

Chapters 3 and 5, a number of RFMOs have adopted trade-related measures as a means of trying to secure compliance with their conservation and management measures.[155] Such trade-related measures fall into three principal categories.

First, and most commonly, there are measures against individual vessels that are included on lists of vessels regarded as having participated in IUU fishing. The lists are drawn up by RFMOs, and the RFMOs' members are then required to apply certain measures against the listed vessels. The required measures usually include, *inter alia*, prohibitions on landing of catches; such prohibitions are related to trade because in effect they reduce access to the market. Although the said prohibitions are directly against individual vessels, they may indirectly have an effect on the flag State of the vessel and so may be seen as trade-related measures against States. Almost all of the major RFMOs have adopted IUU vessel lists and associated measures.

Secondly, but far less commonly, there are measures against named flag States whereby an RFMO's members are required to prohibit the import of certain fishery products from States which have been identified as not complying with that RFMO's conservation and management measures. Although several RFMOs have adopted framework provisions enabling them to adopt such measures, the only RFMO to have adopted measures of this kind in practice is the International Commission for the Conservation of Atlantic Tunas (ICCAT). The ICCAT's measures in this respect currently comprise import bans against Bolivia and Georgia in respect of certain fishery products.[156]

Thirdly, some RFMOs have adopted schemes that require certain documentation to accompany fishery products as they travel along the supply chain, such documentation being intended as evidence that the products have not been caught by IUU fishing. Depending on the scheme in question, the absence of such documentation may then mean that a particular product is not permitted to enter (or leave) the market of an RFMO member. At the very least, the schemes may enable an RFMO to detect evidence of IUU fishing and then take appropriate action. Such RFMO schemes will be referred to in this chapter as 'catch documentation schemes', although not all such schemes go by this label.

The three kinds of RFMO trade-related measure just described have been implemented by the EC in respect of those RFMOs of which it is a member by means of an array of Regulations (see further Chapter 5). In addition, more

---

[155] For a useful survey and review of such measures, see Lack, M, *Catching On? Trade-related Measures as a Fisheries Management Tool* (Cambridge: TRAFFIC International, 2007). See also Lodge, MW, Anderson, D, Løbach, T, Munro, G, Sainsbury, K, and Willock, A, *Recommended Best Practices for Regional Fisheries Management Organizations* (London: Chatham House, 2007), 54–63; and Owen, D, *Practice of RFMOs regarding Non-Members, Recommended Best Practices for Regional Fisheries Management Organizations: Technical Study No 2* (London: Chatham House, 2007), *passim*.

[156] For a description of the EC's implementation of the ICCAT's measures against Bolivia and Georgia, see Owen, D, *Practice of RFMOs regarding Non-Members*, 133–4.

generally, where catch has been taken by a third State vessel on the high seas inside the regulatory area of a competent RFMO of which the EC is a member, Article 28g of the Control Regulation requires Member States to authorize landing only if the species retained on board have been caught in compliance with that RFMO's conservation and management measures.[157] The IUU Regulation, discussed earlier, will repeal Article 28g of the Control Regulation when the former becomes applicable at the beginning of 2010 and will replace it, and parts of the aforementioned array of Regulations, with a wide ranging set of measures for controlling imports.

Some compliance measures in the IUU Regulation relating to imports in the form of direct landings by third State vessels in Member States' ports have already been outlined at the beginning of this subsection. (Others are described later below.) More generally, the IUU Regulation establishes an EC catch documentation scheme labelled as a 'catch certification scheme'. This provides that fishery products[158] may be imported into the EC only when accompanied by a catch certificate validated by the flag State of the fishing vessel from whose catch the products in question have been obtained: that certificate must certify that the catch was made 'in accordance with applicable laws, regulations and international conservation and management measures'.[159] That requirement applies not only where the exporting third State is the flag State, but also where it is not.[160]

In the latter situation, where the catch has simply been transported to the exporting State without undergoing processing there, the importer must provide documentation evidencing this, as well as the catch certificate validated by the flag State.[161] Where the product has been processed in the State of export, the importer must submit to the authorities of the Member State of import not just the catch certificate but also a statement from the processing plant in the exporting State and endorsed by the latter's authorities which, *inter alia*, shows that the product in question was processed from catches that were accompanied by a catch certificate validated by the flag State.[162]

As a general rule, a catch certificate must be submitted by the importer to the competent authorities of the relevant Member State at least three working days before the estimated time of arrival of the imported product.[163] That requirement

---

[157] Reg 2847/93, Art 28g, 2nd indent.

[158] The definition in the IUU Regulation of the term 'fishery products' is not as broad as that used by the authors in the first footnote to this chapter (see section 1 above). See further Reg 1005/2008, Arts 2(8) and 12(5). Of note, the IUU Regulation's definition does not include products listed in Annex I to the Regulation, namely certain molluscs as well as '[f]reshwater fishery products', '[o]rnamental fish', and certain aquaculture products.

[159] Reg 1005/2008, Art 12(2) and (3). Art 12(4) provides, *inter alia*, that within the framework of a cooperative arrangement with a third State (on which see below) a catch certificate may be replaced by 'electronic traceability systems' ensuring the same level of control as a catch certificate.

[160] Reg 1005/2008, Art 14.   [161] Reg 1005/2008, Art 14(1).

[162] Reg 1005/2008, Art 14(2).   [163] Reg 1005/2008, Art 16(1).

does not apply to importers who have been granted the status of 'approved economic operator', who need simply advise of the estimated arrival of the product
at least three days beforehand and keep the catch certificate available to the
authorities for checking.[164] The information required to be provided on a catch
certificate is set out in the IUU Regulation's Annex II.[165]

Catch certificates will only be accepted if the validating flag State has notified
the Commission that it has in place 'national arrangements for the implementation,
control and enforcement of laws, regulations and conservation and management
measures which must be complied with by its fishing vessels' and that its authorities
are empowered 'to attest the veracity' of the information contained in catch certificates and to carry out verification of such certificates at the request of an EC
Member State.[166]

Member States must check the catch certificates required from the importer and
verify compliance with the Regulation's requirements on catch certification.[167]
Article 18 specifies the circumstances in which importation must be refused.
Most, but not all, of these circumstances relate to non-compliance with the
Regulation's catch certification requirements. Reflecting the potential economic
impact on the importer, and possibly others, of decisions to refuse importation, the
Regulation states that '[a]ny person shall have the right to appeal against [such]
decisions . . . which concern him'.[168]

'[W]here appropriate', the Commission is to 'cooperate administratively' with
a third State with the aims of, *inter alia*, ensuring that fishery products imported
into the EC originate from catches made in compliance with the applicable
rules; facilitating the accomplishment by the flag State of its obligations under
the EC's catch certification scheme; and enabling the Commission to conduct
'on-the-spot-audits . . . to verify the effective implementation of the cooperation
arrangement'.[169]

As mentioned above, some RFMOs have adopted their own catch documentation schemes. Article 13(1) of the IUU Regulation provides that where an
RFMO's catch documentation scheme is recognized as complying with the
requirements of the Regulation, a catch document validated in conformity with
such a scheme is to be accepted as equivalent to a catch certificate under the IUU
Regulation. That provision is to apply 'without prejudice' to the various EC
Regulations implementing RFMO catch documentation schemes.[170] In the case
of fishery products imported from a third State other than the flag State, a
re-export certificate of an RFMO catch documentation scheme recognized under
Article 13 may replace the documentation otherwise required.[171]

---

[164] Reg 1005/2008, Art 16(2). Criteria for the granting of approved economic operator status are set
out in Art 16(3), and provisions on the suspension or withdrawal of such status in Art 45(8).

[165] Reg 1005/2008, Art 12(4).   [166] Reg 1005/2008, Art 20(1). See also Art 12(4).

[167] Reg 1005/2008, Arts 16, 17, and 24.   [168] Reg 1005/2008, Art 18(4).

[169] Reg 1005/2008, Art 20(4).   [170] Reg 1005/2008, Art 13(2). See also Art 6(2).

[171] Reg 1005/2008, Art 14(1) and (2).

The EC's catch certification scheme is aimed at preventing fishery products derived from IUU fishing from entering the EC. The IUU Regulation also contains other provisions that may affect the ability of third States to export products to the EC. Article 11(2) requires that if the results of a port inspection 'provide evidence that a third country fishing vessels has engaged in IUU fishing', the port Member State must not authorize that vessel to land its catch. Article 37(5) requires a port Member State to refuse port entry to a third State fishing vessel on the Community IUU vessel list except in cases of *force majeure* or distress; in the latter circumstances, the catch must be confiscated. Alternatively, a port Member State may authorize entry into its ports by such vessels on the condition that the catch is confiscated. Article 37(9) requires that the importation of fishery products caught by fishing vessels on the Community IUU vessel list must be prohibited.[172]

Imports of fishery products caught by vessels whose flag States have been identified as 'non-cooperating third countries' are also generally prohibited.[173] Procedures for identifying, and establishing a list of, such States are set out in Articles 31–33 of the IUU Regulation.[174] In cases where there is evidence that the measures adopted by a third State are undermining conservation and management measures adopted by an RFMO, the Commission may adopt emergency measures, which may, *inter alia*, include a prohibition on fishing vessels registered in that State from having routine access to EC ports (and thereby losing the possibility of landing their catches there).[175] Presumably this provision is intended to apply in cases of States that have not (yet) been placed on the list of 'non-cooperating third countries'.

The IUU Regulation, if properly implemented, may turn out to have a significant impact on the volume and pattern of the EC's imports of fishery products from third States, as around 10 per cent (by value) of such imports are estimated currently to come from IUU fishing.[176] If such products cannot find an alternative market, the Regulation will also make a significant impact on IUU fishing. On the other hand, the catch certification scheme established by the Regulation will impose on third States exporting fishery products to the EC (especially developing States) considerable administrative burdens, perhaps as great as those resulting from the EC's health and quality rules, described above.

It may be asked whether the IUU Regulation is compatible with the EC's WTO obligations, in particular those under the GATT. Any prohibitions on imports adopted under the IUU Regulation would clearly breach Article XI(1) of the GATT, which prohibits quantitative and similar restrictions on imports.

---

[172] See also Reg 1005/2008, Art 18(1)(f).

[173] Reg 1005/2008, Art 38(1). See also Art 18(1)(g).

[174] See also Reg 1005/2008, Arts 34 and 35.   [175] Reg 1005/2008, Art 36.

[176] *Commission staff working document—Accompanying document to the Proposal for a Council Regulation establishing a Community system to prevent, deter and eliminate illegal, unreported and unregulated fishing— Impact Assessment*, SEC(2007) 1336, 17.10.2007, section 2.1.3.

However, any such breaches of Article XI may be justifiable under Article XX of the GATT. This provides that nothing in the GATT shall prevent the adoption by any party of measures, *inter alia*, for the protection of human or animal life or health (paragraph (b)) or 'relating to the conservation of exhaustible natural resources if such measures are made effective in conjunction with restrictions on domestic production or consumption' (paragraph (g)). Such measures must, however, satisfy the requirements of the '*chapeau*' of Article XX, namely that they 'are not applied in a manner which would constitute a means of arbitrary or unjustifiable discrimination between countries where the same conditions prevail, or a disguised restriction on international trade'.

As far as ground '(g)' is concerned, the IUU Regulation is clearly concerned with 'the conservation of exhaustible natural resources', a term that the WTO Appellate Body has held includes renewable marine living resources.[177] The IUU Regulation 'relates to' such conservation because, to employ the analysis of the Appellate Body in the first *Shrimp/Turtle* case,[178] the means (restricting imports from IUU fishing) are reasonably related to the end of conserving what are generally fully or over-exploited fish stocks and seeking to ensure that stocks are managed sustainably.

To be justifiable under ground '(g)', it is also necessary that the IUU Regulation is 'made effective in conjunction with restrictions on domestic production or consumption', ie that there are equivalent restrictions on EC Member States including, in particular, in respect of Community fishing vessels, or, as the Appellate Body has put it, that there is 'even-handedness in the imposition of restrictions, in the name of conservation, upon the production or consumption of exhaustible natural resources'.[179] There are 'restrictions on domestic production' in the form of EC legislation. Such EC legislation includes, *inter alia*, the IUU Regulation itself (although many of the trade-related provisions of this Regulation relate only to third States) and the Control Regulation. Lack of space precludes an analysis as to whether EC Member States are subject to restrictions that are equivalent to those that may be applied to third States under the IUU Regulation. However, some idea of the complexities that may arise in judging even-handedness is provided by the following example relating to the Regulation's provisions on the Community IUU vessel list.

As indicated above, being on the said list could have significant implications related to trade. Article 27(8) of the IUU Regulation states that: 'Community fishing vessels shall *not* be included in the Community IUU vessel list if the flag

---

[177] *United States—Import Prohibition of Certain Shrimp and Shrimp Products*, Report of the Appellate Body, WT/DS58/AB/R (1998), paras 128–34.

[178] *United States—Import Prohibition of Certain Shrimp and Shrimp Products*, Report of the Appellate Body, paras 135–41.

[179] *United States—Standards for Reformulated and Conventional Gasoline*, Report of the Appellate Body, WT/DS2/AB/R (1996), pp 20–1.

Member State has taken action pursuant to this Regulation and [the Control Regulation] against breaches constituting serious infringements as laid down in Article 3(2), without prejudice to the action taken by [RFMOs].' (Emphasis added.) It is questionable whether a comparison can easily be made between the economic impact of being placed on the Community IUU vessel list and the actions referred to in Article 27(8). Furthermore, Article 27(8) places an emphasis on enforcement action taken by Member States, which introduces a need to analyse practice. Overall, in this example, it would probably not be easy to reach a decision on whether or not there was equivalence.

It is also possible that any restrictions on imports from third States provided for in the IUU Regulation could be justified under paragraph (b) of Article XX, which is concerned with the protection of animal life and health. To be so justified, a measure must be 'necessary'. That means that no GATT-consistent alternative is reasonably available and that the measure in question entails the least degree of inconsistency with other GATT provisions.[180]

As mentioned above, both grounds '(g)' and '(b)' in Article XX must also meet the requirements of that Article's *chapeau*. In the first *Shrimp/Turtle* case the Appellate Body found that the USA had not met the requirements of the *chapeau* because it had unilaterally sought to impose a conservation policy (compulsory use of turtle excluder devices in shrimp fishing) for a migratory marine resource (turtles) that was not confined to US maritime zones but was also found in the maritime zones of other States and on the high seas, without first attempting to negotiate a multilateral conservation agreement with those States whose imports it had banned. That amounted to unjustifiable discrimination.[181] On the other hand, in the second *Shrimp/Turtle* case, where Malaysia challenged the way in which the USA had implemented the ruling in the first *Shrimp/Turtle* case, the Appellate Body held that it was sufficient that the USA had tried to obtain an agreement; it was not necessary that an agreement had actually been concluded.[182]

How can the lessons from the two *Shrimp/Turtle* cases be applied in the context of the IUU Regulation? It is necessary to make a distinction at this point, between the trade-related provisions of the IUU Regulation that may be regarded as implementing RFMO compliance measures and those that go beyond such measures. In the former case, any challenge to the provisions in question would presumably involve scrutiny of whether the RFMO compliance measures they implemented met the requirements established by the Appellate Body in the

---

[180] Schoenbaum, TJ in Birnie, P and Boyle, A, *International Law and the Environment* (2nd edn, Oxford: Oxford University Press, 2002), 702 and 710–11 See also Tarasofsky, *Regional Fisheries Organizations and the World Trade Organization*, 13.

[181] *Shrimp/Turtle* case, Report of the Appellate Body, paras 161–76.

[182] *United States—Import Prohibition of Certain Shrimp and Shrimp Products. Recourse to Article 21.5 by Malaysia*, Report of the Appellate Body, WT/DS58/AB/RW (2001).

Shrimp/Turtle cases.[183] In that regard, if the challenging third State was not a member of the RFMO in question, it might not be sufficient that the RFMO itself, and the measures it had adopted, represented a multilateral agreement. In such a case, it would presumably also be necessary to consider what attempts had been made by the RFMO to seek to persuade the State in question to join the RFMO or otherwise cooperate with it.

In the case of those provisions of the IUU Regulation that go beyond RFMO compliance measures,[184] the situation is potentially quite different. In this case, such provisions should probably be regarded as unilateral measures adopted by the EC. Logically the focus should then be on the EC, rather than on any RFMO, as needing to pass the tests established in the *Shrimp/Turtle* cases or, more generally, the tests in the *chapeau* of Article XX. The mere fact that a measure is unilateral does not necessarily mean that it will be found to be incompatible with the *chapeau*.[185] Furthermore, it should not be overlooked that the purpose of the unilateral measure in question would be to ensure compliance with RFMOs' conservation and management regimes. However, regarding trade-related measures to ensure such compliance, the FAO's International Plan of Action on IUU fishing (on which, see Chapters 3 and 5) places emphasis on such measures being adopted on a multilateral basis.[186] It will be interesting to see whether or how the EC seeks to implement the relevant provisions of the IUU Regulation in a way that minimizes the likelihood of a successful challenge under the WTO's Dispute Settlement Understanding.

Even if the provisions of the IUU Regulation going beyond RFMO compliance measures could not be justified under Article XX of the GATT, the question arises whether they could instead be justified as a legitimate countermeasure in international law.[187] In this context it is interesting to note that Schoenbaum states that it would have been 'a permissible countermeasure' for Canada to have adopted 'environmental trade restrictions', such as 'a ban on imports of fish products', against Spain in response to intensive fishing in 1995 by

---

[183] See Tarasofsky, *Regional Fisheries Organizations and the World Trade Organization*, especially at 18–29, for a detailed study of the compatibility of RFMO trade-restrictive measures with WTO obligations. He reaches the conclusion that most such measures are compatible with the GATT and other WTO agreements. See also Roheim, CA and Sutinen, J, *Trade and Marketplace Measures to Promote Sustainable Fishing Practices*, ICTSD Natural Resources, International Trade and Sustainable Development Series Issue Paper No 3 (Geneva: International Centre for Trade and Sustainable Development, 2006).

[184] The differences between the provisions of the IUU Regulation and existing RFMO measures are referred to in general terms in Chapter 5.

[185] See further Schoenbaum in Birnie and Boyle, *International Law and the Environment*, 712.

[186] International Plan of Action, paras 66, 68, and 69. See also the UN Fish Stocks Agreement (introduced in Chapters 3 and 5), Art 20(7) (cf Arts 17(4) and 33(2)).

[187] On the conditions and limitations applicable to the taking of countermeasures, see Articles 49–54 of the International Law Commission's 2001 Articles on State Responsibility, UN General Assembly Official Records, Fifty-sixth session, Supplement No 10 (A/56/10).

Spanish vessels on the high seas adjacent to Canada's EEZ that was 'disrupting Canadian efforts to rebuild fish stocks' and that 'violated several provisions' of the relevant RFMO treaty.[188]

Individual Member State measures

As mentioned earlier in this section, because the EC is a customs union, Member States are not permitted to impose customs duties (or charges of equivalent effect) on fishery products imported from third States. Member States may, however, under Article 24(2) of Regulation 3285/94, adopt prohibitions, quantitative restrictions, or surveillance measures in respect of imports from third States on grounds similar to those in Article 30 EC (discussed in subsection 2.4 above in the context of intra-EC trade), provided that they first notify the Commission. The authors do not know to what extent, if at all, this power has been exercised in practice in respect of fishery imports.

3.3 The regulation of exports

At the time of writing there was very little applicable EC law relating specifically to the export of fishery products. The only such law was legislation implementing RFMO catch documentation schemes (referred to above) and legislation implementing the Convention on International Trade in Endangered Species of Wild Fauna and Flora (CITES, discussed in Chapter 5; and see further subsection 3.1 above). That position will change at the beginning of 2010 when the IUU Regulation, and the EC's catch certification scheme that it establishes, takes effect. The Regulation contains a number of provisions dealing with the export and re-export of fishery products. Article 15 of the Regulation will make the 'exportation' of catches made by 'fishing vessels flying the flag of a Member State' subject to having a catch certificate validated by the flag Member State, but only if that is required within the framework of cooperation under Article 20(4) between the EC and third States relating to catch certification (referred to in subsection 3.2 above). 'Exportation' is defined as 'any movement to a third country of fishery products harvested by fishing vessels flying the flag of a Member State, including from the territory of the Community, from third countries or from fishing grounds'.[189] Article 21 of the IUU Regulation deals with 're-exportation'. It provides that where fishery products are to be re-exported from the EC following their import into the EC accompanied by a catch certificate, the EC Member State from which re-exportation is to take place must validate the appropriate section of the certificate. 'Re-exportation' is defined as 'any movement from the territory of

---

[188] Schoenbaum in Birnie and Boyle, *International Law and the Environment*, 713–14. For some literature on the dispute between Canada and Spain, see Chapter 5.

[189] Reg 1005/2008, Art 2(13).

the Community of fishery products which had been previously imported into the territory of the Community'.[190] The IUU Regulation also contains a separate stricter provision on export and re-export of products from fishing vessels included in the Community IUU vessel list. Export and re-export of such products 'for processing', specifically, is prohibited.[191] This wording implies that the prohibition does not apply where fish is exported for a purpose other than processing (for example, for direct human consumption).

Where the export of fishery products is not subject to the provisions of the IUU Regulation, Regulations implementing RFMO trade-related measures or Regulations implementing the CITES, general EC law relating to the export of goods applies. In principle, such export is free of restrictions.[192] There are two exceptions to this principle that appear to be potentially relevant to fishery products. First, under Article 6 of Regulation 2603/69, 'in order to prevent a critical situation from arising on account of a shortage of essential products, or to remedy such a situation, and where Community interests call for immediate intervention', the Commission, acting at the request of a Member State or on its own initiative, and taking account of the nature of the products and of the other particular features of the transactions in question, may make the export of a product subject to the production of an export authorization. Conditions for the granting of such authorizations are to be laid down by the Commission. As far as the authors are aware, the Commission has never made use of its powers under Article 6 in respect of fishery products. The second potential exception is Article 11 of Regulation 2603/69. This provision allows individual Member States to restrict exports on grounds similar to those in Article 30 EC (on intra-Community trade; see sub-section 2.4 above). Article 11 would therefore allow a Member State to ban exports of fishery products from its territory to a third State that it believed to be a threat to human health. It might also allow a Member State to prohibit the export of illegally caught fish that was not covered by the IUU Regulation on the ground of public policy or the protection of the health and life of animals. The authors are not aware to what degree, if any, Member States have used their powers under Article 11 in respect of fishery products.

Exports of fishery products from the EC to a third State may well have to face customs duties imposed by that third State. However, some of the agreements referred to in subsection 3.2 above under which the EC has reduced or abolished customs duties on imports of fishery products from third States also provide that the third State concerned shall take more or less similar action in respect of exports from the EC. Such agreements include the EEA Agreement[193] and the EC's Agreements with Algeria,[194] the CARIFORUM States,[195] Chile,[196] the Faroe

---

[190] Reg 1005/2008, Art 2(14).   [191] Reg 1005/2008, Art 37(10).

[192] Regulation (EEC) No 2603/69 of the Council of 20 December 1969 establishing common rules for exports, OJ 1969 L324/25, as amended, Art 1.   [193] Protocol 9, Art 1.

[194] Protocol 4.   [195] Art 16 and Annex III.   [196] Art 69.

Islands,[197] and South Africa.[198] Otherwise, where EC exports are to States that, like the EC, are members of the WTO, they will enjoy most-favoured-nation treatment and national treatment under Articles I and III of the GATT.

EC exporters obviously have to comply with any relevant laws of third States relating to imports of fishery products (for example, health and quality standards). If the EC considers that any such national laws violate the WTO obligations of the State concerned, it may initiate proceedings against that State under the WTO's Dispute Settlement Understanding. So far this has been done on only one occasion. In 2000 the EC commenced proceedings against Chile in respect of a Chilean law that prohibited the unloading in Chile's ports of swordfish caught by Community vessels on the high seas of the south-east Pacific. The EC claimed that that law violated Articles V and XI of the GATT (which prohibit restrictions on trade in transit and quantitative restrictions on imports and exports, respectively). A panel was constituted to hear the dispute, but proceedings were suspended in March 2001 when the EC and Chile announced that they had come to a provisional arrangement concerning the dispute: proceedings have remained suspended ever since then.[199] The dispute is linked to the *Chile/EC Swordfish* case before the International Tribunal for the Law of the Sea (discussed briefly in Chapter 5), proceedings in which are also currently suspended.

4 Conclusions

As far as trade in fishery products between EC Member States is concerned, the basic principle is complete freedom of trade, in keeping with the fundamental nature of the EC as a single market. There are, however, some qualifications to that principle. First, the EC may restrict trade between Member States in furtherance of Community objectives. Currently, it does so only in respect of health and hygiene standards and, especially in the light of the IUU Regulation, IUU fishing. Secondly, by virtue of Article 30 EC or the rule of reason enunciated in *Cassis de Dijon*, Member States may unilaterally restrict trade through measures that constitute, or are equivalent in effect to, quantitative restrictions.

The position in relation to trade in fishery products between the EC and third States is quite different and altogether more complex. While there is a general freedom in EC law to export (other than where the fish is the product of IUU fishing or where the export is regulated by the CITES), imports are subject to a

---

[197] Protocol 1, Art 4.

[198] Art 15 and Annex VII. The concessions made by South Africa will not begin to operate until the concessions made by the EC have begun to take effect: as seen earlier, this had not happened as at the end of November 2008.

[199] *Chile—Measures affecting the Transit and Importing of Swordfish*, Dispute DS193. For the most recent information about the continuing suspension of proceedings, see WTO Doc WT/DS193/3/Add. 4, 17 December 2007.

significant degree of regulation. Such regulation serves a number of different and, to some extent, competing purposes: to protect EC fishermen from excessive competition from imports (by means of customs duties, reference prices, anti-dumping and countervailing duties, and, very exceptionally, safeguard measures); to facilitate the access of EC processors to the necessary supply of raw material for processing (by relaxing customs duties on such raw material) while protecting them from undue competition from processed products (by maintaining customs duties on such products); to satisfy the increasing demands of consumers for fish of high quality (by reducing or abolishing some customs duties while maintaining strict sanitary and quality standards); to promote the sustainability of fish stocks (by prohibiting the import of fish taken in IUU fishing); and to fulfil the EC's development obligations (by reducing or abolishing customs duties on imports from developing States). In legislating to regulate imports, the EC has not only to seek to satisfy the differing demands of the various interest groups mentioned, but also has to comply with its international trade law obligations, notably those stemming from its membership of the WTO. Not surprisingly, it has not always succeeded in satisfying these competing demands.[200]

It is of interest to note that the EC has recently begun to acknowledge in agreements with third States that its trade regime for fishery products may have a negative impact on such States. In particular, the EC's relatively liberal import regime may encourage producers in third States to export to the EC rather than helping to provide food for the local population. Conversely, EC exports to third States may have a damaging effect on local producers. These potential dangers are referred to in the first EPA with ACP States that the EC has signed (that with the CARIFORUM States),[201] and are likely also to be considered in any further such agreements.

As mentioned at the end of Chapter 6, the Commission indicated in October 2008 that it would put forward a legislative proposal on reform of the common organization of the markets in fishery and aquaculture products during the second half of 2009. At the time of writing it was not clear whether significant changes to the provisions of the Markets Regulation relating to trade with third States were likely to be proposed.

---

[200] For an interesting discussion of the EC's attempts to resolve the conflicting interests of processors and EC fishermen, see Lequesne, *The Politics of Fisheries*, 134–6.

[201] See CARIFORUM-EC EPA, Arts 37(4), 40(1), and 40(2).

8

Public expenditure in the fisheries sector

1 Introduction

This chapter addresses public expenditure in the fisheries sector. It deals first with two EC financial instruments—the European Fisheries Fund (EFF) and Regulation 861/2006.[1] The latter is complementary in purpose to the EFF and is sometimes referred to as 'the second fisheries instrument', ie second to the EFF. The EFF and Regulation 861/2006 are not the only sources of EC funding for the Common Fisheries Policy (CFP). A further important source is the European Agricultural Guarantee Fund (EAGF), which is discussed in Chapter 6. As noted there, the EAGF funds the market intervention system (ie permanent withdrawal, 'carry-over', 'private storage', and the 'compensatory allowance' for tuna producers) as well as providing some other funding to producer organizations. As noted in subsection 2.1 below, some other Community financial instruments provide support in connection with fisheries, albeit not under the CFP. After dealing with the EFF and Regulation 861/2006, this chapter moves on to consider State aid, ie aid granted by Member States to the fishing industry other than in conjunction with funds from any EC financial instrument.

2 European Fisheries Fund

2.1 Introduction

The EFF was established by Regulation 1198/2006 (hereafter, 'the EFF Regulation'),[2] which was adopted in July 2006 on the basis of Articles 36 and 37 EC. The Commission's legislative proposal for this Regulation was issued two years earlier, in July 2004,[3] on the same date as proposals were issued for new Regulations to govern the EAFG, the European Agricultural Fund for Rural Development (EAFRD), the European Regional Development Fund (ERDF), the

---

[1] Council Regulation (EC) No 861/2006 of 22 May 2006 establishing Community financial measures for the implementation of the common fisheries policy and in the area of the Law of the Sea, OJ 2006 L160/1, Art 1.

[2] Council Regulation (EC) No 1198/2006 of 27 July 2006 on the European Fisheries Fund, OJ 2006 L223/1.

[3] *Proposal for a Council Regulation: European Fisheries Fund*, COM(2004) 497, 14.7.2004.

European Social Fund (ESF), and the Cohesion Fund.[4] The relationship between the EFF and the latter funds is mentioned briefly below.

The EFF Regulation entered into force in September 2006,[5] and is due to be reviewed by the Council by the end of 2013 at the latest.[6] Some specific aspects of the EFF have already been mentioned in earlier chapters of this book; this chapter will consider the Fund more generally. The EFF is now the principal EC fund in the sphere of fisheries, having succeeded the Financial Instrument for Fisheries Guidance (FIFG) as from 1 January 2007.[7] Detailed rules for the implementation of the EFF are set out in Regulation 498/2007 (hereafter, in this section, 'the Commission Regulation'),[8] although the EFF Regulation itself also contains many detailed provisions. The Commission has also issued guidelines, which it calls a 'Vademecum' (ie handbook or manual), to provide advice on the implementation of the EFF.[9] The account that follows in this subsection and in subsection 2.2 below does not address the various additions to, and derogations from, the EFF Regulation that were introduced by Regulation 744/2008,[10] which was adopted in summer 2008 in response to oil price increases affecting the fishing industry. Instead, that Regulation is considered separately in subsection 2.3 below. References in this subsection and in subsection 2.2 below, including in the footnotes, to particular Articles, Annexes, or recitals are to the EFF Regulation unless otherwise stated.

The funding for the EFF falls under the 'Conservation and Management of Natural Resources' heading of the EC financial framework for 2007–13, because of the Fund's close connection with the implementation of the CFP.[11] The EFF

---

[4] COM(2004) 489, on EAFRD and EAGF (now Reg 1290/2005, OJ 2005 L209/1, as amended and corrected); COM(2004) 495, on ERDF (now Reg 1080/2006, OJ 2006 L210/1); COM(2004) 493, on ESF (now Reg 1081/2006, OJ 2006 L210/12); COM(2004) 494, on Cohesion Fund (now Reg 1084/2006, OJ 2006 L210/79); and COM(2004) 492, on ERDF, ESF, and Cohesion Fund (now Reg 1083/2006, OJ 2006 L210/25, as amended and corrected).   [5] Art 106.

[6] Art 105. See also Art 16.   [7] Arts 104 and 103.

[8] Commission Regulation (EC) No 498/2007 of 26 March 2007 laying down detailed rules for the implementation of Council Regulation (EC) No 1198/2006 on the European Fisheries Fund, OJ 2007 L120/1.

[9] EFF Vademecum, available on the website of DG Mare (no document reference number in final published version). On financial aspects of the EFF, see also: Council Regulation (EC, Euratom) No 1605/2002 of 25 June 2002 on the Financial Regulation applicable to the general budget of the European Communities, OJ 2002 L248/1, as amended and corrected, inter alia, Arts 26 and 155–159 (see also Art 10 of Reg 1198/2006); and Commission Regulation (EC, Euratom) No 2342/2002 of 23 December 2002 laying down detailed rules for the implementation of Council Regulation (EC, Euratom) No 1605/2002 on the Financial Regulation applicable to the general budget of the European Communities, OJ 2002 L357/1, as amended and corrected, inter alia, Arts 35a and 228.

[10] Council Regulation (EC) No 744/2008 of 24 July 2008 instituting a temporary specific action aiming to promote the restructuring of the European Community fishing fleets affected by the economic crisis, OJ 2008 L202/1.

[11] Communication from the Commission to the Council and the European Parliament: Financial Perspectives 2007–2013, COM(2004) 487, 14.7.2004, section 3.2, p 18.

Regulation states that '[t]he resources available for commitments from the EFF', also referred to as 'commitment appropriations', for the period 2007–13 are to be €3,849 million at 2004 prices.[12] (This contrasts with the Commission's original proposal of €4,963 million at 2004 prices.[13]) An annual breakdown of this global figure is provided in the Regulation.[14] The commitment appropriation figures provided in the EFF Regulation are to be indexed at 2 per cent per year '[f]or the purpose of programming and subsequent inclusion in the general budget of the European Union'.[15] At 2008 prices, the total commitment appropriations from the EFF are stated by the Commission to be €4,305 million (see further below).

The EFF Regulation 'defines the framework for Community support for the sustainable development of the fisheries sector, fisheries areas and inland fishing'.[16] The terms 'fisheries area' and 'inland fishing' are defined by the EFF Regulation (see subsection 2.2 below). So too is the term 'fisheries sector', which means 'the sector of the economy, including all activities of production, processing and marketing of fisheries and aquaculture products'.[17] In general terms, the Fund aims to contribute to attaining the objectives set out in Article 33 EC as well as the CFP's objectives as set out in secondary legislation (on which, see Chapters 1 and 2).[18] It therefore has social, economic, and environmental roles. More specifically, and in summary, assistance under the EFF aims to promote sustainable marine and inland fishing and aquaculture; a sustainable balance between resources and fleet capacity; competitiveness and viability of operators; protection and enhancement of the environment and natural resources; sustainable development and quality of life; and equality between men and women.[19]

The EFF Regulation recognizes the need for coordination and complementarity between the EFF and other EC financial instruments including, *inter alia*, the EAFRD, the ERDF, the ESF, and the Cohesion Fund.[20] Some of the Regulations governing the latter funds expressly recognize the potential for those funds to contribute to fisheries-dependent areas,[21] and there may also be scope for them to contribute in other ways that are relevant to the fisheries sector. Some of the Regulations contain provisions on coordination and complementarity with the EFF.[22] However, the EFF Regulation makes it clear that expenditure co-financed by the EFF 'shall *not* receive assistance from another Community financial instrument' (emphasis added).[23]

The EFF is based around five 'priority axes' and, as a general rule, works on the basis of co-financing, whereby any given operation is funded not just by the EFF

[12] Art 12(1). [13] COM(2004) 497, 14.7.2004, proposed Art 12(1). [14] Annex I.
[15] Art 12(3). [16] Art 1. [17] Art 3(a). [18] Art 5.
[19] Art 4. On gender equality, see also, *inter alia*, Arts 8(2), 11, and 19(i).
[20] Art 6(2) and (4). See also, *inter alia*, Arts 5, 13, 20(1)(e), 43(1), 44(6), 67(2)(b), and 68(3)(b), as well as *Vademecum*, section 3.1.
[21] Reg 1080/2006, Art 9; Reg 1081/2006, Art 4(2); Reg 1083/2006, Arts 3(3) and 27(4)(b).
[22] Reg 1698/2005, Arts 5(4), 11(3)(e), 16(h), and 60; Reg 1080/2006, Arts 9 and 12(7); Reg 1083/2006, Arts 9(4), 27(4)(g), 27(5)(b), and 37(1)(f). [23] Art 54.

but also by the Member State concerned and by the private beneficiary (see further below).[24] Operations funded by the EFF are to comply with EC legislation, and assistance from the EFF is to be consistent with EC policies, priorities, and activities.[25] However, the EFF Regulation adds that Articles 87–89 EC, ie those on State aid (on which see section 4 below), 'shall *not* apply to financial contributions from Member States to operations co-financed by the EFF and provided as part of an operational programme' (emphasis added).[26] In some cases, the EFF Regulation expressly states that the Fund may be used 'for the purpose of guaranteeing compliance' with certain new requirements under EC law, but only up to the date when such requirements become mandatory (or shortly thereafter, in one case).[27] In two instances, the EFF Regulation expressly refers to use of the Fund for the purpose of exceeding requirements under EC law.[28]

Under Article 2(1), the measures provided for in the EFF Regulation apply to 'the entire *territory* of the Community' (emphasis added).[29] This phrase is unusual in the context of the CFP. In its most restrictive sense, the term 'territory' means those geographical areas that are subject to the territorial sovereignty of the Member States. In the marine environment, that means (just) marine internal waters and the territorial sea (see Chapter 3). However, for current purposes, it will be assumed that 'territory' as used in Article 2(1) is intended to refer to the territory of the Member States as well as to so-called 'Community waters'.[30]

Even interpreted in the broader sense just mentioned, the phrase 'the entire territory of the Community' is potentially rather limiting. Several of the measures foreseen in the EFF Regulation, such as those aimed at improved gear selectivity (see below),[31] could usefully be applied to Community fishing vessels operating *beyond* Community waters. Yet such application would arguably be incompatible with Article 2(1). Furthermore, the wording of Article 2(1) does not fit entirely comfortably with priority axis 1 where the latter provides for support from the EFF in the event of 'the non-renewal of a fisheries agreement between the Community and a third country or a substantial cut in fishing opportunities under an international agreement or other arrangement' (see below).[32] It is unclear why the EFF Regulation, when defining its own scope, adopts a purely territorial approach and

[24] Exceptions to this general rule are mentioned below. In summary: (a) regarding Member State funding, the only exception relates to certain measures under priority axis 5 (see Arts 46(1) and 53(10)). Regarding private beneficiary funding, the only potential exception relates to so-called 'Group 1' operations referred to in Annex II to the EFF Regulation.
[25] Art 6(3) and (2). See also, *inter alia*, Arts 59(a) and (b), 60(b)(ii), and 67(2)(h).   [26] Art 7(2).
[27] Arts 25(8)(a), 28(4), and 34(5).   [28] Arts 25(7)(b) and 26(4)(d).   [29] See also Art 2(2).
[30] The term 'Community waters' is defined in Art 3(a) of Reg 2371/2002 (introduced below) as 'the waters under the sovereignty or jurisdiction of the Member States with the exception of waters adjacent to the territories mentioned in Annex II to the [EC] Treaty'.
[31] See, in particular, Arts 25 and 41.
[32] Art 21(a)(iii). See also Art 15(3)(b), which requires the national strategic plan (on which, see below) to contain, where relevant, certain information regarding 'the strategy for ... the development of fishing activities *outside* Community waters' (emphasis added).

does not also apply itself to Community fishing vessels irrespective of their location. In this respect, it contrasts with the approach taken in Article 1(1) of Regulation 2371/2002 (hereafter, 'the Basic Regulation'; see further Chapter 2).[33]

The EFF's resources are potentially available to both developed and less-developed regions of the EC. However, the allocation of resources must achieve 'a significant concentration' on the least-developed regions, known as regions eligible under the 'Convergence objective'.[34] Article 14 requires the Commission to make an annual indicative breakdown by Member State of the commitment appropriations available for the period 2007–13, on the basis of certain criteria.[35] These criteria are 'the size of the fisheries sector in the Member State', 'the scale of adjustment needed to the fishing effort', and 'the level of employment in the fisheries sector'. Further flexibility is introduced by the requirement for the Commission to take into account 'particular situations and needs and past commitment appropriations'.

Pursuant to Article 14, the Commission adopted a decision in 2006 fixing an annual indicative indication,[36] and has amended it in 2007[37] and 2008[38] to take into account various developments. The amendments on each occasion provide revised tables indicating the funding anticipated from the EFF per Member State for each of the seven years in question. Separate tables are presented for non-Convergence regions, Convergence regions, and both. Whereas the 2007 amendment uses 2004 prices, the 2008 amendment uses 'current prices' which the authors have assumed to mean 2008 prices. On that basis, as mentioned above, the total commitment appropriations from the EFF are €4,305 million at 2008 prices. Of this, €3,252 million (75 per cent) relates to Convergence objective regions and €1,053 million (25 per cent) relates to non-Convergence objective regions.[39]

---

[33] Council Regulation (EC) No 2371/2002 of 20 December 2002 on the conservation and sustainable exploitation of fisheries resources under the Common Fisheries Policy, OJ 2002 L358/59, as amended and corrected.

[34] Art 12(4). See also Art 13. For the definitions of the terms 'Convergence objective' and 'Non-Convergence objective' see Art 3(n) and (o). The 'Convergence objective' regions, excluding those for which funding associated with this status is being phased out as a result of EC enlargement, include the entirety of Bulgaria, Estonia, Latvia, Lithuania, Malta, Poland, Romania, and Slovenia as well as certain regions (including some coastal regions) in Czech Republic, France, Germany, Greece, Hungary, Italy, Portugal, Slovakia, Spain, and the UK (information from the 'Regional Policy' website of the European Commission). [35] See also Art 13.

[36] Commission Decision C(2006) 4332 final of 4 October 2006.

[37] Commission Decision 2007/218/EC of 28 March 2007 on amending Decision C(2006) 4332 final fixing an annual indicative allocation by Member State for the period from 1 January 2007 to 31 December 2013 of the Community commitment appropriations from the European Fisheries Fund, OJ 2007 L95/37.

[38] Commission Decision 2008/693/EC of 13 August 2008 amending Decision C(2006) 4332 fixing an annual indicative allocation by Member State for the period from 1 January 2007 to 31 December 2013 of the Community commitment appropriations from the European Fisheries Fund, OJ 2008 L229/5.

[39] Commission Decision C(2006) 4332, as amended by Dec 2008/693, amended Annex I, Tables 3, 2, and 1 respectively. The amounts are stated to be those derived 'after separating out the amount devoted for technical assistance at the initiative of/and on behalf of the Commission'; this is presumably a reference to Art 46 (on which, see subsection 2.2 below).

Article 52, by cross-reference to Annex II, establishes the 'maximum intensity of public aid'. Annex II is headed 'Aid intensity'. It contains a table which, in respect of the measures covered by the EFF Regulation, identifies 'the limits of public contribution granted to an operation (A), and, where appropriate, by the private beneficiaries (B) ... expressed as a percentage of total eligible costs being the sum of (A) + (B)'. It has to be said that the EFF Regulation is rather confusing in terms of the plethora of terms it uses to describe public monies. There is 'public aid', 'public contribution', 'public expenditure', 'public financing', and 'public financial resources'. The only one of these that is defined is 'public expenditure', which means 'any public contribution to the financing of operations whose origin is the budget of the State, of regional and local authorities, of the European Communities and any similar expenditure'.[40] Thus 'public expenditure' includes Member State funding and EC funding.

As noted above, Annex II refers to 'the limits of public contribution'. Strictly speaking, based on the above definition of the term 'public expenditure', 'public contribution' is wider than 'public expenditure'. In any event, it will be assumed that the term 'public contribution' as used in Annex II means EC funding and Member State funding taken together. Furthermore, because of the prohibition on assistance from other EC financial instruments to expenditure co-financed by the EFF (see above), it will be assumed that the term means, more specifically, the sum of EFF funding and Member State funding.

The method used in Annex II is fairly complex, and depends on the status of the region in question (for example whether or not it is a Convergence objective region), the nature of the operation to be funded, and any special conditions on the balance of public and private contributions.[41] Operations are placed into four categories, Groups 1–4, and operations corresponding to more than one priority axis may fall within one Group. In some cases there is discretion for the management authority in a Member State to decide into which Group a particular operation falls. Broadly speaking, the outermost regions (on which, see Chapter 2) enjoy the highest ceilings for public contribution, followed by Convergence objective regions (and certain Greek islands). In the case of Group 1 (which includes operations under certain Articles from across all five priority axes, and is the only Group to include operations under Articles 23 and 24 on cessation of fishing activities), the public contribution may be as great as 100 per cent of the total eligible costs.

Annex II is perhaps best illustrated by means of a simple example. Under the Annex, for an operation falling within Group 3 (which comprises operations provided for in Articles 37, 38, 39, and 41 in priority axis 3 and Article 44 in

---

[40] Art 3(m); this provision goes on to provide more detail.

[41] Regarding the special conditions in Annex II, see: '(*)' regarding Art 25(3) in priority axis 1; '(**)' regarding, and reflecting, Art 26(2) in priority axis 1; and '(***)' regarding Arts 29 and 35 in priority axis 2. See also the additional provisions regarding Art 25(3) under the heading 'Group 2'.

priority axis 4) taking place in 'Regions not covered by the Convergence objective', the 'public contribution' (referred to as 'A') to the funding of the operation
must be no more than 60 per cent of the total eligible cost, meaning that the
contribution by the private beneficiaries (referred to as 'B') must be at least 40 per
cent. This is represented in the Annex as 'A ≤ 60% B ≥ 40%'. By way of comparison, the figures for a Group 3 operation taking place in 'Regions covered by
the Convergence objective and outlying Greek islands' and in the outermost
regions are 'A ≤ 80% B ≥ 20%'. It can be seen that, in the case of Group 3, the
maximum permissible public contribution is 20 per cent higher for Convergence
objective regions (and outlying Greek islands and the outermost regions) than it is
for other regions.[42]

The EFF Regulation, in Article 53, in turn sets out the maximum and minimum proportion of the total public expenditure that may be contributed by the
EFF itself. As a general rule, the ceiling for the EFF's contribution to the total
public expenditure per priority axis is 75 per cent in Convergence objective
regions and 50 per cent in other regions.[43] That ceiling is subject to significant
uplifts for certain operations falling under specified provisions of priority axis 1[44]
and for the outermost regions and certain Greek islands.[45] The EFF Regulation
also specifies that the overall amount of support granted by the EFF to any individual operation may not exceed 95 per cent of the total public expenditure
allocated for assistance to that operation.[46] The minimum contribution from the
EFF to the total public expenditure is fixed at 20 per cent per priority axis and 5
per cent for the operation in question, irrespective of the nature of the region.[47]

The effect of Article 53 is that, in respect of any Member State's operational programme (on which, see below), for any given priority axis covered by that programme
the overall contribution by the EFF to the total public expenditure must, subject to
any possible uplifts, be no more than 75 per cent for the Convergence objective
regions of that Member State and no more than 50 per cent for its other regions. The
remainder of the total public expenditure is to be met by the Member State.

For example, let us suppose that a Member State, in respect of its Convergence
objective regions, has a total allocation from the EFF for the period 2007–13 of
€150 million to be distributed across the five priority axes. Let us in turn suppose
that the Member State has in mind projects in respect of its Convergence
objective regions that, taking into account private beneficiary contributions and
the requirements of Annex II, need €200 million of public expenditure and that
the Member State wishes to see all these projects funded. Assuming no uplifts,
the maximum contribution by the EFF is €150 million (ie the total allocation

[42] In respect of Group 3, Annex II sets out no special conditions on the balance of public and private
contributions. [43] Art 53(3).
[44] Art 53(7) (uplift for certain operations falling under Arts 24 and 27 and for operations falling under
Art 26(3) and (4)); and Art 53(8) (uplift for operations falling under Art 23). [45] Art 53(9).
[46] Art 53(6). [47] Art 53(4) and (5).

figure referred to above) or 75 per cent of the €200 million, whichever is lower. In this example, both figures are the same, so the EFF contributes €150 million. The Member State would then need to contribute €50 million itself to make up the €200 million of public expenditure required.

Now let us suppose that the Member State has projects in mind in respect of its Convergence objective regions that, after private beneficiary contributions and adherence to the requirements of Annex II, need €300 million of public expenditure and that the Member State wishes to see all these projects funded. Once again, assuming no uplifts, the maximum contribution by the EFF is €150 million (ie the total allocation figure referred to above) or 75 per cent of the €300 million, whichever is lower. The former figure is lower. So the EFF contributes €150 million, and the Member State (wanting to see all the projects realized) must contribute €150 million. The limit on what the Member State can add to the EFF funding is dictated by the minimum limits for EFF contribution referred to above, ie 20 per cent per priority axis and 5 per cent for the operation in question.

Before a Member State may access EFF financing, two key processes must be completed. First, the Member State must adopt a 'national strategic plan' (NSP) covering the fisheries sector. The NSP must: (a) 'contain, where relevant to the Member State, a summary description of all aspects of the [CFP]'; and (b) 'set out the priorities, objectives, the estimated public financial resources required and deadlines for its implementation'.[48] The EFF Regulation lists some matters to which the NSP is to have particular regard,[49] including, *inter alia*, 'the strategy for ... the adjustment of fishing effort and capacity with regard to the evolution of fisheries resources'.[50] The NSP is to be adopted only after an appropriate consultation with relevant partners,[51] and must be submitted to the Commission.[52] In practice, all Member States except one have submitted their NSPs to the Commission.[53] The exception is Luxembourg, which appears not to be covered by the EFF.[54]

Secondly, the Member State must draw up a single 'operational programme', coherent with the NSP, to 'implement the policies and priorities to be co-financed by the EFF'.[55] It is to cover the period 2007–13.[56] The programme must have been drawn up in close consultation with relevant partners, which also have a role in implementing, monitoring, and evaluating the programme.[57] The EFF Regulation lists several 'guiding principles' to be taken into account by the Member State in preparing and implementing its operational programme.[58] These address the economic, social, and environmental aspects of sustainable development, but

---

[48] Art 15(2).   [49] Art 15(2)(a)–(h).   [50] Art 15(2)(a).
[51] Arts 15(1) and 8(5), as well as Art 8 generally.   [52] Art 15(1).
[53] The NSPs are available on the website of DG Mare.
[54] Luxembourg is not listed in the allocation tables in Commission Decision C(2006) 4332, as amended.   [55] Art 17(1).
[56] Art 18(1).   [57] Arts 17(3) and 8(4), as well as Art 8 generally.   [58] Art 19(a)–(k).

start by emphasizing the need to achieve 'a stable and enduring balance between fishing capacity and fishing opportunities'.[59] The Regulation also specifies the programme's contents.[60] In contrast to the NSP, the operational programme must be approved by the Commission.[61] The Commission is to judge the programme against the EFF's objectives, the 'guiding principles', and the Member State's NSP. There is scope for re-examination and revision of an approved operational programme in certain circumstances (see further subsection 2.4 below).[62] The Commission Regulation sets out detailed requirements for the content of operational programmes,[63] building on those in the EFF Regulation.

The operational programme, as approved by the Commission, is the Member State's passport to funds from the EFF: if a measure is not included in the operational programme it will not be co-financed by the EFF. In practice, from November 2007 onwards, operational programmes for all Member States except Luxembourg (see above) were approved by the Commission.[64] To deal with the fact that seven Member States' operational programmes could not be approved in 2007, and to enable the transfer of unused allocations to later years, the EC's Interinstitutional Agreement on budgetary discipline and sound financial management was amended.[65] The authors are unaware whether, in the circumstances, any beneficiary took advantage of Article 55(1) which allows expenditure paid by beneficiaries from 1 January 2007 onwards to be eligible for a contribution from the EFF even where the operational programme has been submitted to the Commission after that date.

The EFF Regulation establishes a 'European Fisheries Fund Committee' to assist the Commission.[66] This is a comitology committee and is provided with various specific roles by the Regulation.[67] It has met several times since its first meeting in September 2006. It has provided favourable opinions on several Commission initiatives relating to the EFF, including, *inter alia*, what became the Commission Regulation (in November 2006) and working papers on indicators for monitoring and evaluation and on *ex ante* evaluation of the EFF (in April 2007).[68]

---

[59] Art 19(a).   [60] Art 20.   [61] Art 17(4)–(6).   [62] Art 18(2) and (3).
[63] Reg 498/2007, Art 3.
[64] See DG Mare press releases, available on the website of DG Mare. The approved operational programmes themselves are also available on the DG Mare website.
[65] Decision 2008/371/EC of the European Parliament and of the Council of 29 April 2008 amending the Interinstitutional Agreement of 17 May 2006 on budgetary discipline and sound financial management as regard adjustment of the multiannual financial framework, OJ 2008 L128/8. The seven Member States were Belgium, Hungary, Ireland, Malta, Poland, Slovenia, and the UK (see Dec 2008/693, recital (3)).   [66] Art 101.
[67] See Arts 18(3), 24(2), 25(5), 27(4), 46(4), 47(5), 55(8), 59(b), and 103(3). See also, more generally, Art 102.
[68] *Working paper on indicators for monitoring and evaluation: a practical guide for the European Fisheries Fund* (Doc/EFFC/8/2007); *Working paper on ex ante evaluation for the European Fisheries Fund* (Doc/EFFC/7/2007). See also Reg 498/2007, recital (35).

In view of the very large amounts of money involved in the EFF, it is not surprising that the EFF Regulation establishes a complex management system involving the Commission and the Member States. The Regulation recognizes this complexity and allows the means used for management to 'vary according to the total amount of public expenditure allocated to the operational programme'.[69] This provision has been implemented by the Commission Regulation.[70] In summary, the management system established by the EFF Regulation comprises the following:[71] evaluation of the operational programme by the Member State or the Commission, as appropriate;[72] provision of information and publicity about, *inter alia*, the availability of financing under the operational programme;[73] management and control of the operational programme (including designation by the Member State of a managing authority, a certifying authority, and an audit authority);[74] monitoring of implementation of the operational programme (including establishment by the Member State of a monitoring committee, to operate in association with its management authority);[75] annual reporting by the Member State's management authority and audit authority to the Commission;[76] annual reporting by the Commission to, *inter alia*, the European Parliament and the Council on the implementation of the EFF Regulation;[77] and annual examination, by the Commission and the Member State's management authority, of progress made in implementing the operational programme.[78] There is also a system of financial management regarding the Community budget,[79] payments made by the Commission to the Member States,[80] and payments made to beneficiaries.[81]

Access to EFF support is restricted by Regulation 1005/2008,[82] on illegal, unreported, and unregulated (IUU) fishing, in certain circumstances. Of particular note, Article 40(3) of Regulation 1005/2008 states that: 'Without prejudice to other provisions laid down in Community law pertaining to public funds, Member States shall not grant any public aid under national aid regimes *or under Community funds* to operators involved in the operation, management or ownership of fishing vessels included in the Community IUU vessel list.'[83] (Emphasis added.) In addition Article 45(7) of the same Regulation states that, in relation to sanctions to be imposed by Member States for so-called 'serious infringements', the Member States may accompany the required sanctions with, *inter alia*, a 'temporary or permanent ban on access to public assistance or subsidies'. Furthermore the Basic

---

[69] Art 9(2).   [70] Reg 498/2007, Arts 2, 28(2), 51, 52, and 53. See also *Vademecum*, section 3.2.
[71] See also Reg 498/2007, Chapters IV–V and VII–X.   [72] Arts 47–50.   [73] Art 51.
[74] Arts 57–61, 70–73, and 87.   [75] Arts 62–66; see also Art 9(2).
[76] Arts 67 and 61(1)(e); see also Art 9(2).   [77] Art 68.   [78] Art 69.   [79] Art 74.
[80] Arts 75–79, 81–84, 86, 88–94, and 97–98. See also Arts 85, 96, and 99–100.   [81] Art 80.
[82] Council Regulation (EC) No 1005/2008 of 29 September 2008 establishing a Community system to prevent, deter and eliminate illegal, unreported and unregulated fishing, amending Regulations (EEC) No 2847/93, (EC) No 1936/2001 and (EC) No 601/2004 and repealing Regulations (EC) No 1093/94 and (EC) No 1447/1999, OJ 2008 L266/1.
[83] Regarding the 'Community IUU vessel list', see Reg 1005/2008, Arts 25–30.

Regulation, in its provisions on adjustment of fishing capacity, makes access to EFF assistance, other than for scrapping of fishing vessels, conditional on Member States' compliance with certain requirements (see further Chapter 4).[84]

2.2 Priority axes

Introduction

The EFF Regulation sets out five priority areas, known as 'priority axes', for potential inclusion in an operational programme, although it is for the Member State to decide what emphasis is to be placed on each axis in its programme. Further details regarding each axis are laid down in the Commission Regulation. In practice, the term 'priority' is misleading, since the Member States' operational programmes may address the five priority axes exclusively.[85] In other words, EFF funding will not be available for operations other than those stemming from the five priority axes. An underlying principle applicable to any of the axes is that '[o]perations financed by the EFF shall not increase fishing effort'.[86] This principle is reflected in several of the individual provisions comprising the priority axes.[87]

The priority axes are as follows: priority axis 1: 'measures for the adaptation of the Community fishing fleet';[88] priority axis 2: 'aquaculture, inland fishing, processing and marketing of fishery and aquaculture products';[89] priority axis 3: 'measures of common interest';[90] priority axis 4: 'sustainable development of fisheries areas';[91] and priority axis 5: 'technical assistance'.[92] Each of these five axes is discussed below by reference to the EFF Regulation and, in some cases, the Commission Regulation and the *Vademecum*.

Priority axis 1

Priority axis 1 addresses the 'adaptation' of the Community fishing fleet. Much of the axis deals with adaptation necessitated by fisheries management measures adopted at the EC level, or sometimes at the Member State or external levels. These include, *inter alia*, measures to reduce capacity and fishing opportunities and to improve the selectivity of fishing gear. However, some of the aid under axis 1 is foreseen for other purposes. For example, the EFF's contribution to equipment and modernization of fishing vessels may potentially relate to improving safety on board, working conditions, hygiene, product quality, and energy efficiency and

---

[84] Reg 2371/2002, Art 16(1). [85] See, *inter alia*, recital (18) and Art 53(3). [86] Art 6(5).
[87] Arts 25(6)(e), 26(4)(d), and 44(1)(b). See also Art 33(7).
[88] Arts 21–27. Reg 498/2007, Arts 4–8 and 26. *Vademecum*, section 4.
[89] Arts 28–35. Reg 498/2007, Arts 9–14 and 26. *Vademecum*, section 5.
[90] Arts 36–42. Reg 498/2007, Arts 15–20 and 26. *Vademecum*, section 6.
[91] Arts 43–45. Reg 498/2007, Arts 21–25 and 26. *Vademecum*, section 7.
[92] Art 46. *Vademecum*, section 8.

the EFF may potentially contribute to 'individual premiums' of young fishermen acquiring ownership of a fishing vessel (see further below).

Article 21 identifies six areas for support from the EFF under axis 1: (a) 'public aid for owners of fishing vessels and fishers affected by fishing effort adjustment plans', where such plans 'form part' of specified initiatives; (b) 'public aid for temporary cessation of fishing activities in accordance with Article 24(1)(vii)'; (c) 'investments on board fishing vessels and selectivity in accordance with Article 25'; (d) 'public aid for small-scale coastal fishing in accordance with Article 26'; (e) 'socio-economic compensation for the management of the Community fishing fleet in accordance with Article 27'; and (f) 'public aid in the framework of rescue and restructuring plans in accordance with the Community Guidelines on State aid for rescuing and restructuring firms in difficulty'.

The term 'fishing vessel' in the EFF Regulation means 'any vessel within the meaning of Article 3 point (c) of [the Basic Regulation]'.[93] Article 3(c) of the Basic Regulation states that 'fishing vessel' means 'any vessel equipped for commercial exploitation of living aquatic resources', and 'living aquatic resources' in turn means 'available and accessible living *marine* aquatic species, including anadromous and catadromous species during their marine life' (emphasis added; see further Chapter 2).[94] The Commission, in its *Vademecum*, concludes that 'vessels operating exclusively in inland waters and aquaculture service vessels are excluded from support under priority axis 1'.[95] The term 'fisher' is defined as 'any person engaging in professional fishing on board an operational fishing vessel, as recognised by the Member State'.[96]

Categories '(a)', '(c)', '(d)', and '(e)' referred to above are discussed next. However, categories '(b)' and '(f)' are not referred to further here. Category '(b)' has a very specific purpose. As can be seen, it cross-refers to Article 24(1)(vii) of the EFF Regulation, which deals exclusively with 'a natural disaster, closures of fisheries decided by Member States for reasons of public health or other exceptional occurrence which is not the result of resource conservation measures'. Category '(f)' relates to rescue and restructuring, which is mentioned briefly in section 4 below on State aid.

Category '(a)' above relates to so-called 'fishing effort adjustment plans', where these 'form part' of specified initiatives. The initiatives in question are as follows: (i) 'recovery plans as referred to in Article 5 of [the Basic Regulation]'; (ii) 'emergency measures as referred to in Articles 7 and 8 of [the Basic Regulation]'; (iii) 'the non-renewal of a fisheries agreement between the Community and a third country or a substantial cut in fishing opportunities under an international agreement or other arrangement'; (iv) 'management plans as referred to in Article 6 of [the Basic Regulation]'; (v) 'measures as referred to in Articles 9 and 10 of [the Basic Regulation]'; and (vi) 'national decommissioning schemes as part of the

---

[93] Art 3(c).   [94] Reg 2371/2002, Art 3(b).   [95] *Vademecum*, section 1.1.
[96] Art 3(b).

obligations laid down in Articles 11 to 16 of [the Basic Regulation] on the adjustment of fishing capacity of the Community fishing fleet'.[97]

The term 'fishing effort adjustment plan' (hereafter, 'FEAP') is clearly important in the context of the EFF and yet neither the EFF Regulation nor the Commission Regulation defines it. It is left to the *Vademecum* to explain its meaning.[98] The latter states that FEAPs 'constitute the main instrument to implement reductions in fishing effort'. It adds that the term 'fishing effort' is as defined in Article 3(h) of the Basic Regulation, ie it is 'the product of the capacity and the activity of a fishing vessel'. This is an important point. Priority axis 1 is about the 'adaptation' of the Community fishing fleet. In principle, adaptation of the fleet (to available resources) may be brought about (primarily) by an adjustment in capacity or activity, or both. Thus 'effort adjustment', in that effort is the product of capacity and activity, is an important means of achieving such adaptation. As with fleet adaptation, effort adjustment may be brought about by adjustment in capacity or activity, or both. A FEAP, despite not referring to 'capacity' in its name, is therefore potentially a plan for reducing, *inter alia*, capacity.

The *Vademecum* adds that Member States may adopt more than one FEAP. It adds that a FEAP should contain: a description of the context, including, *inter alia*, the fisheries concerned; a description of the applicable legal framework (ie 'reference to the legal texts giving support or justification to the plan relating to either conservation measures as provided for in Chapter II and III of [the Basic Regulation] or the non-renewal of fisheries agreement [sic]'); expected results; measures contemplated; and monitoring schemes and revision procedures.

As implied by the *Vademecum*, FEAPs are to be adopted by the Member States rather than, say, by the EC institutions. (In this respect, see further Article 22 of the EFF Regulation discussed below.) In that several of the initiatives '(i)' to '(vi)' listed above are EC initiatives, notably recovery plans and managements plans under Articles 5 and 6 of the Basic Regulation and Commission emergency measures under Article 7 of the Basic Regulation, the reference in Article 21(a) to Member States' FEAPs 'forming part' of such initiatives is rather misleading. It would probably be more accurate to refer to Member States' FEAPs as forming a *response* to the EC initiatives mentioned. In contrast, Member States' FEAPs could more logically 'form part' of those of the initiatives '(i)' to '(vi)' listed above that stem from the Member States themselves, notably 'national decommissioning schemes' and measures adopted by Member States under Articles 8 and 9 of the Basic Regulation.

The *Vademecum*'s explanation of FEAPs, referred to above, is helpful but it is unsatisfactory that no explanation of this kind is found in EC legislation. As far as the latter is concerned, Article 22 of the EFF Regulation, entitled 'Content of

---

[97] Art 22(1)(a). Regarding the initiatives specified in '(i)', '(ii)', '(iv)', and '(v)', see further Chapter 4. Art 7 of the Basic Regulation relates to the Commission's emergency powers and Arts 8, 9, and 10 of the Basic Regulation relate to Member States' delegated powers.   [98] *Vademecum*, section 4.1.

fishing effort adjustment plans', sheds some limited light on the subject. First, in paragraph (1), it requires each Member State to state in its NSP 'its *policy* for adjusting fishing effort' (emphasis added).[99] The said statement does not appear to be the same as a FEAP, not least because it is to be a statement of 'policy', rather than a plan. The Member State is to set out its policy on effort adjustment 'with a view' to fulfilling its obligation under Article 11(1) of the Basic Regulation. The latter obligation relates to *capacity* adjustment rather than *effort* adjustment.[100] The link made in Article 22(1) between effort adjustment and capacity adjustment emphasizes the point made above about the potential for a FEAP, despite not referring to 'capacity' in its name, to be a plan for reducing, *inter alia*, capacity. Article 22(1) adds that Member States are to accord priority to the financing of 'the operations referred to in Article 21(a)(i)', which presumably means those FEAPs that 'form part' of recovery plans established under Article 5 of the Basic Regulation (see further subsection 2.4 below).

Article 22(2) deals with the content of FEAPs. However, all it has to say is that FEAPs 'may include all the relevant measures provided for in this Chapter'. The reference to 'this Chapter' is a reference to Chapter I of Title IV of the EFF Regulation, which is the Chapter on priority axis 1. The term 'measure' is defined as 'a set of operations aimed at implementing a priority axis'.[101] However, the reference to 'all the *relevant* measures' (emphasis added) implies that not all the measures set out under priority axis 1 in the EFF Regulation may be included in a FEAP. Judging what is 'relevant' requires consideration of any given measure provided for in priority axis 1. Clearly, the measures in Article 23 (on permanent cessation of fishing activities) and many of those in Article 24 (on temporary cessation of fishing activities) are particularly relevant (see further below). However, certain measures in Articles 25–27 may also be relevant. In this respect, it is noteworthy that Article 25 makes a specific reference to FEAPs and that Article 27 makes a specific reference to Article 23.[102]

Article 22(3) sets out time limits for the adoption of FEAPs. These reinforce the point made in the *Vademecum* (see above), and implicit in Article 21(a), that a Member State may adopt more than one FEAP. In the cases 'provided for' in Article 21(a)(i), (ii), and (iv), which presumably means FEAPs that form part of recovery plans established under Article 5 of the Basic Regulation, emergency measures adopted under Article 7 or 8 of the Basic Regulation or management plans established under Article 6 of the Basic Regulation, the relevant FEAP 'shall be adopted by the Member States within six months following the date of the Council or Commission decision'. In the cases 'provided for' in Article 21(a)(iii), which presumably means FEAPs adopted in response to the international situations

[99] See also, in this respect, Art 15(2)(a).
[100] On Art 11(1) of the Basic Regulation, see further Chapter 4.   [101] Art 3(j).
[102] Art 25(7)(a) and Art 27(1)(e).

specified therein (see above), the FEAP is to be adopted within six months 'following the notification by the Commission'.

Article 22(4) deals with reporting. It relates to Article 67 of the EFF Regulation, under which Member States are to send the Commission an annual report on the implementation of their operational programmes and a final report by the end of March 2017. Article 22(4) requires that such reports are to include Member States' 'results achieved in implementing their [FEAPs]'.

It may be recalled that one of the initiatives specified in Article 21(a) is 'national decommissioning schemes as part of the obligations laid down in Articles 11 to 16 of [the Basic Regulation] on the adjustment of fishing capacity of the Community fishing fleet'.[103] Under Article 21(a), a FEAP may 'form part' of such a scheme. In such a case, recalling the discussion above on capacity and activity, the FEAP would presumably be focused on *capacity* adjustment, in the context of decommissioning, rather than on *activity* adjustment.

As with FEAPs, the term 'national decommissioning scheme' (hereafter, 'NDS') is not defined in the EFF Regulation or the Commission Regulation and it is left to the *Vademecum* to explain what it means.[104] However, here some confusion arises. Whereas Article 21(a) states that a FEAP may 'form part' of an NDS, the *Vademecum* states, *inter alia*, that 'a [FEAP] could *include* one or more decommissioning schemes for different parts of the fleet' (emphasis added).[105] Some further confusion is created by Article 23 of the EFF Regulation, considered further below, which deals with permanent cessation of fishing activities. Under Article 23, permanent cessation may be supported by the EFF if it 'forms part' of a FEAP referred to in Article 21(a); permanent cessation is to be programmed 'in the form of [NDSs] which shall not exceed two years from the date of their entry into force'.[106] Thus Article 23 states that permanent cessation supported by the EFF is to form part of a FEAP and be programmed as an NDS, but leaves the relationship between FEAPs and NDSs unclear. Overall, it must be said that greater clarity and coherence in references in EC legislation to FEAPs and NDSs would be helpful.

Having discussed the scope of priority axis 1 and general aspects of FEAPs, it is now time to turn to the individual areas in which the EFF may provide support under priority axis 1. Article 23 deals with the first of these—the *permanent* cessation of fishing activities of fishing vessels. As already noted, Article 23 states that the EFF will contribute to financing such cessation only if it forms part of a FEAP referred to in Article 21(a) and that permanent cessation must be programmed 'in the form of [NDSs] which shall not exceed two years from the date of their entry into force'.[107] Article 23, with its focus on *permanent* cessation, emphasizes the point made above that a FEAP, despite not referring to 'capacity' in its name, may be a plan for reducing, *inter alia*, capacity.

---

[103] Arts 11–16 of the Basic Regulation are discussed in Chapter 4.
[104] *Vademecum*, section 4.2.1.   [105] Ibid, point (c); see also points (b) and (d).
[106] Art 23(1) and (2).   [107] Art 23(1) and (2).

Article 23 clarifies that permanent cessation means scrapping; reassignment 'under the flag of a Member State and registered in the Community for activities outside fishing'; or reassignment for use as an artificial reef.[108] The aid that the vessel owner receives under Article 23 is to apply to the vessel's fishing capacity and, where appropriate, the associated fishing licence.[109] The Member State has discretion to set the level of aid taking into account, in summary, vessel price, turnover, age, tonnage, and engine power.[110] The Commission Regulation adds that after permanent cessation involving an EFF contribution, the fishing vessel concerned 'shall be *permanently* deleted from the fishing fleet register of the Community and, where appropriate, the fishing licence associated with it shall be *permanently* cancelled' (emphasis added).[111]

Article 24 of the EFF Regulation enables support 'for fishers and the owners of fishing vessels' for *temporary* cessation of fishing activities.[112] It applies to only certain sources of temporary cessation, and it clarifies that a 'recurrent seasonal suspension of fishing shall *not* be taken into account for the grant of allowances or payments under this Regulation' (emphasis added).[113] The eligible sources are FEAPs under any of the initiatives '(i)' to '(iv)' listed above,[114] as well as 'management plans adopted at national level' (see below), rescue and restructuring plans under Article 21(f),[115] and some types of 'exceptional occurrence' (see above).[116] The Article sets out the 'maximum duration, during the period 2007 to 2013' for which the EFF may contribute to the financing of aid measures. The maximum duration varies depending on the source of temporary cessation, ranging from twelve months extendable by a further twelve months (where the source is a FEAP that forms part of a recovery plan under Article 5 of the Basic Regulation) to three months (in respect of, *inter alia*, a FEAP forming part of Member State emergency measures under Article 8 of the Basic Regulation).[117]

The aid under Article 24 for management plans adopted at the national level is noteworthy. To qualify for aid under Article 24, such plans must have been adopted 'within the framework of Community conservation measures' and must 'provide for gradual reductions of fishing effort'.[118] No further explanation is given of such plans, either in the EFF Regulation, the Commission Regulation, or the *Vademecum*. However, in a note to the European Fisheries Fund Committee, the Commission has clarified that aid for such plans may be granted where: (a) Community conservation measures impose the adoption of such a plan; or (b) Community conservation measures do not impose the adoption of such a plan but 'measures are taken for the establishment of a zero TAC or a closure of a fishery' and Member States elect to adopt such a plan to deal with this.[119] In the case of

---

[108] Art 23(1).   [109] Art 23(1).

[110] Art 23(3). On level of aid, see further Reg 498/2007, Art 4(2)–(4) and *Vademecum*, section 4.2.2.

[111] Reg 498/2007, Art 4(1).   [112] Art 24(1).   [113] Art 24(3).   [114] Art 24(1)(i)–(v).

[115] Art 24(1)(vi).   [116] Art 24(1)(vii).   [117] Art 24(1)(i) and (ii).   [118] Art 24(1)(v).

[119] *Subject: Note of Commission services regarding eligible expenditure in the 2007–13 programming period*, Note No 1, EFFC/14/2007, September 2007, 2 (available via Commission's online register of comitology).

'(a)', the Commission provides Regulation 1100/2007[120] on eel recovery as an example. Indeed, this Regulation states that: 'An Eel Management Plan shall constitute a management plan adopted at national level within the framework of a Community conservation measure as referred to in Article 24(1)(v) of [the EFF Regulation].'[121] In the case of '(b)', a national plan 'consisting in [sic] temporary cessation of the fishing activities alone' will not suffice; instead, any aid under Article 24 'must be accompanied by structural measures that are comparable to the management measures adopted on the basis of Article 6 of [the Basic Regulation]'.[122]

The inclusion of 'management plans adopted at national level' within the scope of Article 24 raises a question about the legal basis for inclusion of such plans within the scope of the EFF. It is Article 21 of the EFF which defines the scope of priority axis 1 as a whole. With one exception, all of the initiatives listed in Article 24 have their basis in Article 21.[123] The exception is 'management plans adopted at national level', which appear to have no basis in Article 21. So what is the status of such plans, mentioned in Article 24 but with no apparent basis in Article 21? Are they legitimately within the scope of priority axis 1 or not? The answer depends on whether Article 21 is taken as being exhaustive of the scope of axis 1 and, if it is, whether the national management plans in question can somehow be implied as falling within the scope of Article 21. Provision on national management plans of the type in question was not included in the Commission's legislative proposal for what became the EFF Regulation.[124] The reality may be that the provision was included in Article 24 during subsequent negotiations without a consequential amendment to Article 21.

Of note, Article 24 does not refer to aid in the case of FEAPs forming part of measures adopted by Member States using their delegated powers under Article 9 or 10 of the Basic Regulation (except to the extent such powers would be needed to adopt national management plans of the type referred to above).[125] The reason for this is not clear. Either of these Articles could potentially be used to adopt a one-off measure of a limited duration involving cessation of fishing activity, but it may be that Article 24 does not envisage the use of these Articles for this kind of purpose.

Article 24 also specifies a maximum limit on the amount of EFF aid available under that Article per Member State over the entire period 2007–13, except in respect of aid for the types of 'exceptional occurrence' specified in Article 24(1)(vii). This limit, exceedable in some circumstances, is the higher of 'EUR 1 million or 6% of the Community financial assistance allocated to the sector in

---

[120] Council Regulation (EC) No 1100/2007 of 18 September 2007 establishing measures for the recovery of the stock of European eel, OJ 2007 L248/17.   [121] Reg 1100/2007, Art 2(12).
[122] On Art 6 of the Basic Regulation, see further Chapter 4.   [123] Art 21(a), (b), or (f).
[124] COM(2004) 497, proposed Arts 26 and 23.
[125] On these delegated powers, see further Chapter 4.

the Member State concerned'.[126] The Commission Regulation clarifies that the phrase 'Community financial assistance allocated to the sector' means 'the EFF contribution to the operational programme of the Member State concerned'.[127]

It is noteworthy that some of the long-term plans adopted under the Basic Regulation classify themselves as either a recovery plan (under Article 5 of the Basic Regulation) or a management plan (under Article 6 of the Basic Regulation), or both, in order to clarify their status for the purpose of EFF funding under Articles 21–24 of priority axis 1. This is the case with the long-term plans for bluefin tuna and Baltic Sea cod, both of which deem themselves, for a given period, to be recovery plans 'within the meaning of' Article 5 of the Basic Regulation 'for the purpose of Article 21(a)(i)' of the EFF Regulation.[128] It is also the case with the long-term plans for North Sea plaice and sole and Western Channel sole, both of which deem themselves to be initially a recovery plan 'within the meaning of' Article 5 of the Basic Regulation 'for the purposes of Article 21(a)(i)' of the EFF Regulation and subsequently a management plan 'within the meaning of' Article 6 of the Basic Regulation 'for the purposes of Article 21(a)(iv)' of the EFF Regulation.[129] (See further Chapter 4 about how long-term plans categorize themselves.)

Category '(c)' in Article 21 relates to 'investments on board fishing vessels and selectivity in accordance with Article 25'. Article 25(1) states that the EFF 'may contribute to the financing of equipment and the modernisation of *fishing vessels of five years of age or more* only under the conditions of this Article and in accordance with the provisions of Chapter III of [the Basic Regulation]' (emphasis added). Paragraph (2) of Article 25 is a broadly worded provision. It states that the EFF contributions referred to in Article 25(1) may relate to investments to improve 'safety on board, working conditions, hygiene, product quality, energy efficiency and selectivity', on the condition that the improvements do not 'increase the ability of the vessels to catch fish'. It adds that: 'No aid shall be granted for the construction of fishing vessels nor for the increase of fishholds.'

The remaining provisions of Article 25 are more specific. Paragraphs (3)–(5) relate to engine replacement, with qualifications that seek to avoid an increase in engine power (see further Chapter 4). Paragraph (6) deals with equipment and modernization works for specified purposes, most of which are relevant to stock conservation or protection of the wider environment. Paragraph (7) relates to investments to 'achieve' gear selectivity in certain circumstances. Paragraph (8) deals with the first replacement of gear for specified purposes, including, *inter alia*, 'for reducing the impact of fishing on non-commercial species'. It is not entirely clear whether the specific paragraphs (3)–(8) are exhaustive of the way in which the more broadly worded paragraph (2) may be implemented. The fact that the

---

[126] Art 24(2).   [127] Reg 498/2007, Art 5(2).
[128] Reg 1559/2007, OJ 2007 L340/8, Art 29; Reg 1098/2007, OJ 2007 L248/1, Art 28.
[129] Reg 676/2007, OJ 2007 L157/1, Art 19; Reg 509/2007, OJ 2007 L122/7, Art 13.

adaptations referred to in paragraphs (3)–(8) seem unrelated to some of the heads referred to in paragraph (2), notably safety on board, working conditions, hygiene, and product quality, suggests that paragraph (2) may be implemented in ways other than those set out in paragraphs (3)–(8).

Category '(d)' in Article 21 relates to 'public aid for small-scale coastal fishing in accordance with Article 26'. The term 'small-scale coastal fishing' is defined by Article 26(1) as 'fishing carried out by fishing vessels of an overall length of less than 12 metres and not using towed gear as listed in Table 3 in Annex I of [Regulation 26/2004]'. The question arises as to how small-scale coastal fishing is covered by priority axis 1 in general. Article 26(3) states that: 'The EFF may contribute to the financing of socio-economic measures provided for under Article 27 in favour of small-scale coastal fishing.' Thus the application of Article 27 to such fishing is clear. However, Article 26 contains no equivalent statements in respect of Articles 23 (on permanent cessation), 24 (on temporary cessation), and 25 (on vessel investment).

Article 26(2) suggests that Article 25 as a whole applies to small-scale coastal fishing: it concedes a greater role for public expenditure '[w]here the EFF provides financing for measures under Article 25 in favour of' such fishing. However, in that Article 25 contains a provision specifically on such fishing, in relation to engine replacement,[130] it is not entirely clear whether Article 26(2) is applying the concession in question just to that specific provision or to Article 25 more generally. Articles 23 and 24 are silent about small-scale coastal fishing, and Article 26 is likewise silent about Articles 23 and 24. The *Vademecum* provides the Commission's interpretation, which is that: '*All* the measures provided for the fleet under priority axis 1 of the EFF are also available for small scale vessels (i.e. permanent and temporary cessation of fishing activities, investments on selectivity and socioeconomic compensation for the management of the community fishing fleet, etc.).'[131] (Emphasis added.)

Article 26 does not simply contain provisions relating to the application of Articles 25 and 27. It also provides for some EFF support for small-scale coastal fishing that is not available elsewhere under priority axis 1. Thus Article 26(4) states that the EFF 'may contribute to the payment of premiums for fishers and owners of fishing vessels involved in small-scale coastal fishing' in order to: '(a) improve management and control of access conditions to certain fishing areas; (b) promote the organisation of the production, processing and marketing chain of fisheries products; (c) encourage voluntary steps to reduce fishing effort for the conservation of resources; (d) encourage the use of technological innovations … that do not increase fishing effort; (e) improve professional skills and safety training'.[132]

In its *Vademecum*, the Commission considers that EFF support regarding items '(a)', '(b)', and '(c)' above (in contrast to items '(d)' and '(e)') 'concerns measures

---

[130] Art 25(3)(a).   [131] *Vademecum*, section 4.5.1.   [132] Art 26(4).

whose objectives can be attained *only* if implemented by individual operators acting collectively or by organisations acting on behalf of them or by other organisations recognised by the Member States as more appropriate for the attainment of these objectives' (emphasis added).[133] However, the Commission notes that any support provided under items '(a)', '(b)', and '(c)' would, by virtue of the wording of Article 26(4), cover 'only the premiums that will be granted to fishers and owners of fishing vessels who participate to [sic] the operation concerned', rather than covering 'any expenditure incurred by the relevant organisation for the operation concerned'.[134] In the Commission's view, the latter could instead be supported under Article 37(l) in priority axis 3 on measures of common interest (on which, see below), which also deals with small-scale coastal fishing.[135]

Category '(e)' in Article 21 relates to 'socio-economic compensation for the management of the Community fishing fleet in accordance with Article 27'. Under Article 27, the EFF may contribute to the financing of socio-economic measures proposed by Member States for 'fishers affected by developments in fishing'. The measures may involve any of the following: (a) 'the diversification of activities with a view to promoting multiple jobs for fishers'; (b) 'upgrading professional skills in particular for young fishers'; (c) 'schemes for retraining in occupations outside sea fishing'; (d) 'early departure from the fishing sector, including early retirement'; or (e) compensation to fishers in specified cases where a vessel falls within the scope of Article 23 (on permanent cessation of fishing activities).[136] In certain circumstances, the EFF may also contribute to 'individual premiums' of young fishers acquiring ownership of a fishing vessel.[137]

Priority axis 2

Priority axis 2 is on 'aquaculture, inland fishing, processing and marketing of fishery and aquaculture products'. The provisions on aquaculture in priority axis 2 are discussed in Chapter 9. Article 33 deals with inland fishing, which is defined as 'fishing carried out for commercial purposes by vessels operating exclusively in inland waters or by other devices used for ice fishing',[138] and will not be addressed further in this subsection, except below in the context of Article 42. Articles 34 and 35 relate to processing and marketing. These Articles are summarized in the context of aquaculture products in Chapter 9; that summary applies likewise to fishery products. Processing and marketing are not dealt with only in axis 2; provisions on one or both of these themes are also found in axes 1 and 3.[139]

Priority axis 3

Priority axis 3 is on 'measures of common interest'. Article 36 does not define this term. Instead, Article 36(1) states that: 'The EFF may support measures of

---

[133] *Vademecum*, section 4.5.2.   [134] *Vademecum*, section 4.5.2.
[135] See also Art 39(1), 2nd para, in respect of 'coastal fishers'.
[136] Art 27(1); see also Art 27(4).   [137] Art 27(2) and (3); see also Art 27(4).
[138] Art 33(1).   [139] See, *inter alia*, Arts 26(4)(b), 36(2)(d), 37(e), (h), and (n), and 40.

common interest with a broader scope than measures normally undertaken by private enterprises and which help to meet the objectives of the common fisheries policy.' It is not entirely clear from this whether the requirements of 'broader scope' and helping to meet the CFP's objectives are supplemental to the term 'common interest' or instead constitute its definition. The Commission's guidance brochure on the EFF suggests the latter, since it refers to 'actions of common interest, *i.e.* whose scope is broader than that of private enterprises and which help to meet the objectives of the common fisheries policy' (emphasis added).[140] However, the Commission's *Vademecum* introduces some confusion when it repeats the text of Article 36(1) and then adds that: 'Measures are "of common interest" when they are contributing to the interest of a group of beneficiaries or the general public.'[141]

The measures falling within priority axis 3 include 'collective actions' (Article 37); 'measures intended to protect and develop aquatic fauna and flora' (Article 38); 'fishing ports, landing sites and shelters' (Article 39); 'development of new markets and promotional campaigns' (Article 40); 'pilot projects' (Article 41); and 'modification for reassignment of fishing vessels' (Article 42).[142] In practice, this is a fairly mixed bag of subjects. In each case, EFF funding is only available if, in addition to any specific requirements, the measure is judged to fall within the scope of Article 36(1) (see above).

Article 37 addresses 'collective actions'. It appears to define these as 'measures of common interest which are implemented with the active support of operators themselves or by organisations acting on behalf of producers or other organisations recognised by the Member States'.[143] In the Commission's view, the term 'other organisations' includes public or private bodies, such as, *inter alia*, non-governmental organizations and scientific or trade organizations.[144]

Article 37 provides a long and varied, but non-exhaustive, list of the aims of such measures. This list includes, *inter alia*, to 'contribute sustainably to better management or conservation of resources', to 'promote selective fishing methods or gears and reduction of by-catches', to 'improve working conditions and safety', to provide 'investments concerning production, processing or marketing equipment and infrastructure', to 'contribute to the objectives laid down for small-scale coastal fishing in Article 26(4)' (see priority axis 2 above), and to 'create producer organisations ...' (on which, see Chapter 6).[145] The Commission Regulation states that support under Article 37 is not to cover costs related to exploratory fishing.[146] The *Vademecum* states that the term 'exploratory fishing' as used in the Commission Regulation means 'the use of various types of fish-searching equipment and

[140] *European Fisheries Fund 2007–2013: A user's guide* (Luxembourg: Office for Official Publications of the European Communities, 2008), p 20.
[141] *Vademecum*, section 6.1; see also bullet points in section 6.4.1.　　[142] Art 36(2).
[143] Art 37, *chapeau*.　　[144] *Vademecum*, section 6.2.1.
[145] Art 37(a), (b), (d), (h), (l), and (n).　　[146] Reg 498/2007, Art 15(1).

fishing gear to ascertain what kind of fish are present in an area, and in which quantities, so as to obtain some idea of the magnitude of the stocks in this area and of the economic viability of their commercial exploitation'.[147]

Article 38 deals with 'measures of common interest intended to protect and develop aquatic fauna and flora while enhancing the aquatic environment'.[148] The measures must be 'implemented by public or semi-public bodies, recognised trade organisations or other bodies appointed for that purpose by the Member State'.[149] They are to relate to 'the construction and installation of static or movable facilities intended to protect and develop aquatic fauna and flora'[150] (such as artificial reefs,[151] but excluding fish aggregating devices[152]); 'the rehabilitation of inland waters, including spawning grounds and migration routes for migratory species';[153] and 'the protection and enhancement of the environment in the framework of NATURA 2000 [sic] where its areas directly concern fishing activities, excluding operational costs'[154] (for example infrastructure and equipment 'for reserves' and preparation of management plans, but not including compensation 'for rights foregone, loss of income and salaries of employees'[155]).

Article 39 covers 'fishing ports, landing sites and shelters'. Under this Article, the EFF may support 'investments in existing public or private fishing ports, which are of interest to fishers and aquaculture producers using them, with the aim of improving the services offered'; 'investments to restructure landing sites and to improve the conditions for fish landed by coastal fishers in existing fish landing sites designated by the competent national authorities'; and 'safety related investments for the construction or modernisation of small fishing shelters'.[156] A non-exhaustive list of purposes for investments in ports and landing sites is provided, including, *inter alia*, measures to improve product quality and 'measures to reduce discards'.[157] The Commission, in its *Vademecum*, states that: 'The construction of fishing ports is excluded from support under Article 39 of the EFF.'[158] The Commission's brochure on the EFF states that the 'small fishing shelters' as referred to in Article 39 are 'for use by fishermen during storms or in case of damage to a vessel'.[159]

Article 40, on 'development of new markets and promotional campaigns', deals with 'measures of common interest intended to implement a policy of quality and value enhancement, development of new markets or promotional campaigns for fisheries and aquaculture products'.[160] As with Article 39, a non-exhaustive list of purposes is provided, including, *inter alia*, 'the supply to the market of surplus or underexploited species which are normally discarded or of no commercial

---

[147] *Vademecum*, section 6.2.2.   [148] Art 38(1).   [149] Art 38(3).   [150] Art 38(2)(a).
[151] Reg 498/2007, Art 16(1). See also *Vademecum*, section 6.3.1.
[152] Reg 498/2007, Art 16(2). See also *Vademecum*, section 6.3.1.   [153] Art 38(2)(b).
[154] Art 38(2)(c).   [155] Reg 498/2007, Art 16(3) and (4). See also *Vademecum*, section 6.3.2.
[156] Art 39(1) and (3).   [157] Art 39(2).   [158] *Vademecum*, section 6.4.1.
[159] *European Fisheries Fund 2007–2013: A user's guide*, p 21.   [160] Art 40(1).

interest'; 'implementation of a quality policy for fisheries and aquaculture products'; 'promotion of products obtained using methods with low impact on the environment'; and 'quality certification, including … the certification of products caught or farmed using environmentally friendly production methods'.[161]

Article 41 covers 'pilot projects'. The pilot projects to be supported must be 'aimed at acquiring and disseminating new technical knowledge' and must be 'carried out by an economic operator, a recognised trade association or any other competent body designated for that purpose by the Member State, in partnership with a scientific or technical body'.[162] They must not be of a 'directly commercial' nature, and any profit generated during their implementation must be deducted from the public aid provided.[163] For pilot projects costing more than €1 million, approval by the Member State must await a prior assessment by an 'independent scientific body'.[164] Categories of eligible pilot project are listed, relating to testing the effects of certain fisheries management measures; 'methods to improve gear selectivity, reduce by-catches, discards or the impact on the environment …'; and 'the technical or economic viability of an innovative technology'.[165] Emphasis is placed on adequate scientific follow-up.[166] In the Commission's view, pilot projects supported under Article 41 'must be truly innovative' and it is not sufficient for the projects to concern '[s]mall technical improvements of well known technologies'.[167] No support is to be granted under Article 41 for exploratory fishing.[168]

Article 42 deals with 'modification for reassignment of fishing vessels'. It states that: 'The EFF may support the modification of fishing vessels for their reassignment, under the flag of a Member State and registered in the Community for training or research purposes in the fisheries sector or for other activities outside fishing. These operations shall be limited to public or semi-public bodies.'

Whereas Article 42 ambiguously refers to 'modification of fishing vessels *for* their reassignment', Article 20 of the Commission Regulation clarifies that support under Article 42 'may be granted for the modification of a fishing vessel *after* its reassignment …' (emphasis added). The latter wording indicates that a vessel must first have been reassigned before Article 42 comes into play. The term 'reassignment' is not defined in the EFF Regulation or the Commission Regulation. However, the reassignment of a vessel to active use outside fishing is envisaged at two other points in the EFF Regulation: in Article 23, where the permanent cessation of fishing activities of a fishing vessel may be achieved by, *inter alia*, 'its reassignment, under the flag of a Member State and registered in the Community for activities outside fishing'[169] (see above) and in Article 33, on inland fishing,

---

[161] Art 40(3).   [162] Art 41(1).   [163] Reg 498/2007, Art 19(3).
[164] Reg 498/2007, Art 19(4).   [165] Art 41(2).
[166] Art 41(2), last para and Reg 498/2007, Art 19(2).   [167] *Vademecum*, section 6.5.1.
[168] Reg 498/2007, Art 19(1).   [169] Art 23(1)(b).

under which the EFF 'may support the reassignment of vessels operating in inland fishing to other activities outside fishing'.[170]

At this point, it is necessary to bear in mind that Article 42 relates to 'fishing vessels' specifically. As noted above, 'fishing vessels' are defined in terms of 'living aquatic resources' which in turn are defined in terms of the marine environment.[171] For that reason, Article 33, on inland fishing, is careful not to use the term 'fishing vessel'. However, for the same reason vessels reassigned from fishing in inland waters could not become subject to support under Article 42. Thus a vessel could become the subject of Article 42 having first been reassigned under Article 23, or perhaps some other route, but not under Article 33.

The Commission Regulation states that EFF support under Article 42 may be granted 'only if that vessel has been deleted *permanently* from the fishing fleet register and, where appropriate, the fishing licence associated with it has been permanently cancelled' (emphasis added).[172] It is not clear which 'fishing fleet register' is being referred to. However, if the vessel had first been reassigned under Article 23 it would anyway have been permanently deleted from the *Community* fishing fleet register (see above).[173] Of some interpretative value, the Commission's brochure on the EFF states in respect of Article 42 that the fishing vessel 'must first be removed from the *Community* fishing fleet register' (emphasis added).[174]

The *Vademecum* provides some useful elaboration on both Article 42 of the EFF Regulation and Article 20 of the Commission Regulation.[175] It states that support under Article 42 is to cover the cost of modifying the fishing vessel 'to make it fit for its new use outside fishing (e.g. training or research) after it has been reassigned' and that the support 'shall be paid to the public or semi-public body (e.g. school or research institute) undertaking the [modification] operation'. The *Vademecum* notes that the (reassigned) vessel in question 'may have been purchased by the public [or semi-public] body, or offered to it for free'. It also considers briefly the relationship between Article 42 and Article 23: support under the latter is paid to the original vessel owner, whereas support under the former is paid to the public or semi-public body.

Priority axis 4

Priority axis 4 is on 'sustainable development of fisheries areas'. The term 'fisheries area' is defined as 'an area with sea or lake shore or including ponds or a river estuary and with a significant level of employment in the fisheries sector'.[176] This axis expressly envisages the involvement of other EC financial instruments and requires that any EFF assistance is complementary (reflecting the principle in

---

[170] Art 33(3).   [171] Art 3(c) and Reg 2371/2002, Art 3(c) and 3(b).
[172] Reg 498/2007, Art 20.   [173] Reg 498/2007, Art 4(1).
[174] *European Fisheries Fund 2007–2013: A user's guide*, p 24.   [175] *Vademecum*, section 6.6.1.
[176] Art 3(e). See also Art 43(3).

Article 6(2) and (4)—see subsection 2.1 above).[177] The assistance in question is 'for the sustainable development and improvement of the quality of life in fisheries areas eligible as part of an overall strategy which seeks to support the implementation of the objectives of the common fisheries policy, in particular taking account of its socio-economic effects'.[178] Thus this axis has a particular socio-economic focus. The priority fisheries areas for support are those with 'low population density', 'fishing in decline', or 'small fisheries communities'.[179]

Article 43 provides a list of objectives for 'measures for sustainable development of fisheries areas'. This includes, in short, maintaining prosperity, maintaining and developing jobs, promoting the quality of the coastal environment, and promoting cooperation between fisheries areas.[180] Article 44 then sets out a longer list of eligible measures and, in addition, permits support for measures provided for under priority axes 1, 2, and 3 (except, in the case of axis 1, Articles 23 and 24 on cessation of fishing activities).[181] Of note, one of the listed eligible measures, namely 'restructuring and redirecting economic activities ...', is qualified by the requirement that these activities do not lead to an increase in fishing effort.[182] Article 45 states that measures under axis 4 are to be implemented by groups 'representing public and private partners from the various local relevant socio economic sectors'.[183] Each such group is to use a bottom-up approach to propose and implement an 'integrated local development strategy' comprising operations corresponding to the measures set out in Article 44.[184] The territory covered by any one group should be coherent and have 'sufficient critical mass in terms of human, financial and economic resources to support a viable [strategy]'.[185]

The Commission Regulation, in seeking to implement the framework created by Articles 43–45, identifies two distinct categories of activity to be funded under priority axis 4. The more procedural category relates to cooperation:[186] the EFF support is to implement 'inter-regional and trans-national cooperation' among the groups in fisheries areas, reflecting both the cooperation objective in Article 43 (see above) and a specific measure on cooperation listed in Article 44.[187] The more substantive category relates to local development strategies:[188] the EFF support is to implement these strategies with a view to achieving the objectives in Article 43 (other than the cooperation objective) through the measures set out in Article 44 (other than the specific measure on cooperation referred to above). In addition to its *Vademecum*, the Commission has prepared some other guidance documents on priority axis 4.[189]

---

[177] Arts 43(1) and 44(6).   [178] Art 43(1).   [179] Art 43(4).   [180] Art 43(2).
[181] Art 44(1), (2), and (3). See also Art 44(4).   [182] Art 44(1)(b).   [183] Art 45(1).
[184] Art 45(2) and (4).   [185] Art 45(3).   [186] Reg 498/2007, Art 21(b).
[187] Art 44(1)(h).   [188] Reg 498/2007, Art 21(a).
[189] (a) *Sustainable development of fisheries areas: guide for the application of axis 4 of the EFF*, 29.5.2006; (b) *Implementing axis 4 of the EFF: some useful questions and suggestions*, 15.01.2007; (c) *Tools for launching axis 4 of the EFF*, 14.02.2008 (all available on the website of DG Mare).

Priority axis 5

Priority axis 5 is on 'technical assistance'. This axis funds three categories of technical assistance. Two of these are at the initiative of the Member State. The first, under Article 46(2), deals with actions under the operational programme relating to 'the preparation, management, monitoring, evaluation, publicity, control and audit' of the programme itself, as well as 'networking'. The reference to 'networking' is intended by the Commission to include, *inter alia*, establishment of national networks of groups selected under priority axis 4.[190] The limit on funding for this category is normally 5 per cent of the total amount of the operational programme; however, exceptionally and 'in duly justified circumstances', this 5 per cent threshold may be exceeded.

The second category at the initiative of the Member State, under Article 46(3), addresses actions under the operational programme relating to 'improvement of administrative capacities of the Member State'. However, this category only applies to those Member States 'all of whose regions are eligible under the Convergence objective'. In practice, this means 'most of the Member States that have joined the [EU] since 2004'.[191] The Commission's view is that this category of technical assistance may be used to improve administrative capacity not only for management of the operational programme but also to 'support activities for other areas of the [CFP] provided that no other Community financing is foreseen'.[192]

The third category of technical assistance, under Article 46(1), is '[a]t the initiative of and/or on behalf of the Commission'. Measures in this category are to be financed by the EFF at 100 per cent, ie with no Member State contribution.[193] Assistance under the EFF in this category is limited to 0.8 per cent of the EFF's annual allocation.[194] It may finance 'the preparatory, monitoring, administrative and technical support, evaluation and audit measures necessary for implementing' the EFF Regulation. A list of measures is provided,[195] including some relating to networking and cooperation throughout the EC. In July 2007, the European Fisheries Fund Committee gave a favourable opinion on the Commission's proposed use of technical assistance in the period 2007–09.

One specific measure, in Article 46(1)(f), is 'the establishment of trans-national and Community networks of actors in the sustainable development of fisheries areas …'. The phrase 'sustainable development of fisheries areas' is the language of priority axis 4 (see above); yet there is no express link made to this axis and the word 'actors' is not used in the Articles comprising axis 4. The *Vademecum* clarifies that the focus of Article 46(1)(f) is the groups established under axis 4 (see above).[196] It explains that there is to be a 'Community network of groups', managed by the Commission. It is envisaged that all groups (at the national level) will be members of the Community network. The national groups, preferably

---

[190] *Vademecum*, section 8.1.   [191] *European Fisheries Fund 2007–2013: A user's guide*, p 27.
[192] *Vademecum*, section 8.3.   [193] Art 53(10).   [194] See also Art 12(2).
[195] Art 46(1)(a)–(f).   [196] *Vademecum*, section 8.1.

through one national network per Member State, are to make available to the Community network information on their actions and results achieved. In turn, the Community network is to, *inter alia*, analyse and publish such information, organize 'trans national meetings', and provide training and technical assistance to national groups.

2.3 Regulation 744/2008

Regulation 744/2008 was adopted in July 2008 to address the then crisis in the fishing industry caused by the unprecedented increase in the price of oil.[197] Aspects of the Regulation are discussed in Chapters 4 and 6 and in section 4 below, but some additional points will be made here. Regulation 744/2008 introduces measures supplementing and derogating from the EFF Regulation (and derogating from the Basic Regulation).[198] The Regulation applies 'only to public aid which has been the subject of an administrative decision by the relevant national authorities by 31 December 2010';[199] some time-frames in the Regulation are even shorter. There is no new money identified to support the measures in the Regulation; instead they are to receive support from the EFF 'within the limits of the commitment appropriations defined for the period 2007–2013'.[200]

Making use of the large majority of the opportunities provided by the Regulation will presumably require existing approved operational programmes to be re-examined and revised under Article 18 of the EFF Regulation (or 're-programmed', as the process is more commonly described). At the time of writing, the authors are unaware of whether, or to what extent, Member States have taken advantage of the said opportunities through re-programming. In any event, in relation to Fleet Adaptation Schemes (see below) under Regulation 744/2008, even if an operational programme were to be re-programmed to reserve a Member State's right to use EFF support for such a Scheme,[201] a Member State would not need to communicate its adopted Scheme to the Commission until the end of June 2009[202] and, assuming the said communication followed swiftly after adoption, the Member State's actual use of the Scheme would then not be known until after that.

Some of the additions and derogations introduced by the Regulation, referred to as 'general measures', relate to Article 24 of the EFF Regulation (temporary cessation of fishing activities), Article 25 (investments on board fishing vessels and

---

[197] *Communication from the Commission to the European Parliament and to the Council on promoting the adaptation of the European Union fishing fleets to the economic consequences of high fuel prices*, COM(2008) 453, 8.7.2008, provides the policy background to Reg 744/2008.   [198] Reg 744/2008, Art 1(2).

[199] Reg 744/2008, Art 2; see also Arts 5 and 11.

[200] Reg 744/2008, Art 3. On financial provisions, including derogations from the EFF Regulation, see also Reg 744/2008, Art 20.   [201] Reg 744/2008, Art 12(7).

[202] Reg 744/2008, Art 12(6).

selectivity), Article 27 (socio-economic compensation), Article 37 (collective actions), and Article 41 (pilot projects).[203] The remaining additions and derogations relate to so-called 'Fleet Adaptation Schemes'.[204] Some aspects of these Schemes, as well as the corresponding derogations from the Basic Regulation, are discussed in Chapter 4. Some additional points are made here.

One potentially important effect, as regards fleet adaptation, of Regulation 744/2008 compared to the EFF Regulation is as follows. Article 23 of the EFF Regulation requires that for permanent cessation of fishing activities to receive support from the EFF, such cessation must form part of a fishing effort adjustment plan (FEAP) 'referred to in' Article 21(a).[205] As noted in subsection 2.2 above, Article 21(a) requires that FEAPs falling within its scope must 'form part' of one or more specified initiatives. Regulation 744/2008, like Article 23 of the EFF Regulation, provides for permanent cessation of fishing activities. However, in contrast to Article 23, this is just for fleets or fleet segments falling below a specified fuel efficiency threshold and for vessels therein meeting specified historical activity levels.[206] Permanent cessation under Regulation 744/2008 is to be effected by means of Fleet Adaptation Schemes.[207]

Regulation 744/2008 specifies that, '[f]or the purposes of Article 23 of [the EFF Regulation]', Fleet Adaptation Schemes 'are assimilated to' the FEAPs referred to in Article 23.[208] The wording 'assimilated to' is rather ambiguous. However, one interpretation is that such Schemes may be regarded as supplementing the reference to FEAPs in Article 23, such that the EFF may contribute to financing of permanent cessation if such cessation *either* forms part of a FEAP referred to in Article 21(a) *or* is provided for in a Fleet Adaptation Scheme under Regulation 744/2008. The effect of this would be that, in respect of vessels in a Fleet Adaptation Scheme, the scope of EFF support for permanent cessation under Article 23 is extended beyond the constraints of Article 21(a). In other words, the adaptation envisaged need *not* be in response to one of the initiatives specified in Article 21(a).

The above interpretation is supported by recital (15) to Regulation 744/2008 which states, *inter alia*, that: 'There is a need to encourage Member States to *further* extend their permanent cessation schemes in order to adjust their fleets to the available resources. Consequently, it is appropriate to allow for *further* contribution possibilities to permanent cessation.' (Emphasis added.) Regulation 744/2008 also states that the requirement in Article 23(2) of the EFF Regulation for permanent cessation of fishing activities to be programmed in the form of national decommissioning schemes 'shall *not* apply to permanent cessation measures adopted in the context of a Fleet Adaptation Scheme' (emphasis added).[209] Thus the procedural

[203] Reg 744/2008, Arts 5–10.   [204] Reg 744/2008, Arts 11–19.
[205] Reg 1198/2006, Art 23(1).   [206] Reg 744/2008, Art 12(3) and (5).
[207] Reg 744/2008, Arts 11–14. Fleet Adaptation Schemes and their associated conditions are discussed in Chapter 4.   [208] Reg 744/2008, Art 14(1).
[209] Reg 744/2008, Art 14(2).

requirement under the EFF Regulation for permanent cessation to be pro-grammed as national decommissioning schemes is removed in respect of vessels in a Fleet Adaptation Scheme.

If the above interpretation is correct, the effect of Regulation 744/2008 is to broaden considerably the scope of EFF support for permanent cessation. Fur-thermore, in respect of vessels included in a Fleet Adaptation Scheme, Regulation 744/2008 allows: (a) public aid for the permanent cessation of fishing activities to be received by owners engaging in so-called 'partial decommissioning';[210] and (b) public aid for temporary cessation of fishing activities to be received beyond the constraints of Article 24 of the EFF Regulation.[211] Overall, it may be said that although Regulation 744/2008 works on the basis of short-term time-frames, its effects may be longer term. However, its *net* impact on capacity remains to be seen. In that respect, the Commission is due to report to the European Parliament and Council on the Regulation's application by the end of 2009.[212]

2.4 Conclusion

As noted in subsection 2.1 above, the total commitment appropriations from the EFF are €4,305 million at 2008 prices. This amount is to be spread over the Fund's priority axes and to be accompanied by funding from the Member States and, in most cases, from private beneficiaries. One important feature of the EFF is that the Member States have discretion as to how they allocate public expenditure across the priority axes. In this respect there is scope for differences between the aspira-tions of a Member State and its fisheries sector, on the one hand, and the ambitions of the Commission on behalf of the EC, on the other hand. The matching of fishing capacity to resources is one area where such differences may be particularly acute and it is the role of the EFF in this regard that will be explored in this concluding subsection.

The EFF Regulation makes several references to the importance of balancing fishing inputs to resources. As noted in subsection 2.1 above, Article 4 (on objectives) states that EFF assistance shall aim, *inter alia*, to promote a sustainable balance between resources and fishing capacity, Article 14 requires the Commis-sion to allocate, on an annual and indicative basis, the EFF's funds amongst the Member States based on, *inter alia*, 'the scale of adjustment needed to the fishing effort' in any given Member State,[213] Article 15 requires the NSP to address, *inter alia*, 'the adjustment of fishing effort and capacity with regard to the evolution of fisheries resources',[214] and Article 19, on 'guiding principles' for the operational

---

[210] Reg 744/2008, Arts 17 and 18.   [211] Reg 744/2008, Art 15; see also Art 6.
[212] Reg 744/2008, Art 22.   [213] Reg 1198/2006, Art 14(b).
[214] Reg 1198/2006, Art 15(2)(a).

programme, emphasizes the need to achieve 'a stable and enduring balance between fishing capacity and fishing opportunities'.[215]

In December 2007, in the context of capacity adjustment by the Member States, the Commission stated that: 'The operational programmes for the period 2007–2013 in the context of the [EFF] offer *an opportunity that cannot be missed* to ease the transition towards a more efficient Community fleet in economic, environmental and social terms.'[216] (Emphasis added.)

Clearly, priority axis 1 of the EFF is the most relevant of the Fund's five axes to reducing fishing capacity. In that regard, Article 19 requires Member States, when preparing and implementing their operational programmes, to 'take into account ... an appropriate allocation of the available financial resources between the priority axes and, particularly, where relevant, an appropriate level of financing for operations under [priority axis 1]'.[217] It is noteworthy that Article 23, on permanent cessation of fishing activities, states that the EFF '*shall* contribute' (emphasis added) to financing the said cessation, whereas all other individual heads of funding with the EFF's priority axes 1–5 use the word 'may'.[218] Furthermore, Article 22 requires Member States to 'accord priority' to the financing of effort adjustments under the recovery plans established under Article 5 of the Basic Regulation;[219] however, it is not entirely clear whether this means priority among (just) the various initiatives set out in Article 21(a) or among the EFF's five axes as a whole.

Operational programmes, to become effective, require the approval of the Commission. In terms of the law, the operational programme is to be judged by the Commission against (simply) the EFF's objectives, the 'guiding principles', and the Member State's NSP.[220] These criteria would seem to leave quite a lot of discretion to the Member State. Of course, the Member State cannot proceed without the Commission's approval and it may be that in practice the Commission, during the course of negotiations, is successful in persuading the Member State to place more emphasis on priority axis 1 than might otherwise be the case. Now that the Member States' original operational programmes have been approved by the Commission, it should be possible to see what attention they have paid to priority axis 1 in practice. At the time of writing no annual report by the Commission under Article 68 was available to provide an analysis of Member States' operational programmes. However, some indications from the Commission on Member States' practice are nonetheless available.

In 2008, the Commission participated in an inquiry into the CFP by the UK's Parliament. In a written memorandum dated February 2008 to the inquiry, the

---

[215] Reg 1198/2006, Art 19(a).

[216] *Annual Report from the Commission to the European Parliament and the Council on Member States' efforts during 2006 to achieve a sustainable balance between fishing capacity and fishing opportunities*, COM(2007) 828, 19.12.2007, section 4, p 11.   [217] Reg 1198/2006, Art 19(c). See also Art 20(1)(b).

[218] Reg 1198/2006, Arts 24–46.   [219] Reg 1198/2006, Art 22(1).

[220] Reg 1198/2006, Art 17(5).

Commission stated that it 'has invited Member States to put more emphasis [in their operational programmes] on the decommissioning of vessels'.[221] In a supplementary memorandum dated May 2008, it added that if Member States had the political will to do so, there was scope for them 'to re-programme the initial allocations [under the EFF] from fleet modernisation or other axis [sic] to fleet decommissioning'.[222]

In July 2008, in the context of what became Regulation 744/2008 (see sub-section 2.3 above), the Commission invited Member States 'to reprogramme their EFF operational programmes in view of adapting the current allocation of funds between priority axes, allowing for a greater concentration on Axis 1 measures in the coming two years'.[223] In a working document on CFP reform issued in September 2008, the Commission stated that: 'The structural funds are not used effectively to help reduce capacity and to mitigate the short-term impacts of conservation measures. There is reluctance to use funds effectively to adapt the size of the fleets and there is a preference to use funds to maintain activity and employment at the cost of sustainability.'[224]

The views of the Commission set out above all post-date its approval of the very large majority, if not all, of the operational programmes. It appears that there is a degree of frustration on the part of the Commission regarding the failure of Member States to place sufficient emphasis on priority axis 1 in their operational programmes, notwithstanding the Commission having approved the said programmes. As noted in subsection 2.3 above, it remains to be seen whether re-programming occurs in the light of Regulation 744/2008. The Commission may well take into account the choices made by Member States under the EFF, including in the light of Regulation 744/2008, when considering, in the context of the reform of the CFP, what changes are needed to the CFP in order to rectify the current imbalance between fishing capacity and fisheries resources. If the EFF, in combination with other existing mechanisms (see Chapter 4), cannot fix the problem, more fundamental solutions under the CFP may be required.

3 Regulation 861/2006

3.1 Introduction

The EFF Regulation is complemented by Council Regulation 861/2006, which was adopted two months prior to the EFF Regulation on the basis of Article 37

---

[221] House of Lords, European Union Committee, 21st Report of Session 2007–08, *The Progress of the Common Fisheries Policy*, Vol II, Evidence, HL Paper 146-II (London: The Stationery Office Ltd, 2008), p 198.   [222] House of Lords, 2008, HL Paper 146-II, p 211.

[223] COM(2008) 453, section 2, p 4.

[224] *Commission Working Document, Reflections on further reform of the Common Fisheries Policy* (2008), section 3, p 6, available on the website of DG Mare.

EC. The Regulation repealed and replaced a Regulation on funding of certain governance-related activities,[225] a Decision on the funding of monitoring and control,[226] and a Decision on the funding of data collection (Decision 2000/439— see further below).[227] It entered into force in July 2006,[228] and applies from the beginning of 2007 until the end of 2013,[229] which is the same period of application as the EFF Regulation. It 'establishes the framework for Community financial measures for the implementation of the [CFP] and the Law of the Sea'.[230] The Regulation abbreviates such measures to 'Community financial measures'; however this section will refer to them simply as 'EC funding'. The existence of Regulation 861/2006 is not expressly acknowledged in the EFF Regulation, but the EFF (then still a proposal) is acknowledged in the explanatory memorandum to the legislative proposal for what became Regulation 861/2006.[231]

Regulation 861/2006 may be contrasted with the EFF Regulation in several ways. Perhaps most significantly, the former is about the funding by the EC budget of *public* functions undertaken by the Commission and the Member States in specified areas under the CFP. Some private beneficiaries are foreseen (for example under Articles 10 and 12, on which see below), but this is in the context of the Commission and the Member States exercising their public functions. Also of importance in comparison to the EFF, there is no pre-stated sum of money available.[232] Instead, '[a]nnual appropriations shall be authorised by the budgetary authority within the limit of the financial framework'.[233]

Regulation 861/2006 works on the basis of co-financing in that Member States' expenditure covered by the Regulation is funded in part by the Member State and in part by the EC. The Regulation requires that actions financed under it are not to receive assistance 'from other Community financial instruments'. It adds that the Regulation's beneficiaries are to provide the Commission 'with information about any other funding received and of ongoing applications for funding'.[234] A system of 'control and evaluation' is established by which the Commission is to ensure that 'the financial interests of the Community are protected'.[235] In respect

---

[225] Council Regulation (EC) No 657/2000 of 27 March 2000 on closer dialogue with the fishing sector and groups affected by the common fisheries policy, OJ 2000 L80/7.

[226] Council Decision 2004/465/EC of 29 April 2004 on a Community financial contribution towards Member States fisheries control programmes, OJ 2004 L157/114, as amended and corrected.

[227] Council Decision 2000/439/EC of 29 June 2000 on a financial contribution from the Community towards the expenditure incurred by Member States in collecting data, and for financing studies and pilot projects for carrying out the common fisheries policy, OJ 2000 L176/42, as amended.

[228] Reg 861/2006, Art 33, 1st para.   [229] Reg 861/2006, Art 33, 2nd para.

[230] Reg 861/2006, Art 1, cf Reg 1198/2006, Art 1.

[231] *Proposal for a Council Regulation establishing Community financial measures for the implementation of the Common Fisheries Policy and in the area of the Law of the Sea*, COM(2005) 117, 6.4.2005, explanatory memorandum, p 2.

[232] Cf Dec 2004/465, Art 5(1) and Dec 2000/439, Art 1(2), which each state a 'financial reference' amount expressed in euros.   [233] Reg 861/2006, Art 25.

[234] Reg 861/2006, Art 26.   [235] Reg 861/2006, Arts 27, 28, and 29(1) and (2).

of fisheries agreements with third countries, the Regulation notes that: 'Under the principle of national sovereignty, only by agreement with the third country may the Commission carry out, or have carried out, financial audits of funds paid to third countries for measures financed ...'[236]

The Commission is to report, at three separate points in time, to the European Parliament and the Council on the implementation of the Regulation.[237] The Commission is to be assisted by the Committee for Fisheries and Aquaculture,[238] which is a comitology committee provided for under Article 30 of the Basic Regulation and which is provided with various specific roles by Regulation 861/2006.[239] Detailed rules may be drawn up to implement specific provisions of the Regulation.[240] Pursuant to this, two Regulations have been adopted by the Commission: Regulation 391/2007 (regarding monitoring and control systems)[241] and Regulation 1078/2008 (regarding data collection and management).[242] Regulation 861/2006 also foresees annual Decisions being adopted by the Commission regarding monitoring and control and data collection (see below).[243]

Article 2 of Regulation 861/2006 states that the Regulation is to apply to EC funding in four areas, namely: (a) 'control and enforcement of CFP rules'; (b) 'conservation measures, data collection and improvement of scientific advice concerning the sustainable management of fisheries resources within the scope of the CFP'; (c) 'governance of the CFP'; and (d) 'international relations in the area of the CFP and the Law of the Sea'. To use an analogy with the EFF Regulation, these four areas may be seen as the 'priority axes' of Regulation 861/2006. It is not entirely clear why 'conservation measures' is included in '(b)' above because the term is not mentioned subsequently in the Regulation.

Article 3 in turn identifies seven 'general objectives', corresponding to the four areas set out in Article 2, that EC funding covered by the Regulation is to support (or 'contribute towards', to use the language of the Regulation). For example, corresponding to 'control and enforcement of CFP rules' in Article 2, the general objective in Article 3 is 'improving the administrative capacity and the means for control and enforcement of CFP rules'.[244] Articles 4–7 then identify 'specific objectives' for four areas that broadly correspond to the four areas listed in Article 2.

[236] Reg 861/2006, Art 28(4).   [237] Reg 861/2006, Art 29(3).
[238] Reg 861/2006, Art 30.   [239] Reg 861/2006, Arts 9(2)(b)(i), 21(1), 23(1), 24(1), and 31.
[240] Reg 861/2006, Art 31.
[241] Commission Regulation (EC) No 391/2007 of 11 April 2007 laying down detailed rules for the implementation of Council Regulation (EC) No 861/2006 as regards the expenditure incurred by Member States in implementing the monitoring and control systems applicable to the Common Fisheries Policy, OJ 2007 L97/30.
[242] Commission Regulation (EC) No 1078/2008 of 3 November 2008 laying down detailed rules for the implementation of Council Regulation (EC) No 861/2006 as regards the expenditure incurred by Member States for the collection and management of the basic fisheries data, OJ 2008 L295/24.
[243] Reg 861/2006, Arts 21 (monitoring and control) and 24 (data collection).
[244] Reg 861/2006, Art 3(a).

The text that follows looks at Articles 4, 5, 6, and 7 in turn, including associated Articles.

Article 4, on control and enforcement, specifies the objective of 'improving the control of fishing activities in order to ensure effective implementation of the CFP within and outside Community waters'. This is to be supported by the EC funding referred to in Article 8, by financing certain broad actions by the Member States, the Commission, and the Community Fisheries Control Agency (CFCA). Article 8 in turn lists expenditure on control and enforcement that is to be eligible for EC funding. The eligible expenditure by Member States, which is set out in Article 8(a), is discussed in Chapter 4. The rate of co-financing by the EC under Article 8(a) is up to 50 per cent of the eligible expenditure, with scope for an uplift for certain actions.[245]

Article 5, on data collection and scientific advice, specifies the objective of 'improving the collection and management of the data and scientific advice required to assess the state of the resources, the level of fishing and the impact that fisheries have on the resources and the marine ecosystem and the performance of the fishing industry, within and outside Community waters'. This is to be supported by the EC funding referred to in Articles 9, 10, and 11 (see the following paragraph). Article 5 makes particular reference to 'providing financial support to the Member States to establish multi-annual aggregated and science based datasets which incorporate biological, technical, environmental and economic information'. This specific point is referred to again in Article 23 (see below).

Under Article 9, EC funding is to apply to Member States' expenditure in collecting and managing 'basic fisheries data' for a multitude of broad purposes specified in the Article. The rate of co-financing by the EC under Article 9 is up to 50 per cent of the eligible public expenditure incurred in carrying out a data programme (see below).[246] Article 10 identifies types of 'studies and pilot projects' that may be carried out by the Commission and that are eligible for EC funding, to a maximum of 15 per cent of the 'annual appropriations' authorized for the actions under Articles 9 and 10. 'Calls for proposals' by the Commission are envisaged under Article 10, and bodies such as universities and public research bodies are envisaged as responding to these.[247] The rate of co-financing by the EC under Article 10 'in the case of measures carried out following a call for proposals' is up to 50 per cent of the eligible costs.[248] Article 11 identifies expenditure regarding scientific advice that is eligible for EC funding, including, *inter alia*, funding of the Scientific, Technical and Economic Committee for Fisheries (STECF) and 'contributions to international bodies in charge of stock assessments' (of which the International Council for the Exploration of the Sea (ICES) may be an example, although this is not mentioned).

Article 6, on governance, specifies the objective 'of involving stakeholders at all stages of the CFP, from conception to implementation, and of informing them

---

[245] Reg 861/2006, Art 15.   [246] Reg 861/2006, Art 16.   [247] Reg 861/2006, Art 17.
[248] Reg 861/2006, Art 17.

about the objectives of, and measures relating to, the CFP, including, where appropriate, their social economic [sic] impact'. This is to be supported by the EC funding referred to in Article 12. Article 12 in turn lists expenditure regarding governance that is eligible for EC funding, including certain costs related to the Advisory Committee on Fisheries and Aquaculture (ACFA) and the Regional Advisory Councils (RACs) and costs of explaining, and disseminating information about, the CFP to third parties.[249]

Article 7, on international relations, specifies objectives relating to fisheries agreements, including fisheries partnership agreements (FPAs), and to the EC's involvement 'in regional and international organisations' (which presumably includes regional fisheries management organizations, although these are not mentioned). These objectives are to be supported by the EC funding referred to in Article 13. Article 13 in turn lists expenditure regarding international relations that is eligible for EC funding, including, *inter alia*, expenditure arising from fisheries agreements and FPAs, the EC's 'compulsory contributions to the budgets of international organisations' as well as other aspects of membership, various 'voluntary financial contributions' at the international level, and more generally 'financial contributions to activities (working, informal or extraordinary meetings of the contracting parties) which uphold the interests of the Community in international organisations and strengthen cooperation with its partners in these organisations'.

Just as with the EFF Regulation, there is provision for EC funding of technical assistance, namely 'expenditure associated with the preparation, follow-up, monitoring, audit and evaluation activities necessary for the implementation and the assessment of the measures within the scope of this Regulation and the achievement of its objectives …'.[250]

3.2 Funding of monitoring and control and data collection

In the areas of monitoring and control as well as data collection, access by Member States to EC funding is made contingent on their fulfilling certain duties. The situation regarding funding of monitoring and control is simpler and will be dealt with first. Member States are required to make annual applications to the Commission for funding; the application is to be accompanied by 'an annual fisheries control programme' containing specified information.[251] For any given project in the programme, the project is to be linked to one of the categories of eligible expenditure as set out in Article 8(a) (see above).[252] There is scope for the funding of major items such as vessels and aircraft.[253]

---

[249] See also Reg 861/2006, Art 18. [250] Reg 861/2006, Art 14.
[251] Reg 861/2006, Arts 19 and 20(1). [252] Reg 861/2006, Art 20(2).
[253] Reg 861/2006, Art 20(3).

Regulation 391/2007 provides detailed rules on the content of national programmes, eligible expenditure, applications for funding, and other aspects of funding. On the basis of annual applications by the Member States, the Commission is to adopt a Decision on funding, giving priority to the most appropriate actions and taking into account 'the performance of Member States in implementing programmes already approved'.[254] The latest such Decision was adopted in October 2008.[255] It sets out co-financing rates, and some maximum contributions, for particular expenditure, and it provides for a total EC contribution for 2008 of approximately €14.8 million.[256]

Regarding data collection, the situation regarding EC funding is more complicated because: (a) in addition to Member States' national programmes on data collection, there is a Community programme; (b) there is a legal framework on such programming that underpins the provisions on data funding set out in Regulation 861/2006; and (c) the latter framework has recently changed. Previously, the underpinning Regulation on programming was Regulation 1543/2000.[257] This Regulation is mentioned here because it still applied at the time that the latest Commission Decision on funding of data collection, Decision 2008/793,[258] was adopted (see further below). Regulation 1543/2000 was repealed and replaced by Regulation 199/2008,[259] which was implemented by Regulation 665/2008[260] and Decision 2008/949 (see further below).[261] So for Decisions on funding of data collection going forward, the underpinning framework is Regulation 199/2008, Regulation 665/2008, and Decision 2008/949.

---

[254] Reg 861/2006, Art 21.

[255] Commission Decision 2008/860/EC of 29 October 2008 on a Community financial contribution towards Member States' fisheries control, inspection and surveillance programmes for 2008, OJ 2008 L303/13.

[256] Dec 2008/860, Annexes I–VIII; figure calculated by adding together the total figures for 'Community contribution' in each Annex.

[257] Council Regulation (EC) No 1543/2000 of 29 June 2000 establishing a Community framework for the collection and management of the data needed to conduct the common fisheries policy, OJ 2000, L176/1, as amended.

[258] Commission Decision 2008/793/EC of 1 October 2008 on the eligibility of expenditure incurred by certain Member States in 2008 for the collection and management of the data needed to conduct the common fisheries policy, OJ 2008 L272/11.

[259] Council Regulation (EC) No 199/2008 of 25 February 2008 concerning the establishment of a Community framework for the collection, management and use of data in the fisheries sector and support for scientific advice regarding the Common Fisheries Policy, OJ 2008 L60/1, Art 28.

[260] Commission Regulation (EC) No 665/2008 of 14 July 2008 laying down detailed rules for the application of Council Regulation (EC) No 199/2008 concerning the establishment of a Community framework for the collection, management and use of data in the fisheries sector and support for scientific advice regarding the Common Fisheries Policy, OJ 2008, L186/3.

[261] Commission Decision 2008/949/EC of 6 November 2008 adopting a multiannual Community programme pursuant to Council Regulation (EC) No 199/2008 establishing a Community framework for the collection, management and use of data in the fisheries sector and support for scientific advice regarding the common fisheries policy, OJ 2008 L346/37.

Regulation 1543/2000 provided for the Commission to define a Community programme on the information needed for scientific evaluations,[262] which the Commission duly did by means of Regulation 1639/2001,[263] and for each Member State to draw up a national programme of collection and management of data.[264] Member States were entitled to apply to the EC for financial assistance in respect of their national plans.[265] The EC financial assistance was to be decided upon in accordance with Decision 2000/439;[266] in that this Decision was repealed and replaced by Regulation 861/2006 (see above), the reference to Decision 2000/439 is presumably to be read as a reference to Regulation 861/2006 for the period between the beginning of 2007 and the end of 2008.[267]

Regulation 199/2008, repealing and replacing Regulation 1543/2000, likewise provides for a Community programme and national programmes. At the EC level, there is to be a 'multi-annual Community programme for collection and management and use of biological, technical, environmental, and socio-economic data' on specified matters, the first such programme to cover the years 2009 and 2010.[268] This programme was adopted by means of Decision 2008/949; the programme itself runs to fifty-one pages in its original format in the *Official Journal*. In turn, and '[w]ithout prejudice to their current data collection obligations under Community law', Member States are to draw up multi-annual national programmes in accordance with the Community programme, the first being for the years 2009 and 2010, and to submit these to the Commission for approval.[269] Regulation 199/2008 states that EC financial assistance for national programmes is to be implemented in accordance with the rules laid down in Regulation 861/2006.[270] This is the same approach as was taken in Regulation 1543/2000 (see above).

However, in respect of funding, Regulation 199/2008 adds two further points. First, it states that: 'The basic data referred to [sic] Article 9 of [Regulation 861/2006] shall cover only those parts of Member States' national programmes that implement the Community programme.'[271] The meaning of this statement is not entirely clear. As noted above, Article 9 of Regulation 861/2006 specifies the categories of data for which EC funding is available to Member States under Regulation 861/2006. However, these categories are very broad. Thus the purpose of the above provision of Regulation 199/2008 may be to limit the scope of EC funding under Regulation 861/2006 to data collection and management by

---

[262] Reg 1543/2000, Art 5(1).

[263] Commission Regulation (EC) No 1639/2001 of 25 July 2001 establishing the minimum and extended Community programmes for the collection of data in the fisheries sector and laying down detailed rules for the application of Council Regulation (EC) No 1543/2000, OJ 2001 L222/53, as amended.   [264] Reg 1543/2000, Art 6(1).

[265] Reg 1543/2000, Art 6(4).   [266] Reg 1543/2000, Art 6(4); see also Art 10(3).

[267] Reg 861/2006, Art 32 and Reg 199/2008, Art 28(1).   [268] Reg 199/2008, Art 3.

[269] Reg 199/2008, Arts 4 and 9(1).   [270] Reg 199/2008, Art 8(1).

[271] Reg 199/2008, Art 8(2).

the Member States that falls into both Article 9 *and* the Community programme. Secondly, Regulation 199/2008 states that: 'Community financial assistance for national programmes shall only be granted if the rules set out in this Regulation are fully respected.'[272] The rules set out in the Regulation are quite extensive, and relate not only to the national programme itself but also to data collection, management, and use. It is notable that the Regulation refers to the rules set out 'in this Regulation' rather than, more specifically, to the rules set out in a particular Chapter or section of the Regulation. The Commission also gives itself powers to suspend, recover, or reduce Community financial assistance in certain circumstances.[273]

Regulation 861/2006 establishes procedures for the provision of '[t]he Community financial contribution to the expenditure incurred by the Member States for the collection and management of the basic fisheries data referred to in Article 9'.[274] The procedures refer first to programming. They refer to a Community programme and to national programmes in the field of data collection (see below), but make no reference to the underpinning framework in this regard in Regulations 1543/2000 or 199/2008. The link is instead made by Regulations 1543/2000 and 199/2008 themselves, as noted above. In respect of Regulation 1543/2000, this link is clarified by Decision 2008/793 (see below), which states that the national programmes as referred to in Regulation 861/2006 'are to be drawn up in accordance with' Regulation 1543/2000.[275] The generic approach adopted in Regulation 861/2006 may have been deliberate, in anticipation of a change of regime from Regulation 1543/2000 to Regulation 199/2008, but that does not prevent it from being rather confusing.

Under Regulation 861/2006, each Member State is required to draw up 'a national programme for collection and management of data'.[276] The programme is to 'describe both the collection of detailed data and the processing *needed to produce aggregated data in accordance with the objectives set out in Article 5*' (emphasis added).[277] A Community programme 'shall be defined' under the comitology procedure, 'covering the essential information needed for scientific evaluations'.[278] Each Member State is to 'include in its national programme the elements relating to it as foreseen under the Community programme …'.[279] Member States 'may apply to the Community for financial assistance for those parts of their national programmes that correspond to the elements of the Community programme with which they are concerned'.[280]

On the basis of the national programmes submitted by the Member States, the Commission is to adopt Decisions each year 'on the Community financial

---

[272] Reg 199/2008, Art 8(3).
[273] Reg 199/2008, Art 8(4)–(7).
[274] Reg 861/2006, Arts 22–24.
[275] Dec 2008/793, recitals (1)–(5).
[276] Reg 861/2006, Art 23(2).
[277] Reg 861/2006, Art 23(2).
[278] Reg 861/2006, Art 23(1).
[279] Reg 861/2006, Art 23(3).
[280] Reg 861/2006, Art 23(4).

contribution to the national programmes', giving priority to the most appropriate actions.[281] The latest such Decision at the time of writing, Decision 2008/793, was adopted in October 2008 and, as noted above, was made by reference to Regulation 1543/2000. It sets out co-financing rates and provides for a maximum Community contribution for 2008 of approximately €31.4 million.[282] Regulation 1078/2008 provides detailed rules on the application by Member States for the Community financial contribution for expenditure for collection and management of data under Regulation 861/2008, by reference to Regulation 1543/2000's successor, Regulation 199/2008. It applies to expenditure incurred by Member States from the start of 2009.[283]

4 State aid

Section 2 above examines the EFF. As seen there, EC aid under the EFF requires a contribution from Member States (except in respect of some aid under priority axis 5).[284] This section deals with aid granted by Member States to the fishing industry separately from any EFF or other EC-financed project, and considers how far it is permissible under EC law for such aid to be granted.

To answer that question it is appropriate to begin by examining the provisions of the EC Treaty dealing with State aid in general, which are set out in Articles 87–89 EC. Article 87(1) stipulates that, except as otherwise provided in the EC Treaty, any aid 'which distorts or threatens to distort competition by favouring certain undertakings or the production of certain goods shall, in so far as it affects trade between Member States, be incompatible with the common market'. Paragraph 2 of Article 87 lists certain types of aid that '*shall* be compatible with the common market', while paragraph 3 list types of aid that '*may* be considered to be compatible with the common market' (emphasis added). The only kind of aid listed in Article 87(2) that is potentially relevant to the fishing industry is aid 'to make good the damage caused by natural disasters or exceptional occurrences'. Article 87(3) lists four types of aid of possible relevance: (a) aid to 'promote the economic development of areas where the standard of living is abnormally low or where there is serious underemployment'; (b) aid to 'promote the execution of an important project of common European interest or to remedy a serious disturbance in the economy of a Member State'; (c) aid to 'facilitate the development of certain economic activities or of certain economic areas, where such aid does not adversely affect trading conditions to an extent contrary to the common interest'; and (d) such other categories of aid as may be specified by the Council.

---

[281] Reg 861/2006, Art 24.

[282] Dec 2008/793, Annexes I and II; figure calculated by adding together the total figures for 'Max. Community contribution' in each Annex. [283] Reg 1078/2008, Art 17.

[284] Reg 1198/2006, Art 53 and, in particular, Art 53(6) and (10).

Under Article 88(1) the Commission is to keep all systems of State aid under review. Article 88(3) provides that the Commission must be informed in advance of all plans to grant aid. Under the first subparagraph of Article 88(2), where the Commission finds that aid is 'not compatible with the common market', it 'shall decide that the State concerned shall abolish or alter such aid' within a specified time limit. If that State fails to do so, the Commission, or any other interested State, may, under the second subparagraph of Article 88(2), refer the matter to the Court. Under the third subparagraph, the Council, at the request of a Member State and if unanimous, may decide that aid which that State is granting or intends to grant shall be considered to be compatible with the common market, in derogation from Article 87 EC or any Regulation made under Article 89 EC (see below), if such a decision is 'justified by exceptional circumstances'. If the Commission has already initiated the procedure under the first subparagraph of Article 88(2), any request made to the Council by a Member State under the third subparagraph of Article 88(2) has the effect of suspending that procedure. Article 89 authorizes the Council to make any 'appropriate regulations' for the application of Articles 87 and 88.

According to Article 36 EC, '[t]he provisions of the chapter relating to rules on competition shall apply to production of and trade in agricultural products only to the extent determined by the Council'. The 'chapter relating to rules on competition' contains, *inter alia*, Articles 87–89. 'Agricultural products' include fishery products (see Chapter 2). Thus, the effect of Article 36 is that the rules on State aid in Articles 87–89 EC apply to 'production of and trade in' fishery products only to the extent determined by the Council.

At the time of writing there were three pieces of legislation in force in which the Council had made such a determination regarding fisheries.[285] The first, in chronological order of adoption, was the basic Regulation on the common organization of the markets.[286] Article 32 of that Regulation stipulates that notwithstanding any provisions to the contrary adopted under Articles 36 and 37 EC, Articles 87–89 EC 'shall apply to production of and trade in the products referred to in Article 1' of the Regulation. In summary, such products include most forms of fresh, chilled, frozen, and processed fish, crustaceans, and molluscs (see further Chapters 6 and 2). There is no definition of 'production' in the Regulation, but 'producer' and 'fishery products' are defined. The former means 'physical or legal persons using means of production to produce fishery products with a view to first-stage marketing of them', while 'fishery products' cover 'products caught at

[285] As noted at the beginning of subsection 2.1 above, some of the EC funds other than the EFF have potential application to fisheries. One of them, the EAFRD, has provisions concerning the applicability of Arts 87–89: see Reg 1698/2005, Art 88. For reasons of relevance and space, this provision is not considered further here.

[286] Council Regulation (EC) No 104/2000 of 17 December 1999 on the common organisation of the markets in fishery and aquaculture products, OJ 2000 L17/22, as amended and corrected.

sea or in inland waters and the products of aquaculture listed' in Article 1.[287] It is reasonable to infer from those definitions that 'production' as referred to in Article 32 includes the production of fishery products by means of fishing at sea and in inland waters, and aquaculture. Thus, the effect of Article 32 is that the EC Treaty's rules on State aid apply to the production of fishery products by means of fishing at sea and in inland waters, and aquaculture, as well as trade in such products. The justification for such application is expressed in recital (37) of the Regulation as follows: 'the establishment of a single market based on a common price system would be jeopardised by the granting of certain aids; therefore, the provisions of the [EC] Treaty under which State aid granted by Member States may be examined, leading to the prohibition of schemes which are incompatible with the common market, should also apply to the fishing industry'. Regulation 104/2000 is the most recent of a series of basic Regulations relating to the common organization of the market in fishery products dating back to 1970. Those earlier Regulations each had provisions similar to Article 32 of Regulation 104/2000.

The second piece of current legislation dealing with the application of the EC Treaty's rules on State aid to the fishing industry is the EFF Regulation (introduced in section 2 above). Article 7(1) of the Regulation states that '[w]ithout prejudice to paragraph 2 of this Article, Articles 87, 88 and 89 of the [EC] Treaty shall apply to aid granted by the Member States to enterprises in the fisheries sector'. 'Fisheries sector' is defined as 'the sector of the economy, including all activities of production, processing and marketing of fisheries and aquaculture products'.[288] Thus, subject to what is said about paragraph 2 below, there is a considerable duplication between Article 7(1) of the EFF Regulation and Article 32 of Regulation 104/2000. Paragraph 2 of Article 7 of the EFF Regulation stipulates that the EC Treaty's rules on State aid shall *not* apply to financial contributions from Member States to operations co-financed by the EFF and provided as part of an operational programme.[289] Under paragraph 3 of Article 7, '[n]ational provisions setting up public financing going beyond the provisions of this Regulation concerning financial contributions, as provided for in paragraph 2, shall be treated as a whole on the basis of paragraph 1', and thus are subject to Articles 87–89 EC. The reference to 'as a whole' is not very clear. Presumably what it means is that where a project is funded partly by a contribution from the EFF and partly by a contribution from a Member State of an amount greater than is allowed under the EFF Regulation,[290] the whole of that Member State's contribution, and not simply that part of the contribution in excess of the level stipulated by the EFF Regulation, is to be assessed for its legality under Articles 87–89 EC.

---

[287] Reg 104/2000, Art 1.   [288] Reg 1198/2006, Art 3(a).

[289] For an explanation of what is meant by an operational programme, see subsection 2.1 above.

[290] The minimum permissible contributions by the EFF are specified in Reg 1198/2006, Art 53(4) and (5). See further subsection 2.1 above.

The third piece of legislation in which the Council has made a determination about the application of the EC Treaty's rules on State aid to fisheries is Regulation 744/2008, which was adopted in the summer of 2008 to address the then crisis in the fishing industry caused by the unprecedented increase in the price of oil (see further subsection 2.3 above and Chapters 4 and 6). Article 4(1) of Regulation 744/2008 provides that the EC Treaty's provisions on State aid do *not* apply to aid granted by Member States as part of projects financed by the EFF under that Regulation. That is similar to Article 7(2) of the EFF Regulation. Article 4(2) of Regulation 744/2008 goes on to provide that 'aid granted by Member States with no financing from Community financial instruments and exceeding the limits laid down in' Regulation 736/2008,[291] which provides that certain forms of aid to small and medium-sized enterprises are permissible (discussed below), 'shall be subject to the application of' Articles 87–89 EC. This is essentially the same position as under Article 32 of Regulation 104/2000 and Article 7(1) of the EFF Regulation.

In broad terms, the cumulative effect of Regulation 104/2000, the EFF Regulation, and Regulation 744/2008 is that State aid to the fishing industry that is not part of a project co-financed by the EFF is in principle subject to Articles 87–89 EC. That means that any such proposed State aid to the fishing industry must be notified to the Commission, which will assess it to see whether or not it is compatible with the common market within the meaning of Article 87 EC. However, some modification to that position has been made by two Commission Regulations that provide that certain types of State aid to the fishing industry are automatically to be considered as compatible with the common market and therefore permissible. Those two Commission Regulations were adopted under Regulation 994/98,[292] which empowers the Commission to declare certain types of State aid as compatible with the common market and therefore permissible.

The first of the Commission Regulations is Regulation 875/2007, which deals with so-called '*de minimis*' exceptions.[293] The Commission had first laid down *de minimis* exceptions in Regulation 1860/2004,[294] which applied to both the agriculture and fisheries sectors. Regulation 875/2007 disapplies Regulation

---

[291] Commission Regulation (EC) No 736/2008 of 22 July 2008 on the application of Articles 87 and 88 of the Treaty to State aid to small and medium-sized enterprises active in the production, processing and marketing of fisheries products, OJ 2008 L201/16.

[292] Council Regulation (EC) No 994/98 of 7 May 1998 on the application of Articles 92 and 93 [now 87 and 88] of the Treaty establishing the European Community to certain categories of horizontal State aid, OJ 1998 L142/1.

[293] Commission Regulation (EC) No 875/2007 of 24 July 2007 on the application of Articles 87 and 88 of the EC Treaty to *de minimis* aid in the fisheries sector and amending Regulation (EC) No 1860/2004, OJ 2007 L193/6.

[294] Commission Regulation (EC) No 1860/2004 of 6 October 2004 on the application of Articles 87 and 88 of the EC Treaty to *de minimis* aid in the agriculture and fisheries sector, OJ 2004 L325/4, as amended.

1860/2004 to the fisheries sector,[295] and substantially increases the levels of aid that had been considered *de minimis* in Regulation 1860/2004, 'in the light of the experience gained by the Commission' in the operation of *de minimis* exceptions in the fisheries sector.[296] Regulation 875/2007, which applies until the end of 2013,[297] provides that '[a]id measures shall be deemed not to meet all the criteria of Article 87(1)' EC (and therefore will be considered permissible) and need not be notified under Article 88(3) EC if the total amount of aid granted to 'any one undertaking' does not exceed €30,000 over any period of three fiscal years.[298] An 'undertaking' is defined as one that is 'active in the production, processing and marketing of fisheries products'.[299] Such products are defined as meaning those products defined in Article 1 of Regulation 104/2000 (see above). The total amount of such aid granted to undertakings by a Member State over three fiscal years must not exceed the level specified for that Member State in the Annex to the Regulation.[300] Those levels range from €138.55 million in the case of France to €0 in the case of Luxembourg (other land-locked Member States are allocated an amount, which is presumably for inland fisheries and/or aquaculture). The amount per Member State represents roughly 2.5 per cent or less of its annual fisheries output.[301] The amounts for France, Italy, Spain, and the UK, each of which is over €90 million, appear generous, and would allow each of those States to provide permitted aid to 3,000 or more undertakings over a three-year period. The *de minimis* exceptions do not apply to: (a) aid in cases where the amount is fixed on the basis of price or quantity of goods put on the market; (b) aid to export-related activities; (c) aid which is made on condition that domestic goods are used rather than imported goods; (d) aid that serves to increase fishing capacity unless it concerns aid for modernization over the main deck, which is permitted under EC law (see Chapter 4); (e) aid for the purchase or construction of fishing vessels; and (f) aid 'granted to undertakings in difficulty'.[302] An explanation for some of those exceptions is set out in recitals (10) to (13) of the Regulation. Although, as mentioned, there is no obligation to notify *de minimis* aid to the Commission under Article 88(3) EC, the Commission may nevertheless request the information necessary to assess whether a Member State has complied with all the conditions laid down in the Regulation.[303] A witness to a British parliamentary committee reviewing the CFP in 2008 argued that *de minimis* exceptions were objectionable because they allowed a Member State, if it wished, automatically to provide 'a de facto subsidy for fuel costs in the fishing industry'.[304] The Committee itself forcefully expressed the view that there should be no relaxation of the current *de minimis* exceptions.[305] Nevertheless, a

[295] Reg 875/2007, Art 6.   [296] Reg 875/2007, recitals (5) and (6).
[297] Reg 875/2007, Art 7.
[298] Reg 875/2007, Art 3(1) and (2). See further Arts 3(3)–(8), 4, and 5.
[299] Reg 875/2007, Art 2(a).   [300] Reg 875/2007, Art 3(4).
[301] Reg 875/2007, recital (6).   [302] Reg 875/2007, Art 1.   [303] Reg 875/2007, Art 4(4).
[304] House of Lords, 2008, HL Paper 146-I, para 79 and HL Paper 146-II, p 71 (evidence of the Royal Society for the Protection of Birds).   [305] House of Lords, 2008, HL Paper 146-I, para 87.

fortnight before the Committee's report was published, the Commission had announced that it was considering, in the context of the crisis then facing the fishing industry in the wake of the huge rise in the price of oil, an increase in the limits of aid that would be considered *de minimis*.[306] However, no further action had been taken by the Commission at the time of writing.

The second Commission Regulation is Regulation 736/2008, which has already been referred to briefly above. The Regulation follows a similar Regulation of 2004,[307] which lapsed at the end of 2006. Regulation 736/2008 itself is to remain in force until the end of 2013.[308] It provides that certain types of State aid to small and medium-sized enterprises (SMEs) 'active in the production, processing or marketing of fisheries products' are automatically considered to be permissible, without the need for examination by the Commission.[309] 'Fisheries products' are defined as 'both products caught at sea or in inland waters and the products of aquaculture listed in Article 1' of Regulation 104/2000.[310] SMEs are defined in Article 2(g) of Regulation 736/2008 as 'small and medium-sized enterprises as defined in Article 2(7) of Commission Regulation (EC) No … /2008 of 2 July 2008 on the application of Articles 87 and 88 of the Treaty declaring certain categories of aid compatible with the common market'. The authors have been unable to discover a Commission Regulation of that date or title. The nearest piece of legislation that they could find was Commission Regulation (EC) 800/2008 of 6 August 2008 declaring certain categories of aid compatible with the common market in application of Articles 87 and 88 of the Treaty (General block exemption Regulation).[311] Support for the view that Regulation 800/2008 is the Regulation to which Article 2(g) of Regulation 736/2008 intends to refer is provided by recital (16) of the latter Regulation, which states that an SME should be defined as in Annex I to Regulation 70/2001:[312] Article 43 of Regulation 800/2008 provides that any reference to Regulation 70/2001 shall be construed as a reference to Regulation 800/2008. The latter defines an SME, in Article 2(7), as an undertaking that fulfils the criteria set out in Annex I to the Regulation. The latter, which runs to three pages, provides, broadly speaking, that an SME is an enterprise that employs fewer than 250 people and has an annual turnover not exceeding €50 million and/or an annual balance sheet not exceeding €43 million.[313] Whatever the correct definition of an SME is for the

[306] COM(2008) 453, p 11.
[307] Commission Regulation (EC) No 1595/2004 of 8 September 2004 on the application of Articles 87 and 88 of the Treaty to State aid to small and medium-sized enterprises active in the production, processing and marketing of fisheries products, OJ 2004 L291/3.   [308] Reg 736/2008, Art 27.
[309] Reg 736/2008, Arts 1 and 3.   [310] Reg 736/2008, Art 2(f).   [311] OJ 2008 L214/3.
[312] Commission Regulation (EC) No 70/2001 of 12 January 2001 on the application of Articles 87 and 88 of the EC Treaty to State aid to small and medium-sized enterprises, OJ 2001 L10/33, as amended.
[313] Annex I complicates matters further by referring in the criteria for an SME not only to 'small' and 'medium-sized' enterprises, but also to 'micro' enterprises: see Art 2.

purposes of Regulation 736/2008 (and the drafting of that Regulation on this point is rather unsatisfactory, compounded by the fact that no correction had been published by end of November 2008, four months after the adoption of the Regulation), 'the vast majority of fishing undertakings in the European Union are SMEs', according to recital (24) of the Regulation.

The types of aid to SMEs that Regulation 736/2008 provides are automatically permissible are the following: (a) permanent and temporary cessation of fishing activities;[314] (b) 'socio-economic compensation for the management of the fleet';[315] (c) 'productive investments' in aquaculture;[316] (d) 'aqua-environmental measures';[317] (e) public health measures;[318] (f) animal health measures;[319] (g) inland fishing;[320] processing and marketing;[321] (h) 'collective actions';[322] (i) protection and development of aquatic flora and fauna;[323] (j) investments in fishing ports, landing sites, and shelters;[324] (k) development of new markets and promotional campaigns;[325] (l) 'pilot projects';[326] (m) reassignment of fishing vessels;[327] (n) technical assistance;[328] and (o) aid in the form of certain types of tax exemption.[329] In every case apart from '(o)' the matters listed parallel a number of the matters that are eligible for assistance from the EFF. Recital (5) of Regulation 736/2008 also explains that the listed types of aid are ones that the Commission has 'systematically approved' under Articles 87 and 88 EC for many years and therefore do 'not require a case-by-case assessment of [their] compatibility with the common market'. To be permissible, each type of aid listed in Regulation 736/2008 apart from '(o)' above must fulfil certain of the conditions applying to assistance from the EFF set out in the EFF Regulation and Regulation 498/2007. Articles 8–23 of Regulation 736/2008 make such conditions applicable by simply cross-referring to particular provisions of those Regulations. They also state, in point (b) of each Article, that 'the amount of aid [given by a Member State must] not exceed, in grant equivalent, the total rate of public contributions fixed by Annex II' to the EFF Regulation. It is not entirely clear how this system of cross-referencing is meant to work since Annex II and many of the provisions of the EFF Regulation and Regulation 498/2007 referred to in Articles 8–23 relate to matters involving, or exclusive to, the EFF.

Various other conditions must also be fulfilled in order for State aid to the fisheries sector of the kinds listed in Articles 8–24 of Regulation 736/2008 to benefit from that Regulation and be considered permissible. First, any aid granted must be 'transparent'.[330] 'Transparent aid' is aid 'in respect of which it is possible to calculate precisely the gross grant equivalent ex ante without need to undertake

---

[314] Reg 736/2008, Arts 8 and 9.   [315] Reg 736/2008, Art 10.
[316] Reg 736/2008, Art 11.   [317] Reg 736/2008, Art 12.   [318] Reg 736/2008, Art 13.
[319] Reg 736/2008, Art 14.   [320] Reg 736/2008, Art 15.   [321] Reg 736/2008, Art 16.
[322] Reg 736/2008, Art 17.   [323] Reg 736/2008, Art 18.   [324] Reg 736/2008, Art 19.
[325] Reg 736/2008, Art 20.   [326] Reg 736/2008, Art 21.   [327] Reg 736/2008, Art 22.
[328] Reg 736/2008, Art 23.   [329] Reg 736/2008, Art 24.   [330] Reg 736/2008, Art 5(1).

a risk assessment'.[331] Certain forms of aid are listed in Article 5 that are considered to be transparent (for example, direct grants and interest rate subsidies), while other forms of aid are listed that are considered not to be transparent (for example, 'aid comprised in capital injections'). Secondly, aid must have an 'incentive effect',[332] a concept that is explained in Article 7(2) and (3). Thirdly, measures financed by State aid and 'their effects' must 'comply with Community law'.[333] Fourthly, a beneficiary of aid must comply with 'the rules of the Common Fisheries Policy' during the grant period. Failure to do so means that the grant must be reimbursed 'in proportion to the gravity of the infringement'.[334] This provision is potentially a useful supplement to those EC rules that seek to ensure compliance with conservation and marketing measures (discussed in Chapters 4 and 6). It is perhaps unfortunate that there is no equivalent provision in Regulation 875/2007 (on *de minimis* exceptions). Fifthly, a Member State must send the Commission summary information about the aid that it has granted in accordance with Regulation 736/2008; publish full details of such grants on the Internet; publish an annual report on its application of the Regulation; and provide the Commission with the information that the latter considers necessary for it to monitor the way in which the Regulation is being applied.[335] Lastly, in applying the provisions concerning the limits on the amount of aid that may be granted, rules regarding the cumulation of aid, set out in Article 6 of Regulation 736/2008, must be observed.

Regulation 736/2008 does not apply to a number of types of aid. They include certain of the types of aid to which Regulation 875/2007 does not apply, namely points '(a)'–'(c)' and '(f)' listed earlier when discussing Regulation 875/2007.[336] In relation to point '(f)', aid 'granted to undertakings in difficulty', that phrase was not explained in Regulation 875/2007. It is, however, defined in some detail in Article 2(i) of Regulation 736/2008. There are a number of types of aid to which Regulation 736/2008 does not apply that have no equivalent in Regulation 875/2007. They are: (a) aid schemes that do not explicitly exclude the payment of individual aid to an undertaking that is subject to an outstanding recovery order following a Commission decision declaring an aid illegal and incompatible with the common market;[337] (b) ad hoc aid in favour of an undertaking that is subject to an outstanding recovery order following a Commission decision declaring an aid illegal and incompatible with the common market;[338] (c) aid for individual projects with eligible expenses in excess of €2 million;[339] and (d) aid for individual projects where the amount of aid exceeds €1 million per beneficiary a year.[340]

Unlike Regulation 875/2007, Regulation 736/2008 does not explicitly exclude from its application aid that increases fishing capacity or aid for the purchase or

[331] Reg 736/2008, Art 2(h).   [332] Reg 736/2008, Art 7(1).

[333] Reg 736/2008, Art 3(4).   [334] Reg 736/2008, Art 3(5).   [335] Reg 736/2008, Art 25.

[336] Reg 736/2008, Art 1(2)(a)–(d).   [337] Reg 736/2008, Art 1(2)(e).

[338] Reg 736/2008, Art 1(2)(f).   [339] Reg 736/2008, Art 1(3).   [340] Ibid.

construction of fishing vessels, which might therefore give rise to concerns about the possibility of fleet capacity being increased. However, the omission of those two kinds of aid from the list of exceptions in Regulation 736/2008 does not mean that a Member State may grant such aid under the Regulation. Since those two kinds of aid are not included among the types of aid listed in Regulation 736/2008 that may be granted to SMEs that are considered permissible, it follows that a Member State cannot grant aid that increases fishing capacity or aid for the purchase or construction of fishing vessels under Regulation 736/2008. It is, of course, always possible for a Member State to consider granting such aid outside the framework of Regulation 736/2008 (and Regulation 875/2007). The position will then be governed by Articles 87–89 EC. The general operation of those provisions in respect of aid that falls outside the framework of Regulations 875/2007 and 736/2008 must now be considered.

State aid to the fishing industry that falls outside the scope of those Regulations, and that is not part of a project co-financed by the EFF as described above or some other EC fund, is subject to review by the Commission under Article 88 EC to assess whether or not it is compatible with the common market and therefore permissible under the EC Treaty. To discover what kinds of aid are likely to be regarded by the Commission as compatible with the common market, one could examine the Commission's Decisions reviewing past aid, which are published on the website of DG Mare.[341] However, that would be a rather cumbersome exercise, and might not give a complete indication of the Commission's views on the permissibility of State aid, which have changed over time.[342] Few of the Commission's Decisions on State aid to the fishing industry have been considered by the Court,[343] so there is no significant jurisprudence on this matter on which one can draw. However, it is possible to have a fairly good idea of what kinds of aid are likely to be regarded as compatible with the common market because the Commission has from time to time issued guidelines on the matter. The current Guidelines date from 2008.[344]

---

[341] For two recent examples of such Decisions, see Commission Decision 2008/936/EC of 20 May 2008 concerning aid granted by France to the Fund for the prevention of risks to fishing and fisheries undertakings (State aid C 9/06), OJ 2008 L334/62, as corrected (in which the Commission found that aid granted for the acquisition of financial options on the futures market and a fuel subsidy were impermissible); and Commission Decision 2008/738/EC of 4 June 2008 concerning the State aid scheme that France intends to implement in favour of the processing and marketing of fisheries and aquaculture products (notified under document number C(2008) 2257), OJ 2008 L249/15 (in which the Commission found that the aid scheme planned by France for subsidizing undertakings processing and marketing fisheries products from the Agri-Food Industries Strategic Intervention Fund was impermissible).

[342] Churchill, RR, *EEC Fisheries Law* (Dordrecht: Martinus Nijhoff Publishers, 1987), 223–6.

[343] The only instances of which the authors are aware are Case 93/84 *Commission v France* [1985] ECR 829; Case C-311/94 *IJssel-Vliet Combinatie BV v Minister van Economische Zaken* [1996] ECR I-5023; and Case C-288/96 *Germany v Commission* [2000] ECR I-8237.

[344] Guidelines for the examination of State aid to fisheries and aquaculture (2008/C 84/06), OJ 2008 C84/10. These Guidelines replace guidelines adopted in 2004: OJ 2004 C229/5.

The Guidelines set out the framework within which the Commission administers the derogations to Article 87(1) EC that are provided for in Articles 87(2) and (3), ie State aid that is or may be considered compatible with the common market and thus permissible.[345] The Commission requires State aid not only to be justified under Article 87 but also to be justified by the objectives of the CFP and to comply with its rules.[346] Furthermore, State aid must not be 'protective in its effect': it must promote the rationalization and efficiency of the production and marketing of fishery products on a lasting basis.[347] In terms reminiscent of Regulation 736/2008, the Guidelines go on to stipulate that a State aid measure must also be consistent with aid funded by the EFF,[348] have an incentive effect,[349] be transparent,[350] and last for no longer than ten years.[351] The Guidelines then list eight types of aid that 'may be declared compatible' with the common market and set out various conditions with which each type of aid must comply if it is to be considered compatible.[352] These types of aid are: (a) aid for categories of measures covered by a block exemption Regulation adopted by the Commission under Regulation 994/98, such as Regulation 736/2008 on SMEs; (b) aid falling within the scope of certain horizontal Commission guidelines on State aid, such as the guidelines on State aid for rescuing and restructuring firms in difficulty;[353] (c) aid for investment on board fishing vessels; (d) aid to make good damage caused by natural disasters, exceptional occurrences, or specific adverse climatic events; (e) aid in the form of tax relief and labour-related costs for Community vessels fishing for tuna outside Community waters; (f) aid financed through parafiscal charges;[354] (g) aid for the marketing of fishery products from the Community's outermost regions; and (h) aid concerning the fishing fleet in the outermost regions.[355] Aid for other measures, including operating aid, is in principle not compatible with the common market and therefore illegal, although a Member State is free to try to make a case that such aid is compatible.[356] Member States were requested to amend their existing aid schemes to conform to the Guidelines by 1 September 2008, and were invited to notify the Commission by 1 June 2008 that they were prepared to do so: failure to respond would be taken as acceptance.[357]

The Court has had occasion to comment on the legal significance of the Commission's Guidelines. In *IJssel-Vliet* the Court was asked by a Dutch court whether a previous version of the Guidelines (adopted in 1988) was binding. The

---

[345] Guidelines, para 1.3.   [346] Guidelines, para 3.1.   [347] Ibid.
[348] Guidelines, para 3.2.   [349] Guidelines, para 3.3.   [350] Guidelines, para 3.5.
[351] Guidelines, para 3.6.   [352] Guidelines, para 4.

[353] OJ 2004 C244/2. As to how the Commission intends to apply those Guidelines to the fishing industry, or at least how it intended to do so in 2006, see *Communication from the Commission to the Council and the European Parliament: On improving the economic situation in the fishing industry*, COM(2006) 103, 09.03.2006, pp 6–8.

[354] A parafiscal charge is one the revenue from which is appropriated to a specific purpose.

[355] Guidelines, paras 4.1–4.8.   [356] Guidelines, paras 3.4 and 4.9.

[357] Guidelines, para 5.2.

Court noted that the Guidelines were based on what is now Article 88(1) EC and were thus 'one element of that obligation of regular, periodic co-operation from which neither the Commission nor a Member State can release itself' and that Member States had been consulted on a draft of the Guidelines.[358] Furthermore, the Netherlands had indicated in a letter to the Commission that it would observe the criteria laid down in the Guidelines, and the Commission had subsequently approved the Dutch national aid scheme in question to the extent that it complied with the Guidelines. Thus, 'as a result of the obligation laid down by Article 93(1) [now 88(1)] of the [EC] Treaty and of its acceptance of the rules laid down in the Guidelines, a Member State, such as the Netherlands, must apply the Guidelines'.[359] The Court reached a similar conclusion in *Germany v Commission*, where the German government had also 'approved' the then current version of the Guidelines.[360] As has been seen above, the present Guidelines request Member States to ensure that their existing aid schemes comply with the Guidelines. A Member State that confirms to the Commission by the due date (1 June 2008) that its aid scheme(s) is (are) in conformity with the Guidelines, or fails to contact the Commission, would, following the reasoning in *IJssel-Vliet*, be bound by the Guidelines. In *IJssel-Vliet* the Dutch court also asked whether the Commission was empowered to adopt Guidelines that required (as the current Guidelines also do) aid to be compatible with the objectives of the CFP as well as with EC competition policy. The European Court held that the Commission was so empowered, noting that it was 'essential' for the Commission to take the CFP into account in assessing State aid to the fisheries sector, and that if the Commission did not do so, 'it would run a serious risk of undermining the effectiveness' of the CFP.[361] In *Germany v Commission* the Court held that where the Commission is assessing the compatibility of State aid with the common market in accordance with its Guidelines and adopts a Decision finding that the aid in question is not compatible, the statement of the reasons for its Decision (which the Commission is required to give by what is now Article 253 EC) need not be as full as would be required if its assessment was not based on the Guidelines.[362]

Apart from the various instruments referred to above, there is one other piece of legislation, not directly connected with Articles 87–89 EC, that deals with State aid to the fishing industry. That is Regulation 1005/2008 on IUU fishing. The relevant provisions are Articles 40(3) and 45(7), which are mentioned in subsection 2.1 above in the context of the EFF. Article 40(3) provides that '[w]ithout prejudice to other provisions laid down in Community law pertaining to public funds, Member States shall not grant *any public aid under national aid regimes* or under Community funds to operators involved in the operation, management or ownership of fishing

[358] C-311/94 *IJssel-Vliet*, paras 37 and 39.   [359] C-311/94 *IJssel-Vliet*, para 44.
[360] Case C-288/96 *Germany v Commission*, paras 64–65.
[361] C-311/94 *IJssel-Vliet*, paras 30 and 32.
[362] Case C-288/96 *Germany v Commission*, paras 85–86.

vessels included in the Community IUU vessel list' (emphasis added).[363] Article 45(7) states that, in relation to sanctions to be imposed by Member States for so-called 'serious infringements', the Member States may accompany the required sanctions with, *inter alia*, a 'temporary or permanent ban on access to public assistance or subsidies'.

As was seen in Chapter 3, subsidies to the fishing industry are considered to be a major reason for the overcapacity of world fishing fleets. While much of the State aid that is or may be considered compatible with the common market under the Guidelines and Commission Regulation 736/2008 is not directed at fishing vessels but at infrastructure development (such as port improvements), processing, marketing, and aquaculture, some of the aid that may be permissible under the Guidelines and Regulation 875/2007 (on *de minimis* exceptions) is capable of having an adverse effect on fleet capacity (in terms of improved catching ability rather than in terms of increased tonnage or engine power[364]) and vessel effort, thereby possibly stimulating overfishing. It is, therefore, a matter of some concern that such State aid continues to be permissible.

It is possible that in future State (and EC) aid to the fishing industry will be curtailed as a result of developments at the World Trade Organization (WTO). Subsidies to the fishing industry were included on the agenda of the so-called Doha Round of trade negotiations that was initiated in 2001. Negotiations on subsidies to the fishing industry have made some progress, but at the time of writing appeared still to be a considerable way from a successful conclusion, along with many of the other items on the Doha agenda.[365]

---

[363] The establishment of a Community IUU vessel list is provided for by Reg 1005/2008, Art 27. See further Chapters 5 and 7.

[364] On the question of measuring capacity in terms other than of tonnage or engine power, see Chapter 4.   [365] For further details, see the website of the WTO.

9

Aquaculture

1 Introduction

The Common Fisheries Policy (CFP) extends to aquaculture. Article 1(1) of the Basic Regulation[1] states that the CFP 'shall cover . . . aquaculture, and the processing and marketing of . . . aquaculture products where such activities are practised [*inter alia*] on the territory of Member States or in Community waters'. Article 1(2) goes on to say that the CFP 'shall provide for coherent measures concerning . . . (f) aquaculture'. Recital (4) of the Basic Regulation, which is reflected in Article 2(1), states that the objectives of the CFP include 'sustainable exploitation of . . . aquaculture in the context of sustainable development, taking account of the environmental, economic and social aspects in a balanced manner'.[2] In furtherance of that objective, the EC 'shall aim to contribute to efficient fishing activities within an economically viable and competitive fisheries and aquaculture industry, providing a fair standard of living for those who depend on fishing activities and taking into account the interest of consumers'.[3] Rather surprisingly perhaps, there is no further mention of aquaculture in the Basic Regulation other than in the context of the Committee for Fisheries and Aquaculture, which is established by Article 30 to assist the Commission: however, the Regulation gives the Committee no specific functions in relation to aquaculture. There is, in fact, no EC legislation that deals comprehensively with aquaculture. Instead, the subject is addressed, to some degree, in a variety of disparate pieces of EC legislation.

There is no definition of aquaculture in the Basic Regulation. A definition is, however, given in the Regulation establishing the European Fisheries Fund (EFF) (discussed in section 8 below).[4] Article 3(d) provides that, for the purposes of that Regulation, 'aquaculture' means 'the rearing or cultivation of aquatic organisms using techniques designed to increase the production of the organisms in question beyond the natural capacity of the environment; the organisms remain the property of a natural or legal person throughout the rearing or culture stage, up to and including harvesting'. The same definition is used in Regulations 708/2007 (on

---

[1] Council Regulation (EC) No 2371/2002 of 20 December 2002 on the conservation and sustainable exploitation of fisheries resources under the Common Fisheries Policy, OJ 2002 L358/59, as amended and corrected.

[2] In contrast to recital (4), Art 2(1) of Reg 2371/2002 does not explicitly refer to aquaculture.

[3] Reg 2371/2002, Art 2(1).

[4] Council Regulation (EC) No 1198/2006 of 27 July 2006 on the European Fisheries Fund, OJ 2006 L223/1.

the use of alien species in aquaculture, discussed in section 5 below)[5] and 834/2007 (on organic aquaculture production, discussed in section 6 below)[6] for the purposes of those Regulations, and an almost identical definition is found in Directive 2006/88 (on health standards for aquaculture, discussed in sections 2, 3, and 6 below) for the purposes of that Directive.[7] According to the Commission, aquaculture in the EC has in practice three major, but quite separate, components: (a) freshwater fish farming (mainly of trout and carp); (b) marine shellfish farming (mainly of mussels and oysters); and (c) marine fish farming (mainly of salmon).[8]

In 2005 aquaculture production in what are now the twenty-seven EC Member States amounted to about 1.27 million tonnes, with a value of about €2.86 billion.[9] This represented, by weight, about 2.0 per cent of total world aquaculture production and about 18.4 per cent of total EC fishery production.[10] Shellfish accounted for about 55 per cent of EC aquaculture production by weight, freshwater fish farming for about 24 per cent, and marine fish farming for about 21 per cent.[11]

The Commission has long been keen to encourage aquaculture in the EC, which it sees as both helping to make up the shortfall from marine catches by Community fishing vessels in meeting consumer demand in the EC for fishery products (and thereby to some degree reducing the need for imports from third States) and as providing employment in the EC's less developed regions.[12] It has therefore taken a number of steps to promote aquaculture. They include, in recent years, the publication of a *Strategy for the Sustainable Development of European Aquaculture* in 2002,[13] holding a public consultation on opportunities for the development of aquaculture during the first half of 2007,[14] and following that up by organizing a conference on 'European Aquaculture and its Opportunities for

[5] Council Regulation (EC) No 708/2007 of 11 June 2007 concerning use of alien and locally absent species in aquaculture, OJ 2007 L168/1, as amended, Art 3(1).

[6] Council Regulation (EC) No 834/2007 of 28 June 2007 on organic production and labelling of organic products and repealing Regulation (EEC) No 2092/91, OJ 2007 L189/1, as amended, Art 2(g).

[7] Council Directive 2006/88/EC of 24 October 2006 on animal health requirements for aquaculture animals and products thereof, and on the prevention and control of certain diseases in aquatic animals, OJ 2006 L328/14, as amended and corrected.

[8] *Communication from the Commission to the Council and the European Parliament: A Strategy for the Sustainable Development of European Aquaculture*, COM(2002) 511, 19.9.2002, pp 3–4. See also Commission, *Background Information. European Aquaculture—Facts and Figures* (2007), available on the website of DG Mare.   [9] Eurostat, *Facts and Figures on the CFP, Edition 2008*, 16.

[10] Ibid.

[11] Commission, *Background Information. European Aquaculture—Facts and Figures*, 7. The figures are for 2004.   [12] COM(2002) 511, pp 3–5 and 11.

[13] COM(2002) 511.

[14] Commission press release, 'Commission launches consultation on a sustainable future for European aquaculture', 11 May 2007, available on the website of DG Mare. Details of the consultation, including a background document, may also be found on that website.

Development', held in November 2007.[15] The Commission's 2002 strategy document was aimed at achieving stability for the aquaculture industry, guaranteeing security of employment, and ensuring the protection of human and animal health and the environment. The document set out action to be taken at various levels—the EC, the Member States, and the industry itself. As far as the EC is concerned, the main actions to be taken should be to create a framework of support for the sustainable development of aquaculture with the structural funds, to stimulate research and innovation, and to ensure a high level of environmental, consumer, and animal protection. As will be seen below, a good deal of progress has been made on these matters since the publication of the strategy document in 2002. In October 2008 Commissioner Borg announced that the Commission would present a revised strategy in early 2009.[16] The following month the Council considered the promotion of aquaculture, engaging in a preliminary exchange of views on the basis of a Presidency questionnaire seeking directions on policy with a view to a renewed EC strategy for the sustainable development of aquaculture.[17]

From the point of view of law, there are a number of matters in respect of which aquaculture may require regulation. The principal such matters include: (a) requiring authorization for the establishment and operation of an aquaculture installation;[18] (b) preventing and controlling disease in aquaculture installations; (c) regulating possible pollution damaging to, or resulting from, aquaculture; (d) controlling the use of alien or genetically modified species in aquaculture; (e) marketing and trade; (f) tuna farming; and (g) public financial assistance for aquaculture. Each of these matters is discussed in turn below.

2 Authorization for the establishment and operation of an aquaculture installation

The siting and construction of an aquaculture installation may require authorization: once an installation has been established, authorization to operate it may also be required. This matter was originally regulated primarily by national law. However, the EC became significantly involved when in 2006 it adopted Directive 2006/88, which introduced a Community system of authorizations for aquaculture

---

[15] Commission press release, 'Conference on European Aquaculture and its Opportunities for Development, Brussels, 15–16 November 2007', 5 December 2007, available on the website of DG Mare. A summary of the conference proceedings may also be found there.

[16] 'Speech by Commissioner Joe Borg at the 10th International Frozen Products Exhibition (Conxemar 2008), Vigo, 7 October 2008', available on the website of DG Mare.

[17] Council of the European Union, 2904th meeting of the Council, Agriculture and Fisheries, 18–20 November 2008, press release, 15940/08 (Presse 335), 19.

[18] 'Aquaculture installation' is not a term of art. The term is used here simply for convenience to refer to any confined enclosure or location where aquaculture is practised.

installations with effect from 1 August 2008.[19] Under this system Member States must authorize every proposed 'aquaculture production business' (hereafter, 'APB') and 'processing establishment slaughtering aquaculture animals for disease control purposes'.[20] An APB is defined as 'any undertaking, whether for profit or not and whether public or private, carrying out any of the activities related to the rearing, keeping or cultivation of aquaculture animals'.[21] A Member State may only grant an authorization if certain conditions are fulfilled.[22] Those conditions are that an APB or processing establishment: (a) keeps a record of all movements of all aquaculture animals and products thereof into and out of the aquaculture installation, the mortality in each epidemiological unit, and the results of the scheme referred to in '(c)' below;[23] (b) implements good hygiene practice to prevent the introduction and spread of disease;[24] (c) applies a risk-based animal health surveillance scheme that is aimed at the detection of any increased mortality in an aquaculture installation and certain listed diseases, taking into account recommendations set out in Annex III of Directive 2006/88 and any guidelines laid down by the Commission;[25] (d) has a system in place that demonstrates that conditions '(a)'–'(c)' above are being fulfilled;[26] and (e) remains subject to supervision by the relevant authorities of the Member State concerned.[27] A Member State may not grant an authorization if the activities of an APB or processing establishment 'were to lead to an unacceptable risk' of disease spreading to other aquaculture installations or to wild stocks of aquatic animals in the vicinity.[28] Where an APB or processing establishment has been authorized, the Member State concerned shall carry out regular inspections and audits of the authorized activity.[29]

There are a number of other pieces of EC legislation that may be relevant to the siting and construction of an aquaculture installation. Foremost among them is the Environmental Impact Assessment (EIA) Directive.[30] The Directive requires a Member State to determine, either through a case-by-case examination or by the application of specified criteria, whether '[i]ntensive fish farming' requires an EIA.[31] That provision was at issue in *Commission v Ireland*, where the Court found that Ireland had failed to transpose this aspect of the Directive fully into Irish law.[32] The Habitats and Birds Directives[33] may also be relevant as to where a proposed

[19] Dir 2006/88, Arts 4–10, 63, and 65.   [20] Dir 2006/88, Art 4(1) and (2) (and Art 3(1)(f)).
[21] Dir 2006/88, Art 3(1)(c). 'Aquaculture animals' are defined in Art 3(1)(b).
[22] Dir 2006/88, Art 5(1).
[23] Dir 2006/88, Art 8(1). Art 8(3) sets out recording obligations for transporters of aquatic animals.
[24] Dir 2006/88, Art 9.   [25] Dir 2006/88, Art 10.   [26] Dir 2006/88, Art 5(1)(b).
[27] Dir 2006/88, Art 5(1)(c).   [28] Dir 2006/88, Art 5(2).   [29] Dir 2006/88, Art 7.
[30] Council Directive 85/337/EEC of 27 June 1985 on the assessment of the effects of certain public and private projects on the environment, OJ 1985 L175/40, as amended and corrected.
[31] Dir 85/337, Arts 2 and 4(2), and Annex II(f).
[32] Case C-66/06 *Commission v Ireland*, judgment of 20 November 2008 (not yet reported).
[33] Council Directive 92/43/EEC of 21 May 1992 on the conservation of natural habitats and of wild fauna and flora, OJ 1992 L206/7, as amended and corrected; and Council Directive 79/409/EEC of 2 April 1979 on the conservation of wild birds, OJ 1979 L103/1, as amended and corrected.

aquaculture installation is sited. For example, a Member State may agree to the establishment of an aquaculture installation only after having ascertained that it will not adversely affect the integrity of a Special Area of Conservation or a Special Protection Area established in accordance with the Habitats and Birds Directives, respectively.[34] This point is illustrated by a judgment of the Court in 2007, in which it found that Ireland had breached the Birds Directive by systematically failing to consider possible impacts on Special Protection Areas when authorizing aquaculture projects.[35] The Water Framework and Marine Strategy Directives[36] may also be relevant to the siting of aquaculture installations, but it is beyond the scope of this chapter to consider their provisions. Both those Directives and the Habitats and Birds Directives are also potentially relevant to the matters discussed in sections 4 and 5 below.

3 Prevention and control of disease in aquaculture installations

In broad terms, fish in aquaculture installations are more prone to disease than fish in the wild because of their concentration in a small and confined location. Salmon farmed in cages in sea water may also spread disease to wild fish through sea lice.[37] In 2004 financial losses in the aquaculture industry due to disease were estimated to be around 20 per cent of the value of production.[38] It is therefore important to try to prevent disease spreading to aquaculture installations and to control it once it has so spread. This matter is dealt with by Directive 2006/88.[39] The Directive repealed and replaced, with effect from 1 August 2008, two Directives which were adopted in 1993 and 1995.[40] Directive 2006/88 was prompted, in part, by developments in aquaculture since the earlier Directives were adopted.[41]

---

[34] Dir 92/43, Arts 6 and 7, subject to the exception in Art 6(4).

[35] Case C-418/04 *Commission v Ireland* [2007] ECR I-10967, paras 235–247.

[36] Directive 2000/60/EC of the European Parliament and of the Council of 23 October 2000 establishing a framework for Community action in the field of water policy, OJ 2000 L327/1, as amended; and Directive 2008/56/EC of the European Parliament and of the Council of 17 June 2008 establishing a framework for community action in the field of marine environmental policy (Marine Strategy Framework Directive), OJ 2008 L164/19.   [37] COM(2002) 511, p 9.

[38] *Proposal for a Council Directive on animal health requirements for aquaculture animals and products thereof, and on the prevention and control of certain diseases in aquatic animals*, COM(2005) 362, 23.8.2005, p 2.

[39] There are a number of Commission Decisions implementing Dir 2006/88, but for reasons of space they are not discussed here.

[40] Council Directive 93/53/EEC of 24 June 1993 introducing minimum Community measures for the control of certain fish diseases, OJ 1993 L175/23, as amended; and Council Directive 95/70/EC of 22 December 1995 introducing minimum Community measures for the control of certain diseases affecting bivalve molluscs, OJ 1995 L332/33, as amended.   [41] Dir 2006/88, recital (4).

Chapter V of Directive 2006/88 deals with the notification and minimum measures for control of diseases in aquaculture installations. Notification must be given where one of the diseases listed in Annex IV to the Directive is present or suspected in aquatic animals or if increased mortality occurs in aquaculture animals.[42] The diseases listed are those that potentially have substantial economic repercussions or a detrimental environmental impact on wild aquatic animals.[43] Where disease is suspected, various measures must be taken, such as sampling, keeping the area concerned under surveillance, control on movement of animals, and an epizootic investigation.[44] Where disease is confirmed, the measures to be taken (which differ slightly between those required for exotic diseases and those for non-exotic diseases) include declaring the area to be infected, prohibiting the movement of animals, removing and disposing of dead and infected animals, and fallowing the aquaculture installation.[45] If those measures are not sufficient, Member States may be authorized to adopt further ad hoc measures by the Commission (subject to possible review by the Council).[46] Where disease is suspected or confirmed in wild aquatic animals, the Member State concerned must monitor the situation and take measures to reduce and prevent the spread of the disease.[47] In the case of diseases not listed in Annex IV that constitute a significant health risk, a Member State may take any necessary and proportionate measures to prevent or control the disease.[48] Chapters VI and VII deal with the steps to be taken and the conditions to be met in order for an area or a Member State to be declared disease-free by the Commission.

Where, as a result of measures taken in response to disease, aquaculture animals have to be slaughtered, Directive 2006/88, like its predecessor (Directive 93/53), does not require compensation to be paid by either the EC or the Member States (although it may be noted that the control and eradication of disease is eligible for aid from the EFF—see section 8 below). In relation to Directive 93/53, it was argued before the Court that the failure of that Directive to require the payment of compensation where fish in an aquaculture installation were slaughtered in order to control disease violated the right to property of the owner of such an installation: the Directive should therefore be declared invalid for its failure to respect fundamental human rights.[49] The Court dismissed that argument, observing that the right to property was not an absolute right, and that restrictions on that right were permitted in the general interest provided that they were not disproportionate or intolerable.[50] That, the Court held, was the case here: slaughtering fish in an affected aquaculture installation was an effective way of restoring normal

---

[42] Dir 2006/88, Art 26(1).

[43] Dir 2006/88, Annex IV, Part I. There are additional criteria for the listing of non-exotic diseases.

[44] Dir 2006/88, Arts 28 and 29.   [45] Dir 2006/88, Arts 30–39.   [46] Dir 2006/88, Art 42.

[47] Dir 2006/88, Art 40.   [48] Dir 2006/88, Art 43.

[49] Joined Cases C-20/00 and C-64/00, *Booker Aquaculture Ltd and Hydro Seafood GSP Ltd v Scottish Ministers* [2003] ECR I-7411.   [50] *Booker*, paras 64–68.

market conditions from which the owner of that installation would also benefit. In any case, disease was an ordinary commercial risk for aquaculture operators, and diseased fish had no commercial value.[51] It therefore followed from all those considerations, in the view of the Court, that the slaughtering of fish in an aquaculture installation in order to control disease, without the payment of compensation to the owner, did not constitute 'a disproportionate and intolerable interference impairing the very substance of the right to property'.[52]

4 The regulation of pollution damaging to, or resulting from, aquaculture

Aquaculture, whether taking place in fresh or salt water, requires a clean and unpolluted environment if it is to flourish. There is one piece of EC legislation which, although it does not explicitly refer to aquaculture, is nevertheless relevant, at least in part, to protecting shellfish aquaculture from pollution. That is Directive 2006/113 on the quality of shellfish waters.[53] The Directive lays down water quality objectives for 'those coastal and brackish waters designated by the Member States as needing protection or improvement in order to support shellfish (bivalve and gasteropod [sic] molluscs) life and growth and thus to contribute to the high quality of shellfish products directly edible by man'.[54] The Directive will be repealed and replaced in 2013 by the Water Framework Directive,[55] although it has been suggested that the adoption of a 'daughter' Directive under the Water Framework Directive may be necessary in order to ensure sufficient protection of shellfish waters from pollution.[56] There is a large amount of other EC legislation concerned with freshwater and marine pollution in general. Although not directed specifically at preventing harm to aquaculture, that legislation may indirectly have such an effect. It is beyond the scope of this chapter to give any details of such legislation.

---

[51] *Booker*, paras 69–93.   [52] *Booker*, para 86.

[53] Directive 2006/113/EC 14, as amended. The Directive was/14, as amended. The Directive was not adopted under Art 37 EC and so does not fall under the CFP. The Directive replaces and repeals Council Directive 79/923/EEC of 30 October 1979 on the quality required of shellfish waters, OJ 1979 L281/47, as amended. A number of Member States were found by the Court not to have implemented the 1979 Directive correctly: see Case C-298/95 *Commission v Germany* [1996] ECR I-6747; Case C-225/96 *Commission v Italy* [1996] ECR I-6887; Case C-67/02 *Commission v Ireland* [2001] ECR I-9019; and Case C-26/04 *Commission v Spain* [2005] ECR I-11059.

[54] Dir 2006/113, Art 1.

[55] Dir 2000/60, Art 22(2). The reference in the latter to Dir 79/923 is to be construed as including Dir 2006/113: see Dir 2006/113, Art 16.

[56] *Minutes from European Aquaculture and its opportunities for development Conference, Brussels, 15 and 16 November 2007* (available on the website of DG Mare), 12.

Aquaculture installations may lead to local pollution of the aquatic environment in various ways, such as the loss of feed, which may contain chemicals or may add excessive nutrients to the aquatic environment; the addition of disease-prevention chemicals to the water in an installation; and natural waste from aquaculture animals.[57] There is no EC legislation that specifically and directly regulates pollution from aquaculture, although Directive 2002/32 sets maximum limits for harmful substances in feeds for aquaculture animals.[58] Otherwise it is possible that some of the EC's rather extensive legislation relating to freshwater and marine pollution may incidentally control pollution from aquaculture installations, but it is beyond the scope of this chapter to seek to identify or discuss such legislation as might be relevant.

5 Controlling the use of alien species in aquaculture

In the past aquaculture in the EC has benefited from the introduction of alien species, notably rainbow trout and Pacific oyster. However, alien species in aquaculture pose a potential threat to ecosystems, for example by spreading parasites and pathogens to native species and by escaping into the wild where they may inter-breed with or displace native wild species, leading to a loss of genetic and species diversity.[59]

The EC legislated to address these issues in 2007 with the adoption of Regulation 708/2007.[60] The aim of the Regulation is to establish a framework whereby the possible impact of alien and locally absent species, as well as of any associated non-target species, on aquatic habitats may be assessed and minimized, 'and in this manner contribute to the sustainable development of the sector'.[61] The three types of species referred to are defined as follows. 'Alien species' are: (a) species of an 'aquatic organism occurring outside its known natural range and the areas of its natural dispersal potential'; and (b) polyploid organisms (ie aquatic organisms in which the number of chromosomes has been doubled through cell manipulation techniques) and 'fertile artificially hybridised species irrespective of

---

[57] OSPAR Commission, *Quality Status Report 2000*, 88 (available on the website of the OSPAR Commission).

[58] Directive 2002/32/EC of the European Parliament and of the Council of 7 May 2002 on undesirable substances in animal feed, OJ 2002 L140/10, as amended.

[59] COM(2002) 511, pp 9–10 and 19; and *Proposal for a Council Regulation concerning use of alien and locally absent species in aquaculture*, COM(2006) 154, 4.4.2006, pp 2–3.

[60] See also Commission Regulation (EC) No 535/2008 of 13 June 2008 laying down detailed rules for the implementation of Council Regulation (EC) No 708/2007 concerning use of alien and locally absent species in aquaculture, OJ 2008 L156/6.   [61] Reg 708/2007, Art 1.

their natural range or dispersal potential'.[62] 'Locally absent species' are defined as species of an 'aquatic organism which is locally absent from a zone within its natural range of distribution for biogeographical reasons'.[63] By 'associated non-target species' is meant any species of aquatic organisms likely to be detrimental to the aquatic environment that are moved accidentally together with alien or locally absent species.[64]

In furtherance of its aim, the Regulation introduces a system of permits, under which an aquaculture operator intending to undertake the introduction of an alien species or the translocation of a locally absent species must apply for a permit from the receiving Member State.[65] 'Introduction of an alien species' in this context means the intentional movement of an alien species to an environment outside its natural range for use in aquaculture.[66] By 'translocation of locally absent species' is meant the intentional movement for use in aquaculture of a locally absent species within its natural range to an area where it previously did not exist because of biogeographical reasons.[67] Movement of a locally absent species within a single Member State normally falls outside the ambit of the Regulation.[68]

The permit system distinguishes between routine and non-routine movements. A routine movement is the movement of aquatic organisms from a source that has a low risk of transferring non-target species *and* which does not give rise to adverse ecological effects,[69] whereas a non-routine movement is any movement of aquatic organisms which does not fulfil the criteria for a routine movement.[70] In the case of a *routine* movement, the receiving Member State may grant a permit subject to requirements for quarantine and pilot release.[71] In the case of a *non-routine* movement, an environmental risk assessment must be carried out,[72] except for movements of alien or locally absent species to be held in closed aquaculture facilities:[73] the latter are facilities where aquaculture is 'conducted in an aquatic medium, which involves recirculation of water and which is separated from the wild aquatic medium by barriers preventing the escape of reared specimens or biological material that might survive and subsequently reproduce'.[74] A permit may only be issued if the risk assessment shows a 'low' risk to the environment,[75] and if the requirements of various other pieces of EC legislation are met.[76] An operator may also be required to comply with any requirements relating to quarantine or pilot release.[77] Where the potential or known effects of a proposed movement are liable to affect neighbouring Member States, the receiving Member State shall notify the Member State(s) concerned and the Commission if it intends to grant a permit: that intended decision may be confirmed, rejected, or amended

---

[62] Reg 708/2007, Art 3(5) and (6).   [63] Reg 708/2007, Art 3(7).
[64] Reg 708/2007, Art 3(8).   [65] Reg 708/2007, Art 6(1).   [66] Reg 708/2007, Art 3(10).
[67] Reg 708/2007, Art 3(11).   [68] Reg 708/2007, Art 2(2).
[69] Reg 708/2007, Art 3(16).   [70] Reg 708/2007, Art 3(17).
[71] Reg 708/2007, Arts 8 and 14.   [72] Reg 708/2007, Art 9(1).
[73] Reg 708/2007, Art 2(6).   [74] Reg 708/2007, Art 3(3).   [75] Reg 708/2007, Art 9(4).
[76] Reg 708/2007, Arts 13 and 19.   [77] Reg 708/2007, Art 15.

by the Commission, subject to possible review by the Council.[78] Any permit granted may be withdrawn at any time if unforeseen events with negative effects on the environment or on native populations occur.[79] Decisions refusing to grant a permit or withdrawing a permit must be justified on scientific grounds or on the basis of the precautionary principle.[80] The Regulation contains provisions on monitoring and on the keeping of a register of introductions and translocations.[81]

The permit system does not apply to some twenty-five alien species of fish and shellfish listed in Annex IV that have commonly been used in aquaculture in the EC;[82] but even in the case of those species (as with all other species used in aquaculture) Member States 'shall ensure that all appropriate measures are taken to avoid adverse effects to biodiversity, and especially to species, habitats and eco-system functions which may be expected to arise from the introduction or trans-location of aquatic organisms and non-target species in aquaculture and from the spreading of these species into the wild'.[83]

It was originally envisaged that Regulation 708/2007 should include measures for containment of farmed salmon, but it was eventually decided not to include such measures as at the time of the adoption of the Regulation the North Atlantic Salmon Conservation Organization's existing guidelines on this matter were being evaluated in the light of experience and scientific progress: it therefore seemed appropriate for the EC to defer legislating on the question.[84] Another omission from the Regulation concerns any reference to genetically modified organisms (GMOs). The Commission had received expert advice that GMOs should be included in the scope of the Regulation, but it rejected that advice because GMOs were already covered by existing and developing EC legislation.[85]

6 Marketing and trade

The discussion in this section deals with two matters: (a) the application of health standards to aquaculture products that are to be placed on the market; and (b) rules relating to the organic production and labelling of such products. Financial support for marketing is discussed in section 8 below. Other aspects of marketing and trade are dealt with by the Regulation on the common organization of the markets[86] and its associated legislation, which are discussed extensively in Chapters 6 and 7 and therefore require no further discussion here.

---

[78] Reg 708/2007, Art 11.   [79] Reg 708/2007, Art 12.
[80] Reg 708/2007, Art 9(4) and 12.   [81] Reg 708/2007, Arts 18, 22, and 23.
[82] Reg 708/2007, Art 2(5). See also recital (11).   [83] Reg 708/2007, Art 4.
[84] COM(2006) 154, p 4.   [85] COM(2006) 154, p 5.
[86] Council Regulation (EC) No 104/2000 of 17 December 1999 on the common organisation of the markets in fishery *and aquaculture products*, OJ 2000 L17/22, as amended and corrected (emphasis added).

EC health standards relating to the marketing of aquaculture products are set out in Directive 2006/88, which, with effect from 1 August 2008, repealed and replaced a Directive of 1991.[87] As mentioned earlier, Directive 2006/88 was prompted by developments in aquaculture: its provisions dealing with health standards, contained in Chapter III of the Directive, also take account of the fact that the EC has become a party to the World Trade Organization (WTO) Agreement on the Application of Sanitary and Phytosanitary Measures, which is less stringent than the 1991 Directive.[88]

Chapter III of Directive 2006/88 lays down health standards where aquaculture products are placed on the market. 'Placing on the market' means 'the sale, including offering for sale or any other form of transfer, whether free of charge or not, and any form of movement of aquaculture animals'.[89] The primary purpose of Chapter III is to ensure that disease is not spread.[90] The Chapter addresses four distinct ways in which aquaculture products may be placed on the market. They are: (a) directly for human consumption; (b) for processing before human consumption; (c) for farming and restocking; and (d) when transported. In all four cases Member States are under a general obligation to ensure that placing aquaculture products on the market does not jeopardize 'the health status of aquatic animals' at the place of destination in relation to the diseases listed in Annex IV to the Directive (as to which, see section 3 above).[91] In the case of placement on the market represented by forms '(b)' and '(c)' above, animals must have a health certificate when introduced into disease-free areas.[92]

Where aquaculture products are placed on the market *directly for human consumption*, all that Directive 2006/88 stipulates, in Article 19, is that such products comply with the requirements for packaging and labelling laid down in Regulation 853/2004.[93] Where products from aquaculture animals of species susceptible to certain listed diseases undergo *processing before human consumption*, they may only be placed on the market for processing if this is done in an area that has been declared free of those diseases and provided that those products themselves originate from a disease-free area, or are processed in an authorized processing establishment under conditions that prevent the spreading of disease, or, if the products are fish, that they are slaughtered and eviscerated before dispatch.[94] Aquaculture animals may only be placed on the market for *farming and restocking* if they are clinically healthy and do not come from an aquaculture installation where there is 'any unresolved increased mortality'.[95] In order to be introduced for farming and restocking in 'a

---

[87] Council Directive 91/67/EEC of 28 January 1991 concerning the animal health conditions governing the placing on the market of aquaculture animals and products, OJ 1991 L46/1, as amended.

[88] Dir 2006/88, recitals (4) and (7).   [89] Dir 2006/88, Art 3(l).

[90] Dir 2006/88, recital (19).   [91] Dir 2006/88, Art 12(1).   [92] Dir 2006/88, Art 14(1).

[93] Regulation (EC) No 853/2004 of the European Parliament and of the Council of 29 April 2004 laying down specific hygiene rules for food of animal origin, OJ 2004 L139/55, as amended and corrected.   [94] Dir 2006/88, Art 18(1).

[95] Dir 2006/88, Art 15(1).

Member State, zone or compartment' that has been declared free of a specified disease, aquaculture animals of species susceptible to that disease must originate from a Member State, zone or compartment that has also been declared free of that disease.[96] Similar provisions apply to species that may be responsible for disease by acting as vector species.[97] Article 13 provides that when aquaculture animals are being *transported*, measures must be taken to ensure that their health status is not altered.

Apart from Directive 2006/88, much general EC food hygiene law applies to aquaculture. However, it is beyond the scope of this chapter to spell out its details.[98]

The use of organic methods of production in aquaculture and the labelling of aquaculture products as organic is dealt with by Regulation 834/2007. Although the Regulation is concerned with organic food production in general, it has a number of provisions specifically relating to aquaculture. The Regulation applies to the following products of aquaculture where such products are placed, or are intended to be placed, on the market: live or unprocessed products; processed products for use as food; and feed.[99] The main rules for organic aquaculture production are set out in Article 15. They address: (a) the origin of aquaculture animals; (b) husbandry practices (which, *inter alia*, must minimize negative environmental impact from the aquaculture installation, including the escape of farmed stock); (c) breeding; (d) feed (which, where derived from aquatic animals, must originate from 'sustainable exploitation of fisheries'); (e) water quality in areas where bivalve molluscs and other species that feed on natural plankton are grown; and (f) disease prevention and veterinary treatment. A number of the general principles that apply to organic production generally have specific relevance for aquaculture. Thus, aquaculture production, if it is to be considered as organic, must be based on the following principles: (a) 'the appropriate design and management of biological processes based on ecological systems using natural resources' by methods that comply with the sustainable exploitation of fisheries and exclude the use of GMOs and products produced from or by GMOs;[100] (b) 'the maintenance of the biodiversity of natural aquatic ecosystems, the continuing health of the aquatic environment and the quality of surrounding aquatic and terrestrial ecosystems in aquaculture production';[101] and (c) the feeding of aquatic organisms with feed from sustainable fisheries or with organic feed composed of agricultural products from organic farming.[102] Normally an aquaculture installation in its entirety must be managed in compliance with the requirements applicable to organic production if it is to qualify as organic. However, in

---

[96] Dir 2006/88, Art 16(1).   [97] Dir 2006/88, Art 17(1).

[98] For a brief survey, see Long, R, *Marine Resource Law* (Dublin: Thomson Round Hall, 2007), 311–14.

[99] Reg 834/2007, Art 1(2).

[100] Reg 834/2007, Art 4(a)(ii) and (iii). The prohibition on the use of GMOs is amplified in Art 9.

[101] Reg 834/2007, Art 5(n).   [102] Reg 834/2007, Art 5(o).

accordance with specific conditions to be laid down by the Commission in implementing legislation, an installation may be split into clearly separate production sites, only some of which may be managed in accordance with organic production methods.[103]

A product may be labelled as 'organic' (or a similar term) only where the labelling or advertising material suggests to the purchaser that the product, its ingredients or feed materials have been obtained in accordance with the rules set out in Regulation 834/2007.[104] The label must include the code number of the national control body and, in the case of pre-packaged goods, the packaging must include the Community logo and an indication of the place of origin of the raw materials of the product.[105]

7 Tuna farming

Tuna farming refers to the practice whereby tuna (primarily bluefin tuna) are caught, either by a vessel or a tuna trap (which is a piece of fixed gear anchored to the sea bed, usually containing a guide net that leads fish into an enclosure[106]), and then transferred to structures where they are kept and undergo further growth. They are then slaughtered and sold, mainly to the Japanese market, where the price of fattened bluefin tuna is substantially higher than that of lean tuna.[107] Bluefin tuna farming has been carried on in a number of Mediterranean Member States since the mid-1990s.[108] By 2001 50 per cent of total tuna catches by vessels from all States using purse seines in the Mediterranean Sea were transferred to tuna farms for fattening.[109]

The question arises whether tuna farming is covered by EC legislation on the general theme of aquaculture. For reasons of space, that matter will not be considered further here. However, there is some EC legislation applying specifically to tuna farming. The principal such legislation is Regulation 1936/2001 (on control measures for highly migratory fish)[110] and Regulation 1559/2007 (on a recovery

---

[103] Reg 834/2007, Art 11.   [104] Reg 834/2007, Art 23(1).

[105] Reg 834/2007, Art 24(1).

[106] This is the definition of tuna trap given in Council Regulation (EC) No 1559/2007 of 17 December 2007 establishing a multiannual recovery plan for bluefin tuna in the Eastern Atlantic and Mediterranean and amending Regulation (EC) No 520/2007, OJ 2007 L340/8, Art 2(e).

[107] Miyake, PM, De la Serna, JM, Di Natale, A, Farrugia, A, Katavić, I, Miyabe N, and Tičina, V, 'General Review of Bluefin Tuna Farming in the Mediterranean Area' Col Vol Sci Pap ICCAT 55(1) (2003) 114, at 115.

[108] Miyake et al, 'General Review of Bluefin Tuna Farming', 116–17. This development is not referred to in the Commission's 2002 aquaculture strategy paper referred to in section 1 above.

[109] Miyake et al, 'General Review of Bluefin Tuna Farming', 116.

[110] Council Regulation (EC) No 1936/2001 of 27 September 2001 laying down control measures applicable to fishing for certain stocks of highly migratory fish, OJ 2001 L263/1, as amended. Amendments to Reg 1936/2001 in 2004 introduced provisions on tuna farming.

plan for bluefin tuna).[111] These Regulations, as far as tuna farming is concerned, implement various recommendations of the International Commission for the Conservation of Atlantic Tunas (ICCAT), the regional fisheries management organization with management responsibility for tuna in the Atlantic Ocean and Mediterranean Sea (see further Chapter 5).

The situation is complicated by the fact that the relevant provisions in Regulation 1936/2001 relate to bluefin tuna 'fattening' farms, specifically, whereas Regulation 1559/2007 relates to both 'fattening' and 'farming' farms for bluefin tuna. In Regulation 1936/2001, the term 'fattening' means 'raising of individuals in cages to increase their weight or fat content with a view to marketing' and a 'fattening farm' is an 'enterprise which raises wild individuals in cages for fattening'.[112] In Regulation 1559/2007, the term 'fattening' means 'caging of bluefin tuna for a short period (usually two to six months) aiming mostly at increasing the fat content of the fish' whereas the term 'farming' means 'caging of bluefin tuna for a period longer than one year, aiming to increase the total biomass'.[113]

It is not clear whether the definition of 'fattening' in Regulation 1936/2001, in that it refers to 'raising of individuals . . . to increase their weight or fat content' covers both 'fattening' and 'farming' as used in Regulation 1559/2007. Cross-references in Regulation 1559/2007 to Regulation 1936/2001 suggest that this may be the case.[114] However, for the sake of clarity, the relevant provisions of these two Regulations will be dealt with separately, starting with Regulation 1936/2001.

Regulation 1936/2001 requires each Member State to send the Commission a list of the fattening farms under its jurisdiction that it has authorized to conduct fattening operations on bluefin tuna caught in the ICCAT area.[115] The Commission will then forward such lists to the ICCAT.[116] Any fattening farms under the jurisdiction of a Member State not on the list may not conduct fattening activities on bluefin tuna caught in the ICCAT area.[117] Annually each Member

---

[111] See also, *inter alia*: (a) Commission Decision 2008/323/EC of 1 April 2008 establishing a specific control and inspection programme related to the recovery of bluefin tuna in the Eastern Atlantic and the Mediterranean, OJ 2008 L110/7 (establishing a 'specific control and inspection programme' applicable from 1 April 2008 to 31 December 2008), *inter alia*, Arts 2(1)(c), 7(1)(b), and 8(1)(b)(i) and Annex I; (b) Commission Regulation (EC) No 530/2008 of 12 June 2008 establishing emergency measures as regards purse seiners fishing for bluefin tuna in the Atlantic Ocean, east of longitude 45 °W, and in the Mediterranean Sea, OJ 2008 L155/9 (applicable for 6 months from 13 June 2008), Arts 1–3 and related litigation pending before the Court at the time of writing (Case T-305/08 *Italy v Commission* OJ 2008 C272/31; Case T-329/08 *AJD Tuna v Commission* OJ 2008 C272/38; and Case T-330/08 *Ligny Pesca di Guaiana Francesco and Others v Commission* OJ 2008 C272/38); and (c) Council Regulation (EC) No 1005/2008 of 29 September 2008 establishing a Community system to prevent, deter and eliminate illegal, unreported and unregulated fishing, amending Regulations (EEC) No 2847/93, (EC) No 1936/2001 and (EC) No 601/2004 and repealing Regulations (EC) No 1093/94 and (EC) No 1447/1999, OJ 2008 L266/1, Art 36(2)(d) and (e).   [112] Reg 1936/2001, Art 3(g) and (i).
[113] Reg 1559/2007, Art 2(g) and (h).   [114] Reg 1559/2007, Arts 20(1), 25(2)(a), and 26(2).
[115] Reg 1936/2001, Art 4c(1), (2), and (4).   [116] Reg 1936/2001, Art 4c(3) and (4).
[117] Reg 1936/2001, Art 4c(5).

State must also send the Commission a list of all vessels flying its flag and registered in the Community that catch bluefin tuna for fattening and of all vessels authorized to provide or transfer bluefin tuna for fattening.[118]

Where bluefin tuna for fattening are transferred from a fishing vessel to a transport vessel, that transfer must be recorded by both vessels. The flag Member State must notify the Commission of the amounts of bluefin tuna caught and caged by vessels flying its flag, as well as details relating to the import and export of bluefin tuna for fattening.[119] Bluefin tuna fattening farms under the jurisdiction of a Member State are required to submit to that State a 'caging declaration' (seventy-two hours after each caging operation) and a 'marketing declaration for the bluefin tuna fattened' (annually), on the basis of which the Member State must notify the Commission annually, in respect of the previous year, the amount of bluefin tuna caged and the amount marketed.[120]

Regulation 1559/2007 has many provisions relevant to bluefin tuna farming or caging,[121] and only those relating more directly to farming itself will be described here. Unless otherwise stated, the provisions described relate to both 'fattening' farms and 'farming' farms (see above). The Regulation requires that before any bluefin tuna is transferred into a cage, the Member State under whose jurisdiction the farm falls must inform the flag State of the catching vessel (if it is a member of the ICCAT or a cooperating non-member, but regardless of whether it is an EC Member State) of the amount caught by that vessel to be transferred to a cage. If the flag State considers that the vessel had 'insufficient individual quota for bluefin tuna put into the cage', or the quantity of fish has not been duly reported and not taken into account for the calculation of any quota that may be applicable, or the vessel is not authorized to fish for bluefin tuna, the flag State shall request the Member State concerned to seize the catch and release it into the sea.[122]

Within one week of a caging operation, the Member State under whose jurisdiction the relevant farm falls must submit a 'caging report', validated by an observer, to the flag State whose flag vessels fished the tuna and to the Commission (the latter forwarding that information to the ICCAT). The caging report is to contain the information included in the 'caging declaration' required by Regulation 1936/2001 (see above).[123] Where a farm is located on the high seas, the above reporting obligation applies, *mutatis mutandis*, to 'Member States where the natural or legal persons responsible for the . . . farms are established'.[124] This reflects a provision in the Basic Regulation about the scope of the CFP, namely that it applies not only to Community waters and Community fishing vessels, but also

[118] Reg 1936/2001, Art 4a(5) and (6).
[119] Reg 1936/2001, Art 4a(1)–(4). Reg 1936/2001, Art 3(h), defines 'caging' as 'placing of wild individuals of any size in closed structures (cages) for fattening'.
[120] Reg 1936/2001, Art 4b and Annex 1a.
[121] Reg 1559/2007, Art 2(f), defines 'caging' as meaning that 'live bluefin tuna is not taken on board and includes both fattening and farming'.   [122] Reg 1559/2007, Art 20(3).
[123] Reg 1559/2007, Arts 20(1) and 25(2)(b).   [124] Reg 1559/2007, Art 20(2).

'without prejudice to the primary responsibility of the flag State, [to] nationals of Member States'.[125] More generally, Member States must take the necessary measures to 'control each caging operation' in farms within their jurisdiction, with a similar *mutatis mutandis* obligation to that just described in the case of farms on the high seas.[126]

Once the tuna is within cages, a further set of obligations arises. Member States must sample tuna in cages by length and weight, and notify the Commission of the results annually.[127] Member States must also ensure that an observer is present during all transfers of bluefin tuna to the cages and during all harvesting of fish from the farm.[128] Article 27 of Regulation 1559/2007 prohibits Community trade, landing, imports, exports, placing in cages for fattening or farming, re-exports, and transhipments of eastern Atlantic and Mediterranean bluefin tuna: (a) that is not accompanied by the required documentation; and (b) where the flag State of the catching vessel does not have a quota, catch limit or allocation of fishing effort or has exhausted its fishing possibilities.[129] In addition under Article 27, trade, imports, landing, processing, and exports from farms that do not comply with ICCAT Recommendation 2006[07] on bluefin tuna farming are to be prohibited.

Article 26(2) of Regulation 1559/2007 provides that each Member State within whose jurisdiction 'the bluefin tuna farm' falls shall take enforcement measures with respect to that farm where it has been established that the farm does not comply with Articles 20 and 25(2) of the Regulation or the provisions of Regulation 1936/2001 outlined above. The reference to Articles 20 and 25(2) of Regulation 1559/2007 is odd as these provisions impose obligations only on Member States or the masters of Community fishing vessels, not on farms.

8 Public financial assistance for aquaculture

This section considers only public financial assistance from the EC; the possibility of separate financial assistance from Member States is discussed in Chapter 8. The EC has provided considerable financial aid for aquaculture since the mid-1960s.[130] By way of illustration, total EC aid for aquaculture for the period 2000–06 inclusive amounted to about €351 million.[131] According to the Commission, EC aid has led to greater investment in, and faster development of, aquaculture in the EC than otherwise would have happened.[132] The current instrument providing

---

[125] Reg 2371/2002, Art 1(1). See further Chapter 2.   [126] Reg 1559/2007, Art 22(2) and (3).
[127] Reg 1559/2007, Art 8.   [128] Reg 1559/2007, Art 25(2).
[129] Processing is also to be prohibited in this instance.
[130] For details of the aid available for aquaculture up to the late 1980s, see Churchill, RR, *EEC Fisheries Law* (Dordrecht: Martinus Nijhoff Publishers, 1987), 216–17.
[131] Eurostat, *Facts and Figures on the CFP, Edition 2008*, 24.   [132] COM(2002) 511, p 6.

for EC aid to aquaculture is Regulation 1198/2006 on the European Fisheries Fund (EFF) (see further Chapter 8). One of the objectives of the EFF is to 'support aquaculture in order to provide sustainability in economic, environmental and social terms'.[133] Assistance from the EFF for aquaculture is dealt with principally in Chapter II of Title IV ('Priority axis 2: aquaculture, inland fishing, processing and marketing of fishery and aquaculture products'). As far as aquaculture is concerned, Chapter II stipulates that the EFF may provide funding for: (a) measures for 'productive investments' in aquaculture; (b) 'aqua-environmental measures'; (c) public health measures; (d) animal health measures; and (e) the processing and marketing of aquaculture products.[134] More detail about the types of aid eligible under each of these heads is spelt out in both Regulation 1198/2006 and a Commission implementing Regulation.[135]

In the case of head '(a)' above, EFF aid may cover investments in the construction, extension, equipment, and modernization of aquaculture installations, in particular with a view to improving working conditions, hygiene, human and animal health, and product quality, provided that such investments contribute to one of the following objectives: diversification to new species and production of species with good market prospects; implementation of aquaculture methods substantially reducing negative impact or enhancing positive effects on the environment compared with normal practices; support for 'traditional aquaculture activities important for preserving and developing both the economic and social fabric and the environment'; the purchase of equipment to protect aquaculture installations from wild predators; and improvement in the working and safety conditions of aquaculture workers.[136] Aid under this head is available only for micro, small, and medium-sized enterprises or for enterprises not falling within the definition of 'micro, small and medium-sized' given in Article 3(f) of the EFF Regulation that have less than 750 employees or with a turnover of less than €200 million, except in the 'outermost regions' (on which, see Chapter 2) and the outlying Greek islands.[137] Aid for 'aqua-environmental measures' (head '(b)' above) covers aid from the EFF to provide compensation for the use of aquaculture production methods that help to protect and improve the environment and conserve nature, provided that would-be beneficiaries commit themselves for at least five years to aqua-environmental requirements that go beyond normal good aquaculture practice.[138] Aid for public health under head '(c)' above relates to compensation to mollusc farmers where, because of public health risks resulting from a proliferation of toxin-producing plankton or the presence of plankton

---

[133] Reg 1198/2006, Art 4(a).   [134] Reg 1198/2006, Arts 28(1) and 34.
[135] Commission Regulation (EC) No 498/2007 of 26 March 2007 laying down rules for the implementation of Council Regulation (EC) No 1198/2006 on the European Fisheries Fund, OJ 2007 L120/1.   [136] Reg 1198/2006, Art 29(1). This provision is elaborated in Reg 498/2007, Art 10.
[137] Reg 1198/2006, Art 29(2) and (3).
[138] Reg 1198/2006, Art 30(1) and (3). Further details as to this type of aid are spelt out in Art 30(2), (4), and (5), and in Reg 498/2007, Art 11.

containing biotoxins, harvesting of molluscs is suspended for more than four months or suspension of harvesting (presumably for a shorter period) results in a loss of income of more than 35 per cent of the annual turnover of the business concerned.[139] Aid for animal health measures (head '(d)' above) is for the control and eradication of certain listed diseases that may occur in aquaculture installations.[140] Lastly, EFF aid for the processing and marketing of aquaculture products (head '(e)' above) is limited to products intended for human consumption, subject to one relatively minor exception, and is to be concentrated on improving working conditions; improving and monitoring public health and hygiene conditions or product quality; producing high quality products for niche markets; reducing negative impacts on the environment; improving the use of little-used species, by-products, and waste; producing or marketing new products; applying new technologies or developing innovative production methods; and marketing products mainly originating from local landings and aquaculture.[141] Furthermore, aid must aim to promote sustainable employment, may only be granted to micro, small, and medium-sized enterprises or other enterprises with less than 750 employees or a turnover of less than €200 million, except in the outermost regions and the outlying Greek islands, and must not be granted for investment relating to the retail trade.[142]

There are a number of conditions relating to the granting of funding by the EFF that are common to several of the heads referred to above. In the case of heads '(a)' to '(d)', Member States must ensure that adequate mechanisms exist to avoid counter-productive effects, particularly the risk of creating surplus production capacity or of 'adversely affecting the policy for conservation of fishing resources'.[143] It is not clear to what this last phrase refers, but it may be alluding to concerns about the adverse effect on wild fish stocks of catching wild fish for use as feed in aquaculture installations.[144] Where aid is being sought for projects under heads '(a)', '(c)', '(d)', and '(e)' for the purpose of 'guaranteeing compliance with standards under Community law on the environment, human or animal health, hygiene or animal welfare', aid may be granted only until the date on which the standards become mandatory for the enterprise concerned.[145]

Some aid for aquaculture from the EFF is also available under priority axes 3 and 4. Under priority axis 3, the EFF may provide funding for measures of 'common interest'.[146] Measures of 'common interest' of relevance to aquaculture include, inter alia: (a) 'collective actions' (which appear to be defined as measures

---

[139] Reg 1198/2006, Art 31. No further details as to this type of aid are set out in Reg 498/2007.

[140] Art 32. Further details as to this type of aid are spelt out in Reg 498/2007, Art 12.

[141] Reg 1198/2006, Arts 34(4) and 35(1).   [142] Reg 1198/2006, Art 35(2)–(6).

[143] Reg 1198/2006, Art 28(5).

[144] For expression of such concerns, see, for example, FAO, State of World Aquaculture 2006, 64–66, available on the website of the Fisheries and Aquaculture Department of the FAO.

[145] Reg 1198/2006, Arts 28(4) and 34(5).

[146] See Chapter 8 for a discussion of the meaning of this phrase.

implemented with the active support of operators themselves or by organizations acting on behalf of producers[147]) which aim to contribute to the transparency of markets in aquaculture products (including traceability) or which aim to develop, restructure or improve aquaculture sites;[148] (b) investment in existing fishing ports, which are of interest to fishers and aquaculture producers using them, with the aim of improving the services offered and relating, *inter alia*, to improving the conditions under which aquaculture products are landed, processed, stored in the ports, and auctioned;[149] and (c) measures intended for the development of new markets and promotional campaigns for aquaculture products.[150]

Under priority axis 4 the EFF may provide assistance for 'the sustainable development and improvement of the quality of life in fisheries areas eligible as part of an overall strategy which seeks to support the implementation of the objectives of the common fisheries policy, in particular taking account of its socio-economic effects'.[151] The term 'fisheries area' is defined as an 'area with a sea or lake shore or including ponds or a river estuary and with a significant level of employment in the fisheries sector'.[152] The 'fisheries sector' includes aquaculture.[153] The measures for the sustainable development of fisheries areas shall seek to maintain the economic and social prosperity of these areas and add value to fisheries and aquaculture products; maintain and develop jobs in fisheries areas; promote the quality of the coastal environment; and promote national and international cooperation between fisheries areas.[154]

As can be seen, much of the aid from the EFF envisaged for aquaculture supports the Commission's 2002 strategy of promoting the sustainable development of aquaculture in the EC, with considerable emphasis on both environmental and social aspects. Under Article 15 of Regulation 1198/2006 each Member State is to produce a national strategic plan covering the fisheries sector, which should set out the priorities, objectives, and estimated public financial resources required for particular aspects of the fisheries sector (see further Chapter 8). Those aspects include, *inter alia*, the sustainable development of the aquaculture sector and the sustainable development of the processing and marketing of aquaculture products.[155]

It may be recalled from Chapter 8 that each Member State is to draw up an operational programme to implement the policies and priorities to be co-financed by the EFF. In preparing and implementing such programmes, Member States are required to take into account various guiding principles. The latter include several that are impliedly applicable to aquaculture as well as two that refer explicitly to aquaculture, namely 'encouragement of operations with high added value through

---

[147] See further Chapter 8.   [148] Reg 1198/2006, Art 37(e) and (g).
[149] Reg 1198/2006, Art 39 and Reg 498/2007, Art 17.
[150] Reg 1198/2006, Art 40 and Reg 498/2007, Art 18.   [151] Reg 1198/2006, Art 43(1).
[152] Reg 1198/2006, Art 3(e).   [153] Reg 1198/2006, Art 3(a).
[154] Reg 1198/2006, Art 43(2).   [155] Reg 1198/2006, Art 15(2)(b) and (c).

the development of innovative capacities that provide for high quality standards and meet consumer needs for fisheries and *aquaculture* products' and 'contribution to a better supply to, and to a sustainable development of, the community [sic] market of fisheries and *aquaculture* products' (emphasis added).[156]

9 Concluding comments

As has been seen, there is now a considerable body of EC law dealing with aquaculture, contained in a variety of pieces of legislation (a good deal of it in the form of Directives), most of it adopted since 2006 (albeit in some cases replacing earlier legislation). There also exists a considerable body of national legislation, in part implementing EC Directives and in part supplementing them, as well as industry codes of practice and various soft law instruments adopted by international organizations.[157] The regulation of aquaculture in the EC, like the regulation of sea fisheries, is therefore a matter of some complexity. This regulatory complexity has been criticized by some in the aquaculture industry[158] and by some Member States[159] for hindering the development of aquaculture.

---

[156] Reg 1198/2006, Art 19(g) and (h).

[157] See, for example: FAO, Code of Conduct for Responsible Fisheries (1995), Art 9 (relating to which, see FAO, *FAO Technical Guidelines for Responsible Fisheries 5. Aquaculture Development* (Rome: FAO, 1997) (both available on the website of the Fisheries and Aquaculture Department of the FAO); and North Atlantic Salmon Conservation Organization, Resolution by the Parties to the Convention for the Conservation of Salmon in the North Atlantic Ocean to Minimise Impacts from Aquaculture, Introductions and Transfers, and Transgenics, on the Wild Salmon Stocks (2003, as amended in 2004 and 2006) (available on the Organization's website).

[158] *Minutes from European Aquaculture and its opportunities for development Conference, Brussels, 15 and 16 November 2007*, 6 and 16–18.

[159] See Council of the European Union, 2904th meeting of the Council, Agriculture and Fisheries, 18–20 November 2008, press release, 15940/08 (Presse 335), 19.

Index

NOTE TO THE READER: Where ranges of pages are stated (eg 1–3), this does not necessarily mean that the matter is dealt with continuously across the pages in question. Instead, it simply means that the matter is dealt with on each of the pages within the stated range.